Scott Titsworth
Dept. of Commu[...]
Southwest Miss[...] [...]sity

Crystal Stratton

LCCC.

THE PRACTICE OF RHETORICAL CRITICISM

SECOND

EDITION

Developed under the
advisory editorship of
Beverly Long, School of Speech Communication
University of North Carolina at Chapel Hill

THE PRACTICE OF RHETORICAL CRITICISM

SECOND

EDITION

JAMES R. ANDREWS

Longman
New York & London

The Practice of Rhetorical Criticism,
Second Edition

Longman, 95 Church Street, White Plains, N.Y. 10601

Associated companies:
Longman Group Ltd., London
Longman Cheshire Pty., Melbourne
Longman Paul Pty., Auckland
Copp Clark Pitman, Toronto

Executive editor: Gordon T. R. Anderson
Production editor: Judith Harlan (with Camilla T. K. Palmer)
Text design: Kevin C. Kall
Cover design: Kevin C. Kall
Production supervisor: Priscilla Taguer

Library of Congress Cataloging in Publication Data
Andrews, James Robertson, 1936–
    The practice of rhetorical criticism/James R. Andrews.—2nd
ed.
       p.   cm.
    Bibliography: p.
    Includes index.
    ISBN 0–8013–0389–3
    1. Rhetorical criticism. I. Title.
PN4096.A5 1990
808.5—dc20
                                       89–34637
                                           CIP

ABCDEFGHIJ—MA—99 98 97 96 95 94 93 92 91 90

Copyright Acknowledgments

James R. Andrews. "The Passionate Negation: The Chartist Movement in Rhetorical Perspective." Copyright 1973. Speech Communication Association.

J. Michael Hogan. "Public Opinion and American Foreign Policy: The Case of Illusory Support for the Panama Canal Treaties." *Quarterly Journal of Speech* 71 (August 1985). Speech Communication Association. Reprinted by permission.

Ronald Lee. "The New Populist Campaign for Economic Democracy: A Rhetorical Exploration." *Quarterly Journal of Speech* 72 (August 1986). Speech Communication Association. Reprinted by permission.

William F. Lewis. "Telling America's Story: Narrative Form and the Reagan Presidency." *Quarterly Journal of Speech* 78, (August 1987). Speech Communication Association.

Wayne Brockriede. "Rhetorical Criticism as Argument." *Quarterly Journal of Speech* 60 (February 1974). Speech Communication Association. Reprinted by permission.

Stephen E. Lucas. "The Schism in Rhetorical Scholarship." *Quarterly Journal of Speech* 67 (February 1981). Speech Communication Association. Reprinted by permission.

Richard Gregg. "A Phenominologically Oriented Approach to Rhetorical Criticism." *Central States Speech Journal* 17 (May 1966). Central States Communication Association. Reprinted by permission.

Michael Calvin McGee. "The 'Ideograph': A Link Between Rhetoric and Ideology." *Quarterly Journal of Speech* 66 (February 1980). Speech Communication Association. Reprinted by permission.

Ernest G. Bormann. "Fantasy and Rhetorical Vision: The Rhetorical Criticism of Social Reality." *Quarterly Journal of Speech* 58 (December 1972). Speech Communication Association. Reprinted by permission.

Contents

Preface

George Campbell wrote in his introduction to *The Philosophy of Rhetoric* that without "eloquence, or the art of speaking...the greatest talents, even wisdom itself, lose much of their lustre, and still more of their usefulness." By wisdom, Campbell observed, "a man's own conduct may be well regulated," but, the art of speaking "is absolutely necessary for diffusing valuable knowledge, and enforcing right rules of action upon others."[1]

For centuries past, as in our own time, men and women have communicated with each other in order to transmit what they have learned and to influence each others' actions. This communication has taken many forms, but undoubtedly much of it has been through public discourse. Campbell's *Philosophy of Rhetoric* was published in London in 1776, a time when some of the greatest orators of the English language—Edmund Burke, William Pitt, Charles James Fox—debated the great questions of empire, and when Americans like James Otis, Patrick Henry, and Samuel Adams brought their persuasive powers to bear on the creation of a new nation. Throughout history, and certainly in the present day, issues of great monument have been and are argued publicly. Living as we do in a rhetorical world, heirs as we are of a rhetorical tradition, it is essential that we understand the operations of public persuasion.

This book is designed to orient the beginning student to the nature and function of rhetorical criticism, to acquaint the student with those elements in the rhetorical situation that warrant serious attention, and to teach the student a useful strategy with which to begin to practice criticism.

Scholars and teachers will recognize a "traditional" perspective in this book. Its focus is clearly on public speeches and it recommends careful critical attention be paid to those aspects of the rhetorical act that have long been recognized as comprising the fundamental ingredients of public persuasion. This work is not, however, a call to return to some past critical age; the author's assumption is that

[1] George Campbell, *The Philosophy of Rhetoric*. Lloyd F. Bitzer, ed. Carbondale and Edwardsville: Southern Illinois University Press, 1963, xlix.

the beginning student should start first with a discreet object for critical scrutiny and with a practical way of examining that object. There should be no methodological or philosophical restraints on the critical imagination other than those of sound scholarship, and this book does not seek to impose any. But there must be some place to begin. As the painter first learns to draw the human figure, to suggest perspective, to appreciate the uses of color, and the like, so the rhetorical critic begins by studying basic factors in persuasion and by practicing the technique of explicating the ways in which those factors interact.

This, then, is not a handbook to guide or direct all critical inquiry. It is meant to launch a critical voyage and not to chart its eventual course: for the rest of his or her life the serious critic, through the study of discourse, of theory, and of the critical works of others, and through the practice of the critical art, will continue to develop abilities, to refine judgment, and to create more perceptive methods and approaches. This book, it is hoped, is a beginning.

Along with mastering basic concepts, the beginning critic will also be given the opportunity, through the study of examples and essays suggesting a variety of critical approaches, to begin to grapple with fundamental and enduring critical issues. For the student whose formal experience with rhetorical criticism will be limited to this one course, this book is designed also as a starting point, a means to equip that student with the basic knowledge and skill to confront rhetoric critically and to understand the usefulness of such a confrontation to him or her as a consumer and producer of communication.

Included in this book are examples of critical studies. In Part II: Critical Case Studies, the texts of Abraham Lincoln's "Second Inaugural" and Richard Nixon's "Address on the Vietnam War" are printed, each followed by critical essays. Students may read the texts and then study the essays on that speech by distinguished contemporary critics. These studies exhibit a variety of approaches, interpretations, and judgments. The exchange between Professors Hill and Campbell highlights important issues for critics and provides some insight into the basic assumptions and methods of practicing critics.

Examples of other critical studies appear in Part III: Critical Examples and offer the student a small sample of the varieties of contemporary critical practice. The samples demonstrate the results of combining imagination and scholarship to reach critical conclusions. These studies are, of course, the work of mature critics, and beginning students are unlikely to emulate them. But the studies do provide points of departure for discussion and may serve as stimulants to students' own critical work.

Again, Part IV: Critical Approaches is only a sample from an extensive possibility of choices. They do represent, however, different perspectives and theoretical formulations of the practice of criticism and should serve as entree into the complex and varied world of critical theory.

In a work of this kind it is impossible to name all those who have contributed to it—either directly or indirectly—since it is the result of what I began to learn as a graduate student and what I have continued to learn over the years from my students and colleagues. Further, this revision has profited from the comments of many teachers of criticism who have generously shared their reactions to the original edition with me. I do, however, wish to thank Professors Harry Sharp, Gary Collier, Martin J. Medhurst and David Henry for allowing me to participate in a seminar on teaching rhetorical criticism sponsored by the Western Communication Association, an experience that helped me sharpen and focus some of my ideas and enrich my own perceptions through the ideas of other participants. And I am especially grateful to my friend and colleague Dr. Karen King Lee for her very helpful advice on the revision of this book. All the assistance I have had in writing this book has surely contributed to its strengths; I know that its shortcomings are solely attributable to me.

I also wish to acknowledge with gratitude Ms. Helen Herrell who assisted me with the preparation of the manuscript and Mr. Trevor Parry-Giles, a dedicated and conscientious research assistant.

James R. Andrews
Bloomington, Indiana

PART
ONE

An Introduction to the Practice of Rhetorical Criticism

1

The Nature
of Criticism:
An Overview

DEFINING CRITICISM

Everyone reacts to things produced by others, but is everyone a critic? The student
who responds to a question about a political speech with, "It was boring"; the
seven-year-old who pronounces the latest offering in the *Rambo* saga "great"; the
parent whose comment on the music that his or her child enjoys is, "It's too loud";
the visitor to an art gallary who observes that a new painting "doesn't look like
anything"—all are reacting to products of human talent and imagination in a
personal and idiosyncratic way. In our common, everyday use of the word, some of
these comments might be labeled "critical."

In common parlance, criticism has become associated with carping, with
tearing down, with the pointed, negative comment. We tend to label one as "too
critical" when we mean that that person appears to be harping on insignificant
details, or objecting for the sake of objecting, or looking for something that is
wrong; in this sense, the "critic" is the builder of roadblocks, the troublemaker, or
the cynic. In our more egocentric moods we see praise as justified evaluation and
blame as unwarranted "criticism."

But such popular notions of criticism are certainly not the basis for defining
the activity of serious critics. In this connection, Marie Hochmuth Nichols points to
John Dewey's observation that "criticism. . . is not fault-finding. It is not pointing
out evils to be reformed. It is judgment engaged in discriminating among values. It
is taking thought as to what is better and worse in any field at any time, with some
consciousness of *why* the worse is worse."[1] One way to define criticism succinctly
would be as *the systematic process of illuminating and evaluating products of
human activity.*

As a *process* of illumination and evaluation, criticism does not result solely in ultimate pronouncements. The critical impulse is not one that leads to destruction, but, rather, is one that builds understanding. The serious study of criticism should be free of the misleading conceptions of "destructive" criticism and "constructive" criticism; criticism in the sense that the term is used here can never be destructive, and to say that it is constructive is redundant. At its best, criticism leads us to a fuller and richer understanding of a particular work as it exists within the context of human endeavor. *The critic of rhetoric focuses his or her attention on human efforts to be persuasive.*

Students of the art of rhetoric have not achieved universal agreement on what the critic of rhetoric should be studying. Nevertheless, both common sense and the evidence presented by what critics actually study suggest that persuasive public discourse is an obvious and sensible object for critical examination. Whereas mature scholars and critics may argue that a variety of phenomena may be studied rhetorically, certainly the best place to *begin* to deal with the problems of rhetorical criticism is with persuasive public discourse. Indeed, such an overwhelming number and variety of persuasive messages are a crucial part of the human experience that most critics devote their sustained attention to them.[2]

RESPONDING CRITICALLY: CONSUMERS OF RHETORIC

It is necessary early on to distinguish between responding critically and being a critic. Learning to respond critically is one of the possible, and very important, outcomes of the study of criticism. Persuasion invites response, and the nature of the responses to any given message can vary widely. Responses can be personal, impressionistic, or global. Many times the response tells more about the person responding than about the message. For example, in a group of people listening to an address by the President of the United States, one listener might respond favorably because that listener happened to be of the same political party as the President, or because the listener found certain of his or her own frustrations echoed in the speech, or because the President sounded so sincere, or because that listener found himself or herself agreeing with what the President said. Another listener might respond negatively to the speech because he or she never did trust the President, or because the speech sounded slow and monotonous, or because the listener found nothing in the speech with which he or she could directly identify, or even because the speech preempted the latest episode of "The Cosby Show."

All of us occasionally respond to the appearances of things rather than to the substance. One can read newspaper columns in which one is told how to dress in order to *appear* successful and confident on the probably valid assumption that potential associates will make a judgment about what we know and what we can do on the basis of how we look. Political advertisements may show a candidate with his shirt sleeves rolled up and his tie loosened, talking with factory workers so as to imply not only that the candidate has a real concern for the problems of ordinary people but also to suggest that somehow he knows how to cope with those problems. Actors or athletes who are famous, or even notorious, for their macho images are made to imply that the secret of their prowess somehow lies in the kind of scented alcohol they splash on their faces after they shave. All of us, no matter how well educated or intelligent we may be, can be influenced in some way by the appearance of things.

To respond critically to a message, however, is to be able to distinguish between what is relevant and what is irrelevant in that message. It is to know what the speaker was trying to do, what the speaker said, and what the speaker meant. It is to make some sense out of the speech by comparing the problem as it is addressed by the speaker with the problem as it is seen by the listener and by others who have experienced the problem; by comparing the solution offered by the speaker with other solutions; and by matching the solution with the dimensions and subtleties of the problem as the listener evaluates them. The listener, responding critically, can ask many questions, such as: Who is the speaker and what does he or she have to gain by giving this speech? What are the circumstances that gave rise to the speech? Did the speaker articulate some purpose or goal in giving the speech? What were the speaker's major points? How did he or she support these points? The listener who responds critically is the listener who tries to decide what the speech is all about, what it means, and what there is in the speech that should lead the listener to make some kind of decision or take some kind of action. The critical listener will realize that ideas and not gray hair denote wisdom; that clear thinking is not dependent on a youthful, handsome profile; that being smooth and glib is not an indication of sound reasoning.

Learning to respond critically is, in part, learning to apply the perspective and the methods of a critic. Some students will become rhetorical critics, serious and continuing students of rhetoric and of the way rhetoric influences and is influenced by human events. Other students who read this book, however, will seek to make intelligent responses to public discourse by adopting a critical stance toward communication. They will *do* criticism not because they hope to become professional critics, but because they hope to acquire the point of view and the skills that will help them to respond critically.

In the final analysis, developing the ability to respond critically will be extremely useful on a personal level. The critical listener will be able to make more informed judgments that will improve the quality of his or her response to public messages. Just as one who studies music can respond to certain musical works with more pleasure and appreciation, and just as one who studies poetry can read works of poetry with a deeper sense of personal satisfaction and identification, one who learns to respond critically to public communication can develop a sound basis for his or her own actions.

IMPROVING COMMUNICATION
SKILLS: PRODUCERS OF RHETORIC

Approaching communication critically involves learning how and why communication is effective. As the student begins to understand the basic factors that underlie rhetorical messages, he or she increases his or her own chances of shaping those factors to advantage. Specifically, knowledge of the operation of rhetoric in the following areas can help to make the student of criticism a better communicator.

Awareness of the impact of the context on a message directs a speaker's attention to the influences operating both outside of and within the immediate

CONTEXT

speaking situation. Such an awareness should help speakers focus their purposes more sharply and highlight the historical, political, and cultural factors that will impinge on the accomplishment of that purpose.

Understanding the nature of audiences will also contribute to the development of the speaker's purpose by helping speakers understand what can and can not be reasonably accomplished. The critic's ability to discern the factors which can influence an audience—their knowledge in relation to the topic, the groups with whom they identify, their receptivity to the message—can be carried over when critics become speakers so that they can tailor their messages to fit audience needs and perspectives.

Appreciating the role of ethos, or speaker image, should lead speakers to discover ways in which they can deal with perceptions that audiences have of them as they approach the speaking situation. Understanding the impact of image will also move speakers to finds ways to use the situation, the message itself, and the delivery of the message to enhance their own ethos.

Analyzing the argument will also enhance a speaker's ability to construct and employ rhetorical structures that use evidence effectively through persuasive reasoning. Attention to the function of language in promoting argument can help speakers make stylistic choices that best fit their purposes and audience expectations.

Interpreting and judging rhetorical acts will heighten the speaker's awareness of the ways in which rhetoric interacts with the values and cultural standards of society. The same intellectual discipline needed by the critic to unearth strategic relationships will help speakers understand the ways in which their own rhetorical efforts fit into the larger rhetorical pattern. Further, such a critical process will aid speakers in forming and adopting not only their own standards of effective communication, but their own standards of ethical communication, as well.

CHARACTERISTICS OF A CRITIC

A critic is a specialist and must be able to communicate to others the results of his or her critical observation and inquiry. A critic combines knowledge with a systematic way of using that knowledge and constantly seeks to refine his or her practice of criticism.

In the most fundamental sense the critic is an educator. He or she confronts a message; his or her reaction to that message is not the same as the reaction of the causal or even the critical listener. The critic seeks to understand what is going on in order to interpret more fully the rhetorical dynamics involved in the production and reception of the message and to make certain judgments about the quality of the message.

All critics do not go about their work in the same way, nor do all critics reach the same conclusion about a particular message. The critical impulse—the impulse to illuminate and evaluate—may be similar in all critics; the demands for system and rigor likewise obtain for all criticism; and whereas all critics seek to ask significant questions and go about answering those questions in a methodical fashion, the questions themselves and the means of answering them are not the same for all critics.[3]

For the beginning critic two considerations are primary. First, it is necessary to understand the kinds of question that appropriately can be raised about a rhetorical message, and, second, it is crucial to develop a methodical way of answering those questions. The remainder of this chapter is devoted to a discussion of the possible function of rhetorical criticism as a way of pointing out the major questions that a critic may address. The remainder of the book presents a framework within which the critic may go about answering these questions systematically.

CRITICAL FUNCTIONS: SEARCHING FOR EFFECT

In what was probably the most influential essay on rhetorical criticism written in this century, Herbert Wichelns observed that rhetorical criticism "is not concerned with permanence nor yet with beauty. It is concerned with effect. It regards a speech as a communication to a specific audience, and holds its business to be the analysis and appreciation of the orator's method of imparting his ideas to his hearers."[4] Certainly the purpose of any rhetorical message is to persuade, to influence human feelings or beliefs or actions in some specific way. When any speaker faces an audience he or she wants members of that audience to *do* something. We think of an "effective" speaker as one who is able to accomplish his or her rhetorical purposes. It is logical and eminently understandable that one possible function of rhetorical criticism is to assess rhetorical effect.

At first glance this function may seem a somewhat simple one, a matter of determining what the auditors did after a speech was given. But just to count the votes at the end of a debate or the number of orders at the end of a sales pitch, or even to consult national polls hardly illuminates a rhetorical message. Nor does it tell us in reality very much about the causal relationship between the message and the actions that followed the message.

In trying to understand effect, the basic question that the critic needs to raise is more complex than simply, "What was the effect of the speech?" The crucial question focuses on the interaction between the message and its total context and is best stated: "What potential did the message have to influence what audience or audiences in what ways?" Answering such a question involves careful analysis, interpretation, and evaluation—processes that are developed in some detail in the following sections of this book. At this point, however, it is appropriate to consider the most relevant factors that engage critics' attention.

To understand rhetorical effect, it is crucial to understand the dimensions of purpose and possibility. A speech functions within a larger context and happens because of things that are happening in the world. A speaker may wish to rally public opinion behind a proposal, create goodwill for an organization or a group in society or a country, or induce members of the audience to take some specified action such as giving money or signing a petition or buying a product. Great oratory often grows out of a series of events that either precipitate a crisis which calls for immediate action or delineates a serious problem which demands a solution. Whatever the circumstances, a rhetorical message is a purposive message; its aim is to get a response from an audience. *The critic who would search for effect must try to discern the purpose of the message, that is to say, what effect is desired by the speaker.* In discovering this purpose the critic will need to know what events brought the speech about, what was or is in the speaker's present position or background that caused him or her to speak at this time, what the speaker actually says in the speech that explicitly defines the purpose, and what there is in the speech that may reveal an unstated purpose.

A speaker's purposes are not always apparent or easy to determine. The speaker may have an underlying purpose that is more pressing and important than the apparent one. It has been argued persuasively, for example, that during a political campaign a speaker's real purpose is to "ingratiate" himself or herself with an audience.[5] Whereas the topic of a speech might be foreign policy and the speaker's purpose may seem to be to convince the audience that the NATO alliance should be strengthened, the speaker's "real" purpose might be to convince that audience that he or she is a well-informed and capable leader.

Once the best case possible for his or her reconstruction of the speaker's rhetorical purpose has been made, the critic will consider the possibilities for effecting that purpose. Here the critic must understand the constraints that are likely to affect the outcome of a speech. For example, political, personal, and social realities may shape or limit the achievement of rhetorical goals. A member of Congress might listen to a particularly well-crafted speech—clear, well-organized, amply documented, and supported—but still vote against the speaker's proposal because of his or her own party's commitment to an opposing point of view. A listener may hear a speech given by someone he or she distrusts and dislikes, and, even though the speaker's ideas may match those of the listener, the listener may respond negatively because of his or her overpowering personal antipathy to the speaker. A speaker favoring a Constitutional amendment that would prohibit abortion would be unlikely to devise any speech that would win support from an audience of members of the National Organization for Women because the social viewpoints of the speaker and listeners are separated by a deep, unbridgeable chasm. This does not mean, of course, that the speaker and the listener must always be in perfect agreement; if that were the case, there would be no such concept as persuasion—there would be no change and no need for change. But it does mean that *persuasion must take place within the limits of the possible*, and one of the critic's tasks is to try to determine what those limits are and the extent to which the speaker has recognized the limits and operated within them. Given this understanding of context, the critic will look to the text of the speech itself in order to discover clues as to the speaker's identification of an appropriate audience or audiences and the ways in which the speaker has sought to move those audiences. Through a careful textual analysis, the critic attempts to understand the ways in which persuasive potential has been exploited.

The critic's search for effect, then, involves him or her in the examination of both external and internal factors. The study of context sheds light on the nature of the issues being addressed, the speaker's relationship to those issues and the speaker's personal potential to exert influence, as well as the audience's relationship to the issues and its potential to influence change in the direction urged by the speaker. An examination of the internal factors, that is, the text of the message itself, should provide insights into how well the speech was crafted—how well arguments were constructed in order to appeal to influential audiences as the critic can best understand those audiences.

Forbes Hill, arguing for Aristotelian criticism, maintains that Aristotle's rhetoric provides a "comprehensive inventory" of the means whereby a speaker can persuade audiences. He asserts that the end of criticism "is to discover whether the speaker makes the best choices from the inventory to get a favorable decision from a specified group of auditors in a specific situation. It does not, of course, aim to discover whether or not the speaker actually gets his favorable decision. . . ."[6] The critic does not make the absolutely causal assessment embodied in the judgment, "The speech was effective"; rather, rhetorical investigation leads the critic to a conclusion concerning the *probable* effectiveness of the message.

Data of various kinds are available to a critic concerning actions taken or statements made following a speech. But the critic must be extremely cautious in dealing with such data. It would be simplistic and misleading, for example, to say that a candidate for political office who won that office did so as the direct result of a speech or even a series of speeches.

In a relatively limited number of cases, students of contemporary speaking have some poll data, usually gathered only after what are considered to be extremely important speeches, but even these data must be viewed with some suspicion. Polls may register impressions of certain audiences at a particular time, but they will never tell the critic that the speaker's use of certain kinds of evidence changed auditors' minds, or that the organizational pattern of the speech functioned persuasively—indeed, such data will not be able to establish any direct relationship between specific rhetorical behaviors and specific outcomes.

Critics also will be able to find a variety of personal reactions to speeches; some listeners will record their responses in their diaries or in letters to friends or even in public statements. But all such manifestations of behavior that occur after a speech are vague and can be extremely unrepresentative, and would constitute unsound bases upon which to argue direct effect. The critic should not ignore such data, but he or she needs to use them with care and to put recorded reactions to speeches into proper perspective.

As Wayne Minnick has observed, "Contemporary testimony and post-speech behaviors best serve the critic if he treats them as establishing hypotheses to be supported rather than as conclusive evidence of effect itself."[7] For the rhetorical critic who would attempt to assess effect, Professor Minnick's conclusion is a sound one: "A hypothetical effect based on testimony and/or post-speech behavior is supported with evidence that the speaker reached an appropriate audience and employed rhetorical methods which, on the face of it, seemed adequate to produce the effect."[8] Furthermore, the probability that the alleged effect actually took place is increased when the critic can demonstrate that "the speaker presented a broadly distributed, rhetorically adequate case in a context which allows the negation of extra-speech events as major causal factors."[9]

Determining effect, in short, is not just finding out what happened after a speech was given; it is a careful examination of the interrelationships between text and context in order to offer the most reasonable explanation for the probable result of any given message.

CRITICAL FUNCTIONS:
ILLUMINATING EVENTS, CONTEXT
AND SPEAKERS

At various times in human history, public discussion and debate of important issues has been a crucial mode of solving or contributing to the solution of the problems faced by human societies. In the English-speaking countries in modern times public discourse has accompanied political and social change; public argument is a part of the Anglo-American tradition.

By turning its attention to such public argument, rhetorical criticism may function to illuminate specific historical events and the social/cultural context in which these events occur. When a rhetorical critic approaches a historical event, he or she does so from a unique perspective. The careful historical investigation of any set of events or period may well reveal hidden forces at work, or at least reveal submerged forces of which the participants in events might be only dimly aware. Examining historical data by looking back on events may lead the historian to discover patterns of behavior and motivations for behavior of which the participants in those events were not fully cognizant. Historical perspective might lead one in a sense to describe what "really" happened.

But events are not always fully or clearly apprehended by those who participate in them. A prime function of rhetoric is to interpret and make meaningful what is in the process of happening. *The reality of one's world at any given moment is the reality as it is perceived.* Speeches afford concrete evidence of how actors living through history perceive what is going on and how they try to shape the perceptions of others. A speaker may judge events imperfectly or incorrectly or may even interpret events deceptively, but what he or she says is an effort to make sense out of events and to project courses of action consistent with that sense.

The critic does not study speeches carefully only to learn what conclusions the speaker reaches or what positions the speaker holds. Also of essential interest to the rhetorical critic is the way in which the speaker attempts to make issues salient and ideas persuasive. Through a careful examination of rhetorical behaviors, the critic should be able to uncover the issues as they are defined and refined at the time of their importance. The critic should be able to discover the implicit and explicit points of clash between differing views. Much rhetorical activity is devoted to the struggle for control of the issues. A careful reading of speeches that focuses not only on the ideational content but also on rhetorical method will uncover the ways in which issues emerge, the ways in which they jostle each other for supremacy, and the ways in which they assume hierarchical values.

Since the rhetorical critic is concerned with rhetorical method, he or she is compelled to come to grips with the totality of a speaker's argument. A full examination of argument can generate insights into the nature of the society in which that argument flourishes. The critic, for example, will search for the uncontested premises of argument. He or she will attempt to uncover those fundamental premises that the speaker perceives as being so basic that they do not need elaboration or justification.

These premises provide clues as to a culture's value structure. This basic structure can be filled in as the critic begins to look at other rhetorical factors. The critic can find much that is instructive in the forms of evidence used by a speaker to determine what that speaker considers to be compelling. This analysis is more than simply identifying forms of support. If, for example, testimony is a predominant form of evidence, it could be enlightening to know the source of *authoritative* testimony. One might, for example, construct the outlines of the social history of the United States by uncovering the time in our own history in which religious leaders, or the founding fathers, or businessmen, or scientists were considered as the ultimate voices of authority.

To be persuasive, a speaker must involves his or her audience in the message itself; the speaker must make that message meaningful or salient to those who listen and must appeal to what the speaker conceives to be the most motivating of audience needs. As the critic examines the rhetorical methods of achieving salience and determines what hierarchical patterns of audience appeals exist, the critic begins to fit into place some of the tiny pieces that make up the mosaic of a culture. *A legitimate function of rhetorical criticism, then, is to try to determine how people argue as a means of describing who those people are.*

Within the general context of culture, rhetorical criticism can also provide specific illumination of individuals through the study of their rhetorical practices. Not only does an examination of the various parts of discourse shed light on the society in which that discourse flourishes, it can also tell the investigator much about the ways in which the particular speaker thinks and the way he or she sees his or her world. Rhetorical criticism can thus contribute much to biographical study since it uncovers the rhetor's ideas in action as he or she seeks to persuade those over whom that speaker would exert influence.

CRITICAL FUNCTIONS:
SOCIAL CRITICISM

If criticism can illuminate historical and cultural contexts, it surely must be able to contribute to the understanding of contemporary events as they are occurring. The rhetorical criticism of contemporary messages may perform what Karlyn Kohrs Campbell describes as a "social function." According to Professor Campbell, "this function requires that critics appraise both the techniques used and the ends advocated in rhetorical acts, in addition to the immediate and long-range effects of both." Campbell goes on to define social criticism as "criticism that evaluates the ways in which issues are formulated and policies justified, and the effects of both on society at a particular historical moment."[10] What Campbell in effect implies is that critics enter the fray of public discussion, using their critical abilities and perspective to become active *participants* in the solution of problems by their careful investigation of rhetoric and its consequences.

The social function of rhetorical criticism is a matter of some controversy.[11] An argument against such criticism might go something like this: The criticism of rhetoric involves the evaluation of *rhetorical* choices. If the function of rhetoric is to persuade, then the critic of rhetoric has as his or her task the discovery of the ways in which, and the extent to which, a message was persuasive. When one begins to make judgments about whether the aims of persuasion are good or bad for our society, or judgments about whether the policies advocated are practical and useful solutions to problems, one ceases to be a *rhetorical* critic and ventures into the realm of other disciplines. This is not to say that the rhetorical critic cannot comment on contemporary affairs; he or she does so, however, as an intelligent, educated observer might do, not as a *rhetorical critic*.

On the other hand, there is a compelling argument that such a view limits too severely the possible functions of rhetorical criticism. When public discussion takes place, *how* the participants in that discussion argue is as important as the conclusions they reach. If rhetoric does, indeed, shape perceptions, then the critic of rhetoric should be able to make evaluative statements concerning the accuracy and the implications of those perceptions as the speaker would have them.

There would be little disagreement that a rhetorical critic may, for example, legitimately focus his or her attention on arguments. The critic can make descriptive statements about the structure of an argument, but the investigation does not end there; an assessment of the quality of an argument is surely within the realm of rhetorical criticism. Quality may be judged upon a variety of standards. The potential effectiveness of the argument is certainly a standard that can be applied, but it is not the *only* standard. Consider the quantity and quality of evidence used to support argumentative conclusions; is the critic's legitimate standard a measurement of how convincing an audience might find the evidence? An argument, after all, is a structure that must be utilitarian as well as pleasing. A house may be well designed, beautiful to look at, and functional; it may sell at a high price and return a substantial profit to the builder, but the firmness of the foundation and the quality of the support beams, which are not readily discernible to the untrained consumer, may be such that the building collapses on the new occupants during the first storm. Building codes are designed to provide some protection for the consumer by demanding expert certification of soundness. Should not the expert in argument be prepared to expose the shaky premises or the tenuous supporting evidence that underpins a conclusion advocating actions that affect our lives?

Such critical response is not as simple as pointing out a deliberate prevarication on the part of the speaker. It is more subtle than that; it may be raising the question of whether a speaker has adequately "proved" a point. For the critic who is concerned only with effect, "adequate" is defined as what an audience accepts, but for the social critic "adequate" can be defined as convincing enough to establish the probable truth of a claim for the discerning, informed, skeptical observer. In establishing probable "truth," the critic becomes a *participant* in the rhetorical process. The critic who is trained in rhetoric knows what *is* persuasive; when that critic enters into a controversy, it is to argue the question of what *should* be persuasive. The rhetorical critic can argue, for example, that the speaker's selective choice of supporting material ignores relevant data and thus distorts perceptions of events, or that the speaker's argument hinges on acceptance of a premise that conflicts with widely held values, or that there is a discongruity between the problem as the speaker outlines it and the solutions to that problem which he or she proposes.

Critics, like other human beings, have a perspective that shapes their perceptions. When they enter into a controversy, they bring with them their own biases and experiences. Complete objectivity in any critical activity is a quixotic goal; certainly in the realm of social criticism the nature of the critic's subjectivity has the potential to distort his or her judgment. The only possible answer to such a problem is to remind ourselves as critics that we have one prime obligation to those to whom we address ourselves—and that is to apply the same rigorous standards to *all* rhetorical efforts we seek to judge. A good critic scrutinizes the position with which she or he agrees just as carefully as opinions that conflict with the critic's own position. Political judgments are inevitably formed in part on the basis of rhetorical messages; what the critic seeks to avoid is making a judgment of rhetorical soundness on the basis of political conviction.[12]

CRITICAL FUNCTIONS:
DEVELOPMENT AND REFINEMENT
OF THEORY

Another primary function of criticism, in a sense, subsumes all others: The criticism of rhetoric contributes to the development and refinement of rhetorical theory. All criticism is implicitly theoretical. *Theory*, like *criticism* and *rhetoric*, is a term that has a variety of specialized and popular meanings. Contrasted with *applied* or *practical, theoretical* connotes for some people a kind of idle speculation on the ideal. However, that is not what is meant by the term when we talk of rhetorical theory. *By theory we mean a body of plausible generalizations or principles that explain a complex set of facts or phenomena.* A theory looks at a series of related events and tries to tell us why things happen as they do; and if the explanation of why things happen is accurate, then that explanation should be able to tell us what *will* happen in a similar set of circumstances. Rhetorical theory, then, can be visualized, in the words of Samuel Becker, as an "explanatory-predictive mosaic."[13]

The mosaic image a very useful one in discussing the relationship between theory and criticism. Pieced together with tiny bits of glass or stone that form patterns, the completed mosaic is a total picture in which the smaller patterns merge into a complete whole. Looked at in that way, all criticism is implicitly theoretical; the more we learn about what happened in one particular situation, that is, the more information bits that can be adduced, the better able we will be to generalize a pattern of rhetorical behavior. As these patterns are formed, and compared and contrasted with other patterns, a basis for predicting what will happen in similar cases is established.

To say, however, that every critical study is *implicitly* theoretical is *not* to say that every study must be *explicitly* theoretical. To demand that all critical studies must make a direct connection with and contribution to some specific theory, would be to devalue a rhetorical analysis that helps us to understand what is *unique* in any given situation. Critical insights that further our understanding of a particular historical event or person are valid and important contributions to knowledge. Furthermore, a critic may better serve theory if he or she tries simply to explicate a rhetorical act on its own terms, thus generating knowledge and insights that can, when viewed in relation to other critical findings, lead the theorist to discover patterns of behavior. That is to say, critical explanations of how rhetoric works in one given case might, in a metaphoric sense, be seen as the "data" with which the theorist will ultimately work; the critic need not, however, attempt in every case to strain for the "theoretical implications" inherent in that case.

Most students of speech communication have had experience in dealing with theory even though they might not be fully aware of it. Take, for example, the study of public speaking. Any good textbook on public speaking is really an embodiment of theory, no matter how "practical" it is alleged to be or perceived to be. When the author of a textbook advises the student on how to prepare for a speech, for example, that author is really laying down certain principles. The author may recommend rules to be observed when organizing a speech, present the characteristics of a good introduction to a speech, explain the ways in which to test the validity of an argument, or suggest that basis upon which evidence ought to be judged, and so forth. What the author of the textbook is really saying is that if that student organizes well, develops a valid argument with good supporting materials, and follows a whole range of suggestions in the text, then the student is likely to be successful in achieving his or her purpose in speaking. That is, the author implicitly asserts that certain patterns of rhetorical behavior will lead to certain results—from the theory (what we know about public speaking) certain procedures are recommended (the practice of public speaking) which should lead to predictable results (getting the desired audience response).

Criticism plays a vital role in this chain of rhetorical events. The critic focuses intensely on the practice of public discourse, and his or her findings may strengthen or weaken the predictive power of any theory or may generate hypotheses upon which new theories can ultimately be built.

CRITICAL FUNCTIONS: PEDAGOGICAL CRITICISM

Every critic is, in some sense, an educator. Rhetorical criticism teaches all of us something about the nature and operations of the persuasive process. In the classroom, however, the teacher-critic is most clearly concerned with applying his or her critical powers to the task of modifying behavior.

It is hoped that all criticism will have some impact on the way people produce and react to messages. But the critical functions we have been examining thus far do not aim at producing such effects immediately or directly. In the educational setting, criticism functions to improve the quality of messages and to increase audiences' awareness of the ways in which they respond (or *should* respond, or *want* to respond) to messages.

The critic's first task as a teacher is to identify and explain the criteria for judgments as to how poorly or how well a student is communicating. A textbook certainly helps the teacher by presenting, in an organized fashion, basic principles that serve as a guide to behavior. The teacher's job is to see that students understand that these principles are just that: They are *generalizations* to be used by the student when planning and executing his or her message. The teacher-critic should never lose sight of the principles; the student must not be allowed to form the impression that there are a raft of techniques, a series of unrelated "helpful hints" to remember when giving or listening to a speech. The critic, rather, points to standards of excellence and illustrates the ways in which and the extent to which these standards are being met in actual student performance.

It is in the pedagogical role that the critic has the opportunity to discuss most fully not only what was happening but what should be happening. The issue is not so much one of raising standards as of helping the student learn what standards are, and applying those standards in creating and delivering a message or responding to a message. The critic in this situation clearly and explicitly matches standards to performance when making a judgment. The specificity of the matching process is crucial. It simply will not do for a critic to tell a student, "Your ideas were not clear." There are standards relating to organizational patterns, development of argument, use of evidence, and language choice, all of which can impinge on the clarity of ideas. The critic, in his or her pedagogical role, must specify these standards and point directly and explicitly to the ways in which their violation contributed to a lack of clarity.

The teacher-critic then takes the next step: suggesting to the student possible strategies for putting these principles into operation. Strategies will grow out of a careful examination of the principles and what went wrong in previous efforts to implement them. Beginning critics, if they are not consciously attuned to the need for careful analysis and the communication of the results of that analysis to the student, are tempted to respond as casual observers rather than as trained professionals. Instead of relating experience to principles and shaping future behavior by helping the student use these principles in devising strategies, the teacher may end up being "critical" in the popular sense and not in the sense we have been using that term. This teacher will respond to the student with the useless observation: "You weren't clear; be clearer when you give your next speech." The true critic, on the other hand, will relate judgments to standards and will communicate specifically the ways in which standards can be made operational in future communication efforts.

SUMMARY

In this chapter, we have said that the rhetorical critic is one who is engaged in the systematic process of illuminating and evaluating persuasive messages. As the critic functions, he or she may be searching for the potential effects of messages, investigating messages to discover the light they shed on events that have occurred or the society that gave rise to the messages, evaluating the social utility or worth of messages, relating the practice of persuasion exemplified in particular messages to theoretical constructs, or seeking to modify the behavior of persuaders and their audiences.

As should be apparent, these functions are not mutually exclusive. The search for effect, for example, may lead to modifications in, or implications for, rhetorical theory; theoretical conceptions may serve as a starting point for the critic who would study persuasive discourse in order to illuminate the underlying values of a society. Certainly one of the best ways to understand the functions of criticism is to see how critics really work. This volume provides the beginning student the opportunity to study the ways in which mature critics have approached this process and to understand the variety of ways in which they have put the functions discussed into critical practice.

Whatever function, or functions, apply in any given critical work, the practicing critic needs to pursue them systematically. What follows in the remaining chapters is an attempt to construct a system. That is to say, the constituents of the rhetorical act that are invariably present are examined in order to explain what is essential for the beginning critic to know about them in order to move to analysis and judgment. Then, the specific elements to be subjected to analysis and a procedure for carrying out the analysis are presented. What the critic must know in using the results of the analysis in making interpretations and judgments is discussed, and, finally, varieties of ways are suggested in which critics can pattern the results of their investigations in order to illuminate and evaluate different aspects of the total rhetorical process.

_____ NOTES _____

1. Cited by Marie Hochmuth, ed., *A History and Criticism of American Public Address*, III (New York: Longmans, Green, 1955), p. 4.
2. See, e.g., discussions of areas for investigation by the rhetorical critic in essays by David Zarefsky, "The State of the Art in Public Address Scholarship," Martin J. Medhurst, "Public Address and Significant Scholarship," and James Arnt Aune, "Public Address and Rhetorical Theory," which appear in *Texts in Context: Critical Dialogues on Significant Episodes in American Political Rhetoric*, Michael C. Leff and Fred J. Kauffeld, eds. (Davis, CA: Hermagoras Press, 1989).
3. The case studies in criticism, which appear later in this book, afford excellent examples. A perusal of the other critical models and of the bibliography of critical studies also suggests this.
4. Herbert Wichelns, "The Literary Criticism of Oratory," reprinted in William A. Linsley, ed., *Speech Criticism: Methods and Materials* (Dubuque, Iowa: Wm. C. Brown, 1968), p. 32.
5. Michael C. Leff and G. P. Mohrmann, "Lincoln at Cooper Union: A Rhetorical Analysis of the Text," *Quarterly Journal of Speech*, 60 (1974), 346–358.
6. Forbes Hill, "Conventional Wisdom—Traditional Forms: The President's Message of November 3, 1969," *Quarterly Journal of Speech*, 58 (1972), 374.
7. Wayne C. Minnick, "A Case Study in Persuasive Effect: Lyman Beecher on Duelling," *Speech Monographs*, 38 (1971), 275.
8. Ibid.
9. Ibid., p. 276.
10. Karyln Kohrs Campbell, "Criticism: Ephemeral and Enduring," *Speech Teacher*, 23 (1974), 10–11.
11. See the Nixon case study in criticism, particularly the exchange between Professor Campbell and Professor Hill, which appears on pages 140–150.
12. A word needs to be said concerning the audience for whom the social critic writes. The principal function of such criticism, since it is by nature a part of the immediate issue, is to have an impact on the outcomes of rhetoric. Accordingly, it is not particularly addressed to other critics and rhetorical theorists. Its publication outlets are not necessarily academic journals. Rhetorical critics, however—for good or ill and for a variety of reasons—rarely publish in popular periodicals; most social criticism of rhetorical acts tends to be undertaken by journalists.
13. Samuel L. Becker, "Rhetorical Studies for the Contemporary World," *The Prospect of Rhetoric*, p. 41.

1. Potential Effects

2. Illuminate possible events, contexts, speakers

3. Evaluating social worth (ethics) of message

4. Theory Build

5. ↑ communication skills

2

Constituents of the Rhetorical Act: Context and Audience

BEGINNING THE CRITICAL PROCESS

One of the rhetorical critic's first problems is deciding where to begin. If one is going to undertake to explicate and interpret the rhetorical dimensions of a particular message, be it a speech, a pamphlet, an editorial, or a proclamation, it makes obvious and good sense to begin with the message itself. The problem arises when it is realized that all the constituents of the rhetorical act are exerting mutual influence on each other even as the act occurs. What the critic must do, in effect, is to freeze an ongoing process, sort out its various elements, and examine sequentially matters that occur simultaneously.

In a speaking situation, for example, there is always a speaker, a message produced by that speaker, an audience responding to that message, and a complex context made up of a multiplicity of factors ranging from prevailing ethical standards and the importance of the issues involved to the size and temperature of the room and the speaker's energy level. The critic has to deal in some way with all these constituents one by one.

Of course, no critic approaches any rhetorical activity from a completely naive point of view: To be a critic in any discipline presupposes some prior knowledge and background. One would hardly be ready to become a literary critic after reading his or her first novel, nor could one decide to be a music critic and then listen for the first time to a symphony. No student could reasonably expect to become a rhetorical critic after reading one speech.

But the student who would master the critical craft must make a beginning. The nature of that beginning partly depends on the background and knowledge which the student brings to the situation. Whereas the text of the speech is a logical place to start, the student who knows something about the historical, political, and social factors that surround a particular speech obviously will understand better what the speaker is saying and what the speaker is trying to do. It is always advisable for the beginning rhetorical critic to start by reading, carefully and thoughtfully, the text of the message to be studied. The close analysis of that text may come later in the critical process, but initial study of the text must precede a systematic investigation of all the constituents. Following the careful reading of the text, the beginning critic, or the critic who is not already fully versed in the subtle and complex background to, and events surrounding, any communication event, will need to move backward, as it were, in order to understand what gave rise to the speech, how the issues involved emerged over time, what their relevance and importance was, and to whom they were significant. Since messages are designed to influence the way people think and act, the critic must come as close as he or she can to a full comprehension of what those who actually experienced the message thought and felt and believed.[1]

RHETORICAL IMPERATIVES: HISTORICAL AND POLITICAL EVENTS

One of the first factors to be considered by the rhetorical critic is the events that made it possible or necessary for a speaker to address an audience at all. People speak in order to solve problems, to gain adherents, to rouse interest and sympathy, or to compel action because there is something going on in the world around them that is in *need* of modification or is threatened and must be defended. In other words, rhetoric grows out of events that a speaker wants us to see as important. Historical and political events and trends can force certain issues into our consciousness; the situation can make it *imperative* that we somehow come to grips with issues. Let us consider some brief examples of such rhetorical imperatives[2] and how they take on special importance for the critic.

In the 1960s black Americans began a concerned and determined effort to gain for themselves the rights that were guaranteed to them by the Constitution and to reverse the economic and social effects of years of discrimination. Laws in several states barred blacks from eating in restaurants, sleeping in motels, and even drinking from water fountains reserved for whites only. Requirements for registering to vote were so stated and interpreted by white registrars as to effectively disenfranchise large numbers of blacks. While exercising their rights to petition and protest, blacks were often assaulted by police or set upon by dogs. Unemployment among blacks far exceeded that of whites, and the road to improvement through special job training and increased education was blocked to many blacks. Black groups, particularly the NAACP, attempted to work through the courts to redress wrongs, and had secured a landmark Supreme Court decision, in *Brown* v. *Board of Education*, that separate schools for blacks were inherently unequal and thus unconstitutional. Black leaders had lobbied for legislation that would improve the lot of their people, and prior to 1963, Civil Rights Acts had passed Congress. But, in spite of these efforts, the plight of most blacks in the United States was still seen as desperate. The tactics of sit-ins, demonstrations, and civil disobedience were employed to dramatize the problems of blacks, to make clear the extent and depth of black feeling, and to set forth clearly black demands.

In response to this surge of black pressure, white leaders reacted in a variety of ways. Labor leaders like Walter Reuther, religious leaders like Eugene Carson Blake, and political leaders like Hubert Humphrey pressed for congressional action. Other, like Alabama Governor George Wallace, tried to assert the right of the states to determine the nature of black-white relationships, particularly arguing for the right of the state to control such matters as education and voting rights. Many whites became alarmed at the potential for violence and frightened by the frustrated outbursts that erupted in major cities.

In 1963, with major civil rights legislation pending in Congress, at a massive rally, Martin Luther King, Jr., gave his most famous speech, "I Have a Dream." A critic would need to know details of those factors that brought forth and surrounded the speech before he or she could begin to appreciate such matters as King's purpose in giving the speech, his major premise concerning the American dream and the argument derived from it, the hopes and fears of those who heard the speech as they stood massed on the Mall in front of the Lincoln Memorial or watched their television sets at home, and the ways in which King's message might succeed. One would need to know about the challenge to King's leadership from militant blacks who were increasingly embittered by brutal treatment and growing more impatient with the results of what King called "creative suffering." One would also need to know the key provisions of the Civil Rights Bill and what efforts were being made to weaken and strengthen it.

RHETORICAL IMPERATIVES:
SOCIAL AND CULTURAL VALUES

In reconstructing rhetorical imperatives, historical and political events obviously must be considered. Social and cultural values and traditions also must be understood as they pertain to a speaking situation. In the civil rights movement, for example, consider the paternalistic myth of the "happy Negro." It was often alleged that blacks were happy with their lot; they didn't want contact with white society; they were content to move in the circles prescribed for them and in accordance with the traditions of white supremacy; the role of whites was to "take care of" blacks; and blacks, when they were not interfered with by "outside agitators," were docile and satisfied. When one recognizes the existence of such a cultural conception, one begins to see the need for black speakers like King to shatter it. And along with the deep-seated racial prejudices and stereotypes embedded in the culture, were conflicting American values that held that all Americans should be treated equally under the law, that ours was a land of equal opportunity, that basic to all religious convictions was the brotherhood of man—values that were available to King and others who sought to awaken the conscience of white Americans. For the critic to understand the rhetorical problems that King had to face, the rhetorical opportunities that were open to him, and the constraints that were placed on him by events in the past and his role in those events and by prevailing attitudes and beliefs, one would have to reconstruct the imperatives that brought King's speech about.[3]

What we are discussing here is much more than a painted backdrop against which the principal scene is played; we are talking about matters that have a direct impact on the very nature of the message itself. The speaker cannot control what is going on in an audience's mind; that is determined by what the listeners have experienced, what they know, and what they believe. The speaker cannot ignore what is important or salient to an audience or assume that what he or she thinks is important will be recognized as such by his or her listeners. So the critic who would assess what the speaker *has* done, working within the limitations imposed by events and by the social and cultural milieu, must know the significant contextual factors that have the potential to influence the message. How could a future critic, for example, hope to render any kind of explanation or judgment about a political speech dealing with foreign policy in 1980 who did not know in detail the impact of the seizure of the hostages in Iran or the Soviet invasion of Afghanistan? Who could hope to shed any light on the rhetorical strategies of Democratic incumbents and Republican challengers who did not appreciate the facts and feelings associated with rising inflation and increasing unemployment?

The rhetorical critic faces certain problems that are somewhat different from those encountered by the historian, although both are engaged in a reconstruction of the past. Whereas the historian may search for an accurate account of what happened, he or she may not be as vitally concerned with *perceptions* of what happened. The historian, for example, may take up the issue of English "tyranny" at the time of the American Revolution and question whether British actions and policy were, indeed, "tyrannical" in regard to political or economic restrictions.[4] The rhetorical scholar is likely to be more interested in how speakers and audiences of the time *interpreted* British actions so that they might be seen and understood as tyrannical. Historians looking back at the Bush–Dukakis Presidential race in 1988 might be able to discover what was "really" happening to the American economy, whether policies advocated by politicians would have or could have had real impact on the deficit. The rhetorical critic will focus attention more directly on attitudes and beliefs—whether mistaken or not—that people held toward economic matters. In short, the "imperatives" we are discussing are those that are imperative to speakers and audience at the time discourse is being produced and not unseen forces at work in human affairs. "Nationalism," for example, may be a rising tide, but for the rhetorical critic the ways in which speakers and listeners translate such a conception into concrete reality becomes of primary importance; attempts to stem nationalism or a willingness to be engulfed by it can only be assessed and understood within the context of some public *consciousness* of it. The critic's historical task, then, is the reconstruction of such a consciousness.

DISCERNING ISSUES

Once the critic can master the swirl of events and perceptions of events and can discern some pattern of conflicting and complementary forces—the rhetorical imperatives—that bring matters to a rhetorical head, then the critic needs to turn his or her attention to the emerging issues as they are molded, shaped, distorted, or sharpened in public debate. What really *is* at issue is a matter of serious concern in any controversy. In the civil rights struggle, for example, was the issue legal, social, and educational equality of opportunity for blacks? Or was it the constitutional right of the states to govern themselves in matters beyond the legal right of the federal government to intervene? Was it civil rights or states' rights? Was the issue whether citizens had the right to peaceful protest with the expectation that the forces of the government would protect them in carrying out this right? Or was it whether an orderly society could tolerate protest capable of, or even designed to, provoke violence or to disrupt the normal functioning of those who were unsympathetic to or disinterested in the movement? Was it civil rights or civil wrongs?

To take a more recent example, what was at issue in the debate in the United States Senate over the confirmation of President Bush's nominee, John Tower, for Secretary of Defense? Was the issue a constitutional one: Should the President have the right to name whomever he chooses to his Cabinet? What is the proper role of the Senate in advising and consenting to Presidential nominations? Was the issue a moral one: Did John Tower's personal conduct render him unfit to hold a high office? Was the issue a practical one: Did John Tower's use of alcohol disqualify him from holding a sensitive governmental position in which he could be called upon at any time to make important decisions affecting the lives of millions of people? Would his past association with defense contractors make him biased in their favor? Was the issue a personal one: Did John Tower's sometimes strained relations with other Senators when he was Chairman of the Armed Services Committee contribute to a personal dislike on the part of some Senators so intense that they wished to deny him the office he so clearly wanted? Various sectors of public opinion tended to coalesce around what each believed to be the "real" issue, and much of the debate centered on what the debate itself was about.

The rhetorical critic must discern in the context the nature of the issues as various parties see them. Consider this historical example for its relevance to perception of issues. During the American Civil War, both the Union and the Confederate States gave much diplomatic attention to the question of the recognition of the Confederate States by the government of Great Britain.[5] Recognition by England would have greatly benefited the South; the federal blockade could be weakened, the shipbuilding activities of the Confederates in England would have been made easier, the North would likely have become embroiled in a war with Britain, and so forth. In England, the ongoing debate over the Government's stance toward the warring sides touched on a variety of issues: Was it in Britain's best economic interests to encourage the permanent separation of a country that was fast becoming a major trade rival? Should the arrogant, uncouth Yankee industrialists be allowed to bully the more courtly, civilized southerners? And, most pertinently, should the federal blockade of the South be allowed to ruin Britain's important textile industry by creating a "cotton famine" in England? Such formulations of the issues certainly tilted toward the South. But those who were sympathetic to the North put the war in a perspective that was ultimately more captivating to most Englishmen when they described the war as one to eliminate slavery. For a nation that had almost singlehandedly eliminated the African slave trade and had abolished slavery in its own West Indian dominions, a nation whose rising working classes exhibited a strong antipathy to slavery even when the cotton famine brought personal hardship, the issue of slavery for Great Britain was an overriding moral consideration. The promulgation of the Emancipation Proclamation by President Lincoln in 1863 helped define the issue for the English clearly as one that rested on the slavery question and thus tilted the balance in favor of pro-Union spokesmen in England. Once the central issue of the debate was defined, the outcome was no longer in doubt.

AN ARGUMENTATIONAL HISTORY

As the rhetorical critic studies the context, he or she must construct what might be called an argumentational history of issues along with his or her reconstruction of events. As events unfold, people interpret their meaning, argue about their significance, and deliberate on their ultimate effect. Any message occurs at some point in this process that goes on until the issues are resolved, or supplanted by other issues, or diminish in perceived relevance. For a critic to make sense out of the context in which a speech took place, he or she must know what the issues were and were perceived to be *at that point*.

An argumentational history goes further than the definition of the issues. Surely the critic approaching a speech would need to know how others had argued the question in the past since the speaker and the audiences would be likely to have such information or at least have been exposed to it. By studying the ways in which particular matters have been argued, the critic can come to understand what kinds of evidence, what appeals to traditional values, what relationships between ideas have been offered in the past and the extent to which such things persist or fade away. How much better an assessment can be made of a rhetorical event when we know whether the arguments and the support for those arguments are original, or whether they have been used so frequently in the past (and gone unchallenged or only ineffectively combated) as to be conceded as "truths," or whether they have been discarded or discredited long ago.

Take, for example, the debate over the teaching of evolution, an issue that some thought had been laid to rest. In the current controversy, those who oppose on religious grounds what they understand to be evolutionary theory no longer argue the question of whether the Genesis story is "true"; rather, they focus on the concept of "theory." The appeal to the ultimate truth of the literal interpretation of the Bible as opposed to "Godless" science, has faded as an appeal to general audiences. The argument now asserts that there are opposing *theories*, and, in the interests of academic freedom and fair play, both *theories* ought to be taught in the public schools. As a part of the attack on what is called "secular humanism" this argument relies less on proof derived from scriptural quotation and more on the implied opposition of God and Christian principles to secular and human interpretations of events. The critic who would understand how such arguments have evolved must understand the social and cultural context *and* the way the arguments have developed to reflect that context.

RHETORICAL CONVENTIONS

Another factor to be considered is one of unique importance to the rhetorical critic. In any given time and place there are rhetorical conventions that apply and communication styles that prevail. Sometimes these are the function of a historical period. In England in the eighteenth and nineteenth centuries, for example, it was not uncommon for a speaker to address the House of Commons in a speech lasting several hours, a practice that few would tolerate in twentieth-century America. The change in the length of speeches is an obvious example of a rhetorical convention that operates within a specific context. These conventions, or common practices, are rooted in audience expectations. A Puritan divine in colonial New England could sermonize for three hours because his audience expected such a lengthy talk; a modern preacher whose sermons consistently ran more than twenty or thirty minutes would probably find his congregations melting away. Modern traditional churchgoers expect that church services will not greatly exceed an hour or so.

Beginning rhetorical critics, when studying texts of speeches that were given in the past, are often struck not only by their length but also by what they perceive as the complexity of the style of these speeches. The matter of prevailing historical styles is a complicated one. Much of what a critic knows about the style of a time comes from his or her immersion in the rhetoric of the period. In the present state of the art of rhetorical scholarship, we have little solid, normative data on stylistic practice. What the critic has, largely, is his or her own impressionistic perceptions of the way in which language was used by speakers in a particular period. (This fact should reinforce the notion that the would-be critic must read widely and extensively in the period in which he or she intends to work.)

The matter of audience expectations goes much deeper than conventions concerning such matters as length and style; we consider these issues further in the discussion of audiences. But it is essential for the critic who embarks on the study of historical rhetoric to bear in mind that what sounds right to the contemporary ear or reads right to the contemporary eye, is not what appeared right to the eighteenth- or nineteenth-century listener and reader.

ETHICS AND CONTEXT

Perhaps one of the most difficult elements contributing to a full understanding of context is the ethical one. If we take the ethics of any group to be a set of behaviors that are judged to be acceptable when measured against some prevailing code of conduct, we can see that what is essential is an understanding of the prevailing code, which, however, is not always spelled out in a specific, concrete fashion. There are, to be sure, "codes of ethics" that professional groups adopt and that are supposed to guide the conduct of their members. The Speech Communication Association, the National Association of Broadcasters, the American Psychological Association, the American Medical Association, and others all have written statements of what they, as a group, consider ethical behavior by members of their profession.

Along with various professionals codes are religious codes—the most notable one in the Judeo-Christian tradition being the Ten Commandments—that are designed to prescribe and circumscribe ethical behavior. But anyone who has studied arguments based on religious principles knows that the precise meaning and application of these codes are subject to wide varieties of interpretation and emphasis. "Thou shalt not kill," for example, seems to be a straightforward injunction, but pacifists have never been able to convince large numbers of people that this commandment applies in *all* cases and in *all* situations.[6] There are also laws that define acceptable behavior. "Conflict of interest" laws, for example, attempt to set out procedures governing the behavior of public officials, particularly in regard to financial matters. These laws are based on the precept that those who are elected to public office should not profit economically through the use of the power derived from holding office. But laws alone do not determine ethical behavior; who has not heard the phrase, often employed by those whose actions generate public suspicion or outrage, "It may be unethical, but it's not illegal."

Of utmost importance to the rhetorical critic is what might be called the ethical tenor of the times, the feelings that most people have concerning what is right or wrong behavior, whether or not such behavior is specifically articulated in any written code. For example, take a speaker who attacks a political leader for giving public offices with no real duties assigned to friends and relatives who are thereby paid from the public treasury for doing nothing. Surely, such a charge, if proven, would do serious damage to a modern American politician's career. Those precise charges were leveled against leading political figures in England in the early nineteenth century by radical speakers, and they were most decidedly true. Yet the practice of giving political supporters and family members honorary jobs that entailed no duties ("sinecures," as they were called) was common at the time, and it engendered few denunciations on ethical grounds from the governing classes of England.[7]

Determining the ethical climate of a period is never easy. Major problems confound any attempts that one might make to discern the ethical climate. In any society, competing ethical standards seem to be held simultaneously; subgroups within a society may hold conflicting standards or emphasize different standards. Societies, like individuals, may seem to profess standards that do not, in fact, guide their actions.

In contemporary American society, for example, we are repeatedly faced with choices for which there may be conflicting ethical precepts.[8] One of the most persistent strains to which Americans have been subjected is that of dealing with the demands placed on them by professed ethical imperatives while, at the same time, experiencing the strong urge to succeed. We are often considered a people with a strong sense of what is expedient. In the past, we have been proud of our lack of doctrinaire politics. As Erik H. Erikson reminds us, "American politics is not, as is that of Europe, 'a prelude to civil war'; it cannot become either entirely irresponsible or entirely dogmatic; and it must not try to be logical. It is a rocking sea of checks and balances in which uncompromising absolutes must drown."[9] We have avoided the rigid adherence to principle at all costs and have seen the virtue of our pragmatism contrasted with the factious, splintered politics of Europe.

In politics and in life, success has been our touchstone. Some students of American culture have observed that the will to get ahead, the need to compete successfully with our fellows, may be bred into us.[10] In this connection, "Bear" Bryant's aphorism that "football is life" may be a most apt metaphor. Facing the forces that would hold them back, Americans combine physical stamina, strategy, determination, and occasionally bursts of enthusiastic drive to reach their goal. To score, to win is essential, and in this process the American may feel compelled, at times, to gouge, kick, and cheat.

For some, this contradiction has been disquieting. In *Young Radicals*, Kenneth Keniston reports on an interview in which a young man describes his family: "It seems to have a lot of tensions in terms of its orientation—what your aspirations are, what they should be or shouldn't be. 'It isn't important that you make money, it's important that you be godly. But why don't you go out and make some money?' A whole series of contradictions. In terms of what I should do, what my life should be like."[11]

On the whole, however, Americans have learned to live with contradiction. As Gabriel A. Almond observed: "Under normal circumstances this conflict does not appear to have a seriously laming effect. It tends to be disposed of by adding a moral coloration to actions which are really motivated by expediency, and an expediential coloration to actions which are motivated by moral and humanitarian values."[12]

An excellent example of this attempt to render these contradictory values compatible appears in John F. Kennedy's Inaugural Address. Why should we help the world's poor who are "struggling to break the bonds of mass misery"? In the words of Kennedy, "not because the Communists may be doing it, not because we seek their votes, but because it is right." The moral coloration is given to what is, after all, expedient policy (the Communists, with whom we are in competition, *are* doing it; we *do* want votes in the sense that we want international support to check and contain our perceived rival and enemy, the Soviet Union). Yet the most interesting thing about this excerpt is that the sentence that immediately follows the one just quoted gives expedient coloration to what has been stated as a moral stance. There can be no doubt of the implication in, "If a free society cannot help the many who are poor, it cannot save the few who are rich." The rich, in this teeming world of the poor, are obviously the Americans, and we are invited to attend to the realization that, although we may be acting out of principle, when the principle operates in such a way as to help save a few—and the few are us—the moral purpose is given a recognizable practical cast.[13]

A critic's examination of the context will also help him or her understand when a debate is perceived as being over moral issues. In such cases, a tolerant examination of opposing arguments is difficult, for certainly virtue cannot tolerate vice; *nothing* is sacred in such a confrontation. "We make no secret of our determination to tread the law and the Constitution under our feet," Wendell Phillips asserted at an abolitionist meeting, at a time when practical political questions were beginning to become overwhelmed and overshadowed by the moral question of slavery.[14] Phillips' fiery colleague, William Lloyd Garrison, in asserting the primacy of the moral issue, epitomized the rejection of moderation. "I *will be* as harsh as truth, and as uncompromising as justice," Garrison told his readers in the January 1, 1831, issue of *The Liberator*. "On this subject, I do not wish to think, or speak, or write, with moderation. No! no! Tell a man whose house is on fire to give a moderate alarm; tell him to moderately rescue his wife from the hands of the ravisher; tell the mother to gradually extricate her babe from the fire into which it has fallen;—but urge me not to use moderation in a cause like the present."[15] When a speaker for a cause envisions a kind of Armageddon, his or her rhetoric reflects the moralist's impatience with expediency. As Barry Goldwater reminded the cheering delegates to the Republican National Convention in 1964, "Extremism in the defense of liberty is no vice. And. . .moderation in the pursuit of justice is no virtue."[16]

The conflict between competitive goals and professed moral values seems to be firmly rooted in our American culture, and the rhetorical critic must be aware of it. The value placed on success in a competitive society has within it the seeds of another conflict. The need to succeed implies a kind of individualistic drive to best others in competition. Yet when a child is reared and judged against the actions of his or her peers, when what constitutes success (particularly in its material dimension) is generally agreed upon, when the methods of attaining success are to some degree prescribed, and when the constraints of the society necessitate teamwork and cooperation, individuality itself is tempered by conformity.

These two elements—individuality and conformity—have existed in a state of tension, pulling at us, shaping, in part, our character. De Tocqueville worried about the conformity induced by the tyranny of the majority, and Frederick Jackson Turner hypothesized that the great American frontier bred the independent qualities of self-reliance. We extolled "rugged individualism" on the one hand and developed the "organization man" on the other.

Any student of the American character would agree that we are more than a sum of separate traits and characteristics; the whole is extremely complex. The qualities of the particular American culture that help to shape the rhetorical behavior alluded to here are not ones a critic can always uncover easily. These qualities are, however, noteworthy and might be helpful in understanding what is going on in a given period of American rhetoric.

As is evident, understanding the prevailing ethical code of any given time is a complex matter. In the final analysis, the most gaping pitfall to be avoided by the rhetorical critic is the assumption that the ethical standards of his or her time, or group, or culture can be imposed on the subject of investigation. The critic who believes in the absolute immutability of ethical standards will have difficulty with the conception that ethical standards are relative to the context in which they flourish. But there can be little argument that the ethical climate that permeates a rhetorical situation will vary from setting to setting, if only with the interpretation and manner of putting ethical conceptions into effect in practical affairs. Certainly the critic is at liberty to apply to discourse any ethical standards he or she wishes, to argue that evils are evils no matter where or when they occur. But to act as if others, removed in time and place, would make similar assumptions, would blind the critic to the ways in which rhetoric actually functioned in a particular situation. The critic may be shocked or repelled by ethical practices or norms, but no sound rhetorical judgments can be made about discourse if the critic fails to understand the prevailing codes.

THE SETTING FOR A SPEECH

We have discussed the larger context in which rhetorical activities take place. Any message occurring in this broad context also takes place within a more particularized setting. The speech is not only occasioned by past and immediate events, by elements that make rhetoric imperative, but it happens at a given moment in time, in certain surroundings, on a discrete occasion. A speech is an event, and the event has the potential for impact on the message and its reception.

First, there is the *public nature* of the occasion, which can shape the expectations that the audience will have and which speakers will feel constrained to meet. An audience will have a sense of what is fitting to be said in the circumstances, which will relate both to the substance and the manner of the speech. Some occasions are ceremonial. They tend to be formal, to have persuasive ends of stimulating feelings of unity, heightening common emotions, or extolling shared values; they tend to concentrate on general or abstract principles. Certain occasions are more frankly issue-oriented, calling for arguments that attempt to move audiences to action or to shape their beliefs. Still other occasions demand that persuasion be muted while the dissemination of information takes precedence.

Contrast, for example, the acceptance speech of a candidate for the presidency given to the nominating convention with the inaugural address of a newly elected President. When the candidate appears before partisan supporters, addressing them and, at the same time, the nation, clearly a "political" speech is expected. This is the right occasion for the speaker to laud the virtues of one's own party and to point to the failings of the opposition. Audiences, both those in the convention hall and those in front of their television sets, know that such an occasion does not call for a careful weighing of all the alternative solutions to problems; it does not call for a modest appraisal of one's own political shortcomings. The clarion sounded in such a speech on such an occasion is a call for a political army to unify, to gird itself to fight for American ideals and against the political enemy who would undermine or fail to live up to those ideals. Most listeners who would readily accept such partisanship in an acceptance speech would be shocked by the same sentiments, expressed in the same way, in an inaugural address. Typically, an inaugural address is an effort to rise above the recently ended political battle and instill a sense of national unity and concerted purpose. For example, John F. Kennedy, in his inaugural address, aptly described the inauguration as a "celebration of freedom," and not a victory of party. The ceremonial occasion of the inaugural, then, raises expectations that are different from the frankly political acceptance speech.

The setting of a speech also has a concrete, specific physical surrounding. It can be indoors or outdoors, in a large auditorium or a small meeting room; it can be given before a small group or large masses of people; it can be amplified by a public address system or heard only by those within earshot of the speaker's voice. The audience may be jammed together, elbow to elbow, or spread thinly throughout the room. The physical surroundings can have a real impact on the way a message is constructed and how it is delivered, again, because of what an audience expects in any given setting.

Everyone has experienced the effects of the setting of a speech on listeners or speakers. One might sit in a dormitory room or in a friend's living room and talk about what's going to happen if tuition costs are to continue to rise; the same person might give a speech in a public speaking class about tuition costs; and the same person might speak on behalf of students at a meeting of the university's board of trustees. Some of the differences in the messages will be determined by audience factors, which are discussed later, but the physical factors of the setting will affect the formality/informality of the discourse, including such matters as language choice, whether the speaker speaks extemporaneously or uses a manuscript, and the nature of audience response and participation. The prescribed behavior of the classroom, for example, rarely leads audience members to cheer or to heckle a speaker. In such a setting the audience does not expect a speaker to exceed a certain level of loudness and would be made uncomfortable or embarrassed by a speaker whom they perceived as "shouting" at them, whereas increased volume may be necessary and deemed quite appropriate at an open-air rally. A political candidate who was asked to state his or her position on the issues at a neighborhood gathering in a supporter's home would not be expected to produce a manuscript and read it to that group; but, called upon to speak at a press club luncheon on the same topic, the candidate may be expected to deliver a manuscript speech.

A critic must understand and appreciate the potential significance of a specific setting, which, like the broader context, will be reflected in a variety of ways in the message. The setting can influence the speaker's delivery, his or her style, and the emotional and intellectual responses of his or her listeners. Students, for example, are often concerned about large lecture classes as opposed to small, less formal classes. Many students believe that the opportunity to respond in a smaller class, the feeling of more direct contact with the instructor, and the fact that in smaller classes students know each other better and are known by the instructor better, all contribute to their ability to respond better intellectually. Consider also Martin Luther King, Jr.'s, "I Have a Dream" speech, for which the setting clearly contributed to the heightened emotional response of the audience. Thousands of people gathered in a large crowd on the Mall facing the statue of Abraham Lincoln as King spoke. The author of this book was in the audience for that speech. At the point in King's speech in which he stressed the need for blacks and whites to work together, a black man standing next to me put an arm around my shoulder and said, "We're in this together, brother." This natural, spontaneous emotional act of response to the speaker was prompted not only by the content of the speech but by the physical surroundings; it would not have been likely to occur in an auditorium. And the presence of such feelings in an audience, along with the opportunity to display them, had an influence on King's speech itself that a perceptive critic understands as he or she analyzes and evaluates the message.

The circumstances of Dr. King's speech suggest another important consideration for the critic in studying the impact of setting. While thousands listened to the speech in Washington, millions watched the speech on television throughout the country. The television viewers may or may not have sensed the emotional environment that surrounded the speech, but they certainly could not experience it in precisely the same way as those who were there. The *medium* through which listeners receive a speech is an aspect of the setting that can profoundly affect the listener's reactions. There are situations, such as King's speech or an inaugural address, in which viewers are looking in on an event; their unseen presence will certainly influence what is going on, but their expectations are colored by the total event. This situation differs somewhat from a speech given, for example, by the President of the United States, directly *to* the American people via television. Nevertheless, whichever case obtains, television itself presents a unique setting for a speech.

For one thing, television viewers tend to be in smaller groups and less subject to the moods, attitudes, and actions of those around them, and would probably be more passive than a live audience. The speaker will receive no stimulation from a television audience that might encourage him or her to become more excited or to "tone down" his or her material, or to combat restlessness by moving rapidly to a new point. The medium itself, because it brings the speaker into the living room, encourages a muted presentation that is more conversational in tone. It also provides a more concentrated focus on the speaker, so that other factors of the *speaker's* setting are either eliminated (there are no other people to look at or outside noises to contend with) or highlighted (the American flag may be unobtrusively, but nonetheless obviously, displayed in the background). Audience attention may be directed toward visual materials, and subtle nuances of delivery, such as facial expression, may be more pointedly brought to listeners' attention. On the other hand, the television audience is far less captive than a live one. A viewer can switch to another channel, or begin to read a newspaper, or even get up and leave to fix a snack or answer the telephone.

Perhaps the most important, and obvious, aspect of the television medium is its highly visual nature, which tends to emphasize what is *seen* at the possible expense of what is *said*. Audiences can form judgments about the speaker's competence, compassion, and intelligence based on what the speaker looks and sounds like, close up, and not only on what he or she says. It has often been observed, for example, that the outcome of the televised debates between Richard Nixon and John Kennedy turned on how Nixon looked, that Nixon's make-up man "did him in." Whether or not this bit of conventional wisdom is true, there is no doubt that practical politicians are very much concerned with their appearances as they are projected on television. The rhetorical critic who limits himself or herself exclusively to the text of such a speech is in danger of overlooking a potentially significant part of the setting that could lead to distorted conclusions about what happened rhetorically.

THE CENTRALITY
OF THE AUDIENCE

Frequent mention has been made of the expectations of the audience. The audience for any message is one of the most important constituents of the rhetorical act with which a critic must deal. Speeches are, by their nature, audience centered; the understanding of the audience is absolutely vital to any critical inquiry.

As the critic reconstructs the context for a message or series of messages, much information about the nature of the audiences addressed will be uncovered. The critic must organize, systematize, and search out missing information to give as complete a picture as possible of those whom the speaker would influence. In order to do this, the critic must first identify immediate and potential audiences, and then examine the primary variables that have a direct bearing on how audiences might receive and act on messages.

IDENTIFYING AUDIENCES

The critic's first consideration is to identify the audience or audiences. In some cases, this task will not be too difficult; it will be obvious that the primary audience is the one actually gathered to hear the speech. Certainly before the advent of mass media this was more likely to be the case. A speech given in the House of Commons in the eighteenth century, for example, was largely addressed to the members present; a speech given at a state convention called for the purpose of ratifying the new United States Constitution was primarily directed at the assembled delegates. But, even in historical cases, speeches were often designed with those in mind who would read about them later. Robert Emmet, the Irish revolutionary, spoke not for the English court that condemned him to hang, but to the larger Irish audience who would hear reports of what he said.[17] Abraham Lincoln, delivering his first inaugural speech, did not address the crowd assembled in Washington as much as the people and leaders of the southern states who had already begun to secede from the Union and those in the border states who might contemplate doing so.[18] Those who failed to take wider audiences into consideration were sometimes confounded by the results. William Seward's speech on the "irrepressible conflict" in Rochester, New York, had a profound effect on those who were not there and who judged the speech as an "abolitionist" one. It thereby helped to thwart Seward's chances to gain the Republican nomination for President.[19]

For any speech, then, there is an immediate audience and a potentially larger one. This is true of messages given in the past, and it is certainly true of modern times when the mass media have the potential to disseminate a speaker's ideas rapidly, sometimes instantaneously, throughout the world. It is obvious, for example, that a major address by the President of the United States may be an attempt to communicate with the American people at large or with segments of the American public, with legislators who will act to effect presidential policy, with foreign governments in alliance with the United States, and with those who are seen as hostile to American interests and intentions. The immediate audience may be the Congress in joint session, students and faculty in a university convocation, television viewers, or the National Press Club. But a far wider audience is likely to be envisioned.

Both the text and the context will direct the critic's attention to the wider audience. The critic who has investigated the imperatives giving rise to rhetoric should know the political, social, and economic issues that are uppermost in the minds of potential listeners. Specific references to foreign policy, for example, alert the critic to the possibility that the speaker wishes to send a message to the leaders of other countries or to supporters or potential adversaries at home. Knowing the context, setting, and content of the speech, the critic can begin to make informed assumptions about the audience the speaker hoped or needed to reach.[20]

AUDIENCE VARIABLES

What a critic needs to know about an audience can be grouped under three essential variables. These elements are "variable" in that their *impact* and significance varies—they may differ in importance and in relevance depending on the rhetorical characteristics of the situation. These variables are the listeners' *knowledge*, their *group identification*, and their *receptivity* to the speech and the topic.

In order for a critic to begin to understand how an audience may respond to a speech, it is essential to understand what the audience knows about the subject under consideration, about current related events, and about the speaker. In addition to knowledge pertinent to the specific rhetorical event, audiences have general knowledge, which may or may not be relevant, that grows out of their educational background and personal experiences. The critic hopes to understand interactions and make reasonable judgments about how well and in what ways speakers have adapted such elements as language choice, basic arguments, supporting evidence, and the like, to audiences; in order to carry out an operational analysis that can lead to a sound judgment, the critic must know what the audience knows.

Take, for instance, the use of historical analogy. A speaker who compares American government policy in Central America with American actions in Vietnam could reasonably assume that the Vietnam experience is recent and general enough for most listeners to have personal knowledge of it. As a speaker delves further into the past, however, his or her audience's knowledge of history may be a function of their educational background. Furthermore, particular audiences can be expected to know more about particular subjects because of their cultural identity, their professional activities, or the perceived impact of the topic on their own lives. Some audiences may know more not only about a given subject, but about current events in general because they tend to read newspapers, watch television documentaries and special reports, or discuss issues with other well-informed people. Also, some audiences will know more about the particular speaker than will other audiences. They may have been that speaker's constituents, or have read things that the speaker has written, or have belonged to the same social or religious organizations, and so forth. The ways in which a speaker capitalized on, or failed to take into account, what an audience *knows* is an important critical concern, one that the critic can assess only if he or she is aware of audience knowledge.

What anyone knows is not only a function of that person's educational level and personal intellectual practices; knowledge is shaped partly by the *groups with which one identifies.* This group affiliation, in addition to furthering knowledge, also influences the way people interpret and use knowledge. Members of the Sierra Club, for example, probably know more about conservation than many other people do; they are likely to read publications, attend meetings, and generally gather specific information that will provide them with more detailed facts about such matters as federal land management policy, criteria for designating wilderness areas, or potential industrial uses of public lands. But along with this knowledge there is also a *point of view* that members of a group tend to share. Catholics, Presbyterians, Episcopalians, Pentecostals, and Jehovah's Witnesses may all "know" the Bible; they may all be able to quote passages or relate the essential ingredients of a particular scriptural narrative. They nevertheless hold widely divergent views of what the Bible means not only theologically but in very practical terms relating to day-to-day human relations. Association and identification with particular groups will predispose audience reactions to messages.

Other group identifications derive from less voluntary factors. One may elect to join the Sierra Club or to change one's religious affiliation, but one cannot change his or her age or sex or ethnic background. Also, it is much more difficult to modify one's social status or economic circumstances than it is to join or drop out of a particular interest group or formal organization. The critic must also be aware of how these group identifications may exert influence on audiences. Polish organizations in Chicago have a cultural and emotional relationship to Eastern Europe that is bound to affect their response to a speaker who addresses the problems of American foreign policy in that area; blue-collar workers threatened with unemployment will view speeches on economic policy from that very personal perspective; older Americans' real stake in the Social Security program will shape their reaction to speeches that deal with that issue. Because the speaker's task is to adapt to a variety of groups within audiences, often groups with *conflicting* orientations, the critic's job of sorting out the possible responses of audiences is likewise difficult. The effective critic must understand the problems that arise from the speaker's efforts to persuade heterogeneous elements within audiences in order to describe and evaluate the speaker's solutions to these rhetorical problems.

Just as listeners' knowledge about a given subject derives partly from the groups with which they identify, both the knowledge and group identification have an impact on the *receptivity of an audience* to both subjects and speakers. The receptivity of an audience depends partly on *saliency*.

An issue or topic is salient to a group when that group sees the subject as important to them, as impinging directly on their lives. The basic act of receiving a message takes some effort on the part of the receiver. To choose to listen to a speech or read a pamphlet or attend a meeting is an act based on some initial receptivity. Most open meetings of school boards, for example, will be sparsely attended. But if there is a threat of some schools being closed, or a plan to redistrict areas served by particular schools in order to change busing patterns, large crowds will very likely be present. Parents will attend these meetings, in spite of conflicting demands on their time and energy, because they believe that their children's education, safety, or social adjustment will be significantly affected by the outcomes of the meetings. Some audiences might not be disposed to take a serious or intense interest in foreign policy, but if they are farmers whose livelihood is affected by a grain embargo, or college students whose education could be interrupted by compulsory military service, certain aspects of foreign policy will be salient to them and will compel their receptivity to a discussion of the issue.

Receptivity in this sense concerns the listeners' willingness to engage themselves as a part of the communication process. The critic must realize that a speaker's rhetorical problem often involves the *creation of saliency*. That is, there are times when audiences or potential audiences do not readily perceive the relevance of issues, or do not see the relevance in the way the speaker wishes them to see it. For example, some listeners may see the "cleaning-up-the-environment" issue as remote to their personal experience, but to those who lived on property contaminated by PCBs, pollution is a very real and harrowing threat. To those living in small towns or relatively nonindustrialized areas, the problem of pollution might be seen as a "big-city" issue that doesn't touch them directly. To some people, environmental controls have relevance because they believe that such controls can affect their health and the health of their children; others see relevance in the issue of government controls that increase manufacturing costs and thus affect them negatively in an economic way. The critic's task is to discern how audiences might answer the question, "Is this issue relevant to me and in what ways?" Then the critic will be better able to analyze the extent to which, and the ways in which, a speaker attempted to solve the saliency problems of the situation.

In conjunction with saliency, receptivity concerns the audience's disposition toward a subject or a speaker; it is important for the critic to understand listeners' attitudes, so that he or she can better uncover rhetorical problems. Certain topics may be received by audiences in a hostile, friendly, or fearful way. (Likewise, audiences can be hostile or indifferent, respectful, or suspicious toward a speaker; this point is developed more fully in the following chapter in the examination of the role of the speaker.) For example, a PTA audience may respond positively toward a speaker dealing with improving the quality of playground equipment; the same audience might approach a speaker dealing with the need to reduce the local school budget with suspicion, or even hostility. A conservative religious group might be negatively disposed to the subject of the church's role in promoting social action. The National Association of Broadcasters might initially be threatened by a discussion of the need for increased government regulation of broadcasting. The National Education Association would be inclined to receive positively a message that dealt with the increased use of national resources to improve the quality of instruction in the public schools.

A painstaking construction of audience variables in a given situation is fundamental to the critical process. In most circumstances, the critic will discover wide variations in the knowledge, group identifications, and receptivity of those who receive messages. But whether the audiences tend to move in the direction of homogeneity or heterogeneity, the message that is designed for them must take into account who they are and where they stand. The speaker will have choices to make and will make them—consciously or unconsciously. The pattern of these choices will contribute to the formation of the speaker's strategy. Understanding precisely what those choices are and judging whether or not they are appropriate— strategically or ethically—is part of the critic's role.

SUMMARY

The critic should realize that the constituents of the rhetorical act discussed in this chapter are those over which the speaker exercises little direct control. A speaker cannot change the past, erase the traditions and values that are part of a culture, escape the technical limitations imposed by television, make an audience of women into men, or convert workers who are fearful of losing their jobs into economically secure people. The context in which a message occurs and the audience or audiences to whom the message is addressed present rhetorical problems or rhetorical opportunities that delineate the boundaries within which a speaker must operate. Rhetoric is the process whereby values may be changed, traditions discarded, class distinctions erased or redefined, and future action shaped. But any given message, at a particular moment in time, is constrained by contextual and audience factors that are then operant. As a painter may be constrained by his or her canvas, a musician by the notes that instruments are capable of producing, and a dramatist by the technical possibilities of stage production, a speaker's possibilities are, in large measure, circumscribed by relevant events and relevant audience variables. The significant challenge for the speaker is to manipulate those factors over which he or she does have more control—for example, the construction of arguments, the selection of evidence, the identification and appeal to values, the language employed, and the manner of delivery—so as to influence real audiences living in real contexts. The critic can only begin to appreciate a speaker's wisdom and skill, or lack of it, when the critic fully comprehends the constraints under which a speaker labors.

Perhaps the best way to epitomize the critic's task in regard to context and audience is to say that the critic must answer the fundamental question: What is there in the rhetorical situation that presents a clear indication of the rhetorical problems that a speaker must solve and the rhetorical opportunities that exist to be used? This chapter has suggested important elements to be dealt with by the critic as he or she goes about answering that overarching question. These elements can be summarized by directing the critic's efforts toward answering the following subsidiary questions:

1. What *political, social, or economic factors*, both historical and immediate, brought the issue into *rhetorical* being?
2. What *cultural values and practices* in the society were relevant to the issue?
3. What *varying perceptions of the issue* existed at the time the message was given?
4. What *rhetorical conventions* shaped audience expectations of how, in what circumstances, and within what limitations the message was to be sent and received?
5. What *prevailing ethical standards* were relevant to the message?
6. What were the particular *circumstances of the setting* for a speech, and in what ways did they determine what a speaker could or could not do?
7. What was the composition of the *immediate audience* to whom a message was addressed?
8. Who was the *larger audience*, or audiences, if any, to whom the message was addressed?
9. In what ways were the *audiences' knowledge, group identifications*, and *receptivity* relevant to the issue being addressed?

As the critic answers these questions, he or she will construct a framework within which analysis, interpretation, and evaluation of the message as it functions rhetorically can take place.

One other constituent of the rhetorical act must be considered before the critic can turn to an intensive investigation of the text of the message itself: the examination of the speaker as a unique constituent in the rhetorical act is the subject of the next chapter.

_____ **NOTES** _____

1. As C. V. Wedgewood observed, "The historian's choice of significant issues is often different from that of contemporaries." *The King's War: 1641–1647* (London: Collins Fontante, 1958), p. 11.
2. The concept of "rhetorical imperatives" is discussed more fully and illustrated in James R. Andrews, "The Passionate Negation: The Chartist Movement in Rhetorical Perspective," *Quarterly Journal of Speech*, 59 (1973), 196–208.
3. See the chapter on "The Unfinished Revolution," in Kurt W. Ritter and James R. Andrews, *The American Ideology: Reflections of the Revolution in American Rhetoric* (Falls Church, Va.: SCA Bicentennial Monograph Series, 1978), pp. 93–117.
4. See, e.g., Gordon Wood, "Rhetoric and Reality in the American Revolution," *William and Mary Quarterly*, 3rd Ser., 23 (1966), 3–32.
5. See examples of critical studies that deal with this issue: Walter R. Fisher, "Gladstone's Speech at Newcastle-on-Tyne," *Speech Monographs*, 26 (1959), 255–262; James R. Andrews, "Coercive Rhetorical Strategy in Political Conflict: A Case Study of the *Trent* Affair," *Central States Speech Journal*, 24 (1973), 253–261; Stanford P. Gwin, "Slavery and English Polarity: The Persuasive

Campaign of John Bright Against English Recognition of the Confederate States of America," *Southern Speech Communication Journal*, 49 (1984), 406–419.

6. See, e.g., James R. Andrews, "Piety and Pragmatism: Rhetorical Aspects of the Early British Peace Movement," *Speech Monographs*, 34 (1967), 423–436.

7. See the example of the radical Henry Hunt's attack on the Tory Prime Minister George Canning in James R. Andrews, "History and Theory in the Study of the Rhetoric of Social Movements," *Central States Speech Journal*, 31 (1980), 276–279.

8. I have developed this point in some detail in "Reflections of the National Character in American Rhetoric," *Quarterly Journal of Speech*, 62 (1971), 316–324, and what follows draws extensively on that study.

9. Erik H. Erikson, *Childhood and Society*, 2d ed. (New York: W. W. Norton, 1963), p. 318.

10. See, e.g., David M. Potter, *People of Plenty: Economic Abundance and the American Character* (Chicago: University of Chicago Press, 1954), p. 49.

11. Kenneth Keniston, *Young Radicals* (New York: Harcourt, Brace and World, 1968), p. 66.

12. Gabriel A. Almond, *The American People and Foreign Policy* (New York: Harcourt, Brace, 1950), p. 52.

13. In *Speech Criticism: Methods and Materials*, ed. by William A. Linsley (Dubuque, IA: Wm. C. Brown, 1968), p. 376.

14. Cited in Robert T. Oliver, *History of Public Speaking in America* (Boston: Allyn & Bacon, 1965), p. 235.

15. Cited in Richard Hofstader, *Great Issues in American History* (New York: Vintage, 1958), I, p. 322.

16. "I Accept Your Nomination," *Voices of Crisis: Vital Speeches on Contemporary Issues*, ed. by Lloyd W. Matson (New York: Odessey Press, 1967), p. 125.

17. See Robert M. Post, "Pathos in Robert Emmet's Speech From the Dock," *Western Journal of Speech Communication*, 30 (1966), 19–25.

18. See Marie Hochmuth Nichols, "Lincoln's First Inaugural Address," *Anti-Slavery and Disunion, 1858–1861: Studies in the Rhetoric of Compromise and Conflict*, ed by J. Jeffery Auer (New York: Harper & Row, 1963), pp. 392–414.

19. Robert T. Oliver, "William H. Seward on the "Irrepressible Conflict,' October 25, 1858," *Anti-Slavery and Disunion*, pp. 29–50.

20. See Forbes Hill's discussion of "target audience" in "Conventional Wisdom—Traditional Form," esp. p. 375.

3

Constituents of the Rhetorical Act: The Speaker

DEFINING ETHOS

"Knowing" any person is an extremely difficult task. All of us present different pictures of ourselves to different people in different circumstances. The roles we play, the settings in which we find ourselves, the expectations of others, our own motives—all contribute to the extremely complex whole that makes up the "real" person. People have many sides, and no one can hope to see all those sides; we rarely understand or are even aware of every facet of our own personalities. When we communicate with others, most of us tend to manipulate, consciously or unconsciously, the aspects of ourselves that we wish others to see; and those who communicate with us form impressions, intended or unintended, of what we are.

We know that we ourselves and those around us define us as students, or as friends, daughters, brothers, lovers, rivals, co-workers, and so forth. At the same time we may think of ourselves and be seen as Christians, or scientists, or Democrats, or vegetarians. And as situations change, what we and others think is most important about us, what is most relevant to the situation, also changes.

If we project these individual human circumstances into the public communication setting, we can see that speakers and audiences interact in such a way as to "define" the person who is sending the message. This "definition" is what is termed the speaker's *ethos* or the composite *perception* an audience has of a speaker. This perception is not a complete, or in all ways an accurate, reflection of a "real" person; it is what an audience *thinks* about a person at any given time. It is formed by a variety of factors to which the critic must turn his or her attention. Chief among these considerations are the context out of which the speech arises and into which it intrudes itself; the speaker's prior reputation; the audience's needs, expectations, and priorities; the content and rhetorical characteristics of the message itself; and the manner in which the speech is given.

CONTEXT AND ETHOS

Considerable attention was given in the last chapter to the elements in the context that can influence a rhetorical interaction. These factors can be viewed from the standpoint of their potential to influence an audience's perception of a speaker. Certain events or trends that gave rise to rhetoric in the first place may affect attitudes toward speakers.

Take, for example, what has come to be known as the Watergate scandal of the early 1970s. The revelations about the inner workings of government, the generally condemned unethical or even illegal actions of political figures, and the sense of violation of the public trust that arose from news accounts and congressional hearings, created serious issues related to honesty and integrity of government, the powers of the presidency, the balance of powers between the branches of government, and a host of related issues that had to be dealt with rhetorically in subsequent political campaigns.

Part of the fallout from the Watergate experience was a profound suspicion of politicians. Any speaker who was a professional politician faced potential hostility from an audience because he or she could be perceived as a part of the whole system that had produced Watergate. Indeed, one of Jimmy Carter's principal assets when he was elected President might have been that he was not associated with the Washington establishment. In other circumstances, his lack of experience would have been a negative factor; given the context of the mid-1970s such a potentially harmful perspective could be turned to the speaker's advantage. Thus, the dissociation of former Governor Carter from professional politicians could have been a factor in shaping a positive ethos for many listeners.[1]

Contrast this with the selection of Dan Quayle by George Bush as his running mate in 1988. The most persistent attacks on Senator Quayle dealt with his competence and experience. Charges that he was "just a pretty face" or a token conservative chosen to mollify the Republican right wing or a young man who had used family influence to avoid the draft, were rooted in the conviction that he was not of potential Presidential caliber. Given that everyone remembered that President Reagan had been shot in an unsuccessful assassination attempt and that the Vice President was just "a heartbeat away" from the Presidency, the experience factor became an important issue—especially when Quayle was contrasted with the older, politically astute Democratic Vice Presidential candidate, Senator Bentsen of Texas. So, what was a political plus for Jimmy Carter twelve years before—a lack of identification with the political establishment—became a negative for a candidate who was perceived as inexperienced because events altered the context in which the political ethos was formed.

Social and cultural elements within a context also can bear on ethos. Even though potential listeners may not know a speaker, they may associate him or her with a group or cause that suggests a network of values. For example, if an audience gathers for a speech in favor of reviving the Equal Rights Amendment, its members may identify the speaker as a feminist. To some audiences this label will suggest an interwoven fabric of positive values: The speaker is in favor of equality; the speaker believes in the right of women to determine their own destinies and control their own bodies; the speaker believes women should have confidence and respect for themselves. For other listeners, a feminist represents threatening or negative values: The speaker is too aggressive and competitive; the speaker scoffs at the values of home and family; the speaker hates men. Of course, neither set of perceptions is likely to be entirely true in any objective sense. What is important is that the audience's social and cultural set, which grows out of its experiences of the imperatives calling forth the rhetoric, can predispose the members to view any speaker in a particular way, and, accordingly, influence the speaker's *ethos*.

Because of the impact of context on ethos, the critic of public addresses needs constantly to be reminded that perceptions of speakers *at the time they spoke* are influenced by that time and are not colored, as the critic's perceptions might be, by subsequent historical events. To have been an abolitionist before the Civil War, for example, was to be labeled a fanatic by most audiences and to ensure a negative ethos in most circumstances. Lincoln, whose popular image of "the great emancipator" has come down to later generations, took great pains to dissociate himself from the abolitionists right up to and including the presentation of his First Inaugural Address.[2] Speakers in England in the early nineteenth century who advocated reform of Parliament in order to enlarge the franchise vehemently denied the merest suggestion that they were "democrats."[3] To be against slavery and for democracy may seem to the contemporary student automatically positive virtues; what the critic must realize is that the context helps determine what is virtuous and thus contributes to the speaker's ethos.

THE SPEAKER'S REPUTATION

Our discussion of contextual factors relates to a speaker's reputation. If one is identified in a particular way with a particular issue, one takes on the generalized reputation that audiences associate with like-minded individuals. But many speakers are, or audiences believe them to be, known quantities. Listeners' awareness of anything that has occurred in a speaker's past can affect their prejudgment of the speaker.

One of the first matters about which an audience is likely to have information is the speaker's *issue orientation*. Because of other speeches, political actions, written works, or reports of positions the speaker has taken, the audience may have some awareness of the speaker's stand on the topic under consideration. Sometimes such information will be relatively concrete. The audience may know, for example, that the speaker voted against a constitutional amendment to prohibit school busing. Sometimes what is known is more vague: The speaker is a "conservative." And sometimes what the audience thinks it knows about the speaker is the result of labels attached by the speaker's opponents: He is a "big spender." The critic's task, then, is to assemble all the available data about a speaker's actions or statements about a particular issue and assess the extent to which and the ways in which these positions were made public and were interpreted by others.

The speaker may also bring to the speaking situation a *public character*. His or her past actions, not only those associated with the specific issue being discussed, will contribute to audiences' impressions of the speaker's sincerity, trustworthiness, judgment, and ethical qualities. A good example of the impact of this aspect of ethos is that of General Dwight D. Eisenhower. Eisenhower, a hero of World War II, was generally regarded as an honest, trustworthy man who was used to solving massive problems. His political position on major issues was virtually unknown when he entered politics; indeed, most political leaders did not even know whether he was a Democrat or a Republican. The fate of Gary Hart, whose relations with women were revealed in some detail by the national media, affords another example. These revelations about Hart's private behavior did not bear directly on his stance on foreign policy or domestic issues; they did, however, cast a shadow on his character sufficient to eliminate him from contention for the Democratic nomination in 1988.

As the critic attempts to reconstruct the public character of a speaker, then, much more is relevant than the speaker's identifiable stand on issues. The speaker's entire public life, as well as that part of his or her private life that is known or has been reported, is significant.

A speaker's reputation is also made up, in part, of an audience's beliefs about the speaker's *intelligence* and *experience*. It is apparent that for some listeners a speaker will be seen as someone who "knows what he's talking about." Aspects of the speaker's past will have established him or her as an authority on the question at hand. Simply being identified in an audience's mind as an expert can enhance a speaker's ethos.

A noted medical researcher, for example, may be expected to be regarded favorably by an audience gathered to hear a discussion of ways to prevent heart disease. Coaching clinics throughout the country attract eager young athletes who are willing to listen with great attention to a famous coach who has established authority by producing a string of winning teams. Eisenhower is an example of one whose favorable image made him trustworthy. During the election campaign of 1952, he was able to strike a responsive chord in the American public with the announcement, "I shall go to Korea." Eisenhower succeeded not because that statement revealed a specific plan for ending the war, but because he was viewed as an authority on military matters who could end a conflict that threatened to drag on endlessly.

An audience's perception of the depth and genuineness of the speaker's interest in them and their problems can also contribute to the speaker's reputation. A speaker's ability, then, is tempered by the audience's conviction of his or her sincerity. Such qualities as consistency, for example, can influence listeners' views of a speaker's sincerity. A speaker who has changed his or her mind on issues can be seen as one who has grown and developed over the years, whose views have matured, or whose experiences have altered earlier convictions or attitudes. On the other hand, such a person may be viewed as an opportunist whose principles are easily adapted to prevailing popular currents of thought. Politicians often belabor one another with statements made in the past. In the New York Primary in 1988, for example, Mayor Edward I. Koch, a supporter of Senator Albert Gore of Tennessee for the Democratic Presidential nomination, was quick to remind the Jewish voters of New York City of what was construed as antiSemitic remarks made four years earlier by Reverend Jessie Jackson, Gore's rival in the primary election. Congressmen from relatively conservative districts are frequently attacked for talking conservatively at home and voting liberally in Washington; such attacks seem clearly designed to call into question the sincerity and integrity of those officeholders.

Experience can relate not only to a speaker's expertise but also to his or her perceived interest in, and identification with, the audience. A speaker and an audience who have shared experiences and common tastes, similar backgrounds or even mutual prejudices, tend to be in sympathy with one another. A speaker who is seen as "one of us" may be viewed in a friendly light in comparison with a speaker about whom the audience is inclined to ask, "What does he know about what it's like to be poor?"—or to be black—or to work for a living—or to be lonely—or whatever.

Audiences can be gullible; their yearnings for solutions to their problems can lead them to believe what and whom they want to believe. History abounds with examples of those who successfully courted audiences through appeals to their fears and desires in order to obtain power. But audiences can be suspicious, too. They can question the motivations of speakers who appear to have something to gain by soliciting their support. Certainly what the audience believes it knows about a speaker's motivations forms a part of the reputation that the speaker brings to a communicative situation. The used car salesman—fairly or unfairly—has become something of a symbol of the speaker whose word is to be discounted since he is perceived as one who has everything to gain and very little to lose in getting a car off the lot. "What's in it for him" is a silent question that listeners can be expected to ask as they listen to a speaker.

AUDIENCE PRIORITIES

A speaker's reputation, then, is made up of an audience's various perceptions of the speaker, based on what it knows or believes about the speaker. But in this case, the whole is certainly not equal to the sum of its parts. A critic cannot simply catalogue the speaker's strengths and weaknesses according to the speaker's character or intelligence or sincerity. What is *important* about a speaker's reputation, and how that reputation works for or against a speaker, is a function of the audience's needs, expectations, and priorities.

A speaker's character, for example, may be judged by his or her public actions, but whether those actions are interpreted favorably or unfavorably depends on the standards of the listeners. This point was made in the preceding chapter, but it is important to reemphasize it here. Some groups may judge a person to be of "good character" because he or she does not smoke or drink whereas others would find such information largely irrelevant to whether the speaker was, for example, a trustworthy manager of public funds. Other elements of a speaker's reputation, which are usually thought of as favorable, may not always be so: There are those who like to believe that experts or intellectuals operate in a theoretical vacuum and lack "common sense." Many political incumbents have faced the charge that their experience in solving national problems flatly disqualifies them from leadership since the problems they addressed over their years in office remain unsolved.

Furthermore, what constitutes an authority is a very relative matter. Some listeners would pay close attention to a distinguished geologist or astronomer on the question of the age of the earth. Others would reject out-of-hand such persons as authorities and rely, instead, on the opinions of an evangelist who had no pretensions to scientific training or knowledge. Whether Carl Sagan or Jerry Fallwell is the best authority on how the earth was formed depends on who is listening.

Authority can also be misplaced, and the critic needs to be aware of the fact that audiences are sometimes disposed to generalize widely. A distinguished physicist, who might rightly be regarded as an expert on certain scientific matters, may receive close attention when he is giving his opinion on political and social matters, on which he may have no more expertise than any well-informed, intelligent citizen. Audiences may have "heroes"—be they scientists, businessmen, or sports figures—whose authority, although logically limited to the field in which they have direct experience and in which they excel, is enlarged by listeners to include virtually any area in which such persons choose to express opinions. Such a phenomenon is the basis for much "endorsement" advertising, for example.

Authority can be spread and misplaced; it can also be disregarded by audiences when they perceive the basic issue as one lying outside the relevant area of authority. We have previously discussed the importance of understanding the ways in which issues are defined and focused. Take, for example, the issue of government regulation of the automobile industry. Some listeners may well concede that a scientist working for the Environmental Protection Agency is an authority on air pollution control, but audiences may dismiss the speaker's advocacy of strict regulation of emission control devices. Although audiences might grant that the speaker knows well the dangers to health and the scientific means of reducing those dangers, they might view the issue as economic, not scientific. Workers in Flint, Michigan, or Kokomo, Indiana, may be more responsive to a speaker whom they regard as an economic or political authority, whose concern is with increasing automobile production. The critic, as a more dispassionate observer, may look at the welter of conflicting arguments and issues and reach a logical conclusion that our ultimate survival may depend on how well we learn to preserve our environment. But the critic does not have to face stockholders who want more profits or a family whose standard of living depends on the wage earner's regular weekly check. What is crucial to listeners *as they see it* is what determines how an issue is focused, and this definition of an issue influences an audience's definition of an authority.

The crucial point here goes back to the definition of ethos. *The perception an audience has of a speaker* is what finally determines ethos; it ultimately rests not on a catalogue of more or less objective personal qualities possessed by the speaker, but, rather, on what is known about those qualities and how they are interpreted by listeners.

ETHOS AND THE MESSAGE

Much of the discussion thus far has been concerned with what an audience knows (or believes it knows) about the speaker prior to a communication event. Part of the critic's task is to understand as fully as possible the ethos a speaker *brings to* a speaking situation. Yet it is also essential that the critic search for and explicate the ways in which the speaker both uses and creates ethos in his or her speech.

The text of the speech itself can reveal the *use of existing ethos* as a persuasive device. A general, for instance, may use an example from his personal experience that reminds his listeners of his military expertise; a political leader may refer to his or her many years of public service; and a business executive may relate a personal anecdote that reveals his or her managerical skills. When President Lyndon Johnson presented his sweeping proposals for a new civil rights law that would effectively end political discrimination in the South, he reminded his audience that his own "roots go deeply into Southern soil," and, as a consequence, he knew "how agonizing racial feelings are."[4] The President was recommending to Congress a bill whose provisions would call forth the bitterest denunciation from southern political leaders. With this statement, Johnson identified himself not as an outsider who disparaged southern traditions, but as a southerner who could cherish his heritage and still demand serious and deep reform. When Prime Minister Winston Churchill, faced with an election challenge from the Labour party, spoke to the British electorate near the end of World War II, he reminded voters of the situation when he had taken office and how he had led the country from "that memorable grim year when we stood alone against the might of Hitler with Mussolini at his tail. We gave all—and we have given all throughout to the prosecution of this war—and we have reached one of the great victorious halting-posts."[5] Speakers, then, will make efforts to exploit what they consider favorable elements of their ethos, and critics will attempt to discover the persuasive potential of such efforts.

It is also possible for speakers to strive to *create* favorable ethos within the speech itself. We have discussed previously some of the forces at work in the context and the audience that can dispose listeners to respond favorably or unfavorably to persuasive messages. As the speaker deals with such forces, he or she may enhance his or her ethos. A speaker with whom an audience can identify is a speaker for whom a positive ethos may be created.

The critic searches for the speaker's attempts to promote identification by discovering: (1) the ways in which the speaker associate himself or his position with an audience's values and, conversely, pictures the opposition as linked to positions upon which an audience looks unfavorably; (2) the ways in which the speaker refutes or minimizes unfavorable aspects of his or her ethos; (3) the extent to which the speaker capitalizes on the positive ethos of those with whom the audience does identify; (4) the ways in which the speaker shows a grasp of the issues that are most important to the audience and a command of facts, information, and interpretations of those issues; (5) the ways in which the speaker seeks to convince audience members that he or she understands their problems and shares their aspirations and concerns; and (6) the ways in which the speaker reveals his or her motivations in order to counter impressions of self-interest.

A speaker may employ any or all of these tactics to enhance the listeners' image of him or her. In responding to speakers, as in so many aspect of life, we often find ourselves relying ultimately on very personal evaluations. On almost any given matter, there is such a welter of confusing and conflicting information that many feel too overwhelmed to make any sense of it. Others simply can't be bothered or are too busy with other things, or can not begin to understand the meaning of masses of data and varieties of incompatible explanations of what those data mean. So we often resolve such difficulties by fixing on a *person* to save us or enlighten us or simply tell us what is best for us to do. Sometimes the results of such dependence are happy; sometimes they are disastrous. But there can be little doubt that reliance on persons we trust is a very potent force in shaping our behavior. The critic who would understand the persuasive impact implicit in a message must assess carefully and thoroughly the ways in which the speaker tries to promote such reliance by listeners.

ETHOS AND DIVERGENT AUDIENCES

One very obvious problem for the speaker, and certainly for the critic, is that a speaker's ethos, by definition, varies with the audience and over time. That is to say, a speaker may have a very positive ethos with one set of listeners and a negative ethos with another. When speakers hope to address mass audiences, this difficulty is compounded.

Major political speeches, for example, must, of necessity, be addressed to people of different ages from different economic and racial backgrounds in different parts of the country. In the case of a major presidential address, not only are many different Americans listening but people and governments throughout the world—some friendly, some unfriendly, some uncertain—are also potential auditors of the message. This complexity may well cause some speakers to attempt to say nothing that offends anyone and thus end up saying nothing. But what is of concern for the critic is the way in which any speaker balances the potential impact of the message on his or her ethos with different groups. In a later section of this book a case study of the varieties and problems of criticism is presented. A speech by then-President Richard Nixon is reproduced, followed by several critical studies of that speech. One of the major issues that emerges from those studies is the question of how Nixon dealt with this very problem of audiences for whom he had divergent images. One solution to the dilemma of differing audiences is offered by a critic who argues, in effect, that Nixon did the most rhetorically wise thing by simply writing off those people whom he had no chance to persuade and concentrating instead on those who were susceptible to his efforts to convince. Another critic takes sharp issue with this assessment, arguing that it was the President's responsibility to answer his critics.[6] No matter what position the critic takes, the fact remains that he or she must grapple with the complexities of ethos, describing and explaining the many facets of the problem as it is faced—or ignored—by the speaker.

THE SPEAKER IN ACTION: ASSESSING DELIVERY

For all that an audience may know or believe about a speaker, for all that a text might reveal about the speaker's efforts to exploit or create audience perceptions, speeches are, after all, actually delivered to an audience. Much of what has been said thus far in this book relates to rhetorical artifacts in general, be they speeches, pamphlets, editorials, or polemical essays. But one of the most obviously unique qualities of a speech is that it is oral and that the audience receives it directly from its originator.

Many speeches are known through reports—either media accounts or through accounts of other people, and many people will hear a two-minute summary of a major speech by a national figure, and, perhaps, see and hear a forty-five-second excerpt from that speech. Nevertheless, a speaker who is actually giving a speech is intimately bound up with the persuasive message itself, and the potential impact of *how* a speaker says what he or she says is inevitably present. Communication researchers W. Barnett Pearce and Bernard J. Brommel observe, "A written message is not the same as the same words spoken aloud...."[7]

The critic who wishes to come to a complete understanding of oral discourse must take delivery into account. Understanding delivery, like understanding everything else rhetorical, can best be done within a full knowledge of the limitations of the situation and the expectations of the audience.

Audiences can and do form impressions of a speaker that have the potential to influence a speaker's ethos on the basis of that speaker's delivery. Rhetorical critics have long assumed that answers to the three basic questions concerning delivery—How does the speaker sound? How does the speaker look? How does the speaker move?—will give us insights into the nature of that speaker's effectiveness and clues to the image he or she would project.[8] Experimental evidence also points to the conclusion that nonverbal elements in a message have some influence on the audience's reception of the message, although research findings do not conclusively establish a precise cause-effect relationship between specific nonverbal action and audience responses.[9]

Empirical observations from our own experience further confirm the conclusion that nonverbal messages are considered as, and designed to be, persuasive. Advertisers go to great lengths to ensure that their products are promoted by, or seen to be used by, or even seen in the same picture with persons they believe will suggest the rugged or sexy or classy image they wish to project for those products. Political hucksters do the same thing, surrounding their candidate with his or her family, showing the candidate engaged in earnest conservation with factory workers, picturing the candidate in a friendly and confidential exchange with the President of the United States (if he's popular). It is only common sense to assume that such efforts seek to create the impression that the candidate holds traditional American family values and that he or she is a friend of the working man and a confidant of the powerful.

What a speaker *does* in front of an audience almost always has some effect on that audience. For example, some listeners tend to respond stereotypically to regional dialects. Depending on where one is from, one may form immediate opinions of the intelligence, energy, and educational level of the speaker whose dialect demonstrates him or her to be from the hills of Kentucky or from Alabama or from Brooklyn. Speakers whose monotonous voices bore audiences seem to have the added disadvantage of being less credible, as well.

Correctly or incorrectly, a speaker's vocal qualities can suggest corresponding personality traits to audiences. The author of a highly publicized study of female sexual behavior came to speak at a large university campus. The speaker startled and dismayed some members of the audience because her breathy, "little girl" voice suggested to many that she could not be taken too seriously. Indeed, audiences tend to associate such vocal quality with immaturity. Though nothing the speaker said either strengthened or diminished the scientific validity of her published findings, some auditors may have felt uneasy about accepting those findings because the credibility of the speaker was tarnished by the immature image her voice helped to project. It seems safe to assume that when audiences judge a speaker's voice to be harsh, or nasal, or deviating in some way from "normal" quality, the speaker's ethos will suffer.

The way that speakers look and how they move also contribute to the formation of audience perceptions. Certainly President Carter's casual cardigans were meant to suggest an informality and directness when he gave his "fireside chats" to the American people. The famous smiles of popular politicians from Franklin Roosevelt to Dwight Eisenhower to Ronald Reagan suggested to some a warmth and sincerity that influenced their perceptions of the speaker's reliability and trustworthiness. We have all observed speakers whose tense, tiny movements seem to indicate tentativeness, or whose exaggerated motions distract us or embarrass us.

In fact, delivery of which we are extremely conscious is likely to be delivery that does not help a speaker's ethos or contribute to the successful communication of that speaker's message. "Distracting" mannerisms do just that—they distract us from the message and irritate listeners.

Of greatest interest to the critic is the relationship between the qualities describing a speaker's delivery and the content of the speaker's message. Audiences tend to be sensitive to whether a speaker's nonverbal behavior seems to contradict or deviate from the intended message. Thus, a speaker whose voice, gestures, and appearance convey the impression of remoteness while the message tries to say that the speaker cares about his or her audience, or a speaker who appears to take lightly a serious topic will have his or her ethos impaired. Elements of delivery thus have the potential to interact with verbal elements. In 1988, for example, George Bush was plagued by the so-called "wimp factor." Questions about his ability to lead were implied by the suspicion that he was not "his own man;" he was a good "second banana," a man with an excellent resumé, but not a striking personality. For his part, Michael Dukakis, was seen as dull—competent but not inspiring. For both men, their acceptance speeches became important to enhancing the "forceful," "dynamic," "inspirational" image considered essential to a credible Presidential candidacy. To an inordinate extent, then, the way the speeches were delivered—as well as what was said in the speeches—became important as a measure of leadership. Both candidates took great pains preparing to deliver the speech (as well as with the text of the speech), and both seemed, through their delivery, to experience some measure of immediate success in improving their images.

The crucial point is that although delivery does seem to influence audience perceptions, it does not seem to be a critical determinant of audience perception in and of itself. What the critic tries to assess is the potential interactions between content and delivery in an effort to uncover aspects that could contribute to the overall perception formed by an audience and, accordingly, could impact on the speaker's ethos.

SUMMARY

In this chapter, the fundamental question raised for the critic's consideration is: *What does the speaker bring to the communication situation, or capitalize on within the situation, that influences the audience's perception of that speaker?* The speaker's ethos can serve to help or hinder his or her persuasiveness, and the critic needs an accurate picture of what that ethos is for any given audience at any given time.

The following series of questions will help to summarize this chapter and will serve as a guide to the critic in reconstructing the ethos of the speaker.

1. What are the *historical and political factors* that can influence the audience's perception of the speaker?
2. What are the *social and cultural elements* within the context that bear upon ethos formation?
3. What is the speaker's *orientation toward the issue* under consideration?
4. How have the speaker's past actions served to form a *public character* perceived by the audience?
5. What is the audience's view of the speaker's *intelligence and experience*?
6. What does the speaker's past suggest to an audience about the speaker's *genuine interest* in its needs and concerns?
7. What factors in the speaker's background are most *salient* to the audience?
8. What devices, techniques, or strategies does the speaker *employ in the message itself* to enhance his ethos?
9. How does the speaker's ethos *vary among potential receivers* of his or her message?
10. What *distinguishing features in the speaker's delivery* can be described, and what is their potential for audience influence?
11. What potential for influencing ethos exists in the *relationship between the content of the speaker's message and his or her delivery*?

NOTES

1. See, e.g., J. Louis Campbell, "Jimmy Carter and the Rhetoric of Charisma," *Central States Speech Journal*, 30 (1979), 174–186; Christopher Lyle Johnstone, "Electing Ourselves in 1976: Jimmy Carter and the American Faith," *Western Journal of Speech Communication*, 42 (1978), 241–249; John H. Patton, "A Government as Good as Its People: Jimmy Carter and the Restoration of Transcendence to Politics," *Quarterly Journal of Speech*, 63 (1977), 249–257.
2. See Nichols, "Lincoln's First Inaugural Address," *Anti-Slavery and Disunion*, p. 401, pp. 403–404.
3. See James R. Andrews, "The Rhetoric of Coercion and Persuasion: The Reform Bill of 1832," *Quarterly Journal of Speech*, 56 (1970), 187–195.
4. Lyndon B. Johnson, "We Shall Overcome," in James R. Andrews, *A Choice of Worlds: The Practice and Criticism of Public Discourse* (New York: Harper & Row, 1973), p. 85.
5. Winston S. Churchill, "The Conservative Programme," *British Public Addresses, 1828–1960*, ed. by James H. McBath and Walter R. Fisher (Boston: Houghton Mifflin, 1971), p. 469.
6. See pp. 121–150.
7. W. Barnett Pearce and Bernard J. Brommel, "Vocalic Communication in Persuasion," *Quarterly Journal of Speech*, 58 (1972), 305.
8. See, e.g., Robert G. Gunderson's classic description of Daniel Webster on the stump in "Webster in Linsey-Woolsey," *Quarterly Journal of Speech*, 38 (1951), 23.
9. See, e.g., W. Barnett Pearce and Forrest Conklin, "Nonverbal Vocalic Communication and Perception of a Speaker," *Speech Monographs*, 38, (1971), 235–241; John Waite Bowers, "The influence of Delivery on Attitudes toward Concepts and Speakers," *Speech Monographs*, 32 (1965), 154–158; David W. Addingtion, "The Relationship of Selected Vocal Characteristics to Personality Perception," *Speech Monographs*, 35 (1968), 492–503; David W. Addington, "The Effect of Vocal Variations on Ratings of Source Credibility," *Speech Monographs*, 38 (1971), 242–247.

4

Understanding Rhetorical Texts: Analysis, Interpretation, and Judgment

THE WHOLE AND ITS PARTS

As difficult as it is to understand the many complex forces at work in the rhetorical environment, beginning rhetorical critics often find the analysis of the text itself more baffling. Yet the text is at the heart of the critic's work: Only through the careful analysis of its intricacies can the critic begin to interpret its overall functioning and judge its rhetorical worth.

As was mentioned earlier, a careful and thoughtful reading of the text should precede examination of other elements in the rhetorical act. Some critics will prefer to carry out a more detailed textual analysis initially, turning then to contextual factors to enlarge their understanding of the text and to refine and enrich their interpretation and evaluation. As the critical process has been described here, the culmination is analysis, interpretation, and judgment. But, in either case, the text itself must be of central critical concern.[1]

The text of a speech is an organic whole. It lives because its parts function together. No sensible student of rhetoric assumes that any persuasive message is produced additively—that is, that logic is added to emotion or that style is added to content in order to produce the final result. Nevertheless, in order to understand the physiology—how all the parts function together—it is necessary to study the anatomy—how each of the parts is constructed. To that end, the critic begins by systematically taking apart the text through an orderly analysis.

ANALYTICAL CATEGORIES

The critic begins to look for features that are fundamentally under the speaker's control. Though the speaker must take contextual features into account in constructing a message, they cannot be readily modified or influenced. The speaker cannot, for example, change the age or sex of his or her listeners; he or she cannot alter historical events or refashion cultural values. And whereas the speaker may be in part responsible for his or her own ethos and certainly can make efforts to manipulate his or her image, an audience's perception of the speaker is not entirely dependent on the speaker's choices. The text of the speech, however, does represent the speaker's *choices*—out of the range of possible material to be used and ways that the material might be put together, the speaker has selected certain material and certain arrangements to accomplish a purpose. In trying to identify these choices, the critic may be guided by certain categories that direct attention to crucial aspects of the discourse.

Argument

Any speech makes certain assertions about reality. The speech grows out of a situation in which the speaker perceives the need to induce listeners to believe or feel or act in certain ways. The speaker has a conclusion he or she wishes to see accepted or a course of action taken. The principal conclusion of the speech, along with the reasons that sustain that conclusion, is the argument of the speech.

Studying the argument of the speech provides the critic with internal evidence of the speaker's purpose. What is the speaker really getting at? What is the speaker trying to do? These questions are best answered through an examination of the speaker's own ideas. The speaker may not clearly or directly state his or her purpose, but the speech itself will surely reveal the speaker's intention.

Perhaps the most famous speech in which the speaker's *stated* purpose is not the purpose revealed by the argument of the speech is Marc Anthony's fictional funeral oration for Julius Caesar in Shakespeare's tragedy. The explicitly stated purpose of simply providing the requisite forms for a decent burial—"I come to bury Caesar, not to praise him"—is revealed as patently opposite to the implicit purpose that the speech itself reveals: to incite the mob to take vengeful action against Caesar's assassins.

The overall argument of a speech is made up of a number of specific arguments, units that in themselves make assertions or draw conclusions; taken together, arguments are designed to achieve the speaker's purpose. The critic who would understand how a speaker thinks and how that speaker wishes to direct the thinking of the audience must consider these units to illuminate the relationship between the fundamental parts of an argument. An argument is made up of a specific bits of information or motivational material that can be called the *data*, a *conclusion*, and some form of *ideational link* between the two. Another way of describing an argument would be to say that it is the process whereby a speaker presents an idea which he or she wishes to have accepted, offers evidence that will promote acceptance, and demonstrates why or how the evidence is sufficient to warrant acceptance of the idea.

It is very important for the critic to realize that the parts of an argument do not dictate its organization and that the speaker will not always explicitly state all the parts of an argument. Indeed, one of the critic's tasks is to identify the implicit parts of an argument and to reconstruct the argument in its entirely in order to understand precisely the relationship between its parts. Only then will the critic uncover the hidden assumptions, the sometimes invisible links in the chain that the speaker hopes to forge. And only then will the critic have the precise data necessary to judge the worth of the argument.[2]

To understand an argument more fully, let us take an example. The following is an excerpt from President Lyndon Johnson's speech on behalf of a civil rights bill that he was preparing to send to Congress in 1963:

> The history of this country in large measure is the history of expansion of that right to all of our people. Many of the issues of civil rights are very complex and most difficult. But about this there can and should be no argument: every American citizen must have an equal right to vote.
>
> There is no reason which can excuse the denial of that right. There is no duty which weighs more heavily on us than the duty we have to insure that right. Yet the harsh fact is that in many places in this country men and women are kept from voting simply because they are Negroes.
>
> Every device of which human ingenuity is capable has been used to deny this right. The Negro citizen may go to register only to be told that the day is wrong, or the hour is late, or the official in charge is absent.
>
> And if he persists and, if he manages to present himself to the registrar, he may be disqualified because he did not spell out his middle name, or because he abbreviated a word on the application. And if he manages to fill out an application, he is given a test.
>
> The registrar is the sole judge of whether he passes this test. He may be asked to recite the entire Constitution or explain the most complex provisions of state law.
>
> And even a college degree cannot be used to prove that he can read and write. For the fact is that the only way to pass these barriers is to show a white skin.
>
> Experience has clearly shown that the existing process of law cannot overcome systematic and ingenious discrimination. No law that we now have on the books, and I have helped to put three of them there, can insure the right to vote when local officials are determined to deny it. In such a case, our duty must be clear to all of us.
>
> The Constitution says that no person shall be kept from voting because of his race or his color. We have all sworn an oath before God to support and to defend that Constitution. We must now act in obedience to that oath.[3]

All the parts of an argument can be seen clearly in this passage. The conclusion of the argument is that black Americans are wrongly being denied their constitutional right to vote simply because they are black. The data offered to support this conclusion are a series of specific examples of devices used to thwart blacks in their attempts to register. There are two explicit links between the data and the conclusion: The barriers to voting are based on race since "The only way to pass these barriers is to show a white skin"; and, to establish racial barriers to voting is wrong since "The Constitution says that no person shall be kept from voting because of his race or color." Implicit links between data and conclusion are also to be found. The argument carries weight when there is a shared assumption that there is no justification for the violation of the Constitution and when there is a shared adherence to the value embodied by the concept of "equality under the law."

In the analysis of arguments, critics often find useful a model that has been adapted from the work of the English philosopher Stephen Toulman.[4] The Toulman model can be useful because it offers a diagrammatic way of looking at the parts of an argument, at how they articulate, and particularly, at how the link between the data and the conclusion may be established–implicitly or explicitly. The parts of the model are as follows:

(D)   *Data*. These are the "facts" as the speaker sees them and presents them to the audience.

(C)   *Claim*. This is the conclusion that the speaker draws from the facts.

(W)   *Warrant*. This is a statement, whether explicit or implied, that justifies moving from the Data to the Claim.

(B)   *Backing*. This is specific information, whether implicit or explicit, that supports the Warrant.

(R)   *Reservation*. This is a statement that identifies possible areas of exception to the Warrant and Claim. (It need not appear in the speech.)

(Q)   *Qualifier*. This is a statement that indicates the degree of certainty with which the Claim may be held.

Put in the form of a diagram, the model would look like this:

On first encounter, the model may seem somewhat complex to the beginning critic. But the subtleties of an argument are not always apparent on the initial reading, and the model is designed to illuminate complexities. Let us consider the model using the Johnson passage once again. The Johnson argument might be diagrammed as follows:

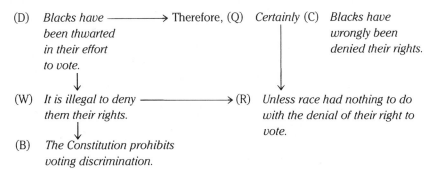

In light of this diagram, the Johnson argument might be restated like this: Blacks have been thwarted in their efforts to vote; *since* it is illegal to do this *because* the Constitution prohibits discrimination, *therefore* blacks have wrongly been denied their rights *unless* it can be shown that they were not barred from voting because of their color.

Although the critic might initially feel that using the Toulman model to lay out an argument is a somewhat intricate process, it is possible through practice to become more adept at diagramming. This method suggests that a very careful reading of the text, guided by some systematic approach to each argument, can uncover the complex relationship between ideas and evidence.

Systematic analysis of arguments also can illuminate for the critic the ways in which individual arguments form links in the chain of reasoning that supports *the* argument of the speech. One might continue with an examination of the Johnson speech, for example, in which the *Claim* of the argument as diagrammed can be seen to become the *Data* for the argument that follows:

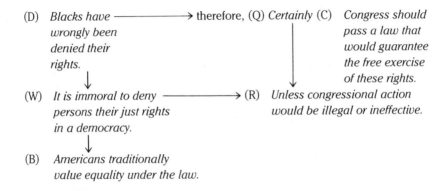

The separate arguments, and the way they relate to each other, form the building blocks of *the* argument of the speech. The careful analysis of these arguments will begin to uncover data that form the basis for the critical investigation of other analytical categories.

Supporting Materials

Within any ideational unit of the speech, the speaker will make some effort to make the conclusion understandable and believable to the audience. The critic's task is to identify the forms of support used and to determine the role played by any supporting device in the development of an argument.

The basic forms of supporting material are generally known to students of rhetoric. Most supporting material could be classified as example, definition, analogy, testimony, statistical data, and scientific results. The analysis of the text leads the critic carefully to classify these forms and to note the extent and nature of their use.

It is of prime importance that the critic realize that, whereas identification of forms of support is necessary, *merely* identifying them leads to no significant insights. To say only that a speaker used numerous examples or relied heavily on statistics does not, in itself, provide much illumination of the discourse. What is significant is the *function* that supporting material performs.

The critic seeks to uncover both logical and psychological dimensions in support for an idea. *Examples* that are specific and real may serve to demonstrate that actual cases do exist; yet, unless their typicality can also be demonstrated or is accepted, their psychological power is generally more formidable than their logical power. Examples help to make vivid and real generalizations that might otherwise be abstract; thus they promote audience identification. *Definition* serves the logical function of explaining what terms mean. It is also basic to audience adaptation since it recognizes the possibility of audience members' technical or educational limitations. It has the potential to reassure an audience that the speaker does have a psychologically positive concern for them and an awareness of their limitations. On the other hand, it could cause an informed audience to view the speaker as partronizing or pompous. *Analogy* is a means of comparing the known or experienced with the unknown or unexperienced. To the extent to which the two ideas or things juxtaposed really are comparable in essential elements, analogies lead to logical predictions of what the unknown will be like. Analogies relate the familiar with the unfamiliar, providing listeners with an identification point from which to move on to what may be more complex or little known to them; the potentially threatening nature of the unknown may thus be reduced. *Testimony* by a relevant expert enhances the logical quality of the conclusions reached by the speaker. It may also serve to promote audience confidence in the speaker by allying him or her with recognized authority. *Statistical data*, when recent and accurate, may logically support conclusions related to such matters as how widespread a particular problem is or the rate at which a problem is increasing. It can also suggest to an audience that the problem is encompassing enough to be likely to affect them. *Scientific results* provide empirical evidence in support of generalizations. Like testimony, scientific results bring to bear the findings of experts in the field under discussion. Both scientific results and statistical data also possess a positive psychological appeal in a society such as ours, which places value on things that may be called "scientific."

The critic, then, examines the discourse to determine what kinds of supporting material were used and to discover how they were used. One procedure that the critic could employ in examining supporting material would be to use a modified Toulman model to uncover function. That is, the critic could focus on a particular piece of support, determine the conclusion that support seeks to justify, and then speculate on the Warrant or Warrants that would be necessary to justify progress from the Data to the Claim. The two following examples, though not exhaustive or detailed, serve to illustrate the process.

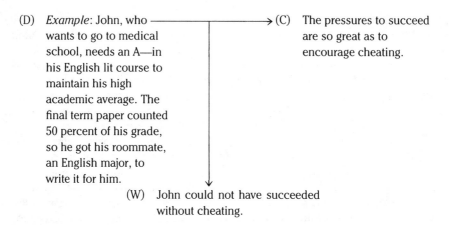

(D) *Example*: John, who → (C) The pressures to succeed
wants to go to medical   are so great as to
school, needs an A—in   encourage cheating.
his English lit course to
maintain his high
academic average. The
final term paper counted
50 percent of his grade,
so he got his roommate,
an English major, to
write it for him.

    (W) John could not have succeeded
        without cheating.

(D) *Analogy*: When a bill → (C) The effect of the present bill
cutting corporate taxes   to cut corporate taxes will
was passed before, prices   be to increase profits while
remained the same while   prices stay fixed.
profits increased.

    (W) Economic circumstances are
        similar and the effect of
        similar bills on profits and
        prices will be the same.

Such an exercise could help the critic describe how supporting materials seem designed to serve the ends of the speaker. It also offers insights into how arguments may be working and will provide the critic with specific data upon which to base observations on the logical soundness and/or psychological appeal of the overall argument of the speech. Such judgments may occur to the critic as he or she proceeds with the analysis of the text. These judgments, however, must be tentative. Only when the analysis of the text is complete and the critic begins to discern patterns and relationships in the discourse itself, and to relate these patterns to the context outside the discourse, can the critic make more definitive judgments.

Structure

As the critic analyzes the arguments that contribute to the goal of furthering the speaker's purpose, the critic will begin to discern the ways in which these arguments are put together in order to suggest relationships between them. Each idea developed by the speaker becomes the backdrop against which the next idea is painted. Thus, the ideas and supporting material of the speech form a pattern that the critic can identify and study to determine how well the speaker appears to be using the form in which the material is presented to move the audience toward acceptance of the persuasive purpose of the speech.

It is probably best for the critic to organize this phase of analysis by constructing a detailed outline of the speech. The critic should seek to identify the main ideas of the speech, arrange supporting material to discover the ways in which it serves to make the ideas believable and understandable to the audience, uncover the transitions and internal summaries that function to tie the ideas together, and isolate the ways in which the speaker sets the context for the speech in the introduction and gives direction to further audience thought and action in the conclusion. Such a reconstruction of the speech should point out for the critic the logical and psychological connections between the parts of the speech.

The critic is then in a position to understand the ways in which the speaker has arranged his or her ideas and material in order to promote such connections for the audience. That is, the critic, understanding how the speaker's ideas relate to each other, can describe the ways in which the speaker patterned those ideas into a meaningful sequence. The sequencing of ideas demonstrates how the speaker perceives, and/or wishes the audience to perceive, the nature of the issues under consideration. For example, if a speaker arranges his or her ideas in a *chronological* pattern, a historical view of the situation is suggested. This form will imply that what has happened in the past leads to the present state of events and provides clues with which to deal with present problems.

Several different patterns of organization are open to the speaker, and different patterns may predominate in different parts of the speech. These patterns are important to understand because they demonstrate the speaker's perspective on the problem and suggest the movement of ideas he or she wishes the audience to follow. A *topical* arrangement of ideas suggests independent ideas, which, taken together, show what the speaker thinks are the most relevant factors in the case. A speaker, for example, may develop economic, military, and political facets of a particular case, implying that moral or social considerations are not germane. A *cause-to-effect* or *effect-to-cause* development emphasizes the consequences of actions and events and can lead to the prediction of outcomes of actions taken by others as contrasted or compared with those advocated by the speaker. A *problem-solution* pattern defines the way the speaker perceives the problem, suggests criteria for the satisfactory solution of the problem, and shows how the speaker's solution meets those criteria. A *climactic* pattern may lead an audience from the most simple ideas to the most complex, or from ideas that are generally accepted and hence likely to be emotionally neutral to those that are more controversial and may generate highly intense emotional responses.

An investigation of the pattern or patterns that can be discerned in the speech points the critic's way to a fuller disclosure of the speaker's point of view with regard to the topic itself and to the speaker's conception of ways to motivate audiences. It should be understood, however, that the speaker may not *present* the speech in such a way that the pattern is immediately apparent. The critic's careful outline of the speech, for example, may show that when the speaker offers an idea that an audience might consider controversial or might react to with some initial antagonism, the speaker is using an indirect approach, carefully reviewing the evidence before fully disclosing the conclusion. In effect, the speaker turns the logical outline upside down, presenting the supporting material before disclosing the main idea that it supports. Another way of looking at this phenomenon might be to say that the critic, in order to see how ideas and evidence relate, prepares a *deductive* outline whereas the speaker may choose to deliver the speech *inductively*.

Style

Style is perhaps the most difficult single constituent of the rhetorical act for the critic. That is because the way in which a speaker uses language—from word choice to sentence construction to figurative devices—is so intimately bound up with the speaker's own personality and perspective, the audience's experiences and expectations, and the demands and constraints of the time that dictate "taste." The analysis of style is also complicated by the fact that it is very difficult to describe in such a way as to identify its unique qualities, and because it is so interwoven with meaning and argument.

Perhaps the overarching question for the critic to attempt to answer when considering style is concerned with the "fitness" of language. Traditionally, the test of good style is that it is clear, correct, appropriate, and exhibits pleasing aesthetic qualities. These criteria all depend on interaction among speaker, audience, and context. What is clear to one audience, to use an obvious example, may not be clear to an audience with less technical expertise or practical experience. Language that is appropriate in a classroom may not be appropriate when used in a formal address. The critic can examine these factors—clarity, correctness, appropriateness, and aesthetic appeal—seeking to discover how the language chosen and put together fits the constraints and expectations of the total situation. But the important thing for the critic to keep in mind in this analysis is that "fit" implies a *relationship*. The style of a speech is the result of the relationship between qualities and their potential to influence audiences.

A significant issue implied in fitness transcends the qualities of good style that have been enumerated. The critic has the additional responsibility to uncover the social, ethical, and logical implications of the use of language.

An argument, for example, may be furthered not only by supporting material. By using a parallel construction, for instance, a speaker may suggest parallel ideas or consequences to his or her audience so that language construction furthers analogy and thus becomes "evidence" in and of itself. As an example, a speaker might allege that "The American determination to insure liberty for all led us to found this nation. To insure liberty we fought each other over the issue of whether or not men and women could be held as property by other men. To insure liberty we twice sent our young men to die on battle grounds of Europe. To insure liberty we must stand ready today to sacrifice our bounty and our blood in whatever part of the world that liberty is threatened." The parallel construction of this segment clearly implies that historical situations are comparable to the present situation; it acts as a "proof" that what was done before must be done again. The critic, in this case, has the right to question whether such a stylistic construction is "fitting" support for the conclusion. The critic's scrutiny of style includes the search for the ways in which style is used to further the argument of the speech.

In his or her effort to understand the operation of style, the critic may focus on a number of specific stylistic elements. Analysis may be directed as discerning the *tone* of the speech suggested by style. Language signals the speaker's attitude —whether serious or light, comic or tragic, sympathetic or hostile, realistic or idealistic—toward the audience and the topic itself. A close study of style can reveal the *level of generality*, ranging from the abstract to the concrete, and the *level of complexity* evident in the choice of mono- or polysyllabic words, the length and configuration of sentences, and the like. The *diction* of the speech is indicated by the way the speaker's language suggests the level of formality with which he or she approaches the audience and the topic. The *texture* of the speech is uncovered by paying close attention to the speaker's stylistic devices; that is, by the way in which the speaker uses such schemes as parallelism or antithesis, figurative language such as similes or metaphors, and imagery.

The critical analysis of style, then, is guided by the careful examination of the *functions* of language in discourse. The critic's goal thus is to describe the ways in which language is *used* to promote the purpose of the speech and the potential influences of this use of language on listeners.

INTERPRETATION

The analysis of a speech provides the critic with a mass of specific detail concerning the way in which the speech has been crafted by the speaker's choices. As the analysis proceeds, the critic will inevitably, if peripherally, begin to assess the meaning of these data and their interrelatedness. But only when the analysis is finished can the critic devote full attention to drawing out and examining the patterns that have begun to emerge from the analysis.

After scrutinizing the argument, supporting material, structure, and style of a speech, the critic knows, if we may return to an earlier analogy, the anatomy of the discourse. Now the critic must make inferences about the physiology of the discourse. This process of inferring *how the discourse works* is interpretation.

Interpretation of a rhetorical work always involves the search for the meaning and function of the various parts of the text as they relate to the context. The critic's task is to explain how the text and context are mutually dependent and mutually effective; only through such an explanation can the critic promote readers' understanding and appreciation for the speech.

Traditionally, critics have sought to interpret a speech by assessing the ways in which the data show that the speaker has identified his or her rhetorical problems and opportunities and has adapted the materials of the speech to meet these circumstances. The audience has assumed a central place in traditional criticism, and the critic has sought to find significance in the speaker's adaptations to a particular audience. This critical focus tends to bear most directly on a speech as a unique event, a situation in which a speaker has a specific purpose to accomplish with a specific group of auditors. A traditional critical interpretation would be addressed to this situation.

Perhaps one of the most potent forces in shaping the thinking of modern critics has been the work of Kenneth Burke.[5] Burke's *dramatic criticism* is based on his conception of human beings as symbol-using animals who act out the social drama that is life by inducing action and shaping attitudes in others through language. For Burke, rhetoric is a means of using language to overcome the divisions that exist between people. He sees "the use of language as a symbolic means of inducing cooperation in beings that by nature respond to symbols."[6] *Identification*, a key term in the Burkeian scheme, is promoted when language is used to reduce divisiveness and to bring the speaker and listener closer together in their conceptions and perceptions of the world around them, the ultimate achievement being a psychological fusion that Burke calls *consubstantiality*.

A rhetor's language choices form a pattern that Burke calls a *strategy*, which is not a term employed exclusively by Burkeian critics. Indeed, almost any critic who describes a pattern of choices made by a speaker could be said to be describing a strategy. A traditional critic could look at a speaker's methods of adaptation to an audience and describe the way these methods work together to promote the speaker's purpose as a strategy. Generally, however, critics tend to consider strategy as a representation of a speaker's deliberate design in persuasion; choices have normally been thought of and written of as if they were *conscious* choices. Burke, who contends that identification "can include a partially 'unconscious' factor in appeal,"[7] conceives of strategies as the means of bringing about identification, and therefore admits the possibility that all strategies are not wholly intentional. The critic who would draw on Burke in interpreting a rhetorical act would seek to discover and illuminate the strategies operating through language that promotes the desired end of identification.

Traditionally, speeches have tended to be examined by critics as discrete entities. And, in a sense they are, the way a century or historical period is discrete, the way a painting or a film is discrete, and the way a person's life is discrete. Speeches have a beginning and ending that can be defined—arbitrarily, to be sure, but still logically. Nevertheless, rhetorical events are part of a *process*; they are influenced by and can influence other events. To understand fully the circumstances surrounding a speech act, the critic will need to understand other speech acts that have a bearing on it. It would be absurd, however, to say that useful criticism cannot result from the intensive investigation of one speech just as it would be ridiculous to assert that a critical analysis of *Hamlet* is not possible without a full analysis of all of Shakespeare's works, of all Elizabethan drama, or of all drama, for that matter. Even so, it surely must be recognized that rhetorical events can be shaped and directed by rhetorical events that have preceded them. Circumstances can circumscribe the limits of rhetorical options, for example, or mold audience expectations.

With this reality of the relatedness of rhetorical acts in mind, some critics have turned their attention to the ways in which situation can exert influence on discourse, that is, that similar contexts can evoke similar rhetorical responses. *Genre* denotes a similar grouping or species, and generic rhetorical criticism is a search for generalities that can be made about discourses in such matters as purpose, style, form, types of proof, and the like. Understanding generic features may lead the critic to a fuller comprehension of what an audience expects in certain situations, and may lead to the formulation of a set of criteria whereby the critic can determine how well any speaker has met those expectations. Mohrmann and Leff in their study of Lincoln, proposed Lincoln's Cooper Union address as an example of the genre of ingratiation,[8] arguing that political speeches are meant to ingratiate the speaker with significant audiences. Such an observation, if it is accepted, has implications for the understanding and evaluation of political speeches.

Acutely aware of the interrelatedness of rhetorical events, other critics have focused on units larger than the single speech and have studied the rhetorical processes involved in debates over important issues, political and other campaigns, and social movements. The obvious difficulty for the critic is in the almost overwhelming amount of rhetorical material that needs to be studied. Movement studies have become a significant area of investigation in rhetoric, but ways of organizing, processing, and interpreting the rhetorical artifacts of these movements are still to be refined.[9] But the critic of movement rhetoric assumes the task of interpreting a significant single rhetorical event in the light of rhetoric that precedes and follows it, seeking to find the meaning of rhetorical strategies in the way discourse progresses over time, the way it influences events, the way it is influenced by events, and how the whole process contributes ultimately to some resolution of the issue that called for movement in the first place.

It is not possible in the limited space available to describe, even as briefly as has been done previously, all the varieties of rhetorical criticism that are yielding useful perceptions of how rhetoric functions. The work of Ernest G. Bormann on fantasy theme analysis, of Thomas B. Farrell on social reality, of Michael Calvin McGee on ideographs, of Walter R. Fisher on the narrative paradigm, of Stephen E. Lucas and Michael C. Leff on textual analysis, are only a few examples of important work that has broken new ground and provided imaginative and illuminating ways of interpreting rhetorical events. Careful study of the results of such inquiries can enlarge the novice critic's view of the possibilities of criticism.[10]

Regardless of the method of interpretation that directs the critic's efforts, it should be recognized that a crucial function of interpretation is to isolate the significant. No critique will evenhandedly discuss every aspect of the discourse that is capable of being discussed. The purpose of an exhaustive analysis of a rhetorical act is not to provide material that demands the critic's attention. Indeed, to consider the analytical categories as some kind of checklist of items that must be discussed is to move toward a sterile, formulaic description that submerges interpretation. On the basis of the data, the critic discovers—and can *substantiate* that discovery—what is most meaningful in the discourse under investigation. Interpretation, by examining and explaining the unique and the meaningful in discourse, is then a creative process that leads to insight and not a clerical chore that simply touches all the bases.

JUDGMENT

In the first chapter of this book criticism was defined as "the systematic process of illuminating and evaluating products of human activity." The final step in the process that has been described thus far is evaluation—reaching a reasoned judgment. "Reasoned" is to be emphasized. The rhetorical critic does not judge a speech on the basis of quick impressions; any critic who has gone through the analytical and interpretive stages of investigation has become intimately aware of the workings of the discourse in its context. It remains to reach a defensible conclusion on the quality of the speech.

A judgment may take different forms. Essentially, the judgment made on a rhetorical act or series of acts depends on the standards of judgment—the criteria—that are employed. In reaching a judgment, and in evaluating the judgments reached by other critics, we must look to the criteria advanced explicitly or implicitly suggested.

The criteria may derive from a variety of perspectives, depending on the critic's perception of his or her function, the nature of the evidence that has been uncovered in the examination of the discourse, or the demands—self- or situationally imposed—on the speaker. Basically, judgments are made on the grounds of audience receptiveness and potential audience effects, logical and intellectual validity, and social consequences. Some critics might wish to say that rhetoric can be judged as an art form; that is the *ultimate* judgment. An artistic work, however, one that is unflawed, is one that encompasses *all* the relevant possible criteria: Rhetoric has truly reached the highest artistic pinnacle when it can be said to be effective, intellectually sound, and of benefit to humanity. That is the perfection toward which the best rhetoric strives, but which cannot frequently be reached.

Even though a speech may be flawed in one sense it can still be judged positively with regard to the other elements that are subsumed under the overriding artistic evaluation. Critics, however, no matter how systematic they are and no matter how rigidly they adhere to the demand that their conclusions be based on soundly arguable conclusions, will differ in their values and in their views of both the nature and role of rhetoric. This being so, certain bases for judgment may be more important to some critics that to others.

Judgments based on audience receptiveness will be determined by the potential effect of the discourse. (We have already discussed in some detail the problems of determining effect.) If a speech is judged effective it is, according to this criterion, "good" speech. Judged by intellectual or logical validity, a speech may be determined to be a "good" if the arguments advanced are sound, based on the best possible evidence available and leading to the conclusions that are warranted by that evidence. Using social consequences as a criterion, a critic would reach a positive judgment about a speech that promoted social welfare and contributed to furthering values that were most conducive to a full realization of the human and humane potential of listeners.

Depending on the critic's point of view, for example, he or she might consider the results of the analysis of a particular argument in different ways. A critic might look at an argument and determine that, since it so closely conformed to the prejudices and beliefs of the audience, it needed little development and was thus a good argument because the conclusion reached would be readily acceptable to the designated listeners. Another critic looking at the same argument might point to the fact that the example used was stereotypical, and even though the audience accepted its stereotypical quality as fact, it was not strong enough to support logically the conclusion drawn from it. A third critic could point out that the examples played on the darker prejudices of the audience and thus reinforced a conception of another group of individuals in such a way as to promote strife and divisiveness.

These perspectives are not mutually exclusive. The same critic might look at material in the speech and evaluate its worth with all three viewpoints in mind. Certain cases might make ethical considerations more relevant than logical ones, and vice versa. The paramount consideration for the critic is that he or she articulate criteria and demonstrate clearly and logically how the rhetorical effort under consideration meets them.

SUMMARY

Analysis, interpretation, and judgment are the principal means whereby the critic pursues his or her art. All these means are part of the process characterized by rigorous and careful examination in which the discourse and its context become the data out of which sound critical conclusions grow.

To summarize these steps and to help the beginning critic organize his or her approach to the rhetorical act, the following set of questions may serve as a guide:

1. What is the principal argument of the speech?
2. What is the implied purpose of the speech? How does it compare with the stated purpose?
3. What are the individual arguments? How are they constructed?
4. What specific forms of support can be identified? How do they function to promote conclusions?
5. What are the main ideas of a speech? How do they relate to the specific materials presented and to each other?
6. What functions do introduction, conclusion, and transitions play in promoting the movement of the speech?
7. Is a predominant pattern of development evident in the speech? Are there subpatterns within the speech?
8. What do the patterns suggest about the speaker's perspective on the issues involved and his or her perception of a desirable audience perspective?
9. How may the speech's tone, level of generality, level of complexity, diction, and texture be described?
10. What function does language appear to play in furthering the argument of the speech?
11. Given the analytical findings, what consistent patterns or strategies emerge in the areas of argument, supporting material, structure, and style?
12. How may these patterns be related to the entire rhetorical situation—context, audience, speaker—in which the rhetorical act took place?
13. What significant rhetorical meaning or meanings can be placed on this act within the rhetorical process of which it forms a part?
14. In what ways and to what extent does the speech engage the audience?
15. In what ways and to what extent does the speech exhibit sound intellectual and reasonable judgment?
16. What are the probable consequences to society of the speech's ideas and information, and the strategic patterns of ideas and information?

_____ NOTES _____

1. This is not to say that the speech itself is always the most important single variable in a context. The critic should not fall into the trap of believing that the speech is always *the* causal factor in whatever follows it. For insights into the impact, or lack of it, of the speech itself, see, e.g., Wayne C. Minnick, "A Case Study in Persuasive Effect: Lyman Beecher on Duelling," *Speech Monographs*, 38 (1971), 262–276; Robert W. Norton, "The Rhetorical Situation is the Message: Muskie's Election Eve Broadcast," *Central States Speech Journal*, 22 (1971), 171–178.

2. The notion of "good" argument, and related questions of judgment, is discussed later in this chapter.

3. *Congressional Record, House of Representatives*, March 15, 1963, 5059–5061.

4. Stephen E. Toulman, *The Uses of Argument* (Cambridge: Cambridge University Press, 1958); see, also, Wayne Brockriede and Douglas Ehninger, "Toulman on Argument: An Interpretation and Application," *Quarterly Journal of Speech*, 46 (1960), 44–53; Charles Arthur Willard, "On the Utility of Descriptive Diagrams for the Analysis and Criticism of Arguments," *Communication Monographs*, 43 (1976), 308–319.

5. See particularly Kenneth Burke, *A Grammar of Motives and a Rhetoric of Motives* (New York: Meridian Books, 1962). An excellent example of Burke's own rhetorical criticism is "The Rhetoric of Hitler's 'Battle,'" in *The Philosophy of Literary Form* (New York: Vintage Books, 1957), pp. 164–189. See, also, Marie Hochmuth Nichol's essay on Burke, "Kenneth Burke and the 'New Rhetoric,'" *Quarterly Journal of Speech*, 38 (1952), 133–144.

6. Burke, *A Grammar of Motives and A Rhetoric of Motives*, p. 567.

7. Kenneth Burke, "Rhetoric—Old and New," *The Journal of General Education*, 5 (1951), 203. For an interesting and perceptive discussion of intentionality, see Robert L. Scott, "Intentionality in the Rhetorical Process," *Rhetoric in Transition: Studies in the Nature and Uses of Rhetoric*, ed. by Eugene E. White (University Park: The Pennsylvania State University Press, 1980), pp. 39–60.

8. Michael C. Leff and G. P. Mohrmann, "Lincoln at Cooper Union: A Rhetorical Analysis of the Text," *Quarterly Journal of Speech*, 60 (1974), 346–358.

9. An entire issue of the *Central States Speech Journal*, 31 (1980), 225–319, was devoted to the rhetorical study of movements. Included in the issue are Leland M. Griffin, "On Studying Movements"; Michael Calvin McGee, "'Social Movement': Phenomenon or Meaning?"; David Zarefsky, "A Skeptical View of Movement Studies"; Stephen E. Lucas, "Coming to Terms with Movement Studies"; Robert S. Cathcart, "Defining Social Movements by Their Rhetorical Form"; James R. Andrews, "History and Theory in the Study of the Rhetoric of Social Movements"; Carol J. Jablonski, "Promoting Radical Change in the Roman Catholic Church: Rhetorical Requirements, Problems and Strategies of the American Bishops"; Ralph R. Smith, "The Historical Criticism of Social Movements"; Charles J. Stewart, "A Functional Approach to the Rhetoric of Social Movements"; Herbert W. Simons, "On Terms, Definitions and Theoretical Distinctiveness: Comments on Papers by McGee and Zarefsky." See also, Suzanne Volmar Riches and Malcolm O. Sillors, "The Status of Movement Criticism," *Western Journal of Speech Communications*, 44 (1980), 275–287.

10. See, e.g., Ernest G. Bormann, "Fantasy and Rhetorical Vision: The Rhetorical Criticism of Social Reality," *Quarterly Journal of Speech*, 58 (1972), 397–407; Thomas B. Farrell, "Knowledge, Consensus, and Rhetorical Theory," *Quarterly Journal of Speech*, 62 (1976), 1–14; Michael Calvin McGee, "The 'Ideograph': A Link Between Rhetoric and Ideology," *Quarterly Journal of Speech*, 66 (1980), 1–16; Walter R. Fisher, "Narration as Human Communication Paradigm: The Case of Public Moral Argument," *Communication Monographs*, 51 (1984), 1–22; Stephen E. Lucas, "The Renaissance of American Public Address," *Quarterly Journal of Speech*, 74 (1988), 241–260; Michael C. Leff, "Textual Criticism: The Legacy of G. P. Mohrmann," *Quarterly Journal of Speech*, 72 (1986), 377–389. See the bibliographies at the end of this book for additional citations.

Afterword:
The Practice
of Rhetorical
Criticism

Herbert Muller once wrote, "...most precious are the works that man has consciously preserved, in defiance of time."[1] Among the most precious works that we have sought to preserve are rhetorical ones, products of human thought and imagination that define the world we live in, make sense of what we have experienced, and influence events that shape our future.

In the crucial civilizing task of preservation, the rhetorical critic plays an important role. For preservation implies not only the physical maintenance of intellectual artifacts but also learning to understand them, to judge their worth, and to apply what is valuable in them to various facets of human activity.

The rhetorical critic's central concern must be with discourse. The introductory principles discussed in this book are designed to focus the beginning critic's attention on rhetorical messages as they exist within social and historical contexts. The complex of interactions that take place between a speaker and his or her audience is never easy to understand fully—indeed, *total* comprehension of any rhetorical exchange is not to be obtained. The critic, nevertheless, strives to come as close to the achievement of that goal as he or she can to contribute his or her mite to the ongoing work of other rhetorical scholars.

Becoming a critic involves the careful practice of a craft. The rhetorical critic "practices" in the sense that any professional does, through the continuous application of specialized knowledge to situations for which he or she is trained. The critic also "practices" in the sense that he or she works at the task in order to enhance proficiency. A rhetorical critic is perpetually a student, learning more about rhetorical theory, reading the great mass of recorded human discourse, studying and assessing the criticism of others, and immersing himself or herself in the social-political-historical milieu in which discourse takes place. Most importantly, however, a practicing rhetorical critic *does* criticism.

The first efforts at criticism will be modest. The critic needs to become familiar with and confident in the use of the data with which he or she habitually works and the tools that will enable the critic to analyze materials with thoroughness, interpret findings with clarity and imagination, and judge discourse with discrimination.

The aim of this book is to provide the beginning critic with a systematic way of undertaking the critical process. Basic to any critical system or methodological approach is the stipulation that the critic be prepared to investigate the texts, the contexts, and their interactions. The critics' proficiency will grow with increased experience and expanding knowledge, and will develop as they apply imaginative and disciplined efforts to understand rhetorical acts. A painter may break exciting new ground with his or her creative use of form, balance, color, or perspective; but form, balance, color, and perspective are fundamental concepts that the artist must understand in order to use them in a novel, or arresting manner. The critic as artist must delve deeply into the components of the communication act, understanding the basic processes of inception, construction, presentation, and reception of rhetorical messages; only then may the critic's findings be communicated to others in a clear, reasoned, and insightful manner.

The questions presented as summaries in the preceding chapters offer a starting point from which to begin to do criticism. New questions or new ways of raising old questions will occur to the critic as he or she gains in maturity. The critic will soon realize that a single piece of criticism rarely answers all the questions; indeed, many questions will be irrelevant or of minor importance in certain cases. But, taken as a whole, they suggest a broad set of topics that are worthy of careful consideration.

The goal, of course, is to write good criticism. Good criticism is that which ultimately promotes a richer understanding of the influence and operation of discourse and contributes to the comprehension and refinement of humane values. Such goals are reached through the systematic and thorough investigation of relevant evidence, which leads to reasoned conclusions based on sound argument, and through the formulation of judgments based on clear, defensible criteria.

The best way to reach these goals is to undertake criticism seriously and to apply rigorous standards of scholarship to the undertaking. Practice will never make the critic perfect, but as we develop in our art we will grow in our own perceptiveness and in our appreciation of the ways in which human beings have sought to solve human problems; we may also contribute to the knowledge of the uniquely human process of communication and to the preservation of the highest standards of human conduct. Such a task is well worth undertaking.

_____ **NOTE** _____

1. Herbert J. Muller, *The Uses of the Past* (New York: Mentor Books, 1954), p. 393.

PART
TWO

Critical Case
Studies

INTRODUCTION

Following are two speeches given by American Presidents at crucial periods in our history. Along with the speeches are critical essays by prominent rhetorical critics.

The first speech, Abraham Lincoln's "Second Inaugural Address", is, as David Zarefsky notes, "justly acclaimed among the masterpieces of American public discourse." Professor Zarefsky's introductory essay, "Approaching Lincoln's Second Inaugural Address," explains briefly the reasons for such an appraisal and then goes on to examine the premises and assumptions underlying the four essays that follow. He raises a question of great importance to students of criticism: Can all the critics be right? Focusing attention on "the standards of argument which are fashioned and used by critics," Professor Zarefsky underlines the importance of this series of studies for students learning to do criticism: "Reading these essays which focus on a single significant text should prompt thought about the assessment of critical practice...."

The second speech, Richard M. Nixon's "Address to the Nation on the War in Vietnam," aroused controversy when it was given and led to critical controversy, as well, when scholars attempted to assess the merits of the speech. The four critical studies presented here demonstrate how different critics can approach the same speech from varying perspectives, with contrasting methodologies, and can reach differing critical judgments. The exchange between two of these critics, Karlyn Campbell and Forbes Hill, affords an excellent illustration of divergent views on the nature, function, and method of rhetorical criticism held by two mature rhetorical scholars.

A B R A H A M
LINCOLN

Second Inaugural Address

When Abraham Lincoln was inaugurated for a second term on March 4, 1865, the great Civil War that had raged for four years was coming to a close. It had been a costly war with casualties ranging between 33 and 40 percent of the forces on both sides. A movement in the summer of 1864 among radicals in his own party to deny Lincoln the nomination had been turned back, and Lincoln had successfully killed a radical plan for reconstruction of the South, the Wade-Davis Bill; but it was clear, nevertheless, that many expected harsh punishment to follow the demise of the Confederacy. Lincoln, while still a leader of a nation at war with itself, not only reviewed the past in this short inaugural address, but, also, looked forward to the trials of reconciliation and reconstruction that would face the country once the peace was won.

Fellow-countrymen, at this second appearing to take the oath of the presidential office there is less occasion for an extended address than there was at the first. Then a statement somewhat in detail of a course to be pursued seemed fitting and proper. Now, at the expiration of four years, during which public declarations have been constantly called forth on every point and phase of the great contest which still absorbs the attention and engrosses the energies of the nation, little that is new could be presented. The progress of our arms, upon which all else chiefly depends, is as well known to the public as to myself, and it is, I trust, reasonably satisfactory and encouraging to all. With high hope for the future, no prediction in regard to it is ventured.

On the occasion corresponding to this four years ago all thoughts were anxiously directed to an impending civil war. All dreaded it, all sought to avert it. While the inaugural address was being delivered from this place, devoted altogether to *saving* the Union without war, insurgent agents were in the city seeking to *destroy* it without war-seeking to dissolve the Union and divide effects by negotiation. Both parties deprecated war, but one of them would *make* war rather than let the nation survive, and the other would *accept* war rather than let it perish, and the war came.

One-eighth of the whole population was colored slaves, not distributed generally over the Union, but localized in the southern part of it. These slaves constituted a peculiar and powerful interest. All knew that this interest was somehow the cause of the war. To strengthen, perpetuate, and extend this interest was the object for which the insurgents would rend the Union even by war, while the Government claimed no right to do more than to restrict the territorial enlargement of it. Neither party expected for the war the magnitude or the duration which it has already attained. Neither anticipated that the *cause* of the conflict might cease with or even before the conflict itself should cease. Each looked for an easier triumph, and a result less fundamental and astounding. Both read the same Bible and pray to the same God, and each invokes His aid against the other. It may seem strange that any men should dare to ask a just God's assistance in wringing their bread from the sweat of other men's faces, but let us judge not, that we be not judged. The prayers of both could not be answered. That of neither has been answered fully. The Almighty has His own purposes. "Woe unto the world because of offenses; for it must needs be that offenses come, but woe to that man by whom the offense cometh." If we shall suppose that American slavery is one of those offenses which, in the providence of God, must needs come, but which, having continued through His appointed time, He now wills to remove, and that He gives to both North and South this terrible war as the woe due to those by whom the offense came, shall we discern therein any departure from those divine attributes which the believers in a living God always ascribe to Him? Fondly do we hope, fervently do we pray, that this mighty scourge of war may speedily pass away. Yet, if God wills that it continue until all the wealth piled by the bondsman's two hundred and fifty years of unrequited toil shall be sunk, and until every drop of blood drawn with the lash shall be paid by another drawn with the sword, as was said three thousand years ago, so still it must be said, "The judgments of the Lord are true and righteous altogether."

With malice toward none, with charity for all, with firmness in the right as God gives us to see the right, let us strive on to finish the work we are in, to bind up the nation's wounds, to care for him who shall have borne the battle and for his widow and his orphan, to do all which may achieve and cherish a just and lasting peace among ourselves and with all nations.

Approaching Lincoln's Second Inaugural Address

DAVID ZAREFSKY

Abraham Lincoln's Second Inaugural Address is justly acclaimed among the masterpieces of American public discourse. A cluster of reasons helps to explain its canonical status in the study of political rhetoric.

To begin with, the speech is an interesting and imaginative response to a historical situation. It followed an election, held in the midst of the Civil War, in which Lincoln's re-election was anything but certain. Democrats had recovered quickly from the debacle of 1860; they had made impressive gains in the 1862 midterm elections, reducing by half the Republican majority in Congress. Many opposed emancipation and wished to abandon the war as futile; certainly they did not support the broader war aims which had evolved in the wake of Antietam. In early 1864 the Administration was beset by eroding public confidence in its prosecution of the war, and doubts were expressed even by Republicans as to whether Lincoln should be renominated or could be re-elected. He prevailed partly through astute management of the platform and his selection as running mate of Tennessee War Democrat Andrew Johnson.

Sensing victory in the face of Republican division, Democrats nominated the deposed but popular Union General George B. McClellan and ran on a peace platform. It was an attractive combination. Fear that it might succeed, together with a succession of good news about the war, led Republicans to close ranks during the fall. Even so, the election was expected to be very close; that Lincoln prevailed with 55% of the popular vote and a landslide in the Electoral College was a surprise probably even to him. By March of 1865, the outcome of the war was no longer in doubt, but there was considerable disagreement about what the nature of the postwar Union should be. Lincoln needed both to acknowledge the seemingly miraculous military and electoral results and also to articulate a course of action which—despite those triumphs—would surely be controversial.

Essential to these tasks was an explanation or accounting for the war, and here again the Inaugural is a fascinating study. It both acknowledges the original justification for war (preservation of the Union) and defines slavery as the underlying root cause. That is a considerable change from Lincoln's position before and during the early years of the war. In 1861, for example, he would have accepted the *proposed* 13th Amendment which would have guaranteed slavery in perpetuity where it already existed. The Second Inaugural completes a slow but steady evolution of Lincoln's thought.

The explanation Lincoln offers fuses the secular and the sacred; he sees the war as Divine punishment for moral offenses. By implication, changing Northern attitudes about slavery and race was a process of atonement for sin, and only when the cleansing had been completed would the "scourge of war" pass away. Seeing God's design in everyday events was a frequent theme in early American discourse. It was important to discern the meaning in calamitous events so that God might call off the plague or so that the people might avert even worse danger.

The speech, then, falls within the genre which Bormann (1977) has called "fetching good out of evil," an adaptation of the jeremiad. But it is also, of course, an Inaugural Address, and it is worthy of study because it ably meets the generic requirements identified by Campbell and Jamieson (1986, p. 205). The speech reconstitutes the audience as "the people" who are not only collectively present on this occasion but recall a similar event four years before. It recalls values drawn from the past, from the commonalities between the two sections of the country to their common dependence on God. At least by implication it sets forth the political principle of a reconstruction policy which is charitable and magnanimous, consistent with Lincoln's belief that the seceding states never really left the Union. And by placing the ultimate course of the war in God's hands, Lincoln clearly acknowledges the limits of Executive ability. The Second Inaugural, then, is a fit subject for generic criticism.

The speech is also noteworthy for its stylistic features, ranging from the awkwardly passive reference to the occasion ("this second appearing to take the oath") to the parallel structure of "Both read the same Bible, and pray to the same

God," to the stark simplicity of "And the war came." Finally, of course, the speech achieves significance in retrospect as a kind of valedictory statement by Lincoln and, with respect to reconstruction, a poignant reminder of the road not taken.

For all that, the speech as a text has not engaged the serious or sustained attention of communication scholars. Even less frequently have several scholars focused on it together, approaching it from different perspectives and with different methods. That is the special value of the essays which follow. They originally were presented at the 1987 joint convention of the Central States Speech Association and the Southern Speech Communication Association. Those present at the program remember stimulating presentations and a fascinating discussion in which the authors often focused on one another's premises and underlying assumptions.

Carpenter's is the most explicitly historical of the essays here. Taking issue with Bormann's (1985) judgment that Lincoln evolved from the "ungenteel style" to a rich and poetic style, Carpenter traces several of the key phrases in the speech to letters and documents during the preceding months in which Lincoln's style was anything but "poetic." He concludes that the "poetic compression" which Bormann identified "*also* evinces pragmatic considerations." The religious motif which has become so celebrated was viewed by Lincoln as a distraction, and may have been intended only to boast that God was on the side of the Union.

Aune attempts to contextualize the Second Inaugural within a larger discourse about American individualism, "which Lincoln both incorporates and subverts." Aune argues that Lincoln transforms the vision of self from expressive and acquisitive to the self as Suffering Servant, and that the Scriptural motif of the speech helps to achieve this transformation of self. He describes how the use of various figures in the text serves to replace one vision of self with another.

Both Leff and Solomon offer close readings of the text, and both assume that the text is not static but that there is significant rhetorical *movement* from beginning to end. They differ in method and, not surprisingly, in the results of the reading. Leff focuses on references to temporality in order to capture the movement through time within the text. He finds movement from the past through the present and toward the future, and a movement from secular time (continuous and irreversible) to sacred time (circular and reversible, because it always calls us back to origins). The underlying dynamic of the speech. Leff believes, is the "creative equivocations" between sacred and secular time which make it possible for listeners to comprehend the agonies of war as part of a Divine plan.

Solomon begins with the premise that, however much the speech has been venerated in the eyes of history, it was unpersuasive in its own time. It did not diminish the Radical Republican desire for retribution against the South. Solomon seeks to explain the contemporary failure of the speech, not by conveniently assuming that the audience was not up to it, but by reference to the progression of the text. Employing methods akin to deconstruction and reader response criticism, she concludes that there is a tension in the text. The second and third paragraphs develop such a moral contrast between the two sections—with the right so clearly on the Northern side—that the listener is not prepared for the "with malice toward none" appeal of the final paragraph. Indeed, if the second and third paragraphs are correctly read, then the last paragraph is out of place in the speech and retribution (or, at least, punishment) is called for.

Solomon explicitly states her goal as achieving "an alternate understanding of [the] 'message'" of the text and demonstrating "that Lincoln's text is open to alternate interpretations." Carpenter likewise wants to find a reading of the text that stands as an alternative to Bormann's. Other critics imply similar goals. Certainly it is a valuable service for critics to demonstrate that significant texts can be read in more than one way, for one of the most valuable functions of criticism is to render received wisdom contingent. But what then? Are all alternate understandings equally sound? Do they all make similar claims upon readers? Affirmative answers to these questions would render criticism nihilistic, unconstrained by the text or even by language itself. But negative answers would seem to imply an absolute authority in the text, denying the influence of the knower on the known, ignoring the wisdom succinctly expressed by Clark (1982, p. 300): "Documents do not speak, they must be spoken for."

This is the central issue in the politics of criticism. All criticism is in a sense ideological, since it is the work of critics who have interests. Yet a vicious relativism undermines the mission of criticism itself, replacing it with polemic. Confronted with different views of the same text, how then do we distinguish interpretation from misinterpretation? In a recent essay (Zarefsky, 1987) I suggested that embracing Brockriede's (1974) view of criticism as argument will yield critical standards. Attention to the *persona* of the critic as arguer and the norms imposed by critics as a discourse community will enable us to specify some of the constraints on acceptable critical arguments. For example, it is reasonable to expect that a critic exploring historical influences on Lincoln would not confine the study to Radical Republicans just because he or she sympathized with the Radical position. And one would not expect such an analysis to include events which occurred after Lincoln's death. The former practice would place the critic in the role of irresponsible partisan; the latter would violate the norm of the critical community that alleged causes must precede their alleged effects.

Most importantly, norms underlying the concept of "rhetorical validity" can help to distinguish sound from unsound critical argument. Sound arguments are addressed to the general audience of critical readers, not just to the adherents of a particular "school" or perspective. They correspond to what is known about context. They open their own reasoning processes to scrutiny. And they maintain the critical conversation (see Zarefsky, 1987, for elaboration of these standards).

A comparison between the Leff and Solomon essays may be instructive here. Solomon's "problem" is the paradox that a speech judged in retrospect as eloquent was unpersuasive in its original context. She counts as a strength of her analysis that it explains this paradox. In contrast, she is relatively unconcerned with the language of the first paragraph, dismissing it as mundane. For Leff it is just the reverse. He appears not to be interested in the effects of the speech but in its internal dynamics and particularly in the search for textual unity around the motif of temporal movement. *His* paradox is, in part, the prevalence in the text of such a seemingly contrived use of the passive voice. The first paragraph of the speech is central to his analysis.

In the case of this example, of course, there is no need to choose. Although the accounts are quite different, Leff and Solomon could both be right. In Griffin's (1952) felicitous metaphor, they are turning the text on a spit, "piercing it now from one angle, now from another." But if the two perspectives were at odds, we would know the grounds on which to choose between them: Does resolving a paradox count as a benefit of a rhetorical analysis? Are the paradoxes accurately identified by Leff and Solomon? Which of the two paradoxes is the more important to resolve? These questions imply standards of argument which are fashioned and used by critics as members of a discourse community.

A more obvious case of conflict might be between Carpenter and Bormann: Did Lincoln, or did he not, "abandon" the ungenteel style? Here the dispute turns largely on the question of whether Lincoln should be viewed in the context of his own discourse in the months preceding the speech, or against the broader sweep of early 19th century trends in public discourse. The heart of the question is what evidence is privileged, and that too is a matter of argument.

Reading these essays which focus on a single significant text should prompt thought about the assessment of critical practice, as well as about the rhetorical artistry of Lincoln's Second Inaugural Address.

References

Bormann, Ernest G. (1977). Fetching good out of evil: A rhetorical use of calamity. *Quarterly Journal of Speech, 63,* 130–139.

———. (1985) *The force of fantasy: Restoring the American dream.* Carbondale: Southern Illinois Univ. Press.

Brockriede, Wayne. (1974). Rhetorical criticism as argument. *Quarterly Journal of Speech, 60,* 165–174.

Campbell, Karlyn Kohrs, and Kathleen Hall Jamieson. (1986). Inaugurating the presidency. In *Form, genre, and the study of political discourse,* ed. Herbert W. Simons and Aram A. Aghazarian. Columbia: Univ. of South Carolina Press.

Clark, E. Culpepper. (1982). Argument and historical analysis. In *Advances in argumentation theory and research,* ed. J. Robert Cox and Charles Arthur Willard. Carbondale: Southern Illinois Univ. Press.

Griffin, Leland M. (1952). The rhetoric of historical movements. *Quarterly Journal of Speech, 38,* 184–188.

Zarefsky, David. (1987). Argumentation and the politics of criticism. In *Argument and Critical Practices: Proceedings of the Fifth Summer Conference on Argumentation,* eds. Joseph W. Wenzel, Malcolm O. Sillars, Gregg B. Walker. (Annandale, Virginia: SCA, 1987).

Lincoln and the American Sublime

JAMES ARNT AUNE

To begin with, I want to steal (and twist to my own purposes) an analogy which Richard Rorty (1985) used in a debate at the University of Virginia against E. D. Hirsch.

Interpreters are much like a band of anthropologists camped uneasily at the outskirts of the village of an unfamiliar tribe. Every time they approach the village, they hear a series of utterances in an unknown language, followed by a barrage of spears.

Now, these are a sharply divided band of anthropologists. They differ widely on how to interpret their situation and the tribe's language. The traditionalist anthropologist wants to ascertain the objective intention of the tribe. (He's concerned that the younger anthropologists aren't as well trained at this as they should be.) So, he does a good deal of research in his portable library on other native langauges in the area. The hermeneutic anthropologist sneaks into the village at night, goes native, and eventually joins the tribe in an attack on the other anthropologists. The deconstructionist is so preoccupied with the interplay of presence and absence in the flight of the spears that she is killed almost instantly. The Marxist is killed when the natives misinterpret his words, "Counter-Hegemonic Praxis," for a battle cry. The pragmatist simply gets the hell out of there.

I'm not sure that interpretation is quite such a dangerous activity as this analogy implies—although it depends on one's critic. Nonetheless, at a time when our common political culture seems to be disintegrating as a result of many factors, there is a kind of existential danger in reading a text such as Lincoln's "Second Inaugural" (1963). We all are in the business, if we look beyond FTE's and the line items on our vitas, of communicating the significance of texts such as this one to our students and colleagues. If we fail to communicate that significance, something more than our own reputations is at stake.

I recently had the privilege of teaching this text to a group of eighteen undergraduates, mostly juniors and seniors, in a course in American Public Address at St. Olaf College. They are the sort of students every teacher dreams of: almost all of them have read Plato, Shakespeare, and the Bible, can write a coherent essay, and aren't interested in how to get a job in public relations. None of them, however, had read the "Second Inaugural," Washington's, "Farewell Address," the Federalist Papers, or King's Letter from Birmingham Jail. Somehow, the process of canon-formation in the liberal arts had failed to touch on public address.

My purpose in this paper is a pragmatic one. I have no wish to establish the priority of my own orientation over those of other readers of Lincoln, but rather to locate our conversation about this text within the larger conversation of American culture. In doing so, I want first to reflect upon the relationship between public address studies and cultural studies, and then to locate Lincoln's "Second Inaugural" within the larger American discourse about individualism, a discourse which Lincoln both incorporates and subverts.

The study of public address exists in the space between social and intellectual history. Its concern, as James Boyd White (1984) puts it, is the "study of the ways in which character and community—and motive, value, reason, social structure, everything, in short, that makes a culture—are defined and made real in performances of language" (p. xi). The ethical and political thrust of public address studies consists in its ability to characterize ways of reconstituting or subverting rhetorical traditions. White says, "As the object of art is beauty and of philosophy truth, the object of rhetoric is justice: the constitution of the social world" (p. xi). Any account of Lincoln's speech, at least from a pragmatic standpoint, must come to terms with the sort of social world it presumes and wishes for.

The constitution of the social world in America, however, has always been somewhat uneasy. Harold Bloom (1976) has described what he calls the distinctiveness of the American Sublime. He swerves away from Kenneth Burke's concern with rebirth in order to emphasize what he calls "the even more hyperbolical trope of self-begetting." This trope, he writes, "is the starting point of the last Western Sublime, the great sunset of selfhood in the evening land" (p. 244). Scholars have paid a good deal of attention to Lincoln's images of rebirth, but I think we can make a case for the priority of images of self in his rhetoric.

There is a growing consensus in American cultural studies, as represented by the work of Bloom (1975, 1976), Bercovitch (1975), and the authors of *Habits of the Heart* (1985), that American public discourse is uniquely characterized by a focus on the individual. One might say that Americans typically use what Bellah, et al., call a "first language" (I would prefer the term "primary rhetoric") of individualism (pp. 20, 134). This primary rhetoric manifests itself in three closely linked, yet contradictory, notions of the self.

First, a divinely anointed self. As Bercovitch points out, our Puritan cultural heritage gave many Americans a sense of the self as chosen by God to create the New Jerusalem in the wilderness. The rhetorical possibilities of this stance towards the self, from the abolitionists to Manifest Destiny to Ronald Reagan, are all too clear.

Second, an expressive self. Here, the self comes dangerously close to being equated with God. Emerson (1983) experiences his epiphany of the "Transparent Eyeball" on a wintry hillside, and sees himself as "part and parcel of God" (p. 10). Thoreau (1968) rejects his communal ties in the name of a higher self. Whitman (1958) finds a "Kosmos" in himself. Shirley MacLaine and David Manning face the surf on a Malibu beach, arms outstretched like Jesus on the cross. They shout in unison, "I am God!" (cited in Gardner, 1987, p. 16).

Third, an acquisitive self. From Benjamin Franklin's autobiography to Henry Ford to my students' T-shirts that read, "He who has the most toys when he dies, wins," American capitalism has encouraged a sense of self as upwardly mobile, free to cast off all commitments in the name of property.

The problem, of course, with these three notions of the self (with the possible exception of the divinely anointed self) is that they don't work well in times of crisis. In rhetorical terms, one might say that Kenneth Burke's notion of identification missed a key feature of much crisis rhetoric: the way it relieves audiences from the burden of having a self. Longinus' notion of the Sublime seems to capture that sense of release from self, that ek-stasis, or ecstasy, when one is taken out of everyday life.

If eloquence consists in a loss of sense of self, how is that loss manifested in Lincoln's "Second Inaugural"? How are character and community, in White's words, defined and made real in this performance of language? Lincoln's speech works by subverting existing American concepts of the self. He translates them into a higher vision of the self by identifying himself and his audience with the self as Suffering Servant, an image which he draws from the prophet Isaiah and the self-understanding of Jesus.

Lincoln felt the burdens of selfhood acutely. His ambition, as Herndon (1961) tells us, "was a little engine that knew no rest" (p. 304). As Bellah, et al., write, "Lincoln conforms perfectly to the archetype of the lonely, individualistic hero. His dual moral commitment to the preservation of the Union and the belief that 'all men are created equal' roused the hostility of abolitionists and Southern sympathizers alike. In the war years, he was more and more isolated, misunderstood by Congress and cabinet, and unhappy at home" (p. 146). Incapable of orthodox religious belief, he nonetheless had, as Niebuhr writes, a deeper biblical understanding of the Civil War than any contemporary theologian (cited in Bellah et al., 1985, p. 147). He also led this country at a time of social dislocation caused by massive capital accumulation. In 1800, the wealthiest 10% of the population controlled around 40% of the wealth. By 1860, they controlled 70%. The average worker's income fell in relation to the cost of living during that period (Porter, 1981, p. 64).

The acquisitive self (in the form of capitalism), the divinely anointed self (in the form of abolitionism), and the expressive self (in the Transcendentalist creed of Self-Reliance) represent the communal tradition which Lincoln subverts in his speech.

As a subversive text, Lincoln's speech exhibits all the characteristics of what Harold Bloom (1975) calls a "crisis poem." Bloom's elaborate map of poetic sub-version requires some elaboration here. First, great poets exhibit what might be called a "will to priority." They are obsessed with carving out imaginative space for themselves, despite their fear that everything important already has been said. Second, great poets tend to fixate on what Bloom calls a precursor, or the Mighty Dead, and do their work by systematically misreading their precursor. Third, the critic can uncover patterns of misreading in a text by paying close attention to figurative echoes of precursor texts as manifested in key images and tropes. Crisis poems tend to follow a pattern: they move from irony (image of presence and absence) to synecdoche (image of part and whole) to metonymy (fullness and emptiness). The poetic self is emptied out, and a new pattern of tropes and images emerges. The poem then moves from hyperbole (height and depth) to metaphor (inside and outside) to transumption (early and late). If the crisis poem makes it through this process, the poet has carved out his or her own imaginative space. This new "strength," as Bloom puts it, is particularly manifested in the creation of a new Sublime, that terrifying and ecstatic sense of uniqueness and priority that we find in attending to a great work of art. The prior text has been transumed, or figuratively subverted (see Aune, 1983, for a more thorough description of Bloom's "map").

My problem with Bloom is in his Emersonian insistence on the priority of the self and that all strong texts exhibit an Oedipal struggle with a precursor poet rather than with a communal tradition of discourse. And yet, Bloom's map is an effective "way into" the subtle figurations of Lincoln's speech. The structure of Lincoln's images accomplishes his larger rhetorical purpose: to empty out the divinely anointed self in the Puritan sense and to replace it with the new, sublime self as Suffering Servant. More audaciously, one might say that Lincoln seeks to transume the Bible itself.

Lincoln's first figure is a sort of flat irony: "little that is new could be presented." "With high hope for the future, no prediction in regard to it is ventured"— a curiously passive and ironic sentence for an epideictic speech.

The second figure is a synecdoche, where he develops an extended image of part and whole: "While the inaugural address was being delivered from this place, devoted altogether to saving the Union without war, insurgent agents were in the city seeking to destroy it without war."

The third figure is metonymy, an image of fullness and emptiness. Instead of praising the heroic efforts of his side in the war, as one might expect, he empties out the possibility of rational choice by the controlling self. As he says, in a magnificent sentence, "the war came." The only active subject is the war itself. No available conception of the American self was able to prevent it. Lincoln has accomplished the first step of his subversion of the individualist tradition.

Fourth, the controlling subject is emptied out further, as a new source of figurative power invades the speech: "Both read the same Bible and pray to the same God, and each invokes his aid against the other. It may seem strange that any men should dare to ask a just God's assistance in wringing their bread from the sweat of other men's faces, but let us judge not, that we be not judged. The prayers of both could not be answered. That of neither has been answered fully. The Almighty has his own purposes." There is a strong, Sublime chill in this passage. I doubt that it has an equal in the history of rhetoric. Lincoln's image of divine height and human depth is a crucial move towards the reconstitution of the self.

Fifth, one then would expect Lincoln to turn his cause into a metaphor for the divine will. He does this in part, with the inside/outside image of casting out the bondsman. Again, a normal epideictic speech would have ended here. Instead, he makes an astonishing move. In a rhetorical question, he asks, if God "gives to both North and South this terrible war as the woe due to those by whom the offense came, shall we discern therein any departure from those divine attributes which the believers in a living God always ascribe to him?" Lincoln doesn't answer the question directly. Instead of rallying his supporters in the name of God, he finally exhorts them to become like God, by exhibiting those divine attributes it has been given to us to know.

The last paragraph of the speech, "to bind up the nation's wounds, to care for him who shall have borne the battle and for his widow and orphan," is clearly a transumption of Isaiah 61:1–4: "The spirit of the Lord God is upon me, because the Lord has anointed me to bring good tidings to the afflicted; he has sent me to bind up the brokenhearted, to proclaim liberty to the captives, and the opening of the prison to those who are bound...to comfort all who mourn in Zion—to give them a garland instead of ashes, the oil of gladness instead of mourning, the mantle of praise instead of a faint spirit...they shall repair the ruined cities, the devastation of many generations" (*The Holy Bible: Revised Standard Version*, 1952, pp. 655–656).

Jesus himself, as Lincoln well knew, read this passage in the synagogue as he began his ministry in Galilee (Luke 4:16–19). Jesus' divine self, as Paul points out in Philippians 2:6–8, is kenotic, emptied out into the form of a servant. Lincoln's transumption both of the Bible and of the American self is complete. We do God's will by imitating the chief attribute of Jesus: becoming a Suffering Servant. The self is divine, but not omnipotent. The omnipotent God of history is unknowable, perhaps dead. But he is resurrected, emptied out, in every human face. If Lincoln's "Second Inaugural" is about the death of the American self, it is also about the death of the American concept of God.

To summarize: in Lincoln's struggle with his own selfhood and with the burdens of American individualism, he offers up, then and now, an image of the self that is neither divinely ordained in the Puritan sense, expressively self-reliant in Emerson's sense, or acquisitive in the capitalist sense. No typology, however forced, can do justice to Lincoln's American Sublime. The other anthropologists may quarrel with my interpretation of Lincoln's cries. Yet, if we move beyond the antiquarian character of much public address study and the formidable new machines for criticism, deconstructionist, Bloomian, or whatever, we are left with the ineffable sublimity of Lincoln's text. If we lose the ability to use and love it, all our efforts here count for nothing. Perhaps the best result of this panel could be to help us understand that, as Wordsworth (1965) writes, "What we have loved, others will love, and we will teach them how" (p. 366). We stand at another crossroads in the history of American individualism. We can see its victims in the streets of every American city. We can only hope for another eloquent, perhaps final, subversion of American selfhood.

References

Aune, J. A. (1983). Burke's late blooming: Trope, defense, and rhetoric. *Quarterly Journal of Speech, 69,* 328–340.

Bellah, R. N. (1985). *Habits of the heart: Individualism and commitment in American life.* Berkeley: University of California Press.

Bercovitch, S. (1975). *The Puritan origins of the American self.* New Haven: Yale University Press.

Bloom, H. (1975). *A map of misreading.* New York: Oxford University Press.

Bloom, H. (1976). *Poetry and repression.* New Haven: Yale University Press.

Emerson, R. W. (1983). Nature. In J. Porte (Ed.), *Essays and lectures* (pp. 5–49). New York. Library of America.

Gardner, M. (1987). Isness is her business. *New York Review of Books*, April 9, 1987, 16–19.

Herndon, R. (1961). *Herndon's life of Lincoln.* (P. Angle, Ed.). New York: Morrow.

The Holy Bible: Revised standard version. (1952). Teaneck, NJ: Cokesbury.

Lincoln, A. (1963). Second inaugural address. In G. R. Capp, Ed., *Famous speeches in American history* (pp. 92–94). Indianapolis: Bobbs-Merrill.

Porter, C. (1981). *Seeing and being: The plight of the participant observer in Emerson, James, Adams, and Faulkner.* Middletown, CT: Wesleyan University Press.

Rorty, R. (1985). Unpublished public lecture, University of Virginia, October 1985.

Thoreau, H. D. (1968). *Walden and civil disobedience: The variorum editions.* (W. Harding, Ed.). New York: Washington Square Press.

White J. B. (1984). *When words lose their meanings.* Chicago: University of Chicago Press.

Whitman, W. (1958). Song of myself. In G. W. Allen, Ed., *Leaves of grass* (pp. 49–96). New York: New American Library.

Wordsworth, W. (1965). The prelude. In J. Stillinger, Ed., *Selected poems and prefaces* (pp. 193–366). New York: Houghton Mifflin. (1952).

In Not-So-Trivial Pursuit
of Rhetorical Wedgies:
An Historical Approach to Lincoln's
Second Inaugural Address

RONALD H. CARPENTER

In an earlier paper, I asked "What happened to the 'historical' in our historical critical method?"[1] You may not have heard that statement, but my answer is obvious. Although rhetorical criticism abounds, historiography largely *has* dropped out of that research. Yes, we look at discourse of the historical past, but the critical focus too often is restricted primarily to texts and telling us what a rhetor *really* said. Few efforts go beyond discourse to primary source correspondence and other memorabilia to tell us what *really* happened—to an optimal extent ascertainable—as causal antecedents of a message or as consequence among respondents. Thus, current rhetorical criticism often is an argument about meanings read out of—or into—discourse, all highly dependent upon the perspective or methodology being applied.

In this context, consider Ernest Bormann's recent critical appraisal of Abraham Lincoln's Second Inaugural Address, in *The Force of Fantasy*. For Bormann, discourse is "romantic" when form is subordinate to content, and freedom of invention and delivery allow the orator to be perceived as "natural," "untrained," and "therefore unspoiled by formal education." And "pragmatic" denotes orators who aspire to "everyday practicality" and "immediate and visible effect" as evidence of "success or failure." Although at times they *might* achieve "eloquence" to match "the best efforts of classically educated Easterners," these rhetors favored "the anecdote, the homey barnyard smile, and the ridiculing, the vituperation, and the castigating elements of the speaking style of the *ungenteel tradition*." Thus, Bormann perceives an evolution. In the 1840s, Lincoln is firmly entrenched in that "ungenteel style." By the mid 1850s, however, he engaged less in that mode of discourse and relied more upon an abasement-atonement motif expressed in "the direct plain style of the Puritan sermon, shorn of much of the excessive overstatement of the circuit rider, in language resonant with the echoes of the vernacular." And Lincoln's Second Inaugural Address, specifically, "resonates and echoes with the meanings created in substantial portions of the American people by generations of audiences sharing fantasies portrayed from pulpits and platforms over the preceding century." Therefore, that speech is "the culmination" and "attained the greatest heights in the tradition of romantic pragmatism" with its "plain, dispassionate, and objective" style.[2]

As a critic of style, I take issue with Bormann. Several stylistic features make this speech anything *but* "plain," "dispassionate," or "in the vernacular." Look at the line about both parties who deprecated war: "one of them would *make* war rather than let the nation survive; and the other would *accept* war rather than let it perish." This double antithesis is as neatly turned an epigram as any from John Kennedy (or Ted Sorenson), such as "if a free society cannot help the many who are poor how can it save the few who are rich." People do not speak *that* artistically in the "vernacular"; so carefully crafted a statement hardly can be called "plain." Nor does "dispassionate" describe "every drop of blood drawn with the lash, shall be paid by another drawn with the sword. . . ." But with different definitions, founded upon imprecise terminology, style is the confounding canon of rhetoric. So rather than dwell on style, I raise these questions about Lincoln as *rhetor* in the Second Inaugural: (1) to what extent does that speech demonstrate his evolution from an earlier, ungenteel predilection to the "poetic compression and richness of emotional evocation. . .lost in the more detailed" and explicit rhetoric about God visiting the war upon a chosen people to discipline them? and (2) to what extent are Lincoln's rhetorical choices, whether conscious or unconscious, *because* of a "fantasy type in the collective memory of many who have shared in the portrayal of various communities of Americans as chosen people?" For answers, Bormann's conclusions will be juxtaposed contrapuntally here with my readings in correspondence and other memorabilia of Lincoln before and after the Second Inaugural.[3]

The Second Inaugural was delivered on 4 March 1865. On 6 December 1864, a reporter named Noah Brooks visited the White House and was invited into the library. There, Brooks found Lincoln "writing on a piece of common stiff box-board with a pencil." When the President finished writing, he handed the statement to Brooks and said "Here is one speech of mine which has never been printed, and I think it worth printing." After signing his name and handing it over, Lincoln recommended this caption for its publication: "The President's Last, Shortest, and Best Speech." Brooks' account of that "best" speech was published in the Washington *Daily Chronicle* of 7 December 1864:

> On thursday of last week two ladies from Tennessee came before the President
> asking the release of their husbands held as prisoners of war at Johnson's Island.
> They were put off till friday, when they came again; and were put off to saturday.
> At each of the interviews one of the ladies urged that her husband was a religious
> man. On saturday the President ordered the release of the prisoners, and then
> said to this lady "You say your husband is a religious man; tell him when you
> meet him, that I say I am not much of a judge of religion, but that, in my opinion,
> the religion that sets men to rebel and fight against their government, because, as
> they think, that government does not sufficiently help some men to eat their bread
> on the sweat of other men's faces, is not the sort of religion upon which people
> can get to heaven."[4]

Thus, three months before his Second Inaugural, Lincoln prefers as "best" discourse in the "ungenteel style," for the statement about "religion" *is* akin to ridicule, castigation, or personal jibe. Moreover, Lincoln's pride in the statement suggests strongly that the gentile Southern ladies evinced some reaction that Bormann would call "the immediate and visible effect" as evidence of "success or failure."

The argument about bread and sweat appeared in the Second Inaugural this way: "It may seem strange that any men should dare to ask a just God's assistance in wringing their bread from the sweat of other men's faces." Why? Yes, Lincoln often applied the sacred on behalf of a secular cause. Indeed, he saw his reelection as Almighty God "having directed my countrymen to the right conclusion" as voters. Nevertheless, the religious motif in Lincoln's "best" speech differs from the shorter, less explicit form of the Second Inaugural. For Bormann, "when a group of people have shared a fantasy theme, they have charged their emotional and memory banks with meanings and emotions that can be set off by a commonly agreed upon *cryptic symbolic cue*" [italics mine]; and therefore, "by not spelling it out but rather arguing the connotations by allusions," Lincoln "gains a poetic compression and richness of emotional evocation. . .lost in the more detailed amplification" of earlier, explicit statements.

As President, Lincoln had more than ample opportunities to engage in discourse. For example, groups often assembled in the evening with a band, marched to the White house, and serenaded the President—after which Lincoln was expected to speak. Even late in the evening, he tended to write those statements out fully and carefully to be read from an open window; and while their composition often led the speeches to be "very highly spoken of," Lincoln was beginning to show the strain, saying about one in November 1864, "Not very graceful, but I am growing old enough not to care much for the manner of doing things." Clearly, Lincoln was committed to felicity of expression in presidential discourse, saying in

September 1864 that anything for the public "must be written with some care, and at some expense of time." For example, instead of saying "one eighth of the whole population were colored slaves, not distributed generally over the Union, but localized in the Southern half of it," Lincoln changed "half" to "part." After all, slave holding Southern states did not comprise "half" of the Union. Why give the Confederacy more credibility than it was due? But by April 1865, Lincoln was somewhat reluctant to make public statements, even declining to comment (after a serenade) with this explanation about the war's ending:

> *That I supposed in consequence of the glorious news we have been receiving lately, there is to be some general demonstration, either on this or tomorrow evening, when I will be expected, I presume, to say something. Just here I will remark that I would much prefer having this demonstration take place tomorrow evening, as I would then be much better prepared to say what I have to say than I am now or can be this evening...just now I am not ready to say anything that one in my position ought to say. Everything I say, you know, goes into print. If I make a mistake it doesn't merely affect me nor you but the country. I, therefore, ought at least try not to make mistakes. If, then, a general demonstration be made tomorrow evening, and it is agreeable, I will endeavor to say something, and not make a mistake, without at least trying carefully to avoid it. Thanking you for the compliment of this call, I bid you good evening.*

For someone with a predilection for care in public statements, too many speaking opportunities are a burden. And along with conduct of the war, other demands were omnipresent upon the President's time and mental energies. Even the most cursory look at Lincoln's correspondence and other memorabilia show a man beset with pleas from those of Southern ladies about their husbands as prisoners to more serious ones about commuting death sentences for deserters. Lincoln had little time for drafting long, elaborate, explicit statements—if they were to be composed carefully. So what Bormann calls "poetic compression" *also* evinces pragmatic considerations.

Lincoln was ambivalent about the Second Inaugural of 4 March 1865. Writing to Thurlow Weed on 15 March, the President said, "Every one likes a compliment. Thank you for yours on...the recent Inaugural Address. I expect[it] to wear as well as—perhaps better than—anything I have produced." Nevertheless, Lincoln had reservations about the religious motif therein! Although "a God governing the World" is "a truth which I thought needed to be told," Lincoln also felt the speech was "not immediately popular"; for "Men are not flattered by being shown that there is a difference of purpose between the Almighty and them." Bormann attributes effectiveness in the Second Inaugural to "the power of the unifying appeal" about "slavery as an offense which God saw fit to visit upon the people...because of their sinfulness." But Lincoln himself felt that such an appeal *detracted* from the speech. So why is it a rhetorical choice on Lincoln's part?

By 4 March 1865, the war was virtually over. The South was shattered: its military and economic resources were depleted; states conquered by Northern armies already were applying for readmission to the Union; and emissaries from Richmond were seeking an audience with Lincoln about negotiating some settlement of the war. Negotiation with the South was distasteful for many Northerners. Although the Civil War brought immense industrial and economic growth to the

North—sufficient to establish the United States thereafter as a world power—so many Northern lives had been lost (remember, the Civil War killed more Americans than all other American wars combined). Even if called "Reconstruction," *retribution* was in order. In letters to Lincoln of 4 February and 21 February 1865, Henry Ward Beecher articulated an imperative need to reject any negotiated settlement, take a hard line, and maintain military morale to continue the war aggressively and punish the South by total victory. Thus, a preliminary meeting *"has been much criticized. The pride of the nation* is liable to be hurt. Anything that looks like the humiliation of our Goverment would be bitterly felt"; as "the Head of a nation, leaving the Capitol, and going *to* the rebels, is an act of condescension"; and "these *rumors of peace*, and this feverish suspense about commissioners and negotiations, is injurious, in so far as replenishing the army is concerned. . . ." Yes, Beecher also saw the Civil War in a religious light, proclaiming "Heresy is purged out. . . . Our Constitution has felt the hand of God laid upon it." Nevertheless, two weeks before the Second Inaugural Address, Beecher recommended urgently to Lincoln that "an address to the army, or to the nation, declaring that *peace can come only by arms*. . .would end these feverish uncertainties and give the spring campaign renewed vigor," for in Beecher's own efforts at an epigram, "it is more dangerous *to make peace than to make war*." So is the Second Inaugural what Bormann's fantasy theme criticism calls a "poetic compression" of abasement-atonement rhetoric about restoration, in "plain" and "dispassionate" style but an unknown degree of intentionality—or a brief but carefully wrought, stylized statement *also* shaped consciously by immediate, pragmatic considerations of time and timing?

Presidential discourse often generates a focal point of responses sometimes discernible in what people quote afterwards, such as Franklin Roosevelt's "the only thing we have to fear is fear itself" or John Kennedy's "Ask not what your country can do for you—ask what you can do for your country." And Lincoln may have had his oft quoted line, at that time, for the Second Inaugural. In response to her request, Lincoln wrote to Mrs. Amanda Hall on 20 March 1865 to reproduce in his own hand the statement which so impressed her: "Fondly do we hope—fervently do we pray—that this mighty scourge of war may speedily pass away. Yet, if God wills that it continue until all the wealth piled by the bondman's two hundred and fifty years of unrequited toil shall be sunk, and until every drop of blood drawn with the lash shall be paid by another drawn with the sword, as was said three thousand years ago, so still must be said: 'The judgments of the Lord are true, and righteous altogether'." Numerous facsimiles were widely circulated, all leading people to believe they had the original. So this may be an essential argument or focus of meaning which impressed Lincoln's readers or listeners in 1865; and I submit that as much as it is about any rhetorical vision as outlined by Bormann, correspondence just quoted above also is evidence that Lincoln was understood simply as saying that God was on the side of the Union in pursuing the war vigorously, and vindictively, to total military victory.

In conclusion, these excerpts of letters to and from Abraham Lincoln might be regarded as so much trivia. In one sense, my endeavor was trivial; for I simply walked to the library, checked out the pertinent volume from a standard collection of Lincoln's works, and expended approximately two hours reading through and placing bookmarks at pages of appropriate correspondence (although more time was spent composing this paper). My pursuit's goal, though, was to illustrate how these materials can complement reading texts of discourse. For our criticism may carry more weight, particularly outside our discipline, as we apply "rhetorical wedgies" gleaned from historiographical research with pertinent, primary sources.

Notes

1. Ronald H. Carpenter, "What happened to the 'Historical' in Our Historical-Critical Method?" a "Spotlight Scholar" Paper at the Southern Speech Communication Association Convention, Houston, 1986.

2. I quote Ernest Bormann from *The Force of Fantasy* (Carbondale: Southern Illinois University Press, 1985), see especially pp. 6, 18, 214, and 225–230.

3. This is not to say that Bormann operates without a sense of history. Indeed, *The Force of Fantasy* is, in the main, intellectual history; for Bormann basically traces a restoration theme in American discourse over the span of two centuries—and the changing manner of its expression from sacred applications to secular.

4. All quotations from Lincoln's correspondence and memorabilia are found in *The Collected Works of Abraham Lincoln VIII 1864–1865*, ed. Roy P. Basler (New Brunswick: Rutgers University Press, 1953), pp. 2, 101–102, 154–155, 318, 333, 356, 367, and 394.

Dimensions of Temporality in Lincoln's Second Inaugural

MICHAEL LEFF

Many of Lincoln's best remembered orations, including the House Divided Speech, the Cooper Union Address, and the Gettysburg Address, exhibit a clear pattern of temporal organization. The introductory remarks establish an orientation divided into past, present, and future, and then the three tenses reappear in the body of the speech, each marking out one of its major divisions. Close reading demonstrates that this progression is more than a device for separating the gross structural units of these discourses. Temporal movement, in fact, seems essential to their rhetorical economy; it frames the action of the various argumentative and stylistic elements, blends them into a unified field of textual action, and projects this field onto the public events that form the subject of the discourse (Leff and Mohrmann, 1974, Leff, 1983, Thurow, 1976, pp. 70–86, Warnick, 1987, pp. 236–239).

Nowhere is this pattern more evident or developed with greater skill than in the Second Inaugural. Yet, the temporal inflections that guide the text are not generally acknowledged in the existing critical literature. The reason, I believe, is that, despite its status as a masterpiece of eloquence, the speech has not often been studied as an artistic whole. Instead the critical focus has centered either on the historical context or on isolated sections that illustrate Lincoln's character or his excellence as a stylist.

Two recent studies attempt to remedy this defect. In a master's thesis devoted entirely to the text, Amy Slagell (1986) presents a careful and expert analysis of its rhetorical structure. And in his book, *Abraham Lincoln and American Political Religion*, Glen E. Thurow (1976) explicates Lincoln's political philosophy through a systematic reading of a number of his orations, including the Second Inaugural (pp. 88–108). Both studies demonstrate that the arrangement of temporal units directs the symbolic movement of the text and that no adequate interpretation can disregard this chronological pattern. My own analysis relies heavily on these earlier works, but I wish to extend and complicate their findings in two respects: first, I will argue that the speech builds to a creative equivocation in the middle of the third paragraph, an equivocation that blends the historical present into a conception of a sacred present; second, I hope to show that this conflation is central to the form of the speech and serves as the vehicle for sustaining its major themes. To establish these claims, I must review the text in the order of its presentation.

The opening paragraph contains no striking ideas or stylistic flourishes; in fact, it has a somewhat awkward appearance. Yet, it seems carefully constructed to achieve Lincoln's purposes and to establish the framework and tone for the speech as a whole. Most obviously, Lincoln introduces the temporal markers that define his perspective. The first sentence contrasts the present occasion with his previous inaugural. The second sentence refers to the past, the third and fourth to the present, and the final sentence looks forward to the future. The same pattern resurfaces in the body of the address: the second paragraph and the first seven sentences of the third deal with the past; the remainder of that paragraph deals with the present, and the concluding paragraph offers advice for future conduct. (See Thurow, pp. 91–92, for a generally similar but more detailed account of the structure of the opening paragraph.)

On a more subtle level, the paragraph establishes a relentless tone of passivity and self-effacement. The first person pronoun occurs only twice (and never again appears anywhere in the speech). And the whole is constructed in what Slagell (p. 11) aptly calls the impersonal passive. The first sentence, for example, reads: "At this second appearing to take the oath of the presidential office, there is less occasion for an extended address than there was at the first" (Basler, 1953, p. 332; all quotations from the speech refer to this edition.) The wording here contrasts sharply with the more personal and direct language of the First Inaugural. And, of course, Lincoln could have made his point more simply by recasting the sentence in a form such as this: On this occasion, I have less need to make an extended address than I did four years ago. But to speak in this way would suggest an orator striving to take command of the situation. Instead, Lincoln creates the impression that the occasion commands him, that it renders him captive and passive. This passive tone recurs throughout the speech.

The second paragraph refers to the past, as Lincoln recounts the circumstances surrounding his earlier inaugural and the outbreak of the war. The prose now changes markedly; it becomes subject to the nuances of artistic control and glides forward through elegantly balanced clauses. Apparently, the orator has gained command of his material, but he has done so only to articulate the passive frame through which he would have us view the historic drama. His point achieves sublime expression as the paragraph rolls to its conclusion: "Both parties deprecated war, but one of them would make war rather than let the nation survive; and the other would accept war rather than let it perish. And the war came." The cadence of this passage instantiates its message. The final clause seems to follow of necessity from what precedes it, even as the war was an inevitable event, manifesting itself regardless of the intentions of the parties involved.

The third paragraph lingers in the past, as Lincoln considers the causes and consequences of the war. Once again events have outrun conscious intentions: "Neither party expected for the war, the magnitude, or the duration, which it has already attained. Neither anticipated that the cause of the conflict might cease with, or even before, the conflict itself should cease. Each looked for an easier triumph, and a result less astounding." With these words, Lincoln completes his history of frustrated political and military efforts. The constraints are everywhere and apply to everyone. Just as Lincoln himself stands passive in the face of the occasion, so also the North and South were made to accept a war they sought to avoid and to suffer consequences they did not anticipate.

It is at this point, in the midst of the third paragraph, that Lincoln changes his temporal orientation. The shift occurs abruptly, and to appreciate it, we must return to the lines quoted immediately above and then attend to the next sentence in the text: "Neither [party] *anticipated* that the cause of the war might cease with, or even before, the conflict should cease. Each *looked* for an easier triumph, and a result less astounding. Both *read* the same Bible, and *pray* to the same God; and each *invokes* His aid against the other" (my emphasis). The italicized verbs indicate how Lincoln suddenly shifts from the past to the present tense, and without benefit of any perceptible transition, Lincoln moves from historic to present considerations. Equally important, Lincoln's perspective begins to change from the secular to the sacred. Up to this moment, the speaker has remained strictly within the confines of secular events, but from this first reference to the Bible through the end of the speech, he becomes sermonic; virtually every sentence quotes, paraphrases, or alludes to a passage in scripture.

Lincoln begins this section mindful of the divisions existing in the current historical situation. He stresses the competitive solicitation of divine aid by the warring parties, and in the ensuing sentence, he verges toward a partisan judgment: "It may seem strange that any men should dare to ask a just God's assistance in wringing their bread from the sweat of other men's faces." The sentence paraphrases Genesis 3:19, where God, casting Adam from Eden, declares that "In the sweat of thy face shalt thou eat bread...." Thus, the South seems the culpable party, for it has sinned by resisting the curse God placed upon all mankind. And at this stage, we might anticipate a call for retribution. But Lincoln quickly arrests the partisan direction of his argument. Paraphrasing Mathew 7:1, he says "let us judge not that we be not judged."

The reference to Mathew draws the text deeply within a religious context. Lincoln has stepped well outside the immediate historical situation, has departed from the political frame which previously governed his remarks. Yet, in an important sense, the text retains a certain logical and emotional consistency. The speaker has prepared us for this transformation. In the previous section, he had argued that the war followed a course of its own; it resisted the plans and purposes of those caught up in its sweep. This understanding of the past almost mandates a present attitude directed toward the supernatural. What men cannot control, they cannot fully comprehend, and the meaning of the war, therefore, must be gauged against something that transcends the tangible interests of the two sides. The prayers of neither, Lincoln observes, have "been fully answered. The Almighty has his own purposes."

The war, then, represents a divine intervention in human history. It is evidence of a mystery that recurrently plays its way through human affairs. And as the orator considers this mystery, his prose remains fixed within the sacred order, his perspective located in a time beyond the flow of historic events. Quoting Mathew 18:7, Lincoln argues that slavery was an offence which came in the providence of God and continued through His appointed time. And in language that recalls the passion of Christ, Lincoln characterizes the war as as a "mighty scourge", an instrument of atonement applied equally to North and South. Thus, the nation has endured redemptive suffering as it has lived through the drama of sin and mortification. It has shared the offence and the punishment meted out in God's time; all have participated in this mysterious relationship between man and God, which renders men responsible for their acts but unable to control their results. The war, then, offers no occasion for human judgment which would encourage one party to inflict further retribution on the other; it is itself a judgment from a higher source, and a redemptive vehicle that, like Christ's passion, purifies and opens the path to unity through spiritual rebirth. The whole process transcends the narrow limits of human understanding, and in the end, we can only accept the fact that, "as was said three thousand years ago, so still it must be said, 'the judgments of the Lord are true and righteous altogether.'"

In sum, Lincoln has shifted both from political to religious themes and from a perspective grounded in secular time to one grounded in sacred time. The thematic shift is obvious and relatively easy to explain. Given the magnitude of the events and Lincoln's immediate political goals, reference to divine purposes seems a logical, if not necessary, strategy. Moreover, as Ernest Bormann (1977) has demonstrated, a religious justification for secular disaster was a standard item in the repertoire of American political orators.

The temporal shift is much more subtle and demands special attention. In order to appreciate its significance, we must first consider the characteristic differences between secular and sacred time. As Eliade (1959) explains the matter, secular time proceeds in a single direction; it is homogeneous, continuous, and irreversible. Sacred time, on the other hand, calls us to a moment of origins; it is a "primordial mythical time made present," and this presence effects an immediate and total unification of the field of experience (pp. 68–69). It manifests itself recurrently as an interruption in our normal sense of temporality, and thus sacred time is cyclical and discontinuous; it is something always there that we occasionally recover.

It follows that our sense of present time is potentially ambiguous. On the secular level, it is an irreversible moment, of somewhat arbitrary duration, that divides past from future. On the sacred level, however, the present becomes recoverable as a return to origins, as an eternal now, a still moment when primal truths emerge in a changless pattern. It is possible, in fact normal, to overcome this ambiguity by dividing the two into wholly separate categories. Thus, the scared, because it has no progressivity, becomes atemporal, and it can serve as a fixed standard for judging the flux of local circumstance. Nevertheless, the experience of the sacred seems explicable only in terms of our experience of something that occurs in normal time—the attention to what is now before us as opposed to what has happened before or will happen later. Perhaps for just this reason, we define the sacred in terms of that which occurs now, in terms of a radically present experience. Consequently, both semantically and conceptually, it is possible to weaken the conventional dichotomy between the temporal and atemporal and to effect at least a partial conflation between the historical present and the present-ness of sacred insight.

This creative equivocation is, I believe, the mainspring of the "Second Inaugural." Lincoln's purpose in the speech is to develop a frame of passive acceptance, a perspective capable of accounting for the horrors of the war and of justifying a conciliatory post-war policy. These purposes almost demand a transcendental strategy, but they do not permit a simple rejection of worldly affairs. A mere imposition of the sacred on the secular would not suffice to encompass the situation. Thus, Lincoln does not juxtapose these contexts, but makes the sacred appear to evolve from the secular, preserving their distinction while leaving them in a state of organic connection. In fact, the whole economy of the speech seems designed to achieve this elision of temporal perspectives. The studiously awkward language of the opening section suggests a present occasion that commands rather than challenges the resources of the speaker. The narration of past events discloses a force at work that confounds human intentions and passes beyond political understanding. Then, in the crucial third paragraph, the past glides into the present as though through its own momentum, and in the historical present, we see the impact of a past that we cannot comprehend on its own terms—a nation divided into two rival factions suffering blindly and issuing unanswered prayers. We are thus forced to contemplate a presence that exceeds our normal temporal experience. Repeatively and progressively, the text coaxes historical time to a point where it rises outside its own horizons. It imparts a character and movement to secular events that render them comprehensible only by reference to an enlarged and passive vision of divine purposes. The frame of acceptance, then, appears less a construction of the speaker than a residue of history; it is an atemporal insight forced upon us by an historical understanding of the limits of human history.

To put this point somewhat differently, Lincoln seems to merge secular time into sacred time through the use of still another dimension of temporality—the timing in the text itself. The text, that is, gathers its ideas, images, and rhythms in a sequence that prepares the auditor to regard the connection between the secular and the sacred as an inevitable process. The two temporal frames remain distinct; yet they seem to inform one another and to co-operate in imparting meaning to events. The mediation between these frames is effected by the rhetorical action of the text itself, which embodies the connection and, in doing so, induces us to accept its plausibility as an explanation of the moral significance of political events.

In the final paragraph, Lincoln turns to the future as he urges his listeners to "strive on to finish the work we are in." The temporal order, then, is moved forward, but in a way that blurs different temporal perspectives. Lincoln does not enumerate specific policies; instead he recommends the elemental virtues of Christianity—the avoidance of malice, the exercise of charity, the binding of wounds, the protection of the unfortunate, and the search for a just and lasting peace (For the scriptural echoes in this passage, see Slagell, pp. 51–54). Clearly, this is a future informed by the orator's vision of the eternal present. The tone of meditation, of spiritual reverie, continues, and Lincoln's language has not fully re-entered the directional flow of secular time. Yet, in the immediate political context, this paragraph indirectly but powerfully articulates a policy; it justifies a course of conciliation and repudiates the more vindicative and partisan stance adopted by many in Lincoln's own party. Thus, the speech ends with a secular prayer that blends the sacred frame of acceptance into the fabric of local political action.

Lincoln did not live to implement his policy; his successor was impeached for attempting to do so, and in the course of time, policy came to be formulated under the sign of the scape-goat rather than the cross. Whatever the turn of events, however, the Second Inaugural retains the power of its mode of articulation. The speech is a verbal act that embodies the limitations of human action. In the perfection of its utterance, it yields to the imperfections of the human condition, and by yielding, transcends them. Lincoln well understood the limits of any single voice in influencing the course of political history. That understanding permeates the speech, drives its symbolic action forward, and leads its author to a mood of reverie from which he only partially returns.

References

Basler, R., ed. (1953). *The collected works of Abrabam Lincoln.* Vol. 8. New Brunswick: Rutgers University Press.

Bormann, E. (1977). Fetching good out of evil. A rhetorical use of calamity. *Quarterly Journal of Speech.* 63. 130–139.

Eliade, M. (1959). *The sacred and the profance: The Nature of Religion.* New York: Harcourt, Brace, Jovanovich.

Leff, M. & Mohrmann, G. P. (1974). Lincoln at Cooper Union: A rhetorical analysis of the text. *Quarterly Journal of Speech.* 60. 346–358.

Leff, M. (1983). Rhetorical timing in Lincoln's House Divided speech. Van Zelst Lecture in Communication. Evanston: Northwestern University.

Slagell, A. (1986). *A textual analysis of Abraham Lincoln's Second Inaugural Address.* M. A. Thesis: University of Wisconsin-Madison.

Thurow, G. (1976). *Abraham Lincoln and American political religion.* Albany: State University of New York Press.

Warnick, B. (1987). A Ricoeurian approach to rhetorical criticism. *Western Journal of Speech Communication.* 51. 227–244.

"With firmness in the right":
The Creation of Moral Hegemony
in Lincoln's Second Inaugural

MARTHA SOLOMON

With malice toward none; with charity to all; with firmness in the right, as God gives us to see the right, let us strive on to finish the work we are in; to bind up the nation's wounds; to care for him who shall have borne the battle, and for his widow, and his orphan; to do all which may achieve and cherish a just, and a lasting peace, among ourselves, and with all nations.

With these words on March 4, 1865, Abraham Lincoln closed his brief, but powerful second inaugural. Arguably among the most frequently cited and praised of presidential inaugurals, this speech has been closely studied as the fullest expression of Lincoln's particular version of American political religion (Thurow, 1976), as a statement of his view of the ultimate meaning of the Civil War (Anderson, 1970), and as an outstanding example of the genre of inaugural addresses (Campbell & Jamieson, 1985). The eloquence and vision, particularly in the final passage, have led most critics to agree with Earl W. Wiley in his essay in the *History and Criticism of American Public Address* who concluded that in the speech Lincoln became "the voice of the people" (1943, p. 874) and with Dan F. Hahn and Anne Morlando who noted "Lincoln, with his call for compassion, was not just ahead of his time; unfortunately, he was ahead of all times" (1979, p. 378). Despite the widespread endorsement of the speech's sentiments and appreciation for its eloquence, some critics have observed that it was a rhetorical failure for the contemporary audience. Edwin Black, for example, contends that the speech's "detachment from chauvinism, its historical perspective, and its pervasive sense of tragedy added to the tone of compassion and its rejection of retributive justice" created "a universe of discourse that few of Lincoln's auditors ever finally achieved" (1978, p. 172). Hahn and Morlando concur that the speech "although today considered a rhetorical masterpiece, was unpersuasive in 1865: his auditors were unable to adjust away from the hatred and malice of wartime toward the love and charity of a Christian peacetime" (1979, p. 378). Both of these views focus on the audience's human limitations as an explanation for the inaugural's contemporary ineffectiveness. But if meaning is created in the interaction between text and reader/listener, another way to understand its apparent rhetorical ineffectiveness is to return to the text with "fresh" eyes to seek in it the sources of its failure.

My goal in this essay is, by approaching this speech from an angle inspired by literary deconstructive theory and reader response criticism, to suggest an alternative understanding of its "message." Working very loosely from the basis suggested by many post-structuralists, I hope to demonstrate that Lincoln's text is open to alternate interpretations and that Lincoln's intentions in creating the text may not have coincided with the auditors' perception of the text's signification. Through these approaches, I will suggest that the speech *as a text* has certain internal tensions and inconsistencies which undercut an analysis of it as a simple, unified message of charity and transcendence. In fact, I will argue that the first three paragraphs implicitly create a moral hegemony at odds with the plea for charity at the end.

Let me clarify my approach: I will treat the speech as text *outside of* and *apart from* Lincoln's personal ideology or concerns. I will not argue what Lincoln thought or felt about the issues at hand; instead I will explore what the text says, *Ding am sich*. Believing that the meaning of a text is established in the exchange between the reader/recipient and the text, I feel that the author has only limited control over how an audience construes his/her message. Establishing the viability of my position is beyond the scope of this essay, although much post-structuralist theory adopts this stance. While my interpretation of Lincoln's message can reflect only my reading of the text, I believe that this alternate view explains in part the speech's apparent ineffectiveness in creating the attitudes in its audience which Lincoln sought.

Briefly, I will argue that Lincoln's depiction of the partisans in the struggle and his interpretation of the war's "moral" meaning accentuated ideological differences and, consequently, developed a moral hegemony that encouraged supporters of the Union both to feel superior to and vindictive toward their Confederate counterparts. To develop my argument, I will probe the text's depictions of the participants in the war and its description of the moral meaning and course of the conflict. I will move through the text, paragraph by paragraph, as auditors and readers would have done, rather than reacting to it globally.

Depicting the War

After the first paragraph which rather mundanely explains his choice of a brief inaugural, Lincoln begins his second paragraph with a generous view of the sentiments of both North and South four years before: "All dreaded it [war]—all sought to avert it." But his next sentence initiates a series of depictions which castigates his Southern opponents. While one group was engaged in a proper ritual (an inaugural address) "devoted altogether to *saving* the Union without war, insurgent agents were in the city seeking to *destroy* it without war, seeking to dissolve the Union, and divide effects, by negotiation." Notice the connotations of the diction in this passage. One side, "devoted" "altogether" to "saving" the "Union" is engaged in an important ritual. "The insurgent agents" were in the city (rather like snakes in the grass) seeking "to destroy" and "divide effects" (a mundane concern for worldly goods and power) through "negotiation," which suggests argument, exchange, and compromise rather than moral principles and transcendence.

The next sentence combines the strategies of the first two. It initially commends both sides—"both deprecated war"—but then distinguishes their motivations and goals. The clause "one would make war" rather than to allow the "Union to survive" clearly attributes belligerence and pettiness to the Confederacy and frames their position not as "peaceable withdrawal" from a union but rather an "unwillingness" to let the nation "survive." In contrast, the other side would, with reluctance, "accept war" rather than see the "nation" "perish." In short, this paragraph has developed distinct depictions of the two sides which suggests the turpitude and belligerence of the South and the North's position as victim and moral agent.

The third, and by far longest section of the address, continues the unfavorable depiction of Southern motivations and behavior before moving into a moral interpretation of the war which further accentuates the criticism of the Confederacy. First, Lincoln defines the issue of slavery. The slaves were, he says, "a peculiar and powerful interest," which somehow was a cause of the war. This definition or labeling again hints at the economic basis of the South's attitude; Lincoln used "interest," a term with economic connotations, rather than the more neutral "concerns." The phrase also highlights the importance ("powerful") of that "interest" and suggests that this significant economic focus is distinctive to and characteristic of the South ("peculiar"). Without denying the accuracy of this depiction, we can nonetheless acknowledge that, as a "terministic screen," it filters out other issues (states rights, for example) and other aspects of the Southern character. For example, from another perspective, historian Richard Hofstadter has observed that

"What the North was waging, of course, was a war to save the Union by denying self-determination to the majority of Southern Whites" (1948, p. 124).

Not only does this economic analysis of slavery oversimplify the South's position, but by identifying it within this speech as the *sole* ground of Southern actions ("to strengthen, perpetuate, and extend this interest was the object for which insurgents would rend the Union") Lincoln implicitly contrasts the base motivation of "the insurgents" with the loftier concerns of "the government," which modestly claimed only a limited right. Moreover, that the South was willing to pursue this concern even to war, which his immediate audience knew to have been personally devastating and economically draining, suggests at best a limited economic perspective and at worst malevolent self-concern.

A bit later Lincoln further castigates the South for its position: "It may seem strange that any man should dare ask a just God's assistance in wringing their bread from the sweat of other men's faces." The implicit deprecation of Southern attitudes contained in the key words "strange," "date," "just God's," belies the explicit admonition "let us judge not that we be not judged." Moreover, Lincoln's hypothetical description of slavery as an offence to God marks the South as sinners who have spurned God's law and, thereby, earned his displeasure.

Before tracing the moral interpretation of the war reflected in the speech, I should note that most previous writers have apparently overlooked this depiction of the South. In fact, to my knowledge only Charles B. Strozier in his psychohistory of Lincoln specifically notes that "at the outset he [Lincoln] established the South's responsibility for the war" (1982, p. 63). Most critics have read the speech as assigning blame equally to both sides for failing to perceive the moral significance of the slavery issue (Thurow, 1976). This "under-reading," may stem from two different sources: (1) a knowledge of the subtlety of Lincoln's attitude and a consequent attempt to read that into the rhetoric of the address; or (2) an attempt to read the entire address in light of the final paragraph. Either reading ignores the rhetorical process of the reader/recipient of this speech who might not have been fully aware of Lincoln's personal philosophy and who would have moved through the speech linearly to the conclusion.

If critics have overlooked Lincoln's depiction of the South, they have concurred in seeing the balance of paragraph three as an attempt to suggest the moral significance of the war. The war was, quite simply, God's "woe due to those by whom the offence [slavery, presumably] came." It reflects God's inscrutable, but fully just and righteous purposes. Both North and South must suffer "the mighty scourge of war" until the moral scales are balanced between the slaves "unrequited toil" and "blood draw by the lash" and the sacrifices necessitated by the conflict. While God has not fully answered the prayers of North or South, each of whom reads the same Bible and prays to Him for success, the termination of the conflict will come at God's appointed time and will reflect the working out of this plan for humankind.

As mentioned earlier many critics have interpreted Lincoln's moral interpretation of the war as faulting North and South equally. For example, William J. Wolf writes, "The judgment fell upon both sides, for slavery was a national and not merely a sectional evil" (1959, p. 185). Certainly, Lincoln's intention may have been to spread blame equally (Trueblood, 1973). But the interpretation of the war provided in the text undercuts this generous view on three fronts. First, it follows the negative depiction of the South discussed above, which clearly castigated Confederate attitudes. This depiction frames and colors the reader/listener's interpretation of Lincoln's later tolerance and forgiveness. Second, but equally important, Northern readers of the text well knew that the "progress of our arms," which in paragraph one Lincoln had averred was going "reasonably satisfactorily" and was "encouraging to all," virtually assured their triumph in the conflict. If, as Lincoln insisted, God's justice would triumph, less subtle and theologically sophisticated listeners could easily have assumed that their imminent victory in the war was an indication of their moral superiority and favor in God's eyes. Finally, the text clearly differentiates quite specific levels of culpability. The South was aggressive and basely motivated in pursuing its economic interests even to war. The North, concerned to preserve the Union, was willing to compromise and acquiesce. The South was, thus, depicted as more aggressive and culpable, less virtuous. If both had sinned, the South's error was more egregious.

In short, within the context of the speech Lincoln's interpretation of the war encourages a perception of moral superiority in his Northern hearers. Because his depiction of the South explicitly castigated their attitudes (which he had oversimplified and distorted), because he pictured the North's role as acquiescent and reactive in the interest of perserving the Union, and because he framed the war as God's judgment for transgression, Lincoln implicitly stimulated the virtually victorious North to perceive its role as more nearly acting out God's will. He created, perhaps inadvertently, a moral hegemony of North over South. If, in the end, he urged his audience to proceed without malice and with charity, he also admonished them to be firm "in the right, as God gives us to see the right," to "strive on to finish the work we are in." Given his depictions of the sides, his admonition could easily be perceived as an affirmation of Northern moral superiority and a depiction of the Union as the agent for God's justice in the struggle.

Conclusion

In their careful discussion of inaugurals Campbell and Jamieson identify four interrelated elements that distinguish the genre. The first two are particularly relevant here. An inaugural, "unifies the audience by reconstituting its members as 'the people' who can witness and ratify the ceremony [and] rehearses communal values drawn from the past" (1985, p. 205). The tensions and internal contradictions within Lincoln's inaugural stem from these characteristics. Because the nation was rent asunder by the war and because the two sides had endured almost four years of alienation and conflict, they were not "a people." They were, instead, *two* people in bitter conflict over values and political philosophy. If they shared a common history and religious orientation, as Lincoln averred, their perceptions of that past and their interpretations of that theology were strikingly different. Both read the same Bible, but found different messages there; both prayed to the same God, but asked disparate things. In short, Lincoln, who was involved in a ritual which one side endorsed and participated in as "the people" with "communal" values, distanced himself from the other group. As Bormann notes "a pressing rhetorical problem for aggregates of individuals moving toward a sense of community is the creation of a common identity." To develop community such persons must feel that they are of an "identifiable group" which differs in some important respects from other groups" (1985, p. 11). Within this text, Lincoln identified two groups with quite disparate values and motivations. His plea for charity and his admonition to eschew judgment were to an audience that had judged the merits of the Southern cause and found them wanting. Moreover, their triumph in arms was easily seen as proof of moral superiority. In sum, Lincoln's rhetoric in the inaugural implicitly encouraged moral hegemony and worked against his sincere plea for charity.

My purpose here has not been to establish a causal link between Lincoln's second inaugural and the painful experiences of the Reconstruction Era. Nor was it to diminish in any way the noble sentiments and eloquence of this speech. Quite simply, I hoped to demonstrate the value of deconstructive approaches for the rhetorical critic. While rhetorical scholars have long distinguished between the implicit and explicit messages in texts, they have not, I believe, fully acknowledged that audience members can decode the same discourse in strikingly disparate way. My reading of this inaugural, I hope, has indicated how a text can be construed very differently yet quite consistently from the "received" meaning. Moreover, this analysis has suggested the dangers of too close an attention to the author and his/her intentions in the text. If meaning develops in the interaction between text and teacher, the author's purposes and intended interpretations may be largely irrelevant in understanding the rhetorical impact of a work. A final caveat emerges from this discussion. As critics, in seeking unity in a text, we overlook the audience's reception of the material. In this case, by focusing on the eloquent final passage and seeing the discourse as framed by it, we neglect the structure of the speech and forget that the first sections framed the last for a contemporary audience. In appreciating and affirming the beauty and nobility of Lincoln's final plea, we forget that plea was to an aggregate of individuals who had experienced a personal and national tragedy. They sought meaning and vindication for their roles in that war. Lincoln offered them both. To paraphrase a later inaugural, Lincoln's audience could clearly discern that "God's work had truly been their own."

References

Anderson, D. (1970). *Abraham Lincoln*. Boston: Twayne.

Black, E. (1978). *Rhetorical Criticism: A study in method*. Madison: University of Wisconsin Press.

Bormann, E. (1985). *The force of fantasy: Restoring the American dream*. Carbondale: SIU Press.

Campbell, K. K. & Jamieson, K. H. (1985). Inaugurating the Presidency. In H. H. Simons & A. A. Aghazarian (Eds.), *Form, genre, and the study of political discourse*. Columbia, SC: University of South Carolina Press.

Hahn, D. F. & Morlando, A. (1979). A Burkean analysis of Lincoln's Second Inaugural. *Presidential Studies Quarterly*, 9.

Hofstadter, R. (1948). *The American political tradition*. New York: Knopf.

Strozier, C. B. (1982). *Lincoln's quest for union*. New York, Basic Books.

Thurow, G. E. (1976). *Abraham Lincoln and American political religion*. New York: Harper & Row.

Trueblood, D. E. (1973). *Abraham Lincoln: Theologian of American anguish*. New York: Harper & Row.

Wiley, E. W. (1943). Lincoln: His emergence as the voice of the people. In W. N. Brigance (ed.), *History and criticism of American public address*. New York: McGraw-Hill.

Wolf. W. J. (1959). *The almost chosen people*. Garden City, N.Y.: Doubleday.

RICHARD NIXON

Address to the Nation on the War in Vietnam

In 1968 Richard Nixon was elected President of the United States following a campaign in which America's involvement in Vietnam was a paramount issue. In the months following his inauguration pressure on President Nixon to solve the Vietnam problem continued to mount, and the protests that characterized the last years of the Johnson administration were unabated. President Nixon had publicly stated that protest would not influence his policy, but a national moratorium on the war held on October 15, 1969, secured intensive media coverage, and a second moratorium was scheduled for November 15. The President's speech on national television on November 3, 1969, was given extensive publicity prior to its delivery and was certainly one of the most important policy addresses of the decade.

Good evening, my fellow Americans:

Tonight I want to talk to you on a subject of deep concern to all Americans and to many people in all parts of the world—the war in Vietnam.

I believe that one of the reasons for the deep division about Vietnam is that many Americans have lost confidence in what their Government has told them about our policy. The American people cannot and should not be asked to support a policy which involves the overriding issues of war and peace unless they know the truth about that policy.

Tonight, therefore, I would like to answer some of the questions that I know are on the minds of many of you listening to me.

How and why did America get involved in Vietnam in the first place?

How has this administration changed the policy of the previous administration?

What has really happened in the negotiations in Paris and on the battlefront in Vietnam?

What choices do we have if we are to end the war?

What are the prospects for peace?

Now, let me begin by describing the situation I found when I was inaugurated on January 20.

—The war had been going on for 4 years.

—31,000 Americans had been killed in action.

—The training program for the South Vietnamese was behind schedule.

—540,000 Americans were in Vietnam with no plans to reduce the number.

—No progress had been made at the negotiations in Paris and the United States had not put forth a comprehensive peace proposal.

—The war was causing deep division at home and criticism from many of our friends as well as our enemies abroad.

In view of these circumstances there were some who urged that I end the war at once by ordering the immediate withdrawal of all American forces.

From a political standpoint this would have been a popular and easy course to follow. After all, we became involved in the war while my predecessor was in office. I could blame the defeat which would be the result of my action on him and come out as the peacemaker. Some put it to me quite bluntly: This was the only way to avoid allowing Johnson's war to become Nixon's war.

But I had a greater obligation than to think only of the years of my administration and of the next election. I had to think of the effect of my decision on the next generation and on the future peace and freedom in America and in the world.

Let us all understand that the question before us is not whether some Americans are for peace and some Americans are against peace. The question at issue is not whether Johnson's war becomes Nixon's war.

The great question is: How can we win America's peace?

Well, let us turn now to the fundamental issue. Why and how did the United States become involved in Vietnam in the first place?

Fifteen years ago North Vietnam, with the logistical support of Communist China and the Soviet Union, launched a campaign to impose a Communist government on South Vietnam by instigating and supporting a revolution.

In response to the request of the Government of South Vietnam, President Eisenhower sent economic aid and military equipment to assist the people of South Vietnam in their efforts to prevent a Communist takeover. Seven years ago, President Kennedy sent 16,000 military personnel to Vietnam as combat advisers. Four years ago, President Johnson sent American combat forces to South Vietnam.

Now, many believe that President Johnson's decision to send American combat forces to South Vietnam was wrong. And many others—I among them—have been strongly critical of the way the war has been conducted.

But the question facing us today is: Now that we are in the war, what is the best way to end it?

In January I could only conclude that the precipitate withdrawal of American forces from Vietnam would be a disaster not only for South Vietnam but for the United States and for the cause of peace.

For the South Vietnamese, our precipitate withdrawal would inevitably allow the Communists to repeat the massacres which followed their takover in the North 15 years before.

—They then murdered more than 50,000 people and hundreds of thousands more died in slave labor camps.

—We saw a prelude of what would happen in South Vietnam when the Communists entered the city of the Hue last year. During their brief rule there, there was a bloody reign of terror in which 3,000 civilians were clubbed, shot to death, and buried in mass graves.

—With the sudden collapse of our support, these atrocities of Hue would become the nightmare of the entire nation—and particularly for the million and a half Catholic refugees who fled to South Vietnam when the Communists took over in the North.

For the United States, this first defeat in our Nation's history would result in a collapse of confidence in American leadership, not only in Asia but throughout the world.

Three American Presidents have recognized the great stakes involved in Vietnam and understood what had to be done.

In 1963, President Kennedy, with his characteristic eloquence and clarity, said: " . . . we want to see a stable government there, carrying on a struggle to maintain its national independence."

"We believe strongly in that. We are not going to withdraw from that effort. In my opinion, for us to withdraw from that effort would mean a collapse not only of South Vietnam, but Southeast Asia. So we are going to stay there."

President Eisenhower and President Johnson expressed the same conclusion during their terms of office.

For the future of peace, precipitate withdrawal would thus be a disaster of immense magnitude.

—A nation cannot remain great if it betrays its allies and lets down its friends.

—Our defeat and humiliation in South Vietnam without question would promote recklessness in the councils of those great powers who have not yet abandoned their goals of world conquest.

—This would spark violence wherever our commitments help maintain the peace—in the Middle East, in Berlin, eventually even in the Western Hemisphere.

Ultimately, this would cost more lives.

It would not bring peace; it would bring more war.

For these reasons, I rejected the recommendation that I should end the war by immediately withdrawing all of our forces. I chose instead to change American policy on both the negotiating front and battlefront.

In order to end a war fought on many fronts, I initiated a pursuit for peace on many fronts.

In a television speech on May 14, in a speech before the United Nations, and on a number of other occasions I set forth our peace proposals in great detail.

—We have offered the complete withdrawal of all outside forces within 1 year.

—We have proposed a cease-fire under international supervision.

—We have offered free elections under international supervision with the Communists participating in the organization and conduct of the elections as an organized political force. And the Saigon Government has pledged to accept the result of the elections.

We have not put forth our proposals on a take-it-or-leave-it basis. We have indicated that we are willing to discuss the proposals that have been put forth by the other side. We have declared that anything is negotiable except the right of the people of South Vietnam to determine their own future. At the Paris peace conference, Ambassador Lodge has demonstrated our flexibility and good faith in 40 public meetings.

Hanoi has refused even to discuss our proposals. They demand our unconditional acceptance of their terms, which are that we withdraw all American forces immediately and unconditionally and that we overthrow the Government of South Vietnam as we leave.

We have not limited our peace initiatives to public forums and public statements. I recognized, in January, that a long and bitter war like this usually cannot be settled in a public forum. That is why in addition to the public statements and negotiations I have explored every possible private avenue that might lead to a settlement.

Tonight I am taking the unprecedented step of disclosing to you some of our other initiatives for peace—initiatives we undertook privately and secretly because we thought we thereby might open a door which publicly would be closed.

I did not wait for my inauguration to begin my quest for peace.

—Soon after my election, through an individual who is directly in contact on a personal basis with the leaders of North Vietnam, I made two private offers for a rapid, comprehensive settlement. Hanoi's replies called in effect for our surrender before negotiations.

—Since the Soviet Union furnishes most of the military equipment for North Vietnam, Secretary of State Rogers, my Assistant for National Security Affairs, Dr. Kissinger, Ambassador Lodge, and I, personally, have met on a number of occasions with representatives of the Soviet Government to enlist their assistance in getting meaningful negotiations started. In addition, we have had extended discussions directed toward the same and with representatives of other governments which have diplomatic relations with North Vietnam. None of these initiatives have to date produced results.

—In mid-July, I became convinced that it was necessary to make a major move to break the deadlock in the Paris talks. I spoke directly in this office, where I am now sitting, with an individual who had known Ho Chi Minh [President, Democratic Republic of Vietnam] on a personal basis for 25 years. Through him I sent a letter to Ho Chi Minh.

I did this outside of the usual diplomatic channels with the hope that with the necessity of making statements for propaganda removed, there might be constructive progress toward bringing the war to an end. Let me read from the letter to you now.

"Dear Mr. President:

"I realize that it is difficult to communicate meaningfully across the gulf of four years of war. But precisely because of this gulf, I wanted to take this opportunity to reaffirm in all solemnity my desire to work for a just peace. I deeply believe that the war in Vietnam has gone on too long and delay in bringing it to an end can benefit no one—least of all the people of Vietnam . . . .

"The time has come to move forward at the conference table toward an early resolution of this tragic war. You will find us forthcoming and open-minded in a common effort to bring the blessings of peace to the brave people of Vietnam. Let history record that at this critical juncture, both sides turned their face toward peace rather than toward conflict and war."

I received Ho Chi Minh's reply on August 30, 3 days before his death. It simply reiterated the public position North Vietnam had taken at Paris and flatly rejected my initative.

The full text of both letters is being released to the press.

—In addition to the public meetings that I have referred to, Ambassador Lodge has met with Vietnam's chief negotiator in Paris in 11 private sessions.

—We have taken other significant initiatives which must remain secret to keep open some channels of communication which may still prove to be productive.

But the effect of all the public, private, and secret negotiations which have been undertaken since the bombing halt a year ago and since this administration came into office on January 20, can be summed up in one sentence: No progress whatever has been made except agreement on the shape of the bargaining table.

Well now, who is at fault?

It has become clear that the obstacle in negotiating an end to the war is not the President of the United States. It is not the South Vietnamese Government.

The obstacle is the other side's absolute refusal to show the least willingness to join us in seeking a just peace. And it will not do so while it is convinced that all it has to do is to wait for our next concession, and our next concession after that one, until it gets everything it wants.

There can now be no longer any question that progress in negotiation depends only on Hanoi's deciding to negotiate, to negotiate seriously.

I realize that this report on our efforts on the diplomatic front is discouraging to the American people, but the American people are entitled to know the truth— the bad news as well as the good news—where the lives of our young men are involved.

Now let me turn, however, to a more encouraging report on another front.

At the time we launched our search for peace I recognized we might not succeed in bringing an end to the war through negotiation. I, therefore, put into effect another plan to bring peace—a plan which will bring the war to an end regardless of what happens on the negotiating front.

It is in line with a major shift in U.S. foreign policy which I described in my press conference at Guam on July 25. Let me briefly explain what has been described as the Nixon Doctrine—a policy which not only will help end the war in Vietnam, but which is an essential element of our program to prevent future Vietnams.

We Americans are a do-it-yourself people. We are an impatient people. Instead of teaching someone else to do a job, we like to do it ourselves. And this trait has been carried over into our foreign policy.

In Korea and again in Vietnam, the United States furnished most of the money, most of the arms, and most of the men to help the people of those countries defend their freedom against Communist aggression.

Before any American troops were committed to Vietnam, a leader of another Asian country expressed this opinion to me when I was traveling in Asia as a private citizen. He said: "When you are trying to assist another nation defend its freedom, U.S. policy should be to help them fight the war but not to fight the war for them."

Well, in accordance with this wise counsel, I laid down in Guam three principles as guidelines for future American policy toward Asia:

—First, the United States will keep all of its treaty commitments.

—Second, we shall provide a shield if a nuclear power threatens the freedom of a nation allied with us or of a nation whose survival we consider vital to our security.

—Third, in cases involving other types of aggression, we shall furnish military and economic assistance when requested in accordance with our treaty commitments. But we shall look to the nation directly threatened to assume the primary responsibility of providing the manpower for its defense.

After I announced this policy, I found that the leaders of the Philippines, Thailand, Vietnam, South Korea, and other nations which might be threatened by Communist aggression, welcomed this new direction in American foreign policy.

The defense of freedom is everybody's business—not just America's business. And it is particularly the responsibility of the people whose freedom is threatened. In the previous administration, we Americanized the war in Vietnam. In this administration, we are Vietnamizing the search for peace.

The policy of the previous administration not only resulted in our assuming the primary responsibility for fighting the war, but even more significantly did not adequately stress the goal of strengthening the South Vietnamese so that they could defend themselves when we left.

The Vietnamization plan was launched following Secretary Laird's visit to Vietnam in March. Under the plan, I ordered first a substantial increase in the training and equipment of South Vietnamese forces.

In July, on my visit to Vietnam, I changed General Abrams' orders so that they were consistent with the objectives of our new policies. Under the new orders, the primary mission of our troops is to enable the South Vietnamese forces to assume the full responsibility for the security of South Vietnam.

Our air operations have been reduced by over 20 percent.

And now we have begun to see the results of this long overdue change in American policy in Vietnam.

—After 5 years of Americans going into Vietnam, we are finally bringing American men home. By December 15, over 60,000 men will have been withdrawn from South Vietnam—including 20 percent of all our combat forces.

—The South Vietnamese have continued to gain in strength. As a result they have been able to take over combat responsibilities from our American troops.

Two other significant developments have occurred since this administration took office.

—Enemy infiltration, infiltration which is essential if they are to launch a major attack, over the last 3 months is less than 20 percent of what it was over the same period last year.

—Most important—United States casualties have declined during the last 2 months to the lowest point in 3 years.

Let me now turn to our program for the future.

We have adopted a plan which we have worked out in cooperation with the South Vietnamese for the complete withdrawal of all U.S. combat ground forces, and their replacement by South Vietnamese forces on an orderly scheduled timetable. This withdrawal will be made from strength and not from weakness. As South Vietnamese forces become stronger, the rate of American withdrawal can become greater.

I have not and do not intend to announce the timetable for our program. And there are obvious reasons for this decision which I am sure you will understand. As I have indicated on several occasions, the rate of withdrawal will depend on developments on three fronts.

One of these is the progress which can be or might be made in the Paris talks. An anouncement of a fixed timetable for our withdrawal would completely remove any incentive for the enemy to negotiate an agreement. They would simply wait until our forces had withdrawn and then move in.

The other two factors on which we will base our withdrawal decisions are the level of enemy activity and the progress of the training programs of the South Vietnamese forces. And I am glad to be able to report tonight progress on both of these fronts has been greater than we anticipated when we started the program in June for withdrawal. As a result, our timetable for withdrawal is more optimistic now than when we made our first estimates in June. Now, this clearly demonstrates why it is not wise to be frozen in on a fixed timetable.

We must retain the flexibility to base each withdrawal decision on the situation as it is at that time rather than on estimates that are no longer valid.

Along with this optimistic estimate, I must—in all candor—leave one note of caution.

If the level of enemy activity significantly increases we might have to adjust our timetable accordingly.

However, I want the record to be completely clear on one point.

At the time of the bombing half just a year ago, there was some confusion as to whether there was an understanding on the part of the enemy that if we stopped the bombing of North Vietnam they would stop the shelling of cities in South Vietnam. I want to be sure that there is no misunderstanding on the part of the enemy with regard to our withdrawal program.

We have noted the reduced level of infiltration, the reduction of our casualties, and are basing our withdrawal decisions partially on those factors.

If the level of infiltration or our casualties increase while we are trying to scale down the fighting, it will be the result of a conscious decision by the enemy.

Hanoi could make no greater mistake than to assume that an increase in violence will be to its advantage. If I conclude that increased enemy action jeopardizes our remaining forces in Vietnam, I shall not hestitate to take strong and effective measures to deal with that situation.

This is not a threat. This a statement of policy, which as Commander in Chief of our Armed Forces, I am making in meeting my responsibility for the protection of American fighting men wherever they may be.

My fellow Americans, I am sure you can recognize from what I have said that we really only have two choices open to us if we want to end this war.

—I can order an immediate, precipitate withdrawal of all Americans from Vietnam without regard to the effects of that action.

—Or we can persist in our search for a just peace through a negotiated settlement if possible, or through continued implementation of our plan for Vietnamization if necessary—a plan in which we will withdraw all of our forces from Vietnam on a schedule in accordance with our program, as the South Vietnamese become strong enough to defend their own freedom.

I have chosen this second course.

It is not the easy way.

It is the right way.

It is a plan which will end the war and serve the cause of peace—not just in Vietnam but in the Pacific and in the world.

In speaking of the consequences of a precipitate withdrawal, I mentioned that our allies would lose confidence in America.

Far more dangerous, we would lose confidence in ourselves. Oh, the immediate reaction would be a sense of relief that our men were coming home. But as we saw the consequences of what we had done, inevitable remorse and divisive recrimination would scar our spirit as a people.

We have faced other crises in our history and have become stronger by rejecting the easy way out and taking the right way in meeting our challenges. Our greatness as a nation has been our capacity to do what had to be done when we knew our course was right.

I recognize that some of my fellow citizens disagree with the plan for peace I have chosen. Honest and patriotic Americans have reached different conclusions as to how peace should be achieved.

In San Francisco a few weeks ago, I saw demonstrators carrying signs reading: "Lose in Vietnam, bring the boys home."

Well, one of the strengths of our free society is that any American has a right to reach that conclusion and to advocate that point of view. But as President of the United States, I would be untrue to my oath of office if I allowed the policy of this Nation to be dictated by the minority who hold that point of view and who try to impose it on the Nation by mounting demonstrations in the street.

For almost 200 years, the policy of this Nation has been made under our Constitution by those leaders in the Congress and the White House elected by all of the people. If a vocal minority, however fervent its cause, prevails over reason and the will of the majority, this Nation has no future as a free society.

And now I would like to address a word, if I may, to the young people of this Nation who are particularly concerned, and I understand why they are concerned, about this war.

I respect your idealism.

I share your concern for peace.

I want peace as much as you do.

There are powerful personal reasons I want to end this war. This week I will have to sign 83 letters to mothers, fathers, wives, and loved ones of men who have given their lives for America in Vietnam. It is very little satisfaction to me that this is only one-third as many letters as I signed the first week in office. There is nothing I want more than to see the day come when I do not have to write any of those letters.

—I want to end the war to save the lives of those brave young men in Vietnam.

—But I want to end it in a way which will increase the chance that their younger brothers and their sons will not have to fight in some future Vietnam someplace in the world.

—And I want to end the war for another reason. I want to end it so that the energy and dedication of you, our young people, now too often directed into bitter hatred against those responsible for the war, can be turned to the great challenges of peace, a better life for all Americans, a better life for all people on this earth.

I have chosen a plan for peace. I believe it will succeed.

If it does succeed, what the critics say now won't matter. If it does not succeed, anything I say then won't matter.

I know it may not be fashionable to speak of patriotism or national destiny these days. But I feel it is appropriate to do so on this occasion.

Two hundred years ago this Nation was weak and poor. But even then, America was the hope of millions in the world. Today we have become the strongest and richest nation in the world. And the wheel of destiny has turned so that any hope the world has for the survival of peace and freedom will be determined by whether the American people have the moral stamina and the courage to meet the challenge of free world leadership.

Let historians not record that when America was the most powerful nation in the world we passed on the other side of the road and allowed the last hopes for peace and freedom of millions of people to be suffocated by the forces of totalitarianism.

And so tonight—to you, the great silent majority of my fellow Americans—I ask for your support.

I pledged in my campaign for the Presidency to end the war in a way that we could win the peace. I have initiated a plan of action which will enable me to keep that pledge.

The more support I can have from the American people, the sooner that pledge can be redeemed; for the more divided we are at home, the less likely the enemy is to negotiate at Paris.

Let us be united for peace. Let us also be united against defeat. Because let us understand: North Vietnam cannot defeat or humiliate the United States. Only Americans can do that.

Fifty years ago, in this room and at this very desk,[1] President Woodrow Wilson spoke words which caught the imagination of a war-weary world. He said: "This is the war to end war." His dream for peace after World War I was shattered on the hard realities of great power politics and Woodrow Wilson died a broken man.

Tonight I do not tell you that the war in Vietnam is the war to end wars. But I do say this: I have initiated a plan which will end this war in a way that will bring us closer to that great goal to which Woodrow Wilson and every American President in our history has been dedicated—the goal of a just and lasting peace.

As President I hold the responsibility for choosing the best path to that goal and then leading the Nation along it.

I pledge to you tonight that I shall meet this responsibility with all of the strength and wisdom I can command in accordance with your hopes, mindful of your concerns, sustained by your prayers.

Thank you and goodnight.

NOTE: The President spoke at 9:32 p.m. in his office at the White House. The address was broadcast on radio and television.

On November 3, 1969, the White House Press Office released an advance text of the address.

1. Later research indicated that the desk had not been President Woodrow Wilson's as had long been assumed but was used by Vice President Henry Wilson during President Grant's administration.

Under the Veneer: Nixon's Vietnam
Speech of November 3, 1969

——————————————— ROBERT P. NEWMAN ———————————————

With the political honeymoon over, with his Congressional critics nipping at his heels and threatening full-scale attacks, and a major outpouring of antiwar sentiment probable on the October 15 Moratorium, Richard M. Nixon announced, on October 13, 1969, that he would make a major address about Vietnam November 3. The advance notice was unusually long for presidential addresses; the stakes in the burgeoning combat were unusually high. Vietnam had broken his predecessor, and Richard Nixon did not care to let himself in for the same treatment.

Part of the tension in October was due to the President's earlier incautious remark that he would not allow his program to be influenced by demonstrations in the streets. This gratuitous irritant to the peace forces guaranteed a massive turnout for the October 15 Moratorium, and it was partially to defuse the Moratorium that the President announced his speech so early. In this effort, the early announcement was perhaps successful; the size of the October 15 turnout remained impressive, but its tone was muted. All but the most violent of the protesters cushioned their stance with an anticipation that on November 3, when the President could speak without appearing to have yielded to pressure, he would announce major steps to end the war.

Even after the Moratorium, announcement of the coming address had its effect on the peace movement. From October 15 until Nixon spoke, plans for the November antiwar events were affected by anticipation of the Presidential speech. Had the prognosis for the November 3 speech been unfavorable, the peace forces would have strained every nerve to mount their greatest effort in mid-November. But Presidential aides let it be known that Nixon had attended to the Moratorium, even though he did not approve it, and the Washington gossip mills were rife with predictions that, on November 3, the President would produce good news for peace. For two weeks, the doves relaxed. Perhaps, thought many, Nixon has really got the word, and the November push won't be necessary after all.

Every channel of public intelligence built up the significance of the November 3 effort. The President was known to be "almost totally preoccupied" with drafting the speech during the last two weeks of October.[1] Whether in the White House, at Camp David, or on the road, he was writing, revising, reflecting. The speech had to "convey an authentic note of personal involvement," rather than appear as a run-of-the-mill ghost-written production; and for this reason, all ten drafts were pristine Nixon. Ray Price, one of the President's top writers, had no idea what was in it: "I contributed nothing—not even a flourish."[2] Evans and Novak, executive-watchers of more than usual competence, noted on the day of the speech: "In stark contrast to his last major speech on Vietnam, almost six months ago, Mr Nixon's talk tonight has been written by one hand alone—the President's hand."[3]

Buildup? On the night of November 3, Caesar himself could not have upstaged Richard Nixon.

In retrospect, expectations were so high that not even the Sermon on the Mount could have fulfilled them. The President had focused the spotlight so long and so carefully that only rhetorical perfection would have been equal to the occasion.

The Background

One of the first questions to be raised about a major address by Nixon, who for years was dogged with the nickname "Tricky Dick," would be "Is he sincere?" Nixon did not survive the political wars by the simple-minded morality of a country parson. He had scuttled Helen Gahagan Douglas, done in Alger Hiss, run interference for Eisenhower, fought Jack Kennedy to a virtual draw, and outlasted Barry Goldwater. He is a politician, which is to say that he has run a gauntlet the parameters of which are set, not by the Marquis of Queensberry, but by the necessities of survival.[4] From such an old pol, some temporizing might be expected.

When, therefore, he claimed, on November 3, to have a plan for peace, which he must unfortunately keep secret due to the perverseness of the enemy, some scepticism was expressed. Did he mean it? Did he really have a secret plan? Did he intend to close out the war, or was this just another maneuver to justify the same old business?

The reaction of the peace forces was largely predictable. Few were more blunt than Nixon's erstwhile nemesis, Senator Kennedy, as quoted by the *Times*:

> I do not wish to be harsh nor overly critical, but the time has come to say it: as a candidate, Richard Nixon promised us a plan for peace once elected; as chief executive, President Nixon promised us a plan for peace for the last 10 months. Last night he spoke again of a plan—a secret plan for peace sometime. There now must be doubt whether there is in existence any plan to extricate America from this war in the best interest of America—for it is no plan to say that what we do depends upon what Hanoi does.[5]

But when it comes to judging the President's sincerity, by all the canons of truth, Mansfield of Montana and Fulbright of Arkansas are superior judges. After five years of dealing with LBJ, they can be counted on to smell a fraud. Both want rapid withdrawal from Vietnam. Both have registered profound opposition to the course of the war. When, after conferences with the President, and caveats about the pace of withdrawal, they nonetheless acknowledge that the President does intend to get out, one must believe them. Both want withdrawal to be programmed independently of what Hanoi does, but both accept as genuine the President's wish to wind down the war.[6]

Were the testimony of the two leading Democratic Senators not conclusive, the ever-watchful White House press contingent, and the major liberal columnists, might be cited in their support. James Reston, whom I shall quote later on matters less favorable to Nixon's cause, regarded Nixon's sincerity as "almost terrifying."[7] And Richard Harwood and Laurence Stern of *The Washington Post* accept as true "that the President, a veteran of the Korean War Settlement, is intent on liquidating the American involvement in Vietnam under a veneer of tough talk."[8] The veneer is highly visible, for all to see; but under it is the intention of winding down the American part of the war in Vietnam. What he said, he meant.

But what is the shape of his commitment to withdrawal? Has he now, after all these years of supporting the anticommunist effort in Indochina, decided that it was a mistake and that we *should* withdraw? Or is he merely bowing to political expediency, withdrawing because he can do no other and still retain power? An understanding both of his rhetoric and of his politics depends on answers to these questions.

There are those who maintain that the President is nonideological, a consummate politician and nothing more. This view is concisely expressed by Edwin Newman of NBC News: "But Mr. Nixon is as he is, and it is as well for him, and perhaps for the country, that he is so little ideological. He is neither embarrassed nor bound by having written in 1964 that the war in Vietnam was a life and death struggle in which victory was essential to the survival of freedom, and by having said in Saigon in April, 1967, that the great issue in 1968 would 'not be how to negotiate defeat but how to bring more pressure to bear for victory.'"[9]

There is indeed much evidence in Nixon's recent behavior to indicate that the anticommunist cold war ideology which he so powerfully embraced has now been modified: the SALT talks are underway with apparently serious intent; economic and travel restrictions applied to China for twenty years have been relaxed, and we are talking to the Chinese in Warsaw; germ warfare has been disavowed; and the military budget is, for the first time in years, on the way down. Does all this add up to a new Nixon, one who can willingly disengage from Vietnam?

Nixon's massive, sustained, vigorous hostility to Ho Chi Minh and his movement simply cannot be wiped out overnight. It was, after all, Nixon who as early as 1954 did his best to launch an American expeditionary force against Ho Chi Minh and in support of the French. On April 16, 1954, Nixon appeared for an off-the-record session before the American Society of Newspaper Editors, meeting in Washington, and said that "if France stopped fighting in Indo-China and the situation demanded it the United States would have to send troops to fight the Communists in that area."[10] This 1954 speech was the first sign that the battle to maintain a noncommunist government in Saigon, whether of French colonials or of French-trained Vietnamese generals, was precisely Richard Nixon's battle. And consistently since, with no exception until the campaign of 1968, he has supported that battle.

One must approach the Nixon rhetoric, then, entertaining the hypothesis that he is disengaging reluctantly, that his heart is not in it, that only the pressure of public opinion has caused him to embrace what he for fifteen years rejected. And one of the strong reasons for believing that the President does have a plan to phase out this war rapidly is the possibility that by late 1970 even the American Legion will be tired of fighting.

A second approach to understanding the President's speech lies in reflection on the various audiences to whom he was speaking.

There were at least three domestic audiences of consequence. First, his friends: the conservative Republicans who voted him into office and the Wallace-ites he is now courting, largely a hawkish group, for whom he had the message, "Do not despair. I'm not heeding the demonstrators. We have to withdraw, but we don't have to give away a thing to the Viet Cong." Second, the "silent majority," some of whom had voted for him and some of whom had voted for Humphrey, many of them fence-straddlers on the war, all of them open, as Nixon saw it, to the plea, "I am winding down this war, but in a methodical and reasonable way which you ought to support." Third, the convinced doves, to whom he said, "Knock it off, I am the President, and disengaging from Vietnam is my bag. I respect your right to dissent, but don't carry it too far." In this latter group the youth, to whom he addressed a specific appeal, probably fit.

Abroad, he was concerned first with the South Vietnamese and other American client states: "We'll keep the faith, we won't desert you, and if the VC get tough again, we'll match them." There was also a clear word for Hanoi and other communist states: "You are going to have to come to terms with Thieu, or we will hang on forever; and if you escalate, the whole ball game is off."

One vital task of criticism is to decide which audience, and which message, was paramount. One is aided in making this decision by the recent publication of a startling book by a Nixon staffer, Kevin Phillips, an assistant to the Attorney General. In *The Emerging Republican Majority*,[11] Philips analyzes socioeconomic data to conclude that the white working-class voters who produced 9,906,473 votes for George Wallace in the last election can be turned into permanent Republicans. This can be done, says Philips, by taking over the Wallace message (which rejects peacenik and Black demands) and peddling it with enough sophistication to retain the present registered Republican clientele. Since the consevative, middle-class sun belt cities are growing at the expense of the Democratic cities in the East, this combination will give the Republicians a permanent majority.

The President has not, obviously, endorsed the book; but it fairly represents the strategy with which he fought the last election, and no repudiation of Phillips has been forthcoming: he assisted Attorney General Mitchell until February 1970. And it was to precisely this group, the Wallaceites, that the "veneer of tough talk" was directed. Nixon's rhetorical strategy was thus influenced by a political strategy: placate the doves not at all, appeal to the patriotism of the silent majority, but above all, show the "lower-middle-class clerks in Queens, steelworkers in Youngstown, and retired police lieutenants in San Diego"[12] *that you are their champion*. This is the rhetoric of confrontation.

It is a rhetoric which the Nixon administration, up to now, has largely delegated to the Vice-President. Careful scrutiny of Nixon's text will provide support for the thesis that he sought confrontation. He made numerous references to humiliation, disaster, and defeat, all of which outcomes he projects on to his opponents; these are fighting words. They were incorporated in the speech against the better judgment of Henry Kissinger,[13] and, according to columnists Evans and Novak, against the advice of Republican leaders in Congress to "give the doves something": "Mr. Nixon rejected that advice because he consciously wanted to split off what he regards as a small minority of antiwar activists from his 'great silent majority' of Americans. He was striving for a polarization of opinion isolating the dissenters and thereby dooming the extremist-led Nov. 15 march on Washington."[14]

This divide-and-isolate strategy was not dictated by the circumstances. The substance of President's plan could have been made palatable to many of his opponents. There were three crucial action programs: (1) avoid precipitate withdrawal; (2) keep the timetable secret; and (3) maintain a noncommunist government in Saigon. Given the division within the peace forces, who ranged from Friends to anarchists, he could easily have explained why the whole timetable could not be announced while announcing the next phase of withdrawal, which he did within six weeks anyway; he could have acknowledged the desirability of broadening the base of the Saigon government; and he could have put a higher priority on a cease fire. Had he done these things, he could have substantially alleviated the fears of many doves.

He not only failed to make these gestures of conciliation, he went far to agitate his opponents. He need not have injected the abrasive discussion of how the war started and how we got involved. He need not have talked as if all his opponents favored precipitate withdrawal. He need not have paraded before us again the controversial domino theory. He need not have done these things, that is, unless he had already decided to write off the dissenters and to start building his "emerging Republican majority" with Wallaceite support. But the decision was his. Anthony Lewis, Pulitzer Prize Winner of *The New York Times*, put it this way: "The puzzle is why he chose to speak as he did. He could so easily have expounded the same policy in less doom-laden rhetoric."[15]

The Argument

There were, according to the President, five questions on the minds of his listeners.

"How and why did America get involved in Vietnam in the first place?

"How has this Administration changed the policy of the previous Administration?

"What has really happened in the negotiations in Paris and the battlefront in Vietnam?

"What choices do we have if we are to end the war?

"What are the prospects for peace?"[16]

After a brief description of the "situation I found when I was inaugurated on Jan. 20th," he turns to what he claims is the "fundamental issue," why and how did we become involved in the first place. This is a surprising candidate for priority in any discussion today. One might have thought that the burning question was how to get out. The President's chief foreign policy advisors, his allies on Capitol Hill, and the memorandum he got from the Cabinet bureaucracy all urged him to skip discussions of the causes and manner of our involvement. Yet the history comes out with top billing. How and to what extent it is distorted is an interesting subject, but not our major concern here. This was a deliberative speech, and the President is arguing for a specific policy.

The substance of his policy argument, scattered throughout the speech, deals with four alternative plans for achieving disengagement. (The possibility of escalation is reserved as a club with which to scare the North Vietnamese into co-operating with Nixon's preferred plan for disengagement, but it is not offered as a full-fledged course of action in its own right).

First, the President could "end the war at once by ordering the immediate withdrawal of all American forces. From a political standpoint, this would have been a popular and easy course to follow." But it is not Nixon's course; it is craven advice, and it draws his most concentrated fire.

It would, for one thing, constitute a defeat. Given Mr. Nixon's historic commitment to a noncommunist South Vietnam, and his visceral reaction to being bested by communists any time on any issue (as revealed in his autobiographical *Six Crises*)[17] it is not surprising that he makes much of this argument. Even though, as he claims, he could blame the defeat on his predecessor, this would not be an honorable course.

Whether acknowledging defeat in Vietnam would be a wise course is another matter. Mr Nixon's mentor, Eisenhowever, recognized that, in the much more defensible war in Korea, we sustained a substantial defeat of MacArthur's objectives of rolling back the communists to the Yalu River. Most Americans seemed to approve a less-than-satisfactory settlement; avoidance of defeat did not then commend itself as the greatest good.

Similarly, in the abortive Bay of Pigs invasion, American-trained troops and American strategy suffered great humiliation. But, as Theodore Draper says of John F. Kennedy, "the President knew how to end the misery, without deception or whimpering, in a way that made him seem to grow in defeat."[18] The trauma of defeat varies with the character of the captain, as de Gaulle proved once again in Algeria. But then Nixon is no Kennedy or de Gaulle.

When one asks, "How can the anguish and terror of a loss in Vietnam be mitigated?" the answer has to be something other than the repeated stress on the necessity of avoiding defeat which we heard from President Nixon November 3. There is a case to be made for the honesty and therapeutic value of admitting that we were in over our heads, that we cannot police the whole world, that we really should not, as the military once told us, become involved in a ground war on the Asian continent.

Nixon does not reject immediate withdrawal solely on the basis of its intrinsic evil as a symbol of defeat. It would also lead to a train of undesirable consequences, all of which he ticks off as reasons for repudiating such a policy. It would damage the credibility of other American commitments; encourage communist aggressiveness everywhere; lead not only to the collapse of South Vietnam but all of Southeast Asia; result in horrendous massacres when the Viet Cong take over; and cause us to lose confidence in ourselves, with "inevitable remorse and divisive recrimination."

It might, indeed, do all of these things. These are consequences which need to be considered, *but they need to be considered only if immediate withdrawal is a serious alternative plan which the President needs to refute*. It is hard to see that it had such status. The sharpest challenge to his policy came from Senator Goodell and those who favored phased but definite withdrawal, with a specific deadline by which all American troops, or at least all combat troops, would be out. The call for immediate and total withdrawal came from a minority faction of the peace movement; and in rebutting it as if it were the most serious challenge to his preferred course, Nixon was drawing a red herring across the trail of his opponents, attacking a straw man whose demolition he could portray as destruction of the dissenters generally. This argumentative strategy seems to have succeeded with the silent majority; it festers and repels when one attends to his rhetoric carefully.

The second alternative plan for disengagement is negotiation. Mr Nixon holds open some slight hope that this might still be the road out; but after a long and frustrating year of meeting with the enemy in Paris, he does not put much faith in it. In this he is undoubtedly correct. North Vietnam has not now, and is not likely to acquire, any faith in negotiated agreements. For those who can remove the distorting lenses of national self-righteousness, which of course always reveal the other part as culprit in scuttling international agreements, the evidence points overwhelmingly to a justification of Hanoi's attitude.[19] But this need not concern us here. Aside from the debater's points Mr. Nixon makes by detailing the substance of U.S. negotiating proposals, and his claim that "Hanoi has refused even to discuss our proposals," this is a blind alley.

The third possible way to get out of Vietnam has the weightiest support behind it, both in the Senate and elsewhere; it is to withdraw steadily with a fixed terminal date. Here is the option upon which attention should have been focused. Here is the real challenge to presidential decision making. If the President were to reason with the most reasonable of his critics, he should have spent the bulk of his energies showing why this plan is disadvantageous compared to his; yet the emphasis it receives is minor.

The few swipes he takes at fixed-schedule withdrawal are instructive. "An announcement of a fixed timetable for our withdrawal would completely remove any incentive for the enemy to negotiate an agreement. They would simply wait until our forces had withdrawn and then move in." This attack is curious indeed. Have we not already written off the prospects for negotiation? Under what possible logic would the enemy be more likely to "wait until our forces had withdrawn and then move in" if they have a terminal point for that wait than if they do not? Is this not likely to happen whether the timetable is secret or public? Here is the core of the dispute between the President and his detractors, and he attends to it with a casual and obfuscating logic that defies belief.

The only other attack on the idea of a *terminus ad quem* for withdrawal is based on its alleged inflexibility; Mr. Nixon does not want to be "frozen in on a fixed timetable." One can accept that some flexibility in such an operation might be in order. This seems not to have deterred our officials from setting up, if not a rigid schedule, at least a terminal date for the accomplishment of other objectives. One must strain one's imagination somewhat to conceive Mr. Nixon incapable of extending a deadline for withdrawal in the face of Vietcong attacks which he defined as serious.

Here is the sum total of the President's refutation of the most serious challenge his program faces. It is hardly worth the candle.

So, finally, we come to alternative number four, the plan adopted and defended by the President. This scenario was worked up by Herman Kahn of the Hudson Institute. The July, 1968 *Foreign Affairs* carried an article by Kahn setting forth his plan for deescalation: build up Arvin, withdraw most American combat units, leave behind a reservoir of between 200,000 and 300,000 men to "deter a resumption of major hostilities."[20] This is now Nixon's plan, with the additional proviso that no long-range schedule be announced.

One needs, at this stage, to view the plan as a whole, inspecting the justifications for it, the reasons for preferring it to alternatives, the rhetoric in which it is clothed. A number of salient points need close scrutiny. As with any policy proposal, the pay off stage is the prediction of future consequences: how will the plan work?

Specifically, one needs to know whether it is probable that (1) the Vietcong and Hanoi will tolerate the presence of 450,000, 400,000 or 350,000 foreign troops while the hated Thieu regime attempts to develop combat effectiveness; (2) the Vietcong and Hanoi will beyond that tolerate the indefinite presence in the country of 250,000 or more occupation troops; (3) the shaky regime in Saigon will really develop political support and military muscle sufficient to keep the communists at bay; (4) the American public, including the great silent majority, the Emerging Republican Majority, and all the rest of us, will tolerate this kind of semi-permanent occupation even if combat casualties drop to zero; and (5) there will be less right-wing recrimination should this plan fail than if there is a fast, clean withdrawal.

The President's defense on all these points deserves the closest inspection. We need, in a situation where Mr. Nixon admits "that many Americans have lost confidence in what their Government has told them about our policy," some indication of the evidence on which these assumed consequences are based, whether it be from the CIA, the military, the State Department, Sir Robert Thompson, or wherever. We need some assurance that the President is capable of what social psychologists call "tough-minded empathy," or the ability to see this plan as Hanoi sees it, and not just from the compulsively optimistic viewpoint of the Department of Defense.

There is nothing. The plan is there, take it or leave it. There is a warning to Hanoi to go along or else. There is a recognition that "some of my fellow citizens disagree" with the plan he has chosen. There is a rejection of demonstrations in the street, an appeal to the young people of the nation to turn their energies to constructive ends, a call for partiotism, a reference to Woodrow Wilson (at whose desk he spoke). In defense of his plan, there is only a contemptible rhetorical device, "My fellow Americans, I am sure you can recognize from what I have said that we really have only two choices open to us if we want to end this war. I can order an immediate precipitate withdrawal of all Americans from Vietnam without regard to the effects of that action. Or we can persist in our search for a just peace through...our plan for Vietnamization." Here it is, all over again, the false dilemma, the black or white position, the collapse of all alternative strategies into the one most offensive and easiest to ridicule. Only two choices: my plan, or the cut-and-run cowardice of the rioters in the streets.

It is, perhaps, a consummation to be expected of the politician who perfected the technique of "The Illusion of Proof."[21]

For the attentive public to accept the Nixon program of open-ended, no-deadline withdrawal, we have got to have answers which he does not provide. Literally dozens of his opponents have protested that he is giving Saigon the best excuse in the world for not broadening its base, for not coming to terms with the Buddhists and General Khanh, for not cracking down on corruption, for not accommodating to the demands of peasants in the countryside. As Reston put it, "For if his policy is to stick with the South Vietnamese until they demonstrate that they are secure, all they have to do is prolong their inefficiency in order to guarantee that we will stay in the battle indefinitely."[22] No defense of the President's plan could ignore the logic of this argument; yet ignore it is precisely what Mr. Nixon did.

Consequences

The announcement that the President would speak about the war on November 3 had consequences in itself. The October Moratorium was weakened; an attitude of "let's wait and see" may have deterred many would-be doves from participating. But the significant consequences were of course after the speech.

The stock market, that sensitive barometer of America's morale and business health, dropped. At 10:30 on the morning of the 4th, prices were down 7.72 on the Dow-Jones industrial average. Stocks largely recovered later in the day, and closed mixed; but the people who handle the money clearly didn't think the President had pulled a coup.

One consequence of the speech, given Nixon's past debilitating relationship with the journalistic fraternity, was a serious lowering of his credibility. Reston put it this way: "The result is that the really important men reporting on the Presidency—not the columnists but the reporters and White House correspondents—are now wondering about the President after his Vietnam speech and his partisan reaction to the elections. He invited them to believe that he would not be like President Johnson, that he would be open and candid. But his approach and reaction to the elections have not been open and candid but personal and partisan. Like Johnson he has dealt with the politics of his problem but not with the problem of Vietnam."[23]

The effects in Saigon were electric. As the *Times* headline read on November 10, "Nixon's Impact: Thieu is Helped Through a Tight Spot."[24] The National Assembly had been raising hell, a motion of no confidence was being discussed in the lower house, and a petition calling for a nationwide referendum was being circulated. Nixon stopped all this. His reaffirmed commitment to stay until there was no more challenge to "freedom" strengthened Thieu's hand immeasurably. Not being one to bite the hand that upholds him, Thieu recorded his gratitude for the press: this was "one of the most important and greatest" speeches made by an American President.[25]

The three domestic audiences identified at the beginning of this essay reacted predictably. Nixon's supporters, the hawks and the Emerging Republican Majority, were delighted. Columnist Joseph Alsop rejoiced hugely: "Whether you agree or disagree with its content, this remarkable speech was one of the most successful technical feats of political leadership in many, many years."[26]

The silent majority was impressed. Gallup, who clocked them in by telephone immediately after the speech, found 77% approving. And in his regular survey of presidential performance, taken November 14–16, approval of the President generally rose 12% over the previous month, to a high of 68%.[27] Although as Gallup noted, there was some question as to the durability of this result, the speech did sell; the "terrifying sincerity" was just what the public wanted to see. But the long pull is yet ahead.

The doves were horror-struck. There had been much reason to believe that the speech would be conciliatory, that the rhetoric would be encouraging. One consequence of the toughness of the speech was that registrations for buses to Washington for the November 13–15 events flooded in;[28] and the ultimate crowd in Washington could be said to be a direct result of Nixon's challenge to the dissidents. The effete ones were not going to take it lying down.

The candid conclusion must be that the President cheered his friends and disheartened his enemies. The peace movement is in disarray, planning no more massive marches, resigned to campus and campaign activities—until the President slips, or Hanoi trips him. As of the end of December, Richard Starnes of Scripps-Howard put it succinctly: "Peace Marchers Give Round to Nixon."[29]

Epilogue

The Nixon style in this speech has been characterized as "tough talk." But this is not the same as saying it was rough; Nixon did preserve the amenities. As Reston put it, "He put Spiro Agnew's confrontation language into the binding of a hymn book."[30] But hymn books are not the only score from which the Administration sings. The cruder, more abrasive tunes are coming steadily from the Vice-President; and it is worth inquiring as to whether the Nixon tune must be heard against the accompaniment of his second in command.

The arguments that have raged in Washington as to whether the Vice-President plays the role of hatchet man to Nixon's above-the-battle dignity just as Nixon was once the hatchet man for Eisenhower, has now largely been resolved. Agnew comes up with his own script. His purple-passioned prose is indigenous, and with the exception of his November 13 blast against the television networks, which according to Clark Mollenhoff "was developed in the White House,"[31] the ideas as well as the language are his.

But even when he is doing his own thing, Mr. Agnew represents the President's true gut feelings.[32] The relationship is one of willing supporter, not ventriloquist's dummy. If Agnew were not around to ventilate the President's pique, someone else would have to be commandeered to put out the purple-passioned prose. The President himself, of course, could do it very well; the summer of 1969 he reverted to a former style with his colorful speeches at General Beadle State College and the Air Force Academy; but the reaction to these by the President's staff was less than enthusiastic, and he has since then turned over the rough talk to the Vice-President.

What we have, then, in the President's speech, is the substance of toughness without the rough style. And the President's text is indeed sanitized. What he might have said, what his style would have been were he not consciously trying to retain the old Republican genteel clientele, one can discover by reading Agnew. The visceral language, the blunt insults, the uncompromising hostilities are missing.[33]

But a presidential address must meet higher standards than campaign oratory or the speeches of lesser figures. Nixon's speech did not meet them. Neither his rhetorical strategies nor his substantive argument were sound. Yet the most likely time for healing and realistic rhetoric has passed. The President's personal involvement in Government decisions will grow, his commitment to what we are doing now will increase, his access to noncongruent intelligence will decrease, the youth will become more alienated. Nixon is not LBJ, and the total closing of filters that occurred in the last days of the Johnson Administration probably will not happen again; but the prospect for improvement is slight. One can always hope that another Clark Clifford is waiting in the wings to restore sanity, or another Eugene McCarthy will appear in the hustings to startle a self-deluded establishment.

A fitting summary of the whole business is provided by Anthony Lewis:

> *The preeminent task of Richard Nixon's Presidency is to heal a nation torn apart by Vietnam. The President knew that when he took the oath of office, and it is no less urgently true today. Part of the process must be to help the American people know, and accept, the unpleasant truths about the war: that we got into it by stealth and for reasons at best uncertain; that the Government we defend in South Vietnam is corrupt and unrepresentative; that in the course of fighting we have killed people and ravaged a country to an extent utterly out of proportion to our cause, and that, in the old sense of dictating to the enemy, we cannot "win." In those terms, Mr. Nixon's speech to the nation last Monday evening was a political tragedy.[34]*

It was not just the speech that was a political tragedy; the speech merely made visible tragic policy decisions—to maintain the goals and propaganda of the cold war, to seek confrontation with those who want change, to go with a power base confined to white, nonurban, uptight voters. Given such decisions, the shoddy rhetoric, the tough talk, the false dilemmas are inevitable. Instant criticism, via the networks, while desirable, cannot begin to do justice to such policies and such rhetoric. They require more searching exploration. As the saying goes, presidential rhetoric is much too important to be left to presidents.

_____ Notes _____

1. Robert B. Semple, Jr., "Speech Took 10 Drafts, And President Wrote All," *The New York Times*, November 4, 1969, p. 17.
2. *Ibid.*
3. Rowland Evans and Robert Novak, "Nixon's Appeal for Unity," (Baltimore) *News-American*, November 3, 1969, p. 7B.
4. For a candid statement of the pressures operating on politicians, and the hard choices they make in the struggle for survival, see John F. Kennedy, *Profiles in Courage* (New York, 1956), ch. I.
5. November 5, 1969, p. 10.
6. Mansfield has generally been more sympathetic to the President's position than Fulbright; the Majority Leader joined Minority Leader Hugh Scott in sponsoring a resolution expressing qualified suport of the President on November 7. See UPI dispatch. "40 Senators Back Cease-Fire Plea," *The New York Times*, November 8, 1969, p. 10.
7. "Nixon's Mystifying Clarifications," *The New York Times*, November 5, 1969, p. 46.
8. "Polls Show the 'Silent Majority' Also Is Uneasy About War Policy," *The Washington Post*, November 5, 1969, p. A19.
9. "One Man Alone," *The New York Times Book Review*, November 23, 1969, p. 10.
10. Luther A. Huston, "Asian Peril Cited; High Aide Says Troops May Be Sent if the French Withdraw," *The New York Times*, April 17, 1954, p. 1. Someone in Paris is alleged to have blown his cover, and Nixon was identified as the "High Aide" the next day. See also Bernard Fall, *Hell in a Very Small Place: The Siege of Dien Bien Phu* (New York, 1966), ch. IX.
11. (New Rochelle, 1969).
12. The categories of Wallace supporters are those of Andrew Hacker in his sympathetic review of Phillips, "Is There a New Republican Majority?" *Commentary*, XLVIII (November 1969), 65–70.
13. Robert B. Semple Jr., "Nixon's November 3 Speech: Why He Took the Gamble Alone," *The New York Times*, January 19, 1970, p. 23.
14. Rowland Evans and Robert Novak, "Nixon's Speech Wedded GOP Doves to Mass of Americans," *The Washington Post*, November 6, 1969, p. A23.
15. Anthony Lewis, "The Test of American Greatness in Vietnam," *The New York Times*, November 8, 1969, p. 32.
16. All quotations from the speech are from *The New York Times* text, carried November 4, 1969, p. 16.
17. *Six Crises* (Garden City, N.Y., 1962).
18. *The Dominican Revolt* (New York, 1968).
19. Probably the best source on American violations of the Geneva Agreement on Vietnam is George M. Kabin and John W. Lewis, *The United States in Vietnam*, rev. ed. (New York, 1969).
20. "If Negotiations Fail," XLVI, 627–641.
21. See Barnet Baskerville, "The Illusion of Proof," *Western Speech*, XXV (Fall 1961), 236–242.
22. James Reston, "Washington: The Unanswered Vietnam Questions," *The New York Times*, December 10, 1969, p. 54.
23. James Reston, "Washington: The Elections and the War," *The New York Times*, November 7, 1969, p. 46.

24. Terence Smith, *The New York Times*, November 10, 1969, p. 2.

25. Terence Smith, "Thieu Hails the Speech: 'One of the Most Important,'" *The New York Times*, November 5, 1969, p. 10.

26. Joseph Alsop, "Nixon Leadership is Underestimated," *The Washington Post*, December 29, 1969, p. A13.

27. George Gallup, "Nixon Support Soars to 68%," *The Washington Post*, November 24, 1969, p. A1.

28. David E. Rosenbaum, "Thousands Due in Capital in War Protest This Week," *The New York Times*, November 9, 1969, pp. 1, 56.

29. *The Pittsburgh Press*, December 26, 1969, p. 15.

30. James Reston, November 5, 1969.

31. E. W. Kenworthy, "Nixon Aide Says Agnew Stand Reflects White House TV View," *The New York Times*, November 16, 1969, p. 78.

32. Robert B. Semple, Jr., "Agnew: The Evidence is That He's Speaking for Nixon," *The New York Times*, November 2, 1969, Sec. 4, p. 3.

33. But the old debator's syndrome is very much present. A good capsule description of what this means is in Earl Mazo and Stephen Hess, *Nixon: A Political Portrait* (New York, 1968), p. 7.

34. *The New York Times*, November 8, 1969, p. 32.

The Quest Story and Nixon's November 3, 1969 Address

——————————— HERMANN G. STELZNER ———————————

The Quest story is a literary genre in which the subjective experiences of life are central. The themes in such stories vary, but the genre is one of the oldest, hardiest, and most popular. Perhaps its persistent appeal is due to "its validity as a symbolic description of our subjective personal experience of existence as historical."[1] The Quest story describes a search for "something" the truth or falsity of which is known only upon the conclusion of the search.

Although the themes and the details change, the form or "the fixity" of Quest stories is fairly stable,[2] one reason why the Quest story is archetypal. When the essential elements of the story interact with the subjective experiences of individuals verbal transactions occur. Occasionally universal human reactions are elicited.

The practical world of political affairs shares many themes with the imaginative world of fiction. When a leader of a body politic and his people seek to resolve a problem, they may be engaged in a Quest. A leader speaks and orders a reality, a form; he offers an *objective* experience of the social, political, or moral life. However, to become viable it must interact with the *subjective* experiences of his listeners. If a given problem, war and peace, for example, occurs frequently enough, perhaps a close examination of all such speeches might yield an archetypal pattern. Thus far, however, the rhetorical criticism of speeches has not proceeded from this perspective. This exploratory effort centers on a single speech.

When President Richard M. Nixon spoke to the nation on November 3, 1969 about the war in Vietnam he indicated how central it was to him, his Administration, and his people: "I did not wait for my inauguration to begin my quest for peace."[3] The connotations of "quest" and Nixon's strong, personal identification with it—"my," not *our* or *the*, convey an orientation and a potential pattern of behavior that suggest that this speech and the archetypal Quest story share similarities.[4] To place the speech within the genre of the Quest story is merely to classify it. But the essential elements of the Quest story may then provide a way into the speech, and they may yield insights that other critical approaches do not obtain. The critical prism refracts light differently as a function of the way it is turned. The light refracted from this angle may be a different "color" from that obtained from some other facet of the prism.[5] Finally, the objective political experience of Vietnam structured by President Nixon and the listeners' subjective experiences of life should interact. What in the chosen and arranged language of the speech increases the probability of a verbal transaction? What goes on in the speech?

The five essential elements of a Quest story are stated here and developed below. These elements also function as a rhetorical partition, providing terms for the analysis and forcing the parts of the analysis to comment on one another. The essential elements are (1) a precious Object and/or Person to be found and possessed or married; (2) a long journey to find the Object, because its whereabouts are not originally known to the seekers; (3) a Hero; (4) the Guardians of the Object who must be overcome before it can be won; and (5) the Helpers who with their knowledge and/or magical powers assist the Hero and but for whom he would never succeed.

1. *A precious Object and/or Person to be found and possessed or married.* Because the conflict in Vietnam was central in the political scene Nixon inherited on his inauguration, he sketches its background in swift, broad strokes; it serves as a refresher for listeners and as a point of departure. He advances five questions that preview the direction his remarks will take: (1) "How and why did America get involved in Vietnam in the first place?" He terms it the "fundamental issue." (2) "How has this Administration changed the policy of the previous Administration?" Centering on this question allows Nixon to capitalize on the public frustration with the Johnson approach and to avoid any serious consideration of the "fundamental issue." (3) "What has really happened in the negotiations in Paris and the battle-front in Vietnam?" Nixon's reports are scattered throughout the speech (4) "What choices do we have if we are to end the war?" This is a central question but Nixon examines only two choices. (5) "What are the prospects for peace?"

Nixon does not make the precious Object immediately clear, withholding its precise nature and character. Instead he alludes to the October 15, 1969 Moratorium and comments briskly and adversely on a peace proposal endorsed by its leaders. Intending to unveil a new view, he weakens the old before announcing it, thus avoiding a direct conflict.

Nixon early makes clear that whatever the policy, it will be influenced by the long view of the national and international scene. He refers obliquely to the young, telling the Now and In generation they must yield to his "greater obligation" to think of the "next generation" and of the "future of peace and freedom in America and in the world." The view is global. Nixon's treatment of time and the next generation suggests that stability and settledness will emerge from the as yet undisclosed precious Object.

But Nixon's statements are not altogether consistent. He appears troubled as he searches for a view that will be acceptable to an anxious audience at home and to the international audience as well:[6] "I had to think of the effect of my decision on the next generation, and on the future of peace and freedom in America and in the world." Three sentences later he offers a view that restricts, if it does not altogether compromise, the breadth of his concern: "The great question is: How can we win America's peace?" If this is indeed the *great question*, what has happened to the world? Has there been a shift in perspective? A possible explanation for these contradictory emphases must be hazarded.

The first statement is not only global; it also emphasizes future time. The second statement is restricted and time is not specifically mentioned. Measured against the first statement the second suggests being accomplished in a shorter time. The second statement springs out of Nixon's need to recognize early emotional stresses and divisiveness at home. It suggests that they can be resolved sooner than later. The long war has often been justified as an international obligation. The national patience has worn thin. Nixon offers something to quiet the impatience. He centers on and satisfies self.

The prized Object is finally announced. It is a "just peace," a "just and lasting peace." Nixon makes clear that the peace his opponents seek cannot be prized. Their method of achieving it and the effects of it tarnish the Object. A just peace is more valuable than a pragmatic peace because it lies beyond men and the moment; it transcends both. Here, of course, is the higher peace of an Upper World and such an Object is potentially persuasive when the opponents in South Vietnam, the Communist North Vietnamese supported by Communist China and the Soviet Union, represent the demonic powers of a Lower World.

Further, if America achieves only an immediate peace, which Nixon defines as the "popular and easy course," she will not have set a goal worthy enough to meet the requirements of a "lasting peace," which concerns "many people in all parts of the world." Peace in Vietnam is not enough; peace in Vietnam must serve the "cause of peace...in the Pacific and the world." The prized Object has been located and defined.

2. *A long journey to find the Object, because its whereabouts are not originally known to the seekers*. The journey takes place in both time and space. For the United States it began "fifteen years ago" when North Vietnam "launched a campaign to impose a Communist government on South Vietnam." Nixon quickly summarizes the actions taken by Presidents Eisenhower, Kennedy, and Johnson who sent men and materials into the conflict.

Time is central in Nixon's analysis. It is partially because the war has been "long and bitter" that he rejects the policy of immediate withdrawal. His many references to its proponents are his open acknowledgment of their strength, but he is certain that a lengthy, bitter military and psychological effort cannot simply stop.

The fifteen long years also condition the peace he will accept. His opposition seeks a pragmatic peace. But the time already spent and still to be spent in the search will further dignify the Object. Nixon makes a "just peace" and an "immediate peace" via withdrawal into antithetical images, a timeless value versus a momentary value; the former has weight, the latter is weightless and ephemeral.

The search for a weightless ephemeral Object cannot be rewarding; it is a journey into Nowhere, a journey "to the end of the night," and the effect would be chaos, Nixon claims. He acknowledges his journey is into a "dangerous" Unknown. But in contrast to the gesture or policy of despair his opponents offer (Nixon resists calling it suicide), his policy has *significant form*. A policy of despair always lacks a reliable and objective narrator. Nixon stresses that the young are idealistic; idealism is antithetical to objectivity and reliability.

However valuable a "just peace" may be, Nixon understands that it must not appear to be beyond reach. Time is both a physical measure and a psychological state, and he senses that to satisfy his listeners he must make the timeless future somehow concrete and reasonably immediate. He announces some of the gains his approach has achieved: "Now we have begun to see the results of this long-overdue change in American policy in Vietnam." The results indicate that both the war and the battle with time can be won.

3. *A Hero*. The precious Object cannot be won by anybody, but only by the one person who possesses the right qualifications of breeding and character. Further, the Quest story presents a Test or a series of Tests by which the unworthy are screened out, and the Hero revealed.

There are two types of Quest Hero. The first has a superior arete manifest to all. No one doubts that he can win the Golden Fleece if anyone can. The second has a concealed arete. He turns out to be the Hero when his manifest betters have failed. His zeal is plodding and pedestrian. He enlists help because unlike his betters he is humble enough to take advice and kind enough to give assistance to people who, like himself, appear to be nobody in particular.

Hero images often appear in public addresses, and they are symbolic. In Nixon's speech both types of Hero appear and his portrayals of them build support for himself and his policy. The Heroes are structured in polar terms, but because they faced a common problem, Vietnam, the polarities are not in direct moral or ethical conflict. The portrayal is not developed as good-bad, strong-weak, right-wrong, but as practical-impractical, workable-unworkable, or feasible-unfeasible. For example, Nixon acknowledges that "many believe that President Johnson's decision to send American combat forces to South Vietnam was wrong." Nixon supports the decision, but observes: "And many others, I among them, have been strongly critical of the way the war has been conducted." His criticism of Woodrow Wilson also centers on practicality, workability and feasibility.

Early in the speech Nixon reports on the efforts of Presidents Eisenhower, Kennedy, and Johnson to achieve success in Vietnam. Immediately following the factual citations, Nixon employs Kennedy for support and refers to him in a special way. About one aspect of American policy, Kennedy spoke, Nixon states, with "characteristic eloquence and clarity," and these are attributes of men of superior arete.

If Kennedy, a Hero of superior arete, appears early in the speech, not until it is almost concluded does Nixon place another figure who is similarly described. Woodrow Wilson, says Nixon, had a "dream for peace." And he "spoke words which caught the imagination of a war-weary world...: 'This is the war to end wars'." Heroes of superior arete can express the affairs of state in apocalyptic terms. They have an imaginative conception of the whole of nature.

These two Heroes are much alike in another way. Kennedy died a tragic death while in office. Listeners need not be reminded. Wilson did not die in office, but Nixon says that he "died a broken man," and he stresses that Wilson's "dream" was "shattered on the hard reality of great power politics." These two examples remind listeners that the leadership offered by visionary Heroes may result in a "tragic fall" if an idealized goal cannot be achieved.

About his policy and himself, Nixon is emphatic; he does not offer a vision beyond his ability to produce: "I do not tell you that the war in Vietnam is the war to end wars." He hopes only to "increase the chance that...younger brothers and...sons" of the men in Vietnam "will not have to fight in some future Vietnam some place in the world."

Nixon knows that he is not a Kennedy or a Wilson, but he does not disassociate himself completely from them. He reports that he, too, is a statesman, aspiring to the title of peacemaker in the world. How? He tells listeners he speaks from the room, "in this room" where Wilson spoke about the "war to end wars." He tells them about Wilson's desk, "at this very desk" Wilson spoke. The desk is in the room and via television in the presence of listeners. Nixon has kept it and apparently works at it. A moral value is not only expressed; it is also displayed.

Nixon also emphasizes the kind of Hero he is by not taking advantage of a fallen Hero, his predecessor. If he supported immediate withdrawal, it would bring defeat, but he could "blame" it on Johnson and "come out as the peacemaker." To achieve peace at another's expense is a low form of honor. Nixon knows that many citizens mistrust Johnson, whose fall is partially explained in moral terms. More than a few citizens believe Johnson capable of the very action Nixon rejects as unworthy of a man of stature. He puts distance between himself and Johnson.

Nixon also equates many of the dissenting young people with the first type of Hero. He delivered this speech two weeks after the first Moratorium (October 15, 1969).[7] Another demonstration was planned for November. Nixon announced his speech far in advance (on October 13, 1969), strategically placing it between the two convocations. That the Moratorium was an eloquent and dramatic statement-act is a value judgment. That it was largely an expression by the young is fact.

That Nixon equates the young with the first type of Hero is clear from evidence in the address. He states that "some" people urged him to order "the immediate withdrawal of all American forces." In Quest stories Heroes of superior arete often ride straight up the golden path to win the prized Object. Nixon alludes to such activity; immediate withdrawal means "without regard to the effects of that action." Further, to ride straight up the path wins the applause of the multitude; it would have been a "popular...course to follow." Nixon acknowledges that the young have "energy and dedication." He also respects their "idealism," a term he specifically reserves for the young.

Nixon and his supporters are the second type of Hero. In 1960 he had jousted with a Hero of the first type, was defeated, and hovered near political death. Patiently and industriously he brought himself back to political health. He and his policy for Vietnam are counterbalances to the first type of Hero. Whatever is done must not risk death—political or any other kind. Withdrawal from Vietnam means "collapse" in all "Southeast Asia." Immediate withdrawal, equated with "defeat," would result in a "collapse of confidence" in America's leadership "not only in Asia but throughout the world." Our collapse would "promote recklessness" and "spark violence" which ultimately would "cost more lives"—more death. An idealistic policy, Nixon suggests, might create a Hell on Earth.

It is interesting to compare Nixon's personal political fortunes with those he has described for the state if the wrong course is chosen. Defeat in 1960 did not mean total collapse for him. Defeat again in California in 1962 did not mean total collapse. Affairs in the world of individual men are reversible. In affairs of state they are not. Or is it that the Hero who has suffered, and understands what to suffer means, wishes to protect his people from the agonies he has personally experienced? He must also know full well that if the nation emerges from Vietnam suffering as he has personally suffered, his place in the history books (the annals of the time) will be dimmed.

Nixon's policy for Vietnam is disciplined, cautious, and pragmatic. He will not go straight up the path. He has provided for options. Realizing that peace might not be achieved "through negotiation" he had ready "another plan." He will work earnestly; even before his inauguration he began his quest. For Nixon peace is not a vision. It is a "concern" and a "goal." Consistent with the type of Hero he is, he asks to be judged by the cumulative effects of his labors, not by the moral intensity of his strivings.

If Nixon's policy is disciplined, cautious, and pragmatic, the language that displays it is hard, rigid, and barren. Word choices are both familiar and unpretentious. Images are absent; the texture is flat.

Noticeably lacking are Biblical images. Yet the speech is directed largely to a silent majority, the generations nurtured on war and Biblical imagery. However, this is a secular war and God does not explicitly support our policy; nor is He explicitly on our side. Three rhetorical considerations explain the absence of such imagery. First, this speech is not so much a war message as it is a message about a war. Second, Vietnam is a small war that Presidents Eisenhower, Kennedy, and Johnson sought to localize and restrain. Nixon, too, aims to deflate it. Biblical images have magnitude, scope, and thrust. Thus, on both logical and aesthetic grounds they are simply "too large" for the problem. Third, Biblical images connote ethical and moral values. Keeping the war secular, and justifying it with political, military, and economic values, deprives the opposition of a potential issue. Further, Nixon does not give the silent majority an opportunity to consciously consider if the Biblical imagery and the Vietnam war are consistent. He avoids constructing for them a potentially disturbing dilemma.

Either type of Hero-president can use the power of the Office to further policies. Nixon reports on many of his efforts. He sent emissaries across the water (another part of the long journey) to the symbolic capital of the civilized—and thus safe—world, Paris, to meet with the North Vietnamese. He himself crossed the water to inspect the unsafe world and to receive firsthand reports about our efforts to stabilize it, a dimension of civilization. Then from Guam, that piece of secure United States territory nearest the conflict, he intoned from afar a shift in foreign policy. The policy is given a potentially potent name, Vietnamization. The phonetic similarities between Vietnamization and Americanization suggest our continued influence and concern. He also announces that other "significant initiatives which must remain secret to keep open some channels of communications" are in progress. Further, he sends a letter to Ho Chi Minh through an unnamed representative who had known Minh personally for 25 years; a dimension of intrigue is added to the effort. In some reports there are signs of hope. Nixon refers to the "deadlock" in negotiations, but perhaps new energies will come from this tired metaphor. He refers to the letter he received from Ho Chi Minh, "three days before his death." The letter says nothing new, but may not its writer's death be read as a hopeful harbinger of some new movement? Of what significance is the report of Minh's death, if not that? In deadlock and in death itself is the potential for rebirth.

Nixon's policy, language, and behavior reveal him as a Hero whose omnipotence and omniscience are limited.

4. *The Guardians of the Object who must be overcome before it can be won.* They may simply be a further test of the Hero's arete, or they may be malignant in themselves.

That the government of North Vietnam is both different from and in opposition to the United States is understood. In the popular mind, North Vietnam is malignant simply because it is communist; external motives are neither necessary to its behavior nor can they ever fully explain its behavior. Nixon does nothing to soften that view. Rather he emphasizes and develops it. An evil government will instigate and support revolutions: in the time past, in the present time, and in the future. Nixon's language is extremely severe: "murdered," "thousands...died in slave labor camps," "civilians were clubbed, shot,...and buried in mass graves," "a bloody reign of terror," and a "nightmare" in South Vietnam describe the North Vietnamese activities; the government is presented as being much worse than an undeveloped version of ourselves. Surely in an address about a war the image of the dual experience, a contest between two sides, friends and enemies, is expected. Nixon emphasizes animality and bestiality.

But the North Vietnamese also present further tests to the Hero and the American people. Nixon details the proposals the United States has advanced. We will work in common and will be openminded. Except for the right of the people of South Vietnam to determine their own future "anything is negotiable." Again and again Nixon remarks on the responses to such proposals. Hanoi has "refused even to discuss our proposals." In Paris a "deadlock" developed. Further negotiation "depends only on Hanoi's deciding to negotiate." The silent, uninvolved, non-participating North Vietnamese made success difficult. Nixon's tone is objective. But to stress his personal exasperation, he concludes with a folksy idiom consistent with his common-sense observation: "Well, now, who's at fault?"

A war message and the Quest story share the presupposition that one side is good, the other bad. But our *objective experience* of social and political life informs us otherwise. The moral ambiguities of political conflicts do not adhere to the proposition. But in war, men stereotype, reserving the good for their side and the bad for their opponents. And any virtues an enemy may possess are ignored.[8]

5. *The Helpers who with their knowledge and/or magical powers assist the Hero and but for whom he would never succeed.* Ideally, all citizens in a democracy will be Helpers, but in a "free society" dissent is recognized and tolerated. However, if dissenters take to the streets they might bind a president and circumscribe his options. In such a situation, what may be of greater danger than a dissenting Chorus is a confused, perplexed, and silent Chorus. To a Hero in need of support a formless and mute Chorus presents problems. How does a Hero-president "divine" what a silent majority will hear? Although Nixon can neither see it nor hear it, he has personal resources. His private vision furnishes him direction.

The rhetorical strategy emerges slowly and develops late. The approach to silent America is through young America, or for purposes of a rhetorical antithesis "shrill America." The young have been described. They are fervent, vocal, idealistic, energetic, and dedicated. These are positive virtues. Nixon counters them with a single negative particular that explains how the young have gone wrong. The positive virtues have been turned "into bitter hatred." Bitter hatred is irrational. It is, Nixon suggests, the tragic flaw in the character of the young.

If a democracy tolerates dissent and if men of station and experience have something to say to those (the young) who have achieved less, it is reasonable to assume that the young will attend to the President. It is also reasonable to assume that the President may speak directly to any audience. Yet when Nixon addresses the young, he casts doubt on these assumptions. He asks permission: "I would like to address a word, if I may, to the young people of this nation." The deliberately artificial idiom creates a cool and distant relationship. A superior depicts himself begging favors of an inferior and in the inversion Nixon discards the rhetorical mask of sociability. He comes close to portraying himself as a "silent American" or still better for his purposes a "silenced American." If the president approaches the young in this fashion, he suggests to others that the young people are a serious problem.

Nixon, however, had stated a policy. He had forcefully declared that he would not be "dictated" to "by the minority." Should other adults adopt his stance? If the connotations of the word "dictate" central to our involvement in Vietnam are extended, the answer is positive. If we are helping South Vietnam to avoid being dictated to by a belligerent minority, surely the people at home can also resist being dictated to.

The stance provides Nixon with an opportunity to give added force to nostalgic values: "I know it may not be fashionable to speak of patriotism or national destiny these days." The negative emphasizes the positive. These values are the beacon lights that confirm the reality of democratic form. They indicate that democracy is not yet, at least, invisible and unrecognizable. A citizenry and a nation unaware of their form live a death.

Together the discussion of the young and of values prepares that audience Nixon has yet to address directly: "So tonight, to you, the great silent majority of my fellow Americans, I ask for your support."[9] Silent America has been invited to speak; it need not ask permission. A formal fashion is preserved. Further, Nixon's private vision rhetorically developed before a public, creates a new form or audience, the "silent majority." The Helpers in the citizen Chorus who were confused are perplexed are made cohesive and real. They are no longer invisible and unrecognizable to themselves. They are also made visible and recognizable to others.

Nixon gives added meaning to patriotism and destiny by commenting on their history and heritage. "Two hundred years ago" America "was the hope of millions" and the "wheel of destiny" has now placed "any hope the world has for the survival of peace and freedom" squarely upon her. Survival suggests life; its absence, death. To his silent majority Nixon says: He who rejects his heritage rejects humanity, and thus himself. Rejection of self is a form of suicide that affects others. A conscious rejection of heritage, humanity, and self by Americans will cause the hopes of others (Vietnamese primarily, but other millions as well) "to be suffocated," still another form of death, perhaps even murder in the first degree.

If history and heritage are rejected, then further tragedy may be expected. Sooner or later we would have "more wars," which "would cost more lives." But Nixon carefully avoids an ultimate conclusion. He does not say that the United States would be overcome. If we desert Asia, we would "lose confidence in ourselves." As we "saw the consequences...inevitable remorse and divisive recrimination would scar our spirit as a people." Here, too, he avoids a final conclusion, but he describes a country peopled by "nameless strangers." The conclusions drawn from Nixon's objective statements are easily cast into images of self-extinction.

When the silent majority speaks, it participates. Constructive action may then occur at home and abroad. But the silent majority speaks not only because it has been asked to. Unless it speaks and participates, it will act much like the North Vietnamese who earlier had been portrayed as nonspeakers and uninvolved participants. The silent majority cannot or will not speak and act like the young; yet neither can it not speak and not act as the North Vietnamese have done. Where then should it place itself? The silent majority will take a middle position, out of choice perhaps, but not until choice has been suggested by the polarities of Nixon's rhetorical structure. For his policy Nixon has a public. He has Helpers.

The resolution of the Vietnam war Nixon terms a quest, a "big" word suggesting magnitude, great risks, and tremendous moments. A true quest has moments so large that they lack definite boundaries and risks of such magnitude that they cannot easily be faced or exactly described by those who must endure them. To look for a paper clip is not a true quest.

Nixon positions the word in the right place—early in the speech. But the word itself is wrong. His policy does differ from those of his predecessors. But it remains one of cautious, subtle modifications. He offers no new imaginative whole; indeed he blunts such considerations. Immediate withdrawal has magnitude, and potentially great risks and moments. Nixon rejects it. Those who call for a serious discussion of war as an important instrument of foreign policy ask fundamental questions of value. They are nearer to Wilson than to Nixon. To the call, Nixon is silent.

Nixon's political narrative also fails as a quest because he does not structure a direct confrontation between himself and the leader of the Guardians of the Object. It is Nixon who prophesies that immediate withdrawal means the loss of Asia and the loss of respect throughout the world. But has Ho Chi Minh or his successor claimed that great a victory growing out of the war? If yes, why doesn't Nixon confront them or him? Let him meet and overthrow the claims of his opponents and show that they are braggadocios. Nixon's prophecy may be correct. But he may also claim more for the Guardians than they claim for themselves. To that extent his political analysis is braggadocian.

Nixon's confrontation with the young is direct. And his listeners have both seen and heard the young. Many believe social unrest at home is an urgent matter. They have again been asked to be patient about Vietnam. Many seem willing, but their frustrations remain intense. Nixon directs them to satisfy them by meeting, testing, and overthrowing the claims of young loud, windy, braggadocios. The strategy adds little nobility or grandeur to his Quest.

Within the development of his Quest, Nixon illustrates how a Hero as one historical personage may move to larger Heroic groups.[10] There was the Great but Woolly Woodrow, Paternal Ike, Dashing John, and finally Black Lyndon. All had opportunities and moments. Now Somber Richard, a different Hero, appears to establish a new Heroic group, the silent majority.

The relationship between Nixon and the silent majority parallels in general outline a standard myth pattern. Nixon fought political battles, lost, and disappeared. He had fallen, becoming a part of the silent minority. During his absence various events caused his followers and others to wonder whether they and their world had fallen. Nixon's risen political body now speaks with a strong voice, uniting and reuniting others with him.

Listeners who sensed the Devil in all around them were assured, if not exhilarated. Traditional values such as the confident love of country, of personal and public honor, of pride in soldiership and citizenship were affirmed. This Hero does not believe that these values are sins. He will confront those who do.

Evaluated in literary terms Nixon's political narrative is obviously not a good Quest story. It is not altogether convincing. There are too many loose ends and too many unanswered questions. It is peopled by flat characters and its language is dull and unimaginative.

This speech was not offered to the public as a literary work. It deals with practical political problems and if evaluated accordingly it accomplishes some objectives. Although divisiveness in the political community remains, Nixon gains an audience and time. He finds listeners who will respond to his words and images. He gains a firmer possession of the policy he lays out before them and makes himself ready for the next series of events he must deal with in Vietnam.

_____ Notes _____

1. W. H. Auden, "The Quest Hero," *Texas Quarterly*, IV (Winter 1961), 82. This analysis borrows much from Auden. The essential elements of the Quest story are Auden's, slightly modified. General accounts of the Quest story and archetypal patterns can be found in numerous works. Maud Bodkin's *Archetypal Patterns in Poetry* (London, 1934) and Northrop Frye's *Anatomy of Criticism* (Princeton, 1957) and *Fables of Identity* (New York, 1963) are indispensable to a study of the method.

2. Wayne Shumaker, *Literature and the Irrational* (Englewood Cliffs, N.J., 1960), p. 135.

3. The text for this analysis is found in *Vital Speeches*, XXXVI (November 15, 1969), 66–70. Each paragraph of the text was numbered, 1–125. Thus this statement appears in paragraph 41 of the text.

4. This speech is the product of Nixon's mind and hand. He "solicited ideas from his large corps of speechwriters but did not order drafts from them...or otherwise use their literary talents." The speech went "through 10 drafts, all written by the President himself." Nixon felt the address "must convey an authentic note of personal involvement. He clearly felt that the speech would not carry such a message if someone else wrote it." These descriptions suggest other dimensions of a "quest." Robert B. Semple, Jr., "Speech Took 10 Drafts, and President Wrote All," *The New York Times*, November 4, 1969, p. 17.

5. For example, see Robert P. Newman, "Under the Veneer: Nixon's Vietnam Speech of November 3, 1969," *QJS*, LVI (April 1970), 168–178.

6. General Ky of South Vietnam is reported to have said before the speech was delivered that it would be addressed to the American audience. See James Reston, "Nixon's Mystifying Clarifications," *The New York Times*, November 5, 1969, p. 46.

7. Unnamed associates of Nixon offer a different interpretation for the timing of the speech. They say that the President had decided as early as August 1969 to give the country an accounting of the war and that he wanted to key "such an accounting...to the first anniversary of the bombing halt in early November." Further, in "the words of one high source," early announcement was necessary to "give Hanoi fair warning and a chance to turn around in Paris." Robert B. Semple, Jr., "Nixon's Nov. 3 Speech: Why He Took the Gamble Alone," *The New York Times*, January 19, 1970, p. 23.

8. Nixon's descriptions of the North Vietnamese are consistent with this observation. He does express emotion apart from intellect and there is a certain automatism in the analysis. However, it is inaccurate to use the metaphor of intoxication, which often designates the complete breakdown of rhetorical control. There is little doubt that what listeners are asked to embrace is in part a projection from Nixon's own emotional life. Insofar as the public scene is concerned, an obsessive repetition of verbal formulas may not stand up in objective discussions of public policy, and the audience may not become as cohesive as the speaker may like.

9. Associates report that Nixon had difficulty developing a satisfactory conclusion for the speech. He had jotted down numerous phrases he wanted to use but could not find room for. One read: "I don't want demonstrations, I want your quiet support." The line in the text seems to have emerged from such jottings. Semple, "Nixon's Nov. 3 Speech...," p. 23.

10. I am indebted to Professor Ernest Bormann, University of Minnesota, who read a draft of this essay and suggested this insightful interpretation.

An Exercise in the Rhetoric of Mythical America

KARLYN KOHRS CAMPBELL

This major policy address on the Vietnam War was, in part, a response to the October moratorium demonstration, despite Nixon's assertion that he would, under no circumstances, be affected by it.[1] The address was followed by an even larger moratorium demonstration in November and by Spiro Agnew's harsh attacks on the news media for their analyses and evaluations of the President's speech.[2] This criticism is an attempt to appraise this discourse primarily in terms of criteria suggested within the address by the President himself.

At the outset the President tells us that there is deep division in the nation partly because many Americans have lost confidence in what the government has told them about the war. In the President's opinion the people of the nation should be told the truth. The three criteria the President explicitly suggests are truth, credibility, and unity, and he later implies a fourth criterion based on responsibility and ethical principles. In other words Nixon tells us that the address is intended to relate the truth, increase the credibility of Administrative statements about the war, unify the nation, and remind us of our duties as Americans.

Two serious misrepresentations cast doubt on the truthfulness of the President. First, he misrepresents his opposition by treating them as a homogeneous group who seek immediate, precipitate withdrawal epitomized by the slogan "Lose in Vietnam; bring the boys home." Hence he also misrepresents the policy options available to him. As the President recognizes, somewhat indirectly, there are four alternatives to the policy of Vietnamization: escalation, immediate and precipitate withdrawal, disengagement through negotiation, and a scheduled withdrawal with a fixed date of termination. He mentions the possibility of escalation only as a threat to Hanoi, should increased enemy activity jeopardize the process of Vietnamization. The primary focus of the President's refutation is immediate, precipitate withdrawal—a justifiable argumentative stance only if the bulk of his opposition supported this policy. Instead most of his critics supported the fourth option—a scheduled withdrawal with a fixed date of termination, such as former Senator

Charles Goodell's proposed disengagement plan, which called for total withdrawal of all American troops in a year's time but continued economic and military aid to South Vietnam at the discretion of Congress and the President.[3] A few critics, such as Eugene McCarthy, advocated a negotiated settlement. But only a small minority of the peace movement supported immediate, total withdrawal. The President's characterization of his opposition is designed to make the alternatives to Vietnamization appear as extreme as possible so that the voices urging them will not be heeded. The misrepresentation of the opposition and the consequent focus on immediate, total withdrawal as the most important alternative allow the President to transform a complex policy question into a simple either-or decision:

> *I am sure that you can recognize from what I have said that we have only two choices open to us if we want to end the war. I can order an immediate precipitate withdrawal of all Americans from Vietnam without regard to the effects of that action. Or we can persist in our search for a just peace through . . . Vietnamization . . .*

The misrepresentation of his opposition makes the only apparent alternative to his policy as unattractive and radical as possible. This strategy may gull the audience, and it may make his speech more persuasive for some listeners, but the technique violates his earlier promise to tell the truth.

The second misrepresentation occurs in relation to what the President calls the "fundamental issue. Why and how did the United States become involved in Vietnam in the first place?" He answers this question with a dubious description of the beginning of the war:

> *Fifteen years ago North Vietnam, with the logistical support of Communist China an the Soviet Union, launched a campaign to impose a Communist government on South Vietnam by instigating and supporting a revolution.*

Now "fifteen years ago" was 1954, the year of the Geneva Agreements that were to unify Vietnam through elections to be held in 1956. Those elections never occurred because the United States supported Diem, who refused elections and attempted to destroy all internal political opposition, Communist and otherwise. The Vietcong did not persuade Hanoi or Peking or Moscow to aid them against Diem until about 1959. By 1965 South Vietnam was clearly losing, the point at which President Johnson decided to send in United States combat forces.[4]

The surprising decision to give top priority to the historical question, in a policy address that perforce must concern itself with the best means of disengagement, merits consideration. The President's attempt to perpetuate the now largely discredited justifications for United States intervention serves at least two functions. First, it allows Nixon to appeal to history and historical values, to the prior decisions of Presidents Eisenhower, Kennedy, and Johnson and to Woodrow Wilson and his dream of a just peace. Nixon's policy becomes the logical outcome of the decisions and values of his predecessors, and Nixon's way becomes the American way. Second, emphasis on the origins of the war structures the argument so that the primary justifications for the policy can be ethical rather than pragmatic. The speech contains no information about how the plan will work, no evidence for the consequences predicted, and no analysis of how the Vietcong or Hanoi will view it. Instead almost all the justifications are ethical; Vietnamization is "the right way." Although the misrepresentation of the beginning of the war may be believed because of the authority of the speaker, the evasion of the hard questions of feasibility and costs is not consistent with the President's promise to tell the truth.

Two major contradictions damage the President's status as a truthteller. Early in the speech he tells the audience that immediate withdrawal would be the popular and easy course, enhancing the prestige of the Administration and increasing its chances of reelection. Yet at the end of the speech it is clear that the President believes his opposition is a "vocal minority" and that his policy represents the will of the "great, silent majority." If so, isn't his policy the popular and easy one with the best chance of returning him to the White House?

Similarly early in the speech Nixon explains that immediate and total withdrawal would be a disaster for the South Vietnamese because it would inevitably allow the Communists to repeat the massacres that followed their takeover of the North.[5] In response former Senator Goodell remarked that this argument rests on the assumption that the South Vietnamese army would be powerless to prevent a complete takeover of the South. Yet at the time of the address the South Vietnamese had over a million men under arms, while the Vietcong had about 100,000, and the North Vietnamese had about 110,000 in the South.[6] If these smaller armies could take over and massacre, then the president's proposed policy of Vietnamization is surely doomed because it assumes that the South Vietnamese army, with American equipment and training, can successfully take over the fighting of the war and defeat both the Vietcong and the North Vietnamese. The two notions seem somewhat contradictory.

The overwhelming questions concerning credibility are, of course, whether the President really had a secret plan for withdrawal and whether he really intended to end the war? The events that followed this address answered these questions for most Americans. Shortly after the address a Gallup poll reported that the Nixon Administration is facing the same crisis in public confidence on the war that confronted the Johnson administration: 69 percent of the Americans feel that the Administration is not telling the American people all they should know about the war, and 46 percent disapprove of the President's way of handling the Vietnam situation.[7] One critic, after careful analysis of the credibility issue, concludes that Nixon had a plan and sincerely intended to end the war. However, even this critic says "that his heart was not in it, that only the pressure of public opinion had caused him to embrace what he for fifteen years rejected,"[8] and that the address seriously lowered his credibility with newsmen.[9]

In an immediate sense the speech may be called highly credible but, at the same time, extremely divisive. Gallup reported that 77 percent of those who heard it gave the President a vote of confidence;[10] still the divisions over the war were not healed. In fact the address played an important part in exacerbating the bitter conflict between what the President termed the "silent majority" and a "vocal minority" fervently seeking to prevail "over reason and the will of the majority." He characterized dissenters as a small group trying to impose their views and dictate policy "by mounting demonstrations in the streets," terms that place them outside acceptable processes for change in a democratic society. He implied that the opposition was a partial cause for the continuation of the war when he said that "the more divided we are at home, the less likely the enemy is to negotiate." Finally he says that "only Americans," presumably only *dissenting* Americans, "can humiliate and defeat the United States." These statements belie the theme of unity and contradict his earlier assertion that "honest and patriotic Americans have reached different conclusions as to how peace should be achieved." In fact one critic has argued that the address was deliberately designed to isolate dissenters from the majority of opinion.[11] If this address is to unify Americans and fulfill the President's Inaugural promise to "bring us together," it will do so only to the degree that the speaker has silenced his opposition or shamed them into acquiescence.

The President also suggests a fourth criterion. The notion of responsibility or obligation appears frequently, and the President emphasizes that his policy is not the easy, but the right, way. An ethical principle seems implicit. However, despite his numerous protestations, the address does not call on Americans to assume responsibility. First, the President never holds the United States responsible in any way for its part in the war despite the role of the United States in undermining the Geneva Agreements. Instead he places all blame for the initiation and escalation of the war on North Vietnam, China, and Russia. Similarly he places all blame for the failure to negotiate a settlement on Hanoi. Praise and blame on such controversial and complicated questions can be assigned so simply and clearly only if the intent is to avoid all responsibility. Second, the President's repeated assertion of *his* responsibility, including his responsibility to choose the best path and lead the nation along it, becomes the individual citizen's *irresponsibility*: The President will decide, the President will lead, and the President will be responsible; while the "silent majority" of "forgotten Americans" will follow, patriotic and undissenting, in the sure knowledge that quiet acquiescence to his considered judgment is the path to victory, peace, and honor.

The powerlessness and frustration felt by dissenters and demonstrators in the face of this rhetoric should be mirrored to some extent in all of us. The President tells us, in effect, there is nothing we can do. By definition, if we are vocal and dissenting, we are the minority whose will must not prevail and to whom no heed will be paid. The only alternative is to join "the great, silent majority" in support of his policy.

In addition as many commentators have pointed out, the policy of Vietnamization, viewed at its worst, is war by proxy in which the Vietnamese supply the bodies while we supply guns, money, and advice.[12] In this sense the policy is a means to avoid the responsibility for making moral judgments about the war. Whether it is viewed as war by proxy or as a long, slow, costly process for ending American involvement, the policy of Vietnamization makes the pace of American withdrawal dependent on decisions made in Hanoi and Saigon and on factors almost wholly beyond United States control. Vietnamization may be "the right way," but it is also a way that limits United States' responsibility severely by placing the burden of decision on others. If the enemy is irresponsible, the threat, although disclaimed, is clear: Troop withdrawals will stop and military action will escalate; and it will be *their* responsibility. As a consequence Americans clearly are not asked to assume moral obligations.

From the point of view of the critic, the most intriguing statements in the speech are these:

> *I have chosen a path for peace. I believe it will succeed. If it does succeed, what the critics say now won't matter. If it does not succeed, anything I say then won't matter.*

The two statements about criticism are cryptic and more than a little mystifying. What does the President mean when he says, "If it does succeed, what the critics say now won't matter"? Presumably he expects the critics to be negative and dissatisfied as they have often been. If they point out weaknesses in the policy, in the arguments, in the truth of what he says, if they point out contradictions and inconsistencies, and if the policy does not succeed, then what? Is the criticism of no matter? Such criticism should provide a partial explanation of why the policy did not work and what was faulty in the decision-making process. The same is true of the criticism of a rhetorical discourse. If the rhetorical act fails, the critics' comments are important because criticism should give some reasons for the failure of the rhetoric. Clearly, however, the President is giving notice that under no circumstances will he be affected by what the critics say, and such warning is precisely the tragedy, for criticism is the mechanism by which to improve the quality of rhetoric and of decision making. But Nixon has been quite bitter about criticism, as was evident in his concession speech of the 1962 gubernatorial campaign in California.[13]

What does the President intend when he says, "If it does succeed, what the critics say now won't matter"? In such a case the President would have proved the critics wrong, vindicating himself and calling the critics' methods and assumptions into serious question. In all likelihood such a moment would be gratifying for the President. However, if we take the rhetorical act as an analogy, can we consider the critical comments inconsequential simply because the address was successful (at least in terms of the Gallup poll)? I think not. It may be futile to warn against the rhetorician who misrepresents, who is self-contradictory, who is divisive while asserting his desire for unity, or who disclaims responsibility while praising the idea of fulfilling moral obligations. But unless we become careful, discriminating critics, questioning and evaluating, we shall be constrained to make poor decisions and supporting policies destructive of ourselves, our society, and the world. In this respect Agnew's attacks on the concept of immediate critical analysis and evaluation are particularly ironic because his protest suggests that the policy and the address are both extremely fragile. The decision worth making and the policy deserving support, as well as the rhetorical act of quality, will withstand, even be strengthened by, critical scrutiny, and such criticism is the essence of democratic decision making.

Finally this address is an example of the perpetuation of American mythology. The President describes a mythical America whose business is the defense of freedom, whose strength has resulted from facing crises and rejecting the easy way, whose greatness has been the capacity to do what had to be done when it was known to be right. This mythical America is the last hope for the survival of peace and freedom in the world; this most powerful nation will not allow the forces of totalitarianism to suffocate the hopes of the peoples of the earth. This is a nation of destiny.

*Non*mythical America presents quite a different picture. *Non*mythical America supports totalitarian governments all over the world. *Non*mythical America is engaged in a war in South Vietnam in which it is systematically destroying the civilian population and agricultural capacity of the country it is ostensibly defending. *Non*mythical America practices a racism that makes a mockery of its mythic principles. The examples could go on and on. Concentrating so on the details of this address—whether this point or that is true or distorted—the critic can so easily forget that all these considerations rest on the speaker's assumption of a mythical America, which always seeks justice, freedom, and right despite difficulty and cost. These considerations become irrelevant and fragmented outside this mythic context. One commentator has made the point that "the only salutary aspect of Vietnam [is] the fact that it is forcing us to examine the misconceptions about ourselves and the world on which postwar American foreign policy has been based."[14]

Although this speech fails to meet the President's criteria of truth, credibility, unity, and responsibility, the most significant criticism is that this rhetorical act perpetuates the myths about America, which must be debunked and shattered if we are to find solutions to the problems that threaten immediately to destroy us. The "silent majority" may want to get out of Vietnam and to save face; it cannot have both—at least not quickly.

To avoid Vietnams of the future we must make a concerted effort to discover and scrutinize *non*mythical America. If in that scrutiny we pay particular attention to the rhetorical discourses that thresh out and formulate ideas of ourselves and our society, we may begin to solve the problems of the *real* America and of this shirinking world. That President Nixon is unwilling or unable to face the *real* problems is precisely the reason why this address is doomed to be so disappointing. It is, as almost every commentator has recognized, just "more of the same."[15]

Notes

1. Cited in "Beyond the Moratorium," *New Republic*, Vol. 161 (October 25, 1969), p. 7.

2. See Chapter 6 in Campbell, *Critiques of Contemporary Rhetoric*.

3. Charles E. Goodell, "Set a Deadline for Withdrawal," *New Republic*, Vol. 161 (November 22, 1969), p. 13.

4. "Nixon's Non-Plan," *New Republic*, Vol. 161 (November 15, 1969), p. 10; Tom Wicker, "In the Nation: Mr. Nixon Twists and Turns," *New York Times*, 9 November 1969, p. E15.

   For a detailed summary of the history of United States involvement in Vietnam, see "Historical Report on U.S. Aggression in Vietnam 1964 to 1967, Testimony by Charles Fourniau" and "Juridical Report on Aggression in Vietnam, Testimony by the Japanese Legal Committee," in John Duffett ed., *Against the Crime of Silence* (New York: O'Hare Books, 1968), pp. 79–90, 105–118.

5. For an analysis of the massacre issue, see Tran Van Dinh, "Fear of a Bloodbath," *New Republic*, Vol. 161 (December 6, 1969), pp. 11–14.

6. Goodell, "Set a Deadline for Withdrawal," p. 13.

7. *Los Angeles Times*, 7 March 1971, p. 11.

8. Robert P. Newman, "Under the Veneer: Nixon's Vietnam Speech of November 3, 1969," *Quarterly Journal of Speech*, Vol. 56 (April 1970), pp. 170–171.

9. *Ibid.*, p. 176.

10. *Los Angeles Times*, 5 November 1969, p. 125.

11. Newman, "Under the Veneer," p. 172.

12. "Nixon's Non-Plan," p. 10.

13. Richard Bergholz, "Nixon Admits Defeat, Indicates Intention to Give Up Politics," *Los Angeles Times*, 8 November 1962, p. 1.

14. Fred Warner Neal, "Government by Myth," *The Center Magazine*, Vol. 2 (November 1969), p. 2.

Conventional Wisdom—Traditional Form—The President's Message of November 3, 1969

—————————————— FORBES HILL ——————————————

More than one critique of President Nixon's address to the nation on November 3, 1969 has appeared,[1] which is not remarkable, since it was the most obvious feature of the public relations machine that appears to have dammed back the flood of sentiment for quick withdrawal of American forces from Southeast Asia. To be sure, the dike built by this machine hardly endured forever, but some time was gained—an important achievement. It seems natural, then, that we should want to examine this obvious feature from more than one angle.

Preceding critiques have looked at Nixon's message from notably non-traditional perspectives. Stelzner magnified it in the lens of archetypal criticism, which reveals a non-literary version of the quest story archetype, but he concluded that the President's is an incomplete telling of the story that does not adequately interact with the listeners' subjective experiences. Newman condemned the message as "shoddy rhetoric" because its tough stance and false dilemmas are directed to white, urban, uptight voters. Campbell condemned it on the basis of intrinsic criticism because though its stated purposes are to tell the truth, increase credibility, promote unity, and affirm moral responsibility, its rhetoric conceals truth, decreases credibility, promotes division, and dodges moral responsibility. Then, stepping outside the intrinsic framework, she makes her most significant criticism: the message perpetuates myths about American values instead of scrutinizing the real values of America.

I propose to juxtapose these examinations with a strict neo-Aristotelian analysis. If it differs slightly from analyses that follow Wichelns[2] and Hochmuth-Nichols,[3] that is because it attempts a critique that re-interprets neo-Aristotelianism slightly—a critique guided by the spirit and usually the letter of the Aristotelian text as I understand it. What the neo-Aristotelian method can and should do will be demonstrated, I hope, by this juxtaposition.

Neo-Aristotelian criticism compares the means of persuasion used by a speaker with a comprehensive inventory given in Aristotle's *Rhetoric*. Its end is to discover whether the speaker makes the best choices from the inventory to get a favorable decision from a specified group of auditors in a specific situation. It does not, of course, aim to discover whether or not the speaker actually gets his favorable decision; decisions in practice are often upset by chance factors.[4] First the neo-Aristotelian critic must outline the situation, then specify the group of auditors and define the kind of decision they are to make. Finally he must reveal

the choice and disposition of three intertwined persuasive factors—logical, psychological, and characterological—and evaluate this choice and disposition against
the standard of the *Rhetoric*.

The Situation

The state of affairs for the Nixon Administration in the fall of 1969 is well known.
The United States had been fighting a stalemated war for several years. The cost in
lives and money was immense. The goal of the war was not clear; presumably
the United States wanted South Viet Nam as a stable non-Communist buffer state
between Communist areas and the rest of Southeast Asia. To the extent that this
goal was understood, it seemed as far from being realized in 1969 as it had been in
1964. In the meantime, a large and vocal movement had grown up, particularly
among the young, of people who held that there should have been no intervention
in Viet Nam in the first place and that it would never be possible to realize any
conceivable goal of intervention. The movement was especially dangerous to the
Administration because it numbered among its supporters many of the elements of
the population who were most interested in foreign policy and best informed about
it. There were variations of position within the peace movement, but on one point
all its members were agreed: the United States should commit itself immediately to
withdraw its forces from Viet Nam.

The policy of the Nixon Administration, like that of the Johnson Administration
before it, was limited war to gain a position of strength from which to negotiate. By
fall 1969 the Administration was willing to make any concessions that did not
jeopardize a fifty-fifty chance of achieving the goal, but it was not willing to make
concessions that amounted to sure abandonment of the goal. A premature withdrawal amounted to public abandonment and was to be avoided at all costs. When
the major organizations of the peace movement announced the first Moratorium
Day for October 15 and organized school and work stoppages, demonstrations, and
a great "March on Washington" to dramatize the demand for immediate withdrawal
from Viet Nam, the Administration launched a counter-attack. The President announced that he would make a major address on Viet Nam November 3. This
announcement seems to have moderated the force of the October moratorium, but
plans were soon laid for a second moratorium on November 15. Nixon's counter-
attack aimed at rallying the mass of the people to disregard the vocal minority and
oppose immediate withdrawal; it aimed to get support for a modified version of the
old strategy: limited war followed by negotiated peace. The address was broadcast
the evening of November 3 over the national radio and television networks.

The Auditors and the Kind
of Decision

An American President having a monopoly of the media at prime time potentially
reaches an audience of upwards of a hundred million adults of heterogeneous
backgrounds and opinions. Obviously it is impossible to design a message to move
every segment of this audience, let alone the international audience. The speaker
must choose his targets. An examination of the texts shows us which groups were
eliminated as targets, which were made secondary targets, and which were prim-

ary. The speaker did not address himself to certain fanatical opponents of the war: the ones who hoped that the Viet Cong would gain a signal victory over the Americans and their South Vietnamese allies, or those who denied that Communist advances were threats to non-Communist countries, or those against any war for any reason. These were the groups the President sought to isolate and stigmatize. On the other hand, there was a large group of Americans who would be willing to give their all to fight any kind of Communist expansion anywhere at any time. These people also were not a target group: their support could be counted on in any case.

The speaker did show himself aware that the Viet Cong and other Communist decision-makers were listening in. He represented himself to them as willing and anxious to negotiate and warned them that escalation of the war would be followed by effective retaliation. The Communists constituted a secondary target audience, but the analysis that follows will make plain that the message was not primarily intended for them.

The primary target was those Americans not driven by a clearly defined ideological commitment to oppose or support the war at any cost. Resentment of the sacrifice in money and lives, bewilderment at the stalemate, longing for some movement in a clearly marked direction—these were the principal aspects of their state of mind assumed by Nixon. He solicited them saying "tonight—to you, the great silent majority of my fellow Americans—I ask your support."[5]

His address asks the target group of auditors to make a decision to support a policy to be continued in the future. In traditional terms, then, it is primarily a deliberative speech. Those who receive the message are decision-makers, and they are concerned with the past only as it serves as analogy to future decisions. The subjects treated are usual ones for deliberation: war and peace.[6]

Disposition and Synopsis

The address begins with an enthymeme that attacks the credibility gap.[7] Those who decide on war and peace must know the truth about these policies, and the conclusion is implied that the President is going to tell the truth. The rest of the *proem* is taken up by a series of questions constructing a formal partition of the subjects to be covered. The partition stops short of revealing the nature of the modification in policy that constitues the Nixon plan. The message fits almost perfectly into the Aristotelian pattern of *proem*, narrative, proofs both constructive and refutative, and epilogue. Just as *proem* has served as a general heading for a synoptic statement of what was done in the first few sentences, so the other four parts will serve us as analytical headings for a synopsis of the rest.

The narrative commences with Nixon's statement of the situation as he saw it on taking office. He could have ordered immediate withdrawal of American forces, but he decided to fulfill "a greater obligation...to think of the effect" of his decision "on the next generation, and on the future of peace and freedom in America, and in the world." Applicable here is the precept: the better the moral end that the speaker can in his narrative be seen consciously choosing, the better the *ethos* he reveals.[8] An end can hardly be better than "the future of peace and freedom in America, and in the world." The narrative goes on to explain why and how the United States became involved in Viet Nam in the first place. This explanation masquerades as a simple chronological statement—"Fifteen years ago..." but thinly disguised in the chronology lie two propositions: first, that the leaders of America were right in intervening on behalf of the government of South Viet Nam; second, that the great mistake in their conduct of the war was over-reliance on American combat forces. Some doubt has been cast on the wisdom of Nixon's choice among the means of persuasion here. The history, writes one critic, "is a surprising candidate for priority in any discussion today....The President's chief foreign policy advisors, his allies on Capitol Hill, and the memorandum he got from the Cabinet bureaucracy all urged him to skip discussions of the causes and manner of our involvement. Yet history comes out with top billing"[9] This criticism fails to conceive the rhetorical function of the narrative: in the two propositions the whole content of the proofs that follow is foreshadowed, and foreshadowed in the guise of a non-controversial statement about the historical facts. Among traditional orators this use of the narrative to foreshadow proofs is common, but it has seldom been handled with more artistry than here.

Constructive proofs are not opened with an analytical partition but with a general question: what is the best way to end the war? The answer is structured as a long argument from logical division: there are four plans to end American involvement; three should be rejected so that the listener is left with no alternative within the structure but to accept the fourth.[10] The four plans are: immediate withdrawal, the consequences of which are shown at some length to be bad; negotiated settlement, shown to be impossible in the near future because the enemy will not negotiate in earnest; shifting the burden of the war to the Viet-namese with American withdrawal on a fixed timetable, also argued to have bad consequences; and shifting the burden of the war to the Vietnamese with American withdrawal on a flexible schedule, said to have good consequences, since it will eventually bring "the complete withdrawal of all United States *combat ground* forces," whether earnest negotiations become possible or not. Constructive proofs close with one last evil consequence of immediate withdrawal: that it would lead eventually to Americans' loss of confidence in themselves and divisive recrimina-tion that "would scar our spirit as a people."

As refutative proof is introduced, opponents of the Administration are char-acterized by a demonstrator carrying a sign, "Lose in Viet Nam"; they are an irrational minority who want to decide policy in the streets, as opposed to the elected officials—Congress and the President—who will decide policy by Constitu-tional and orderly means. This attack on his presumed opponents leads to a passage which reassures the majority of young people that the President really wants peace as much as they do. Reassuring ends with the statement of Nixon's personal belief that his plan will succeed; this statement may be taken as tran-sitional to the epilogue.

The epilogue reiterates the bad consequences of immediate withdrawal—loss of confidence and loss of other nations to totalitarianism—it exhorts the silent majority to support the plan, predicting its success; it evokes the memory of Woodrow Wilson; then it closes with the President's pledge to meet his responsibi-lities to lead the nation with strength and wisdom. Recapitulation, building of *ethos*, and reinforcing the right climate of feeling—these are what a traditional rhetorician would advise that the epilogue do,[11] and these are what Nixon's epilogue does.

Indeed, this was our jumping-off place for the synopsis of the message: it falls into the traditional paradigm; each frame of the paradigm contains the lines of argument conventional for that frame. The two unconventional elements in the paradigm—the unusual placement of the last evil consequence of immediate withdrawal and the use of the frame by logical division for the constructive proofs—are there for good rhetorical reasons. That last consequence, loss of confidence and divisive recrimination, serves to lead into the refutation which opens with the demonstrator and his sign. It is as if the demonstrator were being made an example in advance of just this evil consequence. The auditor is brought into precisely the right set for a refutation section that does not so much argue with opponents as it pushes them into an isolated, unpopular position.

Because of the residues-like structure, the message creates the illusion of proving that Vietnamization and flexible withdrawal constitute the best policy. By process of elimination it is the only policy available, and even a somewhat skeptical listener is less likely to question the only policy available. Approaching the proposal with skepticism dulled, he perhaps does not so much miss a development of the plan. In particular, he might not ask the crucial question: does the plan actually provide for complete American withdrawal? The answer to this question is contained in the single phrase, "complete withdrawal of all United States *combat ground* forces." It is fairly clear, in retrospect, that this phrase concealed the intention to keep in Viet Nam for several years a large contingent of air and support forces. Nixon treats the difference between plan three, Vietnamization and withdrawal on a fixed schedule, and plan four, Vietnamization and withdrawal on a flexible schedule, as a matter of whether or not the schedule is announced in advance. But the crucial difference is really that plan three was understood by its advocates as a plan of quick, complete withdrawal; plan four was a plan for partial withdrawal. The strategic reason for not announcing a fixed schedule was that the announcement would give away this fact. The residues structure concealed the lack of development of the plan; the lack of development of the plan suppressed the critical fact that Nixon did not propose complete withdrawal. Although Nixon's message shows traditionally conventional structure, these variations from the traditional show a remarkable ability at designing the best adaptations to the specific rhetorical situation.

Logical and Psychological
Persuasive Factors

Central to an Aristotelian assessment of the means of persuasion is an account of two interdependent factors: (1) the choice of major premises on which enthymemes[12] that form "the body of the proof" are based, and (2) the means whereby auditors are brought into states of feeling favorable to accepting these premises and the conclusions following from them. Premises important here are of two kinds: predictions and values. Both kinds as they relate to good and evil consequences of the four plans to end American involvement, will be assessed. The first enthymeme involving prediction is that immediate withdrawal followed by a Communist takeover would lead to murder and imprisonment of innocent civilians. This conclusion follows from the general predictive rule: the future will resemble the past.[13] Since the Communists murdered and imprisoned opponents on taking over

North Viet Nam in 1954 and murdered opponents in the city of Hue in 1968, they will do the same when they take over South Viet Nam. Implied also is an enthymeme based on the value premise that security of life and freedom from bondage are primary goods for men,[14] a Communist takeover would destroy life and freedom and therefore destroy primary goods for men.

Presumably no one would try to refute this complex of enthymemes by saying that life and freedom are not primary goods, though he might argue from more and less,[15] more life is lost by continuing the war than would be lost by a Communist takeover, or American-South Vietnamese political structures allow for even less political freedom than the Communist alternatives. Nixon buries these questions far enough beneath the surface of the message that probably auditors in the target group are not encouraged to raise them. One could also attack the predictive premise: after all, the future is not always the past writ over again. But this kind of refutation is merely irritating; we know that the premise is not universally true, yet everyone finds it necessary to operate in ordinary life as if it were. People on the left of the target group, of course, reject the evidence—North Viet Nam and Hue.

A related prediction is that immediate withdrawal would result in a collapse of confidence in American leadership. It rests on the premise that allies only have confidence in those who both have power and will act in their support.[16] If the United States shows it lacks power and will in Viet Nam, there will be a collapse of confidence, which entails further consequences: it would "promote recklessness" on the part of enemies everywhere else the country has commitments, i.e., as a general premise, when one party to a power struggle loses the confidence of its allies, its enemies grow bolder.[17] The conclusion is bolstered by citations from former presidents. Eisenhowever, Johnson, and Kennedy: the statement of the "liberal saint," Kennedy, is featured.

It is difficult to attack the related premises of these tandem arguments. They rest on what experience from the sandbox up shows to be probable. The target group consists of people with the usual American upbringing and experience. Someone will question the premises only if he questions the world-view out of which they develop. That view structures the world into Communist powers—actual or potential enemies—and non-Communist powers—allies. America is the leader of the allies, referred to elsewhere as the forces of "peace and freedom" opposed by "the forces of totalitarianism." Because of its association with freedom, American leadership is indisputably good, and whatever weakens confidence in it helps the enemies. Only a few people on the far left would categorically reject this structure.

The foregoing premises and the world-view fundamental to them are even more likely to be accepted if the auditors are in a state of fear. Fear may be defined as distress caused by a vision of impending evil of the destructive or painful kind.[18] This message promotes a state of fear by the nature of the evil consequences developed—murder and imprisonment of innocents, collapse of leadership in the free world, and reckless aggressiveness of implacable enemies. America is the prototype of a nation that is fearful; her enemies are watching their opportunities all over the globe, from Berlin to the Middle East, yes even in the Western Hemisphere itself. The enemies are cruel and opposed to American ideals. They are strong on the battlefield and intransigent in negotiations. Conditions are such that America's allies may lose confidence in her and leave her to fight these enemies alone. But these circumstances are not too much amplified: only enough to create a state of feeling favorable to rejecting immediate withdrawal, not so much as to create the disposition for escalation.

Nixon claims to have tried hard to make a negotiated settlement, but he could not make one because the Communists refused to compromise. The evidence that they would not compromise is developed at length: public initiatives through the peace conference in Paris are cited, terms for participation of the Communist forces in internationally supervised elections offered, and promises made to negotiate on any of these terms. Then there were private initiatives through the Soviet Union and directly by letter to the leaders of North Viet Nam, as well as private efforts by the United States ambassador to the Paris talks. These efforts brought only demands for the equivalent of unconditional surrender. The citation of evidence is impressive and destroys the credibility of the position that negotiations can bring a quick end to the war.

Nixon does not explicitly predict that the plan for negotiated settlement will not work ever; on the contrary, he says that he will keep trying. But if the auditor believes the evidence, he finds it difficult to avoid making his own enthymeme with the conclusion that negotiated settlement will never work; the major premise is the same old rule, the future will be like the past. Nixon gives another reason, too: it will not work while the opposite side "is convinced that all it has to do is wait for our next concession, and our next concession after that one, until it gets everything it wants." The major premise—no power convinced that victory is probable by forcing repeated concessions will ever compromise—constitutes a commonplace of bargaining for virtually everyone.

Peace is seen in these arguments as almost an unqualified good. Although compromise through bargaining is the fastest way to peace, the other side must make concessions to assure compromise. Reasons for continuing the war, such as an ideological commitment, are evil. There is no glory in war and prolonging it is not justified by political gains made but only by a commitment to higher values like saving lives and preserving freedom. Prolonging the war is also justified as avoiding future wars by not losing Southeast Asia altogether and not promoting the spirit of recklessness in the enemies. "I want," states Nixon, "to end it [the war] in a way which will increase the chance that their [the soldiers'] younger brothers and their sons will not have to fight in some future Vietnam. . . ."

A listener is prone to reject the likelihood of a negotiated peace if he is angry with his opponents. Anger is a painful desire for revenge and arises from an evident, unjustified slight to a person or his friends.[19] People visualizing revenge ordinarily refuse compromise except as a temporary tactic. Nixon presents the American people as having been slighted: they value peace, and their leaders have with humility taken every peace initiative possible: public, private, and secret. The Communist powers wish to gain politically from the war; they have rebuffed with spite all initiatives and frustrated our good intentions by demanding the equivalent of unconditional surrender. Frustration is, of course, a necessary condition of anger.[20] Again, Nixon does not go too far—not far enought to create a psychological climate out of which a demand for escalation would grow.

Nixon announces that his plan for Vietnamization and American withdrawal on a flexible timetable is in effect already. Its consequences: American men coming home, South Vietnamese forces gaining in strength, enemy infiltration measurably reduced, and United States' casualties also reduced. He predicts: policies that have had such consequences in the past will have them in the future, i.e. the future will be like the past. Again, the undisputed value that saving lives is good is assumed. But in this case the argument, while resting on an acceptable premise, was, at the time of this speech, somewhat more doubtful of acceptance by the target group. The evidence constitutes the problem: obviously the sample of the past since the policy of Vietnamization commenced was so short that no one could really judge the alleged consequences to be correlated with the change in policy, let alone caused by it. There is, then, little reason why that audience should have believed the minor premise—that the consequences of Vietnamization were good.

A temporizing and moderate policy is best presented to auditors who while temporarily fearful are basically confident. Nothing saps the will to accept such a proposal as does the opposite state, basically fearful and only temporarily confident. Confidence is the other side of the coin from fear: it is pleasure because destructive and painful evils seem far away and sources of aid near at hand.[21] The sources of aid here are the forces of the Republic of South Viet Nam. They have continued to gain in strength and as a result have been able to take over combat responsibilities from American forces. In contrast, danger from the enemy is receding—"enemy infiltration. . .over the last three months is less than 20 per cent of what it was over the same period last year." Nixon assures his auditors that he has confidence the plan will succeed. America is the "strongest and richest nation in the world"; it can afford the level of aid that needs to be continued in Viet Nam. It will show the moral stamina to meet the challenge of free world leadership.

For some time rumors about gradual American withdrawal from Viet Nam had been discounted by the peace movement. The only acceptable proof of American intentions would be a timetable showing withdrawal to be accomplished soon. Thus the third plan: withdrawal on a fixed timetable. Nixon predicts that announcing of a timetable would remove the incentive to negotiate and reduce flexibility of response. The general premise behind the first is a commonplace of bargaining: negotiations never take place without a *quid pro quo*; a promise to remove American forces by a certain date gives away the *quid pro quo*. For most Americans, who are used to getting things by bargaining, this premise is unquestionable. Only those few who think that the country can gain no vestige of the objective of the war are willing to throw away the incentive. The premises behind the notion of flexibility—that any workable plan is adaptable to changes in the situation—is a commonplace of legislation and not likely to be questioned by anyone. Nixon adds to this generally acceptable premise a specific incentive. Since withdrawal will occur more rapidly if enemy military activity decreases and the South Vietnamese forces become stronger, there is a possibility that forces can be withdrawn even sooner than would be predicted by a timetable. This specific incentive is illusory, since it is obvious that one can always withdraw sooner than the timetable says, even if he has one; it is hard to see how a timetable actually reduces flexibility. Everyone makes timetables, of course, and having to re-make them when conditions change is a familiar experience. But the average man who works from nine to five probably thinks that the government should be different: when it announces a timetable it must stick to it; otherwise nothing is secure. This argument may seem weak to the critic, but it is probably well directed to the target group. The real reason for not announcing a timetable has already been noted.[22]

One final prediction is founded on the preceding predictions—whenever a policy leads to such evil consequences as movement of Southeast Asia into alliance with the enemy and a new recklessness on the part of enemies everywhere, it will eventually result in remorse and divisive recrimination which will, in turn, result in a loss of self-confidence. Guiltlessness and internal unity, the opposites of remorse and recrimination, are here assumed as secondary goods leading to self-confidence, a primary good. The enthymeme predicting loss of self-confidence consequent on immediate withdrawal is summary in position: it seems to tie together all previous arguments. It comes right after a particularly effective effort at *ethos* building—the series of statements developed in parallel construction about not having chosen the easy way (immediate withdrawal) but the right way. However, it rests on the assumption that the long term mood of confidence in the country depends on the future of Southeast Asia and the recklessness of our enemies. Since these two factors are only an aspect of a larger picture in which many other events play their parts, it is surely not true that they alone will produce a loss of confidence. The enthymeme based on this assumption, placed where it is, however, does not invite questioning by the target group. Doubtful though it may look under searching scrutiny, it has an important function for the structure of psychological proof in this message. It reinforces the value image of the danger of facing a stronger enemy in a weakened condition: America itself would be less united, less confident, and less able to fight in the future if this consequence of immediate withdrawal were realized.

Other things being equal, the more commonplace and universally accepted the premises of prediction in a deliberative speech, the more effective the speech. This is especially true if they are set in a frame that prepares the auditor psychologically for their acceptance. There is almost no doubt that given the policy of the Nixon Administration—Vietnamization and partial withdrawal on a flexible schedule not announced in advance—the message shows a potentially effective choice of premises. In some cases it is almost the only possible choice. Likewise the value structure of the message is wisely chosen from materials familiar to any observer of the American scene: it could be duplicated in hundreds of other messages from recent American history.

Several additional value assumptions are equally commonplace. Betraying allies and letting down friends is assumed to be an evil, and its opposite, loyalty to friends and allies the virtue of a great nation. This premise equates personal loyalty, like that a man feels for his friend, with what the people of the whole nation should feel for an allied nation. Many people think this way about international relations, and the good citizens of the target group can be presumed to be among them.

Policies endorsed by the people they are supposed to help are said to be better policies than those not endorsed by them. This statement undoubtedly makes a good political rule if one expects participation in the execution of policy of those to be helped. Policies that result from the operation of representative government are good, whereas those made on the streets are bad. This value is, of course, an essential of republican government: only the most radical, even of those outside the target group, would question it. Finally, Nixon assumes that the right thing is usually the opposite of the easy thing, and, of course, *he* chooses to do the right thing. Such a value premise does not occur in rhetorics by Aristotle or even George Campbell: it is probably a peculiar product of Protestant-American-on-the-frontier thinking. Its drawing power for twentieth-century urban youngsters is negligible, but the bulk of the target group probably is made up of suburbanites in the 35–50 category who still have some affinity for this kind of thinking.

Some shift from the traditional values of American culture can be seen in the tone of Nixon's dealing with the war: the lack of indication that it is glorious, the muted appeal to patriotism (only one brief reference to the first defeat in America's history), the lack of complete victory as a goal. But nowhere else does the culture of the post-atomic age show through; by and large the speech would have been applauded if delivered in the nineteenth century. That there has been a radical revolution of values among the young does not affect the message, and one might predict that Nixon is right in deciding that the revolution in values has not yet significantly infected the target group.

Characterological and Stylistic Factors

Nixon's choice of value premises is, of course, closely related to his *ethos* as conveyed by the speech. He promises to tell the truth before he asks the American people to support a policy whch involves the overriding issues of war and peace— phraseology that echoes previous Nixonian messages. He refrains from harsh criticism of the previous administration; he is more interested in the future America than in political gains; such an avowal of disinterestedness is the commonest topic for self-character building.

Nixon is against political murders and imprisonments and active pushing initiatives for peace. He is flexible and compromising, unlike the negotiators for the enemy. He chooses the right way and not the easy way. He is the champion of policy made by constitutional processes; his opponents conduct unruly demonstrations in the streets. But he has healthy respect for the idealism and commitment of the young; he pledges himself in the tradition of Woodrow Wilson to win a peace that will avoid future wars. He has the courage to make a tasteful appeal to patriotism even when it's unpopular. Such is the character portrait drawn for us by Richard Nixon: restrained not hawkish, hardworking and active, flexible, yet firm where he needs to be. He seems an American style democrat, a moral but also a practical and sensitive man. The message is crowded with these overt clues from which we infer the good *ethos* of political figures in situations like this. Any more intensive development of the means of persuasion derived from the character of the speaker would surely have been counter-productive.

The language of Nixon's message helps to reinforce his *ethos*. His tone is unbrokenly serious. The first two-thirds of the message is in a self-consciously plain style—the effort is clearly made to give the impression of bluntness and forthrightness. This bluntness of tone correlates with the style of deliberative argumentation:[23] few epideictic elements are present in the first part of the speech. Everything seems to be adjusted to making the structure of residues exceedingly clear.

About two-thirds of the way through, the message shifts to a more impassioned tone. The alternative plans are collapsed into two, thus polarizing the situation: either immediate withdrawal or Nixon's plan for Vietnamization and unscheduled withdrawal. From here on parallel repetitions are persistent, and they serve no obvious logical function, but rather function to deepen the serious tone. There is, in short, an attempt to rise to a peroration of real eloquence. The qualities aimed at in the last third of the message seem to be gravity and impressiveness more than clarity and forthrightness. The effort seems to tax the speechwriter's literary skill to the limit, and the only new phrases he comes up with are the "silent majority" and the description of the energies of the young as "too often directed to bitter hatred against those they think are responsible for the war." All else is a moderately skillful pastiche of familiar phrases.

General Assessment

A summary answer can now be given to the question, how well did Nixon and his advisors choose among the available means of persuasion for this situation? The message was designed for those not ideologically overcommitted either to victory over Communism or to peace in any case while frustrated by the prolonged war. It operates from the most universally accepted premises of value and prediction; it buries deep in its texture most premises not likely to be immediately accepted. Enough of the means for bringing auditors into states of fear, anger, and confidence are used to create a psychological climate unfavorable to immediate withdrawal and favorable to Vietnamization. The goals—life, political freedom, peace, and self-confidence—are those shared by nearly all Americans, and connections of policies to them are tactfully handled for the target group. The structure is largely according to tradition: it can best be seen as falling into the four parts, and the right elements are contained in each of the parts. Two minor variations from the traditional are artfully designed to realize evident psychological ends. Conventional wisdom and conventional value judgments come dressed in conventional structure. The style of the narrative and proofs reflects adequately Nixon's reliance on clearly developed arguments from accepted premises; the style of the latter part of the message shows a moderately successful attempt at grandeur. In choice and arrangement of the means of persuasion for this situation this message is by and large a considerable success.

Neo-Aristotelian criticism tells a great deal about Nixon's message. It reveals the speech writer as a superior technician. It permits us to predict that given this target group the message should be successful in leading to a decision to support the Administration's policies. It brings into sharp focus the speechwriter's greatest technical successes: the choice of the right premises to make a version of the domino theory plausible for these auditors and the creation of a controlled atmosphere of fear in which the theory is more likely to be accepted. Likewise, the choice of the right means of making success for peace negotiations seems impossible and the building of a controlled state of anger in which a pessimistic estimate of the chances for success seems plausible. Also the finely crafted structure that conceals exactly what needs to be concealed while revealing the favored plan in a context most favorable to its being chosen.

What neo-Aristotelianism does not attempt to account for are some basic and long-run questions. For instance, it does not assess the wisdom of the speaker's choice of target audience as does Newman, who wanted the President to alleviate the fears of the doves. All critics observe that Nixon excludes the radical opponent of the war from his audience. Not only is this opponent excluded by his choice of policy but even by the choice of premises from which he argues: premises such as that the Government of South Viet Nam is freer than that of North Viet Nam, or that the right course is the opposite of the easy one. Radical opponents of the war were mostly young—often college students. The obvious cliché, "they are the political leadership of tomorrow," should have applied. Was it in the long run a wise choice to exclude them from the target? An important question, but a neo-Aristotelian approach does not warrant us to ask it. There is a gain, though, from this limitation. If the critic questions the President's choice of policy and premises, he is forced to examine systematically all the political factors involved in this choice. Neither Newman nor Campbell do this in the objective and systematic fashion required by the magnitude of the subject. Indeed, would they not be better off with a kind of criticism that does not require them to do it?

Nor does the neo-Aristotelian approach predict whether a policy will remain rhetorically viable. If the critic assumes as given the Nixon Administration's choice of policy from among the options available, he will no doubt judge this choice of value and predictive premises likely to effect the decision wanted. To put it another way, Nixon's policy was *then* most defensible by arguing from the kinds of premises Nixon used. It seems less defensible at this writing, and in time may come to seem indefensible even to people like those in the target group. Why the same arguments for the same policy should be predictably less effective to people so little removed in time is a special case of the question, why do some policies remain rhetorically viable for decades while others do not. This question might in part be answered by pointing, as was done before, to the maturing of the students into political leadership. But however the question might be answered, neo-Aristotelianism does not encourage us to ask it. As Black truly said, the neo-Aristotelian comprehends "the rhetorical discourse as tactically designed to achieve certain results with a specific audience on a specific occasion"[24] in this case that audience Nixon aimed at on the night of November 3, 1969.

Finally, neo-Aristotelian criticism does not warrant us to estimate the truth of Nixon's statements or the reality of the values he assumes as aspects of American life. When Nixon finds the origin of the war in a North Vietnamese "campaign to impose a Communist government on South Vietnam by instigating and supporting a revolution," Campbell takes him to task for not telling the truth. This criticism raises a serious question: are we sure that Nixon is not telling the truth? We know, of course, that Nixon oversimplifies a complex series of events—any speaker in his situation necessarily does that. But will the scholar of tomorrow with the perspective of history judge his account totally false? Campbell endorses the view that basically this is a civil war resulting from the failure of the Diem government backed by the United States to hold elections under the Geneva Agreements of 1954. But her view and Nixon's are not mutually exclusive: it seems evident to me that both the United States and the Communist powers involved themselves from the first to the extent they thought necessary to force an outcome in their favor in Viet Nam. If a scientific historian of the future had to pick one view of the conflict or the other, he would probably pick Nixon's because it more clearly recognizes the power politics behind the struggle. But I am not really intending to press the point that Campbell commits herself to a wrong view, or even a superficially partial one. The point is that she espouses here a theory of criticism that requires her to commit herself at all. If anyone writing in a scholarly journal seeks to assess the truth of Nixon's statements, he must be willing to assume the burden of proving them evidently false. This cannot be done by appealing to the wisdom of the liberal intellectuals of today.[25] If the essential task were accomplished, would the result be called a *rhetorical* critique? By Aristotle's standards it would not, and for my part I think we will write more significant criticism if we follow Aristotle in this case. To generalize, I submit that the limitations of neo-Aristotelian criticism are like the metrical conventions of the poet—limitations that make true significance possible.

Notes

1. Robert P. Newman, "Under the Veneer: Nixon's Vietnam Speech of November 3, 1969," *QJS*, 56 (Apr. 1970), 168–178; Hermann G. Stelzner, "The Quest Story and Nixon's November 3, 1969 Address," *QJS*, 57 (Apr. 1971), 163–172; Karlyn Kohrs Campbell, "An Exercise in the Rhetoric of Mythical America," in *Critiques of Contemporary Rhetoric* (Belmont, Calif.: Wadsworth, 1972), pp. 50–58.

2. Herbert A. Wichelns, "The Literary Criticism of Oratory," in Donald C. Bryant, ed., *The Rhetorical Idiom: Essays in Rhetoric, Oratory, Language, and Drama* (1925; rpt. Ithaca: Cornell Univ. Press, 1958), pp. 5–42.

3. Marie Hochmuth [Nichols], "The Criticism of Rhetoric," in *A History and Criticism of American Public Address* (New York: Longmans, Green, 1955) III, 1–23.

4. Aristotle, *Rhetoric* I. 1. 1355^b 10–14. "To persuade is not the function of rhetoric but to investigate the persuasive factors inherent in the particular case. It is just the same as in all other arts; for example, it is not the function of medicine to bring health, rather to bring the patient as near to health as is possible in his case. Indeed, there are some patients who cannot be changed to healthfulness; nevertheless, they can be given the right therapy." (Translation mine.) I understand the medical analogy to mean that even if auditors chance to be proof against any of the means of persuasion, the persuader has functioned adequately as a rhetorican if he has investigated these means so that he has in effect "given the right therapy."

5. Text as printed in *Vital Speeches*, 36 (15 Nov. 1969), 69.

6. Aristotle *Rhetoric* I. 4. 1359^b 33–1360^a 5.

7. *Aristotle Rhetoric* III. 14. 1415^a 29–33. Here Nixon functions like a defendant in a forensic speech. "When defending he will first deal with any prejudicial insinuation against him. . .it is necessary that the defendant when he steps forward first reduce the obstacles, so he must immediately dissolve prejudice."

8. See Aristotle *Rhetoric* III. 16. 1417^a 16–36.

9. Newman, p. 173.

10. See *Aristotle Rhetoric* II. 23. 1398^a 30–31. This basic structure is called method of residues in most modern argumentation textbooks.

11. Aristotle *Rhetoric* III. 19. 1419^b 10–1420^a 8.

12. For the purpose of this paper the term enthymeme is taken to mean any deductive argument. Aristotle gives a more technical definition of enthymeme that fits into the total design of his organon; in my opinion it is not useful for neo-Aristotelian criticism.

13. Remarkably enough Aristotle does not state this general rule, though it clearly underlies his treatment of the historical example, *Rhetoric* II. 20.

14. See Aristotle *Rhetoric* I. 6. 1362^b 26–27 for life as a good; I. 8. 1366^a for freedom as the object of choice for the citizens of a democracy.

15. The subject for *Rhetoric* I. 7. Chaim Perelman and L. Olbrechts-Tyteca, commenting on this chapter, indicate that there is usually a consensus on such statements as 'life is good'; the dispute is over whether life is a greater good than honor in this particular situation. See *The New Rhetoric: A Treatise on Argumentation*, trans. John Wilkinson and Purcell Weaver (Notre Dame, Ind.: Univ. of Notre Dame Press, 1969), pp. 81–82.

16. See Aristotle *Rhetoric* II. 19. 1393^a 1–3.

17. This principle follows from *Rhetoric* II. 5. 1383ª 24–25.

18. Aristotle *Rhetoric* II. 5. 1382ª 21–22. Aristotle treated the *pathe* as states of feeling that a man enters into because he draws certain inferences from the situation around him: he sees, for example, that he is the type of man who experiences pity when faced with this type of victim in these circumstances. The means of getting a man to draw inferences are themselves logical proofs; hence *pathos* does not work apart from the logical proofs in a message but through them. See Aristotle *Rhetoric* II. 1. 1378ª 19–28 and my explication in James J. Murphy, ed. *A Synoptic History of Classical Rhetoric* (New York: Random House, 1972).

19. Aristotle *Rhetoric* II. 2. 1378ª 30–32.

20. Aristotle *Rhetoric* II. 2. 1379ª 10–18.

21. Aristotle *Rhetoric* II. 5. 1383ª 16–19.

22. Since he gave this speech Nixon has made a general timetable for American withdrawal, thus, presumably, showing that he was not utterly convinced by his own argument. But he has never quite fixed a date for complete withdrawal of all American support forces from Viet Nam; he has been consistent in maintaining that withdrawal as a bargaining point for negotiation with the Viet Cong and North Vietnamese.

23. See Aristotle *Rhetoric* III. 12. 1414ª 8–19.

24. Edwin B. Black, *Rhetorical Criticism: A Study in Method* (New York: Macmillan, 1965), p. 33.

25. Richard H. Kendall, writing a reply to Newman, "The Forum," *QJS*, 56 (Dec. 1970), 432, makes this same point, particularly in connection with Newman's implication that ex-President Johnson was a fraud. "If so, let us have some evidence of his fraudulent actions. If there is no evidence, or if there is evidence, but an essay on the rhetoric of President Nixon does not provide proper scope for a presentation of such evidence, then it seems to me inclusion of such a charge (or judgment) may fall into the category of gratuitous." Newman in rejoinder asks, "Should such summary judgments be left out of an article in a scholarly journal because space prohibits extensively supporting them? Omission might contribute to a sterile academic purity, but it would improve neither cogency nor understanding." I would certainly answer Newman's rhetorical question, yes, and I would go on to judge that view of criticism which encourages such summary judgments not to be a useful one.

The Forum: "Conventional Wisdom —Traditional Form": A Rejoinder

KARLYN KOHRS CAMPBELL

Professor Hill's analysis of Nixon's Vietnamization address in this issue of *QJS*, has added a neo-Aristotelian critique to the roster of criticisms of that speech already published. However, Professor Hill has invited controversy by attacking the methodologies of the other critics, chiefly Professor Robert Newman and myself. I have taken advantage of the opportunity to respond because I think the conflict highlights certain important issues in rhetorical criticism.

Professor Hill legitimates his methodology by appealing to the authority of Aristotle, but in the tradition of heretics, I must demur at several points from his interpretation of the "true faith." I am chiefly concerned with his exclusion of considerations of truth and ethical assessments and with his treatment of the "target audience."

In responding to the exclusion of the truth criterion, I am inclined to appeal to "conventional wisdom" and "traditional form" in interpreting Aristotelian methodology. Thonssen and Baird, for example, treat the evaluation of logical content as one of determining "how fully a given speech enforces an idea; how closely that enforcement conforms to the general rules of argumentative development; and how nearly the totality of the reasoning approaches a measure of truth adequate for purposes of action" (*Speech Criticism*, 1948, p. 334) and specifically call for the rigorous testing of evidence and argument (p. 341). Aristotle himself wrote that rhetoric is valuable "because truth and justice are by nature more powerful than their opposites; so that, when decisions are not made as they should be, the speakers with the right on their side have only themselves to thank for the outcome.... [A proper knowledge and exercise of Rhetoric would prevent the triumph of fraud and injustice.]" (*Rhetorica*, trans. Lane Cooper, I. 1.1355^a 21–24). These statements are at odds with Hill's assertion that "neo-Aristotelian criticism does not warrant us to estimate the truth of Nixon's statements or the reality of the values he assumes..." (p. 385). In fact, there is a puzzling inconsistency in Professor Hill's essay. On the one hand, Newman and I are chided for questioning the President's choice of policy and premises, on the other, Hill himself takes pains to justify the choice of premises, stating that an assessment of the choice of major premises is central to an Aristotelian account. He discusses the truth of the premises used, e.g., "we know that the premise is not universally true, yet everyone finds it necessary to operate in ordinary life as if it were," "they rest on what experience from the sandbox up shows to be probable," and so forth (pp. 378,, 379). Similarly, there are numerous comments indicating Hill's recognition of the highly deceptive nature of this speech in which Nixon said we were to be told the truth, e.g., "this explanation masquerades as...," "but thinly disguised in the chronology...," "this phrase concealed the intention...," and finally, "the finely crafted structure that conceals exactly what needs to be concealed..." (pp. 376, 377, 384). As I see it, Hill is arguing for the truth and acceptability of the major premises while recognizing the deception central to the *logos* of this address. The final statement I have cited makes the point of this critique explicit in regard to questions of truth: what we are to applaud as critics is highly skillful deception and concealment. As a critic, that is a bitter pill I cannot swallow.

The issue I have raised not only involves considerations of truth but ethical assessments, and I propose that an amoral reading of Aristotle is open to question. In the section on deliberative rhetoric to which Hill directs us, Aristotle reiterates that rhetoric "combines the science of logical analysis with the ethical branch of political science..." (I. 4. 1359^b 9–11). Similarly, immediately following the analogy to health care cited by Hill comes the statement that "sophistic dialectic, or sophistical speaking, is made so, not by the faculty, but by the moral purpose" (I. 1. 1335^b 16–18). These statements are coherent parts of a teleology defining man as rational and an ethic stating that moral good consists in acting in obedience to reason (*Ethica Nicomachea*, trans. W. D. Ross, I. 13 1102^b 13–28). It seems to me that Aristotle enables the critic to recognize the skillful use of the faculty, i.e., the best (most effective) choices from the inventory, and to condemn the moral purpose and the rhetorical act as sophistic, perhaps even "shoddy." And Aristotle's description of the nature of deliberative rhetoric provides an additional warrant for combining concerns for truth and ethics. He says that the aim of deliberation is determination of advantage and injury with primary emphasis on expediency (I. 3. 1358^b 22–24), suggesting that questions of practically and feasibility are essential to rational decision-making in deliberative addresses. Consequently, I take it that even an Aristotelian critic, confronting a deliberative speech that seeks to avoid questions of expediency and conceals the true nature of the policy being advocated (which Hill admits), might be justified in making a negative assessment.

Finally, Aristotle says that the deliberative speaker must "know how many types of government there are; what conditions are favorable to each type; and what things...naturally tend to destroy it" (1. 4. 1360^a 20–23), elements relevant to deliberative rhetoric which lead me to object to Hill's assessment of the speech in terms of a "target audience." As he recognizes, political factors and the political context are germane to criticism. There is no dispute that this was a major policy address by the President to the nation. But contrary to Hill's assertion that Aristotelian methodology does not warrant questioning whether or not Nixon should have chosen to ignore parts of his constituency, I submit that Aristotle encourages the critic to recognize that this was not simply a speech by Richard Nixon, but a deliberative address from the Presidency—as institution, symbol, and role—*to all citizens in this republic-democracy*. I am not satisfied that the kind of divisiveness created through this rhetorical act in this political context can be excused by delineating a "target audience." In my critique, I argued that the President eliminated the concept of a "loyal opposition" by creating a dichotomy between the "great silent majority" that supports administrative policy and a "vocal minority" seeking to prevail "over reason and the will of the majority." Aristotle said that the end of democracy is liberty, and if that ambiguous term is to mean anything, it has to include the liberty to dissent from policy without being labeled in terms that suggest that dissent is subversive, if not traitorous. I recognized that Nixon paid lip service to the idea of a loyal opposition ("Honest and patriotic Americans have reached different conclusions as to how peace should be achieved."), but the remainder of the address contradicts this strongly, e.g., "the more divided we are at home, the less likely the enemy is to negotiate" and "only Americans [presumably only *dissenting* Americans] can humiliate and defeat the United States." To assess the speech in terms of a "target audience" is to ignore the special kind of disunity created by the speech which, I believe, is a threat to the political processes of our system of government, particularly when propounded by its chief executive.

As I read Professor Hill's criticism of the analyses of Professor Newman and myself, it seems to me that he believes a major shortcoming of both is a lack of "objectivity." He implies that neo-Aristotelian methodology is "objective," genuinely rhetorical (rather than political or ideological), and, in fact, is the only legitimate methodology—it makes "true significance possible" (p. 386). However, as I understand it, Hill's conception of objectivity requires the critic to remain entirely within the closed universe of the discourse and the ideology or point of view it presents. No testing of premises or data is permitted except that determining the degree of *acceptability* to the immediate audience or, more narrowly, to that part of it that is the speaker's target. This is, of course, commendably consistent with his exclusions of considerations of truth and ethics, but it hardly qualifies as objectivity. It is, in fact, to choose the most favorable and partisan account a critic can render. For example, it is to accept the perspective of the advertiser and applaud the skill with which, say, Anacin commercials create the false belief that their product is a more effective pain reliever than ordinary aspirin. As a consequence, the methodology produces analyses that are at least covert advocacy of the point of view taken in the rhetorical act—under the guise of objectivity. Recognizing that anyone reading my critique of this address will know that I am politically liberal (the same, I think, is true of Professor Newman), my simple rejoinder is that anyone reading Hill's critique will know that he is politically conservative.

The particular point on which he takes me to task, my objections to Nixon's view of the origins of the war, is highly illustrative. Professor Hill writes, "When Nixon finds the origin of the war in a North Vietnamese 'campaign to impose a Communist government on South Vietnam by instigating and supporting a revolution,' Campbell takes him to task for not telling the truth" (p. 385). But Nixon said, "Fifteen years ago North Vietnam, *with the logistical support of Communist China and the Soviet Union*, launched a campaign. . ." (emphasis added). What I said was:

> Now "fifteen years ago" was 1954, the year of the Geneva Agreements that were to unify Vietnam through elections to be held in 1956. Those elections never occurred because the United States supported Diem, who refused elections and attempted to destroy all internal political opposition, Communist and otherwise. The Vietcong did not persuade Hanoi or Peking or Moscow to aid them against Diem until about 1959. By 1965 South Vietnam was clearly losing, the point at which President Johnson decided to send in United States combat forces (Critiques of Contemporary Rhetoric, 1972, p. 52).

Professor Hill has condensed both Nixon's and my own comments about the North Vietnamese campaign *with* alleged aid from China and Russia into the simpler notion of a North Vietnamese campaign to instigate revolution and impose a Communist regime on the South. This condensation, although understandably desirable from a conservative point of view and understandably unacceptable from a liberal viewpoint, hardly qualifies as an objective appraisal of Nixon's characterization of the origins of the war or of my response to it. My point was and is that Nixon wished to disclaim all U.S. responsibility for the events with which we now wrestle in Indochina and place all blame on a monolithic Communist conspiracy. I think it highly doubtful that the "scientific historian" to whom Hill refers would support that characterization.

It should also be evident that I do not agree with Professor Hill that neo-Aristotelianism is the only, or even the best, methodology for rhetorical criticism. As Hill's essay illustrates, such an approach has explanatory power for revealing how a speaker produced the effects that he did on one part of the audience, what Hill calls the "target audience," but it ignores effects on the rest of the audience, and it excludes all *evaluations* other than the speech's potential for evoking intended response from an immediate, specified audience. Because I do not believe that the sole purpose of criticism is an assessment of a discourse's capacity to achieve intended effects, I cannot accept Hill's monistic view of critical methodology. I am strongly committed to pluralistic modes of criticism, considering that the questions the critic asks have such a significant effect on the answers generated, I think we know more about Nixon's rhetorical act because a variety of critical approaches have been brought to it than if Professor Hill's critique stood alone.

The objections I have made so far to Professor Hill's views of criticism and of critical methodology have been, I believe, important ones, but my final objection is, for me, the most important. In describing and defending the uses of rhetoric, Aristotle says that we should be knowledgeable about both sides of a question so that "if our opponent makes unfair use of the arguments, we may be able in turn to refute them," and he continues, to remark that although rhetoric and dialectic, abstractly considered, "may indifferently prove opposite statements. Still, their basis, in the facts, is not a matter of indifference..." (I. 1. 1355ᵃ 30–37). If rhetoric is to be justified, then rhetorical criticism must also be justifiable. For criticism, too, is rhetoric. Its impulse is epideictic—to praise and blame; its method is forensic—reason-giving. But ultimately it enters into the deliberative realm in which choices must be made, and it plays a crucial role in the processes of testing, questioning, and analyzing by which discourses advocating truth and justice may, in fact, become more powerful than their opposites.

The analogy that Professor Hill draws between neo-Aristotelian methodology and metrical conventions as "limitations that make true significance possible" (p. 386) is an interesting one, particularly for an Aristotelian. After all, it was Aristotle who recognized that poetry could not be defined metrically: "though it is the way with people to tack on 'poet' to the name of a metre...thinking that they call them poets not by reason of the imitative nature of their work, but indiscriminately by reason of the metre they write in" (*De Poetica*, trans. Ingram Bywater, I. 1447ᵇ 12–16). Perhaps a more apt analogy is that the strict application of a rhetorical inventory may make the critic a versifier, but not a poet.

The Forum: "Reply to Professor Campbell"

———————————— FORBES HILL ————————————

Professor Campbell's rejoinder states clearly the positions opposed to mine on certain important issues in criticism. I mean the model neo-Aristotelian critique, embodying an ideal form of neo-Aristotelian methodology based on a closer reading of the *Rhetoric* than common to many following Thonssen and Baird, to raise just such issues. They may be grouped in the following three questions: 1) Does neo-Aristotelianism warrant a critic to praise a leader for addressing a target audience and pushing the citizens who are off-target into an isolated and helpless position? 2) Does Aristotle's text authorize excluding considerations of truth from rhetorical critiques, and should such considerations be excluded? 3) Does the text authorize excluding considerations of morality from rhetorical critiques, and should such considerations be excluded? To all parts of these questions I answer yes—though in some particulars it must be a qualified yes. I understand Professor Campbell to answer no in every particular.

Aristotle nowhere uses the concept of target audience. This adaptation of Aristotelian theory to modern conditions is necessary because Aristotle put together his lectures on rhetoric with a group of Athenian students in mind. For them, auditors of a deliberative speech suggested three to five thousand decision-makers gathered in the Pnyx within the sound of the orator's voice. All these decision-makers were male citizens born on that rocky coastland; none were very rich by any standard; few were well-traveled; few had allegiances abroad. In short, they were a highly homogeneous group. That is what Aristotle assumed when he made a demographic analysis into categories of young, old, rich, poor, well-born and powerful. He did not use categories like Greek-descent and non-Greek descent, educated and uneducated, or urban and rural. And he seemed to assume that a speaker will be able to get all sub-groups of auditors to shout assent as did the Achaeans in the epic.

Obviously an American president communicating through the electronic media makes no assumption about getting assent from all his auditors; the audience is not homogeneous enough to permit it. He must start the preparation of his message by trying to decide who his potential supporters are, that is by making a construct of a target audience. Such procedure is entirely in line with Aristotle's, which starts with the question: who is expected to make a decision for or against what? The group expected to make a decision in this case can be only part of that auditing the discourse. When we thus extend Aristotle's method to deal with the greater national audience of a modern country, we are working along Aristotelian lines, not following his *Rhetoric* like a slavish copyist.

Aristotle aside, is it reasonable to demand, as Professor Campbell does, that the President not declare certain groups off-target but promote unity in the nation? It is—up to a point. But if the critic demands that he win over everyone in a policy address to the nation—not a discourse in praise of freedom but a policy address— an unreasonable standard is being maintained. Not Truman, nor even Eisenhower ever met that standard; it was not met save perhaps when Roosevelt asked Congress to declare war after Pearl Harbor. But Roosevelt also derided the money-changers in the temple; was he not acting on the sound precept that someone has to be off-target, that every drama needs an antagonist? Only if the critic wants an American president to fail scrutiny, will he hold up such a standard.

What did Aristotle decree was the role of truth in rhetorical criticism? Professor Campbell interprets the passage about rhetoric being useful since when true and just causes do not win out that must be because of the inadequacy of their advocates' use of rhetoric[1] to mean that Aristotle demands us to determine the truth of an advocate's statements, as part of a critique of his rhetoric. That interpretation is in my opinion incorrect. The passage itself assumes that the same rhetoric used to advocate true and just causes is also used by the advocates of untrue and unjust ones. A little further on Aristotle says that though rhetoric persuades impartially to contrary conclusions, we (i.e., good people like us) should not use it to advocate bad causes (*Rhet.* I. 1. 1355[a] 29–33). A distinction is presupposed here between rhetoric—used to argue either to true conclusions or false—and how a good person uses it—only to argue conclusions he believes to be true. The means of persuasion themselves (enthymemes, examples, and the like) are considered free of truth value, but we who use them should be committed to truth. Rhetoric is the study of our use of the means, not our commitments to ends.

This notion that the means of persuasion are in themselves truth-indifferent fits with other Aristotelian doctrines. Take the well-known distinction between demonstrations and dialectical arguments. The former proceed from premises that are true, primary, immediate, better known than and prior to their conclusions (*Post An.* I. 1 71[b] 20–25; *Top* I. 1. 100[a] 25–30) elsewhere called first principles. The latter assume as starting points premises chosen by the respondent from among those generally accepted (*Top.* I. 1. 100[b] 23–24). Now rhetoric is the counterpart not of demonstrative reasoning but of dialectic. Instead of assuming as premises state-ments accepted by a single respondent, it assumes those believed by the type of people who are in attendance as decision-makers. In a few cases these premises may be first principles, but they seldom are. That is because men debate about human affairs, which are in the realm of the contingent (*Rhet*. I. 2. 1357ᵃ 22–23). Indeed, the more accurately a rhetorician examines his premises, the more likely he is to light on the first principles of some substantive field, and then he will have left the field of rhetoric altogether (*Rhet*. 1. 2. 1358ᵃ 23–26). Another way of putting the distinction between dialectic or rhetoric and the study of demonstrative reason-ings is to say that the former argue from probable premises to probable conclu-sions (*Rhet*. 1. 2. 1357ᵃ 27–28). What does probability mean in this statement? A common Aristotelian synonym is *ta endoxa* (what are today called subjective probabilities), defined in the *Topics* as propositions accepted by all, or by the majority, or by the most distinguished people (*Top*. I. 1. 100ᵇ 22–24).

It is easy to see from this review of Aristotelian doctrine that Aristotle positively commands the critic of demonstrative arguments to inquire whether or not pre-mises are true, but he says that if a rhetorician examines accurately into this question he leaves the field, ceasing to be a rhetorician and becoming some other kind of scholar. Dialecticians are commanded to examine whether the premises are accepted by all or by the majority, or by the most distinguished people; rhetori-cians, by implication, must examine whether the premises will be accepted by the type of people who are decision-makers in this particular case.[2]

A careful look at my critique shows that this is precisely the activity I engaged in. The generalization I worked from is that other things being equal, the more commonplace and universally accepted the premises of prediction and value in a deliberative discourse, the more effective the discourse will be. Applying this principle to Nixon's address, I remarked that "we [the reader, myself, and all other potential members of Nixon's target audience] know that the premise [the future will be like the past] is not universally true, yet everyone finds it necessary to operate in ordinary life as if it were." Professor Campbell accuses me of being inconsistent with my interpretation of what Aristotle demands of a critic by making a judgment about the truth of the premises Nixon used. My remark, taken in context, however, can clearly be seen as a prediction about the acceptability of the premise to potential decision-makers. So can all other comments that taken alone seem to be about the truth of premises or the reality of values.

Only once did I depart from this methodological limitation: when I wrote that Nixon's account of the origins of the war would be preferred by the historian of the future to Campbell's. I was indeed in violation of my own principles. This is, perhaps, as happy an example as could be found of the peril of entering into controversy over the truth of a contemporary speaker's statements.

What is at work in her analysis compelling the conclusion that the United States is responsible for what has happened in Viet Nam is the revisionist theory of the cold war, so popular now in New Left circles. The theory isolates Amer-ica's militant support of the *status quo ante* as the key element disrupting world peace, in contrast to Communist reaction, which is largely defensive. It informs the whole of Professor Campbell's critique. Naturally Richard Nixon does not ana-lyze the situation this way, and of course, that must mean he is guilty of gross misrepresentation.

If a critic will write of Nixon's address from any such point of view, he has the choice of two ways to treat his theme. He can carefully sift the evidence for the revisionist view as it relates to the war in Viet Nam, or he can simply assume statements reflecting this view—like "the truth is that America supports totalitarian governments all over the world"—are to be accepted by his reader. In either case he is not writing rhetorical criticism.

In the broadest sense rhetorical criticism of any kind primarily assesses how a message relates to some group of auditors. In doing this it may, and usually must, secondarily consider some questions about how the message relates to what is known about the external world. Whenever this secondary consideration becomes the greater part of a critique it ceases to be a rhetorical critique—unless, of course, rhetoric is defined to include the universe.

Criticism of any kind, however, rests on established principles of one sort or another. A discourse where many starting-points must be taken on trust is an epideictic speech, or to put it another way, a tract for the faithful. Readers not among the faithful are blocked off from whatever insights about structure and strategies the critique may present. To assess the truth of a contemporary speaker's claims is to take either the scholarly way or the partisan way out of the area of rhetorical criticism. Of course, a critic is just as certainly led out of the area if he judges Nixon accurate in his account of the origins of the war. I hereby apologize for my inconsistency in characterizing Nixon's statement of these origins as more adequate than Campbell's.

It is not always plain whether Professor Campbell thinks that President Nixon fails to tell the truth because he is mistaken or because he deliberately tries to give a false impression. Her rejoinder, though, charges me with applauding deception, which she finds central to the *logos* of the address. I said the finely crafted structure concealed what needs to be concealed, but I avoided using the word deception because it implies a wrongful intention to suppress what the suppressor knows to be true. It demands a judgment on Nixon's intentions, his knowledge of the truth in this case, and the wrongfulness in this case of suppressing the truth. When speaking to my neighbors for George McGovern (as I often have lately; Professor Campbell's inference to the contrary I am a liberal) I easily make these judgments, but when writing rhetorical criticism I avoid them. Both Aristotle and sound critical practice sanction avoidance.

I appeal first to the passage cited by Campbell. Aristotle develops his categorization of rhetoric as the counterpart of dialectic by saying

> [rhetoric's] function is to examine both proof and counterfeit proof, just as dialectic's is [to examine] both real and counterfeit syllogism. For the sophistry is not in the art [dynamics in this context = techne], but in the moral purpose [proairesis]. Except here a man will be a rhetor whether in relation to his art or to his moral purpose, but there [in the case of dialectic] he will be classified as a sophist in relation to his moral purpose, but a dialectician not in relation to the moral purpose, but in relation to his art (Rhet. I. 1. 1355^b 15–21).

Professor Campbell interprets Aristotle as enabling "the critic to recognize the skillful use of the faculty and to condemn the moral purpose and the rhetorical act as sophistic." True, but this interpretation misses the important distinction here drawn: the distinction between artistic judgment and ethical judgment. Built into the language is the proper distinction about dialectic: viewed artistically someone is a dialectician if he understands dialectical method; viewed ethically he is a sophist if he uses this method to bad ends. Employing a non-Aristotelian technique, we might distinguish between *rhetor*$_1$, who understands the art of rhetoric, and *rhetor*$_2$, who uses it purely for self-serving ends. Judgments about *rhetor*$_1$ are rhetorical criticism; those about *rhetor*$_2$ are in the field of ethics.

What the text shows us here follows from an important Aristotelian preoccupation. Whereas Plato wished to bring all arts and sciences (*technai kai epistemai*) under a single deductive system unified by the idea of the good, Aristotle conceived of the arts and sciences as separate and distinct areas of study, each with its own first principles (or probable premises that serve the function of first principles). His great endeavor was to separate all human knowledge into these studies and outline for each the basic principles.[3] He also created hierarchies—political science is for him the architectonic study which coordinate subfields like ethics, the rationale of personal moral choice, and dialectic-rhetoric, the study of methods for arguing about political and ethical subjects (*Nic. Eth.* I. 1. 1094^a 27–30).

What I have just said about the Aristotelian doctrine of the moral neutrality of rhetoric as art and the consequent separation of ethical judgments and rhetorical judgments is not the whole truth; a large section of the *Rhetoric*, (I. 4. to I. 9) is devoted to the value premises from which a speaker may argue. In this section we find a hierarchy of goods—admitted and disputed. We might see the section as an objective description of what people believe—of the value consensus of Aristotle's time. But it clearly is not that; it consists of an adaptation to rhetoric of the rationalized value system of the *Nicomachean Ethics*. Aristotle here commits himself to his own value system. How can he, then, maintain the moral neutrality of rhetoric? Perhaps Campbell is right saying that "an amoral reading of Aristotle is open to question."

Professor Olian in an admirable article, which thoroughly establishes that the dominant thrust of the *Rhetoric* is amoral, maintains that we can see these sections as descriptive and not Aristotle's own value system just so long as we understand that he is describing the values of persons of breeding, wealth, and education (*hoi aristoi*) and not the values of the masses (*hoi polloi*)[4] I will not here attempt a complete examination of this sophisticated view. I only hazard the opinion that if one understands the full context of Aristotle's remarks about the best citizens he will judge that sound ethical principles are discovered by finding they are held by such citizens. But they are verified as being the true principles by an argument from the parts: alternative principles are demonstrably inferior so these must be the right principles. I think that Aristotle establishes by reasoning and not empirically that his value system is the right one.

Aristotle attempts to have matters both ways in the *Rhetoric*. His prologue makes rhetoric the counterpart of dialectic, i.e. amoral. But he introduces the section on value premises by calling it an offshoot (*paraphues*) of the ethical branch of politics. An even better translation might be "a graft onto the ethical branch of politics." He does not say that rhetoric is the mirror-image of ethics; its connection to ethics is not that intimate. But even this way of verbalizing the matter does not quite get him out of contradicting himself.

Friedrich Solmsen, in my opinion the greatest of the twentieth century interpreters of the *Rhetoric*, explained that the first draft of Aristotle's lectures maintained the moral neutrality of the art with consistency. Later drafts, however, introduced the value system precisely because it was needed in any treatment of the art that would be competitive with the completeness of rival sophistic rhetorics all of which laid claim to having ethical foundations.[5] The evidence for this explanation is skimpy, but it has some inherent probability.

As a practical matter it makes for better neo-Aristotelian criticism to interpret the *Rhetoric* as if it were consistently amoral. There are two reasons why. First, no critic can realistically commit himself to Aristotle's value system as a basic inventory of American values and their hierarchy. Aristotle omits thrift, hardworkingness, chastity, piety, honesty, and humility from the list of virtues. (As Lawrence Rosenfield once remarked to me, he does not know about the Protestant ethic.) He omits progress and efficiency from the list of goods. It is by no means plain that happiness in the Aristotelian sense of the term is or should be the ultimate goal for the rational mid-century American. If, then, we are forced to abandon the value system to which Aristotle was committed, what should we do when judging a discourse—commit ourselves to a value system of our own? Or should we try objectively to describe what we think are the value commitments of the target group—the decision-makers in this case?

The second reason why in practice a neo-Aristotelian critic should give an amoral reading to the *Rhetoric* is that if he judges a speaker's values not to match reality, he is inevitably driven to decide the truth on questions that are best avoided: e.g., "who is really responsible for the cold war?" It has already been argued that attempting to answer such questions leads us to take an indefinite leave of absence from rhetorical criticism.

One more minor point: I never advocated critical monism. The several critical methods applied to this address have each produced essays with considerable virtues. Stelzner, in particular, revealed facets of its artistry I had not dreamed of before. Nevertheless, I think neo-Aristotelianism can do more to render a comprehensive assessment on it than other methods. This has something to do with Nixon and his *logographers* being products of highly traditional training. Their tendency is ever to produce another brand of the conventional wisdom structured in traditional forms.

The same is emphatically not true of other discourses. In *Critiques of Contemporary Rhetoric* Campbell prints an essay of Eldridge Cleaver's. By neo-Aristotelian standards that essay must be judged childishly ineffective: the society at large constitutes the body of decision-makers in this case, and these decision-makers will predictably not respond favorably to this selection of means of persuasion from the available inventory. But experience with hundreds of discussions warns me that in some sense Cleaver's essay is a considerable work of art. If neo-Aristotelianism compels a quick negative judgment on it, that is probably because Cleaver plays another kind of ball game from a different game plan. A method that has more explanatory power for Cleaver's game can certainly be found, as Professor Campbell's critique of the essay well shows.

Notes

1. Aristotle, Rhetoric I. 1. 1355[a] 21–24. This paraphrase, like Lane Cooper's translation (used by Campbell), construes a text that is here utterly ambiguous. Literal translation: "Rhetoric is useful because true and just causes are by nature more powerful than their contraries, so that

when decisions do not turn out according to what is fitting, necessarily [they] have been defeated through themselves." What does 'themselves' refer to in this passage? True and just causes? Their contraries? Or must we from our own minds supply 'advocates' of true and just causes' as subject of 'have been defeated' and antecedent of 'themselves'? 'Their contraries' has had defenders, e.g., Victorius and Spengel, cited by Edward Meredith Cope, *The Rhetoric of Aristotle with a Commentary*, rev. and ed. by John Edwin Sandys (Cambridge: at the University Press, 1877), Vol. I, p. 23. But Mr. Cope rightly asks why, if true and just causes are naturally superior, would they be defeated by their contraries? Making 'advocates of true and just causes' the subject brings sense to the argument, but these words certainly have to be supplied out of thin air. I mention this ambiguity because one who would maintain that Aristotle believed determining truth necessary to rhetorical criticism probably needs to give what I consider an incorrect reading of this passage, but he also needs to think the text as we have it here meaningful enough to bear a definitive interpretation. This is probably not the case.

2. See Lloyd F. Bitzer, "Aristotle's Enthymeme Revisted," *QJS*, 45 (Dec. 1959), 407.

3. I have drawn here, on a good popular treatment, John Herman Randall, Jr., *Aristotle* (New York: Columbia Univ. Press, 1960), pp. 32–58.

4. J. Robert Olian, "The Intended Uses of Aristotle's *Rhetoric*," *SM*, 35 (June 1968), 137.

5. Friedrich Solmsen, *Die Entwicklung der Aristotelischen Logik und Rhetorik*, IV, *Neue Philologische Untersuchungen* (Berlin: Weidmann, 1929). For English presentations of material from this book see Forbes I. Hill, "The Genetic Method in Recent Criticism on the Rhetoric of Aristotle," Diss. Cornell 1963, and George Kennedy, *The Art of Persuasion in Greece* (Princeton, N.J.: Princeton Univ. Press, 1963), pp. 82–85.

PART
THREE

Critical Examples

INTRODUCTION

The following studies are examples of rhetorical criticism written by perceptive, mature critics who approach their tasks from different theoretical perspectives and whose work illustrates a variety of critical approaches. Of
course, as the bibliography at the end of this book indicates, the studies
included here represent only a small sample of rhetorical criticism.

Nevertheless, the studies exhibit the richness of critical investigation
and show the decided tendency to critical pluralism that characterizes contemporary scholarship. Written as they are by accomplished professionals,
they are not models that the beginning student can hope to emulate; rather,
they are demonstrations of what serious critics can contribute to our understanding of rhetoric and communication. Beginning critics who study them
carefully will begin to appreciate what kinds of questions can fruitfully be
asked, what techniques of analysis and interpretation can begin to uncover
answers to significant questions, how critical arguments are constructed,
and what fresh insights can be generated. The studies undertake the investigation of different rhetorical artifacts, in different time periods, and with
different goals in view.

The classic study by Michael C. Leff and Gerald P. Mohrmann of Lincoln's speech at the Cooper Union ("Lincoln at Cooper Union: A Rhetorical
Analysis of the Text"), examines the text within the context of Lincoln's
quest for the Republican presidential nomination. Their careful examination
of arrangement, argument, and style in each section of the speech uncovers
Lincoln's attempt to ingratiate himself with his Republican audience by
associating himself and his party with the founding fathers and distinguishing himself from his political rivals.

Martin J. Medhurst ("Eisenhower's 'Atoms for Peace' Speech: A Case
Study in the Strategic Use of Language") examines President Eisenhower's
"Atoms for Peace" speech given before the United Nations' General Assembly in 1953. Arguing that pragmatism, realism, and idealism all played a
part in the promotion of the campaign for the peaceful use of atomic
energy, Medhurst concentrates on the ways in which pragmatic and realistic factors in the rhetorical situation influenced the crafting of the speech.
His careful analysis of the text and the context demonstrates the ways in
which "human agents can shape language and guide perception in accordance with their own purposes."

J. Jeffery Auer ("The Image of the Right Honourable Margaret Thatcher") studies the 1979 General Election campaign in Britain, focusing on the
career of the Conservative leader, Margaret Thatcher, and the part she
played in the campaign. Through an investigation of media sources and
extensive personal interviews, Auer identifies the most salient elements in

Mrs. Thatcher's image and explains the ways in which they relate to political communication in contemporary Britain.

Ernest G. Bormann ("A Fantasy Theme Analysis of the Television Coverage of the Hostage Release and the Reagan Inaugural"), from the perspective of fantasy theme analysis, turns his attention to the live television coverage of the release of the American hostages held by Iran which was taking place at the same time as the inauguration of Ronald Reagan as President of the United States. Identifying the theme of restoration as most significant, Bormann demonstrates how this theme, juxtaposed with television coverage, operates in Reagan's speech to promote the conservative political agenda. (Students may wish to read Bormann's essay, "Fantasy and Rhetorical Vision," which appears later in this book, before reading this article.)

James R. Andrews ("The Passionate Negation: The Chartist Movement in Rhetorical Perspective") investigates the rhetoric of the Chartist Movement, an early working class movement in Britain, to illustrate the way in which a rhetorical critic can study an historical movement. His examination of the context out of which the movement grew and the rhetoric associated with it, leads him to suggest that lines of strategy grow out of the situation and that interacting patterns of advocacy and reaction to that advocacy develop. He argues that the reciprocal shaping of rhetoric and events can best be understood when rhetorical critics focus on popular interpretation of events, seeking to understand the perception of the world around them by those who experienced that world.

J. Michael Hogan ("Public Opinion and American Foreign Policy: The Case of Illusory Support For the Panama Canal Treaties") examines a particular aspect that played a crucial part in the Senate debate over the ratification of the Panama Canal treaties in 1978: the role of "public opinion" as it was perceived and portrayed in that debate. After careful analysis of the debates themselves, along with relevant contextual data, Hogan argues that his examination uncovers the ways in which public opinion was inaccurately, but influentially, depicted as pro-treaty. Further, he explains how this distorted, but politically relevant, depiction was rhetorically constructed.

Ronald Lee ("The New Populist Campaign for Economic Development: A Rhetorical Exploration"), arguing that "the techniques of the new politics has led directly to the discourse of the New Populism," focuses on the rhetoric of the Campaign for Economic Democracy. Lee is interested in the populist tone in political rhetoric and the ways in which populism affects practical politics. In examining New Populist ideology and the ways in which it is transformed into a campaign vision, Lee studies specifically the New Populist rhetoric of Tom Hayden to demonstrate the shift in associational pattern, narrative form, and ideology that is taking place in the discourse of liberal politics.

William F. Lewis ("Telling America's Story: Narrative Form and the Reagan Presidency") attempts to explain both Ronald Reagan's rhetoric and the response to that rhetoric by exploring its dominating narrative form. Lewis maintains that narrative affects political judgment and demonstrates how this is so through an analysis of three characteristics of narrative form: a story-based truth, an emphasis on morality, and a grounding in common sense.

In reading these studies, the student of criticism will find it helpful to structure his or her response to them by reconsidering the basic principles discussed in this book. A suggested pattern for the close and careful reading of these studies is as follows:

1. Read the study carefully. Identify other studies cited in the footnotes that could increase the understanding of the critical work, then read the appropriate cited studies.
2. Summarize the content of the study.
3. Discern the ways in which and the extent to which the study exemplifies particular critical functions, discusses the problems of context and audience, and describes and analyzes the role of the speaker or speakers.
4. Attempt to describe as precisely as possible the method of analysis used, the nature and soundness of interpretations based on that analysis, and the evaluation made along with the implicit or explicit criteria for such evaluations.
5. Enumerate and describe the strengths and weaknesses of the study as a piece of criticism.
6. Consider the implications of the study for the practice of criticism.

Lincoln at Cooper Union:
A Rhetorical Analysis of the Text

—————————— MICHAEL C. LEFF AND GERALD P. MOHRMANN ——————————

When Abraham Lincoln spoke at the Cooper Union on the evening of February 27, 1860, his audience responded enthusiastically, and the speech has continued to elicit praise throughout the intervening years. Biographers, historians, and literary scholars agree that it was "one of his most significant speeches."[1] one that illustrated "his abilities as a reasoner,"[2] and one to which posterity has ascribed his "subsequent nomination and election to the presidency."[3] Ironically, however, this model of "logical analysis and construction"[4] has failed to generate a critical response in kind. Most of what has been written treats of the background, and, too often, the man as myth has intruded; caught up in the drama of the performance, writers find no bit of information too trivial to report, whether it be the price of tickets or the fit of Lincoln's new shoes.[5] Such details can deepen our appreciation of the event, but they do not illuminate the speech as a speech.

Unhappily, little light is shed by those who do comment on the speech text. Nicolay and Hay assert, for example, that Lincoln's conclusions "were irresistibly convincing,"[6] but their sole piece of supporting evidence is a four-hundred word excerpt. And if they happen to be "firmly in the hero-worshipping tradition,"[7] those of sterner stuff fare no better. Basler makes the curious claim that the rhetorical "high-water mark" occurs toward the end of the first section;[8] Nevins mistakenly argues that the speech "fell into two halves";[9] reputable scholars equate summary and quotation with explication;[10] and it is generally accepted that Lincoln demonstrated a conciliatory attitude toward the South.[11]

Certainly all is not dross in previous studies, but wherever one turns in the literature, no satisfying account of the speech is to be found.[12] We are convinced that a systematic rhetorical analysis can help rectify the situation, and what follows is our attempt to accomplish such an analysis. In that attempt, we center on the text of the speech, but our purpose demands some preliminary remarks about the rhetorical context.

Although it was not until after the speech that Lincoln frankly admitted his presidential aspirations, saying, "The taste *is* in my mouth a little,"[13] he had been savoring the possibility for months. The preceding November, he had written that the next canvas would find him laboring "faithfully in the ranks" unless "the judgment of the party shall assign me a different position,"[14] but even as he wrote, Lincoln was grasping for a different assignment, "busy using the knife on his rivals...and doing all he could to enhance his reputation as an outstanding Republican leader."[15] Small wonder that he decided early to "make a political speech of it" in New York.[16] Here was the opportunity to make himself more available to Republicans in the East. The appearance alone would make for greater recognition, but political availability required more; Lincoln had to be an acceptable Republican, and he had to be an attractive alternative to the Democratic candidate.

William A. Seward and Stephen A. Douglas were the presumptive nominees, and they, patently, were Lincoln's antagonists. Moreover, their views on slavery created an intertwining threat that menaced his conception of the party and his personal ambitions. When Seward spoke about a "higher law" and an "irrepressible conflict," he strained Lincoln's sense of moral and political conservatism; these pronouncements smacked too much of radicalism.[17] Douglas, meanwhile, exacerbated the situation with his doctrine of popular sovereignty. Lincoln feared that this siren song would cause wholesale apostasy in Republican ranks, an eventuality all the more likely if the party nominee was tinctured with radicalism. He knew, however, that a middle ground existed, and he long had occupied it with his insistence that slavery should be protected but not extended. Consequently, when Lincoln addressed the Eastern Republicans, both principle and expediency permitted, even dictated, that he speak for party and for self and that he maintain party and self in a position between those taken by Seward and Douglas.

That he took such a course is revealed by an examination of the speech text, but all the external evidence shows a man running hard, if humbly, for political office, and while Lincoln spoke for his party, he spoke first for his own nomination. In fact, the Cooper Union Address is best characterized as a campaign oration, a speech designed to win nomination for the speaker. This identification of genre is basic to our analysis, and the nature of the genre is suggested by Rosenthal's distinction between non-personal and personal persuasion;[18] in the former, the speaker attempts to influence audience attitudes about a particular issue, and ethos is important insofar as it lends credence to the substance of the argument. In the latter the process is reversed. The focal point is the speaker, and the message becomes a vehicle for enhancing ethos. Campaign orations, on this basis, tend to be examples of personal persuasion, for while "the ostensible purpose of a given speech may be to gain acceptance of a particular policy,...the actual purpose is to gain votes for the candidate."[19] In other words, the ultimate goal of the campaign orator is to promote himself as a candidate. Both policies and character are in question, but the treatment of issues is subsidiary to the purpose of creating a general identification between the speaker and the audience. The objective, then, in a campaign oration is ingratiation.

With genre and purpose in mind, we can approach the speech through familiar topics. Addressing himself first to the people of New York, then to the South and finally to the Republican Party, Lincoln divides his speech into three sections, and this pattern of organization invites seriatim analysis of the major dispositional units. Furthermore, argument and style immediately loom as important elements, since they disclose essential characteristics in and significant interrelationships among the main units of the discourse. Consequently, our critique will follow Lincoln's pattern of organization and will have special reference to matters of argument and style. This approach, however, is not without its hazards. The convenience of tracing the natural sequence of the argument may foster fragmentary analysis and obscure the dominant rhetorical motive. Yet to be mindful of the genre is to find a corrective. The central concern is ingratiation, and recognition of this purpose unifies the elements of analysis by giving them a more precise focus; awareness of the ultimate goal becomes shuttle to the threads of structure, argument, and style.

In the address, Lincoln deals exclusively with slavery, and although this inflamatory issue might seem a shaky bridge to ingratiation, the choice is a fitting response to the rhetorical problem. What better point of departure than the paramount issue of the day, the issue with which he was most closely identified, and the issue that had spawned the Republican Party?[20] And Lincoln starts with the very motivation that had driven men to Ripon only a few years before, the question of slavery in the territories. Capitalizing on these initial associations, he counters the emotionalism inherent in the topic by assuming a severely rational posture and enunciating a moderate but firm set of principles. The approach distinguishes him from his chief rivals and solicits an intensified association from Eastern Republicans. These objectives govern the matter and manner of the opening argument, and this argument lays a foundation for subsequent developments in the speech. In the opening section and throughout, Lincoln associates himself and Republicans with the founding fathers and Constitutional principle, and he dissociates rival candidates and factions from those fathers and that principle.

Acknowledging his "fellow citizens of New York," Lincoln begins by adopting a "text for this discourse."[21] The text is a statement in which Stephen A. Douglas had asserted, "Our fathers, when they framed the government under which we live, understood this question just as well and even better than we do now." Defining terms in catechistic sequence, Lincoln maintains that "the frame of government under which we live" consists of the Constitution and the "twelve subsequently framed amendments" and that "our fathers" are "the 'thirty-nine' who signed the original instrument." He then asks, what is the question "those fathers understood 'just as well and even better, than we do now'?" The answer "is this: Does the proper division of local from Federal authority, or anything else in the Constitution, forbid our Federal Government to control as to slavery in our Federal Territories?" The question joins the issue because it is a matter upon which "Senator Douglas holds the affirmative, and the Republicans the negative."

That Douglas should play the foil is most fitting. National newspaper coverage of the 1858 senatorial campaign had linked the two men together, and the debates were to be published in March.[22] Moreover, Lincoln had continued the argument during 1859, worrying whether the Republican Party would "maintain it's [sic] identity, or be broken up to form the tail of Douglas' new kite."[23] Nevertheless, Lincoln knew that Douglas was vulnerable. The Freeport Doctrine had convinced many in the North that the man was only too "willing to subordinate moral considerations to political expediency."[24] Douglas, then, was an established rival, one whom Lincoln perceived as a threat to party unity, and one whose strategic position was open to attack from principle.

On a tactical level, the "text" quoted from Douglas affords Lincoln an ideal starting point. The allusion to the fathers is a symbolic reference with the potential for universal respect, and Douglas' implicit attack upon the principles that had generated the Republican Party creates an antithesis binding speaker and audience together in opposition to a common enemy. This antithesis is a channel for ingratiation: Lincoln makes Republicanism the voice of rational analysis, and the precise terms of Douglas' assertion form the premises of logical inquiry. Moving into the inquiry, Lincoln pursues a vigorous *ad hominem* attack.[25] He accepts Douglas' logic and then turns it against him.

The argument of the first section develops out of a single hypothetical proposition: if the better understanding evinced by our fathers shows that they believed nothing forbade federal control of slavery in the territories, then such regulatory power is inherent in the governmental frame. Lincoln affirms the antecedent with an elaborate chain of inductive evidence. Instances in the induction consist of actions by the fathers before and after they signed the Constitution because the question "seems not to have been directly before the convention."[26] From the Northwest Ordinance of 1784 to the Missouri Compromise of 1820, Lincoln enumerates seven statutes regulating slavery in the territories, and he accounts for votes by twenty-three of the fathers.[27] Twenty-one voted in favor of such regulation. Since these men were bound by "official responsibility and their corporal oaths" to uphold the Constitution, the implication of their affirmative votes is beyond question. To conclude that the twenty-one would have condoned federal regulation if they thought it unconstitutional would be to accuse these fathers of "gross political impropriety and willful perjury," and "as actions speak louder than words, so actions under such responsibility speak still louder."

Emphasizing deeds and "adhering rigidly to the text," Lincoln cannot offer in evidence "whatever understanding may have been manifested by any person" other than the thirty-nine, nor can he cite the sixteen who left no voting records. But the latter include the likes of Franklin, Hamilton, and Morris, and he believes that this group "would probably have acted just as the twenty-three did." In any event, "a clear majority of the whole" understood that nothing "forbade the Federal Government to control slavery in the Federal Territories," and with the remaining fathers probably agreeing, there can be little doubt about "the understanding of our fathers who framed the original Constitution; and the text affirms that they understood the question 'better than we.'"

Lincoln now uses this understanding to discredit arguments based on the fifth and tenth amendments; he says it is "a little presumptuous" to suggest that the fathers embraced one principle when writing the Constitution and another when writing the amendments. And does not this suggestion "become impudently absurd when coupled with the other affirmation, from the same mouth, that those who did the two things alleged to be inconsistent, understood whether they really were inconsistent better than we—better than he who affirms that they are inconsistent?" The touch of sarcasm reveals a more aggressive attitude, but it is justified by the inductive process; Douglas' own criterion forces the conclusion that he does not comprehend the understanding of the fathers. Lincoln will become even more combative before he brings the first section to a close, but some comments on style are merited, and they will lead us into his conclusion.

The style of this section is entirely consistent with Lincoln's severely rational approach. The audience probably did not expect the "rhetorical fireworks of a Western stump-speaker,"[28] but Lincoln is most circumspect. There are none of the "many excuses" that made him a Uriah Heep to some of his opponents,[29] and he avoids all display, indulging neither in anecdotes nor figurative language. The syntax is complex at times, but the complexity is that of legal rather than literary prose, as is evidenced in the following sentence: "It, therefore, would be unsafe to set down even the two who voted against the prohibition as having done so because, in their understanding, any proper division of local from Federal authority, or anything in the Constitution, forbade the Federal Government to control as to slavery in Federal territory."

The preceding quotation, with its echo of the text, points to a noteworthy stylistic element: repetition. Lincoln includes fifteen extended citations of the issue and an equal number from the "text," repetitions that accentuate the single line of argument. He adds to the emphasis by stressing certain key words and phrases. For example, there are over thirty uses of the root "understand," usually in the participial "understanding," and Lincoln alludes to the "fathers" more than thirty-five times. None of these repetitions is blatant or forced because he weaves them into the fabric of the inductive process. Furthermore, the repetitions concomitantly reinforce and control the emotional association with the fathers and their understanding of the Constitution. This point is crucial to an appreciation of Lincoln's rhetorical method. Both the direction of the argument and the symbols expressing it are fiercely emotional; yet, all is enmeshed in an incisive logical and linguistic structure, and while the tone remains rationalistic and legalistic, it also creates a subtle emotive nexus between the Republican audience and the founding fathers.

As noted above, style and argument shift in the concluding paragraphs, after Lincoln already has established his logical credentials. The argument becomes bolder, and the style alters appropriately. When developing the induction, Lincoln refers to the framers of the Constitution as the "thirty-nine," but they become "our fathers" again in the conclusion of the long first section of the speech. And there periods become more polished and sophisticated:

> If any man at this day sincerely believes that a proper division of local from Federal authority, or any part of the Constitution, forbids the Federal Government to control as to slavery in the Federal Territories, he is right to say so, and to enforce his position by all truthful evidence and fair argument which he can. But he has no right to mislead others, who have less access to history, and less leisure to study it, into the false belief that 'our fathers who framed the government under which we live' were of the same opinion—thus substituting falsehood and deception for truthful evidence and fair argument.

This passage completes the negative phase of Lincoln's argumentation. Both matter and manner drive a rational wedge between the speaker and his rivals. Clearly, Lincoln suggests that Douglas may be guilty of deliberate "falsehood and deception," and just as clearly, his own position represents "truthful evidence and fair argument." Lincoln, one of those with "access to history" and some "leisure to study it," attempts to set the record straight. Another direct slash at Douglas, the very source of the text and issue. At the same time, Lincoln indirectly differentiates himself from Seward and his radical posture. Lincoln's position is more to the right, closer to the demands of objective inquiry, closer also to the demands of political availability, and it is important to remark that he achieves this dissociation without recourse to divisive rhetoric. The foray against the man and his position is patent, but it is completely inferential.

Although less obtrusive than the refutation, an equally important constructive movement exists within this part of the oration. Not only does Lincoln distinguish himself from his opponents, he nurtures Republican unity because he makes himself and party the vessels for transmitting the faith of the fathers. Avoiding self-references, he presents himself as the voice of Republicanism, and he caps this appeal with words both to and from the party:

> But enough! Let all who believe that 'our fathers who framed the government under which we live understood this question just as well, and even better, than we do now,' speak as they spoke, and act as they acted upon it. This is all Republicans ask—all Republicans desire—in relation to slavery. As those fathers

marked it, so let it be again marked, as an evil not to be extended, but to be
tolerated and protected only because of and so far as its actual presence among
us makes that toleration and protection a necessity. Let all the guarantees those
fathers gave it be not grudgingly, but fully and fairly, maintained. For this Republi-
cans contend, and with this, so far as I know or believe, they will be content.

At this point in the speech, Lincoln has associated himself and his audience with
the spirit, the principles and the actions of the founding fathers, and in doing so, he
has taken the first steps toward ingratiation.

Comprising nearly half the speech, this initial section is so clearly logical that
it regularly is cited as a demonstration of Lincoln's powers as a reasoner, but to
say no more is to grossly underestimate his achievement. The next section, too,
is remarkable for its logical development, and all that follows in the speech is
anticipated and controlled by the attack upon Douglas. Failure to appreciate this
unity has confounded commentators, and their confusion is strikingly illustrated in
the generally accepted conclusion that Lincoln follows his attack with remarks
"conciliatory toward the South."[30]

The second section does begin with an ostensible change in audience: "And
now, if they would listen—as I suppose they will not,—I would address a few
words to the Southern people." But we learn more about the beholders than the
object when we are told that the next twenty-six paragraphs are filled with "words
of kindly admonition and protest."[31] words of "sweet reasonableness to allay
Southern fears."[32] Presuming that he will not be heard, Lincoln notes that "our
party gets no votes" in the South, and he flatly asserts later that "the Southern
people will not so much as listen to us." These are not idle reservations. They
represent the realistic assessment of an astute politician who knows that the
coming election will be won or lost in the North; it is hardly plausible that this man
would detract from his ultimate purpose by directing nearly forty percent of his
speech to an unavailable audience.

In truth, the audience does not change. Lincoln merely casts the second
section of the speech in the form of a *prosopopoeia*, a figure he had rehearsed five
months earlier in Cincinnati.[33] The device suits his purposes admirably. It enables
him to create a mock debate between Republicans and the South, a debate in
which he becomes spokesman for the party. In this role, Lincoln can strengthen the
identification between himself and the available Republican audience. He is careful
to extend the refutation of Douglas into the second section and thus carry over the
lines of association and disassociation begun earlier in the discourse. If Lincoln
leaves Douglas with little ground on which to stand, he performs the same argumentative service for the South, and the debate he manufactures is far from being
conciliatory.

The *prosopopoeia* develops into another *ad hominem* argument. This time,
however, the presentation is complicated by the need to deal with the collective
contentions of a collective opposition. To provide control, Lincoln again begins by
stressing reason, saying to the South, "I consider that in the general qualities of
reason and justice you are not inferior to any other people." Yet, in the specific
case, rational discourse is stymied because the Southerners never refer to Republicans except "to denounce us as reptiles, or, at the best, as no better than outlaws."
Such responses are unjust to both sides. The proper course would be to "bring

forward your charges and specifications, and then be patient long enough to hear us deny or justify." Obviously, the South is unwilling and unable to follow this procedure, and becoming persona for both Republicanism and reason, Lincoln reconstructs the charges and specifications; these include sectionalism, radicalism, agitation of the slavery question, and slave insurrections.

The putative debate begins: "You say we are sectional. We deny it. That makes an issue; and the burden of proof is upon you." The crux of the matter is whether Republicans repel the South with "some wrong principle." Republican principle, however, is based in the beliefs and actions of the fathers, and Lincoln challenges the South to respond to this fact. "Do you accept the challenge? No! Then you really believe that the principle which 'our fathers who framed the government under which we live' thought so clearly right as to adopt it, and endorse it again and again, upon their official oaths, is in fact so clearly wrong as to demand your condemnation without a moment's consideration." Closing and reinforcing this line of reasoning Lincoln refers to the pre-eminent father: "Some of you delight to flaunt in our faces the warning...given by Washington in his Farewell Address," but if he were to speak for himself "would he cast the blame of that sectionalism upon us, who sustain his policy, or upon you, who repudiate it? We respect that warning of Washington, and we commend it to you, together with his example pointing to the right application of it."[34] Thus, the South claims to be the injured party, but analysis of the charge proves that the wounds are self-inflicted.

Lincoln uses the same refutational method for each of the other issues; first defining the charge with a series of rhetorical questions, he then turns the argument against the adversary. The South proclaims itself the bastion of conservatism and denounces Republican radicalism, but "what is conservatism? Is it not adherence to the old and tried, against the new and untried? We stick to, contend for, the identical old policy...which was adopted by 'our fathers who framed the government under which we live'; while you with one accord reject, and scout, and spit upon that old policy, and insist upon substituting something new." The South alleges that Republicans have made the slavery issue more prominent. True, the issue is more prominent, but this situation arose because the South "discarded the old policy of the fathers." Finally, Southerners complain that Republicans foment insurrection among the slaves, but they can adduce no evidence to support this allegation, cannot "implicate a single Republican" and ignore that "Republican doctrines and declarations are accompanied with a continual protest against any interference whatever" with the institution in the slave states. Indeed, were it not for the loud and misleading protestations of Southern politicians, the slaves would hardly know that the Republican Party existed. Worse yet, the South refuses to acknowledge a simple truth contained in Republican doctrine, a truth articulated "many years ago" when Jefferson indicated that the cause of slave insurrections was slavery itself. Like Jefferson, Republicans would not interfere with slavery where it exists, but Republicans do insist, as the fathers did, that the federal government "has the power of restraining the extension of the institution—the power to insure that a slave insurrection shall never occur on any American soil which is now free."

Finishing his treatment of specific charges, Lincoln builds to a more forceful and aggressive tone, just as he did at the end of the first section. His arrangement of responses to Southern allegations is itself climatic, the issue of insurrections being both last and most critical. Always volatile, this issue had become extremely explosive in the wake of the Harper's Ferry raid and the trial of John Brown, and Lincoln understandably chooses this matter as the instrument for his most extensive defense of party and principle. He is not content, however, to assume a merely defensive posture; the entire pattern of his argumentation reveals a movement from reply to attack that gathers momentum as the discourse proceeds. Thus, having disposed of the insurrection controversy, Lincoln assails, the very character of the Southern position, and he concludes this section with an examination of threats emanating from the South.

The South hopes to "break up the Republican organization." That failing, "you will break up the Union rather than submit to a denial of your constitutional rights." This is a course of "rule or ruin"; the union will be destroyed unless people are permitted to take slaves into the federal territories. But no such right exists in the Constitution, and Southern threats are fruitless. Neither the Constitution nor the Republican Party are so malleable as to bend at the touch of Southern fancy. Not even the Dred Scott decision offers a refuge. That verdict was made "in a divided court, by a bare majority of the judges, and they not quite agreeing with one another in the reasons for making it." The decision rests upon "the opinion that 'the right of property in a slave is distinctly and expressly affirmed in the Constitution,'" but careful analysis shows that this right is not even implied. Surely it is reasonable to expect the Court to retract "the mistaken statement" when apprised of its error. Furthermore, the verdict runs contrary to the judgment of the fathers, those who decided the same question long ago "without division among themselves when making the decision," without division "about the meaning of it after it was made," and without "basing it upon any mistaken statement of facts." Having thus contrasted the babel of the Court with the unity of the fathers and their lineal descendants, Lincoln builds to a striking analogy:

> *Under these circumstances, do you really feel yourselves justified to break up this government unless such a court decision as yours is shall be at once submitted to as a conclusive and final rule of political action? But you will not abide the election of a Republican president! In that supposed event, you say, you will destroy the Union; and then, you say, the crime of having destroyed it will be upon us! That is cool. A highwayman holds a pistol to my ear, and mutters through his teeth, 'Stand and deliver, or I shall kill you, and then you will be a murderer!'*

Adding that the highwayman's threat can "scarcely be distinguished in principle" from "the threat of destruction to the Union," Lincoln completes his *ad hominem* assault against the Southern position, and the *prosopopoeia* ends.

The parallels and interrelationships between the first and the second sections of the speech are evident. Some shifts in invention and style between the two sections are occasioned by the change of antagonist, but it is more significant that Lincoln elects to argue against adversaries in both and that he uses the same fundamental argument to dispatch them all. In both sections, he strives to become spokesman for the party by demonstrating that he is a man of reason and that this characteristic melds himself and party with the principles of the founding fathers. In addition, the same characteristic distinguishes him from other candidates. Finally, each section is based on a severely rational framework and builds to a terminal climax that unifies and heightens logical and emotional dimensions.

Merging style and argument within and between parts of the discourse, Lincoln unquestionably remains in touch with his immediate audience, and he unquestionably has his eye on ingratiation. In the first movement, he separates himself and party from Douglas and Seward; in the second, he favorably contrasts the position of the party with that of its most vociferous opponent.[35] But one further step remains. To this juncture, the identification of speaker, party, and principle has been closely tied to a series of negative definitions. A positive gesture seems necessary, and in the final section of the speech, Lincoln fuses his audience together through more directly constructive appeals.

He begins by saying he will address "a few words now to Republicans," and though he puts aside both text and issue, his remarks evolve naturally from what has proceeded. Once more reason is the point of departure. Having, in the highwayman metaphor, implied a contrast between cool reason and hot passion, Lincoln urges Republicans to "do nothing through passion and ill-temper" that might cause discord within the nation, and, as he draws out the ultimate implications of the Southern position, antithesis becomes the dominant mode of argument and style. The section centers on a contrast between the Republicans and the South (between "we" and "they"); it extends and amplifies the distinction between word and deed that is present throughout the speech: and the argument is couched in and reinforced by antithetical syntax.

Recognizing Southern intransigence, Lincoln still wants his party to "calmly consider their demands" and reach conclusions based on all "they say and do." Pursuing the inquiry, he asks, "Will they be satisfied if the Territories be unconditionally surrendered to them? We know they will not." And "will it satisfy them if, in the future, we have nothing to do with invasions and insurrections? We know it will not." It will not because past abstention has not exempted "us from the charge and the denunciation." To satisfy them, "we must not only leave them alone, but we must somehow convince them that we do let them alone." Experience shows that this is no easy task because Republican policy and actions have been misconstrued consistently. The only recourse seems to be "this and only this: cease to call slavery wrong, and join them in calling it right. And this must be done thoroughly—done in acts as well as words. Silence will not be tolerated—we must place ourselves avowedly with them." Republicans must suppress all "declarations that slavery is wrong," must return "fugitive slaves with greedy pleasure," and must pull down all free state constitutions "before they will cease to believe that all their troubles proceed from us."

Most Southerners, Lincoln admits, would not put the argument in this extreme form. Most would simply claim that they want to be left alone, but "we do let them alone." Consequently, it is apparent that "they will continue to accuse us of doing, until we cease saying." Given the nature of their arguments and the character of their actions, the Southerners cannot stop short of the demand that all Republicans desist from speaking and acting out of conviction. Those who hold that "slavery is morally right and socially elevating" must necessarily call for its recognition "as a legal right and a social blessing." Stripped of its veneer and examined in the cold light of reason, the Southern position reveals the disagreement governing the entire conflict; is also underscores the principle from which Republicans cannot retreat. Lincoln expresses both points in a final antithesis that reduces the issue of slavery to a matter of right and wrong, to a matter of moral conviction:

> *Their thinking it right and our thinking it wrong is the precise fact upon which depends the whole controversy. Thinking it right, as they do, they are not to blame for desiring its full recognition as being right; but thinking it wrong, as we do, can we yield to them? Can we cast our votes with their view, and against our own? In view of our moral, social, and political responsibilities, can we do this?*

Providing no answers because they are only too obvious, Lincoln moves on to merge self and party with the fathers, and Washington is the exemplar.

Style changes appropriately as Lincoln makes his final call for unity. Antithetical elements appear in the penultimate paragraph, but the opposed clauses are subordinated within the long, periodic flow of the final sentence, a flow that builds emotionally to a union with Washington's words and deeds. Lincoln repeats that slavery can be left alone where it exists, but he insists that there can be no temporizing when it comes to the extension of slavery:

> *If our sense of duty forbids this, then let us stand by our duty fearlessly and effectively. Let us be diverted by none of those sophistical contrivances wherewith we are so industriously plied, and belabored—contrivances such as groping for some middle ground between the right and the wrong: vain as the search for a man who should be neither a living man nor a dead man: such as a policy of 'don't care' on a question about which all true men do care; such as Union appeals beseeching true Union men to yield to Disunionists, reversing the divine rule, and calling, not the sinners, but the righteous to repentance: such as invocations to Washington, imploring men to unsay what Washington said and undo what Washington did.*
>
> *Neither let us be slandered from our duty by false accusations against us, nor frightened from it by menaces of destruction to the government, nor of dungeons to ourselves. Let us have faith that right makes might, and in that faith let us to the end dare to do our duty as we understand it.*

This short third section, constituting less than fifteen per cent of the text, is a fitting climax to Lincoln's efforts. Rational principle develops into moral conviction, and the resulting emotional intensity emerges from and synthesizes all that has gone before. Yet the intensity is controlled. Speaker and audience are resolute and principled, but at the same time, they are poised and logical. Others may indulge in "false accusations" and "menaces of destruction," but Lincoln and Republicans will have faith in right and in their understanding.

With this closing suggestion of antithetical behavior, Lincoln harks back to all he has said, and with it, he completes his exercise in ingratiation. Douglas is a pitiful example of one who argues misguided principle in maladroit fashion, and Seward's notion of an irrepressible conflict is at odds with the true spirit of the Republican Party, a party whose words and deeds follow from what the framers of the government said and did. Neither opponent measures up to the new and higher self-conception that the speaker has created for his audience. Furthermore, Lincoln has, by this very performance, demonstrated that he is the one who will best represent party and principle. Starting with reason and principle, he has shunted aside opposition, differentiated between Republicans and the South, and pushed on to unite the party in the faith that will "let us to the end dare to do our duty as we understand it."

The very wording of the concluding paragraphs reflects the organic quality of

Lincoln's quest for unity. "Understand" echoes the "text"; Washington is a synecdochic reminder of the fathers; and the antithetical language recalls dissociations that are fundamental. In examining the discourse, we have attempted to explicate this internal coherence by tracing the sequence of arguments and images as they appear in the text, by dealing with the speech on its own terms. We are satisfied that the analysis has produced a reading that is more accurate than those previously available, a reading that goes farther toward explaining why the Cooper Union Address was one of Lincoln's most significant speeches.

Our interpretation is at odds, of course, with the conventional wisdom concerning his attitude toward the South. Where others have found him conciliatory, we argue that his position on slavery was calculated to win the nomination, not to propitiate an unavailable audience. That he had made "many similar declarations, and had never recanted any of them"[36] unquestionably contributed to the triumph of availability that was to be his, but his position ultimately pointed to an ideological conflict between North and South. Some Southerners took solace from Lincoln's assurances that slavery would be left alone where it existed, but extremists perceived him as the personification of Black Republicanism, even as the source of the irrepressible conflict doctrine.[37] The latter perceptions were distorted. So are ours, if we blink the realities of political rhetoric, and whatever else the speech might have been, it was certainly an oration designed to meet the immediate problems of a political campaign.

This perspective emphasizes that alternatives sometimes really do exclude and that rhetoric may nurture exclusion. Such a perspective may be uncomfortable for those who want to cast Lincoln as the Great Conciliator, but we are convinced that an accurate reading of the Cooper Union Address demands a frank recognition of the immediate rhetorical motives. Despite the mythology, the man was human, perhaps gloriously so, and it does him no disservice to accept this speech as evidence of his political skill, as evidence that "he was an astute and dextrous operator of the political machine."[38] Nor does this acceptance detract from the speech as literature and as logical exposition. The political artistry and the rhetorical artistry are functions of each other, and an appreciation of this coalescence can only enhance our understanding of the Cooper Union Address. And viewing the speech as a whole, we are quite content to close with a slightly altered evaluation from another context: "The speech is—to put it as crudely as possible—an immortal masterpiece."[39]

Notes

1. J. G. Randall, *Lincoln the President* (New York: Dodd, Mead, 1945), I. 135.

2. Howard Mumford Jones and Ernest E. Leisy, eds., *Major American Writers* (New York: Harcourt, Brace, 1945), p. 681.

3. Benjamin Barondess, *Three Lincoln Masterpieces* (Charleston: Education Foundation of West Virginia, 1954), p. 3.

4. R. Franklin Smith, "A Night at Cooper Union," *Central States Speech Journal* 13 (Autumn 1962), 272.

5. The most influential account of this sort is Carl Sandburg, *The Prairie Years* (New York: Harcourt, Brace, 1927), II, 200–216, but the most complete is Andrew A. Freeman, *Abraham Lincoln Goes to New York* (New York: Coward-McCann, 1960).

6. John G. Nicolay and John Hay, *Abraham Lincoln: A History* (New York: Century, 1917), II, 219–220.

7. Richard Hofstadter, *The American Political Tradition* (New York: Alfred A. Knopf, 1948), p. 364.

8. *Abraham Lincoln: His Speeches and Writings*, ed. Roy P. Basler (Cleveland: World, 1946), p. 32.

9. Allan Nevins, *The Emergence of Lincoln* (New York: Charles Scribner's Sons, 1950), II. 186.

10. Randall, pp. 136–137; Basler, pp. 32–33; Nevins, pp. 186–187; Reinhard H. Luthin, *The Real Abraham Lincoln* (Englewood Cliffs, New Jersey: Prentice–Hall, 1960), p. 210.

11. Randall, p. 136; Barondess, p. 18; Nicholay and Hay, p. 220, Nevins, p. 186; Luthin, pp. 243–244.

12. Freeman treats of the text briefly, pp. 84–88, and although Barondess ranges from preparation to audience reaction, pp. 3–30, Hofstadter's observation applies, n. 7 above. Earl W. Wiley discusses the address in *Four Speeches by Lincoln* (Columbus: Ohio State Univ. Press, 1927), pp. 15–27, but he limits analysis to the first section of the speech, a limitation also applied in his "Abraham Lincoln: His Emergence as the Voice of the People," in *A History and Criticism of American Public Address*, ed. *William N. Brigance* (New York: McGraw-Hill, 1943), II, 859–877. In the same volume, the speech is the basis for comments on delivery in Mildred Freburg Berry, "Abraham Lincoln: His Development in the Skills of the Platform," pp. 828–858.

13. Letter to Lyman Trumbull, April 29, 1860, *The Collected Works of Abraham Lincoln*, ed. Roy P. Basler (New Brunswick, New Jersey: Rutgers Univ. Press, 1955), IV, 45.

14. Letter to William E. Frazer, November 1, 1859, *Collected Works*, III, 491.

15. Richard N. Current, *The Lincoln Nobody Knows* (New York: McGraw-Hill, 1958), p. 199. For an indication of Lincoln's activities see *Collected Works*, III, 384–521.

16. Letter to James A. Briggs, *Collected Works*, III, 494.

17. See Letter to Salmon P. Chase, June 9, 1859, *Collected Works*, III, 384; Letter to Nathan Sargent, June 23, 1859, *Collected Works*, III, 387–388; Letter to Richard M. Corwine, April 6, 1860, *Collected Works*, IV, 36.

18. Paul I. Rosenthal, "The Concept of Ethos and the Structure of Persuasion," *Speech Monographs* 33 (June 1966), 114–126.

19. Rosenthal, p. 120.

20. In 1854, "northern whigs persuaded that their old party was moribund, Democrats weary of planting dominance, and free-soilers eager to exclude slavery from the territories began to draw together to resist the advance of the planting power"; Charles A. Beard and Mary R. Beard, *The Rise of American Civilization* (New York: Macmillan, 1937), II, 22. Cf. Don E. Fehrenbacher, "Lincoln and the Formation of the Republican Party," in *Prelude to Greatness* (Stanford: Stanford Univ. Press, 1962), pp. 19–47.

21. We follow the text in *Complete Works*, ed. John G. Nicolay and John Hay (New York: Francis D. Tandy, 1905), V, 293–328; we include no footnotes because aside from unimportant exceptions, citations are sequential. This text is more conservative in typography than that edited and published as a campaign document by Charles C. Nott and Cephas Brainerd. The latter appears in *Collected Works*, III, 522–550; 1860, p. 1. Substantive variations in extant see also the *New York Times*, February 28, texts are minuscule, and this consistency deserves comment. Lincoln ignored suggested alterations in the original (Sandburg, II, 210 and 215–216); he proofread the newspaper copy (Freeman, pp. 92–93); pamphlet copies were available by the first of April (*Collected Works*, IV, 38–39); and Lincoln adamantly resisted editorial changes by Nott (*Collected Works*, IV, 58–59). This evidence emphasizes the care with which he constructed the speech, but it also suggests that he anticipated a wider audience from the outset. Publication practices and his own experience told Lincoln that he would reach many who would not hear him speak.

22. General interest in the debates is underlined by the favorable editorial notice appearing in the Brooklyn *Daily Times*, August 26, 1858, an editorial written by one Walt Whitman; Walt Whitman, *I Sit and Look Out*, ed. Emory Holloway and Vernolian Schwartz (New York: Columbia Univ. Press, 1932), p. 96. For letters referring to publication of the debates, see *Collected Works*, III. 341, 343, 372–374, 515, and 516.

23. Letter to Lyman Trumbull, Dec. 11, 1858, *Collected Works*, III, 345.

24. Harry J. Carman and Harold C. Syrett, *A History of the American People* (New York: Alfred A.

Knopf, 1952), I, 588. Cf. Fehrenbacher, "The Famous 'Freeport Question,'" in *Prelude to Greatness*, pp. 121–142.

25. Logicians often define *ad hominem* as a fallacy resulting from an attack upon the character of a man rather than the quality of argument. In this essay, however, we use the term as Schopenhauer does in distinguishing between *ad hominem* and *ad rem* as the two basic modes of refutation. He differentiates in this manner: "We may show either that the proposition is not in accordance with the nature of things, *i.e.*, with absolute, objective truth [ad rem]; or that it is inconsistent with other statements or admissions of our opponent, *i.e.*, with truth as it appears to him [*ad hominem*]"; Arthur Schopenhauer, "The Art of Controversy," in *The Will to Live: Selected Writings of Arthur Schopenhauer*, ed. Richard Taylor (New York: Anchor Books, 1962), p. 341. See Henry W. Johnstone, Jr., "Philosophy and *Argumentum ad Hominem*," *Journal of Philosophy* 49 (July 1952), 489–498.

26. Lincoln undoubtedly knew that James Wilson, Patrick Henry and Edmund Randolph had discussed the topic (See *Collected Works*, III, 526–527, n. 9.), but he is accurate in asserting that the subject did not come "directly" before the convention.

27. Washington's vote was his signature, as President, on the Act of 1789 which enforced the Ordinance of 1787.

28. Nicolay and Hay, *Abraham Lincoln*, II, 220.

29. See Hofstadter, p. 94; *Collected Works*, III, 396.

30. Randall, I, 136.

31. Nicolay and Hay, *Abraham Lincoln*, II, 220.

32. Nevins, II, 186.

33. *Collected Works*, III, 438–454. Speaking at Cincinnati, September 17, 1859, Lincoln directs so much of his speech across the river "to the Kentuckians" (p. 440.) that one listener complained aloud, "Speak to Ohio men, and not to Kentuckians!" (p. 445.) Interestingly, Nevins appreciates the *prosopopoeia* in this speech, noting that Lincoln was "ostensibly speaking to Kentuckians," II, 56.

34. The varied interpretations of Washington's warning and their longevity are illustrated in debates, early in 1850, over the purchase of the Farewell Address manuscript for the Library of Congress. Much of the debate is reproduced in William Dawson Johnston, *History of the Library of Congress* (Washington: Government Printing Office, 1904), I, 326–340.

35. The second movement continues the implicit attack upon Seward, and all texts indicate a mimicking of Douglas' "gur-reat pur-rinciple" Buchanan also is a victim here, for he had championed popular sovereignty in his "Third Annual Message," December 19, 1859: *The Works of James Buchanan*, ed. John Bassett More (1908–1911; rpt. New York: Antiquarian Press Ltd., 1960), X. 342. Lincoln's efforts were not lost on a New York *Evening Post* reporter who wrote that "the speaker places the Republican party on the very ground occupied by the framers of our constitution and the fathers of our Republic" and that "in this great controversy the Republicans are the real conservative party." His report is reprinted in the *Chicago Tribune*, 1 Mar. 1860, p. 1.

36. Abraham Lincoln, "First Inaugural Address," in *Collected Works*, IV, 263.

37. Michael Davis, *The Image of Lincoln in the South* (Knoxville: Univ. of Tennessee, 1971), pp. 7–40; traces Southern views from nomination through inauguration. See *Southern Editorials on Secession*, ed. Dwight L. Dumond (1931; rpt. Gloucester, Mass.: Peter-Smith, 1964), pp. 103–105, 112–115, 159–162, *et passim*.

38. David Donald, *Lincoln Reconsidered* (New York: Alfred A. Knopf, 1956), p. 65.

39. The original is Randall Jarrell's comment on a poem, Robert Frost's "Provide Provide," in *Poetry and the Age* (New York: Vintage-Knopf, 1953), p. 41.

Eisenhower's "Atoms for Peace" Speech: A Case Study in the Strategic Use of Language

———————————— MARTIN J. MEDHURST ————————————

"Personally, I think this [speech] will be a 'sleeper' as far as this country is concerned—but one of these days when the deserts do bloom, and atomic reactors are turning out electricity where there was no fuel before, and when millions of people are eating who never really ate before . . . the President's December 1953 speech and proposal will be remembered as the starting point of it all."[1]

—C. D. Jackson, Special Assistant to the
President for Psychological Warfare
February 5, 1955

More than thirty years later the deserts have not bloomed, famine is still a reality, and the nuclear reactor, once the hopeful sign of a better tomorrow, stands as a technological indictment of humanity's inability to see beyond the visions of the moment.

Dwight Eisenhower was not the first president to speak of the peaceful uses of atomic energy, yet it was his "Atoms for Peace" speech, delivered in front of the United Nations' General Assembly on December 8, 1953, that marked the public commencement of a persuasive campaign the dimensions of which stagger the imagination. Planned at the highest levels of government, shrouded in secrecy, aided by the military-industrial complex, and executed over the course of two decades, the campaign to promote the "peaceful" use of the atom was conceived in pragmatism, dedicated in realism, and promoted in the spirit of idealism. At each stage of the campaign rhetorical purposes, some lofty, some base, motivated both words and deeds.

Space does not permit a complete explication of this persuasive effort nor even a perfunctory glance at each of its component parts. That must await some future forum. In this essay the pragmatic atmosphere that prompted Eisenhower to deliver a speech advertised as a step away from the nuclear precipice will be described. At the same time, the realist assumptions and motives that reveal Eisenhower's true purposes for delivering his "Atoms for Peace" speech on December 8, 1953 will be explicated.

The argument has three parts. First, that despite American protestations to the contrary, Eisenhower's "Atoms for Peace" speech was, in fact, a carefully-crafted piece of cold war rhetoric specifically designed to gain a "psychological" victory over the Soviet Union. It was part of an American peace offensive launched, in part, as a response to an ongoing Soviet peace offensive.

Second, that the speech creates one audience on the level of explicit argument, but a much different audience when the implicit arguments are examined. Explicitly, the speech is addressed to the world at large, particularly those non-aligned nations in the midst of industrialization. It is aimed at that amorphous animal called world opinion. Implicitly, it is addressed to the Soviet Union, partly as warning, partly as challenge.

Third, that the speech is intentionally structured to invite the world at large to understand "Atoms for Peace" as a step toward nuclear disarmament. In addition to the internal structure, the persuasive campaign carried on immediately before and after the speech was designed explicitly to portray "Atoms for Peace" as part of the free world's (read America's) commitment to nuclear arms control. That the speech was not, in fact, related to disarmament talks but was, rather, an attempt to gain a psychological, cold war victory will be demonstrated.

CONCEIVED IN PRAGMATISM

To understand fully how "Atoms for Peace" evolved to the form in which it was delivered, one must return to the opening weeks of the Eisenhower administration, specifically the events of February, March, and April of 1953. Three events are particularly worthy of note.

In February, a top secret report commissioned by President Truman was delivered to the new Secretary of State, John Foster Dulles. Known internally as the Oppenheimer Report, the document "declared that a renewed search must be made for a way to avert the catastrophe of modern war" (Donovan, 1956, p. 184). Essential to this goal, the report held, was "wider public discussion based upon wider understanding of the meaning of a nuclear holocaust" (Donovan, 1956, p. 184).

As discussion of the policy implications of the Oppenheimer Report ensued, a new factor changed the complexion of American foreign policy: Stalin died. Announced to the world on March 6, 1953, the death of Stalin was viewed as a unique opportunity for advancing the cause of freedom, both in the occupied countries of Europe and within the Soviet Union itself. As historian Louis Halle puts it, the hope was "widespread throughout the West, that the Soviet state, unable to resolve the problem of the succession, would fall into confusion and helplessness upon Stalin's removal from the scene" (Halle, 1967, p. 312). Nowhere was this hope more evident than within Eisenhower's inner circle.

C. D. Jackson, Special Assistant to the President for cold war strategy (also known as psychological warfare), and the man who would later be primarily responsible for the drafting of "Atoms for Peace," viewed the death of Stalin with both elation and alarm. On March 4, 1953, Jackson wrote to General Robert Cutler, head of the National Security Council:

> *This morning's developments, both in Moscow and in Washington point up both a great need and a great opportunity. As to the need, it is hardly an exaggeration to say that no agency of this government had in its files anything resembling a plan, or even a sense-making guidance, to cover the circumstances arising out of the fatal illness or death of Stalin . . . . It is both fair and safe to say that, left to itself, the existing machinery will be incapable of assuming the initiative and moving on the first really great opportunity that has been presented to us.*
>
> *Conversely—and this is the opportunity—if we do not take the initiative and capitalize on the dismay, confusion, fear, and selfish hopes brought about by this opportunity, we will be giving the enemy the time to pull himself together, get his wind back, and present us with a new monolithic structure which we will spend years attempting to analyze . . . .*
>
> *In other words, shouldn't we do everything possible to overload the enemy at the precise moment when he is least capable of bearing even his normal*

*load.... During the present moment of confusion, the chances of the Soviets
launching World War III are reduced virtually to zero, and will remain in the low
numbers so long as the confusion continues to exist. Our task, therefore, is to
perpetuate the confusion as long as possible, and to stave off as long as possible
any new crystallization.*

*It is not inconceivable that out of such a program might come further opportuni-
ties which, skillfullly exploited, might advance the real disintegration of the Soviet
Empire (Jackson, 1953a).*

Thus was set in motion a systematic plan to "exploit" the weakness perceived
to accompany a Soviet transfer of power. Within the week plans were being laid,
amidst much internal dissension, to take advantage of the historical moment.
Against the wishes of John Foster Dulles, Jackson convinced the President to
launch an American peace offensive and, with the assistance of Walt Rostow and
Emmet Hughes, began to draft a major foreign policy address designed, in Rostow's
words, "to hold up a vision of the specific long-range objectives of American
diplomacy but to make the negotiations designed to achieve that vision contingent
upon a prior Korean settlement" (Rostow, 1982, p. 7).

After "some fourteen drafts" (Rostow, 1982, p. 7) the "Age of Peril" speech was
delivered before the American Society of Newspaper Editors on April 16, 1953. It
was the opening shot in the psychological warfare advocated by Jackson as a
means "to preempt a possible Soviet peace offensive" (Rostow, 1982, p. 4). The
speech laid out American objectives: settlement in Korea, peace in Indochina,
unification of Germany, an Austrian peace treaty, and, in one line, the peaceful use
of atomic energy. The atom for peace, long sought after by scientists and visionar-
ies, had now joined the cold war effort.

Having launched the offensive, Jackson, at Eisenhower's direction, continued
to probe for opportunities to exploit the situation. In an effort to line up the
American public behind the offensive and to prepare them for the twilight struggle
that lay ahead, Jackson and Hughes were charged with producing drafts of what
came to be known as Operation Candor—a straightforward report to the American
people on the destructive capacity of nuclear weapons.

Both Eisenhower and Jackson agreed with the findings of the Oppenheimer
Report: that the public must come to understand the full implications of nuclear
war. Moreover, the Soviet peace offensive and public weariness with the Korean
War made incorporation of the American audience behind the U.S. effort an absolute necessity lest Americans, in the words of Konrad Adenauer, be tempted "to
succumb to the blandishments of a detente which for the time being was nothing
but a pipedream" (Adenauer, cited in Rostow, p. 50). It was time to be completely
candid with the American public concerning the possibility of mutual destruction, a
possibility that now defined the very nature of superpower politics.

Numerous drafts of the Operation Candor speech were produced from late
April to early October of 1953. None proved adequate to the task at hand. Furthermore, in the intervening months the situation had changed radically once again. On
July 26 a Korean truce had been signed; the war was over. Two weeks later, on
August 12, 1953, the Soviet Union tested their first hydrogen bomb. Unbeknowst to
the American public, the type of thermonuclear weapon tested by the Soviet Union
indicated that they were much closer to the capacity for delivering a hydrogen
bomb than anyone imagined.[2] The need for "Candor" was now greater than ever.
The public must be prepared for the worst, but there were problems.

On September 2, Jackson wrote to Gordon Arneson at the State Department: "I am afraid that the Candor speech is slowly dying from a severe attack of Committee-itis" (Jackson, 1953b). Though Jackson tried to establish new guidelines for production of the speech, the difficulty of the concepts involved along with a well-publicized leak to *Washington Post* columnist Stewart Alsop (1953, p. 23), resulted in the death of Operation Candor. On September 28, 1953, James Lambie distributed the following memo to the twenty people who were by then involved in the Candor question: "C. D. Jackson asks me to use this outworn method (rather than the more expeditious one of going directly to Stewart Alsop) to make sure you are apprised of the following: Subject Operation, *as a series* of connected and integrated weekly talks is canceled. The President may deliver a single speech of his own in the general area to have been covered by subject series. As of now, however, no final decision has been taken as to such a speech by the President— what, when or whether."[3]

Though no "final decision" had been made, Eisenhower wanted to continue the search for an appropriate speech, though with a different emphasis. Consulting with Jackson, Cutler, and Admiral Lewis L. Strauss, Chairman of the Atomic Energy Commission, Eisenhower proposed, in a very general sort of way, an international pool of fissionable material that could be used strictly for peaceful purposes. It was this idea, first shared with his three top advisors on September 10, that eventually matured into "Atoms for Peace."[4]

The story of the evolution of Project Wheaties, the code name given to the newly-resurrected "Atoms for Peace" speech, is an essay unto itself and must not detain us here. Suffice it to note that starting with the first complete draft on November 3, 1953, "Atoms for Peace" went through eleven major revisions before its presentation on December 8. The last four drafts were completed at the Big Three conference at Bermuda from December 4–7, with the final draft being edited on the flight from Bermuda to New York City on the afternoon of December 8. There is much to be learned from examination of the eleven drafts of the speech, but that, too, is a separate essay. I turn now to the speech delivered by Eisenhower at 4:30 p.m., December 8, 1953, in front of 3500 delegates, guests, and media representatives at the United Nations building in New York City.

DEDICATED IN REALISM

The address was a masterpiece of "realpolitik," long before the term became fashionable. Every line was included (or excluded) for a purpose, and that purpose was strategic advantage, whether defined in terms of placing the Soviet Union at a psychological disadvantage, or in terms of preparing the American audience for an "age" of peril, or in terms of ingratiating the foreign audience.

From the outset, the public posture of the U.S. was that this was *not* a propaganda speech, but a serious proposal that could, if accepted by the Soviets, lead to a climate more conducive to nuclear disarmament. As Eisenhower himself would later maintain in his memoirs, "if we were successful in making even a start, it was possible that gradually negotiation and cooperation might expand into something broader" (Eisenhower, 1963, p. 254). Possible yes, but not probable. Indeed, given the relative strengths of each side's nuclear forces, the relative scarcity of mineable uranium within the U.S.S.R., and the diplomatic tradition which held that serious proposals were made through private, not public channels, it seems clear that any public offer would have had a propaganda *effect* by placing the Russians on the spot in front of a world-wide audience. Even if the American offer was sincere, it placed the U.S.S.R. in a position of either accepting the offer (and thereby implicitly testifying to America's long-professed desire for peace) or rejecting the offer (and thereby appearing to the world at large as an aggressor unwilling to explore a plan that, as presented by Eisenhower, would benefit directly the underdeveloped nations as well as the cause of international peace).

The beauty of "Atoms for Peace," as conceived by Jackson and Strauss, its primary authors, was precisely that it would place Russia in an awkward position and allow America to gain a psychological advantage on the stage of world opinion. As Jackson wrote to Eisenhower on October 2, 1953: "It must be of such a nature that its rejection by the Russians, or even prolonged foot-dragging on their part, will make it clear to the people of the world...that the moral blame for the armaments race, and possibly war, is clearly on the Russians" (Jackson, 1953c).

Analysis of the Test

Eisenhower's speech follows a three-part pattern progressing from the present danger, to past efforts toward reconciliation, to a vision for the future. Each section features an America striving after "peace," a term that occurs twenty-four times in the address.[5] One might logically expect a deliberative speech structured chronologically to proceed from past to present to future. Why does Eisenhower violate expectations by starting with the present? There are several reasons.

First, the primary purpose of the speech is psychological advantage rather than historical narration. The story is important only insofar as it provides the context for the perceived psychological gains. Four such gains are paramount: to warn the Russians against nuclear attack on the United States; to alert Americans to the potential destructiveness of a nuclear exchange; to position the United States as a peacemaker and friend in the eyes of the developing nations; and to place the Soviet Union in a policy dilemma by issuing to them a public challenge.

Second, had Eisenhower started with the past he would have encountered two disadvantages: he would have been forced to start with a recitation of failure that would have set the wrong tone for the speech by drawing immediate attention to Russian intransigence, thereby establishing an atmosphere of confrontation, precisely the opposite of what needed to be done if the psychological advantage were to be obtained. Further, by elevating the past to the position of primacy, the president would have been forced to bury to present in the middle portion of the speech. This, too, would have been disadvantageous inasmuch as one of the primary purposes of the address is to issue an implicit warning to the Russians who, it was held widely in military circles, would soon possess the requisite number of nuclear weapons to launch a preemptive strike against the United States. Eisenhower wants to feature the warning, not bury it in the midst of an historical narrative.

Finally, by holding the past efforts at reconciliation until the middle portion of the speech, Eisenhower is able dramatically to juxtapose the failures of the past with his visionary plan for the future. The rhetorical disposition adopted adds argumentative force to the atoms-for-peace proposal by highlighting the significant departure from past plans represented by the new proposal for an international pool of fissionable materials dedicated to peaceful purposes. If the past was characterized by suspicions leading to fear, the future is presented as an opportunity leading to hope.

Atomic Strength of the United States

In the introductory paragraphs the term "hope" or its derivative occurs five times. "Never before in history," claims Eisenhower, "has so much hope for so many people been gathered together in a single organization. Your deliberations and decisions during these somber years have already realized part of those hopes."[6] After paying homage to the organization, Eisenhower asserts that it would not be "a measure of this great opportunity merely to recite, however hopefully, pious platitudes." He realizes, he says, "that if a danger exists in the world, it is a danger shared by all—and equally, that if hope exists in the mind of one nation, that hope should be shared by all."

Thus, in his opening statement, Eisenhower prepares the audience for a speech about the way out of the atomic dilemma that confronts humanity. At this point it would be easy to slip into a chronological pattern, starting with past efforts to solve the dilemma, the state of present negotiations, and, finally, his new plan for the future. A second alternative might be to review, in summary fashion, the hopes of the past and then to continue without pause into discussions of his plan. Eisenhower chooses a third way.

He begins by speaking of the present. "I feel impelled to speak today in a language that in a sense is new—one which I, who have spent so much of my life in the military profession, would have preferred never to use. That new language is the language of atomic warfare." Thus does Eisenhower launch the first part of the body, a section that might well be labeled "The Nuclear Capability of the United States of America," by confronting the audience with the paradox of a warrior who hates to speak of war, thereby distinguishing the persona of the General from that of the statesman. The General spoke the language of war; the President speaks the language of peace.

Though ostensibly a recitation of the extent to which nuclear weapons have proliferated both in size and number since 1945, the opening section is, in reality, a series of veiled warnings to the Soviet Union. Though ostensibly informative in intent, the opening section is really an exhortation whose central message is that the Soviet Union should reconsider any plans it might have for launching a preemptive strike against the United States.

The entire section is a series of warnings under the guise of a dispassionate report as demonstrated in the following chart:

1. *Explicit Argument:* Today, the United States' stockpile of atomic weapons, which, of course, increases daily, exceeds by many times the explosive equivalent of the total of all bombs and all shells that came from every plane and every gun in every theatre of war in all of the years of World War II.

   Implicit Argument. Be assured that we are not reducing our weapons program despite reported cutbacks in the defense budget. We are building more nuclear weapons every day and will continue to do so as long as we must.

2. *Explicit Argument*. The development has been such that atomic weapons have virtually achieved conventional status within our armed services. In the United States, the Army, the Navy, the Air Force, and the Marine Corps are all capable of putting this weapon to military use.

Implicit Argument. If you think you can hope to prevail over us merely by knocking out our Air Force bases and missile silos, you are woefully mistaken. We are capable of launching a retaliatory nuclear strike against you with any branch of our services.

3. *Explicit Argument*. Our earlier start has permitted us to accumulate what is today a great quantitative advantage.

Implicit Argument. You may have enough nuclear devices to hurt us, but we have a lot more and can outlast you in any nuclear exchange.

4. *Explicit Argument*. The free world...has naturally embarked on a large program of warning and defense systems. That program will be accelerated and expanded.

Implicit Argument. Don't think for a moment that we are letting down our guard. We are prepared both militarily and psychologically.

5. *Explicit Argument*. But for me to say that the defense capabilities of the United States are such that they could inflict terrible losses upon an aggressor—for me to say that the retaliation capabilities of the United States are so great that such an aggressor's land would be laid waste—all this, while fact, is not the true expression of the purpose and the hope of the United States.

Implicit Argument. Think not that the land of Mother Russia will remain inviolate. It will not. We will inflict damage so great that it will make your losses in WW II seem like child's play.

That the movement from explicit to implicit argument was a conscious and intentional strategy is clear from the documentary history. On October 23, 1953, for example, Secretary of State John Foster Dulles sent a "personal and private" memorandum to Eisenhower in which he advises that the speech should "make clear our determination, so long as this danger exists, to take the necessary steps to deter attack, through possession of relatiatory power and the development of continental defense" (Dulles, 1953).

The speech drafts leading up to the December 8 address make it abundantly clear that the writers, principally Jackson and Strauss, are attempting to retain the threat of retaliation while, at the same moment, couching that threat in language that becomes successively less confrontational. In other words, the rhetoric of the drafts proceeds from bold, outright threats to implied warnings couched in the language of peaceful intentions. By comparing the last "Operation Candor" draft completed on or about October 1, 1953, by presidential speechwriter Emmet Hughes, with the final draft delivered by President Eisenhower on December 8, 1953, the movement from explicit to implicit argument can be clearly observed.

Candor Draft 10/1/53

We are today armed with bombs a single *one* of which—with an explosive equivalent of more than 500,000 tons of TNT—exceeds by more than *30 times* the power of the first atomic bombs that fell in 1945. . . . Each *year* sees this mass increase with a power that is many times greater than that of *all* explosives dropped by the aircraft of *all* the Allied nations in World War II.

Candor Draft 10/1/53

Any single *one* of the many air wings of our Strategic Air Command could deliver—in *one* operation—atomic bombs with an explosive equivalent greater than *all* the bombs that fell on Germany through *all* the *years* of World War II.

Any *one* of the aircraft carriers of our Navy could deliver in *one day* atomic bombs exceeding the explosive equivalent of *all* bombs and rockets dropped by Germany upon the United Kingdom through *all* the years of World War II.

We have certain knowledge that we can not only increase greatly the power of our weapons but also perfect their methods of delivery and their tactical use.

These, then, are measures of the fantastic strength we possess.

Candor Draft 10/1/53

We possess detailed evidence of the progress, over the past four years, of the Soviet Union's development of atomic and thermo-nuclear weapons.

We know that in this period the Soviet Union has exploded six atomic devices—and quite recently, one involving thermo-nuclear reaction.

We know, too, how the amassing of these weapons can be speeded by the implacable methods of police state and slave labor.

We know—above all else—this fact: Despite our own swift perfection of new

Wheaties Draft 12/8/53

Today, the United States' stockpile of atomic weapons, which, of course, increases daily, exceeds by many times the explosive equivalent of the total of all bombs and all shells that came from every plane and every gun in every theatre of war in all the years of World War II.

Wheaties Draft 12/8/53

The development has been such that atomic weapons have virtually achieved conventional status within our armed services. In the United States, the Army, the Navy, the Air Force, and the Marine Corps are all capable of putting this weapon to military use.

Wheaties Draft 12/8/53

Our earlier start has permitted us to accumulate what is today a great quantitative advantage.

weapons, despite our vast advantage in their numbers—the very nature of these weapons is such that their desperate use against us could inflict terrible damage upon our cities, our industries and our population.

Candor Draft 10/1/53

The second decision is to devise for America a defense system unmatched in the world. Such a system—entailing the most developed use of radar, interceptor aircraft, anti-aircraft artillery and guided missiles—is in the making.

The building of this defense will be pressed with uncompromising vigor. . . . Our defenses will be built with vision, care, common sense—and a frank readiness to spend whatever money or energy such a logical program demands.

Wheaties Draft 12/8/53

The free world. . . has naturally embarked on a large program of warning and defense systems. The program will be accelerated and expanded.

Candor Draft 10/1/53

. . .we declare clearly that if—and wherever—United States forces are involved in repelling aggression, these forces will feel free to use atomic weapons as military advantage dictates.

Any such use of atomic weapons would be strictly governed by a clear order of priority.

(1) They would be used immediately against military forces operating against us or our allies.

Wheaties Draft 12/8/53

But for me to say that the defense capabilities of the United States are such that they could inflict terrible losses upon an aggressor—for me to say that the retaliation capabilities of the United States are so great that such an aggressor's land would be laid waste—all this, while fact, is not the true expression of the purpose and the hope of the United States.

The evolution of the speech drafts from early October to early December evidences a shift away from straightforward assertion to implicative argumentation. That the implications are, in most cases, similar or identical to the authorial intentions of the original Candor draft can be seen by comparing the October 1, 1953 draft with the implicit arguments found in the December 8 address.

That the Soviets are likely to have understood the argumentative implications in ways roughly similar to the reconstructions above is a function both of timing and of access. For four months prior to the December 8 address, the American media ran story after story about governmental, military, and scientific concerns about a possible nuclear confrontation. Not only were such concerns easily picked up through environmental cues, but the Soviets were also given advanced warning about the December 8 speech and instructed to pay close attention and to take seriously what the President said.

In a top secret cable sent from Chip Bohlen, U.S. Ambassador to the Soviet Union, to Secretary of State John Foster Dulles, Bohlen apprised the Secretary of his talk with Russian Foreign Minister Vyacheslav Molotov: "The purpose of my visit to him," cabled Bohlen, "was to draw the attention of Soviet Government in advance to great importance which my Government attached to this speech . . . I concluded by saying there was no need to stress to him (Molotov) the immense importance of whole question of atomic weapons and repeated the hope that Soviet Government would receive this suggestion as seriously as it was made" (Bohlen, 1953).

In addition to the special visit of Bohlen to Molotov, the Soviet Union's representative to the United Nations, Andrei Vishinsky, was provided an advance copy of the entire address. Vishinsky, as one reporter noted, "appeared to be the only delegate with a copy of the speech" (James, 1953, p. 3). Thus, through both public and private sources, the Soviets were encouraged to listen closely to "Atoms for Peace."

The dichotomy between the arguments as explicitly stated and those same arguments' implications is matched by the dichotomous audiences created by each argumentative level. The audience created by the explicit argument is the world-at-large, the non-nuclear powers who, as spectators in the deadly game of superpower politics, have a legitimate interest in the state-of-the-standoff as perceived by the U.S. President.

A secondary audience for this explicitly argued content is the American public. Operation Candor was originally planned as a series of addresses to the domestic audience, and Eisenhower explicitly states at the outset of the address that these are "thoughts I had originally planned to say primarily to the American people." Though no longer the primary target audience, the American public will still be informed of the terrible destructive capacity of the U.S. arsenal, and thus Eisenhower is able to accomplish multiple goals simultaneously.

But while the audience for the explicit content is clearly the world at large, the target for the implicitly argued content can be none other than the Soviet Union. Why, in a speech ostensibly devoted to "peace," should Eisenhower spend fully twenty percent of his time issuing veiled warnings to the U.S.S.R.? The reasons are many.

According to C.I.A. estimates the Russians would, within a matter of months, have enough nuclear weapons to launch a preemptive strike against the United States. Knowledgeable sources within the scientific, political, and military establishments believed such an attack to be likely (Herken, 1980, p. 325; Menken, cited in "Briton Warns U.S.," 1953, p. 15; Urey, cited in Strauss, 1962, p. 228). Furthermore, the U.S.S.R. had exploded their first thermonuclear weapon and had immediately followed that test with a series of atomic tests lasting well into September. In the space of ninety days the Soviets had tested as many nuclear weapons as in the previous four years combined. Doubtless the sudden spate of activity could be read as a prelude to an all-out attack.

Hence, Eisenhower conceives his task not only to be the articulation of the atomic pool idea, but also the conveying of a strong warning, implicit though it is, that a "surprise attack" by an "aggressor in possession of the effective minimum number of atomic bombs" would be met with "swift and resolute" action. Though he informs the world of the terrible atomic might of the United States of America, he also exhorts the U.S.S.R. to behave itself or suffer the consequences.

Western Deeds and Desires

Having given his "report" on the present state of United States atomic strength, Eisenhower then makes a long, almost Churchillian, transition into the second major section of the speech—the past record of the Western Alliance in both word and deed. To stop with the recitation of the atomic dilemma, says Eisenhower, "would be to accept helplessly the probability of civilization destroyed—the annihilation of the irreplaceable heritage of mankind handed down to us generation from generation—and the condemnation of mankind to begin all over again the age-old struggle upward from savagery toward decency, and right, and justice. . . . So my country's purpose is to help us move out of the dark chamber of horrors into the light."

But again, it is not the light of the future to which Eisenhower moves, not to the atoms-for-peace plan. Instead, the President turns to the recent past and a recitation of the actions undertaken by the United States and her allies in an effort, he claims, to restore peace and justice to the world. While the explicitly argued content again functions as a report to the world, the implications of the report, the "conclusions" to be drawn by the world audience, are that the Soviet Union has been intransigent.

"Let no one say that we shun the conference table," says Eisenhower. "On the record has long stood the request of the United States, Great Britain, and France to negotiate with the Soviet Union the problems of a divided Germany. On that record has long stood the request of the same three nations to negotiate an Austrian Peace Treaty. On the same record still stands the request of the United Nations to negotiate the problems of Korea."

Eisenhower's method is clear. He seeks to establish the willingness of the Western powers to negotiate, and thereby implies the intransigence and bad faith of the U.S.S.R. Moreover, by positioning the Soviets in the role of spoilers in the recent past, he increases the pressure on them to respond favorably to future entreaties, specifically the plan he is about to announce, a plan no peace-loving nation could reasonably refuse.

Eisenhower seeks to leave no route of escape as he concludes the second section by observing: "There is a record, already written, of assistance gladly given by nations of the West to needy peoples, and to those suffering the temporary effects of famine, drought, and natural disaster. These are deeds of peace. They speak more loudly than promises or protestations of peaceful intent." Once again, Eisenhower seeks to back the Russians into a corner. In effect, he is saying to them, as the whole world watches, "put up or shut up." In the final section of the speech he gives them their chance.

An International Atomic Energy Agency

Eisenhower introduces his atoms-for-peace proposal by quoting a portion of the United Nations resolution passed by the General Assembly only three weeks earlier: "that the Disarmament Commission study the desirability of establishing a subcommittee consisting of representatives of the Powers principally-involved, which should seek in private an acceptable solution. . .and report on such a solution to the General Assembly and to the Security Council not later than 1 September 1954."

By opening his final section with a quote from the United Nations, itself,

Eisenhower accomplishes two goals: first, he establishes a frame of reference with which all delegates are familiar and, ostensibly, with which the vast majority agree; second, he invites the audience to understand his comments within the context of *disarmament*. This fact becomes particularly salient as one seeks to understand precisely what Eisenhower meant by his atoms-for-peace proposal. At the very least, it is clear that the President immediately invites his ostensible audience, the world at large, to believe that what he is about to say has something to do with nuclear disarmament, the subject of both the U.N. resolution and of the first section of the President's own speech.

That such an interpretation could not have been missed by the delegates is assured by the sentence immediately following: "The United States, heeding the suggestion of the General Assembly of the United Nations, is instantly prepared to meet privately with such other countries as may be 'principally involved,' to seek 'an acceptable solution' to the atomic armaments race."

Having committed himself to the exploration of arms control, Eisenhower makes a crucial transition that both shifts the ground from which he originally opened his final section of the speech and commences his challenge to the Soviet Union, a challenge which, whether accepted or rejected by the U.S.S.R., will, it is believed, result in a great psychological victory for the United States: "It is not enough to take this weapon out of the hands of the soldiers. It must be put into the hands of those who will know how to strip its military casing and adapt it to the arts of peace." Thus begins Eisenhower's argument for the development of atomic energy for peaceful purposes.

After proclaiming that "peaceful power from atomic energy is no dream of the future," but rather is "here—now—today," Eisenhower launches into the heart of the atoms-for-peace proposal: "The Governments principally involved, to the extent permitted by elementary prudence, to begin now and continue to make joint contributions from their stockpiles of normal uranium and fissionable materials to an International Atomic Energy." This Agency, said Eisenhower, "could be made responsible for the impounding, storage, and protections of the contributed fissionable and other materials."

"The more important responsibility of this Atomic Energy Agency," he continues, "would be to devise methods whereby this fissionable material would be allocated to serve the peaceful pursuits of mankind. Experts would be mobilized to apply atomic energy to the needs of agriculture, medicine, and other peaceful activities. A special purpose would be to provide abundant electrical energy in the power-starved areas of the world."

The appeal is clearly to those non-nuclear nations represented in the U.N. audience, particularly those to whom power, and agriculture, and medicine are pressing needs. To the world audience of 1953 this would have included the vast majority of member states. The pledge is equally clear: to share of our abundance, in this case our nuclear know-how, with those nations less fortunate. But there is one condition attached.

"The United States would be more than willing," Eisenhower continues, "to take up with others 'principally involved' the development of plans whereby such peaceful use of atomic energy would be expedited. Of those 'principally involved' the Soviet Union must, of course, be one." The proposition could hardly have been put in a more explicit manner. Eisenhower challenges the Soviets to join in an international effort to aid U.N. member nations, and he does so right in front of them so there may be no mistake about his offer. The challenge shifts the burden of proof squarely onto the shoulders of the Soviets. If they really are interested in peace, then here, says Eisenhower, is the perfect chance to demonstrate their commitment.

The International Agency, Eisenhower pledged, would have four tasks:

1. To "encourage world-wide investigation into the most effective peacetime uses of fissionable material";
2. To "begin to diminish the potential destructive power of the world's atomic stockpiles";
3. To "allow all peoples of all nations to see that...the great powers of the earth...are interested in human aspirations first, rather than in building up the armaments of war";
4. To "open up a new channel for peaceful discussion, and initiate at least a new approach to the many difficult problems that must be solved...."

"Against the dark background of the atomic bomb," he concludes, "the United States does not wish merely to present strength, but also the desire and the hope for peace...To the making of these fateful decisions, the United States pledges before you—and therefore before the world—its determination to help solve the fearful atomic dilemma." The section ends, as it had begun, with allusions to atomic disarmament. Indeed, the implicit message to the assembled delegates is that atoms-for-peace, in addition to helping non-nuclear nations reap the benefits of nuclear energy, is a step toward and a mechanism for converting the means of war into instruments of peace. It is a different approach to the whole disarmament problem and the "awful arithmetic" to which Eisenhower had earlier referred.

The implied content of this final section is directed exclusively toward world opinion. The implications to be drawn by the world-wide audience are roughly as follows:

1. The United States is making a serious offer to share its nuclear materials and expertise with the international community.
2. The United States is doing this because it wants to reduce the risks of war and increase international cooperation.
3. If the "principally-involved" parties all cooperate, then there will be an advance in the quality of life all over the globe.
4. The powers of nuclear energy are near-miraculous and the cures mentioned by Eisenhower are immediately available if only the Soviets will cooperate.

The explicit message directed to the Soviet Union is this: Here's the plan; it will benefit the entire world community whose eyes now rest on you. Will you cooperate? Eisenhower places a challenge squarely before the Soviets and dares them—in front of the whole world—to accept the challenge or suffer the consequences that will be wrought, not by the military might of the United States, but by the psychological weight of world opinion turned sour.

EXTERNAL REACTION

As Eisenhower finished his speech there was a "burst of applause" (Hamilton, 1953, p. 2) that swelled to a crescendo. Even Soviet representative Andrei Vishinsky joined in the chorus. The next day Eisenhower's proposal was bannered across the nation's leading newspapers, and the effort to decipher precisely what he meant began.

Thomas Hamilton, writing on the front page of the *New York Times*, observed that "implicit in the President's speech was the realization that the United Nations would have to make a new start if the seven-year-old deadlock on international atomic control was ever to be broken" (Hamilton, 1953, p. 1). Hamilton recalled the failure of the Baruch Plan in 1946, and linked Eisenhower's atoms-for-peace proposal to that earlier effort. In Hamilton's opinion the speech clearly was aimed at moving disarmament talks off dead center.

The editorial page of the *Washington Post* also viewed Eisenhower's proposals as precursors to disarmament: "If the nations of the world—meaning Russia and the Western Allies—could cooperate on the diversion of nuclear materials for peaceful purposes, the groundwork might be laid for cooperation on genuine disarmament" ("The Choice," 1953, p. 10). The proposal was viewed as being part of the long-term process of disarmament.

Reaction on Capitol Hill was, if anything, even more infused with apocalyptic visions of peace. Representative James E. Van Zandt (R-PA) claimed that Eisenhower had "sounded the clarion call to all nations to beat the atomic sword of destruction into plowshares by harnessing the power of the atom for peaceful pursuits" ("Ike's Speech Praised," 1953, p. 16). Similar reactions were voiced throughout the corridors of official Washington.

Such reactions, in themselves, should not be surprising in light of the fact that the "correct" interpretation of the speech was carefully orchestrated and planted in the various media organs by none other than C. D. Jackson. It was Jackson who provided advance copies of the speech, then classified top-secret, to Ernest K. Lindley of *Newsweek*, Roscoe Drummond of the *New York Herald Tribune*, and James Shepley of *Time* magazine (McCrum, 1975, pp. 45–46). It was Jackson, who, in his capacity as a member of the Operations Coordinating Board, designed the campaign to "exploit" the speech, a campaign that included use of "leaders of opposition parties," the Voice of America, Radio Free Europe, the C.I.A., and other "non-attributable instrumentalities" (Jackson, 1954). The message, regardless of medium, was the same: "Atoms for Peace" is a serious peace proposal that could lead to control of the atomic armaments race.

Despite Jackson's best efforts, not all opinion leaders bought into the official "line" on the speech. On such group was the leadership of the Canadian government. Reporting from Ottawa, a correspondent for the *New York Times* noted that "as the speech was interpreted here, President Eisenhower's proposal for an international body and a common stockpool of fissionable material was limited to peaceful uses of atomic energy and could not have any decisive effect on the question of the use of atomic weapons in war" ("Canadians Await Details," 1953, p. 3).

Here was the crucial point. Was the atoms-for-peace proposal a serious effort to take the first step toward disarmament or was it not? If it was not intended as a step toward disarmament why was it given in the first place and, why was it placed within the general context of nuclear destruction and within the specific context of the ongoing disarmament debate at the U.N.? Clearly, the structuring of the speech invites the listeners to associate atoms-for-peace with the general disarmament debate.

INTERNAL DEBATE

If Eisenhower's precise meaning was, despite Jackson's best efforts, a matter of some speculation on the international scene, it was no less obscure within the administration's own inner circles. The debate over what the president meant to say started even before the speech was delivered. As early as mid-October there was fierce disagreement between Jackson and the State Department over the advisability of making any speech at all. As Candor evolved into Wheaties, early in November, the disagreements within the administration began to crystalize.

Jackson chronicled the struggle in his personal log. On November 17, 1953, he wrote: "Meeting in Foster Dulles" office with Lewis Strauss. Unfortunately Bob Bowie invited in. Subject—Wheaties, and UN appearance on December 8. Dulles went into reverse, ably needled by Bowie—he didn't like UN idea; he didn't like Strauss' proposal; he didn't like anything. Bowie kept repeating that this was not the way to do things—quiet, unpublicized negotiations were the only thing that would get anywhere with Ruskies" (Jackson, 1953d).

But quiet diplomacy was anything but what Jackson had in mind. On November 21, 1953, Jackson wrote to Sherman Adams concerning "what we have in mind for December 8," and warning that "if this is *not* properly orchestrated, and these things are dribbled out without organized impact, we will fritter away what is probably the greatest opportunity we have yet had" (Jackson, 1953e). Jackson suggested six specific steps to Adams for insuring proper orchestration. One of these was that "every single one of the Departmental and Agency PR heads should be constantly worked with to see that they keep the news coming out of their departments beamed on a pre-determined frequency" (Jackson, 1953e). Jackson's concern was the psychological victory to be gained and the supposed benefits flowing therefrom. But the State Department had not yet rested its case.

On November 23, 1953, Bob Bowie sent his criticisms of the latest Wheaties draft (draft #4) to Secretary Dulles: "I question whether the proposal on atomic contributions by the United States and the Soviets will have its intended effect. Many people, and probably the Soviets, will treat it as a propaganda tactic rather than a serious proposal if it is made in this way. If serious results were hoped for, many would expect us to attempt private discussions with the Soviets as a beginning" (Bowie, 1953a).

Bowie's reservations came to fruition two days later at a "big meeting in Foster Dulles' office." According to Jackson's log, "red lights started blinking all over the place. Joint Chiefs and Defense have laid their ears back" (Jackson, 1953f). After a one-day Thanksgiving break, the group met again in Dulles' office. The "real problem," as Jackson recorded in his log, "is basic philosophy—are we or are we not prepared to embark on a course which may in fact lead to atomic disarmament? Soldier boys and their civilian governesses say no. Foster Dulles doesn't say yes or no, but says any atomic offer which does not recognize ultimate possibility is a phoney and should not be made. Strauss and I say we won't be out of the trenches by Christmas, or next Christmas or the next one, but let's try to make a start and see what happens. Foster considers this mentally dishonest (he should talk!)" (Jackson, 1953g).

Dulles was not the only one with reservations. His Policy Planning Staff head, Robert Bowie, was also deeply disturbed. As he wrote to Dulles on November 30, 1953: "The only serious point of substance is the one about which we have talked: whether the United States wishes to achieve full-scale atomic disarmament if that should prove possible. My own view is that we definitely should. But unless this is our view I do not think this speech should be made" (Bowie, 1953b). Bowie's opinion was not heeded. Eisenhower made the speech with no consensus among his inner circle as to precisely what, if anything, the United States would do if confronted with the possibility of disarmament.

CONCLUSION

The speech, as delivered, reflected the Jackson-Strauss position which held that disarmament, while desirable, was not an immediately realizable goal. The purpose for giving the speech was, therefore, not to establish a framework for talks about control of nuclear weapons, but instead was an effort to position the United States with respect to the peaceful uses of atomic energy and to bid the Soviets in a public forum to adopt that position, thereby gaining a psychological victory whatever the Russian response might be.

Jackson's memo to the Operations Coordinating Board on December 9, the day following the speech, is instructive: "It will be particularly important to impress upon world opinion the sincerity with which the United States seeks international security through the reduction of the arms burden, while at the same time avoiding any premature stimulation of false optimism regarding immediately realizable disarmament, which cannot be fulfilled under present conditions of international tensions' (Jackson, 1953h). From Jackson's point of view there was no doubt that the speech, though clothed in the language of disarmament, was not, itself, a vehicle for such disarmament, at least not at the present time.

That Eisenhower's speech raised the hope of turning weapons into plowshares can hardly be denied. That the majority of those in the inner circle who crafted the speech intended that nothing *more* than hope be offered can also hardly be denied. Though the public "exploitation" of the speech emphasized peace and negotiation, the backroom decision was that the United States would not "be drawn into separate negotiations with the Soviets on the elimination or control of nuclear weapons alone. For our part," says a summary of a top secret meeting held on January 16, 1954, "we intend to discuss only the peaceful uses of atomic energy" (O.C.B., 1954).

The summary of the January 16, 1954 meeting goes on to note that "Secretary Dulles reiterated that we should try through these discussions to get across to friendly nations the idea that the disagreement over the control of the atomic weapons was not a bilateral difference of opinion between the United States and the U.S.S.R., but rather was a split between the U.S.S.R. and the remainder of the free world" (O.C.B., 1954). If this could be accomplished, if the Soviet Union could be isolated as the foe who refused to cooperate with the rest of the world, then the psychological victory would be won. This was the great, and arguably the primary, purpose for the "Atoms for Peace" speech of December 8, 1953.

By employing both implicit and explicit argumentative techniques, Eisenhower was able to accomplish his goals. He warned the Soviet Union against a preemptive strike; he portrayed the United States as the friend and benefactor of the developing world; and, most importantly, he placed the Soviet Union in a policy dilemma by challenging the U.S.S.R. to accept his atoms-for-peace proposal. Throughout the speech and the subsequent campaign to "exploit" it, the administration portrayed the December 8 speech as a serious offer to negotiate the problems of the nuclear age with any potential adversary. That the speech was, in reality, not such an offer at all testifies to the ease with which human agents can shape language and guide perception in accordance with their own purposes.

Language is not self-explanatory. It is a reflection of the goals, motives, and values of those who choose to use it as an instrument by which to realize their ends. This study demonstrates how a particular group of rhetors used language to address multiple audiences for divergent purposes while, at the same moment, maintaining that the audience was one and the purpose straightforward. Criticism, at this level, is the study of how language is used by humans to channel response, and is, in the case examined, a paradigm both of linguistic deception and strategic posturing at the highest levels of government.

Notes

1. Letter from C. D. Jackson to Merlo Pusey, 5 February, 1955. C. D. Jackson Papers, Box 24, Dwight D. Eisenhower Library.

2. According to Robert A. Devine, "on August 12, 1953, American officials detected the first Soviet hydrogen explosion.... What neither Eisenhower nor Strauss revealed, however, was that the Russian device had used dry hydrogen isotopes that did not require unwieldy refrigeration. The Soviets now appeared not only to have caught up with American nuclear technology but to have moved closer than the United States to a deliverable hydrogen bomb." See Devine (1978), *Blowing on the wind: The nuclear test ban debate 1954–1960.* New York: Oxford University Press, pp. 16–17.

3. Memo from James M. Lambie to R. Gordon Arneson, Edmond Gullion, Brig. Gen. P. T. Carroll, Emmet J. Hughes, Abbott Washburn, Roy McNair, William V. Watts, Ralph Clark, Ray Snapp, W. B. McCool, Jack DeChant, George "Pete" Hotchkiss, Edward Lyman, Maj. Gen. A. R. Luedecke, George Wyeth, Lt. Col. Edwin F. Block, William H. Godel, Fred Blachly, Mrs. Jeanne Singer, William Rogers, 28 September 1953, White House Central Files (WHCF), Box 12, Dwight D. Eisenhower Library.

4. Given the chronology of development of the *idea* for atoms-for-peace, it seems likely that Eisenhower picked up the general concept from a series of articles appearing in the *New York Times* from August 12–14, 1953. The three-part series written by William L. Laurence included the following lines: "The first international conference on atomic energy for industrial power voted unanimously at its closing session today in favor of establishing an international nuclear energy association, open to nuclear scientists of all the nations of the world, including the Soviet Union and other countries behind the Iron Curtain.... The purpose of the association would be to promote the peaceful uses of atomic energy through the exchange of knowledge by the various participating countries on subjects not related to military applications." See Laurence (1953, August 14). Atom scientists favor world pool of ideas. *New York Times*, p. 1.

5. The total count of twenty-four includes "peace" and its derivatives "peaceful" and "peacetime."

6. All quotations from Eisenhower's "Atoms for Peace" address are from the text as printed in *Public Papers of the President of the United States, 1953*. Washington, D.C.: Government Printing Office, pp. 813–822.

References

Alsop, S. (1953, September 18). Candor is not enough. *Washington Post*, p. 23.

Bohlen, C. (1953). Unpublished cablegram from Chip Bohlen to J. F. Dulles. John Foster Dulles Papers, Box 1, Dwight D. Eisenhower Library.

Bowie, R. R. (1953a, November 23). Unpublished memo from Robert R. Bowie to Secretary Dulles. John Foster Dulles Papers, Box 1, Dwight D. Eisenhower Library.

Bowie, R. R. (1953b, November 30). Unpublished memo from Robert R. Bowie to Secretary Dulles. John Foster Dulles Papers, Box 1, Dwight D. Eisenhower Library.

Briton warns United States of atomic attack. (1953, August 12). *New York Times*, p. 15.

Canadians await details. (1953. December 9). *New York Times*, p. 3

Donovan, R. J. (1956). *Eisenhower: The inside story*. New York: Harper and Brothers.

Dulles, J. F. (1953). Unpublished memo from J. F. Dulles to Eisenhower. John Foster Dulles Papers, Box 1, Dwight D. Eisenhower Library.

Eisenhower, D. D. (1963). *Mandate for change*. Garden City: Doubleday.

Halle, L. J. (1967). *The cold war as history*. New York: Harper and Row.

Hamilton, T. J. (1953, December 9). Eisenhower bids Soviets join United States in atomic stockpile for peace. *New York Times*, pp. 1–2.

Herken, G. (1980). *The winning weapon: The atomic bomb in the cold war 1945–1950*. New York: Alfred A. Knopf.

Ike's speech praised generally on "Hill". (1953, December 9). Washington Post, p. 16.

Jackson, C. D. (1953a, March 4). Unpublished memo from C. D. Jackson to General Robert Cutler. C. D. Jackson Papers, Box 37, Dwight D. Eisenhower Library.

Jackson, C. D. (1953b, September 2). Unpublished memo from C. D. Jackson to Gordon Arneson. White House Central Files, Confidential File, Box 12, Dwight D. Eisenhower Library.

Jackson, C. D. (1953c, October 2). Unpublished memo from C. D. Jackson to the President. C. D. Jackson Papers, Box 24, Dwight D. Eisenhower Library.

Jackson, C. D. (1953d, November 17). Unpublished log entry. C. D. Jackson Papers, Box 56, Dwight D. Eisenhower Library.

Jackson, C. D. (1953e, November 21). Unpublished memo from C. D. Jackson to Sherman Adams. C. D. Jackson Papers, Box 23, Dwight D. Eisenhower Library.

Jackson, C. D. (1953f, November 25). Unpublished log entry. C. D. Jackson Papers, Box 56, Dwight D. Eisenhower Library.

Jackson, C. D. (1953g, November 27). Unpublished log entry. C. D. Jackson Papers, Box 56, Dwight D. Eisenhower Library.

Jackson, C. D. (1953h, December 9). Unpublished memo from C. D. Jackson to members of the Operations Coordinating Board. C. D. Jackson Records, Box 1, Dwight D. Eisenhower Library.

Jackson, C. D. (1954, February 16). Unpublished memo from C. D. Jackson to members of the Operations Coordinating Board. White House Central Files, Confidential File, Box 13, Dwight D. Eisenhower Library.

James, M. (1953, December 9). President's plan stirs doubts in U.N. *New York Times*, p. 3.

McCrum, M. (1975, May 15). Unpublished oral history interview, Dwight D. Eisenhower Library.

Operations Coordinating Board. (1954, January 16). Summary of O.C.B. Meeting. White House Central Files, Confidential File, Box 12, Dwight D. Eisenhower Library.

Rostow, W. W. (1982). *Europe after Stalin: Eisenhower's three decisions of March 11, 1953*. Austin: University of Texas Press.

Strauss, L. L. (1962). *Men and decisions*. Garden City: Doubleday.

The choice on the atom. (1953, December 9). *Washington Post*, p. 10.

The Image of the Right Honourable Margaret Thatcher

—————————————— J. JEFFERY AUER ——————————————

In the British General Election on May 3, 1979, Mrs. Margaret Hilda Thatcher[1] retained her House of Commons seat as the member from Finchley by a margin of 7,878 votes out of 55,468 cast, just slightly more than double her majority of 3,911 in the last previous General Election in 1974. Because in this election there was a nationwide 5.2 percent swing to the Conservative Party, the Tories altogether received 339 seats (up from 282), against 268 for the Labour Party (down from 307), 11 for the Liberal Party (down from 14), and 17 for all other minor parties (down from 29). Thus Mrs. Thatcher, the Leader of the Opposition since her election in November 1974, as leader of the Conservative Party, became Prime Minister on May 5 for the "Forty-Eighth Parliament of the United Kingdom of Great Britain and Northern Ireland and the Twenty-Seventh Year of the Reign of Queen Elizabeth II." Incidentally, Mrs. Thatcher also thus became principal author of Queen Elizabeth's twelve-minute speech at the State Opening when the new Parliament was convened on May 15, 1979.

Since a parliamentary majority of 43 seats provides a substantial cushion against adverse results in any by-elections made necessary by the death or resignation of any Conservative member, and because traditional party discipline makes any significant loss by rebellion almost unthinkable, it appears likely that the Conservative Party will remain in office, and that Mrs. Thatcher will occupy No. 10 Downing Street for the maximum of five years that is permitted, under British law, between general elections. Therefore what we can know about the Right Honourable Margaret Thatcher—her political personality and her public persuasion, up to her assumption of the chief parliamentary role in Great Britain—should be recorded now.

As in the United States, so in Britain, the perceived images of parliamentary leaders are thought by voters to reveal true character and, in the case of candidates, qualification for office. An individual's image consists of a composite projection of a variety of inherent and acquired characteristics. Some of these may be strictly political and projected largely by oral messages: he believes in capital punishment, she is opposed to abortion; he expresses liberal views, she is a fiscal conservative, and so on. Other characteristics reveal personality, typically projected in non-verbal communication: physical appearance, manner of speaking, projection of life style, manifestation of integrity, empathy, and so on. Collectively these characteristics seem to reveal an individual's style, the way in which as a leader he or she would make those necessary choices, identified by John F. Kennedy after seventeen months in office as choices "among men, among measures, among methods."[2] Thus the images of candidates provide perceptions that help determine how prospective voters think and feel about them.

It is possible, of course, that an individual's image may be projected differently in a variety of social contexts: in campaigning a person may not appear the same in public meetings, telecasts, and one-on-one conversations. Sometimes these differences may result from deliberate efforts to manipulate one's image (to try to give the appearance of being more determined, more understanding, or more "plain folks," for example). At other times the media itself may make the difference (some people do well with formal addresses but are not facile in television interviews, for example). It is also true that images are viewed differentially by those who perceive them. An image might be constant, but be seen as more or less positive according to the influence on the beholder of such factors as education, experience, social aspirations and economic status.

Those who undertake to examine images in political communication must be aware of these differences both in the circumstances of projection and in the perceptions of their beholders. Where it is impossible to obtain adequate survey data for quantitative conclusions the most rewarding procedure is to attempt to observe as many elements as possible of an individual's image and in a variety of contexts, and then to identify and discuss, using whatever resources may be available, those constituents of the image that are judged to be most salient.

What follows is based upon a study of political communication in Britain over a period of approximately eight weeks prior to the May 3 General Election, supplementing observations of parliamentary debate and public persuasion by reading contemporary British newspapers, periodicals and books; and especially by a series of interviews with both Labour and Conservative members of Parliament, party political advisers and press secretaries, newspaper editors and broadcast journalists;[3] and by talking informally with a variety of British citizens, ranging from innkeepers and civil servants to pensioners and at least one sergeant-major in Her Majesty's Royal Marines.

As a representative of the Finchley constituency for twenty years, a government minister for seven years,[4] and Leader of the Opposition for four and a half years, the public eye has long enough been on Mrs. Thatcher to permit characterizations of the five most salient elements of her political personality, as revealed in her public image.

CULTURAL IDENTIFICATION

Those who live in the public eye inevitably invite critical comment. Because so many of the criticisms of Mrs. Thatcher, even by her political friends, are at least indirectly related to her cultural background, it must be noted first of all.[5]

She grew up in Grantham, in Lincolnshire, a market town hitherto notable only as the home of King's School where Isaac Newton propounded the laws of gravity some three hundred years ago. One grandfather was a shoemaker, the other a railway guard. Her mother, Beatrice Stevenson, had a dress-making shop before her marriage. Her father, Albert Roberts, was a largely self-taught man whose formal education ended at age twelve when he became a grocer's apprentice. By the time Margaret, the Roberts' second daughter, was born on October 13, 1925, the family occupied a flat, without hot water or an indoor toilet, over the grocery shop that he by then owned. In due course Roberts acquired a second shop and found time to serve his community as mayor, justice of the peace, a member of the libraries committee, and on the governing board of the local girls' school and the boys' school. The family all were devout members of the Firkin Street Methodist Church; Albert was a lay preacher, and he also served as a trustee for some ten other churches in Lincolnshire. And he became a Rotarian. In short, Margaret Thatcher's father was a striver, and he strove successfully into the middle class society of Grantham.

Along with middle class membership in the pre-war East Midlands counties of England went middle class morality. Some of this was traditional Sabbath-keeping: there was no dancing in the Roberts home on Sunday, nor tennis, swimming, cinema, or walking in the parks. Some of it was grandmotherly admonition: "Cleanliness is next to Godliness." "If a thing's worth doing it's worth doing well." Some of it was religious instruction, as Margaret Thatcher recalled it: "Everything had to be clean and systematic. We were Methodists and Methodist means method. We were taught what was right and wrong in considerable detail. There were certain things you just didn't do and that was that." Some of it was a closeness of the family: "most of the things we did we tended to do together," whether it was activity at the church, helping out in the grocer's shop, or going every Thursday evening to university extension lectures on current affairs. And always it was a sense of duty, "very, very strongly engrained into us. Duties to the church, duties to your neighbour and conscientiousness were continually emphasized." All in all, as Margaret Thatcher has said, her upbringing was "rather puritan," but if she ever regretted that fact there was no sign of it in her first message back home after being elected Leader of the Conservative Party: "I always believe that I was very lucky to be brought up in a small town with a great sense of friendliness and voluntary service."

Morality of the kind just suggested has, to some extent, gone out of fashion all around the world. To many it now has a distinctly rural and folksy cast, it seems old-fashioned. And of course it was before the high and family fractionating mobility of the automobile, and the substitution of the television tube as a conversational partner. Among the Thatchers conversation was highly regarded; at home after the Sunday evening service there were friends for supper and religious talk, in the grocer's shop proprietor and customers exchanged political views, and at school her classmates knew Margaret as a good debater. Out of all this talk came reinforcement for the middle class virtues of honesty, self-reliance, neighborliness compounded by real concern for others and, always, hard work: High on the list of chores was decision-making: "You make up your own mind," admonished her father, "you do not do something or want to do something because your friends are doing it." And one step further: "You do not follow the crowd because you're afraid of being different—you decide what to do yourself and if necessary you lead the crowd, but you never just follow."

Paul Johnson, former editor of *The New Statesman*, ticked off for Tricia Murray the virtues of Margaret Thatcher. "First of all and most important of all, she is a Christian. She *does* believe in the ten commandments. She *does* make very clear distinctions in her mind between what is morally right and wrong...with complete passionate intensity and conviction and I think it evokes a very definite response among ordinary people.... They like to hear someone at the top of public life speak out for these ordinary things that they were brought up on and regret seeing disappear in our rapidly changing society...."[6] She would be, Johnson wrote elsewhere, "the first fully-committed Christian prime minister since Lord Salisbury." But this does not mean that Christianity is a matter of party politics:

> She emphasizes that neither Labour nor Conservatives have a private line to the
> deity (or, for that matter, to the devil). But she does claim...that the Judaeo-

Christian system of ethics, its view of human conduct and the organization of
society for nonmaterial ends, is a central element in the historical traditions which
have shaped the British political system.[7]

Few graduates of the Grantham Girls School sought higher education at Oxford, but at age seventeen Margaret Roberts was enrolled in Somerville College, in the long run heading for a legal degree, but in the short run majoring in chemistry and, after graduation, securing a position in the development department of a plastics manufacturer in Essex.

Science majors, especially women whose male classmates were at least a year older, worked hard at their studies. But Margaret Roberts found time for one extracurricular activity: the Oxford University Conservative Association. It is doubtful that she would have been more attracted to the Oxford Union, but in any case it was not for another twenty years that it saw fit to admit women. Men, meanwhile, were unrestricted. Edward Boyle, for example, became president of the Conservative club, and was succeeded by Margaret Roberts, but he was also a member of the first postwar Oxford debate team to tour America. It cannot be said that Margaret entered Oxford as a dedicated Conservative, though it is clearly the general imprint that Grantham might make. Indeed, as she told Murray, "I joined the Conservative Club right from the beginning simply because I was interested but it was really no more than that. Whatever club you joined, there was an eventful life evolving round it and most of the students joined one or more of the associations."[8]

Even though socializing may have been a part of the rationale for joining the Conservatives, Margaret Roberts threw herself into its political activities. In 1945 when the war ended she campaigned for Quintin Hogg, a successful candidate, though overall Labour overwhelmed the Conservatives and the heroic Churchill became ex-Prime Minister. It was not too long after, Mrs. Thatcher recalls, someone said to her, "I feel that what you would really like to do is to be a member of Parliament," and "that was the very first time that it had occurred to me that perhaps one day I could, if the chance ever came."[9] But first there was the Oxford degree to complete, then the research job with B X Plastics, residence in Colchester, membership in the local Conservative Association, and attendance at party conferences representing the Oxford Graduates Association.

"My ideas," said Margaret Thatcher, "took form at Oxford."[10] Aside from her education in chemistry, where she took respectable second class honors, the Oxford influences appear to have affected most of her views on politics and on religion. She had come from a home where her father was an Independent, but Conservative-leaning, and where both parents exemplified the Non-conformist work ethic that nourished the rising middle class. At Oxford, 1943–1947, the forces of both scientism and socialism were strong and pervasive, and while the inductive and experimental methods of the former were professionally attractive, the collectivism of the latter was philosophically disturbing. Essentially her negative reaction to socialism had a stronger religious base than a political one. This was reflected in a speech at St. Lawrence Jewry, in London, on March 30, 1978:

I never thought that Christianity equipped me with a political philosophy, but I
thought it did equip me with standards to which the political actions must, in the
end, be referred. It also taught me that, in the final analysis, politics is about

personal relations, about establishing the conditions in which men and women can best use their fleeting lives in this world to prepare themselves for the next. Now all this may sound rather pious. But I still believe that the majority of parents want their children to be brought up in what is essentially the same religious heritage as was handed to me. To most ordinary people, heaven and hell, right and wrong, good and bad, matter.[11]

From that base it seems an easy step for Margaret Roberts of academic Oxford to become the Margaret Thatcher of everyday politics and attack the socialist wing of the Labour Party for wanting every decision a political one: "I hate the things which I believe deny each and every person's right to dignity and respect, and their right to live their own lives in their own way, provided it doesn't harm anyone else.... I dislike the way the party has sold itself to socialism, to nationalisation, to almost a Marxist philosophy."[12]

Because there is a strong Christian theme that runs through Thatcher's political thinking, it may be significant to identify its origins. In Grantham, as has been said, she and her family were staunch Methodists, and at Oxford she regularly attended meetings of a student Methodist group. But also at Oxford she began to read religious treatises, with special attention to C. S. Lewis; thus began, in one biographer's view, her gradual move away ("higher and higher," she said) from Methodism, from fundamentalist to sacerdotal views.[13] When Margaret Roberts married Denis Thatcher in 1951 it was in a Methodist church, but when the twins were born in 1953 they were baptized in an Anglican church.

The conception of Mrs. Thatcher as a middle class high achiever, with upper class affiliations through education, politics and religion should by no means suggest that she is not personally a warm, compassionate and decent person. Brian Walden, thirteen years a Labour MP, now chief presenter for the ITV Weekend World, but himself a product of a deprived background, is very emphatic:

> *She isn't a snob—she really isn't. I know that traditionally by all appearances, she ought to be and I also know that successful people of lower class origin are often the worst snobs because they are insecure. For some reason, she isn't insecure and she isn't a snob.... She has as much or as little interest in Dukes as in housewives. There is no element of the English vice which is disliking people not for what they are but for what they seem to be. There is no element of that in her at all.*[14]

Unfortunately the English vice of which Walden complains is still very much in evidence. As was said at the outset, much of the criticism of Mrs. Thatcher that is heard in conversation and from the platform, and that is read in the press, relates at least indirectly to her cultural background. She is criticized for what she seems to be, for the image that she indeed sometimes projects, and not necessarily for what she is. The focus is not so much upon substance as upon her style.

THE SOUND OF "CLASS"

It is about matters of style that English snobbishness is most apparent. In his foreword to the 1978 volume that updates Nancy Mitford's 1956 *Noblesse Oblige*, H. B. Brooks-Baker, managing director of Debrett's Peerage, contends that "England is among the least snobbish and class-conscious countries," but "this does not mean that snobbishness is rare in England. On the contrary, it is prevalent to some degree in most areas of society," and can be observed in the way that middle-classes often imitate in vain "the peculiar characteristics of language and behavior which come naturally to the English upper-classes."[15] The class distinction is reflected in the categories of "U" (Upper Class) and "non-U" (not Upper Class); that "not only means that one speaks with the right accent, but...also means that a person must choose the right word or phrase." While these two matters of style are "vitally important," Brooks-Baker also notes that "clothes, clubs, vocations and hobbies are also U and non-U, as well as such things as the way in which a person walks."[16] Richard Buckle's essay in the same volume illuminates the general point with the specific complaint that "Mrs. Thatcher, who may or may not be our next Prime Minister, pronounces 'involved' with a long 'o', as in 'vote'."[17]

Whatever the exact accent and word choice patterns of lower middle class Grantham, those of Margaret Roberts were influenced by childhood elocution lessons and, during her first years out of Oxford, reported her plastics company employer Stanley Booth, "she tended to iron out of herself her human character-istics, trying hard even then to become a politician, teaching herself artificial speech."[18] If indeed she did try to sound like one of the elite by modifying her vocal behavior, including accent, emphasis patterns, inflections, and precision of phrasing, she did not bring it off, at least in the eyes of that elite. Over and over one hears and reads in England a common set of terms used by professional political commentators, and Members of Parliament from both parties, to describe Mrs. Thatcher's communication characteristics. To be sure that these terms are under-stood in the way that Englishmen use them, they are presented here along with definitions taken from the most recently published and up to date Oxford English dictionary.[19] According to these informants, all themselves members of the elite, Mrs. Thatcher's speech is:

> Plummy—*"full of plums...sounding affectedly full and rich in tone"*
> Toffee-nosed—*"snobbish, pretentious"*
> La-di-da—*"having an affected manner of pronunciation"*
> Starchy—*"Stiff and formal in manner"*

And her words mark her as:

> Suburban—*"having only limited interests and narrow-minded views"*
> Privet hedge personality—*see suburban*

The thrust of these commonly used labels, of course, is to tax Mrs. Thatcher with *affectation*—"behavior that is put on for display and not natural or genuine, pretence." Specifically, of course, this means that as she engaged in upward social mobility she tried to sound more and more like the elite. It is not unnatural anywhere to want to fit the expectations of one's peers, though it is probably more common in America than in Britain that one moves from non-U to U.

The attitudes reflected in the terms just cited are of long standing as applied to Mrs. Thatcher, but they came most conspicuously into use at the time of her 1975 challenge to Edward Heath for the Leadership of the Conservative Party. As Patrick Cosgrave reported that contest, Ian Gilmour, owner of the *Spectator* and Secretary of State in the Heath cabinet, even carried his opposition outside the party confer-ence and to his constituents who heard him phrase "a dig against what was rapidly coming to be thought of as Margaret Thatcher's suburban image." "We cannot," said Gilmour at Amhersham, "retreat behind the privet hedge into a world of narrow class interests and selfish concerns."[20] At the outset of the 1979 General Election campaign there were still notes of concern, as in a not unfriendly review of her career by Philip Rawstorne:

> The well-groomed appearance, the cultivated accent, suggested a Southern sub-urban outlook, a scale of values which would strike few sympathies outside its own trimly hedged world. Many Tories having taken a leap in the dark [by electing her as leader], were disturbed by the distance from their immediate past at which they had apparently landed.... [But] the aggression with which she won her position and the abrasiveness caused in part by the tensions of main-taining it have been softened.[21]

It may be appropriate to ask whether American journalists would find kindlier terms with which to describe Mrs. Thatcher's political personality insofar as it is reflected in her communicative behavior. Here are fair samples from the most widely circulated American reports on Mrs. Thatcher in the election campaign. For the International Edition of *Newsweek*, John Nielsen and Anthony Collings thought "Thatcher still suffers from a humorless, doctrinaire image."[22] Peter Webb and Collings later wrote of "her combative speeches and abrasive style."[23] And Angus Deming, Tony Clifton, Allan J. Meyer and Collings heard "a strong-willed, some-what shrill and prickly suburban matron," though admittedly "she tried to alter her image, speaking softly and avoiding controversial details on just how she would make her new-right government work."[24] The *Time* team headed by Bonnie Angelo summed up the Thatcher campaign by saying that her "sometimes hectoring, sometimes condescending manner irritated many voters.... [She had] an upper-class accent acquired by elocution lessons.... She had, and still has, two faces that are startlingly different: prim and tart-tongued in public, she is also a home-body who delights in comparing prices with other housewives.... Because of her authoritarian air, she sometimes appears to be rather like a headmistress dealing sternly with rowdy students."[25]

To sum up this matter, Kenneth Hudson's perceptive volume on *The Language of Politics* is helpful. He cites the common English term "Officer Class" v. "Not Officer Class Material," used to identify those whose education and family back-ground make it apparent that "command has been placed in the right hands." To sound like Officer Class requires distinctive accents and vocal subtleties. Among recent Prime Ministers only Edward Heath was a middle class product and he lacked the true U Officer Class voice. In common with Heath, says Hudson, Mrs. Thatcher acquired the upper class accents too late in life for them to sound genuine. "A connoisseur of such matters can spot the difference immediately and so, one suspects, can quite a large proportion of the electorate. The imitation is too perfect, yet the subtleties are missing." Although Hudson does not question her sincerity, he notes that "the main disadvantage of the accent which is not quite right is that it is liable to give an impression of insincerity, of an actor playing a part."[26] In short, there are grounds for viewing Mrs. Thatcher as "plummy" and putting on the "la-di-da," as one prominent journalist said of her.

Mrs. Thatcher is, of course, well aware of what many critics have said about her speech behavior and her political personality. In a widely read interview with

Kenneth Harris, published in *The Observer*, he reported that "I sometimes hear it said [and from some Conservatives] that your manner, your voice, even your looks, have a kind of middle-class quality which diminishes your appeal to the electorate as a whole." Her reply:

> *Absolutely poppycock! Isn't it ridiculous? It would be far better if such critics got on with the job of putting across Conservative views and philosophy, and did a little more converting themselves. I am what I am, and I will stay that way. I just hope to improve in communicating as I go along.*

Harris pursued the topic of communication: "What do you think about your image on television? Do you work on your image on television?" No, she said, she doesn't work on it, but just tries to be more relaxed. "You can't alter your own personality. You just can't. You don't try to. If you discovered some irritating mannerisms that you didn't previously know about, of course you'd try to get rid of them, because if you don't, people will be distracted by them and not listen to what you're saying."[27] There is some evidence that Mrs. Thatcher accepts criticism of her speaking. Brian Walden, former Labour MP and now a television presenter, has encouraged her to be more spontaneous, in part to loosen her up and shed some of her studio dignity. Monty Modlyn, a longtime BBC announcer and interviewer, and now with LBC, advised Mrs. Thatcher that her style "was too much like a grande duchess and that her rather high pitched speaking voice should be altered since she was giving the impression that she spoke posher than the Queen." And Janet Brown, a television and cabaret entertainer, one of whose popular impersonations has been of Mrs. Thatcher, gave her suggestions on more effective script reading and phrasing of lines. "One of her great strengths," concluded Brown, "is that whatever criticism is levelled at her, she tries so blooming hard to put it right."[28]

TORY PERSUASION

"The trouble with politicians," Mrs. Thatcher said in an interview with Anthony King, "is we have to speak more often than we have something to say. And by the time you've been speaking two, three, four or five times a week, while Parliament is sitting, not always in the House, but the many organizations you have to speak to, you feel a bit stale." The remedy, she proposed, is that "you must try to find in politics a different approach. There's not much new to say in politics, there hasn't been for years, but it's the approach that's individual and different."[29]

Margaret Thatcher has made a political career out of taking "a different approach."

Her 1959 maiden speech in the House of Commons violated the polite tradition of introducing one's self by a few noncontroversial remarks, perhaps on the features of one's constituency. Instead it was a twenty-seven minute speech, "delivered without a note,"[30] arguing for her Private Member's Bill that would require local council meetings to be open to citizens and to journalists (what has been called in America a "sunshine" law). It was reported to be "Front Bench quality" and it "drew plaudits from Ministers as well as Opposition spokesmen."[31]

Her 1975 speech to the National Press Club in Washington overturned the tradition that no one ever speaks ill of his or her own country when abroad, and laid out the problems of Britain and the spirit in which she approached them:

> *In my country, at present, we have serious problems; it would be foolish to ignore them. We have, to a more intense degree than many other countries, a combination of rising prices, falling output and unemployment. And we have a sense of losing our way. The problem is not a technical one. It is one of the life and death of the national spirit. We are in the midst of a struggle for human dignity.*
>
> *It is not my job, nor the job of any politician, to offer people salvation. It is part of my political faith that people must save themselves. Many of our troubles are due to the fact that our people turn to politicians for everything.*[32]

Her three speeches on foreign policy and defense (July, 1974, at Chelsea; January, 1976, at Kensington; and July, 1976, at Dorking) challenged not only the position of Roy Mason, the British Defense Secretary, but also the policy of Henry Kissinger, the American Secretary of State, and specifically the practice of *detente* at the Helsinki conference. For this the Russian press labelled her "The Iron Lady," and Warsaw radio shifted the figure to say "she flutters like an iron butterfly."[33]

Her impromptu speech to a group of journalists with whom she was touring a computer factory near London during the recent campaign was a surprise lecture on science. She volunteered to explain to her companions what they were looking at, because "if you don't know it'll be deadly dull." Then came a briefing on the use of silicone chips in making small computers that could be used in moving data for decision making into field units and away from the central corporate office, and this conclusion:

> *The political point is that the age of centralization and massive Big Brother computers is going, and you can have small computers with microprocessors on the spot, so that decisions can be taken on the spot. That is very much more interesting than pumping it all up there, having a few powerful chaps up there, and not being able to use your nous [common sense] locally.*

As some of the journalists started to move on, she called "I haven't finished with you chaps. Here we all are in a science factory. You've all been concentrating on the possibility of the first woman Prime Minister in Downing Street. What you have failed to observe, which I must point out to you in all modesty, is that I will be the first person in No. 10 Downing Street to have a science degree."[34]

Overall Mrs. Thatcher speaks with good effect. Because they are so often generalities, her arguments frequently sound like slogans, but they are theme-related and the linkages are always apparent. Kenneth Hudson suggests that the flavor of much Conservative speaking has always been non-ideological (in contrast with Labour), and characterized by "plain statement on topics where straightforward, direct language is out of fashion."[35] One can easily select examples from the Thatcher speeches: "I gather from the radio I am called a reactionary. Well, there is a lot to react against." "Free choice is ultimately what life is about...from saying we are all equal it is only a small step to saying that we cannot make any choice for ourselves." "The balance between power and responsibility in the trades union movement needs to be restored as between employer and employee."[36]

Her style is fairly undistinguished, other than by the square-jawed, uncompromising phraseology of her convictions. The style is seldom marked by the figures of speech, metaphors, and graphic phrases that seem to fit so smoothly together in the speaking of British elites. Perhaps it is simply that the speaking experience in the Oxford Conservative Association is no match for that in the Oxford Union.

Whatever shortcomings there may be in Mrs. Thatcher's public speaking, they are not the result of inattention. Like all British politicians, she knows the importance of quality in public discourse. The distinguished academic student of politics, Jean Blondel, writes of the essential talents of politicians: "They must be able to grasp quickly the main points of a question with which they are not familiar...they must be able to speak reasonably fluently in public, they must be able to argue a case in debate with some cogency, they must be able to retort quickly and see the flaw in the other man's argument."[37] Few practitioners of communication could be less in agreement on political issues than William Rees-Mogg, editor of *The Times*, and Anthony Wedgewood Benn, MP and Labour Minister of Energy. But on at least one point they are agreed: both of these former presidents of the Oxford Union affirm that at least fifty percent of a politician's success in England depends upon his ability in public speaking.[38] This truth Margaret Thatcher also recognizes, and there is ample testimony from her associates that she works very hard indeed at anything she thinks is important, and speeches are in that category.

Like most political leaders in America, in England at least the top bracket people (Prime Minister, Leader of the Opposition, and cabinet members) receive some assistance in the preparation of their speeches. Some of Mrs. Thatcher's predecessors used very little help. Sir Harold Wilson, Prime Minister, 1964–1970 and 1974–1976, testified that "I never used any drafting, or speech contributions, until the 1974 elections, when I was faced with two or three or even five and six a day, plus a hand-out for each day's press conference."[39] Edward Heath, Prime Minister, 1970–1974, however, had Michael Wolff on his staff as a speechwriter, and at least five other persons were regular aides in turning out complete speech drafts for him. Though he always intended to rework the drafts, there was never enough time, and so "at the last minute the adequate draft was looked at, reluctantly approved and unenthusiastically delivered."[40] The two political heroes of Margaret Thatcher are earlier Prime Ministers, Winston Churchill and Harold Macmillan, and she tends to follow their speechwriting practices. Churchill, for example, "relied on civil servants and other functionaries to provide briefing material, but preferred to actually compose [his speeches himself], often moving from draft to draft and taking several days over the polishing and revision."[41]

It is important to recognize in this matter that "the man in the street" in London, and even the average university intellectual, is unaware of the pervasiveness of the professional speechwriter in political and business circles; they take it for granted that the speaker himself writes what he speaks. Even politicians who may hire the services of ghostwriters keep very quiet about it for the practice is thought to be infra dig. The exception is understood to be the Prime Minister, the Leader of the Opposition, or a major spokesman; for such persons some speechwriting aid is understandable and acceptable, provided, as Roger Evans put it, "that you always sound like yourself; and Mrs. Thatcher always sounds like Mrs. Thatcher, whereas, unfortunately, Ted Heath, when he was in office—he really did sound like his speechwriters."[42] To sum up the matter, it appears that Mrs. Thatcher's speech preparation procedure is something like this:[43]

1. She holds a general discussion, sometimes more like an informal seminar,

on a subject, and having a speech rather than a policy paper or a policy decision as the goal. Outside experts frequently take part.

2. Her views are expressed (a) to a speech writing aide, or (b) to an expert on her shadow staff, and "she explains the destination she wants the argument to reach and the track along which it is to go." If instructing the former, the end product will probably be a draft of the speech; if the latter, the product will be a brief, similar to that used by a lawyer, including all of the relevant factual information, and organized but not phrased as it might be used in an oral presentation.

3. This product, first draft or brief, is now subjected to criticism and further discussion. If pertinent documentation is missing, it is asked for, and if an unfamiliar quotation is used, its context must be produced. Then the aide is asked to have another go at it, or Mrs. Thatcher may herself undertake the second draft.

4. Still another session, and until she is satisfied the draft continues to be amended. One speechwriter who worked with her recalls spending eight to ten hours getting the last three or four pages of a manuscript just right, when the subject was extremely controversial and the feelings of the audience unusually tender. In any case, when the speech is ready, it has on it the authentic stylistic stamp of the Leader.

There is some reason to believe that Mrs. Thatcher, as Prime Minister, will wish to make somewhat less use of civil servants for the preparation of briefs of facts and figures than some of her predecessors. It is expected that instead she will have a larger political staff at No. 10 Downing Street, and draw upon its members for any speechwriting help she may need. Interestingly enough, if that proves to be the case, it will be because predecessor Wilson in March 1974 initiated the practice of appointing political advisers, both in his own office and for his Cabinet ministers. In a list of seven examples of areas in which they would work, he designated one as "speech writing and research."[44]

As the 1979 General Election campaign got underway, Mrs. Thatcher's speechwriting team included a number of part-time aides, but only two regular members. One was Patrick Cosgrave, historian and biographer, political columnist, former staff member of the *Spectator* and now free lance writer, who has served off and on for the last few years as a writer for Mrs. Thatcher. The other was Professor Douglas C. Hague, deputy director of the Manchester Business School, former consultant to the National Economic Development Office, and member of the Price Commission. Now, he told the press, he would advise Mrs. Thatcher on economic developments and write some of her speeches.[45]

The substantive source for Mrs. Thatcher's campaign speeches was a party document, called a manifesto. Each party issues one, and generally it is shorter than the American party platform and cast in more general terms. It is written "in a very woolly fashion," says one political scientist, because in recent years it has become a ritualistic enterprise, not so much to influence the electorate as to provide the party faithful with a compact reference work on policies, and to reassure them that "the party image" has not been changed.[46] Under the Thatcher leadership, however, the manifesto has taken on a new significance. Issues identified in it are the themes of campaign speeches, and policies it lays out are seriously intended to provide a blueprint for action by the Conservative government.[47] Mrs. Thatcher in some ways may strive to do the accepted thing in public life, but her personal style would seem to preclude performing rituals for their own sake. "If a thing is worth doing, it's worth doing well," her grandmother used to tell her.[48]

An overview of the substance of the Tory persuasion in the recent election is therefore provided by the manifesto that refused to accept the inevitability of Britain's decline and said so in language that might well have been Thatcher's: "We think we can reverse it, not because we think we have all the answers but because we think we have the one answer that matters most. We want to work with the grain of human nature, helping people to help themselves—and others. This is the way to restore that self-reliance and self-confidence which are the basis of personal responsibility and national success." Five tasks would be performed by an elected Tory government:

1. Control inflation and set a fair balance between rights and responsibilities of trade unions, to restore national economic health.
2. Reduce income taxes at all levels, to ensure that "hard work pays, success is rewarded and genuine new jobs are created."
3. Uphold Parliament and maintain law and order, to improve the nation's social health.
4. Help people become home-owners, provide better education, and focus welfare services on the truly needy, to support family life.
5. Work with allies and strengthen national defense, to protect national interests in a world of turmoil.

It doubtless was not by chance that a major opinion poll on April 2 revealed that the electorate thought that these were the issues, and in this order, that the General Election should be about: Prices/inflation, Unemployment, Trade unions/strikes, Taxation, Law and order, Common Market. A breakdown of the responses revealed that exactly the same ranking was given to these issues by three significant groups: women, 18–24 year olds, and trade unionists.[49]

The strategy for making the Tory persuasion effective struck many English as too American in style, i.e., controlled exposure with less emphasis upon party rally speeches and more on formal television appearances, and wide coverage for "telly news" programs of personal appearances in shops and factories, chats with the elderly, and the informal strolls called "walkabouts" in shopping centers and residential neighborhoods. Indeed, its great reputation for television commercial work apparently led to the selection of the firm of Saatchi and Saatchi to handle Tory publicity, and to the inevitable references to "The Marketing of Margaret Thaatchi."[50] Doubtless it was the agency's advice, agreed to by party publicity director Gordon Reece, himself formerly a television producer and marketing director of EMI, that led Mrs. Thatcher to decline an invitation to make a joint appearance on television with Prime Minister Callaghan. Labour was quick to try for a point: "We can only assume that the Opposition Leader does not believe Conservative policies will stand up to such detailed public scrutiny," said the party's general secretary, Ron Hayward; and the political editor of Labour's daily paper suggested that voters were thus denied on opportunity to see how Mrs. Thatcher would react under pressure. An editorial in the *Evening News* defended Mrs. Thatcher's decision. After all, it said, "Mr. Challaghan could probably sell a second-car to Richard Nixon if he had a mind to," and there was no point in facing that kind of competition. Besides, "issues and policies, rather than personalities decide elections," and "salesmanship or TV technique" is no basis for deciding upon the best Prime Minister, any more than a Callaghan-Thatcher "race around Smith Square, or a game of Scrabble."[51]

Whoever may have had the right on the issue of an American-style television confrontation, Labour strategy included no personal attacks upon Mrs. Thatcher. When Robert Mellish suggested, in the Prime Minister's "Question Time" in the House of Commons, that everything possible should be done to "ensure that Mrs. Thatcher appear as frequently as possible on television, because her appearances could only be of advantage to Labour," he was mildly rebuked by Mr. Callaghan. That same evening, in a campaign warmup speech to the Parliamentary Labour Party, Callaghan instructed his colleagues to resist any temptation to make a personal campaign against Mrs. Thatcher.[52] It was freely speculated that at base this gentlemanly approach was taken as a precaution against angering women voters by anything that might appear to be "male chauvinist piggery." More than that, however, it was based also upon the assumption that nothing Labour could say would be as devastating to Mrs. Thatcher as the mistakes they were sure she would make before the campaign was over. "Maggie'll blow it," they were confident, perhaps with an intemperate public outburst about immigration, capital punishment, or some equally divisive topic.

In the campaign, television did play, to the dismay of many, a greatly increased role. In keeping of course with the British tradition of even handedness, even the substantially greater financial resources of the Tories[53] could not purchase additional television programs, but only spend more money on the production of their "fair share" allotment. In an agreement worked out by the political parties, BBC and the independent broadcasters, the Labour and Tory parties were each allocated five ten-minute television broadcasts; seven radio broadcasts, matched schedules of five and ten minutes; and all television broadcasts were scheduled for the same hour and on all networks. Mr. Callaghan and Mrs. Thatcher were each scheduled for one forty-minute live television session when viewers could put their own questions to them. Unlike the American custom, there were no election eve political broadcasts.[54] Independently, of course, the candidates were free to accept invitations—and they did—to appear for interviews on the televised "Jimmy Young Show," and Robin Day's "Election Call" program of candidate responses to telephoned questions from listeners and Mr. Day's own firmly posed follow-ups.[55]

To the regret of Labour hopefuls, Mrs. Thatcher committed no blunders, and she did demonstrate an improved understanding of how to carry the Tory message effectively. In 1974 the party manifesto was entitled *Firm Action for a Fair Britain*, and it proclaimed that "The choice before the nation today, as never before, is a choice between moderation and extremism."[56] In 1979 the election was still a choice, but by now she created the feeling that it might be between two extremes, Labour's radical socialists and the right-wing Conservatives. "I seek confrontation with no one," she said in a speech at Swansea about curbing union power, "but I will always strenuously oppose those at home whose aim is to disrupt our society and paralyze our economy, just as I will always stand up to those who threaten our nation and its allies from abroad." In Birmingham she used another issue to make clear the contrast in party approaches when she recalled that she had a few years earlier warned her country about Soviet expansion and that the Russians had called her an "Iron Lady." As the audience shouted its approval she put a new line into her prepared speech: "Britain needs an Iron Lady!"[57] All of these things she communicated in her formal campaign speeches, and with gestures, as *Guardian* political reporter Simon Hoggart described how she suited the actions to the words in a speech at Nottingham:

> *A slapping hand indicated Government spending, cupped hands meant improved industrial output, and arms held up with the hand bent over signified the inflation rate. A fist clenched with the thumb up meant reduced taxation. When she got down to a complicated explanation of the theory of debased coinage and the money supply the gestures were so elaborate that if she had held a ball of wool they would have knitted a Fair Isle jersey as she spoke.*[58]

In general she ignored the subject of gender. Some women might say "it's time a woman got the chance to run the country," and some men might say "I'd 'a preferred a bloke," but she would make no issue of it. When one lady apologized for her husband who, she thought, felt so strongly that "woman's place is in the kitchen, not the House of Commons," that he would abstain sooner than vote for any woman, Mrs. Thatcher asked the lady to remind her husband that "one of our great success periods was under Queen Elizabeth I. Why, great heavens, if your husband had thought the same thing then, we might never have beaten the Spanish Armada."[59] On other occasions she also remembered Queen Victoria, and suggested that "Women in power have done very well for Britain."[60]

About half of her campaigning time was spent in her own constituency of Finchley; the rest was working the marginal constituencies, where a shift of one percent of the votes might rescue a seat from Labour, an effort that involved travelling over three thousand miles, delivering more than thirty speeches to local audiences, and spending days on walkabouts. She became increasingly skillful at explaining, sometimes in crisp teacherly fashion, what had gone wrong with Britain and how to right it. English political reporter James Lewis grumped that "it was not, on the whole, an edifying campaign, and the winning party will have to pay the penalty of living with its words until the voters forget, as they generally do, who said them." But when American reporter David S. Broder encountered her on the forty-minute "Ask Mrs. Thatcher" BBC television program, he found her no slouch. "She handled a series of pointed and probing questions from some obviously well-coached voters with a skill few U.S. politicians could match. Watching her, you could see why she was one of the youngest Tories elected to Parliament in the 1959 election and the first of her freshman class to achieve cabinet status."[61]

"KEN WHAT A WOMAN MAY BE?"

"Even your looks," said Harris to Thatcher, are thought by some to have "a kind of middle class quality." To discuss this topic here is not sexist; it is a recognition that a very real issue in the 1979 General Elections was how Margaret Thatcher looked—as a woman—in terms of common assumptions about a woman's ways of thinking, a woman's whims, a woman's sensitivity—and as a woman who might become Prime Minister. There was not a print or broadcast journalist, a Member of Parliament, or a political staff member who was unwilling to be interviewed on this issue; nor was there one who thought it unimportant. It was as freely discussed on the streets and in the press.[62]

It was about two centuries ago when Samuel Johnson assured Boswell that "a woman preaching is like a dog's walking on his hind legs. It is not done well; but you are surprised to find it done at all." The tolerance of Englishmen for women in public life is somewhat greater this century, but for each individual woman there is a predictable scrutiny.

Hardly anything is written or said about the appearance of avuncular James Callaghan, Labourite Prime Minister, 1974–1979, but there has been much on "what does 'she' look like?" Well, she is small but not petite, blonde and of fair complexion, carefully coiffed and immaculately dressed, often somewhat stern of visage but generally attractive, poised and seemingly self-confident. Whether Callaghan's checked tie clashes with his striped shirt was not commented on by journalists during the campaign, but it was reported regularly "what 'she' is wearing." She often used to wear hats, and they were caricatured by London newspaper cartoonists, along with the pearls and swooping manner that had characterized so many Tory women, but a shorter hairstyle has outmoded her hats anyway. She eschews flashy jewelry; pictures show her wearing a variety of earrings, but almost always the same relatively simple bracelet, and one decorative ring. She also avoids fussy clothes; most often she appears in fairly simple dresses or well tailored suits. How Mrs. Thatcher looks and what she wears are, in the long run of history, and even today, trivial matters. But to the readers of the London daily tabloids and at least some of the women's magazines, they seem to be matters that matter, and they are duly reported. For example, when addressing an audience in her Finchley constituency she complimented the women present on wearing blue, although "'I feel terribly guilty I am not wearing blue, but I am going to the television studios and the background is bright turquoise—so I have to wear brown. We girls must think about these things,' Mrs. Thatcher said with a smile."[63]

More significant than visual images in terms of developing a political personality is the impact upon candidates of public stereotypes and prejudices. Just being a woman, in England more than in America, jeopardizes a political career. Even though women gained complete voting equality in 1928, in the elections between the wars an average of only seven women were chosen for the House of Commons, and in the elections since 1945 an average of twenty-four.[64] During the Fifties the belief was that voters were less likely to vote for a woman than for a man, though this was more apparent among Conservative than among Labour candidates. In the two elections in the Sixties Conservative women candidates continued to be less successful than men of their party, but Labour women did somewhat better than the men. Studies of elections in the Seventies show that the bias against Conservative women candidates has disappeared, although the public myth of unequal treatment of women candidates persists.[65]

Where there is inequality, however, is in the selection of candidates. Given a knowledge of electoral history, of course, fewer women are inclined to seek nominations, and the persistence of the myth of male bias in the General Election reenforces them. Thus the proportion of women among all parliamentary candidates has never risen above 7 percent, and although the total number of women candidates increases, about the same total get elected (the high was 27 out of the 635 members of the House of Commons in the government that was dissolved in

March 1979), and thus the percentage of those women who run and are elected has declined almost by half in the past decade.[66] The net result is that about 4 percent of the MPs are women, usually a majority being Conservative when that party is in control, and Labour when that party controls. In either case it is traditional for the Prime Minister to appoint one woman member as a minister.[67] This gives women a fair proportion of their number in the House, but far less than in the electorate.

Among the voters at large women number slightly over half, and of those a majority—as in all democracies for which data is available—now regularly support the most conservative party. (Since women live longer than men, there is a special tilt toward the right, and it is thus estimated that the average Conservative lives long enough to take part in thirteen general elections, and the average Labour voter only in twelve.)[68] Nevertheless, as between the two major parties, women find it harder to be selected for nomination by Conservative constituency parties than do women seeking nomination by Labour constituencies.[69]

Political analysts in England attribute the low rate of participation by women to a mix of institutional influences that are political and social.[70] The political institutional barrier is simply that there has been skepticism about the potential of women for effectiveness in politics, and if any woman survives that basic male prejudice it is likely to be only in a constituency that is "safe" for the other party anyway. Margaret Roberts encountered this barrier in 1948. Her friend John Grant, manager of Blackwell's bookshop at Oxford, proposed to John Miller, chairman of the Dartford constituency, that she would make a good candidate. At first Miller was opposed to the suggestion, on the grounds that Dartford was an industrial south of London area with a traditional 20,000 vote majority for the Labour party candidate. A year later, nevertheless, and perhaps because of the bleakness of Conservative prospects, Margaret Roberts, the only female applicant, was given the nomination. As could have been expected, she lost in the general elections of both 1950 and 1951, but the youngest candidate in the country had the satisfaction of reducing the Dartford Labour majority by nearly half. In 1954 she put in for the seat at Orpington, but was not nominated, an outcome that did not greatly upset her since the year before, "with her usual efficiency," as one friend put it, she produced twins. When they were only four months old she sat for and passed her Bar finals; and it is not insignificant that she opted for legal work as a barrister (entitled to represent clients in higher courts) rather than as a solicitor (who ordinarily does not function as a courtroom advocate).

In 1957 Margaret Thatcher was ready to try politics again, and she applied for the nomination at Beckenham. Here she encountered the second of the institutional influences that tend to bar women from politics. While the selection committee at Dartford had seemingly welcomed a bright and attractive young woman, Beckenham saw no political virtue in motherhood: "You are a woman with young children, and we don't think you ought to contest an election."[71] At Maidenstone there was a similar response, but in 1958 success came at Finchley in north London, where in 1955 there had been a Conservative majority of over 12,000 votes. In that constituency she first stood for election in 1959 and was elected with an increased majority, to enter Parliament and the Conservative government of Harold Macmillan.

Although Margaret Thatcher continuously held her seat in Finchley, and by an increased majority in the May 1979 General Election, her successes have not been typical of women in politics. In the House of Commons that was dissolved in March there were twenty-seven women, but there are only nineteen in the House that assembled in May. (Most of the losses, of course, were Labour members, including the greatly respected Mrs. Shirley Williams and the young and impressive Mrs. Helene Haymen.)[72] Among the Thatcher department ministers there is only the one obligatory woman, Mrs. Sally Oppenheimer.

Although private Conservative party polls by March, 1979, showed Mrs. Thatcher attracting 50 percent of the women, while Prime Minister Callaghan was favored by only 30 percent,[73] her special appeal to women is not that she is a feminist. In her first press conference after being selected Leader of the party in 1975 she responded to a question about "Women's Lib" by asking "What has it ever done for me?"[74] In 1979, at a press conference in Glasgow on April 26, she was unchanged: "I don't like strident females. I like people who have ability and who don't run the feminist picket too hard. If you get somewhere it is because of your ability as a person, not because of your sex."[75] One is left with the assumption that Margaret Thatcher believes that if she could achieve so can other women, and without special legal assistance. "I think the fact that a woman had become Prime Minister would do something that no amount of legislation could," she told Tricia Murray. "It's practice that matters now far more than law. I would think it would be a tremendous boost to many women, especially those trying to reach the top in whatever sphere."[76]

The feminists responded mainly by writing critical letters to the newspapers.[77] Although during her national campaign tour Thatcher was generally protected against heckling, the feminists succeeded in making their rebuttal in person when a small group surrounded an election day meeting in Finchley, carrying banners and chanting, "We want women's rights, not a Right wing woman."[78]

The women that Margaret Thatcher appeals to are clearly not the feminists, but they are the housewives who read the major women's magazines, notable in England for their large circulations and longtime retention. Traditionally these publications have avoided articles that were in any way political, and have refused political advertisements. In recent years, however, they have been willing (or persuaded) to carry extensive interviews with Mrs. Thatcher.[79] In general these pieces have been devoid of any outright political pitch, but concentrated on the Thatcher "philosophy" about such matters as running a home and raising a family, and also having a public career. As longtime press secretary Derek Howe put it, Mrs. Thatcher declines to give bread recipes, but she is happy to talk about the importance of bread.[80]

The image of Thatcher the housewife is also promoted in her formal speeches and in informal walkabouts. She at least appears to enjoy making forays into shopping centers (followed by television news cameras) and comparing products and prices with other housewives. Certainly she smiled generously for a picture that made the front page of the *Daily Express*, holding up a large bag of groceries representing what one Tory pound bought in 1974, and another small bag to show how little the Labour pound would buy in 1979.[81] An American reporter was surprised by a typical Thatcher exercise in Birmingham: at the Cadbury chocolate factory she chatted with a worker who was to be married in a few days, discussing how to set up a routine for running a home and still keeping her job. "You've got to dovetail in all your shopping and think ahead the whole time, haven't you? And

when you've had a full day's work you don't want to go back to an untidy house."
Household budgets and planned housekeeping could become a habit, she assured
the young woman, just as they had in the Thatcher household.[82]

One final element of the Thatcher political personality that doubtless aggra-
vates the feminists, but seems not to bother her, is the way that her male colleagues refer to her as having male qualities of mind and male instincts for politics.
From a series of interviews by Tricia Murray it is easy to find examples:[83]

> *Lord Pannell, an MP from 1949 to 1974, recalled that in the famous 1975 contest
> that replaced Heath as Conservative Leader, "when the chips were down, she was
> the only one man enough in the Conservative Party to stand for the leadership."*
>
> *Sir Harold Wilson, an MP since 1945, and Labour Prime Minister, 1964–1970
> and 1974–1976: "Women politicians vary a great deal, as indeed do men, but you
> occasionally find that a woman politician is more of a man than any of the
> men…and I would say it's probably true of Mrs. Thatcher…who obviously
> possesses a great deal of feminine charm and good looks but who at the same
> time is as determined and relentless as any male politician."*
>
> *Andrew Faulds, a Labour MP who once referred to her as "that bloody woman" in
> a parliamentary debate: "I think she may need to put up a tough appearance to
> compensate for the fact that she's not a man…. Politics is more naturally a
> man's world. I think some women hold their own very well but I think they lessen
> their femininity and womanhood by holding their own very well—she's one of
> them."*

Within the Shadow Cabinet, Mrs. Thatcher assured Kenneth Harris, there are
no men or women, just politicians. "I'm not conscious of them as men at all," she
said. "Don't mistake me: I see A as taller than B; I see X as more handsome than Y.
What woman wouldn't? What man wouldn't have such perceptions about women?
But I don't see me and my colleagues in an 'I'm a woman, you are men relationship.' I'm conscious of my colleagues as different personalities. The differences
between them are so great that—it may sound strange—you hardly notice that they
are men and you are a woman."[84]

A SENSE OF CONVICTION

In one respect, however, Mrs. Thatcher does differ markedly from most of her male
colleagues. It is undoubtedly the most distinctive feature of her personal style and
deserves specific though brief notice: she is a self-pronounced "conviction politician." For a long time she had described herself as a reformer, bent on reversing
what she saw as the national decline resulting from the radicalism of the Labour
Party. But there were many who doubted that in a real contest she would hold so
staunchly to her equally radical conservative views; surely she would temper them
under campaign fire. In the spring of 1979, with an election inevitable at least
by fall, she reacted to the doubters in a statement given wide circulation in *The
Observer*: "I'm not a *consensus* politician or a *pragmatic* politician. I'm a *conviction* politician. And it's my job to put forward what I believe, and try to get people to
agree with me."[85] Throughout the campaign she refused to waffle on her ultimate
ends, though she was sometimes unclear about the means. The nation had had
enough of consensus on the middle road, even though some of her right wing

Conservative colleagues still travelled it. In a rousing campaign speech at Cardiff, in the Welsh country of Prime Minister Callaghan, and in her own sharp style, she said it all again: "I am a reformer and I am offering change." From the evangelical Welsh background she took her mission: "If you've got a message, preach it." Though she was in solid Labour territory she gave witness of the strength of her beliefs:

> *I am a conviction politician. The Old Testament prophets didn't say "Brothers, I want a consensus." They said: "This is my faith, this is what I passionately believe. If you believe it too, then come with me."*[86]

No Prime Minister in more than three decades had been so blunt in staking out an uncompromising position; some Tory ones had supported capitalism only softly, and some Labour ones had talked socialism in mild terms. They were all male politicians. Impatience with consensus-seeking and intensity of conviction may not be sex-related qualities, but among her peers it is Margaret Thatcher who clearly has them both.

For some voters the Thatcher style has been refreshing and for others frightening. Within the customary margin of error, the public opinion polls from the dissolution of Parliament to the General Election told the story. Relying upon published reports of polls by MORI (Market and Opinion Research International), just before the campaign began in earnest (slow getting underway because of the death of Airey Neave and the Easter holiday), the fallen Labourites commanded only 38 percent, the Liberals 10 percent, and the Conservatives 51 percent, a substantial majority that would easily sweep them into office if it could be maintained.[87] Without much variation during the campaign Labour steadied into a final "day of election" poll figure of 39.8 percent, the Liberals increased substantially to 13.5 percent and the Conservatives gradually declined to 44.4 percent, still enough to provide an ample margin of victory.[88]

Meanwhile the Conservative Leader fared far less well than her party. Just before the campaign began, those polled on the question of who would make the better Prime Minister gave 42 percent to Callaghan and 40 percent to Thatcher.[89] (At the same time a separate poll revealed that 47 percent were satisfied with Thatcher's leadership of the party, and 38 percent dissatisfied, a healthy shift from the 43 percent–45 percent figures in early March.)[90] By mid April the "better Prime Minister" question showed 45 percent for Callaghan, 37 percent for Thatcher.[91] The trend continued in a poll reported on April 25: 46 percent Callaghan, 33 percent Thatcher; by April 28 the report was 50 percent Callaghan, 31 percent Thatcher.[92] And in one final "day of election" poll that also offered the option of David Steel, the Liberal party Leader, Callaghan rose to 57 percent, Steel received 28 percent, and Thatcher fell sharply to 23 percent.[93]

One of the conclusions that may be drawn from these divergent figures, showing the Conservative party much stronger than its Leader, is that *Guardian* political columnist Peter Jenkins was correct when he told Robin Day on BBCI, as the election returns were being reported, that "she has fought less than a brilliant campaign."[94] The editor of *The Economist* looked at both sides of the coin: "Mrs. Thatcher has not had a good campaign, while Mr. Callaghan has had a very good one."[95] A derivative conclusion may also be drawn by saying that among the voters at large Mrs. Thatcher's political personality, the image that she projected, failed to generate a high degree of either confidence or enthusiasm.

Americans who reflect upon this matter must remember, however, that Mrs. Thatcher, wherever she may have campaigned, was not actually running for national office and did not solicit personal electoral support from the voters at large. The retention of her seat in the House of Commons depended only upon being "first past the post" (i.e., a plurality) in the five-candidate race in the 55,468 vote constituency of Finchley. The retention of her position as Leader of the Conservative party was not at stake at all, for it is dependent upon receiving a majority of votes of the parliamentary members of the party. And succeeding James Callaghan and becoming the new Prime Minister depended upon having enough other Conservative candidates winning election to constitute a House of Commons majority. Thus the question of how Mrs. Thatcher's personality was perceived by the voters at large was not a critical issue. What was important in the election was that the personality of each competing candidate for 635 constituency seats—including Mrs. Thatcher in Finchley—be favorably perceived.

Americans should also be interested in the way Mrs. Thatcher dealt with the matter of political personality. It came up when she received an invitation to appear in a face-to-face confrontation with Prime Minister Callaghan on two peak time television broadcasts. A presidential style debate would be alien to British broadcasting traditions of "presenting the whole policy of a party to the nation. . . . Personally, I believe that issues and policies decide elections, not personalities. We should stick to that approach. We are not electing a president, we are choosing a government."[96]

Mrs. Thatcher was, of course, quite correct in her assessment. Had the election been American style, obliging her to seek voter approval nationwide, the results of the "who would be the better Prime Minister" polls show that she would still be Leader of the Opposition. Had the election turned upon the question of who projected the most compelling image, Mr. Callaghan would still be the Prime Minister. But of course Callaghan's relaxed and avuncular, familiar and comforting image, so well projected on television, was not at issue; and neither was Thatcher's intense and proper, reserved and deliberately disturbing image. If anything, it could be said that British voters at large were willing to gamble on Mrs. Thatcher's political personality. What they were betting on was that a set of Tory policies and proposals would be better than the perceived failures of the Labour government. The British voters often, so their politicians and political scientists say, vote against the government instead of for the opposition. They did it again in May 1979.

One might well conclude this report by saying that it is reassuring to see a democracy function so that it may truly be said that the great decision was made upon "issues and policies . . . not personalities." It is an affirmation of Edmund Burke's advice to his British countrymen more than two hundred years ago: "Not men, but measures."

Notes

1. Mrs. Thatcher prefers to be called Mrs. Thatcher, and that governs the style of this report. Only London tabloid headline writers call her "Maggie."
2. John F. Kennedy, Foreword, *Decision-Making in the White House: The Olive Branch or the Arrows* (New York: Columbia Univ. Press, 1963), p. xii.

3. Interviewees are listed alphabetically and identified by positions held on the interview dates: Barbara Beck, secretary to Helene Hayman, Labour MP, March 9; Anthony Wedgewood Benn, Labour MP, Secretary of State for Energy, March 8; Patrick Cosgrave, historian, freelance political journalist, speechwriter for Mrs. Thatcher, March 14; Robin Day, BBC political interviewer, Radio 4 "Election Call" moderator, March 16; Barbara Hardy, Professor and Chairman, Dept. of Literature and Language, Birkbeck College, University of London, March 15; Kenneth Harris, associate editor, *The Observer*, April 3; Derek Howe, press secretary to Mrs. Thatcher, March 8; Robert Rhodes James, Conservative MP, March 16, April 4; Bryan Magee, Labour MP, April 3; James D. McCaffery, press secretary to Mr. Callaghan, April 2; Thomas McNally, political adviser and speechwriter for Mr. Callaghan, April 4; Eric Parsloe, president Eric Parsloe Industrial Communications, April 2; William Rees-Mogg, editor, *The Times*, March 9; Peter Riddell, economics correspondent, *Financial Times*, March 15; Jo Ryder, secretary to Kenneth Harris and Douglass Cater, *The Observer*, March 12, 14. While I have drawn heavily and generally upon the education provided me in these interviews, I have tried to be discreet in ascribing quotations.

4. 1961–1964, Minister of Pensions in Harold Macmillan's government; 1970–1974, Minister of Education in Edward Heath's cabinet.

5. Published sources with reasonably complete and biographical information are Patrick Cosgrave. *Margaret Thatcher: A Tory and Her Party* (London: Hutchinson, 1978); George Gardiner, *Margaret Thatcher* (London: Kimber, 1975); Russell Lewis, *Margaret Thatcher: A Personal and Political Biography* (London: Associated, 1975); Ernie Money, *Margaret Thatcher: First Lady of the House* (London: Frewin, 1975); Tricia Murray, *Margaret Thatcher* (London: W. H. Allen, 1978). Unless otherwise noted, biographical information used here is drawn from Cosgrave and from Murray.

6. Interview with Murray, pp. 77–78.

7. Paul Johnson, "Margaret Thatcher," *Illustrated London News*, May 1979, p. 45.

8. Murray, p. 41.

9. Murray, p. 42.

10. Cosgrave, p. 138.

11. Interview with Murray, pp. 148–150.

12. Murray, p. 145.

13. Cosgrave, p. 136.

14. Interview with Murray, pp. 83–84.

15. Richard Buckle, ed., *U and non-U Revisited* (London: Debrett's Peerage, Ltd., 1978), p. xi.

16. Buckle, p. xvi.

17. Buckle, p. 86.

18. *Newsweek* International Edition, May 14, 1979, p. 51.

19. *The Oxford Paperback Dictionary*, Joyce M. Hawkins, compiler (Oxford: Oxford Univ. Press, 1979).

20. Cosgrave, pp. 62–63. Gilmour speech in Trevor Russell, *The Tory Party: Its Policies, Divisions and Future* (Middlesex: Penguin, 1978), pp. 163–164.

21. *Financial Times*, March 31, 1979, p. 30.

22. *Newsweek* International Edition, April 9, 1979, p. 24.

23. *Newsweek* International Edition, April 30, 1979, p. 10.

24. *Newsweek* International Edition, May 14, 1979, p. 50.

25. *Time*, May 14, 1979, pp. 31, 32, 34.

26. Kenneth Hudson, *The Language of Politics* (London: Macmillan, 1978), pp. 51–55.

27. *The Observer*, February 16, 1979, p. 33.

28. In interviews with Murray: Walden, pp. 89–90; Modlyn, p. 104; Brown, pp. 121, 123.

29. Hudson, p. 105.

30. Johnson, p. 45.

31. Cosgrave, p. 114. Her bill did ultimately become law and made its contribution to overcoming government secretiveness, which has been called one of the two principal weaknesses in postwar Britain. Peter Calvocoressi, *The British Experience, 1945–75* (New York: Pantheon, 1978), p. 228.

32. Cosgrave, p. 191.

33. Cosgrave, pp. 198–208; Murray, pp. 9–10.

34. *Christian Science Monitor*, May 3, 1979, p. B19.

35. Hudson, p. 70.

36. *International Herald Tribune*, April 23, 1979; *Financial Times*, March 31, 1979; *Financial Times*, March 30, 1979.

37. Jean Blondel, *Voters, Parties and Leaders: The Social Fabric of British Politics* (Hamondsworth: Penguin, 1977 rev. ed.), p. 30.

38. Interviews with Rees-Mogg and Benn.

39. Harold Wilson, *The Governance of Britain* (London: Sphere, 1976), p. 114.

40. Douglas Hurd, *An End to Promises: Sketch of A Government, 1970–1974* (London: Collins, 1979), p. 76.

41. Hudson, p. 124.

42. Transcript of William F. Buckley, Jr., "Firing Line's British Correspondents," broadcast taped in London, June 27, 1978.

43. Based upon interviews with Cosgrave, Howe, Riddell and Hardy; Cosgrave, pp. 25–26.

44. Wilson, pp. 245–246.

45. Letter from Patrick Cosgrave, April 14, 1979; *Financial Times*, April 6, 1979.

46. Geoffrey Alderman, *British Elections* (London: Batsford, 1978), pp. 26–28.

47. In the first months of her administration even some persons who know her well were not prepared for the faithfulness of her proposed legislation to manifesto promises.

48. Murray, p. 17.

49. *Financial Times*, April 14, 1979.

50. See Tom Baistow, *The Guardian*, April 30, 1979, p. 12.

51. Hayward in *Evening News*, April 3, 1979; Terence Lancaster, *Daily Mirror*, April 5, 1979; editorial in *Evening News*, April 3, 1979.

52. *The Guardian*, March 30, 1979; Alan Watkins, "Maggie's Nerve is the Target," *The Observer*, April 1, 1979, p. 14.

53. *Financial Times*, March 15, 1979.

54. *Evening Standard*, April 4, 1979. Proportional allocations were also made to Mr. David Steel and the Liberal Party.

55. *Evening Standard*, April 9, 1979; *Financial Times*, April 14, 1979.

56. David McKie, Chris Cook and Melanie Phillips, *The Guardian/Quartet Election Guide* (London: Quartet, 1978), p. 13.

57. *International Herald Tribune*, April 23, 1979.

58. *Manchester Guardian Weekly*, April 29, 1979, p. 4.

59. *International Herald Tribune*, April 25, 1979.

60. Interview with Bonnie Angelo, *Time*, May 14, 1979, p. 33.

61. Lewis in *Manchester Guardian Weekly*, May 6, 1979, p. 3; Broder in *International Herald Tribune*, April 25, 1979, p. 4.

62. Representative articles in the daily press: Ian Aitkin, "Callaghan Vetoes Abuse of Thatcher," *The Guardian*, March 30, 1979; Leonard Downie, Jr., "Mrs. Thatcher Faces Issue of Being... Mrs. Thatcher," *International Herald Tribune*, April 23, 1979; Anne Edwards, "Will Men be Fair to the Lady?" *The Sunday Express*, April 1, 1979; George Gale, "Maggie's Double Challenge: She is something new and disturbing—not just because of her ideas, but because of her sex," *Daily Express*, March 29, 1979; Alan Rapheal, "Jim's Ray of Election Hope," *The Observer*, March 25, 1979.

63. *Daily Telegraph*, April 2, 1979.

64. Richard Rose, *Politics in England Today* (London: Faber & Faber, 1974), p. 149.

65. Alderman, pp. 84–85.

66. Alderman, p. 84.

67. Rose, p. 149.

68. Iain McLean, *Elections* (London: Longman, 1976), pp. 58–59. Also see Alderman, p. 168.

69. Alderman, pp. 83–84.

70. Rose, p. 149. Also see Blondel, pp. 53–54, 58, 168.

71. Johnson, p. 45.

72. The Conservatives fielded 31 women candidates, three fewer than in 1974, and increased their MPs from seven to eight; Labour fielded 52 women candidates, as against 38 in 1974, and had a net loss of seven, electing only eleven.

73. Interview with Derek Howe.

74. Cosgrave, p. 14.

75. Reuters despatch, *International Herald Tribune*, April 27, 1979.

76. Murray, p. 147.

77. See representative anti-Thatcher feminist letters, *The Guardian*, May 3, 1979, p. 11.

78. Michael White, "Thatcher Pushed and Jostled at Rally," *The Guardian*, May 3, 1979, p. 28.

79. It should be noted that with typical British even-handedness there have also been interviews with Mrs. Callaghan, but of course she was not running for office.

80. Interview with Howe.

81. *Daily Express*, April 25, 1979, p. 1.

82. Takashi Oka, *Christian Science Monitor*, May 3, 1979, p. B2. Also see Ferdinand Mount, *Spectator*, May 5, 1979, p. 4.

83. In Murray: Pannell, p. 109; Wilson, pp. 112–113; Faulds, p. 138.

84. Interview, *The Observer*, February 16, 1979, p. 33.

85. Interview with Kenneth Harris, *The Observer*, February 25, 1979, p. 33.

86. *Manchester Guardian Weekly*, April 22, 1979.

87. *Daily Express*, April 4, 1979.

88. *Financial Times*, May 3, 1979. The official results showed Labour at 36.9 percent, Liberals at 13.8 percent, and Conservatives at 43.9 percent. See *Manchester Guardian Weekly*, May 13, 1979.

89. *Daily Express*, April 4, 1979.

90. *Daily Express*, April 4, 1979; *The Guardian*, March 9, 1979.

91. *Daily Express*, April 25, 1979.

92. *Daily Express*, April 25, 1979; *The Guardian*, April 28, 1979.

93. *International Herald Tribune*, May 2, 1979. The MORI poll that day reported Callaghan at 46 percent, Thatcher at 38 percent, and "don't know" at 11 percent. See *Evening Standard*, May 3, 1979.

94. BBCI election night broadcast, May 3–4, 1979.

95. *The Economist*, May 5, 1979, p. 13.

96. *Financial Times*, April 4, 1979, p. 10.

A Fantasy Theme Analysis of the Television Coverage of the Hostage Release and the Reagan Inaugural

——————————— ERNEST G. BORMANN ———————————

The profound changes in the way members of a mass audience view the world as a result of television coverage of the breaking news have come gradually and almost imperceptibly. Most people have been watching television news for so long that they have learned how to participate in its dramatizations until it has become second nature to them. Most find the process natural and are unaware of how different the world seems to them today when compared to the social realities of the pre-television public. On occasion, however, some coverage of news events has such a startling effect on the viewing public that it reveals the stark outlines of what television news coverage has contributed to the development of social knowledge. The attempt of the major networks simultaneously to cover the release of the American hostages from Iran and President Reagan's inaugural address on January 20, 1981 provided a critical incident which threw the nature of the changes into sharp relief.

For the rhetorical critic using fantasy theme analysis to study political communication on the electronic media the nature of television's instantaneous coverage of the breaking news has become a more and more important puzzle.[1] Many scholars have documented the dramatic or theatrical features of news coverage and, yet, in other respects the camera shows the viewer pictures of events as they happen.[2] The dramatic nature of televised news and public affairs invites fantasy theme analysis but such analysis is inappropriate to the critical study of the direct experience of events.

The intertwined coverage of the hostage return and the inaugural address provided a good opportunity to test the usefulness of fantasy theme analysis in examining television journalism because the two big stories coming to climaxes at the same time taxed the dramatizing ability of the medium and made it easier for a critic to bring the tacit and seldom examined dimensions of TV coverage to conscious analysis.[3]

In this essay I make a rhetorical critical analysis of the television coverage of the hostage release and Reagan's inaugural address using the method of fantasy theme analysis to examine how the dramatization of unfolding events on television creates a social reality for those who are caught up in the portrayal.[4]

My critical analysis compares the subliminal impact of the public affairs coverage of the inaugural and the hostage release on television to the way Reagan and his speechwriters employed the recurring and powerful fantasy type of restoration to meet the needs of a conservative political and economic movement in the 1980s. The comparative analysis examines how the intertwining of the hostage coverage with the portrayal of the inaugural address worked to reinforce and amplify the core fantasy of the speech.

TELEVISION NEWS COVERAGE
AND SHARED FANTASIES

Fantasies are dramatizations of events not in the here-and-now experience of speaker and listener. This is a crucial element in the symbolic convergence theory of communication.[5] The immediate experience of the inaugural might be chaotic and confusing. Eye-witness observers might hear sirens on the street and cease to listen to the speech while they crane their heads to see what has happened. There might be a confused murmur or shouting from some of the crowd. An airplane might fly overhead. Messages that contain rhetorical fantasies cast there-and-then events in narrative frames and provide a structured, understandable, and meaningful interpretation of what happened. The speaker will attribute motives, purposes, and causes to the people in the story and will fit the events into a meaningful sequence of events. Fantasies always provide an organized artistic explanation of happenings and thus create a social reality which makes sense out of the blooming buzzing confusion of the experience.

Later eyewitness accounts of the inaugural by someone who was there are clearly fantasy themes. Newspaper accounts of the inaugural are also clearly fantasy themes. But much TV coverage of the return of the hostages and the inaugural was instantaneous. The viewer could see and hear the president give the speech on the TV monitor. Thus, TV coverage of breaking news is often not composed of fantasies as I have defined them.

Still, the way television journalism has evolved news coverage resembles the dramatizing messages in small groups and other public communication much more than it does the direct personal experience of the event. Television coverage, like a rhetorical fantasy, presents a structured narrative composed of personae in dramatic action.[6]

Television news coverage is in many respects an exercise in creative dramatics in which a cast of familiar characters assembles (anchor persons, on-the-spot reporters, background commentators, and so forth) and improvises a drama according to a stock scenario depending upon the news event. Professional television journalists know how to improvise on camera the scripts of a presidential inaugural or an act of international terrorism. Audience members, too, have learned how to interpret and appreciate such performances.[7] Knowing the essential story line makes it easier for the members of the audience to follow along and make sense out of what is happening.

The whole news production is stitched together artistically by the director who like a film editor cuts, switches, dissolves, runs split screens, and so forth. The end result of the television coverage is an interpretative dramatization that provides the possibility of audience participation much like the sharing of a fantasy in other situations. Although coverage of breaking news events is instantaneous for some segments and although it insinuates into our subconscious the impression that we are experiencing the here-and-now, we are, in fact, presented with a complex, recursive set of images, stories nested within stories, formed, interpreted, artistic, concocted. When we are drawn into these scripts we share the social reality they portray with their implied values, motives, and explanations.

When one of the big events around which the television news team is improvising the drama is a rhetorical affair such as an acceptance speech, a rally speech, or an inaugural speech, the nesting involves fantasy themes within the speech itself. Thus, at one level we get scripts portrayed by network personalities, at another level we get the inaugural speech drama with the personae of the president, the chief justice, spouses, and so forth, and then when President Reagan dramatized the persona of "Martin Treptow—who left his job in a small-town barber shop in 1917..." we reach the level of the fantasy theme within the speech.[8]

At each level we may participate sympathetically in the drama. We can identify or empathize with the kindly powerful persona of a Walter Cronkite and chuckle when some background commentator makes a snide remark about how well the actor Reagan will read his lines. We can then refuse to empathize or identify with the persona of Ronald Reagan when the director cuts to coverage of the inaugural ceremony and speech. Or we can be repelled by the journalist who makes a satirical crack about the Reagan persona and identify with that persona when the direct coverage of the speech begins and also share the fantasy about the persona of Martin Treptow, the common man hero in Reagan's peroration, when we move down to the level of the fantasy within the speech.

TELEVISION COVERAGE
AND THE SUBLIMINAL
SUGGESTION OF RESTORATION

In the speech itself Reagan redramatized a version of one of the most venerable and powerful fantasy types in the history of American public address. He used the fantasy type of "Restoration." According to Reagan's restoration theme, the original founders of the new nation set the basic values and standards of the United States. Subsequent failures of the government and the society to meet these standards were not evidence that American institutions and American society were outmoded, structurally flawed, or inherently at fault. Rather, the problems stemmed from a falling away from the authentic and true basis of society as established by the founders. Reagan's restoration fantasy directed the nation to return to its original basis and rightness.

How did the dramatizations the teams of public affairs broadcasters presented on television on the occasion of the hostage return and the inaugural support and amplify the renewal and return theme of the speech itself?

To answer this question I have to spell out in greater detail an explanation of how we have learned to process data when we watch television. The anlaysis comes from the way computer scientists who are studying artificial intelligence deal with such problems.[9]

The technical term for the process of keeping track of the nested stories and fitting them together into some kind of cognitive scheme is a *push-down stack*. A crude sort of push-down stack is furnished by a cafeteria tray holder in which clean trays can be pushed down for storage and as a customer takes off the top tray another pops up. Here is the way it works in terms of watching television. You are in your living room talking to someone when something on the television screen catches your attention. You push down (mentally) to participate in the television program. After a bit you pop back up and continue your conversation with the other person. Or you push down again into the television program where Walter Cronkite is discussing the hostage release. Cronkite takes you to Wiesbaden for an on-the-spot report and you push down to Wiesbaden. From Wiesbaden the on-the-spot reporter takes you to a telephone report from a Reuter's reporter in Tehran, so you push down into the telephone account after which you pop back up to Wiesbaden and then you pop back up to Cronkite who continues. But how do you keep all that straight? How can you remember to allow Cronkite to pick up his commentary where he left off before we pushed down to Wiesbaden? We locate the information in a stack. The stack keeps track of where we were in each unfinished task (in computer terms the *return address*) and the relevant facts at the time we pushed away (in computer terms the *variable bindings*).

We are generally pretty good at stacking because most of us have learned to watch television news coverage over many years. Still, if we pop back to our conversation in the living room when we have stacked three or so levels and then push down into the world of the TV screen after some minutes we often have to ask, "What's going on?"

If the coverage was only of the hostage release or only of the inauguration most Americans probably could have pushed, popped, and stacked and kept track of what was going on. They could have processed the information without getting the disturbing feeling of confusion and overload that many commented on. But when the two coverages were intertwined so viewers might have to pop down from Cronkite to a reporter watching President Carter walk to the inauguration platform and then pop directly to an on-the-spot report from Algeria where a camera was supplying pictures although the voice-over was coming from a commentator somewhere else, and they then popped back to Cronkite, viewers found it difficult to remember the right return addresses and the right variable bindings.

The juxtaposition of the push-down stacks of the coverage of the hostage return and the preinaugural speech coverage created a montage of images and sounds which on occasion communicated chaos and confusion. What was happening? Had the hostages been released? A press service flashed such a report but it was wrong. Had the airplanes left? Were they being held until Reagan took the oath of office? All this pushing, popping, stacking created a montage which aroused emotions such as suspense, despair, hope, and weariness. Over the months the hope and despair over the hostages had created a symbolic climate conducive to getting the hostage problem out of the consciousness of the viewers, and letting them turn to something else, to start anew with a different drama, one less frustrating and more hopeful.

Into this atypically complicated and confusing coverage in which even the anchor personae seemed unsure and confused at times, the directors cut to the level of the Reagan inaugural speech and held there. Suddenly viewers were invited to participate in only one familiar script which portrayed an ordered, structured social reality where a confident persona was in control.

The script editors in the control room could hardly have done a better job of portraying the speech itself if the Reagan people had written the video directions. They did not interrupt the speech once to go to "our man in Wiesbaden" or anyplace else. They did not even distract the viewer by superimposing a running tape to the effect, "There are reports that the hostages are leaving Iran. No official confirmation as yet." More importantly, their selection of shots, their montage, was reverential and supportive.

I will give only one example of how one director selected shots to support Reagan's script.[10] Towards the close of the speech Reagan noted that this was the first time the ceremony was held on the West Front of the Capitol. Then he said, "Standing here, one faces a magnificent, vista, (*The director called up a long shot of the magnificent vista.*) opening up on this city's special beauty and history. At the end of this open mall (*The director had the camera pan up the open mall.*) are those shrines to the giants on whose shoulders we stand. Directly in front of me, the monument to a monumental man: (*Cut to a shot of Washington's monument*). George Washington, father of our country. . . ." After an encomium to Washington Reagan said, "Off to one side, (*Cut to a shot of the Jefferson Memorial.*) the stately memorial to Thomas Jefferson." After some words of praise for Jefferson, Reagan continued, "and then beyond the reflecting pool, the dignified columns of the Lincoln Memorial (*Camera moves to Lincoln Memorial*)." When Reagan next directed his audience's attention to the "sloping hills of Arlington National Cemetery with its row upon row of simple white markers bearing crosses or Stars of David. . ." The director had the camera focus on the cemetery.

Under the pressure of the demands of enacting the intertwining plots the news teams at times seemed to lose control of the improvisations. As the directors cut back and forth from the inaugural ceremony script prior to the speech itself and to the hostage terrorist script the leading players such as the anchor personae and the background color commentators and on-the-spot reporters did their best but in the overall integration of various segments of the production the result often seemed to be chaotic. David S. Broder, columnist for the *Washington Post*, had this response: "My head—like yours—is swimming in the vivid images of the hostages' release and homecoming, overlaid on the pageantry of the change of governments. . . . We have seen history unfolding through the camera lens in that special way—of instant replays laid atop each other—that fills the consciousness with a montage of dramatically intense scenes and almost obliterates understanding."[11]

By accident or luck or both, the juxtaposition of the halting and sometimes confusing overlay of images from one script on to another with the confident and smooth presentation of the inaugural itself served to draw the viewer into participation in a restoration fantasy.

The anchor personae in television news programs are stock characters of unusual power who rule a magical world in which they can whisk the viewer to anyplace on the globe and call forth a host of spirits to do their bidding. For the anchor personae on this occasion, however, the demands of trying to enact two scripts at the same time sometimes resulted in viewer confusion and overload. Indeed, the actors themselves seemed on occasion to be confused and overloaded. Were they now in the inauguration script or were they playing the hostage return scenario? Or were they trying to integrate the two as subplots in some larger drama? Compared to the usually poised but now harried network professionals the Reagan persona while delivering the inaugural appeared more in charge of things. He was even, apparently, in charge of calling some of the camera shots as in the case of the supporting images of the shrines to the heroes of the past.

The powerful persona's message was one of restoration and renewal. After the speech the viewers popped back to the level of the anchor personae and, while the reporters in the booth commented about the speech and about the next steps for the new president, the director called up images of various prominent personae milling around the inauguration site. They then cut to shots of President Carter and his wife leaving the Capitol. The anchor personae called in the on-the-spot reporters. The directors held the shot of the Carters entering their limousine and then pulled back to show the caravan of the former president moving down the Avenue.

The on-the-spot reporter for CBS remarked that the transition was now complete and then the director cut back to Walter Cronkite who returned to the hostage script. While there were a few moments of uncertainty as the various news services and sources gave conflicting reports as to whether or not the hostages were free, within a few minutes of the departure of the Carter persona all networks were reporting that the hostages were airborne. No sooner had the Reagan and Carter personae completed the acting out of the transfer of power than the confusion was dispelled, the hostages were free and now the inaugural script was essentially complete and the coverage could switch to the playing out of the hostage script and the viewer could concentrate on the triumphant journey of the hostages from tyranny to freedom. Here was joy; here was relief; the bad times of the hostage crisis were over. A new day had dawned.

Although Reagan's inaugural does not contain references to the hostages the television coverage associated his persona with their release in montages which conveyed the powerful suggestion at the fringes of awareness that there was a new actor on the world's stage, an actor who had no sooner taken over control than events began to fall into ordered and structured form.

The Carter persona symbolized the hostage crisis. The drama of the swearing in of the new president enacted the transfer of power. The new presidential persona was then mingled in montages with the personae of the hostages as they left Iran. The confusing, complicated, chaotic events of the hostage crisis aroused strong desires for explanation and meaning. But most viewers had neither the time nor the means to study and understand these events. When they saw them acted out by personae on the television screens in simple scripts they could understand; they had an explanation. To be sure, the explanation was one which suffered from the logical fallacy of *post hoc ergo propter hoc* and assumed that the Carter and Reagan personae had great power to influence the course of events but in those regards the explanation was typical of the way masses of people usually make sense out of complicated questions. Reagan emerged from the coverage as the persona who symbolized a new day dawning.

The suggestion worked hand in glove with the content of Reagan's message that what was needed was not a move to new and dangerous programs nor a continuation of the status quo but rather a change that would restore the basis of past national greatness—a great leap forward to be accomplished only after a firm step backward. The identification suggested that just as the release of the hostages returned us to the more tranquil precrisis times of the *status quo ante* so too the new administration would return us to the more satisfying days of economic boom times and American world power.

With the television coverage working at a subliminal level to support Reagan's central fantasy it becomes important to examine critically the way that his speechwriters artistically adapted the restoration fantasy type to the audience and occasion of the 1981 Presidential Inaugural.

REAGAN'S SPEECH AND
THE RHETORICAL DEVELOPMENT
OF RESTORATION

The restoration fantasy type has been a continuing and powerful religious rhetorical form in this country. The fantasy type was imported to the new world by the first Puritan settlers, who wished to purify the church and restore it to its old piety. In the 1820s and 1830s another Christian restoration movement emerged under the leadership of Alexander Campbell and grew rapidly. The Campbellites sought to restore on the nineteenth-century American frontier the patterns of primitive Christianity as they dramatized them.[12]

But the restoration fantasy type has been equally important in political rhetoric. While the Disciples of Christ were seeking to restore the primitive Christian Church, Andrew Jackson's partisans were arguing for a restoration of the political system of the United States to its true and basic foundations. The core drama of the

Jacksonian persuasion as Marvin Meyers demonstrated was restoration.[13] In Jackson's rhetoric the "real people" whom he personified as a class of industrious folks such as planters, farmers, mechanics and laborers, "the bone and sinew of the country," have been exploited by antirepublican forces who were "intriguers and politicians" and their lackeys "who thrive on political consolidation, chartered privilege, and speculative gain." They created the vicious national bank as "but one of the fruits of a system at war with the genius of all our institutions."

They distrust the popular will and their ultimate object "is the consolidation of all power in our system in one central government."[14] Marvin Meyers sums up the Jacksonian persuasion: "Jackson's appeal for economic reform suggests at bottom a dismantling operation: an effort to pull down the menacing constructions of federal and corporate power, and restore the wholesome rule of 'public opinion and interests of trade'.... Yet, if Jackson gives promise of catching every man's particular enemy in a broad aristocracy trap, does he not promise still more powerfully a reformation and a restoration: a return to pure and simple ways?"[15]

The restoration theme has appeared again and again down through history from Andrew Jackson to Ronald Reagan. Lincoln used the restoration drama widely. In Lincoln's version the Dred Scott decision and Douglas's Doctrine of Popular Sovereignty were part of a conspiracy by pro-slavery forces to fasten slavery on the country forever and what was needed was to reform and restore the country by returning slavery to its original place in the constitutional view of things, namely, keeping the soil of the territories free and defining it as a moral evil on the way to extinction.[16]

How does Reagan use the restoration fantasy type? In Reagan's drama the "real people" of Jacksonian persuasion are to be found in a special group that knows "no sectional boundaries or ethnic and racial division.... It is made up of men and women who raise our food, patrol our streets, man our mines and factories, teach our children, keep our homes and heal us when we are sick—professionals, industrialists, shopkeepers, clerks, cabbies and truck drivers. They are, in short, We the people, this breed called Americans."

Like Jackson, Reagan sees the problem as resulting from the consolidation of government and from the belief that "society has become too complex to be managed by self-rule, that government by an elite group is superior to government for, by and of the people." Reagan, like Jackson, will dismantle the over-blown governmental machinery and restore it to its original form. He said, "It is my intention to curb the size and influence of the federal establishment" and a bit later he adds that he intends "to make it work—work with us, not over us; to stand by our side, not ride on our back." After portraying the current evils and suggesting the proper remedy, Reagan appeals to the American people, "So, with all the creative energy at our command, let us begin an era of national renewal." A bit later he adds, "Steps will be taken aimed at restoring the balance between various levels of government." And he goes on to claim that, "It is time to reawaken this industrial giant, to get government back within its means and lighten our punitive tax burden."

And then the final appeal. "As we renew ourselves here in our own land, we will be seen as having greater strength throughout the world. We will again be the exemplar of freedom and the beacon of hope for those who do not now have freedom."

How does the fantasy of restoration, of a return to the basis of the foundation of government, function rhetorically? The restoration fantasy contains a mixture of reform and conservatism. It allows those who participate in it to eliminate the imperfections of the here-and-now without converting to an entirely new rhetorical vision. The restoration fantasy is conservative in the most fundamental sense of keeping intact the major structural features of the unifying elements of the older American visions and dream.

A rhetoric of unity and conservatism needs to celebrate the entire community and for that purpose it requires a common heritage. What Reagan's restoration fantasy implied was a need to return the nation to its original basis and greatness. The result of sharing such a fantasy is a celebration of the founding of the government. The United States had been founded on a universal and perfect basis of freedom and therefore it is adequate to all the demands of the present and future if the posterity of the founders are but wise enough to restore the country to its original basis whenever new conditions and corruption from evil human design or error cause problems. Such a present problem was the monstrous consolidation of the Federal Government. Interestingly enough it was the very same consolidation represented by their Federalist political foes and the evil national bank that the Jacksonians saw as the reason for the problems of their day.

A crucial feature of the restoration fantasy type is the reliance on unifying personae drawn from already established rhetorical visions. The conservative speaker who decides to adapt the fantasy type of restoration to present conditions has a simpler task than the radical who wishes to destroy the structures of society and who tries to envision a utopian new future. The revolutionary rhetor needs to create fantasy chains which will establish new heroes and destroy those of the established visions. Conservative rhetors can usually rely on established heroes. Their task is to blow on the old coals and start the fires anew. The conservative persuasive speech can succeed by telling the people what they already know and believe. The conservative need only make a judicious selection of old heroes and remind the audience of their virtues and good actions. The rhetorical means for such allusions is usually the encomium, a statement of high praise of the individual.

Long elaborate encomiums filled with fantasy themes in which the individual is the sympathetic protagonist serve to stimulate fantasy sharing and create rhetorical visions with their heroic persona. Once the rhetorical vision is established speakers can use the inside joke phenomenon to mention or allude to the heroic persona and trigger meanings and emotions reminiscent of those aroused by the original sharing.[17]

The speaker needs to only mention the name of Thomas Jefferson to those who share a rhetorical vision in which Jefferson's persona symbolizes all that is good about representative democracy to arouse the proper response for the restoration drama. On the other hand, the audience may contain people who have shared a fantasy in which Jefferson is a symbol of the hypocrisy which typifies a racist society because he fathered a child by his slave and sold his own child into slavery.[18] Those whose rhetorical vision includes Jefferson as a villain will be repelled by an encomium on him and the unifying function of the restoration fantasy will backfire.

Speechwriters for a presidential inaugural which stresses restoration must adapt wisely to the audience and the occasion in selecting personae to symbolize past glories. They must also take care not to use too few for if they do the renewal of commitment may be too weak for the occasion. On the other hand, if they use too many the audience members may grow bored. The nineteenth-century ceremonial orator could often successfully use many long encomiums during the course of a leisurely oration of an hour or more on the 4th of July or some similar occasion because the audience members were connoisseurs of a style of communication in which such devices were expected and appreciated.[19] The twentieth-century speaker is well advised to use only a few heroic personae and blend them into brief montages suitable to the quickened pace of television coverage.

Jacksonian rhetoricians often pronounced encomiums on the leaders of the Revolutionary War period with a special emphasis on Thomas Jefferson. Reagan pronounced an encomium on "one of the greatest among the Founding Fathers, Dr. Joseph Warren." His brief allusion to Warren was unlikely to result in a sharing of a fantasy about him and the number of people watching on TV who participated in a rhetorical vision in which Joseph Warren was established as a central heroic persona was probably quite small. The speechwriters probably erred in using the Warren persona. Much more effective was Reagan's closing section of the inaugural in which he used the brief encomiums of Washington, Jefferson, and Lincoln. When the television directors reinforced Reagan's words with a suitable montage of images the effect was strengthened.

The speechwriters' selection of Washington, Jefferson, and Lincoln ran the risk of being banal but these three symbols had the virtue of appealing to the broadest base of rhetorical visions. If there still is an appreciable national saga these three personae probably represent the most unifying symbols of that saga.[20] They can stand for the former greatness of the country which the speaker seeks to restore without much danger of triggering feelings of repulsion from viewers whose vision portrays them as villainous.

All who share the fantasy of a golden age when a group of founders possessing the wisdom of demi-gods laid down a perfect (or most perfect to date) system for society have a common bond, a symbolic connection with the period of the founders and the founders themselves. They share a history and such a common history is a necessary part of becoming a community.

The restoration fantasy worked most powerfully for members of the television audience who still participated in a national saga which sees the United States as the great experiment in self-government (". . . government for, by and of the people" ". . . to preserve this last and greatest bastion of freedom. . ."), a special nation chosen by God or Providence to be a beacon, a City on the Hill, for the world ("I believe God intended us to be free." "We will again be the exemplar of freedom and the beacon of hope for those who do not have freedom."), which sees the free enterprise system and individual initiative as superior to other ways of organizing the economy (". . . we unleashed the energy and individual genius of man. . . ." "There are entrepreneurs with faith in themselves and faith in an idea who create new jobs, new wealth and opportunity.").

There are, of course, a substantial number of rhetorical visions in the United States which contain fantasies that denigrate and ridicule the older national saga as unrealistic, hypocritical, chauvinistic, and jingoistic. Members of such rhetorical visions may well have been repelled by the restoration fantasy as portrayed by network coverage of the Reagan inaugural and may find Reagan's use of code words drawn from it and allusions to it as irrelevant emotionalism or "mere rhetoric." Those who no longer share in the older national saga nor in any of the rhetorical visions which are antithetical to it may not have been irritated or disturbed by the coverage but were likely to be apathetic and unmoved by it.

Does the old restoration fantasy type which was such a powerful and popular narrative frame for rhetoricians in the 1830s still have persuasive force in the 1980s? Of course a complete answer to such a question would require data from an extensive and expensive public opinion poll.[21] There are, however, some intriguing hints that a sympathetic chain reaction spread through large segments of the populace, even into unexpected corners. On the PBS program "Washington Week in Review" one of the network persona, Haynes Johnson, summed it up this way. (Johnson was a hardbitten, cynical newsman, an apparent participant in the "inside-dopester" rhetorical vision typical of professional journalists.)[22] "President Reagan read his lines superbly and the inaugural address sharing the screen with the joyous news of the release of the hostages brought us all together in a unity we haven't felt for many years."

Certainly the compositor of the *Minneapolis Tribune* seemed to share the fantasy. The front page of that newspaper on January 21, 1981 juxtaposes the two events and stresses the renewal theme. The layout suggests the identification between the new Reagan persona now in power and the end of the hostage crisis. Excerpts from letters to the editor from the January 25th Minneapolis paper indicate how the fantasy worked to arouse positive emotional responses:

> *It was a very long time in coming but Americans were hit by two waves of hope in one day: a new president and the homecoming of the hostages. The prescribed medicine for a weary country couldn't have been better.*[23]

> . . .

> *I had tears in my eyes at hearing that our people had finally come to the end of what must have been a terrible hardship, and one that will live with them forever. Also, tears of joy upon hearing President Reagan's speech. I can't remember having been so moved in years.*[24]

Television coverage of the breaking news is surrounded with the aura of objectivity and reality. The rhetorical vision of many news people includes the fantasy that they report the facts objectively and that their duty is to inform the public. Viewers may well accept the suggestion that news programs differ from imaginative dramatic fare because such programs create the illusion that they report the facts realistically. Television coverage of breaking news may present pictures of things as they happen as was the case in a number of on-the-scene reports of the inaugural and the hostage return and this camera eye view of events heightens the illusion of factuality. The pictures, however, are stitched into dramatically improvised scenes. The viewer sees an artistic, interpretative, organized portrayal of social reality.

Scholars using fantasy theme analysis employ a common theoretical base and a set of clearly defined technical concepts that enable them to compare and contrast findings from study to study and to accumulate knowledge about communication practices in general. Television is a major source of social knowledge and the rhetorical critical study of such knowledge can make a large contribution to the understanding of communication in a mass media society. If fantasy theme analysis can be applied to such messages it will appreciably enlarge the scope of the method and make possible the application of findings from studies of rhetorical fantasies in other contexts to them. The joint coverage of the inaugural and the hostage return provided a good opportunity to test the usefulness of fantasy theme analysis in the critical study of public affairs and news programs on television. This study applied the findings from a number of previous fantasy theme studies to the television coverage of these important news events. Had the two events not been intertwined it would be more difficult to discern that a fantasy theme analysis of the inaugural coverage on television differed from a similar criticism of the text of the speech that could be found in the newspapers the next day. With the intertwining it became clear that not only was the restoration fantasy type a part of the content of the speech; it was also enacted by the television coverage of the "hard news" of that historic day.

Notes

1. For studies which brought the problem into focus see Charles R. Bantz, "Television News: Reality and Research," *Western Speech Communication*, 39 (1975), 123–130; Ernest G. Bormann, "The Eagleton Affair: A Fantasy Theme Analysis," *Quarterly Journal of Speech*, 59 (1973), 143–159.

2. For representative studies using a dramatistic orientation towards television news and particularly television coverage of politics see Edward Jay Epstein, *News from Nowhere* (New York: Vintage Books, 1974); James E. Combs, *Dimensions of Political Drama* (Santa Monica, Ca.: Goodyear Publishing, 1980).

3. A number of commentators at the time of the broadcasts reported their perceptions of the overload conditions. David S. Broder, columnist for the *Washington Post* wrote, "I don't know about anyone else, but my senses and emotional circuits are suffering from drastic overload." *Minneapolis Tribune*, 28 January 1981, p. 12A; Don Morrison, columnist for the *Minneapolis Star*, wrote in a similar vein, "Surely, it was one of the strangest days in the national experience. Yesterday presented a turbulent swirl of simultaneous events, each competing for what should have been our undivided attention and, together, turning everyone's fever chart of emotions into a jagged up-and-down blur. . . . Well, of course we cared about the hostages and the inauguration but we have just gone through a severe case of blow-by-blow electronic overload, exciting but chaotic." 21 January 1981, p. 3B.

4. For the technique of fantasy theme analysis see Ernest G. Bormann, "Fantasy and Rhetorical Vision: The Rhetorical Criticism of Social Reality," *Quarterly Journal of Speech*, 58 (1972), 396–407.

5. For an explanation of the symbolic convergence theory of communication see Ernest G. Bormann, *Communication Theory* (New York: Holt, Rinehart and Winston, 1980). The symbolic convergence theory and fantasy theme analysis differ from many other dramatistic approaches to communication in that they do not explain direct experience. Rather fantasy theme analysis examines messages which dramatize events in the past, in the future, or at some other place. For other dramatistic approaches such as those of Burke, Duncan, Berger, and Goffman see James E. Combs and Michael W. Mansfield, eds., *Drama in Life; The Uses of Communication in Society* (New York: Hastings House, 1976). For a critique of viewing direct social experience as theatre see Sheldon L. Messinger, Harold Sampson, and Robert D. Towne, "Life as Theatre: Some Notes on the Dramaturgic Approach to Social Reality," in Combs and Mansfield, pp. 73–83.

6. *Persona* is a technical term in fantasy theme analysis. One prominent term for a somewhat similar concept is *image*. Image as a concept does not catch the richness of the function of characters in fantasy themes, however. Image implies a static quality. Image also implies a hard reality which is more or less reflected by the image. Persona implies the public role or

face presented in the dramatized messages and may or may not be similar to the individual that people experience in direct social interaction. Persona also implies a dynamic changing characterization which unfolds during the sharing of fantasies about the persona. Persona does not imply that there is a "real" person whose reality is more or less reflected by the persona which is a shared social construct with which people may sympathize, empathize, or identify.

7. Additional evidence for shared scripts comes from cognitive psychologists who have found that individuals organize their cognitions around scripts and from scholars working with artificial intelligence studies of computers who have used scripts as the organizing principle to program computers to respond intelligently to questions. See, for example, R. P. Abelson, "Script Processing in Attitude Formation and Decision Making," in J. S. Carroll and J. W. Payne, eds., *Cognition and Social Behavior* (Hillsdale, N.J.: Lawrence Erlbaum Associates, 1976); R. Schank and R. P. Abelson, *Scripts, Plans, Goals, and Understanding* (Hillsdale, N.J.: Lawrence Erlbaum Associates, 1977).

8. All quotations from Reagan's inaugural address are taken from the text as reported in the *Minneapolis Tribune*, 21 January 1981, p. 9A.

9. With some modifications I take my analogy comparing the processing of television news fantasies with computer data processing from Douglas Hofstadter, *Godel, Escher, Bach: An Eternal Golden Braid* (New York: Vintage Books, 1980), pp. 127–129.

10. This example is taken from CBS television's coverage. NBC's director took a shot of the long vista with Washington's Monument in the background but did not cut to each monument in turn. However, the overall shot selection on NBC was also supportive of the content.

11. Broder.

12. For a fantasy theme analysis of how the Disciples of Christ used the restoration fantasy see Carl Wayne Hensley, "Rhetorical Vision and the Persuasion of a Historical Movement: The Disciples of Christ in Nineteenth Century American Culture," *Quarterly Journal of Speech*, 61 (1975), 250–264.

13. *The Jacksonian Persuasion* (Stanford: Stanford University Press, 1960).

14. Meyers, p. 20.

15. Meyers, p. 25.

16. Lincoln developed rhetorical changes on the fantasy type in great and repetitive detail during the Lincoln-Douglas debates. See Paul M. Angle, ed., *Created Equal? The Complete Lincoln-Douglas Debates of 1858* (Chicago University of Chicago Press, 1958).

17. For a study of the inside-joke phenomenon in mass media communication see Ernest G. Bormann, Jolene Koester, and Janet Bennett, "Political Cartoons and Salient Rhetorical Fantasies: An Empirical Analysis of the '76 Presidential Campaign," *Communication Monographs*, 45 (1978), 317–329.

18. "And Jefferson, author of the *immortal declaration of* 1775,...was a slave holder to the day of his death, the *father* of a *slave daughter*, who was sold in the *New Orleans Market for a thousand dollars*." from Susan B. Anthony's "No Union With Slaveholders" in Ernest G. Bormann, ed., *Forerunners of Black Power: The Rhetoric of Abolition* (Englewood Cliffs, N.J.: Prentice-Hall, 1971), p. 194.

19. For an analysis of communication styles and how they function see Bormann, *Communication Theory*.

20. *Saga* is a technical term in fantasy theme analysis and refers to detailed narratives of the achievement and events in the life of a person, a group, a community, an organization, or a nation. To function, the saga, like the fantasy, must be shared. People residing within the borders of a country may share a number of different and conflicting rhetorical visions but unless there is a national saga to which most or all citizens are committed they will not form a national community.

21. The methodology required to integrate public opinion polling and marketing research with symbolic convergence theory is in the process of being worked out. See John F. Cragan and Donald C. Shields, *Applied Communication Research: A Dramatistic Approach* (Prospect Heights, Ill: Waveland Press, 1981) and Ernest G. Bormann and David L. Rarick, "Uses of Q Methodology and Phone Survey Techniques in a Study of Rhetorical Visions During Campaign, 1980," paper presented at the Central States Speech Association Convention, Chicago, April, 1981.

22. For a study of the "inside-dopester" rhetorical vision of the professional media journalist see Bormann, "The Eagleton Affair."

23. *Minneapolis Star*, 25 January 1981, p. 14A.

24. *Minneapolis Star*, 25 January 1981, p. 14A.

The Passionate Negation: The Chartist Movement in Rhetorical Perspective

—————————————— JAMES R. ANDREWS ——————————————

In 1781 Abigail Adams wisely observed that "It is from a wide and extensive view of mankind that a just and true estimate can be formed of the powers of human nature."[1] Much recent research and criticism in rhetoric has attempted to take such a broad view, either to establish a theoretical framework or to produce insights which illuminate rhetorical transactions. Rhetorical scholars have recently concerned themselves, for example, with the study of movements and have become increasingly convinced of the fruitfulness of such a field of investigation.[2] In this paper, I propose to identify, clarify, and apply a rhetorical perspective on the study of an historical movement, for the recent literature in rhetorical studies suggests to me that there is a particular way in which the rhetorical critic can view such a phenomenon. Specifically, the essay will focus on an important working-class movement of nineteenth-century England: Chartism.

A RHETORICAL PERSPECTIVE

The sociologist Amitai Etzioni has recently written of the "iron law of sociology that states that the fate of all popular movements is determined largely by historical forces they do not control."[3] Etzioni probably overstates the case; Lloyd Bitzer provides balance when he argues that a myriad of factors interact to produce the context in which movements live, and from these interrelationships exigencies develop. An exigence, according to Bitzer, "is an imperfection marked by urgency," and becomes rhetorical "when it is capable of positive modification and when positive modification requires discourse or can be assisted by discourse."[4] Exigencies may or may not actually produce rhetoric, but the critic must understand and identify *rhetorical imperatives* and *strategic indicators* that arise from the context. Rhetorical imperatives are situations or events which *compel* certain people to take some kind of concrete action. The isolation and examination of these imperatives can provide significant information regarding the ultimate goals of the movement and the nature of those who create and sustain it. Factors in the context which suggest the rhetorical form that the movement will take are strategic indicators. That is, the historic situation has imbedded within it group experiences, group perceptions, and a network of values which influence the way adherents of the movement will attempt to exploit communication channels and the ways in which they will identify crucial agents of change.[5]

Given the insight which the understanding of rhetorical imperatives and strategic indicators provide him, the critic then may turn to an investigation of *patterns of advocacy and reaction.* As the movement develops it identifies itself or becomes identified with a philosophy and with specific goals and thus may become itself a rhetorical imperative for others who are compelled to act in a hostile or conciliatory way, either through physical repression or discourse. Robert Cathcart has argued that a movement is defined rhetorically at this point. He describes as the "essential attribute" the "creation of a *dialectical tension growing out of moral conflict*" and maintains that "the formulation of a rhetoric proclaiming that the new order, the more perfect order, the desired order, cannot come about through the established agencies of change. . .in turn, produces a counter-rhetoric that exposes the agitators as anarchists or devils of destruction."[6] The moral nature of the conflict is emphasized since rhetorical imperatives are filtered through perceptions of the contemporary value system as well as being ordered in some hierarchical fashion by those involved according to their experience and the saliency of the imperatives. It is important, however, for the critic to recognize that patterns of advocacy and reaction may also include strong elements of the practical-impractical argument in that strategic choices may contribute to a rhetorical form that is susceptible to attack: the "sympathetic enemy" may abhor (or feign to abhor) the condition which gave birth to the movement, but dismiss the solution proposed (and, in consequence, most likely the movement itself,) as visionary or impractical.[7] Furthermore, the patterns not only of advocacy but of reaction as well will be formed and modified by tensions within the movement itself. As Herbert Simons has observed, "Movements are as susceptible to fragmentation from within as they are to suppression from without."[8]

As the rhetorical patterns of the movement develop, as the movement itself matures, as it engages widespread attention, as it declines, as it ceases to exist as a recognizable, cohesive force, a series of *influential relationships* may be observed. The movement's rhetorical interpretation of imperatives influences a variety of concurrent actions throughout the life of the movement and after, but the success or failure of the movement to achieve specific goals at a particular point in history is not a sufficient measure of its rhetoric. It has already been argued that movements invite response in order to exist as movements at all. But the intrusion of problems or issues, reflecting both the imperatives and the strategies employed by the movement, have the potential to provide a continuing source of motivation and rationale for modifications within society at large. Furthermore, influential relationships are reciprocal: changes in the social condition may make the imperatives less important or less salient, new imperatives may take precedence, rival movements deriving from the same imperatives may sap the initial movement's energy and will. Moreover, the movement leaves behind it a rhetorical legacy: the strategies it employed, the values it embodied, the heroes and villains that it created, form some part of the historical-cultural heritage and may prove an important source of invention for future spokesmen, further causes.

I would suggest, then, that a critic could fruitfully examine an historical movement from a rhetorical perspective through an investigation of rhetorical imperatives, strategic indicators, patterns of advocacy and reaction, and influential relationships. An examination of the Chartist Movement, which must here be more suggestive than exhaustive, will hopefully serve to make this perspective more clear.

RHETORICAL IMPERATIVES
OF THE CHARTIST MOVEMENT

To England the nineteenth century brought growth and change; it was an age of bustle, of unrest, of paradoxes. Industrialization was the great fact, and what Dr. Andrew Ure termed "the blessings [of] physico-mechanical society" were everywhere apparent. The railroads snaked their way throughout the countryside and travel and commerce benefited. The population boomed, particularly in the urban and industrial centers. It doubled in England and Wales between 1801 and 1851; London grew 145.5 percent during the same period, and the great manufacturing county of Lancashire, dominated by the smokestacks of Manchester, increased its population by 201.4 percent in the first half of the century.[9]

But with the blessings came the curse. Among the laborers who supported the industrial complex were great masses who faced, at best, a life of monotonous drudgery and, at worst, frightful privation. The Chartist, Thomas Cooper, was shocked to learn that weavers' earnings were four shillings and sixpence per week.[10] And even this sum was not always reached, for in 1837 the weavers declared in a petition that their income was but one and a half pence per day.[11]

Although living conditions had improved over those of the eighteenth century, squalor and disease still haunted the working classes. In 1842 the Poor Law Commission sponsored a *Report on the Sanitary Conditions of Labouring Population* which pointed out that in Leeds, for example, the drainage system was so poor that it was not uncommon for drains to back up repeatedly, once so badly that "many of the inhabitants were floated in their beds"; many streets were without water or "out-offices"; inhabitants of some neighborhoods had to use cesspools constructed under their doors; streets were so badly paved, if paved at all, as to be hazardous.[12]

The working class did not accept its situation with equanimity. A song current in Manchester in the 30's demonstrates both the bitterness and the pathos of the laboring poor:

> *How little can the rich man know*
> *Of what the poor man feels,*
> *When Want, like some dark demon foe,*
> *Nearer and nearer steals!*
> . . . .
> He *never saw his darlings lie*
> *Shivering, the flags their bed;*
> He *never heard that maddening cry*
> *"Daddy, a bit of bread!"*[13]

The situation in which the working classes found themselves gave rise to sporadic, violent response. Politically powerless, the lower orders often were prone to react through extra-legal means. During the early part of the century, before the Chartist movement came into being, erratic outbursts occurred throughout England. Before the end of the war with France, for example, the discontented "Luddites" smashed weavers' frames in Nottinghamshire, causing more troops to be quartered in the Luddite areas in 1812 than had gone to the Peninsula with Wellesley in 1808; in the midland and northern counties there were over 1,200 regular horse and foot stationed.[14] In 1816 a mob in Loughborough attacked the Heathcote and Borden mill, smashing fifty-three frames and inflicting six thousand pounds damage. At the Nottingham Assizes six men were sentenced to death and three to transportation for their part in the assault, and Luddism seemed to subside.[15]

In spite of firm government repression, however, spontaneous uprisings continued to occur throughout the first years of the century. It is important to understand that these outbreaks, motivated though they were by hunger and distress had, nevertheless, strong rhetorical overtones. For the violence was directed not only at appropriating needed commodities, but also at defying, even cowing authority. In Brandon in 1816, for example, the mob protested against the high cost of bread and meat by levelling the house of the local butcher, Mr. Willit, to the ground. The Sheriff and a local banker testified that the unruly men had marched about the streets waving a banner inscribed, "Bread or Blood."[16] Such a direct ultimatum was implicit in all the disturbances; actions were meant to be seen as symbolic of what might result if authority did not move to change conditions. While the imperatives often did not produce discourse, they did call forth coercive rhetorical acts as perhaps the only discernible options open to the oppressed.

Agitation by the working class for relief in the early nineteenth century did take other rhetorical forms. The famous demonstration at St. Peter's Fields, Manchester, the scene of the "Peterloo Massacre," was a peaceful attempt to promote parliamentary reform.[17] And in collaboration with the middle classes in the first years of the 1830's, the working classes worked for the reform of the House of Commons even though they seemed to play their most important role as bogeymen: their violent attacks on the enemies of parliamentary reform served as concrete evidence for the Whig claims that only reform would avert revolution.[18] There can be little doubt that the masses of workingmen believed that the Reform Bill of 1832 would do great things for them. Yet from the vantage point of the twentieth century it is difficult to understand the expectations of great feats from a parliament so moderately and mildly reformed. The middle classes had, indeed, enhanced their power in the national councils, but the working classes remained without an effective political voice. "A Reformed Parliament," Charles Greville observed in 1833, "turns out to be very much like any other parliaments."[19]

Not only was the Reformed Parliament to prove unresponsive to lower class demands, it was this same parliament that passed the hated Poor Law Amendment Act of 1834. To the lower classes, this act seemed a cruel, almost calculated attempt to deprive them of the means of even marginal subsistence. Its administration represents an undoubted imperative which lay beneath Chartist agitation.

Up until 1834 what was known as the Speenhamland System of poor relief was common in the southern and eastern parts of England and, to a lesser extent, existed in parts of the north. Under this plan wages were supplemented by outdoor relief so that the worker, in times of high prices and low wages, could count on some minimum income related to the price of bread and the size of his family. On the surface, the plan seemed a reasonable, humane one. In practice, such a scheme tended to depress wages even further and to impose a crushing burden on the local rate payer.

Parliament's action in 1834 was an attempt to remedy this situation by abolishing outdoor relief altogether except for the aged or infirm. A system of "unions," some 600 in number, was set up to receive the indigent, but the dreaded and often dreadful workhouses offered cold comfort to the needy. Indeed, they were not meant to, for the Poor Law Commissioners believed that any relief system must insure that the pauper was always worse off than the poorest labourer.[20] Cole and Postgate argue that the Commissioners were preoccupied with agricultural labourers and "forgot, or ignored, the fact that in the industrial districts the old Poor Law served quite a different purpose—that of relieving unemployment due to the fluctuations of trade, and also that of preserving from literal starvation the handloom-weavers and other domestic producers whom the factory system was throwing rapidly upon the industrial scrap-heap. The removal of outdoor relief could not help unemployed factory workers or miners to find employment when the times were bad: nor could it do anything at all to raise the wages of the miserable handloom-weavers."[21] Well might Dickens' Christmas charity solicitors answer Scrooge's question, "Are there no workhouses?" with the horrified response, "Some cannot go there, others would rather die." The Unions were popularly known as "Bastilles" and symbolized for the poor the utter depths of human degradation and despair.

For those who formed and supported the Chartist movement these aspects of nineteenth-century English life were particularly salient. The laboring poor, suffering economic distress intensified by the new Poor Law and unmitigated by the Reformed Parliament from which so much was expected, were compelled to take some action.[22] Sir Charles Napier, who commanded the Northern district of the army took the measure of the problem: "...the doctrine of slowly reforming when men are starving is of all things the most silly; famishing men cannot wait."[23] From these imperatives the rhetoric of Chartism emerged. The ultimate goal of the movement, accordingly, had to be the alleviation of economic distress, and the context out of which it grew readily explains why the movement was the first almost exclusively working class movement. Furthermore, the needs and experiences of the working classes as well as the political realities which surrounded them, help to explain the rhetorical strategies which evolved.

STRATEGIC INDICATORS

The context that I have briefly and selectively reviewed suggests certain important features which help to explain the lines of strategy which the movement developed. The strategy was directly influenced by the Chartists' perception of the focus of power, their relationships with the middle class, and by lower class experiences with and perceptions of the role of violence in promoting change.

It was apparent in nineteenth-century England that the House of Commons was the seat of political power. The entire agitation for parliamentary reform had been predicated on the conviction that the alteration of the composition of parliament was the surest way to modify the condition of life generally. This was the message of the 1832 reformers and it had been absorbed and believed by the lower classes. And it was essentially a correct view. As Richard Cobden observed in discussing the strategy of the Anti-Corn Law League (the middle-class agitational rival of Chartism), "...the present construction of the House of Commons...forbids us hoping for success. *That House must be changed before we can get justice.*"[24]

The optimistic hopes that the lower classes placed in the 1832 Act proved illusory. So to bring about improvement of the quality of life for the lower classes, the Chartists proposed complete and radical reconstruction of the House of Commons. In effect, the strategy of parliamentary reconstruction became an end in itself, a secondary goal which was prerequisite to the ultimate goal. The movement took its very name from the "People's Charter," which set forth six demands: (1) universal manhood suffrage, (2) the ballot, (3) payment of members of Parliament, (4) elimination of the property qualifications for members of Parliament, (5) formation of equal electoral districts, and, (6) annual parliamentary elections. The experience of the past led Chartists to believe that democracy—and the Charter did embody what we have come to identify as basic elements of democratic government—was the only remedy for their ills. Paradoxically, their understanding of the focus of power also led the Chartists to try to influence as best they could the existing House of Commons drastically to reconstruct itself.

Their realization of the source of power, their experiences with the 1832 agitation, and their perceptions of their employers colored the Chartists' strategy with regard to the middle classes. The middle classes appeared to have betrayed them, yet the only spokesmen that working men had in the House were middle class radicals.[25] The uneasy relations with the middle class were aggravated by the variety within the ranks of Chartism itself. Asa Briggs points out in *Chartist Studies* that there were three major social groups who comprised the movement's membership.[26] First, there were the superior craftsmen who were in communication with the "respectables" of the middle classes, but who, at the same time, were somewhat suspect by the lower orders of the working class. Second, there were the factory operatives who were mainly concentrated in the northern centers of the textile industry. Third, there were the domestic outworkers such as handloom weavers, framework knitters, and nailmakers. The existence of subclasses within the working classes contributed to misunderstandings and outright feuds among the Chartists. The tensions between the working class and the middle class and within the working class itself indicate the serious strategic problems that the movement was to face, and it is understandable that contradictory strategies would develop. This was especially true with regard to the role of violence in promoting the movement's aims.

When a group is without political, social, or economic power, it is not surprising that they turn to physical violence. When only the hope of intimidation exists it will be exploited. Thus it had been with the disorganized, erratic outbreaks in the past. Certainly the lessons of 1832 would not have been entirely lost on the lower classes, nor would the more remote, but more potent, example of the French Revolution. But threat and action are not the same. What plagued the Chartists, who never, after all, advocated the outright overthrow of existing institutions, but, rather, their radical amendment, was when and under what circumstances to encourage violence, or at least threaten it, and how to control violence so that the whole repressive weight of government was not brought to bear to destroy the movement. Such considerations were bound to be a confounding factor in the development of a coherent strategy as the movement progressed.

PATTERNS OF ADVOCACY
AND REACTION

Various groups developed in the 1830's with the purpose of bettering the lot of the laboring poor, but it was with the writing of the Charter itself that the movement crystalized and became a more coherent force. In 1838 William Lovett, a leading figure in the London Workingmen's Association, drafted the Charter in the form of a parliamentary bill. The next year a convention, which brought supporters from all parts of the country, was called in London. The Convention drafted a petition which embodied the principles and program of the Charter and presented it to the House of Commons in May, 1839.

The basic goal seemed to be to impress parliament with the overwhelming support which the petition enjoyed, and a campaign to get great numbers of signatures was undertaken. Pressure on parliament was the key to action, and the demonstration of widespread support would intensify that pressure. Agitation for the Reform Bill seemed to Chartists an admirable model to follow. As one Chartist spokesman claimed, "in 1832 the working classes by their moral and physical organization beat the Tories for the sake of the Whigs—by the same means they can in 1837 beat both Whigs and Tories for the sake of themselves."[27] Thus agitation took the form of the canvassing and presentation of gigantic petitions, mass meetings in working class districts, and, to a limited and markedly unsuccessful extent, some attempts to influence parliamentary elections.[28]

Advocacy of the Charter, through petitions and mass meetings, were generally agreed upon tactics within the movement. But the strategic problems, which have already been discussed, distorted the patterns of advocacy and invited strong reactions. The conduct of the Convention of 1839 affords an example of the pattern that Chartist agitation followed and clearly indicates the internal dissension over means which were exploited by the opposition.

Even before the national meeting was convened in February of 1839, a serious rupture had occurred. The Chartists of Birmingham, London, and Scotland (more closely allied with the middle class and used to seeking the aid of middle-class parliamentary radicals) became alarmed at the pyrotechnics of their counterparts in the manufacturing districts of the north of England. In the fall of 1838, in Lancashire and Yorkshire, mass torchlight meetings heard speakers such as J. R. Stephens discourse on the virtues of an armed populace, a giant demonstration in Hartshead Moor listened while Feargus O'Connor, the "lion of the North," talked menacingly on the benefits of tyrannicide. In O'Connor's newspaper, *The Northern Star*, this strongly suggestive note appeared: "The National Guards of Paris have petitioned for an extension of the Suffrage, and they have done it with arms in their hands."[29] The moderates were aghast. The Edinburgh Chartists passed a resolution which strictured the use of violent language and physical force. In turn, O'Connor and others denounced these "moral philosophers" while Stephens sneered at the Birmingham enemies of physical force as "old women."[30]

By the time the delegates assembled there were serious differences as to the scope and purpose of the Convention itself. J. P. Cobbett introduced a motion that attempted to limit the Convention to a body that would exist only to shepherd the National Petition through Parliament. Some of the more radical members, however, were already beginning to think of the Convention as a kind of legislative alternative to parliament itself, a body more truly representative of the people, and the motion was defeated. To imply that the Convention might be more than an agitational body was unacceptable to moderates, and Cobbett quit the Convention. His defection was the first of many by the moral force wing of Chartism, and the Convention gradually came under the sway of the less temperate delegates.

The Convention, racked by dissension, plagued by indecision, and torn between the Scylla of Government repression and the Charybdis of inaction, failed to provide decisive leadership. They moved their seat from London, where the proximity to the Home Secretary and the Metropolitan Police made members somewhat apprehensive, to Birmingham, and finally back to London again. They passed a resolution calling for a general strike without providing for any kind of strike fund; moderates vainly pointed out that such action was a direct invitation to the strikers to plunder for subsistence. Reports from the country that indicated that such a strike would be impossible to organize and carry out successfully caused them to rescind the action. There was much discussion of the Convention's right to adopt "any means whatsoever" to secure the demands set forth in the Petition, and one speaker pointed out that signatures on a petition meant nothing unless they were "the signatures of millions of fighting men who will not allow any aristocracy, oligarchy, landlords, cotton lords, money lords, or any lords to tyrannize over them longer."[31] From the Convention came strong words but no clear, well planned course of action. Mass meetings continued throughout the country. Some Chartist leaders were arrested. There were wild tales of general insurrections in the making, and doubtless many Chartists, particularly in the North, were busily arming themselves. Arrest of many of its leaders and defections among the moderates thinned the ranks of the Convention. In August of 1839, a month after Parliament had rejected the Petition, the "Peoples Parliament" finally dissolved itself amid bitter recriminations among the members.

Disagreements over physical force were an inevitable disintegrating factor within the movement. Given the right circumstances, the threat of violence may coerce ameliorative action even if it does not convince the opposition. Moderate reformers may use the threat, even while deploring it, as a spur to reform.[32] But in the Chartists' case it alarmed authority without intimidating it and poisoned relations with the powerful middle-classes. In such a situation only out and out revolution held the promise of immediate success, and there was very little real revolutionary sentiment among the Chartists. As Hovell astutely observed in *The Chartist Movement*, "...there was little sincerity in the physical force party. To a large section of it...the appeal to arms was a game of bluff calculated to terrorize the governing classes into submission. To another section it was even less than this; it was simply a blatant device to attract attention."[33]

The pressures exerted on the movement by the physical-moral force conflict resulted in a number of rhetorical fissures and counter pressures. Moderate spokesmen had to devote some considerable energy and attention to disavowing violence and placating the middle and governing classes. The millionaire radical, Thomas Attwood, was a firm friend of the Chartists, and spoke in their behalf in the House of Commons. His speech on introducing the Petition on June 14, 1839 is typical of moderate attempts to keep the Chartist agitation on a legal and parliamentary footing. "Although he most cordially supported the petition, was ready to support every word contained in it, and was determined to use every means in his power in order to carry it out into a law," Attwood announced to the House, "he must say, that many reports had gone abroad, in regard to arguments said to have been used in support of the petition on different occasions, which he distinctly disavowed." Attwood asserted that "He never, in the whole course of his life, recommended any means, or inculcated any doctrine except peace, law, order, loyalty, and union." And, "he washed his hands of any idea, of any appeal to physical force." Attwood's declaration that "every argument which justice, reason, and wisdom dictate," would finally secure a favorable public reaction without physical force embodies the hope and the strategic philosophy which activated moderate Chartists and their allies.[34] It also exposes the kernel of the issues around which debate on and within the movement revolved. The Charter itself, with all its political and social ramifications, and the means to attain enactment of the Charter, define the real points of clash and not the conditions of the poor which brought about the agitation in the first place. Naturally, the miserable plight of the poor was discussed, but the situation is analogous to a debate in which the need was barely alluded to after the first constructive speech, and the debate became riveted on the plan.

The ruling classes reacted to the new imperatives created for them by the emergence of Chartism. In some cases they naturally responded repressively. Chartist leaders were arrested from time to time, the movement's activities were kept under police surveillance, and when actual rioting broke out the military was used decisively. At other times, the Chartists were considered more eccentric than threatening, or at least of such insufficient importance to warrant serious retribution or rebuttal. For example, on Attwood's motion of July 12, 1839 to go into a committee of the whole House to consider the National Petition, scarcely anyone who *voted* against the motion, troubled to *speak* against it even though it was swamped by a vote of 235 to 46.[35]

But the masses could seriously disturb the equanimity of the governing classes. As Charles Kingsley observed, "young men believed (and not so wrongly) that the masses were their natural enemies, and that they might have to fight, any year or any day, for the safety of their property and the honour of their sisters."[36] The explicit democracy of the Charter called forth the most strenuous rhetorical reactions on the part of Chartism's enemies. The defense of property and traditional institutions, and the preservation of parliamentary independence were the principal thrusts of the counter-rhetoric.

In the debate in the House of Commons on May 3, 1842, may be seen the microcosm of anti-Chartist rhetoric.[37] Thomas Duncombe, the radical associate of the Chartists, moved that the petitioners be heard at the bar of the House. Thomas Babington Macaulay, the great Whig proponent of reform in 1832, led the attack on the Charter. He saw universal suffrage as "fatal to all purposes for which Government exists, and for which aristocracies and all other things exist, and that it is utterly incompatible with the very existence of civilization" (p. 46). And then Macaulay came to the heart of the argument: "I conceive that civilization rests on the security of...property" (p. 46). The conservative argument was based on the real conviction that those who did not hold property themselves would be most unlikely to protect it. Indeed, the effect of granting the franchise to the uneducated, easily influenced masses, would be governmental "spoliation," according to Macaulay (p. 50). Underlying the argument was the tacit recognition that there were social imperfections, but the means suggested by the Chartists to remedy them were attacked as horrendous. Lord John Russell continued and expanded Macaulay's theme. The condition of the poor, he argued, was not at issue, rather the existence of the ancient and venerable institutions of the country were at stake.

John Arthur Roebuck, while speaking in defense of the motion, had dismissed the Chartist leader Feargus O'Connor as a "malignant" and "cowardly demagogue" (p. 54). Opponents quickly seized on this untimely reference. Russell argued that if a cowardly, malignant demagogue could gain ascendance over the Chartist movement, would not he and his kind be likely to be elected to a democratic parliament? Sir Robert Peel asked who would speak at the bar if the motion carried? Would it be the cowardly and malignant demagogue? The Charter, according to Peel, was incompatible with the monarchial form of government which had, he asserted, brought to the people of England greater liberty and happiness than to any other people in the world.

The counter-rhetoric clearly labelled the Chartist spokesmen as despoilers of England's property and her greatness. It implied that mob rule, that is democratic rule, would make servile politicians who catered to every whim of a rapacious and uninformed electorate. The independence of Members of Parliament was a firmly entrenched value in early Victorian England. The historian Norman Gash maintains that "the highest respect. . .was reserved for the independent politician, in the sense not of one who was outside party but of one who was in party solely because of his conscientious opinion and perhaps traditional association." Gash goes on to explain, "Integrity was held to be inseparable from intellectual independence; and intellectual independence inseparable in the long run from financial independence. All members and all candidates claimed to be independent in their opinions and votes because it was the contemporary ideal of what a politician should be, however far removed from reality that ideal was."[38] In the context of this ingrained value, the call for payment of members, annual parliaments, and members to be responsive to the whims of a large constituency, could easily be pictured as the destruction of the cherished traditions of English liberty.

Cast in this devil role, political Chartism was vulnerable. It could never realistically hope to achieve from the early Victorian House of Commons so sweeping a political change. Its own strategy was a weapon used by its enemies against it. Its own divisions made the accomplishment of its ultimate social goals exceedingly difficult. Mark Hovell has summed up the situation this way:

> They were well agreed in the diagnosis of the obvious social diseases of their time; they could unite in clamouring for the political reforms which were to give the mass of the people the means of saving themselves from their miseries. Beyond this, however, the Chartist consensus hardly went. It was impossible for them to focus a united body of opinion in favour of a single definite social ideal. The true failure of Chartism lay in its inability to perform this task. Political Chartism was a real though limited thing; social Chartism was a protest against what existed, not a reasoned policy to set up anything concrete in its place. Apart from machinery, Chartism was largely a passionate negation.[39]

The "machinery," from the rhetorical point of view, was what was crucial, however, for that is where the debate focused. Yet from the negation, from the protest against what existed, there were discernible influences.

INFLUENTIAL RELATIONSHIPS

Economic and social conditions both influenced and were influenced by the Chartist movement. As severe depressions reversed and the standard of living became better, support dwindled. On the other hand, agitation was most severe when times were harder. The basic evils persisted, but as legislation to limit working hours was passed, as increased world trade caused a rise in wages, and as the Anti-Corn Law movement drew off support, particularly from the better-off workers, the imperatives became less salient.[40] G. D. H. Cole has observed that "the League's [the Anti-Corn Law League] success seemed to give the lie to the Chartist contention that without the Charter nothing could be done to improve the condition of the people. The passing of the Ten Hours Act carried the same moral; and during the 'fifties the Chartists decisively lost their hold on the main body of the working class."[41]

But the Chartists, if not successful in the impossible task of getting Parliament to adopt its political program, did infuse into the situation imperatives which demanded some kind of action. Cole and Postgate claim that Chartist rhetoric influenced other reforms. "These three great advantages," they wrote, "the repeal of the Corn Laws, the Ten Hours Act, and the softening of the Poor Law—were secured under the pressure of the torchlight meetings, the riots, insurrectionary plots and strikes of Chartism. To that extent Chartism was not a failure."[42]

The coercive threat of Chartism made other alternatives seem more attractive, yet Chartist influences may be observed in other areas as well. They left a rhetorical legacy, a memory of strategies which failed and hopes that did not materialize, a stock of arguments to be exploited in other ways and the example of working-class leadership and its problems and advantages. Some historians have seen in Chartism the seeds of Trade Unionism, indeed, of the British labor movement itself.[43] In regard to the influence of the movement Mark Hovell wrote: "In tracing the influence of Chartism on later ideals we must look to the individual rather than the system, to the spirit rather than the letter. But it would be unjust to deny the variety and the strength of the stimulus which the Chartist impulse gave towards the furtherance of the more wholesome spirit which makes even the imperfect Britain of today [1918] a much better place for the ordinary man to live in than was the Britain of the early years of Victoria. The part played by the Chartists in this amelioration is not the less important because, as with their political programme, the changes to which they gave an impetus were effected by other hands than theirs."[44]

In human history events crowd upon events, and the meaning we extract from collective experience is bound to the perspective from which we view the past. Rhetorical scholars, long interested in discrete transactions, are becoming increasingly convinced that we can apply our rhetorical perspective to a more diverse set of occurrences in order to uncover rhetorical meaning in history. If we view history in our own unique way, we may begin to understand not only the reciprocal shaping of rhetoric and events, but the impact of events-as-perceived on the course of history. As rhetorical critics examine movements we are compelled by the nature of our perspective to see that imperatives depend on perception and saliency and not on typicality. A "balanced" historical view, for example, may be necessary to paint an accurate picture of life in early Victorian England, but the rhetorical scholar looking at this period needs to understand the milieu of those who suffered in it; that is, to distill that which would truly be rhetorically imperative. What becomes relevant is not so much historical forces, trends, or even specific events; relevance for rhetorical critics depends on popular interpretations of phenomena. This exploratory study of Chartism suggests to me that rhetorical scholars who focus on man's perception and interpretation of his world may, indeed, be best equipped to understand and explain movements which have shaped our history.

Notes

1. *The Adams-Jefferson Letters*, 2 vols., ed. Lester J. Cappon (Chapel Hill, North Carolina: Univ. of North Carolina Press, 1959), II, 420.

2. The rhetorical study of historical movements surely begins with Leland M. Griffin, "The Rhetoric of Historical Movements," *QJS*, 38 (Apr. 1952), 184–188. Professor Griffin's essay, "A Dramatistic Theory of the Rhetoric of Movements," in *Critical Responses to Kenneth Burke*, ed. William H. Rueckert (Minneapolis: Univ. of Minnesota Press, 1969) is a later statement which modifies his earlier views. Other studies which deal with various theoretical and methodological aspects of movements include: Dan F. Hahn and Ruth M. Gonchar, "Studying Social Movements: A Rhetorical Methodology," *Speech Teacher*, 20 (Jan. 1971), 44–52; Robert S. Cathcart, "New Approaches to the Study of Movements: Defining Movements Rhetorically," *Western Speech*, 36 (Spr. 1972), 82–88; and the particularly important study by Herbert W. Simons, "Requirements, Problems, and Strategies: A Theory of Persuasion for Social Movements," *QJS*, 56 (Feb. 1970), 1–11. Examples of studies of particular movements are: Leland M. Griffin, "The Rhetorical Structure of the 'New Left' Movement: Part I," *QJS*, 50 (Apr. 1964), 113–135; James R. Andrews, "Piety and Pragmatism: Rhetorical Aspects of the Early British Peace Movement," *Speech Monographs*, 34 (Nov. 1967), 423–436.

3. "The Women's Movement—Tokens vs. Objectives," *Saturday Review*, 20 May 1972, p. 35.

4. Lloyd F. Bitzer, "The Rhetorical Situation," *Philosophy and Rhetoric*, 1 (Jan. 1968), 3, 6–7.

5. Bitzer has defined the "rhetorical audience" as "those persons who are capable of being influenced by discourse and of being mediators of change" (*ibid.*, 8). I would be inclined to consider, in this connection, the agents of change as those who could be influenced by *action*, which may include discourse, but which may take other forms.

6. "New Approaches to the Study of Movements: Defining Movements Rhetorically," 87.

7. I have discussed the problem of impracticality and its relationship to strategy in "Piety and Pragmatism: Rhetorical Aspects of the Early British Peace Movement."

8. "Requirements, Problems, Strategies: A Theory of Persuasion for Social Movements," 11.

9. *Annual Register*, 93 (1851), 450–451.

10. Thomas Cooper, *The Life of Thomas Cooper* (London: Hodder and Stoughton, 1882), pp. 137–139.

11. Donald Read, "Chartism in Manchester," *Chartist Studies*, ed. Asa Briggs (London: Macmillan, 1959), p. 32.

12. Edwin Chadwick, "The Sanitary Condition of the Labouring Poor," *Society and Politics in England*, ed. J. F. C. Harrison (New York: Harper and Row, 1965), pp. 152–156.

13. Cited by Read, p. 32.

14. R. J. White, *Waterloo to Peterloo* (London: William Heinemann, 1957), 111.

15. *Ibid.*, pp. 115–117.

16. *Annual Register*, 58 (1816), 66–69.

17. For a detailed discussion of the St. Peter's Field meeting see White, 176–192. See also, Charles W. Lomas, "Orator Hunt at Peterloo and Smithfield," *QJS*, 48 (Dec. 1962), 400–405.

18. I have discussed this point in some detail in "The Rhetoric of Coercion and Persuasion: The Reform Bill of 1832," *QJS*, 56 (Apr. 1970), 187–195.

19. *The Greville Memoirs*, ed. Roger Fulford (New York: Macmillan, 1963), p. 102.

20. "The 1834 Poor Law Report," in *Society and Politics in England*, pp. 147–148.

21. G. D. H. Cole and Raymond Postgate, *The British People, 1746–1946* (London: Methuen, 1961), p. 278.

22. A severe economic depression in the late '30s and '40s intensified the problem and made it even more imperative. The effects, circumstances, and degree of severity differed in different parts of England, but the industrial county of Lancashire was among the hardest hit. By June of 1837, in the Manchester area alone fifty thousand workers were unemployed or on short time. See Read, p. 31.

23. Sir W. Napier, *The Life and Opinions of General Napier* (1857), II, 22. Cited in Asa Briggs, *The Age of Improvement, 1783–1867* (London: Longmans, Green, 1959), p. 309.

24. Letter to J. B. Smith, 1840, cited in Norman McCord, *The Anti-Corn Law League, 1838–1846* (London: Allen and Unwin, 1958), p. 82.

25. Men like Thomas Attwood and Thomas Duncombe were allies of the Chartists but were successful members of the middle class themselves. "Orator" Hunt was the only working class man to be elected to the unreformed House of Commons, and Feargus O'Connor, the only avowed Chartist to be elected, was not returned until 1847.

26. Briggs, pp. 4–5.

27. Quoted in the Lovett Scrapbook, Vol. I, cited by Briggs, *The Age of Improvement*, p. 305.

28. Between 1837 and 1852 Chartist candidates did stand for election in several constituencies, particularly in the General election of 1841 and in the bi-elections in 1842, 1844, and 1845. The General election of 1847 saw a number of Chartists on the hustings and O'Connor won a seat at Nottingham. He, however, was the only Chartist ever returned, and the contesting of elections was never a major tactic of the Chartist movement. For details concerning this form of the Chartist political activity see G. D. H. Cole, *British Working Class Politics, 1832–1914* (London: Routledge, 1941), pp. 19–24.

29. *The Northern Star*, 8 Sept. 1838.

30. Mark Hovell, *The Chartist Movement* (Manchester: Manchester Univ. Press, 1918), p. 120. Hovell's book is probably the best account of the earlier phases of the Chartist movement. His chapter on "The People's Parliament," 116–135, provides a wealth of detail based on contemporary sources.

31. *Ibid.*, p. 127.

32. I have argued elsewhere that this was the case in 1832. See "The Rhetoric of Coercion and Persuasion: The Reform Bill of 1832," esp. 192–194.

33. Hovell, p. 305. The tension between physical force and moral suasion seems to me to be one of the most striking of consistent characteristics of movements; certainly parallels with the Black Power movement, for example, seem apparent.

34. *Hansard's Parliamentary Debates*, Third Series, LXVIII, 14 June 1839. In the debate on the petition in 1842 Duncombe also spent considerable time trying to establish the respectability of Chartism, linking the movement historically not only with radicals of the past, but also with aristocratic Whig reformers. *Hansard's Parliamentary Debates*, Third Series, LXIII, 3 May 1842.

35. Hovell, p. 164.

36. Cited by George Rude, *The Crowd in History, 1780–1848* (New York: London, Sydney: John Wiley and Sons, 1964), p. 182.

37. Quotations are from *Hansard's Parliamentary Debates*, Third Series, LXIII, 3 May 1842, 39–88.

38. *Politics in the Age of Peel* (London: Longmans, Green, 1953), p. 109.

39. *The Chartist Movement*, p. 303.

40. Alfred A. Funk has recently shown how the Anti-Corn Law proponents increasingly focused their arguments on the injustice of high food costs for laborers, an attractive argument for the lower classes. See "Chain of Argument in the British Free Trade Debates," *QJS*, 58 (Apr. 1972), 152–160.

41. *British Working Class Politics*, pp. 22–23.

42. *The British People*, pp. 315–316.

43. See Cole and Postgate, p. 316 ff.

44. *The Chartist Movement*, p. 310.

Public Opinion and American Foreign Policy: The Case of Illusory Support for the Panama Canal Treaties

———————————————— J. MICHAEL HOGAN ————————————————

Americans have a "moral conception" of public opinion that deems it "mandatory that the will of the people prevail."[1] Yet on occasion we also uphold the Hamiltonian notion that policies, especially in foreign affairs, should be insulated from the "prejudices," the "intemperate passions," and the "fluctuations" of the popular will.[2] In one of those curious contradictions of American politics, we at once want our foreign policies dependent upon and protected from the "will of the people." But which impulse actually prevails in American political practice?

For many years diplomatic historians simply assumed that public opinion did in fact determine American foreign policy. For instance, Thomas Bailey concluded that "the American people, exercising their democratic privilege and enjoying freedom of speech and press, have shaped their own foreign policies."[3] In the 1960s and 1970s, however, other diplomatic historians challenged this assumption. According to revisionists, such as Gabriel Kolko, "the close and serious student of modern American foreign relations" could "rarely, if ever, find an instance of an important decision made with any reference to the alleged general public desires or opinions."[4] Revisionists held that American policy-makers promoted the economic interests of an elite, while an indifferent public was duped into quiescence with appeals to "a broader social welfare and erstwhile consensus."[5]

The first generation of survey research, in the 1950s, seemed to confirm that the general public was too uninformed, disinterested, and easily manipulated to play a significant role in the conduct of American foreign policy.[6] But empirical research in the 1960s and 1970s indicated that Americans were more aware, concerned, and politically active than they had been in previous years.[7] These findings led political scientists to develop situational theories of public opinion. As the research accumulated, it became clear that the role of public opinion could be described only in particular historical contexts or in regard to the changing national agenda and political dialogue.[8]

Case studies in the rhetoric of American foreign policy have linked foreign policy decisions and arguments to the constraints of domestic politics.[9] Yet rhetorical theorists often reject a situational perspective on public opinion in favor of general, lachrymose theories of the public's demise. Gerald Hauser and Carole Blair articulate the premise undergirding such theories, arguing that the realities of contemporary western industrialized societies—increased mobility, a lost sense of community, and even "wholesale narcissism"—have rendered "the liberal democratic conception of the public...only an ideal, a fiction at best." They tell us that we now have a "government of, by, and for special interests," while "the people" have been "reduced to a depoliticized estate" that renders "mass loyalty to a government which does not include them in its decision-making process."[10]

It cannot be denied that American policy-makers sometimes act contrary to public opinion. Yet American history is also replete with examples of policies best explained by deference to the people, and the attitudinal and institutional reasons for this fact are well understood. Those who treat the people as a fiction simply ignore this country's history of leadership by eminently ordinary people weaned on an ideological tradition of deference to "the people." The concept of popular sovereignty was infused with "extraordinary meaning" by America's Founding Fathers, and our system of representation, our relatively unrestrained press, and our free and open elections have all served to sustain the practical sovereignty of the people, even in times of public quiescence.[11]

Yet theories of the public-as-fiction correctly maintain that public opinion can have no impact on policy-making independent of how it is perceived by political leaders. As Michael C. McGee argues, *politically relevant* public opinion is discovered, not through survey research, but through analysis of rhetorical documents containing history as "mediated or filtered" by political leaders.[12] Those who speak philosophically about genuine democracy side-step the question of *how* political leaders might come to "know" the "will of the people." They fail to consider in any practical sense the mechanisms or processes by which the public might communicate with policy-makers. They seem to assume, in Bernard Cohen's words, that objective public opinion may be "absorbed, by osmosis, into the political bloodstream."[13]

Policy-making does not always reflect public opinion—especially on foreign affairs—because our political philosophy is ambivalent, allowing policy-makers to justify the "national interest" taking precedence over "the will of the people" in certain situations. Furthermore, the empirical problems of "knowing" public opinion may bedevil even policy-makers intent on obeying its dictates. American policy-makers routinely assume that "the will of the people" may be discerned through "scientific" polling, yet the conceptual and technical limitations of polls call this assumption into question. Polls typically do not distinguish between strong and weak opinions, between rational and irrational opinions, or among shades of opinion on particular issues. Even slight differences in methodology—differing methods of sampling and data collection or slightly differing questions—can make enormous differences in findings. And once statistics are gathered they still may be interpreted in very different ways, especially by politicians with partisan concerns.[14]

This essay aims to demonstrate both the reality of the public's influence on American foreign policy and some of the problems caused by our political philosophy and by our imperfect methods for assessing public opinion. It examines one major foreign policy controversy in which the public played a major role. It reveals how Senate proponents of the Panama Canal treaties of 1977 used claims of a "turnabout" in public opinion to entice recalcitrant Senators to support ratification. Early in the debate, those favoring the treaties conceded that the public overwhelmingly opposed the treaties and argued that the Senate should not be guided by public opinion grounded in emotionalism and ignorance. Later, however, treaty proponents began to speak of a shift in public opinion, a shift in which the public allegedly came to support the treaties with certain pivotal amendments.

In retrospect, however, the "turnabout" proved illusory—the product of wishful thinking and poorly worded and misinterpreted polls. Senators who wished to support the treaties accepted uncritically claims that the public would support the treaties if they were amended to "guarantee America's right to defend the canal." Numerous polls supported these claims. But most of the pollsters' questions failed to distinguish between the amendments actually adopted by the Senate and much stronger language unsuccessfully advocated by conservative Senators. As a result, people who supported the treaties *only* with stronger defense guarantees apparently were counted as treaty supporters. This became apparent as polls following the debate—polls assessing public opinion on the treaties as actually amended— revealed that opposition had "returned" to the position found at the start of the debate.

THE TREATIES AND THE DEBATE

The Panama Canal was a thorn in the side of American policy-makers for many years, especially since World War II. International pressures during the Cold War led American officials to look favorably upon Panamanian demands for control over the waterway, but domestic pressures against "giving away" the canal constrained them from bowing to world opinion. Jimmy Carter became the first President to pursue vigorously the idea of transferring control over the canal to the Republic of Panama. By the fall of 1977, the negotiations he initiated upon assuming office produced a pair of new treaties to replace the Panama Canal treaty of 1903.[15]

The first of the treaties, called the Panama Canal Treaty, acknowledged Panama's sovereignty over the Canal Zone. Under its provisions the United States and Panama were to share responsibility for operating and defending the canal until the year 2000, while total control was shifted gradually to Panama. The second treaty, the Treaty Concerning the Permanent Neutrality and Operation of the Panama Canal (the Neutrality Treaty), provided a permanent regime of neutrality after the year 2000 "in order that both in time of peace and in time of war [the canal would] remain secure and open to peaceful transit by the vessels of all nations on terms of entire equality." In recognition of its contribution in building the canal, the United States was entitled to expeditious transit for its vessels in time of military need. The Neutrality treaty also stipulated that the U.S. and Panama would act together in defending the canal's neutrality should the need arise.[16]

The treaties provoked one of the most vigorous public debates over foreign policy in American history. The so-called New Right led the opposition, spending millions of dollars on direct-mail, political advertising, telethons, and personal appearances by Ronald Reagan and other conservative advocates. The Carter administration countered with its own public relations campaign, beginning with an elaborate series of ceremonies, meetings, and parties to mark the signing of the pacts in Washington on September 6, 1977. Subsequently the administration orchestrated more than 800 speeches and interviews by government officials and other notable Americans, while Carter himself gave dozens of speeches and interviews on Panama, including his second "fireside chat." The administration also recruited a number of influential political, business, and religious organizations to help sell the treaties to the American people.[17]

The controversy culminated in the historic Senate debate in February, March, and April 1978, the second longest treaty debate in American history. For the first time, radio carried deliberations of the Senate to the American people. For the first time in fifty years, the Senate considered treaties article-by-article as a Committee of the Whole. And also for the first time in half a century, the Senate amended a treaty against the public wishes of the President.[18]

But while the Senate debate was historically momentous, it did little to enhance the Senate's reputation as the world's greatest deliberative body. Marquis Childs called the debate "an intolerable charade. . . . since all the arguments pro and con have been rehearsed a dozen times."[19] Senator Patrick Leahy of Vermont agreed, saying the proceedings resembled "the plot line of a television soap opera. You could listen to the debate for several days, leave for a week or two, and come back to it having missed very little."[20]

The repetitiousness of the debate reflected the relatively settled state of Senate opinion on the treaties' merits. The long public controversy had polarized opinion on the treaties, with two camps advancing "mutually exclusive worldviews" in competing "rhetorical visions."[21] Most Senators, like Americans generally, either identified with a nostalgic, "Cold War" vision and viewed the treaties as symbolic of weakness, or they embraced a new, "anti-imperialistic" vision and viewed the treaties as beneficent and just.

But to say that most Senators already had judged the treaties is not to say that the debate was superfluous. Although the prospects for ratification were dim at the outset, the Senate ultimately did ratify the treaties in two separate votes, announcing the end of nearly eighty years of American control over the legendary canal.[22] On March 16, the Senate ratified the Neutrality treaty by a vote of 68 to 32—a two-thirds majority with one vote to spare. After an additional month of debate, the Senate ratified the second treaty, the Panama Canal treaty, by exactly the same vote.[23] How does one explain this outcome? How did a static debate produce a dramatic turnaround in Senate opinion?

Most observers agree that two amendments to the Neutrality treaty account for the shift from opposition to support for the treaties. The amendments, known as the leadership amendments, presumably clarified America's right to defend the canal and to have priority passage in military emergencies after the year 2000. A number of Senators who had opposed the treaties became active supporters of the amended version. Charles Percy, for instance, demanded that the military guarantees be made a "formal and binding part of the treaties" and declared: "I could not support the treaties otherwise. With these changes, however, I believe our interests would be well protected."[24] Similarly, Robert Stafford of Vermont stated on February 27 that the original treaties did not "serve the best interest of the United States" and that he would not "vote for ratification of either treaty as submitted." But with the two amendments, he proclaimed, "I shall support ratification."[25] Similar public statements by Senators Baker, Brooke, Heinz, and Sparkman, along with the fact that only two votes could have changed the outcome, testify to the importance of the leadership amendments.[26] Over three-quarters of the lawmakers actually co-sponsored the changes. Clearly, the leadership amendments proved crucial to the outcome. Seldom does a single factor play such an important role in the resolution of a major Senate debate.

THE DEBATE OVER MILITARY PROVISIONS

The Neutrality treaty and its military provisions took center stage almost as soon as the Foreign Relations Committee began its hearings on the Panama Canal treaties in the fall of 1977. Amid reports that Panamanian officials interpreted America's rights of defense and military transit differently from the administration, committee members qualified opening statements supportive of the treaties to demand that these rights be clarified.[27] Appearances before the committee by treaty negotiators Sol Linowitz and Ellsworth Bunker did little to reassure its doubtful members. Linowitz told the committee that the original language of the treaty left the United States "in a position to assume that the canal's permanent neutrality is maintained" and set no limitation "on our ability to take such action as we may deem necessary in the event the canal's neutrality is threatened or violated from any source." He also claimed that a "special provision" authorizing "expeditious passage" of American warships in an emergency constituted "a preferential right to expeditious transit of our naval vessels whenever we consider this necessary."[28]

But continued complaining by committee members eventually forced President Carter and General Torrijos of Panama to issue a "Statement of Understanding" on October 14, 1979. This document reaffirmed the right of the United States to defend the neutrality of the canal but explicitly denied that this could be interpreted as a right of intervention in the internal affairs of Panama. The statement also interpreted the right of "expeditious passage" to mean that American warships, "in case of need or emergency," could go "to the head of the line of vessels in order to transit the Canal rapidly."[29]

Members of the Foreign Relations Committee remained skeptical because the "Statement of Understanding" was not a legally binding addition to the Neutrality treaty.[30] Skepticism increased after committee members visited Panama for talks with Panamanian officials.[31] Thereafter, debate in the Foreign Relations Committee focused not on whether to add the language to the treaty itself but on the exact form the addition should take.[32] Majority Leader Robert Byrd and Minority Leader Howard Baker eventually settled the matter by announcing that they would support the treaties only if they were amended with the exact language of the statement. Once it became clear that both the Panamanians and the administration would tolerate these "leadership amendments," the Foreign Relations Committee voted to approve the treaties by a vote of 14–1.[33]

When debate commenced on the floor of the Senate in February, Majority Leader Byrd defended the first of the two leadership amendments by arguing that it would make it "as clear as the sun in a cloudless sky" that the U.S. could "take whatever action is necessary" to defend the canal against "any threat no matter from whence it may come."[34] Senator Frank Church led the defense of the second amendment, concluding: "It provides that our naval ships and auxiliary vessels will not have only priority passage, but the right to go to the head of the line. We determine it; what more do we want?"[35]

Treaty opponents obviously wanted more. They wondered *how* the U.S. would exercise its right to defend the canal, since the treaties provided for removing all U.S. troops and bases by the year 2000.[36] They also argued that the amendment would give Panama a "veto" over any U.S. action in the Canal Zone once it became Panamanian territory, since it prohibited interference in the "internal affairs" of Panama.[27] Finally, they pointed out that the amendment merely incorporated the "Statement of Understanding," which had not silenced Panama's differing interpretations of key provisions. Most important, it remained unclear whether the U.S. would need Panama's permission to defend the canal.[38]

Treaty opponents argued that the second leadership amendment, while theoretically guaranteeing the right of priority passage during emergencies, neither described nor defined "emergency"; nor did it specify who would decide whether an emergency existed. "What might be an emergency to us in our country," Senator James Allen argued, "might not be an emergency to Panama." Since Panama would control the canal's operation, the practical effect would be that "Panama would determine whether there was an emergency."[39]

The Senate rejected attempts by conservatives to modify the first leadership amendment with language more clearly asserting America's right to defend the canal with or without the permission of Panama. The Senate then adopted the first leadership amendment on March 9 by a vote of 84 to 5; the second was adopted by a vote of 85 to 3. But these votes did not end controversy over the leadership amendments. Indeed, the amendments remained at the top of the agenda during a full month of additional debate because of a reservation proposed at the last minute by Senator Dennis DeConcini of Arizona.

The DeConcini Reservation aimed to clarify the Senate's understanding of the first leadership amendment. It called for the Senate to attach non-binding language to the Neutrality treaty affirming America's right to take unilateral action in Panama to restore operations of the canal if it were closed for any reason after the year 2000.[40] If one accepted the administration's rhetoric uncritically, of course, the reservation was unnecessary. The administration had insisted all along that the Neutrality treaty guaranteed the right stipulated by the reservation, and the first leadership amendment presumably reiterated that guarantee. So why did the Panamanian Government denounce the reservation in the U.N. and threaten to reject the treaties if the Senate adopted it? Why did Panamanian citizens take to the streets in protest and refer to the reservation as "the DeConcini corollary to the Brezhnev doctrine"?[41] The answer would seem obvious: treaty opponents had been correct all along that the Panamanians interpreted the Neutrality treaty and the leadership amendments differently from the administration.

Eventually the Panamanians calmed down when the Senate leadership reworded the Panama Canal treaty with language designed to both "preserve DeConcini's language and nullify it."[42] This "verbal mirage," fashioned in private consultations, which included State Department officials, Senators Byrd and Church, and representatives of the Panamanian government, affirmed that "any action taken by the U.S." would be "only for the purpose of assuring that the Canal shall remain open,...and shall not have as its purpose nor be interpreted as a right of intervention...or interference with [Panama's] political independence or sovereign integrity."[43]

Despite the fact that this language merely echoed the leadership amendments, it seemed to please all concerned. But the controversy over the reservation raised an interesting question about the motivations behind support for the leadership amendments. Why did the leadership amendments, despite their obvious failure to resolve ambiguity over American military rights, motivate so many Senators to support the treaties? The answer lies more in perceptions of public opinion than in any supposed merits of the amendments. An examination of how pro-treaty Senators popularized the notion that the leadership amendments assuaged a hostile public reveals perhaps the decisive factor in ratification of the treaties.

PUBLIC OPINION AND POLITICAL
PHILOSOPHY

Both political philosophy and empirical questions concerning public opinion played important roles in the debate over Panama, as Senators debated both the propriety of "the people" dictating foreign policy and the state of public opinion and its discernible trends. The first major national poll on the issue came in June 1975, and for the next two years pollsters charted every response to the progression of events. Eventually no fewer than twenty-five national public opinion polls showed everything from a nearly ten-to-one majority against the treaties to a majority in favor of the pacts.[44]

In the early stages of the controversy, polls showed overwhelming opposition to relinquishing the canal.[45] Treaty opponents also noted a remarkable flood of mail to Senate offices confirming the message of the polls. A compilation of Senate mail by the American Conservative Union showed that some Senators received as many as 4,000 communications on Panama in a single week, with opposition running from 90 to 100 percent. Senator Orrin Hatch alone had received 3,000 communications as of August 1977, only three of which supported the treaties.[46]

In response, pro-treaty Senators initially took argumentative refuge in philosophical rationales for acting contrary to "the will of the people." Senator Joseph Biden of Delaware, for instance, argued that "we spend too much time on what the public opinion polls say." He urged his colleagues on the Foreign Relations Committee to "decide what is good and what is not good" and to "stop listening so much to the polls and talk about the issues."[47] Senator Robert Byrd expanded the argument on the floor of the Senate, insisting that courageous public servants must sometimes risk political fortune in the best interest of a mistaken constituency. The "easy vote," he argued, would be "to vote against the treaties," for there was "no political mileage to be gained" in supporting them. But he claimed "a responsibility not only to follow . . . and to represent" his constituents but also "to inform them and to lead them when, in my judgment, . . . it is in the best interests of the United States that the treaties be approved." Senators owed constitutents more than deference, he concluded; they owed them "a judgment, an honest judgment, a sincere judgment, a considered judgment." Byrd and other pro-treaty Senators quoted Edmund Burke as their authority on the proper philosophy of representation: "Your representative owes you not only his industry but also his judgment, and he betrays rather than serves you if he sacrifices it to your opinion."[48]

The philosophical rationale for independent judgment went hand-in-hand in pro-treaty rhetoric with claims that the public was too ignorant and emotional about the Panama Canal treaties to exercise good judgment. Byrd again led the way here, by wondering aloud: "How many of those who urge us to oppose the treaties have actually read the content of these treaties?"[49] Senator Pell argued that public opposition could only be based on "false impressions about the basis of our current presence in the Canal Zone," about "America's interests in the canal" and how they "are protected in the proposed new treaties," and about "our realistic choices in considering these treaties."[50] Others cited polls showing that Americans knew few details of the treaties' provisions as evidence of the irrationality of opposition.[51] According to treaty proponents, "offended sensitivities and ruffled chauvinism" caused hostility toward the treaties, and they blamed a demagogic campaign by the Radical Right.[52]

Treaty opponents had plenty of ammunition to fight the battle over political philosophy. While pro-treaty Senators quoted Burke, Senator William Scott marshalled testimony from a long list of American political heroes, including Thomas Jefferson, John Adams, John Marshall, Daniel Webster, and Abraham Lincoln, all reminding his colleagues that "sovereignty resides in the people." He asked them to "remember that we are here in a representative capacity as servants and not masters of the people."[53] Scott and other treaty opponents professed faith in the seemingly mystical corporate wisdom of "the people." As Senator Curtis put it: "The American people sometimes have a notion and an intuition that is right. They have been endowed with that. They can sense when something is wrong."[54]

Other treaty opponents agreed in principle that an ignorant or overly emotional public should not guide the actions of the Senate, particularly on a matter of foreign policy.[55] But in opposition to treaty supporters, they argued that the public was concerned and informed about the Panama Canal treaties. Orrin Hatch challenged characterizations of the public as ignorant by saying: "I think the people of this country are not as foolish as many of our leaders think they are."[56] He argued that "the vast majority" of the people had "more knowledge about these treaties than any of my protreaty colleagues have been willing to admit."[57] Paul Laxalt went further, arguing that he had "never seen more knowledge exhibited by the public generally throughout the country [on] an issue."[58] Senator J. Bennett Johnston of Louisiana emphasized that the issue was not a technical question requiring "great study." It was not "an issue of a complicated weapons system" like the AWACS control plane, cruise missiles, or B-1 bombers. The Senate could "trust the collective judgment" because the Panama Canal was "a very simple, straightforward issue." Johnston concluded: "I am frank to say that I have no special knowledge that is of such an esoteric nature, of such a difficult or technical nature, that my constituency cannot understand it."[59]

Thus the controversy over political philosophy and public opinion was not simply a contest between champions and opponents of deference to "the people." Both sides agreed that public opinion should not shape policy-making when an issue is too complex, too technical, or too shrouded in secrecy to be understood by the average citizen, and both sides disavowed deference to a misinformed or emotional public. The debate over public opinion on the Panama treaties ultimately boiled down, not to a dispute over the philosophy of popular sovereignty in America, but to questions about the nature of public opinion on the issue.

PUBLIC OPINION AS
AN EMPIRICAL ISSUE

As the debate over the Panama Canal treaties progressed, pro-treaty Senators began to sound more sanguine arguments about public opinion. Instead of evoking the philosophical rationale for ignoring the people, they set out to prove that the public had changed its mind. Specifically, they argued that an "educational process" had begun to "gradually turn around this public opinion."[60] As administration spokesmen appeared before the Foreign Relations Committee to report on their "very extensive program of explanation," pro-treaty Senators began to speak of an emerging "trend" toward public support for the treaties.[61] By November 1977, Majority Leader Byrd was telling the press about a national "shift of opinion" on the treaties, and in January Charles Percy claimed that the shift had begun to show up in congressional mail—a sure indication that people were "really beginning to think."[62] In January 1978 pro-treaty Senators noted that the Gallup Poll showed for the first time a plurality of Americans favoring the treaties: 45 percent of the public reportedly now favored the treaties, while 42 percent remained opposed.[63] Senator Church noted a similar trend in Patrick Caddell's polls and attributed the shift to education about the treaties.[64]

Pro-treaty Senators attributed the "turnabout" in public opinion to more than just "education," however. They principally credited the leadership amendments. George McGovern provided one of the earliest explanations of the connection between public opinion and the amendments during the hearings of the Foreign Relations Committee. He noted that "two or three recent public opinion polls" confirmed that most Americans opposed the original treaties. But when pollsters asked about amending the treaties, an "overwhelming majority" of Americans—"I think a 2-to-1 majority"—came to favor the treaties. McGovern called it "important to show that even in the absence of very much education and information on this subject, by margins of 2 to 1 the American public supports those two treaties as we now propose to modify them."[65]

Other pro-treaty Senators elaborated on the "turnabout" on the floor of the Senate, citing still more polls showing the positive impact of "information" and the leadership amendments.[66] A *New York Times*/CBS News poll cited by Senator Dick Clark was typical of the polls indicating that the amendments produced a "turnabout" in public opinion. The poll showed that the American people opposed the original treaties by a margin of 49 to 29 percent. But the figures shifted to 63 to 24 percent in favor of the treaties when respondents were asked: "Suppose you felt that the treaties provided that the United States could always send in troops to keep the canal open to ships of all nations. Would you then approve of the treaties?"[67] Pro-treaty Senators concluded from such data that the public had been "overwhelmingly opposed to these treaties as they were submitted," but would "support [them] as . . . the Senate may amend them."[68] Senator Byrd even conceded that the amendments added little or nothing to the original treaties, but he urged their adoption anyway because they went "a long way toward alleviating the concerns of the American people."[69]

In developing these arguments, pro-treaty Senators created a portrait of an attentive and dynamic public. They suggested that an initially hostile public rather suddenly came to favor the treaties because of "education" and because of the leadership amendments. Ultimately they claimed that their decision was not only "right" but also supported by "the people."

Anti-treaty Senators, of course, were not about to concede that any "turnabout" had taken place. They could not let claims of a trend toward public support for the treaties go unanswered, for they had been championing the doctrine of deference to "the people." Hence, they too changed their strategy and began attacking the evidence of a "turnabout." They denied claims by Senator Percy and others that congressional mail had begun to reflect a change in public opinion. They insisted that the "overwhelming majority" of letters still opposed the treaties, citing figures ranging from "95 pecent" to "1,000 to 1" against the pacts.[70] The major battle, however, contested the public opinion polls. Treaty opponents cited both state and national polls to show that no "turnabout" had occurred despite administration "propaganda" and a pro-treaty bias in the "major news media."[71]

State-wide polls provided the most startling figures. Senator Hatch cited a poll in Utah showing a persistent margin of nearly four-to-one against the treaties, while Senator Scott reported that his own poll in Virginia revealed that 87 percent of the people opposed the agreement.[72] National polls cited by treaty opponents also showed persistent and overwhelming opposition to the treaties. After pro-treaty Senators began talking of a "turnabout," treaty opponents spoke mostly of figures from the Opinion Research Corporation (ORC)—a "very distinguished and reliable polling organization"—because it had asked "fair" questions on Panama for the preceding four years.[73] As the "most comprehensive survey ever taken on the question of the Panama Canal," the ORC's four-year survey certainly would show any trend toward public support for the treaties. But instead, the ORC survey showed the opposite; opposition to giving up "ownership and control" of the canal actually had risen from 66 percent in 1975 to 72 percent in February 1978.[74]

More important, the ORC data exposed the fallacy in pro-treaty arguments about the impact of the leadership amendments on public opinion. Treaty opponents admitted that the findings shifted "dramatically to nearly 50–50" when pollsters asked the question: "What if the treaties are amended to allow for continued U.S. defense of the canal after the year 2000?"[75] But only the ORC had taken into account the controversy over whether the leadership amendment provided such a guarantee. The ORC recognized that anti-treaty Senators had tried to substitute stronger language for the leadership amendments, language asserting America's right to act unilaterally in defense of the Canal. Rather than ask respondents only if they supported treaties amended to "guarantee America's right to defend the canal," the ORC questioned respondents specifically about the leadership amendments *versus* the stronger language. The results showed that only 18 percent of the public favored the leadership amendments, while 68 percent favored the stronger language.[76] "When given a fair choice of alternatives," treaty opponents noted, the "overwhelming sentiment of the American public...was for an amendment...which gives the United States the right to act "by itself' in defense of the canal."[77]

THE ILLUSORY TURNABOUT

Treaty opponents persuaded few of their colleagues with the ORC data. Instead, the pro-treaty portrait of public opinion prevailed, influencing the procedures and the outcome of the Senate debate. Belief in the "turnabout" first influenced the Foreign Relations Committee, where a pro-treaty majority dictated procedures for the floor debate which promoted ratification. While arguing that Senators could assuage hostile constituencies by co-sponsoring the leadership amendments, the committee reported a "clean" resolution of ratification for the Neutrality treaty; the committee left the amending process up to the full Senate acting as a Committee of the Whole.[78] The unusual procedure allowed all treaty supporters to argue to "skeptical constituents that they had refused to rubber-stamp the treaties, insisting instead on strengthening the protection of American interests."[79] The Carter administration promoted this strategy by refusing to endorse the leadership amendments. One While House aide called Carter's public opposition to the amendments a tactical move designed to allow Senators to "go back home and say they made us do something we didn't want to.... Now they can vote for the treaties."[80] And in the end, the strategy worked. More than 75 Senators co-sponsored the leadership amendments, with many of them stating publicly that they would have opposed the agreement without the changes. Obviously, the amendments proved the key to the outcome. If only two Senators had voted differently, the treaties would have been defeated.

The pro-treaty portrait of public opinion also prevailed outside the Senate. Senator Helms correctly predicted that the American media would not report the ORC survey.[81] Instead, major media reported that public hostility toward the treaties had been overcome by "education" and by the leadership amendments. On January 13, 1978, *NBC Nightly News* reported that while "most Americans" opposed the original treaties, "65 percent of the public would approve ratification if the United States reserved the right to intervene militarily in emergencies."[82] On February 1, *The New York Times* reported that the treaties had yet to win the approval of a majority of Americans but that a "change in opinion since last summer [had] created a political climate" more favorable to ratification.[83] Going a bit further, *Time* reported in February that public opinion had shifted from "2-to-1 opposition" to a "majority" in favor of the pacts, and later *Time* noted a shift in Gallup's poll from 30 percent to 45 percent in favor of the treaties. "Few times in recent history has a President mounted such a strenuous campaign to influence public opinion," *Time* commented, and the administration could "claim substantial credit" for the "turnabout."[84] Similarly, *Newsweek* claimed that the "remarkable turnabout" revealed by Gallup would boost Carter's image and make the Panama campaign "the model on which the Administration will base its future campaigns for passage of other key legislation."[85]

President Carter gave the myth of a "turnabout" in public opinion its ultimate expression in a victory address following Senate ratification of the treaties. The Panama Canal treaties, he proclaimed, now had a "firm base in the will of the American people."[86] Over the next several months, however, Carter's statement, along with the entire pro-treaty case, was belied by numerous public opinion polls. Rather than revealing that the Panama Canal treaties had a "firm base in the will of the people," later polls—polls assessing attitudes toward the treaties as *actually* modified by the leadership amendments—revealed "the public's fundamental distaste for what had been wrought."[87] The Harris poll of April 1978 showed that only 37 percent of the public believed ratification of the amended treaties was a "good thing for the United States," while 44 percent did not "feel that way." A better question by Harris in June ("All in all, do you favor or oppose the treaties on the Panama Canal passed by the U.S. Senate?") produced even higher figures in opposition: 35 percent in favor and 49 percent opposed. Also in June, the Roper poll asked Americans whether the Senate should have approved the Panama Canal treaties, and only 30 percent said yes, while 52 percent said no. Finally, NBC News polled Americans in September and found the greatest opposition yet; only 34 percent of the respondents said they approved of the Senate's action, while 56 percent said they did not approve.[88]

How does one explain these findings? Perhaps there had been another "turnabout" in public opinion. Perhaps many Americans came to favor the treaties during the debate only to change their minds again. But there is another, more likely, explanation: that there had never been a "turnabout" in the first place. In retrospect, it appears that the anti-treaty portrait of public opinion had been correct all along. Pro-treaty forces apparently misinterpreted polls showing support for treaties amended to "guarantee America's right to defend the canal" as support for the Carter-Torrijos treaties with the leadership amendments. Data from the ORC, of course, would explain such a misinterpretation. They indicate that Americans who actually favored the treaties only with the sort of amendments rejected by the Senate were mistakenly counted as treaty supporters by pollsters who failed to discriminate between the leadership amendments and the stronger amendments proposed by conservatives. Many people might have answered "yes" to a pollster who asked only if they would favor the treaties if they were amended to "guarantee America's right to defend the canal." Many Senators who opposed the treaties also claimed they would have supported them if there had been real guarantees of America's right to defend the canal. Some pro-treaty Senators had even cited polls assessing support for an amendment allowing the U.S. to "intervene" in Panama as support for the leadership amendments.[89] This constituted an even more obvious misinterpretation for the leadership amendments explicitly renounced any right of "intervention."

Once the Senate ratified the treaties with the leadership amendments, the illusion of a "turnabout" in public opinion could not be maintained. When respondents were asked to judge the final product of the debate, those favoring stronger guarantees of military rights "returned" to the anti-treaty column, and opposition to the treaties "returned" to almost exactly the same level found by pollsters at the beginning of the debate.[90] Undoubtedly many pro-treaty Senators honestly believed in the "turnabout" in public opinion on the Panama Canal treaties. Nonetheless, the fact that the "turnabout" was illusory raises some troubling questions, both about the Panama Canal treaties, and about the role of public opinion in American foreign policy generally.

CONCLUSION

Adoption of the leadership amendments as a palliative for hostile public opinion raises serious questions about the integrity of the Panama Canal treaties. The administration insisted all along that the leadership amendments merely reiterated America's right to act unilaterally in defense of the canal, while the Panamanian reaction to the DeConcini Reservation revealed that they disagreed. Since the amendments so obviously failed to clear up confusion over this matter, one must wonder if the Senate sacrificed the clarity of the agreement for political reasons. Will the new relationship between the U.S. and Panama, a relationship that depends heavily upon goodwill and cooperation, be jeopardized by renewed bickering over the meaning of the treaties in the future? More important, will Panamanian and American diplomats someday be called upon in the midst of a military emergency to resolve the confusion left by the Senate?

The role of public opinion in the Senate debate over Panama addresses larger, more timeless issues about the conduct of foreign affairs in a democratic society. The episode could be cited as proof that policy-making elites rhetorically create fictional publics in order to justify *a priori* decisions. Most of the political, business, and religious "establishment" in America—indeed, most of the educated elite—favored the treaties, and they were negotiated and submitted to the Senate despite polls showing overwhelming public opposition.[91] During the Senate debate, public opinon was, in effect, rhetorically reconstructed to favor the treaties despite the fact that the polls, at best, were inconclusive. One might argue that the conception of public opinion that most influenced the Senate decision was indeed a "fiction" created by treaty proponents.

But fictional publics are not necessarily "lies" by manipulative politicians. Distortions of "real" public opinion may result from errors of interpretation rather than from strategic manipulation by ruling elites. During the Senate debate over Panama, there were empirical bases for believing in the "turnabout" in public opinion. Senators who cited the "turnabout" to justify their votes may have been guilty of nothing more than wishful thinking, ignorance about the mechanics of polling, or befuddlement in the face of voluminous and conflicting evidence. The proliferation of scientific polling in recent years has not eliminated uncertainty in policy-makers' judgments about public opinion. Public opinion remains an elusive phenomenon; the most accurate portrait of public opinion still may be lost among numerous inaccurate portraits. The debate over Panama reveals how subtle differences in questions asked by pollsters can lead to very different conclusions. It also shows how a major issue can prompt so many polls with such widely varying findings that virtually any characterization of "the people" can be justified.

The debate over Panama does not give cause for hand-wringing over the plight of representative democracy in modern America. Indeed, the debate reaffirmed the extraordinary sensitivity of American policy-makers to public opinion, for even those who considered the public misguided remained reluctant to support the treaties until there were signs that "education" and changes in the treaties produced public support. The debate over the Panama Canal treaties does indicate, however, that policy-makers could be more aware of how differing methods of sampling, data collection, and interpretation make some polls better than others. And it shows that policy-makers should be more skeptical that any poll reveals fully the true state of objective public opinion.

Notes

1. Robert F. Berkhofer, Jr., *A Behavioral Approach to Historical Analysis* (New York: The Free Press, 1969), p. 162; Lee Benson, "An Approach to the Scientific Study of Past Public Opinion," *Public Opinion Quarterly*, 31 (1967–1968), 522.

2. Alexander Hamilton, "On the Powers of the Senate," in *The Debates in the Several State Conventions on the Adoption of the Federal Constitution*, ed. Jonathan Elliot, 2nd ed., 5 vols. (1888; rpt. New York: Burt Franklin Reprints, 1974), II, p. 301.

3. Thomas A. Bailey, *A Diplomatic History of the American People* (New York: F. S. Crofts, 1940), pp. 756. Even critics of foreign policies shaped by public opinion, such as Hans Morgenthau and George Kennan, assumed that American foreign policy *did* reflect public opinion. They suggested, as Ernest May has noted, that "this should not be so—that policies should come to a larger extent from calculation by experts." Ernest R. May, "An American Tradition in Foreign Policy: The Role of Public Opinion," in *Theory and Practice in American Politics*, ed. William H. Nelson (1964; rpt. Chicago: Phoenix Books, 1967), p. 102.

4. Gabriel Kolko, *The Roots of American Foreign Policy: An Analysis of Power and Purpose* (Boston: Beacon Press, 1969), p. 13.

5. Joyce Kolko and Gabriel Kolko, *The Limits of Power: The World and United States Foreign Policy, 1945–1954* (New York: Harper and Row, 1972), pp. 333–334.

6. The classic study is Angus Campbell, Philip E. Converse, Warren E. Miller, and Donald E. Stokes, *The American Voter* (New York: John Wiley and Sons, 1960).

7. See Norman H. Nie, Sidney Verba, and John R. Petrocik, *The Changing American Voter* (Cambridge: Harvard University Press, 1976). Cf. Gerald Pomper, *Voters' Choice: Varieties of American Electoral Behavior* (New York: Harper and Row, 1975), pp. 5–12.

8. See W. Lance Bennett, *Public Opinion in American Politics* (New York: Harcourt, Brace, Jovanovich, 1980), esp. pp. 12–16; Pomper, *Voters' Choice*, pp. 8–12.

9. See Robert P. Newman, "Lethal Rhetoric: The Selling of the China Myths," *Quarterly Journal of Speech*, 61 (1975), 113–128; Robert P. Newman, "Foreign Policy: Decision and Argument," *Advances in Argumentation Theory and Research*, ed. J. Robert Cox and Charles Arthur Willard (Carbondale: Southern Illinois University Press, 1982), esp. pp. 321–323; Philip Wander, "The Rhetoric of American Foreign Policy," *Quarterly Journal of Speech*, 70 (1984), 339–361.

10. Gerald Hauser and Carole Blair, "Antecedents to the Public," *Pre Text*, 3 (1982), 140–141.

11. Gordon S. Wood, *The Creation of the American Republic, 1776–1787* (New York: W. W. Norton and Co., 1969), p. 383.

12. Michael C. McGee, "In Search of 'the People': A Rhetorical Alternative," *Quarterly Journal of Speech*, 61 (1975), 249.

13. Bernard C. Cohen, *The Public's Impact on Foreign Policy* (Boston: Little, Brown and Co., 1973), p. 11.

14. For a detailed discussion of problems of methodology and interpretation in polling see Charles W. Roll and Albert H. Cantril, *Polls: Their Use and Misuse in Politics* (Cabin John, MD: Seven Locks Press, 1980), pp. 65–135.

15. See U.S., Congress, Senate, Committee on Foreign Relations, *A Chronology of Events Relating to the Panama Canal*, by Congressional Research Service, Library of Congress, Committee Print, 95th Cong., 1st sess. (Washington D.C.: GPO, 1977), pp. 24–34.

16. "The Message of the President Transmitting the 1977 Panama Canal Treaties to the Senate, September 16, 1977," in U.S., Congress, Senate, Committee on Foreign Relations, *Background Documents Relating to the Panama Canal*, by Congressional Research Service, Library of Congress, Committee Print, 95th Cong., 1st sess. (Washington D.C.: GPO, 1977), pp. 1514–1553.

17. See J. Michael Hogan, "The 'Great Debate' Over Panama: An Analysis of Controversy Over the Carter-Torrijos Treaties of 1977," Diss. University of Wisconsin-Madison, 1983, pp. 149–187.

18. U.S., Congress, Senate, Committee on Foreign Relations, *Senate Debate on the Panama Canal Treaties: A Compendium of Major Statements, Documents, Record Votes and Relevant Events*, by Congressional Research Service, Library of Congress, Committee Print, 96th Cong., 1st sess. (Washington D.C.: GPO, 1979), pp. 10–11.

19. Marquis Childs, "McIntyre's Stand Against the Radical Right," reprinted from *The Washington Post* in U.S., Congress, Senate, Committee on the Judiciary, *Panama Canal Treaties [United States Senate Debate], 1977–1978*, 3 parts, Committee Print, 95th Cong. (Washington D.C.: GPO, 1978), II, 3491. Hereafter cited as *Debate*.

20. Quoted in Robert G. Kaiser, "What Is (and Isn't) Said in Canal Debate," reprinted from *The Washington Post* in *Debate*, III, 5249.

21. Craig Allen Smith, "New Myths and Old Realities: Jimmy Carter, the 'New Right,' and the Panama Canal," paper presented at the annual meeting of the Speech Communication Association, 1983, p. 9. Cf. Thomas A. Hollihan, "The Public Controversy Over the Panama Canal Treaties: A Fantasy Theme Analysis of Foreign Policy Dramas," Diss. University of Nebraska-Lincoln, 1978.

22. A survey of Senators in the summer of 1977 showed thirty-seven in favor of the treaties (only eleven strongly in favor) and twenty-five opposed, with the rest undecided. As the floor debate was about to begin, Howard Baker commented: "I cannot count the votes to consent to ratify these treaties at this moment." See Angus Deming, et. al., "The Canal: Time to Go?" *Newsweek*, 22 August 1977, pp. 30–31; Baker in U.S., Congress, Senate, Committee on Foreign Relations, *Panama Canal Treaties: Hearings . . . on the Panama Canal Treaty and the Treaty Concerning the Permanent Neutrality and Operation of the Panama Canal, . . . ,* 5 parts, 95th Cong. (Washington D.C.: GPO, 1977), V, 33. Hereafter cited as *Hearings*.

23. See Committee on Foreign Relations, *Senate Debate on the Panama Canal Treaties: A*

Compendium, pp. 347–414, 484–486; "How the Treaty Was Saved," *Time*, 1 May 1978, pp. 12–15; *Debate*, III, 5584–5585.

24. *Debate*, I, 850.

25. *Debate*, II, 2036–2037.

26. *Debate*, I, 1291–1292, 1706; II, 3561–3563; *Hearings*, V, 54. See also Senator Brooke in *Debate*, II, 3669–3672; Senator Baker in *Hearings*, V, 32; the accounts of pro-treaty decisions by Senators Baker and Bentsen in Committee on Foreign Relations, *Senator Debate on the Panama Canal Treaties: A Compendium*, pp. 518–519.

27. See Senator Allen's remarks and Paul Ryan's article of September 11 in *Debate*, I, 121–123; Senator Dole in *Debate*, I, 226–228; Senators Javits, Baker, Clark, Case, and Secretary Vance, in *Hearings*, I, 3–4, 7–8, 30–32.

28. *Hearings*, I, 23.

29. Committee on Foreign Relations, *Background Documents*, p. 1620.

30. See Senators Church, Clark, and Case in *Hearings*, I, 455–456, 465–466, 486. See also the administration's interpretation in *Hearings*, III, 682–683.

31. See U.S., Congress, House, Committee on Foreign Affairs, *Congress and Foreign Policy—1978*, by Congressional Research Service, Library of Congress, Committee Print, 96th Cong. (Washington D.C.: GPO, 1979), pp. 192–193; "Squaring Off on the Canal," *Time*, 30 January 1978, p. 31; Don Holt and Ron Moreau, "The Other Lobbyist," *Newsweek*, 13 February 1978, p. 20; Committee on Foreign Relations, *Senate Debate on the Panama Canal Treaties: A Compedium*, pp. 513, 516–519.

32. The committee first sought to add a new article to the Neutrality treaty. But when Panamanian officials objected, the committee voted to recommend two amendments. See Committee on Foreign Affairs, *Congress and Foreign Policy—1978*, p. 194.

33. See Baker in *Debate*, I, 1291–1293; Byrd and Baker in *Hearings*, V, 3–4, 23, 32; Richard Steele, et. al., "Heading for a Win?" *Newsweek*, 13 February 1978, p. 20.

34. *Debate*, I, 1410, 1413.

35. *Debate*, II, 3417.

36. See Senator Hatch in *Debate*, I, 1412.

37. Senators Allen and Griffin in *Debate*, I, 1547, 1848; II, 3234.

38. Senator Griffin in *Debate*, II, 2798–2840, 3237–3238.

39. *Debate*, I, 1848.

40. See Committee on Foreign Relations, *Senate Debate on the Panama Canal Treaties: A Compendium*, pp. 403–405.

41. Walter LaFeber, *The Panama Canal: The Crisis in Historical Perspective*, 2nd ed. (New York: Oxford University Press, 1979), p. 246; "Last Test of a Battered Treaty," *Time*, 24 April 1978, p. 22; Richard Boeth, et. al., "Canal Showdown," *Newsweek*, 24 April 1978, p. 28.

42. Boeth, et. al., "Canal Showdown," p. 26.

43. Richard Boeth, et. al., "Victory on the Canal," *Newsweek*, 1 May 1978, p. 23.

44. Bernard Roshco, "The Polls: Polling on Panama—Si; Don't Know; Hell, No!" *Public Opinion Quarterly*, 42 (1978), 551–562.

45. Senators Helms, Thurmond, and Hatch in *Debate*, I, 62, 96, 560–561, 847; Philip Crane, *Surrender in Panama: The Case Against the Treaty* (New York: Dale Books, 1978), p. 105.

46. Crane, *Surrender in Panama*, pp. 105–108.

47. *Hearings*, I, 161–162.

48. *Debate*, I, 1252–1253. See also *Debate*, I, 1898; II, 2062–2063, 2455, 3746.

49. *Debate*, I, 1253.

50. *Debate*, II, 2210.

51. Senator Sarbanes in *Debate*, II, 3312–3313.

52. Senators McIntyre and Hatfield in *Debate*, II, 2286–2293, 2302–2303.

53. *Debate*, I, 1251; II, 3596–3597.

54. *Debate*, II, 3346.

55. Senators Allen and Hatch in *Debate*, I, 1853; II, 2141, 2455.
56. *Debate*, I, 1319.
57. *Debate*, I, 1781.
58. *Debate*, I, 1897.
59. *Debate*, I, 2009–2010.
60. Senator Pell in *Hearings*, I, 5. See also Senator Glenn in *Hearings*, V, 24–25.
61. Ellsworth Bunker in *Hearings*, I, 467.
62. Committee on Foreign Relations, *Senate Debate on the Panama Canal Treaties: A Compendium*, p. 513; *Hearings*, V, 17.
63. Senators Byrd, Church, Sarbanes, and Riegle in *Debate*, I, 1255–1256; II, 2551, 3312, 3634.
64. According to Church, Caddell's surveys showed the public opposing the treaties by a margin of 61 to 25 percent in August 1977. But in December, "as the public came to understand the treaties better," opposition had dropped to 49 percent while support had risen to 35 percent. By February, opposition had dropped further to 46 percent, while the number of people supporting the treaties continued to rise to 37 percent. See *Debate*, II, 2550–2551. See also Senator Stevenson's discussion of the Gallup and NBC News polls in *Debate*, II, 3726.
65. *Hearings*, V, 28.
66. See the discussion of William Schneider's study in *Debate*, II, 3306–3311; Senator Church's discussion of the leadership amendments and the Gallup poll in *Debate*, II, 2551; Senator Byrd's discussion of the CBS-Time and NBC News polls in *Debate*, II, 3204.
67. *Debate*, I, 1504.
68. *Debate*, I, 1257.
69. *Debate*, II, 3211.
70. Senators Helms and Hatch in *Debate*, II, 2248, 2994. See also Senators Scott and Thurmond in *Debate*, I, 1623; II, 2986, 3596.
71. Senator Helms in *Debate*, II, 3300.
72. See *Debate*, II, 2140–2141; I, 1251.
73. Senators Helms and Hatch in *Debate*, II, 2987, 3298, 3657.
74. Senator Helms in *Debate*, II, 3298–3306.
75. Senator Melcher in *Debate*, II, 3736.
76. Senator Helms in *Debate*, II, 3301.
77. Senator Laxalt in *Debate*, II, 3369.
78. See Committee on Foreign Affairs, *Congress and Foreign Policy—1978*, pp. 194–195.
79. I. M. Destler, "Treaty Troubles: Versailles in Reverse," *Foreign Policy*, no. 33 (1978–1979), 50. See also "Opening the Great Canal Debate," *Time*, 20 February 1978, p. 19; "Drug Debate: A Bust," *Time*, 6 March 1978, p. 22; Committee on Foreign Relations, *Senate Debate on the Panama Canal Treaties: A Compendium*, p. 520.
80. Steele, et al., "Heading for a Win?" p. 20.
81. *Debate*, II, 2992.
82. Walter LaFeber, "Covering the Canal, Or, How the Press Missed the Boat," *More*, 8 (1978), 27.
83. LaFeber, "Covering the Canal," p. 27.
84. "Opening the Canal Debate," p. 20; "Carter Wins on Panama," *Time*, 27 March 1978, p. 9.
85. Steele, et al., "Heading for a Win?" p. 18.
86. Jimmy Carter, "Address to the Nation," 18 April 1978, in U.S., Department of State, *Bulletin*, May 1978, p. 52.
87. Roshco, "Polling on Panama," p. 562.
88. Roscho, "Polling on Panama," p. 562.
89. Senator Church in *Debate*, II, 2551; Senator Byrd in *Debate*, II, 3204.
90. Roshco, "Polling on Panama," p. 562.
91. See William Schneider, "Behind the Passions of the Canal Debate," reprinted from *The Washington Post* in *Debate*, II, 3310–3311.

The New Populist Campaign
for Economic Democracy:
A Rhetorical Exploration

RONALD LEE

The tension between historical populism and its contemporary counterpart in the rhetoric of such politicians as George McGovern, Jimmy Carter, and Gary Hart has been called the populist "paradox."[1] Earlier populists were called "calamity howlers," "demagogues," and "members of a lunatic fringe." They were throughout advocates of agrarian reform.[2] Populists of the moment are part of the establishment and even as they may promote reform, they are not tied exclusively to agrarian issues. Populism is no longer a pejorative term.

The term's rehabilitation has been so thoroughgoing in recent years that fundamentally opposed political movements searching for legitimacy have self-consciously taken up populist trappings. On the left, progressives have rejected radical orthodoxy and launched the Campaign for Economic Democracy. On the right, social activists frustrated with the impotence of conventional conservatism have organized a movement widely identified as the New Right. With the waning influences of party, narrow factions are no longer effectively screened from meaningful political participation. To take advantage of this emerging opportunity, these movements must find ways to address the persistent commitments of the political culture without undue compromise.

The "New Populism" is the chief rhetorical product of the anti-party age. Anti-elitism, which is the very core of populism, has become attractive with the advent of party reform.[3] With the increasing importance of open primaries, candidates are encouraged to exploit fully Madison Avenue marketing techniques which permit communication with the voter unmediated by party.[4] This new situation creates a disincentive for the continued employment of the comfortable rhetoric of coalition-building and hastens the construction of messages directed toward factional interests.[5] In other words, the techniques of the new politics has led directly to the discourse of the New Populism.[6]

Political perspectives are related traditionally to various modes of presentation.[7] The introduction of new political incentives has stressed the comfortable affinity between explanatory form and ideological commitment. The resulting discourse is not simply the product of the causal connection between situation and message. Rather it is a complex interaction among electoral demands, available patterns of expression, and ideology.

The recent proliferation of ideological "news" and "neos" reflects the struggle between electoral opportunity and philosophical purity. Because the "new populism" is a product of an increasingly open system, the means of ideological adaptation rest on the alleged effects of enlarging the spheres of participation. I will argue that the tension between participation and instrumental change is the major force in the developing rhetorical character of American politics.

In what follows, the "new populism" is explored through a self-conscious case of new political practice. Unlike earlier opposition movements, the leaders of the Campaign for Economic Democracy painstakingly considered the implications of conventional electioneering. This case provides an opportunity to examine the thus far neglected new populist expressions of the left. In this examination, I will describe the refashioned ideological commitments of the new populist left, portray the transformation of this vision from ideological tract to electoral narrative in Tom Hayden's Campaign for Economic Democracy, and explore the relationship between electoral practice and institutional legitimacy.

NEW POPULIST IDEOLOGY

The new populist vision redefines the post-Vietnam experience in America and in so doing demonstrates the continuing vitality of the progressive impulse in domestic life. Proponents of this vision believe that the conditions which led to the gutting of previous lefts' agendas have changed. Because the vision recalls the American populist experience of the last century, activists argue that the "irony of what befell the agrarian radicals was that they would have failed even if they had made no tactical errors of any kind, for their creed centered on concepts of political organization and uses of democratic government that were already too advanced to be accepted in the centralizing, culturally complacent nation of the Gilded Age."[8] But these theorists hold that circumstances are no longer sufficient to block progressive political change. "To the extent that these explanations for the failure of the American Left have merit," Mark Kann wrote, "they have considerably less merit today than yesterday."[9]

Four dimensions of the New Populism's ideological vision emerged from examination of works by leftist theoreticians. I have chosen those facets of populist ideology that are most relevant to the rhetorical difficulties faced by proponents of radical orthodoxy. Each of these dimensions is designed to bring progressives' tactics in closer alignment with electoral reality.

Activism. The defining characteristic of activisim is the reinterpretation of the "Me Decade." Rather than an era of complacency, the new populists see the rise of a "backyard revolution" which "by the beginning of the 1980's" had become a "renaissance in citizen activism...beginning to be visible at every hand." The evidence is found in the "over 500,000 mutual aid groups of different kinds which had come into existence, with total membership of more than 15 million." The new populists see virtually every element of local cooperation as testimony "to the growth of a democratic culture." These include "women's health clinics, art fairs, neighborhood newspapers, housing rehabilitation projects, cooperative athletic programs," and many others.[10]

Leftist historical interpretation of the agrarian revolt in the nineteenth century bolstered the relationship between a "cooperative crusade" and the emergence of a radical democratic consciousness. Historian Lawrence Goodwyn, the key left revisionist, concluded that "the Populists did have a greater sense of self as democratic citizens and a more hopeful view of democratic possibilities than that which is culturally licensed within the modern progressive societies around the globe, either socialist or capitalist."[11]

This construction maintains that the consciousness needed for progressive action lies in "doing." "Politics is not about solutions to problems," Milton Kitler said. "Politics is always about the discovery of common ground, about equality, about being together, about the future."[12] Democratic free space, whether in the grange hall meetings of the previous century or the block clubs of the 1980's, provides a place "for incubating alternative conceptions, ideas, and values, for deepening the definition of protest from defense of what exists into a struggle for new conceptions of rights and possibilities, and at times for generating revolutionary hopes and expectations."[13]

This construction, then, finds justification for revising the portrait of the post-Vietnam years in the numerous individual examples of local citizen cooperation. Proponents find this picture comforting, first, because it affirms the impact of the sixties by refuting the dominance of seventies narcissism, and, second, because it aruges that Americans are again receptive to progressive politics.

Crisis. America faces a crisis in "world view" personified by the contrast between "General Armstrong Custer...archetype 19th century *Man* of the American West" and "Henry David Thoreau, the opposite of Custer, who denounced both the corporate-industrial age from Walden Pond and the Mexican War from a prison cell."[14] For the new populists, the Thoreau who "questioned the very value of the age" was incarnate in the agrarian resistance which stood "at almost the very last moment before the values implicit in the corporate state captured the cultural high ground in American society itself."[15] But the Custer myth stands in the path of inevitable historical forces—the end of empire, the depletion of finite resources, the intolerable ecological cost of growth—which will usher in the post-materialist age.

New Populism differs from orthodox Marxism because it emphasizes culture over capital. It is not just the economic limits of growth that will lead the transformation to the post-materialist age, but the very high moral costs incurred by polluting the values and traditions of the American society. Tom Hayden argues that "the pretense, hypocrisy and emptiness of the affluent society" directed a generation of Americans "inward for their world view."[16] It is a new moral ethic more than an altered economic state that dominates the vision of the new age. Its symbols are conservation, quality, imagination to oppose commitment to growth, consumerism, and greed which marked the frontier ethic. "The emerging morality," Hayden proclaims, "will begin by recognizing an ancient truth—that the great moral and religious philosophers throughout history have tended to promote inner, rather than outer, rewards, modesty rather than status hunger, love rather than domination."[17] New left populism is as concerned with the Protestant Ethic, which fuels self-interest, as with the economic consequences of capitalism.

Tradition. For the left, Marxist economic analysis has always provided a lens through which to view the world. The view of the new populist left is different. The socialist myth of the "New Man" is the antithesis of populism. "The Marxist notion of a 'most radical rupture' with traditional ideas," Ralph Miliband noted, "signifies a break with all forms of tradition, and must expect to encounter the latter not as friend but foe."[18] Marx and Engels in the *Communist Manifesto* argued that "all fixed, fast frozen relations, with their train of ancient and venerable prejudices and opinions, are swept away, all new formed ones become antiquated before they can ossify."[19]

In stark departure, the new populists hold that social change comes not from class consciousness but from the contradiction between tradition and public policy. The uprising in Poland and the civil rights movement in America, for example, both relied heavily on the traditions of the Christian Church.

In theory, embracing tradition sets aside the socialist creed of "radical rupture" and embraces cultural values as an indispensable element in social change. In practice, the language of radical orthodoxy has been set aside because mass political movements in America have not been built on Marxist models. Americans have been moved by their commitment to tradition and not by their rejection of it.

Participation. The new populists contend that political common ground can be found in an emergent contradiction. The political process is increasingly open, at least in formal terms, and the economic system is increasingly closed. Americans have seen the enfranchisement of nearly all potential voters, the reform of the nominating process in both major parties, the revision of seniority systems in legislatures, and the establishment of public hearing requirements for regulatory agencies. On the other hand, "the capitalism in which everyone owned his or her property, in which consumers directly faced sellers, in which there was a kind of Economic Democracy has been replaced by impersonal corporatism which is dangerously independent of democratic control."[20] It is in the tension between these two trends that the new populist *topoi* appear. As Carnoy and Shearer explain, "the very same arguments that for two centuries support[ed] the ceding of political choice to the mass people rather than its retention by a single individual or a small group, also provide the rationale for production and investment decision making by workers and consumers, not by individual capital owners or their managers."[21]

Economic participation is to be gained through electoral participation. America's tradition will allow change only through democratic mandate. Out of this commitment emerges a two-step process: first, involvement in consequential electoral activity and, second, electoral success to fashion a more progressive long-term national agenda. The left, on this view, can never be a significant force in American life as long as it continues to trivialize itself with mere ideological posturing. "Winning," wrote Harry Boyte, "is the lifeblood of grass roots organizing, the only way that those accustomed to defeat and disunity can be welded into a powerful collective acting in their own behalf."[22]

The ideological vision of the new populists, then, is composed of a revisionist view of the post-Vietnam era (activism), a perception of changing political values in the wake of altered economic conditions (crisis), the rejection of socialist orthodoxy for a populist view of social change (tradition), and, finally, a commitment to electioneering with a radically democratic message (participation).

TRANSFORMATION OF
THE IDEOLOGICAL VISION

The difference in substantive commitments of the New Populism from the orthodox radicalism of earlier lefts explains only part of the rhetorical transformation. The transformation is not wholly, or even perhaps essentially, a process of making new factual claims, but rather of adjusting the facts to a different mode of presentation.

The historical context of the transformation is foreshadowed by the relationship of Hegel and Marx. Hegel's idealism led to a conservative view of the state and a protective posture toward the German monarch. Consequently, Marx's radicalism required a revolutionary reappraisal of his mentor's work. Hegelian dialectic, through Marx's materialism, was, as Engels expressed it, "placed upon its head; or rather, turned off its head, on which it was standing, and placed upon its feet."[23] The form of Marx's account of history was fundamentally different from the emplotment of Hegel's optimistic view of reason as the guiding force in Universal History.

Populism requires a vision that in most important respects places history back on its feet, or depending on one's viewpoint, back to its head. If the New Populism is defined by its electoral commitments, it must be structured to facilitate translation from ideology to campaign vision. Hence, the two key rhetorical transformations ought to assume alternately dissonant and consonant presentational forms. In other words, the *ideological* transformation from Marxism to populism should reveal a *shift* in mode, but the *tactical* transformation from populist ideology to campaign vision should disclose two related but distinct levels of discourse in *similar* modes.

Metonymy to Synecdoche

The visions sustaining Marxism and populism are quite different, and these differences are manifest in the form of presentation. Because the dominant organizing trope of an historical interpretation governs the pattern of association, tropological comparison reveals ideological commitments. Each of the four master tropes is a perspective on the world and, therefore, is invaluable for emphasizing the relationship between form and content.

Marxism is essentially metonymic. A "metonymy" is defined as "a figure of speech which consists of substituting for the name of a thing the name of an attribute of it or something closely related."[24] Metonymic association would employ "scepter" for "sovereignty" or the "bottle" for a "strong drink."[25] This tropic operation is reductionist. It speaks to the intangible (sovereignty, strong) in terms of the tangible (scepter, bottle). To borrow an example from Kenneth Burke, social science metonymically reduces action to motion. When empirical methodology is applied to human relations, these relations are discounted to regularities in behavior and, as a result, the "substance" of being human is a casualty to reduction.[26]

Synonyms associated with Marxism suggest its metonymic form—"scientific socialism," "economic determinism," "materialist conception of history," and so on. Each word pair conveys the reduction of the noun (socialism, determinism, history) to an adjectival force (scientific, economic, materialist). This reductionist process is at work in all the key terms of Marxist analysis. *Alienation* describes people's separation from their work, from their own products, and from their fellows.[27] *Class consciousness* is a separation of societal interests and a reduction of revolutionary progress to the activities of a "chosen people."[28] The *labor theory of value* explains the traditionally synthetic equation "product A = product B" in metonymic form. All of the potential contributions to commodity value are reduced to the amount of labor employed.[29] The concept of *historical materialism* holds that historical development is determined, or reducible to, "the mode of production of the material means of existence."[30] Consequently, at least for orthodox interpreters, the mode of production, or the Base, determines the nature of social relations in the Superstructure.

By constrast, the New Populism is synecdochic in form. Synecdoche is a form of "representation," but a representation which integrates part with whole rather than metonymically reduces the qualitative to the concrete.[31] Synecdoche represents the form of the microcosm by a macrocosm relationship. "One could thus," Burke explained, "look through the remotest astronomical distances to the 'truth within,' or could look within to learn the 'truth in all universe.'"[32] But a synecdoche is often confused with a metonymy because they may both appear as part-whole relationships. For example, the phrase "he is all heart" is generally read as a synecdoche because the qualities of the heart are "presumed to inhere in the totality" of the subject. If it were read metonymically, the phrase would reduce the humanness of the subject to the material phenomenon of the organic pump.

For the new populist, American political culture has within it the "germ" required to grow a truly democratic society. The synecdochic form is evident in the dimensions of the populist ideology. *Activism* optimistically notes an "insurgent spirit" of democracy spreading in the civic culture. Combining a number of disparate sociological phenomena, activism posits an irresistible evolution of popular control over formally private spheres of power. And finally, paralleling the stages in Hegelian history, each successive manifestation of the democratic spirit is less fettered than the one that came before.[33] Each critical period of populist history— the 1880s, the 1960s, and the 1980s—gains in strength. The first was co-opted by industrial capitalism, the second by the reform of the advanced welfare state, and the last will succeed because the post-materialist culture will merge with the democratic impulse in the American political tradition.

The *crisis* dimension identifies a critical social change which will remove the impediments to leftist success. The end of the growth ethic will fatally weaken the mechanisms of accomodation and allow for a democratization that is more than a set of formal structures of representation. Crisis will remove the impediment to a fuller integration of reason and politics.

Tradition is an obvious integrative symbol. It is an ideological stance which commits the activist to tradition as the seed of change. Tradition does not belong only to the select, a striking contrast to class consciousness, but to all of those who have a sense of America's democratic history.

The *participation* dimension integrates the means of change with the ends of change. The goal of populism is to increase the control people have over the conditions that affect them. The method of achieving true democracy is by exercising fully the democratic rights citizens already enjoy.

The tropic patterns of association distinguishing the two visions correspond to dramatistic structures. The shift from Marxism to populism features a shift from the tragic frame to the comic frame.

Tragedy to Comedy

In Burkean terms, "the corresponding" dramatistic terminology "for the featuring of materialism" is "scene."[34] Burke argues that "with materialism the circumference of scene is so narrowed as to involve the reduction of action to motion."[35] It is, after all, the scenic elements of economic circumstance which lead to alienation and not the free action of human agents. Such a mechanistic view of history creates a tragic dramatistic structure. As the progressive upward march of technology provides humans with better tools to control the forces of nature, there is a simultaneous downward spiral of disintegrating social relations as workers are more intensely exploited to provide the surplus labor value which fuels the capitalist economy.

In *Anatomy of Criticism*, Northrup Frye writes that "reductive formulas...have often been used to explain tragedy." "One of these," he maintains, "is the theory that all tragedy exhibits the omnipotence of an external fate. And, of course, the overwhelming majority of tragedies do leave us with a sense of supremacy of impersonal power and of the limitation of human effort."[36] Just as Christ could not escape the crucifixion and Oedipus was fated by circumstances to enter an incestuous relationship, so history is the inexorable descent of society into estranged relations and violent revolution. The fact that Jesus was released in resurrection, Oedipus in blindness, and the proletariat in utopian socialism, does not alter the essential tragic plot structure.

Whereas scene is dominant in the materialist conception of Marx, the agent is the driving force of the new populist drama. Burke wrote, "idealistic philosophy starts and ends in the featuring of properties belonging to the term, agent." "Idealistic philosophies," he observes, "think in terms of...'consciousness,' 'will,'...the 'subjective,' 'mind,' 'spirit,'...and such 'superpersons' as church, race, nation, etc. Historical periods, cultural movements, and the like, when treated as 'personalities,' are usually indications of idealism."[37]

The new populist drama emphasizes people and their defining traditions as the force of history. The leading characters are the farmers of the last century, the activists of the turbulent sixties, and this decade's progressive populists. It is a movement of a people and a tradition and not the force of material conditions. Participation symbolizes human initiative as the central motive of the drama rather than the ironclad laws of scene.

Of course, any drama that portrays the progressive march of reason through history will not be tragic. Frye describes the mythos of comedy: "The movement of comedy is usually a movement from one kind of society to another. At the beginning of the play the obstructing characters are in charge of the play's society, and the audience recognizes that they are usurpers. At the end of the play the device in the plot brings hero and heroine together causes a new society to crystallize around the hero, and the moment when this crystallization occurs is the point of resolution in the action, the comic discovery, *anagnorisis* or *cognitio*."[38]

Comic societies "include rather than exclude" and move "toward happy endings" upon which audiences pronounce the social judgment that this is the way it "should be."[39] This is the form that the populist narrative assumes. Various "blocking characters," represented by corporate elites and other nonprogressive interests are in control, but the forces of democracy press for the unification of the political, economic, and social life to create a new society that conforms to the values of the people. Electoral activity is viewed as the process of unification. Comedy provides a rhetorically attractive electoral form because it is consistent with citizen hopes and avoids the unpleasant tragic themes of materialism.

The populist strategy of presenting a world the audience is already believed to be striving for is in stark contrast with the orthodox Marxist commitment to "radical rupture." It is only by adopting a new set of principles personified in the "New Man" of socialism that the tragic story of Marxism finds relief in a utopian vision of the communist state. This is because the "scene," the brutalizing exploitive forces of capitalism, has turned people into brutes. People are not striving to become socialists during the course of the action but do so only after the tragic fall. In the comic structure of populism people rise progressively to "participatory democracy."

TOM HAYDEN'S CAMPAIGN VISION

Thus far, I have argued that the left's New Populism has necessitated a series of rhetorical/ideological transformations: adoption of a vision built on the radical democratic tradition of American populism: presentation in a narrative form emphasizing the integration of social and economic relations rather than their separation; and recitation of a drama in comic form. Each of these changes in form and content was required to build a theory of politics which could spawn an electorally (rhetorically) attractive campaign vision.

The shift from theory to practice is akin to the linguistic move from a sentence's underlying deep structure to its surface structure. The deep structure represents the basic meaning of the sentence, but the surface structure conveys the sentence's sound. This is the connection between ideology and practice I wish to emphasize; ideology sets the limits of meaning and the doing of practical politics presents this meaning within the strictures of available campaign strategy. Just as a single deep structure can account for a variety of different sentences, a single ideology can spawn a variety of seemingly distinct political campaigns. Of course, in the pursuit of victory, a campaign's strategic considerations may overwhelm the philosophic commitment to ideology. If this, in fact, turns out to be the case, such a situation deserves pointing out so that proper ethical judgments may be made. This is important in the present case because the new populists have been accused of insincerity.[40]

The New Populism is closely associated with the Campaign for Economic Democracy in California. Tom Hayden's successful bid for an Assembly seat in the state legislature has been the most widely publicized achievement of the populist movement to date. Examining the discourse surrounding the 44th district race can answer two key questions: How was the new populist vision translated into the world of practical politics? Was this translation formally and substantively consistent with populist ideology?

Hayden's campaign provides remarkably good material for assessing the transformation of the left. First, Hayden as theorist is well acquainted with populism's philosophical commitments and, therefore, Hayden the candidate should provide a clear blueprint of the new populist's campaign style. Second, Hayden's background, although a problem for the campaign, intensified the tension between left and center. The campaign's managers were forced to employ strategies to deal with this exigence.[41] In other words, the situation created an atmosphere in which exaggerated emphasis was put on the defining qualities of the New Populism. Third, Hayden was blessed with the financial and, unquestionably, the intellectual resources to exploit fully the new populist vision.

Tom Hayden's New Populist Rhetoric

Because the 44th District Assembly race was a referendum of the personal qualities and political history of the Democratic candidate, Hayden needed to supply an interpretation of his "radicalism" acceptable to the voters of Santa Monica. This explanation had to be consistent with a candidacy that represented the New Populism incarnate in California as the Campaign for Economic Democracy. These tensions were addressed, in part, by the allegorical text of a popular campaign pamphlet entitled 'Growing Up *with* America: The Life Story of Tom Hayden." It is a political biography of Tom Hayden interwoven with an idealized account of postwar American history. Allegorically, it is the story of contemporary American populism. Seen from these two perspectives the discourse makes two claims: first, Hayden is an idealist and not a radical because he acted from principles inherent in the American tradition; and second, the New Populism is consistent with American values and its programs are logical extensions of traditional principles. This intersection between practice and ideology turns on the biography's treatment of the relationship between scene and agent, purpose and agency.

Scene-Agent Ratio

At the cornerstone of "Growing Up *with* America" is an argument about political motives. The problem of explaining Hayden's past was not so much a matter of accounting for what he did but why he did it. Participation in civil rights and anti-war activity was not necessarily radical but it might have been. For the voters in the 44th District, there was much to admire in Tom Hayden's record of commitment and much to fear from a radical in sheep's clothing.

The pamphleteer's strategy is not so subtly tipped off by the cover designer's use of italics in the title. Typically, one grows up *in* a place and not *with* the place. Although we realize the scene is not static, the traditional use of "in" emphasizes the changes in the agent (growing up) and de-emphasizes the scene as anything more than passive background. Hayden, however, stresses that his development is interpretable only as it fits into the fabric of contemporary history.

The recovery from the Great Depression and the Second World War helped form Tom's values. "Out of these deep sacrifices grew deep convictions. People learned that hard work could make the world a better place. Even against powerful odds, justice and democracy could win out." Later, circumstances afforded the young Hayden an opportunity to act on these values: "For Tom Hayden and millions of other students, the growing civil rights movement and the election of Kennedy represented a chance to act on the values they had learned from their parents. Through involvement and hard work, they could make the world a better, more just place to live. It was an idealistic, hopeful time." The scene nurtured the important qualities of the agent. Yet, the force of ideas explained the motive for political action. "Above all," the narration concludes, "Tom still believes in a 'participatory democracy' in which citizens have a voice in the decisions affecting their lives. For 22 years, he has proven his commitment to this central ideal."[42]

This construction addresses the paradox that populist theoreticians have found so troubling in radical orthodoxy. As Harry Boyte puts it, "people are and must be that to which capitalism tends to reduce them."[43] This view cannot coexist with an ideology that holds tradition and participation as key elements of liberation. The pamphleteer chooses to address this difficulty by featuring the "correlation between the quality of the [scene] and the quality of the inhabitants."[44] Because the scene-agent ratio does not prescribe behavior but instead reflects externally the agent's internal feeling, it permits integration of a critique of culture with a program of individual political action. The text explains Hayden's early activism as an extension of his upbringing, which sympathetically mirrors his intentions, and his current politics as a product of his own ideals.

Noting the extremes of this tension is useful. A philosophy that is individualist holds that "the individual—not external forces—is the source of new ideas that enable society to make changes." All explanations of the social are reducible to accounts of individual goals and actions. Conversely, the anti-individualist position maintains that "the great tradition of culture holds each one of us in its powerful embrace."[45] Explanations of individual action make reference to social context and not the motives of agents.

To characterize the discourse as a middle course between the force of the individual and the environment is to comment that the rhetorical displays the markings of modern liberalism. After all, it was John Dewey who wrote, "We can recognize that all conduct is interaction between elements of human nature and environment, natural and social."[46] Liberal thinkers highlight human nature *and* social nurturing. The new populists preserve the agent's freedom by emphasizing the role of reason. Such a view is idealistic without adopting a conservative philosophy erected on innate characteristics of human nature.

Consequently, the rhetorical strategy of "Growing UP *with* America" is consistent with the precepts of the New Populism. The twin forces of individual responsibility, activisim and participation, and social nurturing, crisis and tradition, are present in Hayden's political history. In this sense, the New Populism is a significant departure from orthodox leftist theories of politics.

Purpose/Agency Collapse

Given all the changes in ideology embraced by the new populists, they still seek alterations in American political life that are too extreme for the vast majority of the electorate. As already noted, the New Populism is more about adopting new methods of activism than about abandoning old ends. The way out of this difficulty is to create a vision that permits a focus on means: and thus allows Hayden to avoid the distractions of radical discourse. The campaign strategists were able to accomplish this by formulating a teleological argument for American progress. In so doing, they collapsed the distinction between purpose and agency.

Teleology is the "theory of purposiveness in nature: characteristically, certain phenomena seem to be best explained not by means of prior causes, but ends or aims, intentions or purposes."[47] Teleological explanation "seems typical of living or organic things" and thus the use of an organic metaphor to describe politics is evidence of the rhetor's commitment to this form of political justification.

The phrase "Growing Up *with* America" captures the organic metaphor around which the discourse is constructed. Hayden's "growing" unfolds in developmental stages: traditional post-War upbringing, young idealist acting on the fervor of principle, and responsible adult bringing maturity to political leadership. The first section describes Hayden's "Roots in Middle America"; the middle section discusses the important events of Hayden's idealistic period including his civil rights and anti-Vietnam activism; and the final section presents the mature Hayden's family life and political work.

The seed of Hayden's maturity was planted by his parent's America of forty years ago. Like many young men, Hayden's adolescent and college years were filled with idealism and only the sobering influence of family and community responsibility brought the realism of adulthood. Similarly, the populism of the previous century, the activism of the sixties, and the progressivism of the eighties all grew from the same democratic seed and each was more mature than the one that came before.

Progress is the key defining symbol for traditional liberal discourse. This tradition, historian Morris Cohen writes, is "associated with the evolutionary philosophy that everything develops through stages...progress was associated with a growth of reason and enlightenment and a decline in superstition and violence."[48] New Populism is distinguished by its variant on this theme. The purpose and agency of progress are collapsed into the slogans "participatory" and "economic democracy." For the populist left, politics is essentially about "doing" and not about solutions to problems. Of course, there are problems the left wants to solve but the vision of a better society is in citizen empowerment and not in specific new proposals. Populists live with the hope that the rise of such a "democratic consciousness" will lead to progressive political ends. Their vision allows them to work on the instrumental end of "participation" and leave the ultimate ends unspoken. Progress is participation.

This was a useful tactic for Hayden in the circumstances surrounding the 44th District Assembly campaign. The belief that real democracy can have radically instrumental effects is difficult for a political opponent to counter. Attacking participatory government is attacking the vision of those who will decide the election.

ELECTORAL PRACTICE AND INSTITUTIONAL LEGITIMACY

Each exemplar of important oppositional campaigns in this century has been decisively undermined by its electoral commitments. Whether the "cooperative crusade" of Henry Wallace or the *Newer World* of Robert Kennedy, a marked dilution of the language of radical orthodoxy accompanied the left's move from tract writing to campaigning. Former Vice-President Wallace ran as the heir to the Roosevelt legacy and was, subsequently, destroyed by Truman's co-optation of his reformist agenda and the public's repudiation of his radical associates. Senator Kennedy ran against the foreign policy commitments of his brother's New Frontier to "go anywhere, pay any price" and for a "participatory" system that rejected the bureaucratic centralization inherent in the Great Society. But he did so with a message which borrowed key New Left symbols and denounced the ideological baggage that made these terms troublesome. In both cases, opposition groups, stripped of reformist support by electoral activity, were politically isolated and easy prey for the state's law enforcement apparatus. The Wallace defeat was followed by the national repudiation of communism and the 1968 debacle in Chicago presaged the vigorous application of legal remedies by the Nixon Justice Department.[49] This pattern of appeasement and repression has been described by sociologist Armand Mauss as a recurrent feature of the American radical movement cycle. "The society itself," Mauss argues, "devises a series of routine measures for coping with the movement, including new laws and penalties on the one hand, combined with new forms of co-optation, on the other."[50]

A dozen years ago Simons, Chesbro, and Orr assessed the uneasy relationship between "The Movement" and the McGovern campaign.[51] The left's venture into electoral politics was rightly described as naive. A decade later, fully aware of the fate of the New Left, the new populists have created an infinitely more sophisticated approach to electioneering. Aware of the possibility of a sellout by a conventional candidate, they have sent their own standard bearer into the fray; concerned about the possibility of co-optation, they have fashioned a "participatory" vision which accounts for system accommodation; and committed to raising a consequential voice in American politics, they have rejected minor party status and used the reform rules of the Democratic Party to seek office.

Despite this more thoughtful approach, I think the new populist effort is bound to fail. It will fail for the same fundamental reason it has always failed. Oppositional movements are co-opted by the constraints inherent in electoral activity. This conclusion is built on two claims: (1) situational constraints assure that electoral practice will function to preserve institutional legitimacy; and (2) the New Populism, although sophisticated in form, cannot overcome these constraints.

The ideological transformations from orthodox radicalism to populism forced the adoption of a conventional vocabulary and shaped the electoral narrative into a traditional liberal form. The key question for the new populists was posed by political scientist Carl Boggs: "At what point does adaptation to the 'American Heritage' become a synonym for adaptation to bourgeois hegemony?"[52] The two key functions of the new populist rhetoric are indistinguishable from other co-optive rhetorics.

(1) *The new populist rhetoric instrumentalizes participation.* The new populists collapse the purpose/agency distinction and regard "democracy" as both a use and ultimate value. Consequently, they hypothesize that a change in the mode of politics will provide sufficient cause for a massive change in political consciousness. This commitment to participatory democracy is not limited in the core vision by any particular policy commitments. Interestingly, all previous oppositional efforts were committed to increasing participation and each pressed for enfranchisement of various disaffected groups. However, these past efforts were directed at the limits of formal *representation*. But the new populists seek to build systems for *participation*. They insist that the move from representation to participation is not merely another incremental step but a revolutionary transformation of the political system. The American Republic becomes the American Democracy and the private corporation becomes the public sphere of citizen politics.

This distinction, when pressed by the demands of electoral politics, collapses. Like all previous practitioners, Hayden was forced to define participation instrumentally. Citizen participation is the solution to inequitable utility rate structures, exploitative apartment rents, irresponsible toxic waste management, unmonitored foreign investment, and unfair residential tax assessments. For example, the difficulties with utilities, according to Hayden, can be corrected by strengthening "the consumer's voice...in the regulatory process." When translated into policy, these participatory structures vary little from other forms of repsentation. "This would be an effective guarantee of consumer representation," Hayden claims, "only if the utilities were prohibited from supporting candidates for the board with contributions, if the consumer board members were explicity mandated to represent the consumer interest only, and if the board is funded by voluntary ratepayer contribution."[53] Likewise, the toxic waste problem will yield to the participation of the common citizen. A headline in *The Economic Democrat* captures the conventional nature of the proposal: "Local Power Grows with Public Disclosure."[54]

Participation functionally "stresses votes and influence rather than autonomous popular struggles."[55] "Economic democracy" becomes a symbol for engaging in interest group politics. Within the realm of the campaign, participation does not challenge the dominant ideology but rather strengthens the forms of representation.

(2) *The new populist rhetoric rehabilitates radical opposition.* The discourse rehabilitates key political symbols and provides a rhetorical halfway house for those temporarily residing outside the "official" politics. "Therapy," Berger and Luckmann wrote, "must concern itself with deviations from 'official' definitions of reality, it must develop a conceptual machinery to account for such deviations and to maintain the realities thus challenged."[56] The practice of the New Populism makes this possible.

In contrast with previous examples (Wallace, Kennedy, McGovern), the new populist is not reaching out to factional opposition but moving voluntarily back to conventional politics. Hayden and his associates came to the electoral enterprise with an already rehabilitated language. The ideological vision specifies the transformation of "capitalism" to "corporatism," "socialism" to "economic democracy," "class" to "tradition," and so forth. But all this was done because the dominant political language is the only ticket out of powerlessness.

Hayden's assent to use the language of the "official" politics was rewarded by the pronouncement that he had returned to good health. The notice of his improved condition appeared in the newspaper story announcing the election returns: "Hayden win puts him in political mainstream."[57]

But more interesting systemically is the invigoration of traditional symbols. The terms "democracy" and "participation" were reaffirmed as instrumental values in American life. The left provided a service by attesting to the vitality of the electoral system. Whether in fact the New Populism has any progressive outcome, it has played a role in strengthening the very means of accommodation that it so despises. In so doing, we can only marvel at the sophisticated strategies of co-optation that continue to gut each new radical agenda in America.

CONCLUSIONS

This case of populism raises a number of issues, three of which are sufficiently general to deserve formulation here. One issue concerns the relationship between the New Populism and other American populist movements. To explain this populism, we must resist the temptation to collapse the doing and the study of politics. Too often, and the equivocation of "movement" and "social movement" is a good example, we equate technical determination with popular meaning. "Populism," like "movement," is persuasively defined by political actors.[58] The New Populism's rhetorical sanitizing operation cleanses the public memory of unpleasant images of demagoguery, racial bigotry, and other unsavory historical associations. This populism is presented as the "true" populism undistorted by corrupt forces of mediation. Consequently, the dimensions which pleasingly emphasize the wisdom of the people's will are the core rhetorical themes. The steps in the evolutionary development of left populism reflect careful historical selection. Revisionist histories of the critical "populist moment" in American history emphasize the early stages of agrarian populism, an idealized rendering of the 1960's, and a progressive interpretation of the "Me Decade."

A second concern involves a more general account of new political expressions. Recent treatments of the "new" liberal and conservative rhetorics have frequently fallen prey to the seduction of an overly simple process of ideological change.[59] Transformations are neither sufficiently explained by the causal arrow pointing from situation to ideology nor from ideology to situation. Situations do constrict the latitude of ideological revision and ideological visions do influence the shape of political situations, but the determination of *form* mediates both causal processes.

I am not treating a particular form as an *a priori* element. The shifts from modern liberalism to neo-liberalism, from economic conservatism to social conservatism, and from socialism to Economic Democracy are a product of a series of new electioneering incentives. The altered landscape calls for appeals in a different discursive form. "Every president from 1968 to 1980," William Schambra contended, "was compelled to accommodate that [populist] sentiment with decentralist rhetoric and programs; no one became president during this period without denouncing centralized, bureaucratic government, and promising to reinvigorate the states and small, local communities."[60]

The chicken and egg arguments in the political communication literature are legend.[61] So with an eye to steering clear of the hen house, I recommend that critics of these new political expressions refrain from form and content separations in generating explanations of rhetorical/ideological changes in the political dialogue.

Finally, issues of practical politics are raised. Why have the conservative expressions of the New Populism been more influential than the liberal manifestations? The New Right has, after all, captured the political news for much of the eighties. In one sense, this is intuitively surprising because the Democratic Party has experience with "populist" campaigns waged against the Johnson and Nixon Administrations by McCarthy, Kennedy, Wallace, and McGovern. Explanations have been offered that deal with infrastructure: the conservative use of sophisticated media operations, particularly the use of direct mail; the Republican Party's narrower ideological range; demographic shifts in population and the declining base of the New Deal coalition; and so forth. All of these arguments probably have a degree of validity. But beyond these situational explanations, determinations of form provide another perspective.

Modern liberalism is most familiar to us as the rhetoric of Roosevelt's "New Deal" and Johnson's "Great Society." The paternal language of liberal politics supplies a comforting portrait of national nurturance. Populism is antithetical to the images of top-down social reform. The discourse of "small republicanism" with "precedence of the [concrete] community over the government" comes more easily to conservatives.[62] Consequently, it is not unexpected that conservative exploitation of the new politics could come more quickly.

This essay examined the Campaign for Economic Democracy to illustrate the rise of a populist tone in the rhetoric of ordinary politics. The relatively drastic nature of the shift in associational pattern, narrative form, and ideology in this case illustrates a process of less startling changes taking place in more centrist perspectives. Tom Hayden's New Populism presages future shifts in the discourse of liberal politics.

Notes

1. Howard S. Erlich, "Populist Rhetoric Reassessed: A Paradox," *Quarterly Journal of Speech*, 63 (1977), 140–151.

2. Robert G. Gunderson, "The Calamity Howlers," *Quarterly Journal of Speech*, 26 (1940), 401–411; Charles W. Lomas, "Dennis Kearney: Case Study in Demagoguery," *Quarterly Journal of Speech*, 41 (1955), 234–242; and Robert W. Smith, "Comedy at St. Louis: A Footnote to Nineteenth Century Political Oratory," *Southern Speech Communication Journal*, 25 (1959), 122–133.

3. Even the most casual canvas of the conflicting treatments of populism reveals a commitment to the demands of the common people: "The belief that the majority opinion of the people is checked by an elitist minority"; "Any creed or movement based on the following premise: *virtue resides in the simple people, who are the overwhelming majority, and in their collective traditions*"; and "Populism proclaims the will of the people as such is supreme over every other standard." See Harry Lazer, "British Populism: The Labour Party and the Common Market Parliamentary Debate," *Political Science Quarterly*, 91 (1976), 259; Peter Wiles, "A Syndrome, Not a Doctrine: Some Elementary Theses on Populism," in *Populism: Its Meanings and National Characteristics*, eds. Ghita Ionescu and Ernest Geller (London; Weidenfeld and Nicholson, 1969), p. 166; and Edward A. Shils, *The Torment of Secrecy* (London: William Heinemann, 1956), p. 98.

4. David L. Swanson, "The New Politics Meets the Old Rhetoric: New Directions in Campaign Communication Research," *Quarterly Journal of Speech*, 58 (1972), 31–40.

5. Nelson W. Polsby, *The Consequences of Party Reform* (Oxford: Oxford University Press, 1983).

6. This new message has been analyzed in the 1968 and 1972 presidential campaigns of Robert Kennedy and George McGovern. See Bernard Brock, "1968 Democratic Campaign: A Political Upheaval," *Quarterly Journal of Speech*, 55 (1969), 29; Ronald Lee, "The Rhetoric of the 'New Politics': A Case Study of Robert F. Kennedy's 1968 Presidential Primary Campaign," Diss. University of Iowa, 1981; and Herbert W. Simons, James W. Chesebro, and C. Jack Orr, "A Movement Perspective on the 1972 Presidential Election," *Quarterly Journal of Speech*, 59 (1973), 168–179.

7. See Hayden White, *Metahistory* (Baltimore: Johns Hopkins Univ. Press, 1973), pp. 1–42.

8. Lawrence Goodwyn, *Democratic Promise: The Populist Moment in American History* (New York: Oxford University Press, 1976). p. xxiii.

9. Mark Kann, ed., *The Future of American Democracy: Views from the Left* (Philadelphia: Temple University Press, 1983), p. 12.

10. Harry C. Boyte, *The Backyard Revolution* (Philadelphia: Temple University Press, 1980), p. 4.

11. Goodwyn, p. xiii.

12. "An Interview with Milton Kotler," *Social Policy*, 12 (1982), 32.

13. Harry C. Boyte, "Building the Democratic Movement: Prospects for a Socialist Renaissance," *Socialist Review*, 8 (1978), 22.

14. Tom Hayden, "American Identity: The Frontiers of Custer and Thoreau," in *The Future of American Democracy*, ed. Mark Kann (Philadelphia: Temple University Press, 1983), pp. 65, 67.

15. Hayden, p. 67; Goodwyn, p. xii.

16. Hayden, p. 69.

17. Hayden, p. 74.

18. Ralph Miliband, *Marxism and Politics* (Oxford: Oxford University Press, 1977), p. 44.

19. Karl Marx and Fredrich Engels, *Communist Manifesto: Socialist Landmark* (London: George Allen and Unwin, 1948), p. 124.

20. Tom Hayden, "Economic Democracy: A Vision for the 80's," *CED News*, Sept. 1979, p.3.

21. Martin Carnoy and Derek Shearer, *Economic Democracy: The Challenge of the 1980's* (Armonk, NY: M. E. Sharpe, 1980), p. 3.

22. Boyte, *The Backyard Revolution*, p. 51.

23. Fredrich Engels, *Ludwig Feuerbach and the End of Classical German Philosophy*, Vol. 11 of *Selected Works* (Moscow: Foreign Languages Publishing House, 1962), p. 387.

24. "Metonymy," *O.E.D.*, 1933 ed.

25. "Metonymy," *Random House Dictionary of the English Language*, 1967 ed.

26. Kenneth Burke, *A Grammar of Motives* (rev. ed., Berkeley: University of California Press, 1969), p. 65.

27. Karl Marx, *Economic and Philosophic Manuscripts of 1844*, in *The Marx-Engels Reader*, ed. Robert C. Tucker, (2nd ed., New York: W. W. Norton, 1978), pp. 70–81.

28. Karl Marx, *Capital, Volume One*, in *The Marx-Engels Reader*, pp. 309–312.

29. Karl Marx, *Alienation and the Social Classes*, in *The Marx-Engels Reader*, pp. 133–135.

30. Karl Marx, *The German Ideology*, in *The Marx-Engels Reader*, pp. 163–175.

31. Burke, pp. 507–511.

32. Burke, p. 508.

33. George Wilhelm Hegel, *The Philosophy of History*, trans. J. Sibree (New York: Dover, 1956), p. 18.

34. Burke, p. 128. I realize that a close reading of *A Grammar of Motives* reveals that Burke does not consider Marx a "mechanical" but a "dialectical materialist" or, as he puts it, an "idealistic materialist." See Burke, pp. 200–202. But a sophisticated view of Marxism is difficult to present in the popular channels of political discourse. Consequently, the new populists view materialism as a rhetorical problem.

35. Burke, p. 131.

36. Northrup Frye, *Anatomy of Criticism* (Princeton: Princeton University Press, 1957), p. 209.

37. Burke, p. 171.

38. Frye, p. 163.

39. Frye, pp. 166–167.

40. The strategy of Hayden's Republican challenger was to make such allegations. In addition, some analysts have made charges of political hypocrisy. See John H. Bunzel, *New Force on the Left* (Stanford, CA.: Hoover Institution Press, 1983).

41. "The issue is Democrat Tom Hayden. The question is whether Hayden is still so burdened with his early-day image as an over liberal, anti-Vietnam activist with anti-business, anti-private property leanings that he is unable to win election in what may be the most liberal Assembly district in California." In Will Thorne, "Hayden Appears Real Issue in Assembly Race," (Santa Monica) *Evening Outlook*, 28 Oct. 1982, Sec. D, p. 1. Throughout the campaign, opposition groups attacked Hayden's radical past. In the closing days, four prisoners of war, led by a Santa Monica Medal of Honor recipient, accused Hayden of "trying to rewrite history." They claimed he was misleading the voters by suggesting that he went to Hanoi to help negotiate the release of POWs rather than aid the North Vietnamese. In a more bizarre episode, a Santa Monica man demanded that Hayden apologize to Vietnam veterans. In order to dramatize his grievances, he threatened to spike the produce of two local supermarkets with LSD. See Will Thorne and Rich Seeley, "Ex-POWs, Dornan Rip Hayden Over Wartime Trips to Hanoi," *Evening Outlook*, 29 Oct. 1982, Sec. A, p. 1; and Rick Martinez, "Markets Target of LSD Threat," *Evening Outlook*, 2 Nov. 1982, Sec. A. p. 1.

42. *Growing Up with America: The Life Story of Tom Hayden* (Santa Monica: Friends of Tom Hayden, 1982), pp. 3, 5, 21.

43. Harry C. Boyte, "Populism and the Left," *Democracy*, 1 (1981), 56.

44. Burke, p. 8.

45. David L. Miller, *Individualism* (Austin: University of Texas Press, 1967), pp. 3, 76–77.

46. John Dewey, *Human Nature and Conduct* (New York: Henry Holt, 1922), p. 18.

47. "Teleology," *A Dictionary of Philosophy*, 1979 ed.

48. Morris R. Cohen, *The Meaning of History*, (2nd ed, LaSalle, IL.: Open Court, 1961), p. 265.

49. See Richard J. Walton, *Henry Wallace, Harry Truman and the Cold War* (New York: Viking Press, 1976); and Jack Newfield, *Robert F. Kennedy: A Memoir* (New York: Berkely, 1969).

50. Armand Mauss, "On Being Strangled by the Stars and Stripes: The New Left, and Old Left, and the Natural History of American Radical Movements," *Journal of Social Issues*, 27 (1971), 193–194.

51. Herbert W. Simons, James W. Chesebro, and C. Jack Orr, "A Movement Perspective on the 1972 Presidential Campaign," *Quarterly Journal of Speech*, 59 (1973), 168–179.

52. Carl Boggs, "The New Populism and the Limits of Structural Reforms," *Theory and Society*, 12 (1983), 356–357.

53. Tom Hayden, *The Economic Democrat*, April/May 1982, p. 3.

54. Boggs, p. 349.

55. Boggs, p. 349.

56. Peter L. Berger and Thomas Luckmann, *The Social Construction of Reality* (New York: Oxford University Press, 1975), p. 113.

57. Will Thorne, "Hayden Win Puts Him in Political Mainstream," *Evening Outlook*, 4 Nov. 1982, Sec. A, p. 1.

58. See Charles L. Steveneson, *Ethics and Language* (New Haven: Yale University Press, 1944), ch. 9.

59. There are a number of titles that might be included on such a list. But I am particularly thinking of Michael Weiler's "The Rhetoric of Neo-Liberalism," *Quarterly Journal of Speech*, 70 (1984), 362–378; and Martin Medhurst's "Resistance, Conservatism, and Theory Building: A Cautionary Note," *Western Journal of Speech Communication*, 49 (1985), 103–115.

60. William A. Schambra, "Progressive Liberalism and American 'Community,'" *The Public Interest*, no. 80 (1985), 44.

61. See, for example, "Colloquy: Perspectives on Political Communication," *Human Communication Research*, 8 (1982), 366–389.

62. Clyde N. Wilson, "Citizens or Subjects?," in *The New Right Papers*, ed. Robert W. Whitaker (New York: St. Martin's Press, 1982), p. 109.

Telling America's Story: Narrative Form and the Reagan Presidency

WILLIAM F. LEWIS

By 1980, AMERICA had lost its sense of direction. Economic troubles, a series of foreign policy failures, and corruption in its government had created a national malaise. Then Ronald Reagan came onto the scene with a vision of America that reinvigorated the nation. His great skills as a communicator and his commitment to fundamental ideals were just what the nation needed. We were once again proud to be Americans.

This familiar and well accepted story follows the pattern of many political success stories in which the hero rescues the country from a time of great trouble. This story is special, however, in that Reagan is said to have accomplished the feat through the power of his speaking and, eventually, to have been brought down when that power failed him. After more than five years in office, Reagan was still referred to as "the Western world's most gifted communicator."[1]

Objection to Ronald Reagan did not originate with the discovery of the Iran arms deal, however. Despite Reagan's consistent popularity and continuing praise for his speaking,[2] there has been a substantial segment of a critical public who not only remained unpersuaded by the President, but were offended by his persuasive manner. What is seen by his supporters as clear direction has been attacked by opponents as "ideology without ideas."[3] While it has been noted often that Reagan has provided a renewed sense of confidence and security in the country, expressions of fear about his ineptitude or his willingness to risk war have been frequent. Despite his continuing high levels of approval, a whole genre of literature against Reagan has developed.[4] What makes these books a genre is not just that they share a common opposition to Reagan and his policies, but also that they share a common approach to their criticisms. Reagan is accused repeatedly of being unrealistic, simplistic, and misinformed. Ronald Dallek, for example, claims that Reagan's anti-Communist foreign policy is "a simplistic and ineffective way to meet a complex problem."[5] He explains Reagan's repeated policy mistakes as a manifestation of his psychological make-up and concludes that his ideology and policy-making are "nonrational."[6] The sense of these criticisms is epitomized in the mocking tone of a *New Republic* editorial that, in the course of bemoaning Reagan's historical ignorance, comments that: "Ronald Reagan has never let the facts get in the way of a good story."[7]

Similar themes recur frequently in the scholarly evaluation of Reagan's rhetoric. His effectiveness is widely recognized, but while Reagan is praised by some for his strategic prowess and for his ability to inspire the American public,[8] others find his success problematic. How, it is asked, can he be so popular when he is uninformed, irrational, and inconsistent?[9] The dominant explanation has been that Reagan manipulates his language, his strategy, or his style to make himself and his policies appear to be attractive.[10] While the power of rhetoric to affect appearances has been demonstrated amply, this insight provides only a partial explanation for the nature of Reagan's rhetoric and the response to it. It does not account satisfactorily for the differences in perception and judgment among Reagan's various audiences, for the difference between support for Reagan and support for his policies, or for the fact that journalistic and scholarly analysis debunking his competence and sincerity was largely irrelevant through most of his presidency.

The purpose of this essay is to account for the distinctive reputation, style, and effect of Ronald Reagan's discourse by providing a consistent and sufficiently comprehensive explanation for the contradictory perceptions of his speaking and for the related paradoxes of this "Great Communicator's" presidency. To construct this account in terms of his discourse requires an explicit awareness of the distinction between a "rational" and a narrative perspective.[11] Narrative theory can provide a powerful account of political discourse, and it is essential for explaining Ronald Reagan's rhetoric, for it is the predominance of the narrative form in Reagan's rhetoric that has established the climate of interpretation within which he is seen and judged.

The frequency of Reagan's story-telling has been widely noted[12] and some perceptive commentaries have demonstrated his consistency with dominant American myths,[13] but what remains to be emphasized is that story-telling is fundamental to the relationship between Reagan and his audience. Stories are not just a rhetorical device that Reagan uses to embellish his ideas; Reagan's message is a story. Reagen uses story-telling to direct his policies, ground his explanations, and inspire his audiences, and the dominance of narrative helps to account for the variety of reactions to his rhetoric.

There is general agreement about the course of the Reagan presidency—the story of his ascendency has now become the story of his rise and fall—but explanations differ. Those who have criticized Reagan using the standards of technical reasoning and policy-making are likely to contend that his rhetoric is simplistic, untrue, or irrational and to lament the lack of public response to his patent deficiencies.[14] They are likely to explain Reagan's successes as being the result of rhetorical manipulation and to explain the Iran/*contra* crisis as being the inevitable result of his continuing lack of realism.[15] Those who listen to Ronald Reagan as a story-teller are likely to emphasize Reagan's character and to praise him for providing vision, reassurance, and inspiration to the American public.[16] They are likely to see Reagan as having struck a responsive chord and to explain the Iranian crisis as a weakening of Reagan's previously strong grasp on public leadership.[17] Reactions diverge because listeners perceive Reagan and his speeches differently, and because they apply different standards of judgment to what they perceive.

This essay will (1) explicate the varieties of narrative form active in Reagan's discourse to help explain his presidency and the reactions to it; and (2) discuss some of the moral and epistemic consequences of Reagan's use of narrative, and of the narrative form itself.

NARRATIVE FORM
IN REAGAN'S RHETORIC

Reagan tells two kinds of stories that differ in scale and purpose, but that work together to establish the dominance of narrative form in the creation and in the interpretation of his rhetoric. *Anecdotes* define the character of an issue at the same time that they illustrate, reinforce, and make his policies and ideas more vivid. *Myth* structures his message.

Anecdotes are the quick stories, jokes, or incidents that are the verbal counter-part of the visual image. The anecdote is intended to spark interest, and its meaning is established in reference to some larger frame of understanding that is either specified within a discourse or assumed in an audience. In this way, the story of Albert Einstein's difficulty in understanding the 1040 form[18] defines a relationship to the tax code—given a belief that complexity is likely to be the reflection of excessive bureaucracy and that government ought to be accessible to all citizens without requiring special expertise. Similarly, Reagan's story of the Supreme Court decision that, he says, prevented New York children from praying in their cafeteria[19] defines a relationship to the issue of school prayer—given a belief that religious belief is a necessary part of moral order and that people ought to be able to act in private without governmental restriction. In both these instances, a simple story carries a clear message to those whose experience leads them to accept the story as either true or as true-to-life and whose values lead them to accept the moral. As one would expect, Reagan uses anecdotes more often when speaking to audiences that are expected to be uniformly Republican or conservative.

Myth informs all of Reagan's rhetoric. In the broad sense in which it is used here, myth refers to "any anonymously composed story telling of origins and destinies: the explanations a society offers its young of why the world is and why we do as we do, its pedagogic images of the nature and destiny of man."[20] Reagan's myth applies not to the origin of the world, but to the origin of America;

not to the destiny of humanity, but to the destiny of Americans. It is a simple and familiar story that is widely taught and widely believed. It is not exactly a true story in the sense that academic historians would want their descriptions and explanations to be true, but it is not exactly fiction either. As Jerome Bruner wrote of myth in general, "its power is that it lives on the feather line between fantasy and reality. It must be neither too good nor too bad to be true, nor must it be too true."[21] Myth provides a sense of importance and direction and it provides a communal focus for individual identity.

America in the Story

Reagan never tells the whole of his American story at any one time, but the myth that emerges in his speeches is familiar and easily stated:

> *America is a chosen nation, grounded in its families and neighborhoods, and driven inevitably forward by its heroic working people toward a world of freedom and economic progress unless blocked by moral or military weakness.*

Reagan portrays American history as a continuing struggle for progress against great obstacles imposed by economic adversity, barbaric enemies, or Big Government. It is a story with great heroes—Washington, Jefferson, Lincoln, Roosevelt—with great villains—the monarchs of pre-Revolutionary Europe, the Depression, the Communists, the Democrats—and with a great theme—the rise of freedom and economic progress. It is a story that is sanctified by God[22] and validated by the American experience.[23] All the themes of Reagan's rhetoric are contained in this mythic history—America's greatness, its commitment to freedom, the heroism of the American people, the moral imperative of work, the priority of economic advancement, the domestic evil of taxes and government regulation, and the necessity of maintaining military strength. The story fulfills all the requirements of myth—it is widely believed, generally unquestioned, and clearly pedagogical. And Reagan tells the story extremely well. His message is always clear, his examples are chosen well, and his consistent tone of buoyant optimism and unyielding faith in progress complements the picture of continuing success that is proclaimed in the myth. Finally, it provides a focus for identification by his audience. Reagan repeatedly tells his audiences that if they choose to participate in the story, they will become a part of America's greatness.

Reagan's version of the course and direction of American history pervades all of his rhetoric, but he tells his story most clearly on those occasions when he intends to be most inspirational. The character of the myth and the moral implications that he draws from it can be seen clearly in Reagan's Second Inaugural Address.[24]

The key to understanding the Second Inaugural is to see it as a story. Like all of Reagan's rhetoric, the logic of the speech is a narrative logic that emphasizes the connection between character and action, not a rational logic that emphasizes the connections between problems and solutions. In this speech, Reagan establishes the identity of America and the American people, that identity establishes the direction for America's story, and the direction implies the actions that should be taken. By making intelligible the *public* identity of the audience members (as Americans), the narrative makes those who accept this identity accountable to a system of values and virtues that are used as standards against which to judge policies.

The center of the speech is itself a story. Reagan describes "two of our Founding Fathers, a Boston lawyer named Adams and a Virginia planter named Jefferson." Though they had been "bitter political rivals," Reagan told of how "age had softened their anger" as they exchanged letters and finally came together to the extent that "in 1826, the 50th anniversary of the Declaration of Independence, they both died. They died on the same day, within a few hours of each other. And that day was the Fourth of July." The cosmic harmony of this story is perfectly in keeping with the mythic frame of the speech, and the "important lesson" that Reagan draws from the story is perfectly in keeping with the dominant theme. Reagan concludes his story with a quotation from one of Jefferson's letters to Adams recalling their mutual struggle "for what is most valuable to man; his right of self government." In this story, America represents a single message for all time and for all people. History has been transformed into a lesson that transcends the contingencies of circumstance.

For Reagan, America's meaning is to be found as much in the future as it has been in the past. Seeking to perfect the ultimate American goal of individual freedom, he says, will guarantee peace and prosperity: "There are no limits to growth and human progress, when men and women are free to follow their dreams"; "Every victory for human freedom will be a victory for world peace." Progress toward freedom is tied directly to economic progress by linking unrestrained individual action to economic productivity: "At the heart of our efforts is one idea vindicated by 25 straight months of economic growth: freedom and incentives unleash the drive and entrepreneurial genius that are the core of human progress." The powerfully future-oriented, forward-looking perspective is summed up in his conclusion: America is "one people under God, dedicated to the dream of freedom he has placed in the human heart, called upon now to pass that dream on to a waiting and a hopeful world."

The only impediments to the fulfillment of this dream that Reagan identifies are those that America imposes on itself.[25] For a time, said Reagan, "we failed the system." We suffered through times of economic and social stress because "we yielded authority to the national government that properly belonged to the states or to local governments or to the people themselves." These were temporary difficulties, however. By renewing our faith in freedom "we are creating a nation once again vibrant, robust, and alive." The other great risk that Reagan identifies is military weakness. "History has shown," he states, "that peace does not come, nor will our freedom be preserved, by good will alone."

Reagan's Second Inaugural is based upon a story of America's origins and its quest for freedom. In it, Reagan shows the dire consequences of being distracted from the quest and the rewards and potential glory of regaining faith and direction. He defines the values that are needed (unity, freedom, strength) and he outlines the policies that will aid in pursuit of the goal. Finally, he ties together the past and the future and calls upon Americans to dedicate themselves to living this story.

The Audience in the Story

In the same way in which Reagan's stories give meaning to America, they define what it means to be an American. The narrative form offers a special kind of identification to Reagan's audience because each auditor is encouraged to see himself or herself as a central actor in America's quest for freedom. To accept Reagan's story is not just to understand the course of an American history that is enacted in other places by other people, it is to know that the direction and outcome of the story depends upon you. Proper action makes the audience member into a hero; inaction or improper action makes the listener responsible for America's decline. The narrative logic that defines the nature of heroism in Reagan's rhetoric was the central theme of his First Inaugural Address.[26]

America is defined as the greatest country in the world. It "guarantees individual liberty to a greater degree than any other," it is the "last and greatest bastion of freedom," and, consequently, it has "the world's strongest economy." To be heroes, the audience members must act in ways that will contribute to America's goals. The narrative defines their virtues—determination, courage, strength, faith, hope, work, compassion—and Reagan identifies their character.

In his most explicit and extensive consideration of heroism, Reagan makes it clear that America's real heroes are its ordinary people—the factory workers and the farmers, those who market goods and those who consume them, those who produce ("entrepreneurs" are given special mention here as elsewhere), and those who give to others.[27]

The idea of the American hero is epitomized in the story of Martin Treptow, "a young man...who left his job in a small town barbershop in 1917" to serve in WWI. "We're told," said Reagan, "that on his body was found a diary" in which he had written: "America must win this war. Therefore I will work, I will save, I will sacrifice, I will endure, I will fight cheerfully and do my utmost, as if the issue of the whole struggle depended on me alone." The character of the individual and the values that he holds are defined by their contribution to America's struggle. If the audience accepts Reagan's description of the nature of that continuing struggle, then they will be encouraged to accept the same kind of values, actions, and commitments that Treptow accepted in his struggle. In this case, Reagan's use of anecdote defines the character that best fits his story of America. World War I is taken to exemplify America's struggle for freedom against hostile forces; Treptow exemplifies the common man; the dedication of the soldier exemplifies the dedication to country and the fighting spirit that are necessary to prevail in the struggle; and the diary entry exemplifies the commitment to act upon these principles (work, save, sacrifice, endure) and the attitude that is appropriate to the fight ("cheerfully"). Significantly, the story is presented as true, but the primary sense of its accuracy is that it represents a larger truth. "We're told" is a weak claim to factuality, but the application of the story in a Presidential Inaugural is a strong claim to moral legitimacy.

Reagan's definition of American heroism is primarily, but not exclusively, economic. The key to heroism is effective action in the ongoing struggle to achieve freedom and prosperity. Reagan encourages identification on the ground of a general commitment to the America of his story and discourages distinctions based on differences in politics or interests.[28] The stories he tells as President feature the audience members as Americans rather than as members of different political parties, and *Time* magazine supports the sharing of this perception when it cites as typical the comment by "a retired brewery worker from San Antonio" that: "He really isn't like a Republican. He's more like an American, which is what we really need."[29]

Reagan in the Story

Some of Reagan's critics have attempted to portray him as a dangerous man, seeing him either as a demagogue[30] or a warmonger.[31] Other critics have marveled at his ability to retain his role as a critic of government even after he became its symbolic head and have worried about his detachment from the policies of his own administration[32] or about his lack of accountability.[33] Such criticisms, however, fail to take account of the nature of the public perception that is encouraged by the narrative form.

To understand the response to Reagan it is necessary to see the understand Reagan-in-the-story, not Reagan-the-policy-maker or even Reagan-the-speaker. Since the story is the dominant mode through which the political situation is interpreted, Reagan will not be perceived or judged as a politician or a policy-maker or an ideologue unless that is the role that is defined for Reagan as part of the story. In the story that emerges through his speeches, however, Reagan plays two roles that have succeeded in encompassing the perspective of his critics. As a character in the story, Reagan is a mythic hero. He embodies the role of the compassionate, committed political outsider; he is the active force that has arrived to help right the prevailing wrongs and to get things moving again. As the narrator of the story, Reagan is portrayed as simply presenting the nature of the situation. There is no artifice and no threat in this style of realistic narration; Reagan-as-narrator just presents things as they are.

Reagan's character has been a dominant focus among those who attempt to explain the impact of his rhetoric. One explanation for Reagan's success is that he has "character"—that is, he projects an image of "manly effectiveness."[34] Reagan is said to be "the political embodiment of the heroic westerner,"[35] both in his appearance ("tall, lank, rugged"[36]) and in his character traits ("honesty and sincerity, innocence, optimism, and certainty"[37]). He is compared with other Presidential heroes such as Thomas Jefferson, Theodore Roosevelt, and Franklin Roosevelt, whose virtues were those of the visionary and the man of action.[38] In this respect, he is said to contrast with the "softer" Democratic candidates who have opposed him. Reagan has been able to establish the perception of his competence through "tough talk, vigorous promises, and his emphasis on immediate solutions."[39] Reagan's opponents are said to have been pushed by the contrast into appearing "impractical, ineffectual, and effete."[40] Such descriptions reveal Reagan's success in establishing himself as a variation on a dominant type of American mythic hero—strong, aggressive, distant, in control, and in Reagan's case, able to see the situation clearly and to explain it to a confused public.[41]

The most familiar form of attack on Reagan's character attempts to reveal a true Reagan behind a constructed mask. "Character" becomes a criticism of Reagan when he is accused of playing a role as he did during his movie career. The criticism appears in a number of related forms—he is said to be a "performer," a "host," an "image," to be playing a "game of cultural make-believe," or to be "using" his role to manipulate the public and to more effectively pursue his political or ideological or personal goals.[42] This use of "character" as artifice will succeed as a criticism only if Reagan is perceived as constructing a fictional persona. It cannot succeed if his persona is seen as matching or expressing his "real" character. The criticism of Reagan as an artificial creation, however, neglects his role as narrator of the story. Reagan's story, and his role in the story, are presented as a realistic and sensible portrayal of the normal and ordinary course of events. The combination of Reagan's calm demeanor,[43] his frequent reference to familiar situations to explain complex or threatening events,[44] and his reliance on American commonplaces[45] combine to create an air of reassuring certainty that has suggested to some commentators that Reagan would be more aptly compared with Harding or Eisenhower than with Theordore or Franklin Roosevelt.[46]

If criticisms of Reagan's character are not adjusted to fit the story, they are likely either to be dismissed or to be reinterpreted—sometimes with unexpected results. The charge that to elect Reagan was to risk war, for example, was unsuccessful for Carter in the 1980 presidential election and for Gerald Ford in the 1976 California primary because these attempts at criticism were perfectly consistent with the strong character that Reagan had established in his story and with the story's assumption that strength is a necessary precondition of peace. From the point of view of the story, Reagan's emphasis on increases in weapons, his assertion of the need to stand up to the Soviets, and his willingness to risk war in pursuit of the higher goals of freedom and democracy reinforced his repeated declaration that "peace is the highest aspiration of the American people," and that he, personally, wanted nothing so much as a peaceful world.[47] The result was that, in both of these elections, the charges made against Reagan did more harm to the accuser than to Reagan. In 1976, Ford's ads were even used by the Reagan campaign.[48] Similarly, Reagan can continue to use "government" as a character in his stories and to oppose himself and his audience to the Federal government after being President for more than one full term because Reagan's role in the narrative situation is to give meaning to the country and its government; he and his vision may inspire and shape policy, but he is not held responsible because designing the particulars of policy will not be seen as his role from within this perspective.

The dominance of the story is also revealed by those occasions in which Reagan's character has been called into question. In the first debate with Walter Mondale during the 1984 presidential campaign, his advisors attempted to prepare him with sufficient information and detail, but this tactic was unsuccessful because it did not accord with the character of Reagan in his own story. In the second debate, his advisors resolved to "let Reagan be Reagan."[49] The failure of this attempt to alter Reagan's "character" to meet the demands of his critics and the success of his return to his "normal" style in the second debate confirms the acceptance of Reagan's story and of his role in it. In the Iran/*contra* affair, Reagan's apparent willingness to deal with an archetypal enemy and to compromise his previously firm stance against terrorism seemed completely inconsistent with the character he had established. There seemed to be only two "rational" explanations (from the point of view of the story): either that Reagan was not responsible for the actions or that his character had changed. Hence, one response to the crisis has been to question Reagan's control over his subordinates and another has been to inquire into his mental and physical health. Neither of these explanations, however, is consistent with the story's image of presidential leadership. The story can encompass Reagan's critics, but it is vulnerable to his own inconsistencies.

Reagan's story encourages his audience to see America as a chosen nation leading the world to freedom and economic progress, to see Reagan as a friendly, well-motivated leader and as a narrator of the American story, and to see them-selves as heroes in the unfolding drama of American greatness. In Reagan's rhetoric, the nature of the world, his policies, his values, his character, and the character of his audience are defined together by the story that he tells. The consequences of this reliance on narrative form need to be considered carefully.

CONSEQUENCES OF REAGAN'S USE OF NARRATIVE FORM

In a 1984 review essay on "Narrative Theory and Communication Research," Robert L. Scott observed that despite the suggestive correspondences between narrative forms and rhetorical functions, "no rhetorical critic . . . has pressed along the lines suggested thus far by narrative theorists."[50] At the same time, Walter Fisher pro-posed a theory of human communication based on narrative. Fisher argued that traditional investigation of communication was regulated by the "rational world paradigm," which presumed that rational communicators managed a world that "is a set of logical puzzles which can be resolved through appropriate analysis and application of reason conceived as an argumentative construct."[51] Fisher found this approach to be more incomplete than wrong. Specifically, he objected to its inability to grasp the manner in which symbolization is a universal though non-rational characteristic of human nature, and to its imposition of ideological restric-tions upon the process of moral choice. In contrast, Fisher offered the "narrative paradigm," which presumes that humans are essentially story-tellers who act on the basis of good reasons derived from their experience in a world that is "a set of stories which must be chosen among to live the good life in a process of continual recreation."[52]

The distinction between narrative and "rational" forms of consciousness is well grounded in the literature of narrative theory. Drawing from the texts of history, literature, and anthropology, these theorists have shown the narrative is a distinc-tive and distinctively important means of giving meaning to events. The important question for political discourse parallels Hayden White's inquiry into historical narrative: "With *what kind of meaning* does storying endow" political events?[53] The answers provided by narrative theorists suggest that narrative is a fundamental form of human understanding that directs perception, judgment, and knowledge. Narra-tive form shapes ontology by making meaningfulness a product of consistent relationships between situations, subjects, and events and by making truth a property that refers primarily to narratives and only secondarily to propositions; narrative form shapes morality by placing characters and events within a context where moral judgment is a necessary part of making sense of the action; and narrative form shapes epistemology by suggesting that all important events are open to common sense understanding.

These characteristics of narrative suggest an explanation for the apparent incongruity of a President with high levels of personal support despite opposition to his policies, and it explains the particular way in which support and opposition to Reagan has been expressed—*Reagan's exclusive and explicit reliance on a single story has dominated the realm of political judgment.* The story is the primary basis for defining the situation, morality is the primary basis for justifying public policy, and common sense is the primary basis for analyzing political issues.

Narrative Truth

Reagan's stories are sometimes presented as fictional, sometimes as fact. In either case, their appropriateness to political discourse depends upon their consistency with the historical world of the audience. If the story is not true, it must be true-to-life; if it did not actually happen, it must be evident that it could have happened or that, given the way things are, it should have happened. When narrative dominates, epistemological standards move away from empiricism. History is more likely to be seen as a literary artifact, fiction is more likely to be seen as a mimetic representation of reality, and the two forms "cross" in the historicity of the narrative form.[54] Understanding this shift in perspective is essential to understanding Reagan's rhetoric and the reactions to it.

As Bennett and Feldman found in their examination of story-telling in jury trials, "judgments based on story construction are, in many important respects, unverifiable in terms of the reality of the situation that the story represents."[55] The story becomes increasingly dominant as the empirically defined context for the story becomes increasingly distant from confirmation by either experience or consensus. Bennett and Feldman identify two situations in which "structural characteristics of stories become more central to judgment": (1) if "facts or documentary evidence are absent," or (2) if "a collection of facts or evidence is subject to competing interpretations."[56] Both of these conditions are typically present in major political disputes.

Even the most obviously fantastic stories make a claim to truth for the order that they impose on a chaotic world. To support the claim that fairy tales give meaning to a child's life, for example, Bruno Bettelheim quotes the German poet Schiller as saying that, "deeper meaning resides in the fairy tales told to me in my childhood than in the truth that is taught by life."[57] Events become meaningful in stories and meaning depends upon the significance of the events within the context of the story. As a consequence, the perception of truth depends upon the story as a whole rather than upon the accuracy of its individual statements. Louis O. Mink argues that a historical narrative "claims truth not merely for each of its individual statements taken distributively, but for the complex form of the narrative itself."[58] The "complex form" of the narrative makes isolated events and individual statements meaningful. Mink concludes that "the significance of past occurrences is understandable only as they are locatable in the ensemble of interrelationships that can be grasped only in the construction of narrative form."[59]

The variety of technical terms developed here all lead to a single basic conclusion: somehow we must recognize that stories admit to a dual evaluation. Alasdair MacIntyre studies moral discourse in terms of *verisimilitude* and *dramatic probability*.[60] Fisher uses *narrative fidelity* and *narrative probability* to express a parallel distinction.[61] In other words, each theorist sees narrative credibility (and narrative power) as having both substantive and formal properties.

An examination of the reaction to Reagan's dominant narrative suggests that the two properties are interdependent, and recognizing the reflexive quality of his narrative suggests an explanation for the difference in claims about the truth of his rhetoric: the kind of "narrative probability" established in Reagan's explicitly narrative and mythic rhetoric has affected judgments of "narrative fidelity." Because his story is so dominant, so explicit, and so consistent, political claims are likely to be measured against the standard of Reagan's mythic American history rather than against other possible standards such as technical competence or ideological dogma. In this way, the story's dominance has diminished the significance of claims about Reagan's factual inaccuracies. For example, in the 1984 campaign Reagan claimed that the tax proposal being advanced by the Democrats would be equivalent to adding $1,800 to the tax bill of every American household.[62] The figure was questioned widely, but the charge of inaccuracy never affected Reagan's credibility or popularity. The meaning of the general story was more important than the particular figure. If Reagan's estimate erred by 10% or by 100% that would not affect the meaning of his story—that the Democrats were, once again, offering a "massive tax and spending scheme" that threatened American economic progress—so the error could be dismissed as trivial.

In addition, relying on the internal relationships established in stories to determine the truth discourages direct denial or refutation and encourages the audience to discover their own place in the story. One reason for the lack of success of many of Reagan's critics has been their tendency to attempt to refute Reagan's assertions.[63] Those most successful in confronting Reagan, such as Mario Cuomo, have been those few politicans who offer alternative stories. The argument must be adjusted to the narrative paradigm—for example, by making the "city on a hill" a "tale of two cities"—or it is likely to be seen as trivial or irrelevant.

The stories that have caused the most trouble for Reagan are those which are least in accord with the generally accepted understanding. In a speech to the VFW during the 1980 campaign, for example, Reagan referred to the Vietnam War as "a noble cause." Despite the approval of the immediate audience, the story complicated his national campaign because of its inconsistency with the general understanding of Vietnam as an unjust war in which America played an ignoble role.[64] Similarly, Reagan's difficulties with the Bitburg ceremony stemmed from his account contradicting the received understanding of America waging war to destroy the evils of Nazi conquest. Neither of these cases resulted in lasting damage to Reagan's popularity or credibility, however, because he was able to show that his actions were consistent with his story of America.[65] The distinctiveness of the Iran/*contra* affair is that Reagan's actions have been interpreted as being inconsistent with Reagan's own story. Trading arms for hostages was not seen as consistent with standing up to terrorism; providing arms to Iran was not seen as consistent with strong opposition to America's enemies. Because it was perceived as being inconsistent with the established story of the Reagan presidency, the effects of the Iranian arms deal have been general and severe.[66] Even a story that is powerfully resistant to outside criticism cannot survive inconsistency with itself.

Reagan's stories are not completely self-contained—if they could not be interpreted as representing real events in the real world they would be vulnerable to charges that they are merely fantasies conjured up by the conservative imagination[67]—but this is a special kind of reality. The basis for accepting the referential value of Reagan's stories is not empirical justification, but consistency with the moral standards and common sense of his audience.

Moral Argument

Narrative form shapes interpretation by emphasizing the moral dimension of understanding. As Hayden White says of historical narrative, "story forms not only permit us to judge the moral significance of human projects, they also provide the means by which to judge them, even while we pretend to be merely describing them."[68] White takes the "moral impulse" to be a defining characteristic of narrativity,[69] Fisher uses *moral* argument to distinguish that form of public argument most suited to narrative,[70] and Alasdair MacIntyre makes the connection between narrative, personal identity, intelligibility, and accountability fundamental to his attempt to rescue ethical judgment from what he sees as the sterile standards of enlightenment thinkers.[71] The nature of the narrative form is said to be moral because stories make events intelligible by imposing a temporal order that leads to some end that defines the moral frame of the story and because the nature of the characters and events in the story will be defined with reference to that purpose.

Ronald Beiner explains and exemplifies the moral impulse of narrative in political discourse. "In attempting to define a conception of the human good," he writes, *"we tell a story."*[72] Not all stories work equally well, but rich and penetrating stories are what we look for in the work of political theorists and in the statements of politicians. The quality of the story will make it more or less effective in disclosing some truth about the human condition. And different stories will suggest different truths, not all of which will be consistent with each other. "For instance," Beiner continues, "if we wish to expound the necessary place of political freedom in a meaningfully human life, we may wish to tell a story about how the union organizers of Solidarity in Poland, against all odds, forced a remote party machine to listen to the voice of the Polish people."[73] Or we may recall the heroic acts and noble sentiments of the American Revolution as conservative spokesmen like Reagan often do. Or we may reverse the focus and tell of the horrors of repression and segregation in South Africa. The significant point here is that whatever story is told will provide a moral direction and that this is especially true for narratives that are presented as historical fact.

The heavily moral orientation of Reagan's rhetoric helps to account both for the character of his rhetoric and for the character of the response to it. Reagan characteristically justifies his policies by citing their goals, while critics of his policies characteristically cite problems of conception or implementation. Reagan's moral focus has worked well because the shift of emphasis to ends rather than means pre-empts arguments about practicality and because it provides Reagan with a ready response by transforming opposition to policy into opposition to principle. The difficulties of reaching the goal are not ignored, but in this idealistic framework they take on the status of technicalities—potentially bothersome, but not really fundamental to judging policies or people.

The focus on goals has also led to two sorts of criticisms. Reagan is accused of overlooking the impact that means can have on ends,[74] and of assuming that stating the goal is equivalent to its achievement.[75] These tendencies can be seen clearly in the justification and defense that Reagan provides for his policies.

Reagan's justification for the Strategic Defense Initiative in the 1985 State of the Union Address provides a good example of the ways in which a moral emphasis can influence public argument. There is, said Reagan, "a better way of eliminating the threat of nuclear war" than deterrence:

> It is a Strategic Defense Initiative aimed at finding a non-nuclear defense against ballistic missiles. It is the most hopeful possibility of the nuclear age. But it is not well understood.

Some say it will bring war to the heavens—but its purpose is to deter war, in the heavens and on earth. Some say the research would be expensive. Perhaps, but it could save millions of lives, indeed humanity itself. Some say if we build such a system, the Soviets will build a defense system of their own. They already have strategic defenses that surpass ours; a civil defense system, where we have almost none; and a research program covering roughly the same areas of technology we're exploring. And finally, some say the research will take a long time. The answer to that is: "Let's get started."[76]

The pattern of response is revealing. While the objections cited by Reagan are primarily pragmatic (expense, Soviet response, time), Reagan's justifications are made in terms of the goals of the program. Reagan does not deny that this program might "bring war to the heavens," he cites the goal of the program as sufficient justification; he does not deny its expense, he invokes the goal of saving lives. The relationship between means and ends is skewed to an exclusive focus on goals as a means of judgment. If the move from practicality to principle is accepted, it makes the policy immune from most objections. From this point of view, the only reasonable explanation for opposition is the one that Reagan cites, the policy must not be "well understood."[77]

The same combination of an exclusive focus upon ends defined within a particular historical narrative has resulted in charges that Reagan "has been pushing his civil-rights policies with a campaign of 'astonishing misrepresentation.'"[78] Reagan's response to such criticisms is that they are the result of "misperceptions" and "misunderstandings."[79] While his critics cite his factual errors and what they see as inconsistencies between his statements and the actions of his administration, Reagan relies on the story of his life and his story of America to counter the accusations. When questioned about his negative image among black leaders, for example, Reagan responded with a reference to his character (that is, to the character of Reagan-in-the-story): "it's very disturbing to me, because anyone who knows my life story knows that long before there was a thing called the civil-rights movement, I was busy on that side."[80] In his Second Inaugural, he again used reference to the past to make racial equality a part of America's story: "As an older American, I remember a time when people of different race, creed, or ethnic origin in our land found hatred and prejudice installed in social custom and, yes, in law. There is no story more heartening in our history than the progress that we've made toward the 'brotherhood of man' that God intended for us." From the narrative point of view, it is sufficient to have the appropriate character, and to believe in the appropriate goals. The proper results are the consequence of the story's progression.

Common Sense

Narrative truth assumes a type of knowledge that differs from the knowledge produced within and sanctioned by rational argument. Both Mink and White claim that narrative is the basic medium of common sense.[81] MacIntyre and Fisher identify narrative with the received wisdom of the community and contrast that to the "elitist" and "technical" knowledge of the academic and political establishment.[82] Since narrative makes sense of experience, the sense that is made will be grounded in the presuppositions of those who accept the narrative, and those presuppositions are common sense. Persuasive narratives, then, both express and assume a knowledge that is shared by the community.

The emphasis on common sense is significant for, as Clifford Geertz in anthropology and Alasdair MacIntyre in philosophy have shown, "common sense" is a culturally defined set of rules and expectations.[83] Just as reliance on a common morality de-emphasizes practical and technical concerns, reliance on a common understanding de-emphasizes objections based on claims to special knowledge or expertise. Common sense is so obvious to those who accept it that disagreement with its implications will often seem irrelevant, impractical, or unintelligible. Hayden White notes approvingly that "one of its virtues is the conviction that informs it: agreement with its dicta is the very mark of goodwill."[84] In this way, common sense insulates its claims from alternative conceptions; it consists of an unreflective, self-evidently "true" set of beliefs that are used to make sense out of situations and events. Common sense establishes a transparent realism—a common sense statement is what everyone knows; a common sense judgment is what any sensible person would do.

Reagan's reliance upon common sense as a standard for understanding and judgment has been noted both by commentators and by Reagan himself,[85] and the consequences of the emphasis on common sense on his expression and his analysis are evident in the style, the logic, and the attitude of his rhetoric. In brief, the common sense grounding that is an element of Reagan's dominant narrative suggests a pattern of understanding that parallels Geertz's informal categorization of the "stylistic features, marks of attitude" of common sense.[86] Reagan's rhetoric employs a simple, familiar, and personal style; a logic grounded in practical analogy; and an attitude that offers a singular perspective, unquestioned assumptions, and definitive portrayals.

Reagan's style encourages the perception that political problems are accessible to solution by the common action of ordinary people. Since common sense is "thin," political understanding requires no mysterious or arcane perceptiveness; things are as they appear.[87] The simplicity of apparently complex issues has been a continuing theme in Reagan's rhetoric. In the so-called Reaganomics speech, he declined to present "a jumble of charts, figures, and economic jargon"; his Strategic Defense Initiative was "not about spending artithmetic"; his proposal for Tax Reform was " a simple, straightforward message"; on Nicaragua, "the question the Congress of the United States will now answer is a simple one"; and on arms control, "the answer, my friends, is simple."[88]

One consequence of Reagan's simple style of common sense rhetoric is that he has been subject to charges of being simplistic throughout his political career. In a revealing response to that claim in his Inaugural Address as governor of California, Reagan said: "For many years, you and I have been shushed like children and told there are no simple answers to complex problems that are beyond our comprehension. Well, the truth is there *are* simple answers—just not easy ones."[89] Much of Reagan's relationship to his audience is contained in this "common sense" observation. The reference to "you and I" places Reagan and the audience together against the unspecified forces that oppose the participation of the people in political decision-making and the reference to "simple answers" opens up the political process. Character and style combine to reinforce the presumption that will and courage, not intelligence or expertise, are required to solve difficult political problems.

Aristotle noted that comparison with the familiar allows us to understand the unfamiliar[90] and the assumptions of common sense move that observation farther: unfamiliar events and complex situations are seen to be "really" like the simple and familiar understandings and beliefs of the groups.[91] Reagan often uses a "common sense" logic of practical analogies to explain and to justify his policy choices. In his Acceptance Address at the 1980 Republican Convention, for example, Reagan said: "I believe it is clear our federal government is overgrown and overweight. Indeed, it is time for our government to go on a diet."[92] And in his first speech on "Reaganomics," he met his opposition with common sense: "There were always those who told us that taxes couldn't be cut until spending was reduced. Well, you know, we can lecture our children against extravagance until we run out of voice and breath. Or we can cure their extravagence by simply reducing their allowance."[93] In Reagan's 1986 address on Nicaragua, the Nicaraguan government is referred to as "a second Cuba, a second Libya," while the *contras* are said to be "freedom fighters" who are "like the French Resistance that fought the Nazis."[94] By using the daily dilemmas of diets and allowances and the widely accepted evils of the Nazis and Cuba as parallels to current American policy-making, Reagan suggests that what might have been seen as complex and distant problems are amenable to simple and familiar (if not always pleasant) solutions. As he concluded later in the "Reaganomics" speech, "All it takes is a little common sense and recognition of our own ability."[95]

Since common sense is assumed to be "natural," the correctness and universality of the perceptions and judgments that Reagan propounds is also assumed.[96] His is not a carefully weighed reflection involving doubts and reservations; Reagan presents the picture clearly and incontestably and the actions follow naturally from his descriptions. In his Address to the Nation on Defense and National Security (the so-called "Star Wars" speech), for example, Reagan began by stating that further defense cuts "cannot be made" and that there is "no logical way" to reduce the defence budget without reducing security. In his description of Soviet power he stated that "the...militarization of Grenada...can only be seen as a power projection into that region" and that "the Soviet Union is acquiring what can only be considered an offensive military force." The appropriate actions are just as clear: "it was obvious that we had to begin a major modernization program," "we must continue to restore our military strength"; and with regard to his proposal: "Are we not capable of demonstrating our peaceful intentions by applying all our abilities and our ingenuity to achieving a truly lasting stability? I think we are. Indeed we must."[97]

This sense of unquestioned truth explains why the observations of theorists about common sense in general apply so smoothly to Reagan's rhetoric—a "maddening air of simple wisdom" exercises Reagan's critics and "comfortable certainties" reassure his supporters.[98] Since common sense justification relies on doing what any sensible person would do based on what everyone knows to be true, a narrative frame may encourage those within it to see intelligence in practical terms and to emphasize sensibility over intellectual analysis. The differing perspectives help to explain why his supporters can recognize that Reagan is "no rocket scientist" and still respect his intelligence,[99] at the same time that his opponents lament what seems to them to be his obvious intellectual weakness. Technical accomplishment has its place in a common sense perspective—expertise is useful, even essential, in making applications and in completing the details of policy—but one need not be a nuclear engineer or a tax accountant to know that nuclear strength ensures peace or that simplicity brings fairness.[100]

Consequences for Policy: Incommensurable Frames

Fisher's description of the rational and narrative paradigms neatly summarizes a major difference in perspective. From the point of view of the rational world paradigm, a story should be substantively true so that it can be used as evidence by example or analogy, or it should be vivid enough to illustrate the problem or its possible solution. In either case, stories are not considered likely to be able to carry the knowledge one needs to analyze and solve a problem. From the point of view of the narrative paradigm, a story should be a good story judged by internal aesthetic criteria and by external criteria of "fit" with the audiences' experience and morality. In any case, it is likely to best express what one really needs to know to get by in the world. The two perspectives clash over standards for evidence and the appropriate basis for judgment.

The rhetorical critic should consider that any discourse can be described differently according to these competing though not contradictory accounts. Furthermore, the critic should consider that different auditors may respond differently to the same message because they are applying these different standards of apprehension.

The incommensurability of these two frames of reference is illustrated neatly in Walter Mondale's attack on Reagan's fiscal policy in the 1984 presidential campaign. In his acceptance address at the Democratic Convention, Mondale called for "a new realism." He challenged Reagan to "put his plan on the table next to mine" and then to "debate it on national television before the American people," and he contrasted Reagan's approach with "the truth" five times including his memorable promise to raise taxes: "Let's tell the truth. . . . Mr. Reagan will raise taxes, and so will I. He won't tell you. I just did."[101] Calls for realism, debate, and truth are fundamental to rational analysis, but they taken on a different meaning from within the narrative paradigm.

In the Second Inaugural and in the related speeches that followed,[102] Reagan offered two directions for reducing budget deficits. First, "a dynamic economy, with more citizens working and paying taxes," and second, an amendment that would "make it unconstitutional for the federal government to spend more than the federal government takes in." Both these strategies are grounded in the *telos* of Reagan's narrative. Working individuals tend naturally toward economic success unless blocked by barriers constructed by government. The federal government, on the other hand, will tend naturally toward expansion and will increase taxes and spending unless blocked by a permanent control that is beyond its power to change.[103] From the point of view of the rational paradigm, tax increases are the logical solution because adding revenue would correct the imbalance between income and expenditure. From the point of view of Reagan's story, tax increases are illogical because they would frustrate the individual initiative that is the basis for economic growth and they are immoral because they would violate the natural order by restraining individuals to benefit government. From the rational point of view, a Balanced Budget Amendment is irrelevant because it addresses a principle without dealing with the underlying problem. From the point of view of Reagan's narrative, the amendment is logical because the federal government will never act contrary to its natural character without some outside restraint and it is moral because it is directed toward the quest for individual freedom.

The dispute over tax policy reveals different structures of perception that lead to different policy conclusions. The distinctive character of these differences is that they are defined by Reagan's reliance on narrative form. It is not just the nature of the particular story, but the reliance on story-telling that defines the relationship of those who accept Reagan's rhetoric to a complex of significant issues. A narrative perspective uses consistency with the story as the primary measure of truth, emphasizes moral standards for judgment, and features common sense as the basis for making political decisions.

CONCLUSIONS

When Reagan is seen as a story-teller and his message is seen as a story, it becomes evident why he was so successful in "re-invigorating" the country—his story gave a clear, powerful, reassuring, and self-justifying meaning to America's public life. And it is evident why Reagan's personal popularity consistently exceeds support for his policies—to accept the story is to see Reagan both as a hero exemplifying the virtues of manly efficacy and as a realistic narrator telling things as they are; it makes sense to rely on Reagan-in-the-story. The reason that charges against Reagan's lack of compassion or his militarism have been ineffectual is that the nature of social justice and peace, and the appropriate means for their achievement, are defined from within his story. The reason that repeated charges of ignorance and factual error have not affected either Reagan's popularity or his credibility is that truth is judged in the context of the story and the story is judged for its fit with popular morality and common sense. In short, Reagan demonstrates the enormous appeal of a narrative form handled with artistry by a major public figure.

Reagan also demonstrates how limiting reliance on a single, unquestioned narrative structure can be when applied to the range of national and international concerns that comprise American political discourse. The effectiveness of Reagan's transcendent narrative depends upon establishing the story as the primary context for understanding people and events. Such a self-contained communication form is effective because it is clear, complete, and (therefore) reassuring. In addition to its evident effectiveness, however, such a narrative is also fragile and dangerous.

A dominant narrative structure is fragile because the requirement of internal consistency is permanent, while the ability of people responding to events to maintain that consistency is inevitably partial and temporary. The fragility of Reagan's story became evident in the public response to the Iran/*contra* affair. Since Reagan's character and his actions were perceived as a part of his story and were judged on the basis of their consistency with that story, his credibility was intact as long as he remained consistent. Perceived inconsistency with the standards that he had established, however, was devastating and the effects were immediate and (apparently) lasting.[104]

Reagan's dominant narrative is dangerous because its assertion of permanence assumes both insularity from material conditions and isolation from social commentary. His mythic rhetoric appeals to a tradition of belief and action that lends credence to the virtues and actions that are justified by his historical sense, but the justification is limited by Reagan's limited notion of history. An essential part of Alasdair MacIntyre's consideration of the ethical role of narrative thinking is that "a living tradition...is an historically extended, socially embodied argument, and an argument precisely in part about the goods which constitute that tradition."[105] When Reagan treats American history as a clearly defined set of actions with a clear and constant set of lessons to be applied to present action and future policy direction, he isolates his vision from historical reinterpretation and from current controversy. Reagan's consistency provides his audiences with a clear, simple, and familiar framework within which to encompass complex or unfamiliar problems. Yielding to this enticing vision can be dangerous, however, because the assumption of the story's truth hides its contingent nature and its implicit ideology. Adherence to a single story with a single point of view can make good judgment more difficult by reinforcing the legitimacy of a single set of social stereotypes and by promoting an exclusively American point of view on international problems.[106]

A related danger concerns the role of the public in Reagan's version of America's story. Relying on the (presumably) established moral code and the (presumably) accepted common sense of the American people to establish the legitimacy of the story implicitly denies the legitimacy of either change or challenge with the result that the story's participants are driven to a posture of passive acceptance.[107] Ironically, Reagan's story of an actively heroic American public forces those who accept it into the position of being listeners rather than creators. At most, the individual becomes a participant in a pre-established historical frame.

The application of narrative theory to Reagan's rhetoric also raises some broader questions regarding narrative and political judgment. Fisher's assertion of the moral superiority of the narrative paradigm[108] is not confirmed. Reagan's story-telling does emphasize moral argument and it does act as an explicit counter to technical elitism, but, as just noted, it may also damage public morality. This examination of Reagan's rhetoric suggests that Fisher's reliance on the Aristotelian dictum that "the 'people' have a natural tendency to prefer the true and the just"[109] may be a mystification that requires a more careful examination of the ways in which stories are accepted or rejected. Reagan has shown that powerful appeals can be made to popular belief and popular morality through the narrative form, but the acceptance of his story and the durability of his popularity also seem to show that there is a preference for clarity over complexity, for consistency over aberration, for positive direction over acceptance of limitations, and for self-justification by the derogation of one's enemies. Goods internal to the story need to be consistent with the moral judgment of the audience, and truths that are accepted within the story need to be consistent with the common sense of the audience, but it is not clear from examining this case in which narrative form is dominant that narrative is likely to provide a morality or truth that is superior to other forms of discourse or to combinations of other forms.

There are other disturbing problems as well. Despite identifying two "paradigms," Fisher assumes that rational and narrative modes of thinking are fundamentally compatible.[110] He argues that considerations of narrative fidelity can subsume the skills and requirements of logic. But this examination of Reagan's rhetoric and the responses to it suggests that the narrative and the rational perspectives can be distinctive and incommensurable. One need not claim that narrative is irrational to distinguish its characteristic form of rationality from that of the "rational world" paradigm. Having made the distinction between these two modes of thought clear, it becomes difficult to accept Fisher's conclusion that narrative offers a superior and fully encompassing alternative.[111]

Americans have listened to Ronald Reagan as President for almost a decade, usually with admiration, but often without agreement. Some have heard poor arguments and marveled at his ability to delude his audiences; others have heard good stories and dismissed his errors as trivial. And while the Iran/*contra* crisis has diminished the credibility of Reagan's presidency, it has not altered the forms of understanding through which he is heard. Until the differences in judgment are identified as differences in perspective, there will be little ground for common discussion and little motivation for self-analysis.

Notes

1. Mary McGrory, ". . . and growls from the training camp," *Des Moines Register*, 6 September 1985, 12A. Paul Erickson begins his book on Reagan with the judgment that, "Ronald Reagan is by far the most persuasive political speaker of our time." *Reagan Speaks* (New York: New York University Press, 1985), 1.

2. "More Popular Than Ever," *Time*, 12 August 1985, 17.

3. Sidney Blumenthal, "The Reagan Millenium," *New Republic*, 19 November 1984, 12.

4. The books cover a range of policies and perspectives, some are explicitly political and were designed to influence election campaigns: Edmund G. Brown, *Reagan and Reality* (New York: Praeger, 1970); Brown and Bill Brown, *Reagan: The Political Chameleon* (New York: Praeger, 1976); Mark Green and Gail MacColl, *There He Goes Again: Ronald Reagan's Reign of Error* (New York: Pantheon Books, 1983). Others respond to specific issues: Robert Scheer, *With Enough Shovels: Reagan, Bush, and Nuclear War* (New York: Random House, 1982); Strobe Talbott, *Deadly Gambits: The Reagan Administration and the Stalemate in Nuclear Arms* (New York: Knopf, 1984). Fred Ackerman, *Reaganomics: Rhetoric vs. Reality* (Boston: South End Press, 1982). Joan Claybrook, *Retreat From Safety: Reagan's Attack on America's Health* (New York: Pantheon, 1984). Others attempt more thorough or scholarly appraisals of Reagan's statements and policies: Ronald Dallek, *Reagan: The Politics of Symbolism* (Cambridge: Harvard University Press, 1984); Ronnie Dugger, *On Reagan: The Man and his Presidency* (New York: McGraw-Hill, 1983).

5. Dallek, 178.

6. Dallek, viii.

7. "Innocence Abroad," *The New Republic*, 3 June 1985, 7.

8. Martin Medhurst, "Postponing the Social Agenda: Reagan's Strategy and Tactics," *Western Journal of Speech Communication* 48 (1984): 262–276; Henry Z. Scheele, "Ronald Reagan's 1980 Acceptance Address: A Focus on American Values," *Western Journal of Speech Communication* 48 (1984): 51–61; Bert E. Bradley, "Jefferson and Reagan: The Rhetoric of Two Inaugurals," *Southern Speech Communication Journal* 48 (1983): 119–136; Walter Fisher, "Romantic Democracy, Ronald Reagan, and Presidential Heroes," *Western Journal of Speech Communication* 46 (1982): 299–310.

9. Richard L. Johannesen, "An Ethical Assessment of the Reagan Rhetoric, 1981–1982," *Political Communication Yearbook 1984*, eds Keith R. Sanders, Lynda Lee Kaid, and Dan Nimmo (Carbondale: Southern Illinois University Press, 1985), 226–241; C. Thomas Preston, Jr., "Reagan's 'New Beginning': Is it the 'New Deal' of the Eighties?" *Southern Speech Communication Journal* 49 (1984): 198–211; Gregg Phifer, "Two Inaugurals: A Second Look," *Southern Speech Communication Journal* 48 (1983): 378–385.

10. David Zarefsky, Carol Miller-Tutzauer, and Frank E. Tutzauer, "Reagan's Safety Net for the Truly Needy: The Rhetorical Uses of Definition," *Central States Speech Journal* 35 (1984): 113–119; Richard E. Crable and Steven L. Vibbert, "Argumentative Stance and Political Faith Healing: 'The Dream Will Come True," *Quarterly Journal of Speech* 69 (1983): 290-301. In his explanation of Reagan's approach to Soviet-American relations Robert L. Ivie found that "a flawed policy is being perceived as successful because of how it is symbolized." "Speaking 'Common Sense' About the Soviet Threat: Reagan's Rhetorical Stance," *Western Journal of Speech Communication* 48 (1984): 40. Sarah Russell Hankins concluded that "the presidential choice in 1980 was an attempt to align the human with the illusion of the heroic." "Archetypal Alloy: Reagan's Rhetorical Image," *Central States Speech Journal* 34 (1983): 34. Similarly, Martha Anna Martin wrote that "the cumulative language, if not the reality, suggested that Carter was an 'unfit' leader." "Ideologues, Ideographs, and 'The Best Men': From Carter to Reagan," *Southern Speech Communication Journal* 49 (1983): 19. Gary C. Woodward makes a parallel claim about Reagan's populist appeal: "Populism has taken on a cosmetic and ironic purpose...pretending to serve the 'public interest', but serving what may be very private interests indeed." "Reagan as Roosevelt: The Elasticity of Pseudo-Populist Appeals," *Central States Speech Journal* 34 (1983): 57–58.

11. Walter R. Fisher, "Narration as a Human Communication Paradigm: The Case of Public Moral Argument," *Communication Monographs* 51 (1984): 1–22.

12. See, Erickson, esp. chapter 3, "Analogies, Allegories, and Homilies," 32–50; David Stockman, *The Triumph of Politics* (New York: Harper & Row, 1986), 90.

13. Martin Medhurst demonstrates the way in which Reagan employs the theme of America as a nation that was set apart, by God. As he notes, "the theme of a people set apart is...a standard *topos* of civil-religious discourse in America." Medhurst, 270. Both Erickson and Johannesen suggest that Reagan's rhetoric uses the form of the jeremiad and the substance of American civil religion. *Reagan Speaks*, 86–93; Richard Johannesen, "Ronald Reagan's Economic Jeremiad" *Central States Speech Journal*, forthcoming. Janice Hocker Rushing argues that "the mythic milieu of the ['Star Wars'] speech is the transformation of the Old West into the New Frontier." "Ronald Reagan's 'Star Wars' Address: Mythic Containment of Technical Reasoning," *Quarterly Journal of Speech* 72 (1986): 417. Perhaps the most notable development of this idea is Gary Wills, *Reagan's America* (New York: Doubleday, 1987).

14. For example, in commenting on Reagan's arms negotiations in Iceland, Anthony Lewis wrote: "Ronald Reagan has never been more breathtaking as a politician than in the weeks since Reykjavik. He has pictured failure as success, black as white, incompetence as standing up to the Russians. And according to the polls, Americans love the performance." Quoted in Thomas Griffith, "Being Too Easy on Reagan," *Time*, 17 November 1986, 88.

15. This has been evident paricularly in the response of the press. A *Time* magazine editorial, for example, offered the following explanation: "A frustrated Washington press corps had felt itself ignored by a public that did not want to hear criticism of a popular President. But the sudden and steep decline in Reagan's popularity suggests that all along the public had recognized, in a man it admired, how casually he minded the store, and how willfully he could deny facts or distort them." Thomas Griffith, "Watergate: A Poor Parallel," *Time*, 29 December 1986, 57.

16. As even the *Washington Post* conceded, "this president has given tens of millions of people in this country a feeling that safe, stable times are returned and that fundamental values they hold dear are back in vogue and unashamedly so" (January 22, 1985).

17. Since the narrative logic of Reagan's story makes his actions in the arms deal difficult to explain, the dominant response has been to remove Reagan from the story either by suggesting that he had no control over the actions of his subordinates or by suggesting that Reagan himself had changed and questioning his mental or physical health.

18. In his campaign speeches, Reagan told the story as a humorous example. In Milwaukee, for example, he said, "Our pledge is for tax simplification, to make the system more fair, to make it easier to understand. Do you know that Einstein has admitted he cannot understand the Form 1040? [*Laughter*]." *Weekly Compilation of Presidential Documents* (hereafter, *WCPD*), 8 October 1985, 1381. In his speech to the nation he told the story in slightly different form: "We call it America's tax plan because it will reduce tax burdens on the working people of this country, close loopholes that benefit a privileged few, simplify a code so complex even Albert Einstein reportedly needed help on his 1040 Form, and lead us into a future of greater growth and opportunity for all." "Tax Reform," 28 May 1985, *WCPD*, 704.

19. "A Debate on Religious Freedom," *Harper's*, October 1984, 15, 18.

20. Rene Wellek and Austin Warren, *Theory of Literature* (New York: Harcourt, Brace, & World, 1956), 119.

21. "Myth and Identity," in *Myth and Mythology* ed. Gilbert Murray (1959; rpt. Boston: Beacon, 1968), 279.

22. Reagan frequently refers to America as a nation "chosen by God." In the 1987 State of the Union Address, for example, Reagan said that "our nation could not have been conceived without divine help" and that "The United States Constitution...grew out of the most fundamental inspiration of our existence: that we are here to serve Him by living free." "The State of the Union," *WCPD*, 27 January 1987, 63, 64.

23. In the 1985 State of the Union Address, for example, Reagan supports his confidence in American abilities by saying, "Two hundred years of American history should have taught us that nothing is impossible." "The State of the Union," *WCPD*, 6 February 1985, 146. Reagan's conception of the American experience closely parallels the "American monomyth" that Robert Jewett and John Shelton Lawrence have found pervading the productions of popular culture. *The American Monomyth* (Garden City, NY: Anchor Press/Doubleday, 1977), xx.

24. All quotations from Reagan's Second Inaugural Address are from the "50th American Presidential Inaugural," *WCPD*, 21 January 1985, 67–70.

25. In the 1985 State of the Union Address, Reagan said, "There are no constraints on the human mind, no walls around the human spirit, no barriers to our progress except those we ourselves erect." "The State of the Union," 141.

26. All quotations are from "Inaugural Address," *Public Papers of the Presidents: Ronald Reagan, 1981*, (Washington, D.C.: GPO, 1982), 1–4.

27. Reagan's language features particular actions and concrete situations that will be familiar to all Americans and that encourage most to see themselves in his description: "Those who say that we're in a time when there are no heroes, they just don't know where to look. You can see heroes every day going in and out of factory gates. Others, a handful in number, produce enough food to feed all of us and then the world beyond. You meet heroes across a counter, and they're on both sides of that counter. There are entrepreneurs with faith in themselves and faith in an idea who create new jobs, new wealth and opportunity. They're individuals and families whose taxes support the government and whose voluntary gifts support church, charity, culture, art, and education. Their patriotism is quiet, but deep. Their values sustain our national life." "Inaugural Address," 2.

28. Unity of interests and goals is a major and continuing theme in Reagan's rhetoric. In welcoming the debate on tax reform, for example, he also stated that "it should not be a partisan debate for the authors of tax reform come from both parties, and all of us want greater fairness, incentives, and simplicity in taxation." "Tax Reform," *WCPD*, 28 May 1985, 707. In urging support for the *contras* in Nicaragua he quoted "Senator Scoop Jackson" as saying: "On matters of national security, the best politics is no politics." "Nicaragua," *WCPD*, 16 March 1986, 374. The quotation was also used in the 1986 State of the Union Address, *WCPD*, 4 February 1986, 139.

29. "Every Region, Every Age Group, Almost Every Voting Bloc," *Time*, 19 November 1984, 45.

30. For example, Edmund G. Brown classes Reagan's speeches with "the unreasoned attacks of simplistic self-servers who pander the lowest urges that plague our troubled people," in Brown and Bill Brown, *Reagan: The Political Chameleon*, 8.

31. Dugger, for example, charges that, "[Reagan] has long been allied with the most bellicose elements in the American military establishment; now he is using the power and glory the White House gives him to bring about...a mortally dangerous shift in U.S. nuclear strategy." *On Reagan*, xiv.

32. Stanley Hoffman, "Semidetached Politics," *New York Review of Books*, 8 November 1984, 34–36.

33. Reporters have repeatedly expressed their frustration with Reagan's "Teflon Presidency." For example, Tom Wicker, "A smile, a quip and no mud on his shoes..." *Kansas City Times*, 31 May 1984, A-18; Sidney Blumenthal, "Reagan the Unassailable," *New Republic*, 12 September 1983, 11–16.

34. Martin, 21. She uses the phrase in a comparison of Reagan with Theodore Roosevelt.

35. Hankins, 41.

36. Fisher, "Romantic Democracy," 302.

37. Fisher, "Romantic Democracy," 302.

38. See, Bradley, "Jefferson and Reagan: The Rhetoric of Two Inaugurals"; Martin, 18–23; Woodward, 44–58.

39. Martin, 22. Fisher reached an almost identical conclusion about Reagan's "manly" character: "Reagan's tough stands on America's military posture and his decisive views on domestic problems gave substance to the perception." "Romantic Democracy," 302.

40. Martin, 15.

41. This role matches the recurring character of the American hero in popular culture identified by Jewett and Lawrence in *The American Monomyth*, xx, 195–196.

42. Christopher J. Matthews, "Your Host, Ronald Reagan," *New Republic*, 26 March 1984, 15–18. Robert J. Kaiser, "Your Host of Hosts," *New York Review of Books*, 28 June 1984, 38–41. Hankins, 42: Reagan is "one step removed...we are content to have him play the part." Martin, 24: "Ironically, the media age had no Teddy Roosevelt to offer. Instead, the 1980's offered an actor whose identification was with pseudo-heroism as filtered through film of his ranch, his horses, possibly even his ability as a 'nice' guy to defeat the guy in the black hat (the Ayatollah and the Communists), Hollywood version."

43. Illustrated most vividly in his reaction to the assassination attempt. Reactions of critics and admirers converge in an appreciation of Reagan's response after being shot. Fisher, "Romantic Democracy," 307–308; Kaiser, 39.

44. For examples, see below in the discussion of common sense.

45. See Ivie for a discussion of Reagan's appeal to American "common sense" about the Soviet Union. Scheele documents Reagan's reliance on American values.

46. Kaiser, 41. French sociologist Michael Crozier believes that Reagan's "soothing style" is a perfect fit for the country's "craving for normalcy." *The Trouble with America* (Berkeley: University of California Press, 1984), 57–60.

47. "Inaugural Address," 20 January 1981, 3. For examples of Reagan's emphasis on the value of "peace" in his Acceptance Address at the 1980 Republican Convention, see Scheele, 56.

48. Lou Cannon, *Reagan* (New York: G.P. Putnam's Sons, 1982), 281–282; Jack W. Germond and Jules Witcover, *Blue Smoke and Mirrors* (New York: Viking Press, 1981), 243, 224–225.

49. See, Rushing, n. 62.

50. Robert L. Scott, "Narrative Theory and Communication Research," *Quarterly Journal of Speech* 70 (1984): 200.

51. Fisher, "Narration," 4.

52. Fisher, "Narration," 8.

53. "The Narrativization of Real Events," *On Narrative*, ed. W.J.T. Mitchell (Chicago: University of Chicago Press, 1981), 251.

54. Paul Ricoeur, "The Narrative Function," *Hermeneutics and the Human Sciences*, ed. and trans. by John B. Thompson (Cambridge: Cambridge University Press, 1981), 289–296.

55. W. Lance Bennett and Martha S. Feldman, *Reconstructing Reality in the Courtroom* (New Brunswick: Rutgers University Press, 1981), 33.

56. Bennett and Feldman, 89.

57. *The Uses of Enchantment* (New York: Vintage Books, 1976), 5.

58. "Narrative Form as a Cognitive Instrument," in *The Writing of History* ed. by Robert H. Canary and Henry Kozicki (Madison: University of Wisconsin Press, 1978), 144.

59. Mink, 148.

60. Alasdair MacIntyre, *After Virtue*, 2nd ed. (Notre Dame: University of Notre Dame Press, 1981), 200.

61. Fisher, 8.

62. Reagan made the claim repeatedly in his campaign speeches, often adapting the particulars to the place where he was speaking. In one week, for example, the gave the Democrat's version of Vince Lombardi's famous statement about winning to an audience in Milwaukee ("They're saying, 'Tax increases aren't everthing. They're the only thing.' ") and he re-defined "shrimp" for an audience in Gulfport, Mississippi ("To you, it's a livelihood; to them, it's your paycheck after they get their hands on it."). *WCPD*, 8 October 1984, 1380, 1405.

63. Sidney Blumenthal suggests that attempts by the press to refute Reagan's errors have been largely ineffectual because Reagan's world view is based on a "unifying vision" which facts "can never fatally undermine." "Reagan the Unassailable," 14.

64. Cannon, *Reagan*, 271–272.

65. William Safire's assessment of Reagan's speeches at Bitburg and Bergen-Belsen demonstrates how the message of Reagan's general story was able to dominate doubts about the propriety of his particular actions: "In driving home the lessons of history, his incredible series of blunders turned out to be a blessing.... [H]e drew the central lesson clearly: 'the freedom must always be stronger than totalitarianism, that good must always be stronger than evil.'" "I am a Jew...'" in *Bitburg in Moral and Political Perspective*, ed. Geoffrey H. Hartman (Bloomington: Indiana University Press, 1986), 212–213.

66. *Time* emphasized the damage to Reagan's credibility: "it seems almost certain that whatever comes out of the many investigations now in progress, Reagan will emerge as a diminished President, his aura of invincibility shattered, his fabled luck vanished, his every policy regarded with new suspicion." "Who Was Betrayed," *Time*, 8 December 1986, 19.

67. Significantly, exactly these charges were made against Reagan. See, for example, Benjamin Barber, "Celluloid Vistas: What the President's Dreams are Made of," *Harper's*, July 1985, 74–75; Sidney Blumenthal, "The Reagan Millenium," *New Republic*, 19 November 1984, 12–14; Green and MacColl, 8–15.

68. "The Narrativization of Real Events," 253.

69. "Where, in any account of reality, narrative is present, we can be sure that morality or a moral impulse is present too." "The Value of Narrativity in the Representation of Reality," in Mitchell, 22. (Quoted approvingly by Fisher, "Narration," 10.)

70. Fisher, "Narration," 12.

71. *After Virtue*, chapter 15, "The Virtues, the Unity of a Human Life and the Concept of a Tradition," esp., 218.

72. *Political Judgment* (Chicago: University of Chicago Press, 1983), 126.

73. Beiner, 126.

74. Jonathon Jacky, "The 'Star Wars' Defense Won't Compute," *Atlantic*, June 1985, 18–30.

75. John Kessel notes that Reagan's aides are sensitive to these problems because his "optimism...often leads Reagan to overlook difficulties that bar the path to achievement." "The Structures of the Reagan White House," *American Journal of Political Science* 28 (1984): 233.

76. "The State of the Union," 6 February 1985, 145.

77. Reagan has used a similar strategy in dealing with the opposition to other issues as well. Theodore Windt and Kathleen Farrell, for example, came to the following conclusion about Reagan's support for his 1981 tax cut: "If the rhetoric took hold in the public consciousness, then anyone opposing him would be perceived as being unfair or as one willing to perpetuate waste and fraud to save some special interest program." "Presidential Rhetoric and Presidential Power: The Reagan Initiatives," *Essays in Presidential Rhetoric* (Dubuque, IA: Kendall/Hunt, 1983), 316.

78. James Nathan Miller, "Ronald Reagan and the Techniques of Deception," *Atlantic*, February 1984, 64.

79. Miller, 62.

80. Quoted in Miller, 68.

81. Mink emphasizes the cognitive element of the common understanding. White adds that the meaning of historical narrative also presumes a common base of moral legitimacy. "The Narrativization of Real Events" in Mitchell, 253.

82. MacIntyre, "Epistemological Crises, Dramatic Narrative and the Philosophy of Science," *Monist* 60 (1977): 453–473; Fisher, 9–10.

83. Clifford Geertz, "Common Sense as a Cultural System" in *Local Knowledge* (New York: Basic Books, 1983): 73–93; and MacIntyre, "Epistemological Crises," 453–454.

84. "The Narrativization of Real Events" in Mitchell, 254.

85. Ivie, "Speaking Common Sense' Reagan's reliance on common sense has also been noted outside of the United States. In a conversation about Reagan between François Mitterand and Marguerite Duras, Mitterand says "He is a man of common sense" (10), and Duras says later "He governs less with his intellect than with common sense" (12). In "Mitterand and Duras on Reagan's America" *Harper's*, August 1986, 10–14.

86. Geertz identifies five "quasi-qualities" of common sense: naturalness, practicalness, thinness, immethodicalness, and accessibleness. "Common Sense as a Cultural System," 84–92.

87. Some critics have taken this implication of his style to be a quality of Reagan's rhetoric. Edward Chester observed that, "when one encounters an address by Ronald Reagan, the appearance coincides with the reality." "Shadow or Substance?: Critiquing Reagan's Inaugural Address," in *Essays in Presidential Rhetoric*, 303.

88. "Address to the Nation on the Economy," 5 February 1981, *Public Papers*, 79; "Address to the Nation on Defense and National Security," WCPD, 23 March 1983, 437; "Tax Reform," 705; "Meeting with Soviet General Secretary Gorbachev in Reykjavik, Iceland, " WCPD, 13 October 1986, 1377.

89. Inaugural Message, Governor of California, January 5, 1967. Quoted in "Reagan" by Lou Cannon, *The Pursuit of the Presidency, 1980*, ed. Richard Harwood (New York: Berkeley Books, 1980), 253.

90. *Rhetoric*, 1410b.

91. For example, Reagan concluded a major address on Soviet-American relations with a story that began as follows: "Just suppose with me for a minute that an Ivan and an Anya could find themselves, oh, say, in a waiting room or sharing shelter from the rain or a storm with a Jim and Sally." "Soviet-American Relations," WCPD, 16 January 1984, 44–45. International relations between two superpowers are represented by (reduced to?) the familiar circumstances of a chance meeting between two couples and we discover (as common sense always confirms) that people are pretty much the same everywhere.

92. "Acceptance Speech by Governor Ronald Reagan, Republican National Convention, Detroit, Michigan, July 17, 1980," in *The Pursuit of the Presidency, 1980*, 419–420.

93. "Address to the Nation on the Economy," 5 Feburary 1981, 81.

94. "Nicaragua," WCPD, 16 March 1986, 371, 373.

95. "Address to the Nation on the Economy," 83.

96. This assumption is so clear that the beliefs often need not even be stated. As Richard Allen, Reagan's former national security advisor, wrote: "Ronald Reagan may no longer *say* that communists lie and cheat, but he believes that they do—and so does the rest of informed mankind." Quoted in "Damage-Control Diplomacy," *Newsweek*, 7 February 1983, 27.

97. WCPD, 23 March 1983, 437, 438, 440, 442.

98. Geertz, 85; Mink, 129.

99. Cannon, "Reagan," *Pursuit*, 270. "Reagan consistently has confounded those who have underestimated him. There is a kind of small-town common sense about him that serves him well and shows in moments when it is least expected" (270).

100. In the 1980 campaign, Carter's "intelligence" was subordinated to Reagan's "good sense." The fact that he knew more than Reagan became a liability when the perception grew that "his particular brand of 'intelligence' was more suitable to the world of academic test-taking than to the pragmatic world of presidential decision-making." Martin, 15.

101. "Mondale Accepts Presidential Nomination," *Congressional Quarterly*, 21 July 1984, 12–14.

102. "Fiscal Year 1986 Budget," WCPD, 2 February 1985, 117–118; "Overhauling the Tax System," WCPD, 28 May 1985, 703–707; "The State of the Union," WCPD, 4 February 1986, 136–137; "The State of the Union," 1987.

103. ". . .we must take further steps to permanently control government's power to tax and spend. We must act now to protect future generations from government's desire to spend its citizens' money and tax them into servitude when the bills come due." "50th Presidential Inaugural," 21 January 1985, 68. The natural tendency of government expansion is a continuing theme in Reagan's rhetoric. See, for example, his "Address to the Nation on the Economy" delivered in his first year as President: ". . .government—any government—has a built-in tendency to grow." 5 February 1981, *Public Papers*, 80.

104. Just one month after the initial revelations, *Time* reported: "A New York *Times*/CBS poll last week showed the President's approval rating plunging 21 points in the past four weeks, from 67% to 46%. That is the most dramatic one-month drop since presidential opinion polls began 50 years ago. The survey found that 53% of the voters think Reagan knew 'money from the Iranian arms sale was going to help the *contras*, even though the President insists that he did not." "Under Heavy Fire," *Time*, 15 December 1986, 21–22. A *Newsweek* report on Reagan's 1987 State of the Union speech, for example, offered the following general (and

typical) assessment of the effect of the Iran/*contra* affair on public perception: "It didn't add up to a sudden crisis, but somehow he seemed on the edge of irrelevance." "Going Nowhere Fast," *Newsweek*, 9 February 1987, 24. See, James Reston, "Reagan administration already being spoken of in the past tense," *Des Moines Register*, 24 February 1987, 6A.

105. *After Virtue*, 222.

106. Stanley Hoffman, for example, worries that national pride may be manifest in "self-righteousness and a sense of moral superiority" and that Reagan's rhetoric may have encouraged "a desire not to be bothered or battered by data." "Semidetached Politics," 36. Similarly, George Ball has expressed concerns about the lack of consideration of the effects of "Star Wars" program in other parts of the world. "The War for Star Wars," *New York Review of Books*, 11 April 1985, 41.

107. Janet Rushing found a similar result in her examination of Reagan's "Star Wars" address: "Reagan's 'Star Wars' address cuts off its auditors as effectively and completely as if it were couched in the most convoluted esoterica." Rushing, 428. Our explanations differ, however. While she attributes the audience's acquiesence to the important role of "technoscience" in that issue, this analysis suggests that the passivity of Reagan's auditors is a concomitant of his narrative form and is not a reaction to technical discourse or limited to technical issues.

108. See Fisher's discussion of the responses to Jonathon Schell's *The Fate of the Earth*, "Narration," 11–15.

109. Fisher, "Narration," 9.

110. The assumption is expressed repeatedly in Fisher's first article on the narrative paradigm: "The narrative paradigm does not deny reason and rationality; it reconstitutes them, making them amenable to all forms of human communication" (2); "In truth,...the narrative paradigm...does not so much deny what has gone before as it subsumes it" (3); "when narration is taken as the master metaphor, it subsumes the others" (6); "Both forms...are modes for expressing good reasons—given the narrative paradigm—so the differences between them are structural rather than substantive" (15).

111. Fisher's assertion of the universality of the narrative paradigm is clearest in "The Narrative Paradigm: An Elaboration," *Communication Monographs* 52 (1985): 347–367. Fisher's reading of the contemporary social scientific and humanistic literature confirms his opening observation that "there is no genre, including technical communication, that is not an episode in the story of life (a part of the 'conversation') and is not itself constituted by *logos* and *mythos*.... Put another way: Technical discourse is imbued with myth and metaphor, and aesthetic discourse has cognitive capacity and import" (347). All of the theorists and philosophers that he considers are found to be helpful (in greater or lesser measure) in confirming Fisher's thesis. The extent to which important differences in background, perspective, and assumptions are glossed, however, suggests that Fisher may be demonstrating how these approaches can be viewed from within the narrative perspective rather than establishing the dominance or universality of this "metaparadigm" (347).

PART
FOUR

Approaches to Criticism

INTRODUCTION

Students who have read the critical studies in this book will realize that there are many different ways of doing rhetorical criticism. The following essays are not critical studies, but, rather, they are discussions of ways to approach the critical act and/or suggestions for theoretical perspectives from which criticism may be viewed. These essays, of course, are but a small sample of the many works that have been written about criticism. The essays do not cover all the "schools" of criticism nor do they represent all the dominant critical methodologies. They are, however, a starting point for discussion about the interesting questions that underlie criticism.

Wayne Brockriede ("Rhetorical Criticism as Argument") maintains that any criticism that is useful must function as an argument. Such criticism will be informative, make clear the grounds for judgment, and promote the kind of intellectual confrontation that leads to an enlarged understanding of rhetorical experiences.

Stephen E. Lucas ("The Schism in Rhetorical Scholarship") offers an insightful review of the development of rhetorical scholarship leading to the important observation that "good criticism does not result from doggedly following a set of formulary procedures, but from the full, free interplay of intelligence with the critical object," with the goal of explaining how rhetoric works.

Richard B. Gregg ("A Phenomenologically Oriented Approach to Rhetorical Criticism") was one of the early critics of rhetoric to draw on the postulate that "behavior is not so much a function of an external event as it is a product of the individual's perception of that event." Criticism derived from this premise would focus on the larger context, provide valuable insights into human motivation, and suggest realistic ways of describing rhetorical strategy.

Michael Calvin McGee ("The 'Ideograph': A Link Between Rhetoric and Ideology") describes political consciousness in collectivities. He argues that, in practice, "ideology is a political language composed of slogan-like terms signifying collective commitment." These terms McGee calls "ideographs." He maintains that that the ideology of a community is established by the use of ideographs in rhetorical discourse.

G. P. Mohrmann and Michael C. Leff ("Lincoln at Cooper Union: A Rationale for Neo-Classical Criticism") explain the approach they used in their essay on Lincoln's speech at the Cooper Union. (The essay appears in the preceding section.) Their approach which, as they point out, is "rooted in the rhetorical theory of antiquity," is to suggest a conception of genre that "can help invigorate critical inquiry based on classical models."They conclude with the observation that "The progress of rhetorical criticism may depend more on the ability of critics to induce principles from actual critiques than on a concern with abstract issues."

Ernest G. Bormann ("Fantasy and Rhetorical Vision: The Rhetorical Criticism of Social Reality") extrapolates the process by which small groups fantasize to create a common culture to the ways dramatizations in public messages spread through a larger public. "The composite dramas which catch up large groups of people in a symbolic reality," Bormann calls a "rhetorical vision." He argues that "the most important cultural artifact for understanding the events may not be the things or 'reality' but the words or the symbols," and asserts that discovering and explaining rhetorical visions is a useful critical function. (This essay provides the theoretical foundation for Bormann's study of the television coverage of the Iran hostage release and the Reagan Inaugural which is reprinted in the preceding section of this book.)

Reading and discussing these essays should help the student to refine his/her own thinking about some fundamental issues raised in this book, important issues that focus on such questions as:

How should rhetorical criticism be defined?

What are the functions of rhetorical criticism?

How may the context be understood and how does it interacts with the rhetorical act itself?

In what ways and to what extent are the audience and the speaker central to the analysis of rhetoric?

What methods of analysis are most appropriate for uncovering data helpful in answering questions, illuminating events, and making sound arguments?

What are the limits of and possibilities for critical interpretation of rhetorical acts?

What is the nature of critical judgment and the criteria relevant to such judgment?

Rhetorical Criticism as Argument

——————————— WAYNE BROCKRIEDE ———————————

The argument of this essay is that *useful* rhetorical criticism, whatever else it may be, must function as an argument.

By "criticism" I mean the act of evaluating or analyzing experience.[1] A person can function as critic either by passing judgment on the experience or by analyzing it for the sake of a better understanding of that experience or of some more general concept or theory about such experiences. Marie Nichols, Edwin Black, and other writers may well be right in claiming that criticism necessarily involves evaluation, judgment, discrimination among values.[2] Others perhaps could make a case that criticism necessarily involves analytic description, classification, or explanation. I do not need to deny either claim when I make a distinction between criticism that has explicit evaluation as its primary purpose (even though analysis is probably implicit in the judgment) and criticism that aims primarily at explicit analysis of the rhetorical experience, (even though value judgments are probably implicit in the description, classification, or explanation of that experience).

Although the relationship between criticism and argument is applicable to any kind of human experience, the focus of this essay is on the criticism of rhetorical experience. I see "rhetoric" broadly as including experiences involving written as well as spoken discourse, non-verbal as well as verbal symbols, movements as well as individual events, and functions other than those implied by a narrow conception of persuasion. Rhetoric is the relationship of persons and ideas within a situation.[3]

By "argument" I mean the process whereby a person reasons his way from one idea to the choice of another idea. This concept of argument implies five generic characteristics:[4] (1) an inferential leap from existing beliefs to the adoption of a new belief or the reinforcement of an old one; (2) a perceived rationale to justify that leap; (3) a choice among two or more competing claims; (4) a regulation of uncertainty in relation to the selected claim—since someone has made an inferential leap, certainty can be neither zero nor total; and (5) a willingness to risk a confrontation of that claim with one's peers.[5]

These characteristics can be viewed either from the point of view of a critic-arguer or a reader-confronter, either of whom can determine whether from the perspective of these five characteristics an argument has been made or is in process. One should never forget that a *person*, whether a critic or a confronter, is involved in argument and will determine whether an experience constitutes an argument. For it is a *person* who makes an inferential leap, perceives a rationale, makes a choice, regulates an uncertainty, and risks a confrontation.

This definition, involving five characteristics considered organically rather than additively, implies an argument-nonargument continuum. Any concrete rhetorical experience may embody these characteristics in varying degrees. Any characteristic may operate too minimally for a critic or a confronter to place the experience very near the argument end of the continuum, even though other characteristics may function more nearly optimally. Perhaps an inferential leap is made but is too narrow or too uninteresting for a critic or a confronter to call it an argument. Perhaps a rationale is implied but is not strong enough or clear enough for a critic or a confronter to justify the label of "argument" (see note. 8 for an example). Or all of the characteristics of argument may operate, but a critic or a confronter may believe that the experience, considered as an organic whole, fails to constitute an argument.

This definition of argument places near the nonargument end of the continuum several kinds of rhetorical experience sometimes thought of as argument. For example, neither the assertion of a true believer's insistence on a non-negotiable position nor the syllogistic entailment of a conclusion through manipulating premises within a closed system function significantly as an argument. If a claim is virtually a foregone conclusion, one which for any reason is not seen as open to dispute, then it is much more nearly nonargument than it is argument: no significant inferential leap has been made; little or no rationale has been asked for or given; only one claim is seen as worth considering thoroughly; that claim is accepted with certainty or virtual certainty; and no one has taken much risk of confrontation, if any.

My point is this: a critic-arguer or a confronter-reader may perceive a rhetorical experience as embodying the five characteristics in varying degrees. A rhetorical experience will not seem much of an argument if that person thinks it virtually ignores one or more of the characteristics, nor will it seem much of an argument if he thinks it includes most or all of the characteristics but in a limited way. A *significant* argument is one which, from the point of view of a person, collectivley achieves the five characteristics of an argument adequately.[6] In this essay I shall argue that useful rhetorical criticism must function as *significant* argument whether the criticism is an evaluation or an analysis of a rhetorical experience.[7]

1

Some evaluative rhetorical criticism does not meet adequately many of the five characteristics of argument. When a critic only appreciates the rhetoric or objects to it, without reporting any reason for his like or dislike, he puts his criticism near the nonargument end of the continuum. The reader of an appreciation has no rational basis for judging whether he should agree with the evaluative leap to praise or blame. When a critic aims at a primarily evaluative function and fails to make a significant argument, his work is not useful beyond the simple report that critic A has made evaluation X.

On the other hand, when an evaluating critic states clearly the criteria he has used in arriving at his judgment, together with the philosophic or theoretic foundations on which they rest, and when he has offered some data to show that the rhetorical experience meets or fails to meet those criteria, then he has argued. A reader has several kinds of choices: he can accept or reject the data, accept or reject the criteria, accept or reject the philosophic or theoretic basis for the criteria, and accept or reject the inferential leap that joins data and criteria.

Such a critical evaluation has all five characteristics of an argument. An inferential leap is made from data to evaluative claim. The claim is based on criteria, which provide a rationale for the inference. The critic's claim can be compared with others that may compete with it. People who respond to the evaluation can regulate their uncertainty about their own evaluation. By exposing to public scrutiny the rationale for the evaluation, the critic risks confrontation.

This last characteristic is especially important. By inviting confrontation, the critic-arguer tries to establish some degree of intersubjective reliability in his judgment and in his reasons for the judgment. The person who appreciates, who evaluates without arguing for the evaluation, assumes the attitude of the Latin adage, *de gustibus est non disputandum*, about taste there is no disputing. A reader can take or leave the appreciation, but even if he takes it he has no good way of knowing whether the judgment he holds in common with a critic has the same or a different basis. When a critic becomes an arguer and takes the risk of arguing a judgment, he invites a reader to confront that judgment. If the argument meets the test of confrontation, some degree of intersubjective reliability has been established. Reliability can also be established with reference to the reasons for the judgment.

If an evaluative argument fails the test of confrontation, and if the arguments of the critic and the counterarguments of the confronter are clear enough, the reasons for the disagreement may be uncovered, issues may be joined, and a debate over the differences may be instructive. Such a debate may enhance an understanding of the concrete rhetorical experience, it may contribute to a better understanding of rhetoric, or it may achieve both goals.

Two examples of critical evaluations that make significant arguments may clarify my distinction between this sort of criticism and what I have called appreciation. After setting the stage for John Jay Chapman's "Coatesville Adress," Edwin Black concludes that an appraisal of it must be high (p. 89). Had he made that statement without offering reasons for the judgment, the criticism would have little value. As Black himself had commented earlier in the book, we are interested in such statements only "if we are curious about the state" of the critic's "glands" (p. 7). What gives Black's judgment utility is the significant argument he offers for that judgment.[8] Without such an argument, evaluative criticism has little worth.

If the critic goes one step further and reveals the philosophic and theoretic bases for the criteria applied, the evaluation becomes an even more significant argument because it invites a reader to confront the criticism with greater precision. In his criticism of the Coatesville Address, Black's book itself serves to disclose the foundations for the criteria he had applied. A second example of evaluative criticism that reveals philosophic and theoretic underpinnings for the criteria employed is Karen Rasmussen's critique of Richard Nixon's presidential campaign of 1972. She characterizes his rhetoric as employing a strategy of avoidance and concedes its success when evaluated by the criterion of the landslide results of the election. Then she judges the strategy negatively by applying criteria she draws from a humanistic philosophic position and from theoretical constructs that relate to a decision-making process.[9] By making clear the criteria she had used and by explicating their philosophic and theoretic foundations, she makes a significant argument, one that can be confronted. Her criticism, therefore, like Black's, has a utiity that mere appreciation lacks.

2

Two of the three kinds of analyses I shall discuss, description and classification, can be found near the nonargument end of the continuum. A third, explanation, functions as a significant argument.

Description rarely functions as a significant argument because the person who reads it frequently is not given enough help to make an inferential leap, nor is such a person offered a rationale for the leap, and consequently the reader is confronted with no choice in the regulation of uncertainty about the rhetorical experience described. When a critic reports what a speaker said in a speech, presents a résumé of a speaking career, narrates one or more rhetorical experiences, or something of the sort, without making a claim (explicit or implicit) that increases a reader's understanding of that experience, the description is not a significant argument and is not useful criticism.

Unfortunately, much of twentieth-century public address criticism fits into such a mold. As early as 1956, Albert J. Croft surveyed studies of rhetorical criticism, especially M.A. theses and Ph.D. dissertations, and discovered that they often amounted merely to collections of "facts and opinions dealing with the biography of the speaker, the historical background of the speech, and the nature of the listening and reading audience." Such studies were inventories of "the speaker's propositions as they occur in representative speeches."[10] The frequency of such descriptions has no doubt declined during the last eighteen years, but such criticism is still written.

Descriptive analysis *could* function as a significant argument if the critic were to draw conclusions from the data and argue their merit, or if he were to present the data enthymematically so the consumer of the criticism would be able to find an unstated but implied claim and/or an unstated but implied rationale for it. But most descriptions stop short of making or implying a significant argument; the critic merely presents the data in a kind of standard chronological or tropical pattern.

The problem with the description that fails to state or imply an argument is that a reader wonders what the material is supposed to tell him. Since presumably most readers know less about the rhetorical experience and have less interest in it than the critic does, they may fail to find their own arguments in the loosely arrayed data and justifiably wonder if the critic has not abdicated his responsibility for making sense of the experience.

Classificaiton also rarely functions as a significant argument because it, too, fails to involve the five characteristics of an argument. When a critic seems to argue that a speaker used *ethos*, *pathos*, and *logos*, or used various organizational patterns, or used several stylistic devices—and then offers examples of such usages, the critic makes no inferential leap; he is moving toward a predetermined conclusion within a closed system. Once a critic accepts a category system categorically, no matter whose, and once he makes an *a priori* decision to apply it compulsively when analyzing a rhetorical experience, he is engaging merely in a form of the self-fulfilling prophecy: he finds examples of things he knew all along he was going to find and merely puts them into appropriate cubbyholes. Such use of anybody's category system tells a reader very little about a rhetorical experience or about rhetoric.

My complaint with this kind of criticism is not that a critic uses categories; no critic can manage in any kind of analysis without having some categories in his head. My objection is that he uses a category system slavishly, determined to force a concrete rhetorical experience into the confines of a closed system, a system that is closed because the critic will not allow himself to discover or create new categories while in the process of his analysis. This use of a classificatory scheme is near the nonargument end of the continuum because it involves no inferential leap (or at best a slight one), little if any rationale, no choice (except the forced choice of whether to toss an instance into one bin or another), not much regulation of uncertainty, and very little risk of confrontation.

Criticism by classification also fails to answer the so-what question. Why should a reader care whether a speaker used a grand, middle, or plain style; an inductive or a deductive order of developing ideas; and so forth. Unless these statements are related to an evaluation or an explanation of a dimension of the rhetorical experience or of a concept of rhetoric, they are not useful beyond proving one more time that human beings can classify phenomena, something most readers will already know.

Explanation, a third kind of analysis, is useful precisely because the critic argues. Whereas an evaluative critic is primarily concerned with passing judgment on the experience, the critic who explains is primarily trying to account for how an aspect of the rhetorical experience worked by relating it to something more general than itself.[11] Three principles characterize critical explanations and turn them into significant arguments and, thus, useful criticism. All three of these principles sharply differentiate an explanation from a description, and the latter two of them distinguish it also from a classification.

Criticism by explanation necessarily requires a comparison between the experience under scrutiny and a more general concept or category system.[12] Such concepts or category systems may already be in existence and ready to be used, or they may be invented by the critic. The critic says, in effect, that a general idea about rhetoric can illuminate a concrete rhetorical experience he is studying. He has a battery of searchlights available from which he chooses the ones that can help him light up the rhetorical experience. Without comparing the experience with a more general idea, the critic can only describe what has happened and, thus, has no significant argument to advance. If he places the experience within the context of a more general set of ideas, the critic can go beyond description into either classification or explanation.

A second principle distinguishes explanation from classification as well as from description. Although explanation and classification both involve a comparison, the latter merely relates the experience to a category system in a compulsive, deductive, *a priori* way. Before he starts his work, the classifying critic selects the system he will use, looks at the concrete experience from the single perspective of that system, operates the categories as a series of molds, and pours into them the data he gets from his investigation of the experience. The explaining critic, on the other hand, proceeds more inductively and selects his concepts, categories, and dimensions while in the process of studying the rhetorical experience, taking pains to pick those most appropriate for his purposes. With a head full of ideas to apply, possible multiple perspectives to take, with no commitment to any *a priori* category system, he looks at what he is analyzing and chooses the perspectives and ideas that best help him understand the object of his criticism. After making his choices, he is then ready to argue the convincingness of his explanation with references to the perspectives and categories he has used.

A third principle also sets explanation apart from the other two modes of analysis. In criticism by classification, for example, the category system sits like a series of passive receptacles waiting for someone to plug in the data. The critic who makes an explanatory argument, on the other hand, does so by marrying data from the experience with some general concept or category system. He makes an *active* use of both partners and creates an *active* interaction between them. The explanation is a product of inferences that grow out of that interaction. Under the control of an explaining critic, the data collected about a rhetorical experience and concepts drawn from his knowledge of rhetoric behave symbiotically and reach out actively as they collaborate in the creation of an explanation.

Explanation involves all five of the characteristics of argument. The claim cannot be reached without making an inferential leap. The idea that certifies that leap gives a reader a rationale for making it. The resulting explanation must compete with alternative explanations or complement them. Since an inferential leap has been made, the explanation makes no claim of certainty, but to the extent that the argument is convincing it can alter a reader's degree of uncertainty. The explanation gives a reader an argument to confront. Because the critic has argued, the reader can develop a better understanding of the rhetorical experience analyzed.

3

Criticism by explanation, if the argument is focused a bit differently and if emphases are shifted slightly, can also satisfy another goal—that of gaining a better understanding of rhetoric itself. I have been discussing explanatory criticism from the point of view of using some general concept or category system as a vehicle for learning something about a concrete rhetorical experience. What I shall now argue is that explanation can involve the use of knowledge about a concrete rhetorical experience as a way of learning something about concepts of rhetoric.

This second kind of explanation comes in two forms, based on two different functions—to validate present concepts or to discover new ones. Both forms require a significant argument. The critic who *validates* present concepts argues that a study of one or more rhetorical experiences can support a theoretical position or some generalization within such a theory.

For example, in his study of the presidential campaign of 1860, Don E. Beck wondered whether the social judgment-ego involvement approach to attitudes of Sherif, Sherif, and Nebergall could explain what happened to Stephen A. Douglas during that campaign.[13] The prediction stemming from his approach is that ego-involved persons distort messages in one of two ways. If a message is close to someone's position, he will tend to *assimilate* it in the direction of his own position. If a message is too distant to assimilate, the ego-involved person will tend to *contrast* it and see it as even more distant from his own position than it is.[14]

By examining reactions in the north and in the south to the speaking of Douglas, Beck supported his hypothesis that one explanation for some of Douglas' difficulties during the campaign was that ego-involved auditors contrasted him. Many northerners saw Douglas not as taking a moderate position somewhere between those assumed by Lincoln and Breckenridge; rather, they contrasted him as a southern sympathizer little better than Breckenridge. Many southerners saw Douglas not as a moderate but as an abolitionist little better than Lincoln. Beck concluded that ego-involved auditors behaved as the Sherif formulation a century later might have predicted they would.[15]

The other form of explanatory criticism that moves from an understanding of a concrete experience in the direction of a better understanding of a rhetorical concept or generalization functions in the context of *discovery*. Critical discoveries may occur when critical validations fail. If a critic finds that some of his interpretations and explanations for a rhetorical experience are not consistent with theoretical expectations, he may want to hypothesize some that may be.[16]

For example, when criticizing the structure of the Truman Doctrine speech of 1947, Robert L. Scott and I observed that the speech did not follow the traditional model of a logical brief.[17] In that model each major contention supports directly the proposition; each contention, in turn, is supported by arguments and subarguments; and these, finally, are supported by evidence. Furthermore, a speaker is supposed to say everything he is going to say about one topic before moving to the next. Judged by that model the structure of Truman's speech fails, and Truman violates frequently the principle of putting all of an argument in one place.

We wondered whether a model derived from the concept of musical counterpoint might more appropriately explain, in part, how Truman's auditors might have responded positively to the speech structured as it is. Contrapuntal form may be defined as the combination of "two or more melodic lines in a musically satisfying way."[18] Each of the melodic lines may recur several times in a musical composition in company with different combinations of other themes that also come and go. We identified ten themes in Truman's speech and viewed them as motifs that developed horizontally in several places, combining with other themes that also developed similarly. After tracing the motifs, we engaged in some speculation about the extent to which speeches structured along the contrapuntal model could have good effects on understanding, attitude change, and behavioral influence.[19] In short, our study hypothesized a new approach to an understanding of rhetorical discourse and invited others to confront and pursue the possibilities.

4

In discussing the role of argument in evaluative and analytic criticism, I have argued that some kinds of criticism fall near the nonargument end of the continuum—for example, evaluative appreciation, description, and classification; and that other kinds more nearly square with the five characteristics of argument I enumerated earlier—for example, evaluations in which criteria and philosophic and theoretic positions are identified and used and explanations, whether a critic explains a concrete rhetorical experience or whether he tries to make a contribution to the validation or discovery of general concepts of rhetoric. What remains is to assume the responsibility for making explicit my primary argument of this essay. Critics who argue are more *useful* than critics who do not. My case rests on two advantages.

First, critics who make significant arguments are more informative than those who do not. What one learns from an appreciation is only that a critic has pronounced a judgment about an experience. What one learns from a description is only that certain data are available and that possibly the reader may arrange them so something else can be learned. What one learns from a classification is the unsurprising news that various kinds of data can be dumped into various kinds of bins.[20]

On the other hand, a reader learns from an argued evaluation the grounds on which that judgment rests. He learns from an explanation that a critic's interpretation can be related to a concept or a category system so a reader can make some sense of a concrete rhetorical experience or can add a bit of confirmation to a current concept of rhetoric or initiate a process of discovery that may lead to a new concept.

Second, and probably more importantly, when a critic assumes the responsibility and risk of advancing a significant argument about his evaluation or explanation, he invites confrontation that may begin or continue a process enhancing an understanding of a rhetorical experience or of rhetoric. The evaluative appreciator provides nothing much to confront except to invite a reader to say "taint" to the critic's "tis." The describer who does not present or imply a significant argument can be confronted only with the accuracy of the description. The classifier who does not present or imply a significant argument gives a reader nothing to confront except the appropriateness of the categories and of the sortings of the data.

But when a critic advances a significant argument about a concrete rhetorical experience or about a general concept of rhetoric, a reader can confront it usefully. If he tries to disconfirm the critic's argument and fails to do so, the intersubjective reliability of that argument is increased. If he can disconfirm or cast doubt about the critic's argument, that argument must be abandoned or revised. The product of the process of confrontation by argument and counterargument is a more dependable understanding of rhetorical experiences and of rhetoric.

Notes

1. The literature on rhetoric in recent years has used a battery of words in specialized ways that renders each of them less than ideal as a general label for what I here call the "concrete rhetorical experience." Traditionally, such experience has been called a "discourse," but this word rules out events in which discourse is either absent or unimportant. Malcolm O. Sillars prefers the word "act" in his "Rhetoric as Act," *QJS*, 50 (Oct. 1964), 277–284, but this word seems to rule out campaigns, movements, and processes—although Sillars himself does not exclude these in his broad definition of "act." The same objection applies to a word like "event' or "happening." In addition, if a person accepts John Stewart's distinctions between act, interaction, and transaction, as I do, then "act" is not a sufficiently general term to refer to all rhetorical experiences. See Stewart's introduction to *Bridges Not Walls* (Reading, Mass.: Addison-Wesley, 1973), pp. 8–17. For this same reason "interaction" and "transaction" are also special genre of rhetorical experience and so are incapable of covering the range of phenomena I want to cover. Some people use "situation" as the generic term, but Lloyd F. Bitzer's influential essay, "The Rhetorical Situation," *Philosophy and Rhetoric*, 1 (Jan. 1968), 1–14, narrows the scope of situation to "an actual or potential exigence which can be completely or partially removed if discourse...can...bring about the significant modification of the exigence" (p. 6). Although "experience" is admittedly a very general term, I need that generality and can think of no better word to provide it. When qualified as "rhetorical experience," it refers to instances when people and/or ideas relate together in a concrete context. Hopefully that phrase includes rhetorical discourse, act, event, movement, campaign, process, interaction, transaction, or exigence-producing situation.

2. Professor Nichols quotes John Dewey as saying that criticism "is judgment engaged in discriminating among values," and she notes three aspects of the critical process, one of which is " judicial act of determining what is better or worse" (p. 4). Furthermore, an emphasis on evaluation is implied when she uses the term also in her statement of the other two aspects of criticism. See "The Criticism of Rhetoric," in *A History and Criticism of American Public Address*, ed. Marie Hochmuth [Nichols] (New York: Longmans, Green, 1955), III. 1–23.

In his *Rhetorical Criticism: A Study in Method* (New York: Macmillan, 1965), Professor Black distinguishes the critic from the scientist by saying that in addition to the traits those two have in common, the critic differs from the scientist in seeking "to judge the thing justly" (p. 4), and he also speaks of "the inextricable involvement of criticism with moral values" (p. 9).

3. For a more comprehensive discussion of this view of rhetoric, see my essay on "Dimensions of the Concept of Rhetoric," *QJS*, 54 (Feb. 1968), 1–12.

4. In an earlier draft of this essay I used the phrase "necessary conditions" instead of "generic characteristics." I still believe that at this moment "argument" in any significant sense requires all five characteristics. The phrase "necessary conditions" is unfortunate, though, because it may imply that I view argument as a closed concept, one not capable of input, change, or growth. I do not wish even to suggest the possibility of such an implication, and I should hope the five characteristics I enumerate should reinforce my affirmation that argument is an open concept.

5. These characteristics are not usefully applied one-by-one as a kind of checklist to help one see if something "adds up" to an argument. Rather, they are interrelated dimensions of the concept of argument and may, each of them, serve usefully as an entry point or as a mode of emphasis in criticizing a rhetorical experience. They do not "add up" to an argument. Rather, they bear holistically the marks of family resemblance, they achieve a gestalt, they justify the surname of argument.

6. I am indebted to Karen Rasmussen, Dept. of Communication, Univ. of Utah, for considerable help in working out the ideas of the last three paragraphs of the introduction.

7. The claim itself is not novel. Edwin Black argues that "a critical statement. . .is one for which reasons can be given, reasons that may gain the agreement of rational people to the statement" (pp. 7–8). Lawrence W. Rosenfield, in his "Anatomy of Critical Discourse," *Speech Monographs*, 35 (Mar. 1968), 50, calls criticism a "special form of reason-giving discourse." What may be novel in my essay is the perspective of argument it reveals, the development of an argument for the less-than-novel claim by relating it to two general types of criticism, the contention that two explicit advantages result when a critic makes an argument, and in general the explication beyond assertion of the claim that criticism ought to be a significant argument if it is to achieve any useful evaluation or explanation.

8. At one point Black reports that Edmund Wilson had commented that the speech is "strange and moving." See Wilson's *The Triple Thinkers* (New York: Oxford Univ. Press, 1948), p. 159. Wilson's appreciation moves a bit in the direction of becoming an argument, which suggests I should not push very far any rigid distinction between argument and nonargument. Wilson applies two criteria to the speech and in one sense offers, therefore, "reasons" for praising the speech, but he does not present much in the way of data or rationale. Black, on the other hand, develops a detailed argument in behalf of his "high appraisal" of the speech and thus gives a reader who may hold a competing evaluation of the speech something substantial to confront.

9. "Nixon and the Strategy of Avoidance," *Central States Speech Journal*, 24 (Fall 1973), 193–202.

10. "The Functions of Rhetorical Criticism," *QJS*, 42 (Oct. 1956), 283.

11. In the third section of this essay I shall argue that explanation can take two forms, the one I am now discussing in which a general concept helps to explain a concrete rhetorical experience and the one I shall discuss later in which an understanding of a concrete rhetorical experience may contribute to a better explanation of the general concept.

12. In his "Anatomy of Critical Discourse," Rosenfield also emphasizes the importance of comparison in rhetorical criticism. Near the end of his essay he discusses two kinds of comparison, model modality and analog modality. Although the latter is an interesting mode that functions especially in the context of discovery (see Section 3 of my essay), I shall not pursue that form of comparative criticism even though I believe it constitutes an argument as I am using that term (see pp. 67–68 of Rosenfield's essay). My discussion of criticism by explanation bears some similarities to Rosenfield's discussion of a model modality, in which "the critic starts by generating some sort of paradigm which he will use as a basis of comparison" (p. 66). Although at times Rosenfield appears more interested in the evaluative function of criticism, he also implies that his model modality has some utility in analysis when he concludes that "the model modality finds its optimal use in confirming or qualifying rhetorical theory" (p. 68), an argument I shall make in Section 3 under the heading of the context of validation.

13. "The Rhetoric of Conflict and Compromise: A Study in Civil War Causation," Diss. University of Oklahoma 1966.

14. This explication appears in several places, for example, Carolyn W. Sherif, Muzafer Sherif, and Roger E. Nebergall, *Attitude and Attitude Change* (Philadelphia: Saunders, 1965), pp. 14–15.

15. Notice the relationship between the two forms of explanation. Beck's study can illustrate explanation as discussed in the preceding section of this essay if a reader considers that Beck has accounted for one rhetorical dimension of Douglas' campaign by viewing it through the lens of Sherif's general conception of attitude. The same study also illustrates the second form of explanation, the one I am now considering, if the reader sees Beck as providing a bit of validation for Sherif's approach by applying it to the 1860 presidential campaign. The first form of explanation aims at saying something insightful about the experience itself; the second intends a contribution to some geneal conception of rhetoric. The same kind of relationship is also present in the final example of my essay.

16. This point of view is somewhat similar to a position expressed by John Waite Bowers in his "Pre-Scientific Function of Rhetorical Criticism," in *Essays on Rhetorical Criticism*, ed. Thomas R. Nilsen (New York: Random House, 1968), pp. 126–145. Instead of positing a relationship between criticism and experimental studies (which Bowers tends to equate with science) in which the former serves the latter, however, I see a relationship between these two kinds of research techniques in which both collaborate in the development of more reliable knowledge (science). The experimenter in his laboratory can make superb arguments about internal validity, but the contrived conditions of the laboratory situation present problems when he tries to generalize to the world beyond the laboratory. The critic can strengthen claims of external validity by seeing if the experimenter's findings are useful in explaining uncontrolled phenomena that actually happen outside the laboratory. Science needs all the help it can get. It can get some help from experimental research. It can also get some help from criticism in uncovering hypotheses to be investigated (discovery), something Bowers concedes, and also in adding confirmation or requiring modifications of existing theory (validation), something Bowers does not allow for unless the critic learns to make "successful predictions in controlled situations" (p. 141). The argument that criticism can contribute to science in these two ways is developed in more detail in my essay on "Trends in the Study of Rhetoric: Toward a Blending of Criticism and Science," in *The Prospect of Rhetoric*, ed. Lloyd F. Bitzer and Edwin Black (Englewood Cliffs, N.J.: Prentice-Hall, 1971), pp. 129–138.

17. Wayne Brockriede and Robert L. Scott, *Moments in the Rhetoric of the Cold War* (New York: Random House, 1970), pp. 27–36.

18. Kent Kennan, *Counterpoint: Based on Eighteenth-Century Practice* (Englewood Cliffs, N.J.: Prentice-Hall, 1959), p. 2.

19. Brockriede and Scott, p. 36.

20. Please remember that description and classification *per se* are not activities a critic must shun; they may be important prerequisites to explanatory argument. Nor do I claim that a critic must make claims that are blatantly explicit when he draws them from description or classification; if he knows his readers well enough, he may choose to let them complete the enthymeme. My objection is to the critic who describes and classifies so that few if any readers will ever discover any argument.

The Schism in Rhetorical Scholarship

STEPHEN E. LUCAS

The relationship between history and criticism in the study of public address is a perennial issue intimately connected with the nature, scope, methods, and purposes of rhetorical analysis. In recent years, thought on the issue has taken a notable turn, as both a cause and consequence of the remarkable upheaval in rhetorical scholarship since the late 1950s. There appears now to be crystallizing a keen sense of schism between history and criticism, as the two are increasingly, characterized—formally and informally, in published writings and private collo- quies—as conflicting rather than complementary activities.[1] Unfortunately, that characterization has neither proceeded from nor produced decisive consideration of the nature of criticism or history as scholarly enterprises. This essay seeks to explore the growing schism in rhetorical scholarship and to point the way toward a new, more discerning view of the affiliation between history and criticism in the study of public address—partly in the interest of lexical precision and conceptual refinement, partly in hopes of putting to rest a dispute that has for too long diverted attention from the substance of scholarship to its classification.[2]

1

The present disjunction between history and criticism is best seen against the traditional view that the study of history is an indispensable aspect of the process of rhetorical criticism. This view may be traced back to Herbert Wichelns' seminal essay, "The Literary Criticism of Oratory." Wichelns' task was twofold: to differenti- ate rhetoric from literature, and to ground rhetorical criticism in the unique nature of rhetorical discourse. How he resolved these tasks is best captured in his famous injunction that the outlook of rhetorical criticism "is patently single. It is not concerned with permanence, nor yet with beauty. It is concerned with effect. It regards a speech as a communication to a specific audience, and holds its business to be the analysis and appreciation of the orator's method of imparting his ideas to his hearers." To Wichelns, the locus of rhetorical criticism was the oration itself, and the burden of the critic was to appraise the artistic proofs "that secure for the speaker ready access to the minds of his auditors." But such appraisal could not be properly conducted unless the critic comprehended thoroughly a number of extrinsic historical factors—particularly the immediate audience to whom the discourse was presented and the effect of the discourse upon that audience. Consequently, said Wichelns, it was necessary "to summon history to the aid of criticism."[3]

The inextricable connection between history and criticism adumbrated by Wichelns shortly became axiomatic. In 1933 William Brigance affirmed that it was not possible to study oratory "without studying the historical foundations on which it rests" and called for *"combined historical* and *critical* study of orators and oratorical literature." In 1937 Donald Bryant argued that since rhetorical criticism "gains its value from its primary concern with considerations of audience-speaker- occasion," it "must depend almost entirely upon historical knowledge for its effectiveness." The most detailed rendering of this position came just more than a decade later, in Thonssen and Baird's enormously influential *Speech Criticism*. This work viewed speeches as manipulative instruments that lose their vitality when considered apart from their original historical milieu. The "core of any satisfactory method of rhetorical analysis" was therefore historical, and the successful critic "must, in effect, put on the garment of the past" to explicate the origins, circum- stances, and consequences of particular speeches.[4]

In short, history and criticism were seen as inseparable partners whose "union is indissoluble."[5] Studies in public address were labeled "history and criticism," while the methodology employed in such studies was identified as "historical-critical." So powerfully were the two allied that forty years after Wichelns' pathsetting essay the orthodox view remained that the rhetorical analyst "must also be a student of history...if he is to comprehend public address and its role in society, and if he is to make lasting critical contributions to his discipline."[6]

Despite its durability, however, the traditional partnership had long showed signs of strain. Even in its halcyon days a handful of dissenters had warned that it was becoming more and more unequal—that criticism was all too often being subordinated to history in the study of public address. The strongest early statement came from Loren Reid. Writing in 1944, Reid declared that rhetorical criticism entailed more than simply narrating the circumstances under which a speech was delivered, recounting a speaker's ideas, or classifying a speaker's rhetorical techniques. In Reid's view, many so-called rhetorical critics were actually producing "second-rate history" rather than criticism. During the early 1950s a few other writers voiced similar concern. Among them was Marie Hochmuth, who seconded the familiar view that rhetorical criticism could not proceed apart from thorough consideration of the speaker and the historical setting. But, she held, consideration of such extrinsic matters was only a preliminary task that did not itself constitute rhetorical criticism. According to Hochmuth, history and criticism served different purposes. Students of public address should be wary of allowing their interest in purely historical matters to divert them from the responsibility to produce criticism.[7]

These early salvos prefigured what was to become an all-out fusillade. By the mid 1960s the imbalance between history and criticism had become an absorbing theme of the growing band of revisionists who sought to revitalize the study of public address, which, in the estimation of one essayist, had "reached a place where it was saying painfully little to the humanities, the social sciences, or itself." Whereas criticism and history had once been percived as inseparable allies, the revisionists tended to portray them not only as separable but as antagonistic. Representative of this position was Anthony Hillbruner's lamentation that "much of what passes for rhetorical criticism today, unfortunately, is rhetorical history." The paramount deficiency of traditional rhetorical analysis was said to be a misguided and enfeebling preoccupation with speeches as historical artifacts. W. Charles Redding put the indictment succinctly when he bemoaned the "heavy reliance upon historical data and historical research techniques" in the study of public address. As a result, said Redding, "rhetorical scholars have too often moved out of rather than more deeply into their own subject."[8]

The dissatisfaction with conventional rhetorical analysis vitiated the traditional connection between history and criticism at almost every turn. Rejection of the customary view that the controlling aim of rhetorical criticism was to appraise a speaker's success in achieving certain effects with a particular audience on a specific occasion meant that it was no longer obligatory to ground rhetorical analysis in penetrating study of the historical setting, or to pursue the "historical" task of determining the results of a given discourse. The corresponding call for close textual analysis in the fashion of literary criticism further severed the ties between the study of rhetorical discourse and examination of its historical environment. So too did the growing interest in ideological criticism, which seemingly could be conducted with litte reference to anything other than the ideas articulated by public speakers and writers. And the call to focus upon contemporary rhetorical events further encouraged belief that the long-standing junction between history and criticism was outmoded and illusory (as if contemporary history were not history at all).

Two recent essays disclose how deeply the rift between criticism and history has embedded itself in the thinking of many rhetoricians. According to Bruce Gronbeck, it is profoundly mistaken to seek to unite historical and critical approaches to public address under a uniform methodology. He argues that rhetorical history and rhetorical criticism are essentially disparate activities that "must pursue different goals, ought to be judged by differing criteria, and usually employ varying sources of evidence." Studies of public address, therefore, ought "to be predominantly *either* exercises in rhetorical history writing or critical ventures into interesting[,] problematic, or insightful aspects of discourse." Barnet Baskerville does not etch nearly as radical a division between history and criticism, although he does agree that there are fundamental distinctions "between a piece of writing which is essentially 'historical' in intent and one which might be called an essay in 'rhetorical criticism.'" More important, Baskerville bemoans what he deems a fashionable "glorification of the critic" and "tacit denigration of those who are merely rhetorical 'historians.'" Like Gronbeck, Baskerville insists that historical scholarship is a worthy undertaking and that rhetoricians should feel free to engage in exclusively historical research and writing.[9]

And so the matter stands. As rhetorical analysts have reconsidered the nature, scope, and practice of their enterprise, they have tended to destroy the accord between history and criticism effected during the formative years of rhetoric as an academic discipline. Let us now take stock of the major grounds upon which distinctions between history and criticism have been advanced.

2

One way rhetorical analysts have differentiated "history" from "criticism" is by using the former to refer to investigation of matters external to rhetorical discourse and the latter to refer to examination of discourse itself. The division, of course, parallels that between literary criticism and literary history and may be seen as implicit even in Wichelns' landmark essay of 1925. By the 1940s it was becoming explicit.[10] In the last quarter-century it has become commonplace. Even writers who insist that students of public address must attend to the full range of extrinsic factors—the speaker and his or her training, the climate of opinion and events, the audience and its attitudes, the effects of the speaker's discourse—frequently contend that all these factors, vital as they may be, are actually "excursions into the fields of history, sociology, or biography," and thus are, "strictly speaking, extraneous to rhetoric." This line of thought has reached its fullest extension in Gronbeck's definition of rhetorical criticism as "any examination of discourse and rhetors which essentially or primarily is *intrinsic*,...which finds most of its confirming materials *inside a rhetorical artifact*." Rhetorical history, on the other hand, he identifies as "any examination of discourse or rhetors which essentially or primarily is *extrinsic*,...which finds most of its confirming materials *outside a rhetorical artifact*."[11]

Such distinctions are of meager benefit. For one thing, they raise the problem of deciding what proportion of a study must be devoted to intrinsic considerations in order to qualify for classification as "rhetorical criticism." More important, they tend to be based more on *what* rhetorical analysts look at than on *how* they look at it. If they explore the intrinsic features of rhetorical discourse, they are said to be engaged in rhetorical criticism; if they explore contextual or biographical factors extrinsic to rhetorical discourse, they are said to be engaged in rhetorical history. Obviously, the strength of such a distinction rests upon maintaining a firm separation between rhetorical discourse and elements extrinsic to it. Theoretically, such a separation may be tenable. In practice, however, it breaks down. Because rhetorical discourses are human creations that function only in particular environments, from which they can only be separated artificially, rhetorical analysts usually acquire at least "some general understanding of the author and his age."[12] Among the questions they characteristically seek to answer are: "What was the context (no matter how broadly or narrowly conceived) in which the discourse functioned?"[13] "What were the origins of the discourse?" "How did it reflect the mind of its author?" "What relationship did it bear to its audiences (contemporary or historical)?" "What kinds of consequences (immediate or long-range) did it help bring about?" "What is its standing in relation to other discourses of a like nature?" In pursuing these and similar questions, the rhetorician moves naturally and easily between the discourse and its interaction with a myriad of complex and dynamic extrinsic forces.

A variety of rhetorical analysis in the past few years has been to engage, somewhat on the model of literary criticism, in close reading of rhetorical discourse—to explicate its "meaning" or to demonstrate how it "functions." Such readings, it would appear, may confidently be classified as intrinsic, since they purport to deal with the internal operations of discourse, apart from any special consideration of its author or historical milieu. In fact, however, they can seldom proceed profitably without serious attention to extrinsic matters. For rhetorical discourse invariably occurs within a particular world; and not only within a particular social, political, religious, economic, and intellectual world, but also within a special rhetorical world, with its own vocabulary, conventions, preconceptions, idioms, patois, and the like. To understand what a rhetorical document means or to ascertain how it functions, one must recapture "the full wealth of association, implication and resonance, the many levels of meaning," which a language contains in a given society at a given time.[14] This is particularly vital when dealing with texts remote from us in culture or in time. But even as we move closer to our own age, we must be exceedingly cautious about reading the likes of Webster, Lincoln, Bryan, Theodore and Franklin Roosevelt, even John Kennedy, as our contemporaries—about assuming that their languages are identical with our language, that their rhetorical praxes are also our own. To explicate satisfactorily what a rhetorical text means or how it functions, we need to comprehend the very identity of that text as inextricably interwoven with its world. And that comprehension demands historical understanding that inescapably involves the rhetorician directly and earnestly with forces, persons, and documents extrinsic to the text under scrutiny.

This interpenetration of intrinsic and extrinsic factors is pronounced even in the one area in which they have been presumed to be most distinct—the study of rhetorical effect. In traditional criticism no task was deemed more important than "to determine the immediate or delayed effect of the speeches upon specific audiences, and, ultimately, upon society."[15] In recent years, many writers have relieved the critic of this obligation, arguing that "influence is an extra-ordinarily difficult thing to establish, much less to measure," and that, in any event, ascertaining influence "is not a critical but an historical undertaking." This position has perhaps been put most forcefully by Wayland Parrish, who, after contending at some length that the "actual influence" of rhetoric is "seldom discoverable," concluded that "the totting up of such responses as are discernible is a task for a historian, a clerk, or a comptometer, not for a rhetorician."[16]

Underlying such a stark division of labor is an assumption that influence "may be identified and measured without antecedent analysis or even knowledge of the discourse" that produced it.[17] And that assumption in turn necessarily presupposes a view of rhetorical effects essentially as overt, measurable outcomes such as getting the votes or winning a verdict.[18] But such outcomes are exceptional rather than commonplace and, even when present, may not be attributable to the discourse in question. Moreover, to think of rhetorical influence as a unidimensional, linear phenomenon that can in some sense be totted up is to distort the nature of a highly convoluted process and to deter consideration of a wide range of significant consequences that cannot possibly be "measured" or determined "precisely"— such as the on-going impact of a mosaic of messages on multiple audiences; the repercussions of discourse in modulating the future rhetorical and ideological options open to its author or the cause he or she espouses; the ways of thinking, acting, and believing fostered by rhetorical communication; the self-persuasion that may accompany efforts to persuade others; the role of popular discourse in the creation, fortification, and decay of cultural norms and social identities; the influence of rhetorical acts on the evolution of conventional modes of public communication.[19]

That these and similar kinds of consequences cannot be verified with exactitude does not mean that they should remain unexplored. To attain absolute confirmation about any subject as mutable, diverse, and variegated as rhetorical influence is virtually impossible; probability, not certainty, is the best that can reasonably be expected. Claims regarding the consequences of discourse are almost unavoidably provisional and can be "proved" only by effectively marshalling the evidence and warranting the inferences upon which they are based. In assessing effect the rhetorician turns to available extrinsic evidence such as newspaper reports, election results, opinion polls, diaries, private correspondence, reminiscences, and the like. But these will not, in and of themselves, divulge what the effects were, for effects cannot be determined merely by citing the impressions of people who listened to an orator or by counting the number who read a pamphlet or voted for its author. Rather, such extrinsic data must be weighed against each other, against what was rhetorically possible in a given situation, and against the rhetorical capabilities of the discourse itself. Only in the rarest of cases is it possible to reach a satisfactory assessment of effect without close analysis of the discourse that contributed to it.

To take but a single example, consider Thomas Paine's *Common Sense*, first published in Philadelphia in January 1776. The extrinsic evidence attesting to the pamphlet's influence is considerable and weightly. Although there is no exact accounting of circulation figures for Paine's work, it was widely reprinted throughout America and within three months sold some 120,000 copies among a free population of less than three million persons. To reach a comparable figure today, a political tract would have to sell approximately ten million copies within 100 days. In addition to such manifest indications that *Common Sense* reached an extraordinary proportion of the politically relevant population, there are numerous testimonies from Paine's contemporaries, Whig and Tory alike, that the pamphlet was an important factor in hastening the onset of independence.[20] Given such evidence, one could reasonably conclude—without ever reading *Common Sense*—that it exerted a powerful impact upon the development of revolutionary thought and action during the first half of 1776. But the conclusion is unsatisfactory, for it leaves unanswered most of the important questions about the role of *Common Sense* in the "terrible wordy war"[21] over independence. And those questions must remain unanswered until one looks exactingly at the pamphlet itself, at its capacity within the rhetorical situation, and at its relationship to other writings on both sides of the controversy.

Once that is done, one begins to see that "the effect" of *Common Sense* was in reality a complex and multifarious phenomenon, that the pamphlet had many distinct, yet interrelated, consequences.[22] It initiated widespread public discussion of independence as a potentially acceptable alternative to continued British rule. This was particularly vital in moderate colonies such as Pennsylvania, where even the word "independence" remained opprobrious as late as the beginning of 1776. *Common Sense* removed that opprobrium, taking pro-independence Whigs off the defensive and allowing them to campaign openly and vigorously for separation. Moreover, the case for American autonomy that Paine injected into the public arena was distinguished by both its comprehensiveness and its audacity. It encompassed a range of topics from the origins of government to the courage of colonial militiamen, and in the process it assailed one after another of the accepted political presuppositions which underlay the apprehension of many colonists about independence. But it did so with consummate skill. *Common Sense* was so well conceived, so soundly structured, so engagingly written, so perfectly timed that it thoroughly dominated public discussion of independence. Its shadow hung over all subsequent writings on the subject, and few authors—whether for or against severing the bond with England—strayed far from the topics introduced in Paine's pamphlet. It did not, however, single-handedly create an irresistible public surge in favor of leaving the empire. It did not convert Tories (nor was it designed to). It no doubt crystallized the thoughts of some Americans who had been leaning toward separation, and it surely helped convince a fair number of previously uncommitted and skeptical colonists that independence was necessary and possible. For other Americans it contributed to the creation of a store of public arguments that could be used to rationalize a decision for independence if and when such a decision was forced upon them.

In addition, the influence of *Common Sense* extended far beyond its immediate context, for it pioneered "a style of thinking and expression different to what had been customary" in America.[23] Unlike most pamphlets of the Revolution, *Common Sense* was not penned in the gentlemanly mode of public address that had dominated American political literature through most of the colonial period. It was, rather, the most influential precursor of the popular mode of public address that came to prevail in the new republic. That the great popularity of Paine's tract was due in some measure to its form and style was widely acknowledged at the time. Not surprisingly, it spawned imitators. Of course, few Americans—even among the gentlemanly elite—possessed Paine's remarkable verbal resources and stylistic abilities, and fewer still could match his piquant prose. But even the least talented scribbler could imitate the most obvious formal and stylistic attributes of *Common Sense*—its forthright address to ordinary citizens, its colloquial idiom, its disdain for literary convention, its direct appeal to popular emotions. Ineluctably, the pamphlet helped produce a new kind of political discourse in America—a kind of discourse that helped deepen and strengthen the democratizing aftershocks of the upheaval in British-American relations.

Much more could be said about the multifaceted nature of rhetorical effects in general and about the impact of *Common Sense* in particular.[24] But the point should be clear: in the study of influence—as in other aspects of rhetorical inquiry—the putative division between instrinsic ("critical") and extrinsic ("historical") analysis is overdrawn and misleading. So too, as we shall see next, are most efforts to discriminate between history and criticism on grounds that the latter, unlike the former, entails evaluation of rhetorical works.

3

Special concern in this century about the evaluative dimension of rhetorical criticism can be dated from publication of Loren Reid's "The Perils of Rhetorical Criticism" in 1944. After reviewing the shortcomings of scholarship in public address over the preceding two decades, Reid concluded by advising that the rhetorical critic "must take to heart his primary and inescapable responsibility as a critic: to interpret, to appraise, to evaluate; to say here the speaker missed, here he hit the mark; sometimes to speak with restraint when others applaud, sometimes to bestow praise when others have passed by." During the past three decades this conception of rhetorical criticism as necessarily judicial has been reiterated by an impressive range of writers, including Thonssen and Baird ("The chief business of the rhetorical scholar...is the evaluation of a speech or speeches"), Barnet Baskerville ("By its very nature, all criticism is judicial"), Marie Hochmuth (criticism "involves a judicial act of determining what is better or worse"), Edwin Black ("At the culmination of the critical process is the evaluation of the discourse or of its author"), Robert Cathcart ("The end sought in criticism is a *judgment* of the work under consideration"), Anthony Hillbruner ("The highest role to which the critic can aspire is the passing of judgment"), Lawrence Rosenfield ("criticism does eventuate in, or at least has as an ultimate objective, assessment"), Karlyn Campbell ("'good' criticism...makes clear and unmistakable judgments about the quality, worth, and consequences of the discourse"), and Walter Fisher ("the most fundamental task of the critic is to make evaluative judgments").[25]

From this notion that criticism entails evaluation has derived a second major view of the distinction between criticism and history in the study of public address. Unlike the rhetorical historian, whose objectives are commonly described as "largely descriptive in character," the rhetorical critic is said to use history "for the more important job of judgment." This distinction has been developed most fully by Ernest Bormann. The critic, Bormann observes, uses "the same tools of scholarship as the historian." Both critics and historians develop viewpoints toward their subjects and seek structure in the works they examine. Their ultimate goals, however, differ greatly. The controlling aim of historians is to explain past rhetorical events, not to render judgments about them. If an historian makes such judgments, "they will tend to be tangential to his main concern." The critic, on the other hand, "to do his job fully," must assess the critical object against "standards of excellence" that have "a certain universality and permanence." The rhetorical critic recognizes the historical context of the work under scrutiny, but, says Bormann, may well overlook that context in appraising the work "against some artistic standard."[26]

Insistence that criticism must be evaluative is, of course, not unique to rhetoricians. It has long recurred among literary critics and may be traced back at least to Aristophanes, who sought to determine in what order of excellence the poets should be ranked, and on what basis. But there is another view of criticism, one that possesses an equally ancient and illustrious heritage—the view that criticism does not seek to judge but to explain.[7] And this view also has its adherents among students of rhetoric. Some may be interpreted as adopting this view inasmuch as they do not expressly identify evaluation as incumbent upon rhetorical critics.[28] Others unconditionally admit to the realm of rhetorical criticism studies that are not explicitly judicial. Wayne Brockriede, for instance, recognizes both "criticism that has explicit evaluation as its primary purpose" and "criticism that aims primarily at explicit analysis." Donald Bryant offers an equally inclusive conception when he states that "all analytic, interpretive, particularizing, or generalizing examinations of the arts broadly conceived—individual works, kinds, elements, aspects, and authors—are essays in criticism." Phillip Tompkins, moving from Bryant's well known definition of rhetoric, describes rhetorical criticism as "the *process of explicating a specific attempt* (whether successful or unsuccessful) to adjust ideas to people and people to ideas." Such explication, Tompkins argues, is neither coequal with nor demanding of evaluation.[29]

Not only do rhetoricians disagree over the role of evaluation in criticism, but there appears to be at least a trace of ambiguity regarding the matter within the writings of some who claim that criticism must be judicial. Even Edwin Black, who is frequently cited as the leading champion of judicial criticism, seems to adopt a somewhat equivocal stance. In the opening chapter of *Rhetorical Criticism* Black explains that critics must go "beyond perception" to "appraisal"—"beyond seeing a thing" to "attaching a value to it." Later, however, he appears to adopt a view of criticism as explication, when he states that "criticism has no relationship with its subject other than to account for how that subject works; it demands nothing but full disclosure."[30]

The ambivalence of many scholars about the role of evaluation in rhetorical criticism is further evident when we turn from what rhetorical critics say they do to what they actually do in their published works. Theories of rhetorical criticism often have little to do with the way criticism is practiced. In fact, relatively few essays in "rhetorical criticism" truly entail *explicit* evaluation as either a necessary or sufficient procedure. In this respect, the apparent attitude of most rhetoricians is well stated by Redding, who, while reiterating that the "*total* enterprise of criticism" is "'the full, evaluated apprehension of the critical subject," argues strongly for the value of critical studies "that frankly concentrate upon analysis."[31] In practice, if not in theory, most rhetorical critics produce scholarship that is essentially analytic rather than judicial.

To be sure, there are two senses in which all essays under the aegis of "rhetorical criticism" may be denominated as implicitly, if not explicitly, judicial, and it is precisely these senses that most writers appear to have in mind when they assert that criticism is necessarily evaluative.[32] First, it may be argued that perception itself is evaluative; that facts are never neutral and have no objective existence apart from the frame of reference of the person who apprehends them. According to this relativist theory of perception, we view the world through the distorting lenses of our individual experiences, aspirations, and values. Every perception is a construction; every observation is an interpretation; every experience is infused with value judgments. So too is ordinary language, which we use to order and communicate our perceptions. Seen from this point of view, rhetorical criticism—like any other human endeavor—is never value-free and is always "to some extent evaluative, judgmental, and subjective."[33]

A second position, consanguineous with the first, holds that there is no sharp line to be drawn between explanation and judgment, that "in most explanations a judgment of some sort is necessarily implied." This is the stance of Scott and Brock, who hold that rhetorical critics must pass judgment "in some way or another, implicitly or explicitly." Despite the efforts of many critics "to ignore the evaluative purpose of criticism," they can never escape evaluation entirely, for "the descriptive act, in and of itself, implies that the phenomenon as described is worth attending to." Black enunciates a similar view. In his estimation, "evluation of the discourse or of its author" should represent "the culmination of the critical process." But, he suggests, even in the absence of such overt terminal judgment, rhetorical criticism is ineluctably judicial:

> *Even the purely technical objective of understanding how a discourse works carries the assumption that it does work, and that assumption is an assessment. Similarly, to understand why a thing has failed is at least to suspect that it has failed, and that assumption is an assessment. There is, then, no criticism without appraisal; there is no "neutral criticism." On[e] critic's judgment may be absolute and dogmatic, another's tentative and barely commital; but however faint the judicial element in criticism may become, it abides.*[34]

However accurate these views of the ubiquity of evaluation, they are of little value in distinguishing between history and criticism in rhetorical scholarship.[35] There is a crucial difference between explicit evaluation in rhetorical criticism and evaluation as an inescapable part of all perception and interpretation. To say that rhetorical critics must forth rightly judge rhetorical works against some set of criteria is one thing. To say that rhetorical critics can never escape some sort of evaluative process no matter how they try is quite another. The latter position rests upon such a broad construction of "evaluation" as to rob the term of any special meaning.[36] More important for present purposes, it does not provide ground by which to separate rhetorical criticism from rhetorical history (or from any other mode of humanistic scholarship). The perception of the rhetorical historian is inherently no more pure or unmediated than that of the critic. The facts of history are always refracted through the mind of the historian, whose point of view enters irrevocably into every observation he or she makes. As Charles Beard put it, "no historian can describe the past as it actually was," for the observation, selection, and ordering of materials must inexorably be determined by each scholar's "biases, prejudices, beliefs, affections, general upbringing, and experience." Neither can historians escape the value laden connotations of the ordinary language they use to present their views of the past. It naturally follows that implicit evaluation is as unavoidable for historians as for critics. Friedrich Meinecke, the great German historian pointed out that even the "mere selection" of most historical facts is "impossible without an evaluation":

> *The historian selects his material not only according to general categories . . . but also according to his living interest in the concrete content of material. He lays hold of it as something having more or less of value, and in this he is evaluating it. The presentation and exposition of culturally important facts is utterly impossible without a lively sensitivity for the values they reveal. Although the historian may, in form, abstain from value-judgments of his own, they are there between the lines and act as such upon the reader.*[37]

Not only is some sort of implicit evaluation as inescapable for rhetorical historians as for critics, but it may be argued that rendering more-or-less explicit verdicts about the artistry, worth, or efficacy of rhetorical acts need not be arbitrarily divorced from the province of rhetorical history—particularly since such verdicts are likely to be cursory and haphazard unless grounded in penetrating historical understanding of what was valuable or possible in any given rhetorical transaction. Before the rise of professionalized history in the late nineteenth century, the writing of history was widely regarded as a judicial enterprise that, in the words of Charles W. Eliot, "shows the young the springs of public honor and dishonor; sets before them the national failings, weaknesses, and sins; warns them against future dangers by exhibiting the losses and sufferings of the past; enshrines in their hearts the national heroes; and strengthens in them the precious love of country."[38] Today the view that a principal task of the historian is to judge the thoughts, actions, and precepts of earlier times has few adherents. Yet it has some,[39] and in certain varieties of history—most notably biography and military history—such judgment is not at all uncommon. As military historians judge the effectiveness and implications of the battlefield tactics of wartime commanders, or as biographers evaluate the standards and achievements of historical figures, so may rhetorical historians make similar assessments about the rhetorical activities of speakers and writers. Indeed, many notably rhetorical studies so thoroughly blend description, interpretation, and evaluation as to make efforts to categorize them discreetly as either "history" or "criticism" nugatory and misleading.[40]

But even if it be granted that rendering explicit assessments of the effectiveness, artistry, and ethics of public address is exclusive to rhetorical criticism, the procedures by which one reaches such terminal judgments usually require substantial historical acumen. This is most obvious of pragmatic judgments, which entail the historical tasks of placing rhetorical acts firmly in context and gauging their impact upon readers and listeners. It is less obvious of artistic judgments, which seek to assess the quality of discourse "as a self-contained unit, without regard for any particular audience."[41] But as we have seen, it is seldom possible to deal satisfactorily with the internal operations of public address without serious attention to historical factors extrinsic to the text itself. Moreover, as Black has observed, because the standards against which critics commonly seek to assess rhetorical quality are based upon their presumed capacity to achieve desired results with audiences, what passes for a formalistic judgment of artistry "is usually a pragmatic judgment at bottom."[42]

A somewhat similar conclusion may be drawn about ethical judgments, which deal with the truth of a rhetor's claims, the propriety of a rhetor's techniques, or the moral consequences of a rhetor's discourse. Since we only hold people responsible for acts of volition, the burden of rhetorical critics is more to assess the *truthfulness* of a claimant than the truth of his or her claims. Making the former assessment is not simply a matter of comparing what a rhetor said either with what was known to be true by the rhetor's contemporaries or with what is now known to be true. Rather, it is a matter of testing a rhetor's statements against what *the rhetor* believed to be true when he or she advanced them. And this demands the same kind of historical skill utilized by the biographer. Likewise, assessing the ethics of a speaker's persuasive techniques necessitates determining what those techniques in fact were and weighing whether their use was ethical in the historical situation in which they were employed. Finally, evaluating the moral consequences of discourse requires the prior task of estimating what impact it actually had upon readers or listeners. In each case, reaching moral judgment—as with reaching pragmatic or artistic judgment—entails historical industry and understanding.

It would appear, then, that the judicial aspects of rhetorical criticism do not provide a secure purchase point for divorcing criticism from history in the study of public address. Nor does an examination of method reveal fundamental fissures between historical and critical scholarship in rhetoric.

4

Although one reads much of "historical method" and "critical method," as if there were grave differences between the two, there is typically little distinction when it comes to the study of public address. Rhetorical critics and historians employ essentially similar methods inasmuch as the central task of each is making inferences about probabilities on the basis of limited data. In this general sense, both may be said to use the critical method, and in fact historians commonly designate their method as "critical" and identify the process of interrogating and evaluating historical evidence as "historical criticism."[43] Beyond this, historians are wedded to no special method. Indeed, it may be argued that "history has no method or methods" at all if one defines method in its strict sense as a settled, systematic mode of procedure in which one step produces a specifiable result and is necessarily followed by another step, which also produces a specifiable result, and so on until the process is complete and yields the final product. Using the term "method" in this fashion, one can sensibly speak of, say, the open-hearth method of making steel, or the various methods of teaching children how to swim, but not the method of historical inquiry. As Jacques Barzun explains, "history resists any genuine application of method."

> *The handbooks say: consult your sources, test and authenticate them, assemble the ascertained facts, write your report, and give clear references. After publication another volume is classified as history on some library shelf. But all this is hardly more than a general description of the work of intelligence, such as is performed by every student and professional, with or without a method. Method for the*

historian is only a metaphor to say that he is rational and resourceful, imaginative and conscientious. Nothing prescribes the actual steps of his work.

Nor should it. Historians ought to be *methodical* in selecting, ordering, and criticizing evidence, but the key to successful historical scholarship is not the rigid use of orthodox procedures, but the resourcefulness and judgment of the individual historian, who "had better keep his mental activity unrestricted" by formal methods, which only constrain the mind by dictating in advance the operation of thought upon its material.[44]

The parallels between this conception of method in history and prevailing ideas about method in rhetorical criticism should be so patent as to require little elaboration. Rhetorical critics employ the critical method broadly conceived, but, like rhetorical historians, reject the uniform application of predetermined formulas, which are most likely to produce scholarship that is dull, mechanical, unimaginative, and commonplace. "There are," Fisher notes, "as many approaches to rhetorical criticism as there are useful things to say about the rhetorical process." Indeed, so powerful is the commitment to critical pluralism that most rhetorical critics today eschew even the term "method," preferring instead to talk of critical "orientations," "approaches," and "perspectives." And whatever particular orientation, approach, or perspective an individual critic elects is not prescribed beforehand, but depends upon the purposes of the critic and the nature of the rhetorical work under scrutiny. Eventually, of course, 'some schema must control the analysis" if criticism is to avoid being "totally whimscial and subjective." Yet good criticism does not result from doggedly following a set of formulary procedures, but from the full, free interplay of intelligence with the critical object. The main ideal of criticism is, in Kenneth Burke's words, "to use all that is there to use." If there is a method of rhetorical criticism (or of rhetorical history), it is simply what mathematical physicist P. W. Bridgeman describes as the "scientific method"—"nothing more than doing one's damnedest with one's mind, no holds barred."[45]

Of course, "method" need not be construed only in its strict sense. Indeed, the term is commonly used more broadly—to refer to the general procedures by which various kinds of scholars go about their work. It is likely this usage that most writers have in mind when they refer to differences between historical and critical method in the study of public address. But however clear such differences may appear in the abstract, they are usually difficult to detect in practice. The procedures employed by most rhetoricians are not readily set apart as "critical" versus "historical." Critics at times offer explicit evaluations of rhetorical transactions; so at times do historians. Historians at times make causal inferences about the influence of rhetorical acts; so at times do critics. Critics at times focus intently upon the internal operations of discourse; so at times do historians. Historians at times attend closely to the context of public communication; so at times do critics. From verifying the authenticity of texts, to plumbing the intentions of their authors, to comprehending the context in which rhetoric occurs, to explicating the discursive and social processes by which it functions, to assessing its artistry, worth, or consequences, rhetorical critics and rhetorical historians employ essentially similar scholarly procedures. What differs from study to study are not so much the methods employed, but the research questions asked and the skill with which they are answered.

These resemblances in method come as no surprise when one considers the extent to which rhetorical critics and historians share common epistemological premises. Both deal with contingencies and both recognize the elusiveness of Truth. Neither are engaged in a search for universal laws. Both seek to elucidate tendencies or probabilities. Although some writers have bemoaned an objectivistic bias in historical approaches to public address,[46] most historians are fully aware that "there can be no 'pure' history—history-in-itself, recorded from nobody's point of view, for nobody's sake. The most objective history conceivable is still a selection and an interpretation, necessarily governed by some special interests and based on some particular beliefs."[47] Historians can never recapture the past just as it was. All they can know of the past depends upon the available evidence, and the selection, interpretation, and evaluation of that evidence will inevitably be influenced by the personal values and professional skill of individual historians. Both critics and historians strive to explicate rhetorical events as wisely, as fully, and as objectively as possible. But neither can be completely value-free and neither offer absolute interpretations. Both must impose their own constructions on their material and on their readers.[48]

Given these methodological and epistemological likenesses, historical and critical studies in public address naturally share common rhetorical characteristics. Critics and historians alike typically work with at least some conception of audience in mind, and both unavoidably interpose themselves between the rhetorical event and their readers. Both strive to persuade readers to see rhetorical events in certain ways, and both confront the compositional demands of arrangement, emphasis, clarity, and vividness in writing convincing accounts of their subjects. Neither, however, deal with questions through controlled experimental investigation, and the discourse of both possesses the spread, richness, and ambiguity of ordinary language. Rhetorical critics and historians alike gain their greatest insights through the exercise of creative imagination, and the work of both is often judged by literary as well as scholarly standards.[49]

Yet neither are chiefly concerned with producing works that are merely persuasive or whose distinguishing feature is high literary merit. The central, irreducible obligation of both critics and historians is to deal with subjects as faithfully, as accurately, as impartially as the limitations of human nature and ordinary language allow. Neither expected their claims to be accepted on faith, and both carry the responsibility of making reasoned assertions that are evidentially and inferentially warranted. Both are bound by the dictates of intellectual honesty and are subject to the highest imperatives of liberal scholarship. History and criticism alike are, to borrow Droysen's words, "not 'the light and the truth,' but a search therefor, a sermon thereupon, a consecration thereto."[50]

5

The acute sense of schism between history and criticism in rhetorical scholarship is relatively recent. As disenchantment with conventional approaches to the study of public address deepened and strengthened, more and more rhetoricians differentiated between criticism and history and called upon their colleagues to produce the former rather than the latter—by which they usually meant writing studies that concentrated upon intrinsic features of rhetorical discourse, evaluated rhetorical works or their authors, and/or followed critical rather than historical methods. As we have seen, however, these distinctions are far from immutable and sometimes blur to the point of disappearing altogether. Consequently, we may conclude with Everett Hunt, who once dismissed quarrels between history and criticism as akin to "the bitter complaints of Jason, who, in denouncing Medea, wished that men could get children without women."[51]

But the conclusion is a bit premature, for, like many truisms, it camouflages a tangled skein of complex issues. I do not mean to claim that because rhetorical history and rhetorical criticism share common characteristics there are no meaningful differences between them. Distinctions between the two may capture somewhat disparate approaches, purposes, and intellectual viewpoints. Yet the very nature of rhetoric militates against a sharp distinction between historical and critical inquiry. Dwelling upon the supposed differences between them has for many years been a kind of red herring that has fastened attention upon the categorization of scholarship rather than upon its quality. In the study of rhetorical discourse, history and criticism are most profitably seen as reciprocal modes of understanding. The boundary between the two is usually so fluid and indistinct that to insist upon a firm partition is fruitless.[52]

Nor do I wish even to intimate that we ought to return to the traditional paradigm of "history and criticism." Although that paradigm predicated a close working relationship between criticism and history, it was nonetheless informed by many of the current misconceptions about the nature of critical and historical inquiry in public address. For one thing, it portrayed the two as fundamentally discrete kinds of intellectual activities. For another, although it insisted that rhetorical criticism could not be written without a strong reliance upon history, it mistakenly implied that adequate rhetorical history could quite easily be written without regard for criticism. Moreover, the traditional paradigm was based upon a severely restricted view of rhetoric and of rhetorical analysis. It generally posed the wrong questions about rhetorical phenomena and went about answering them in myopic and unsophisticated ways.

The breakdown of the conventional archetype of "history and criticism" and the emergence of manifold new approaches has enriched both the diversity and quality of rhetorical scholarship. But the durability of whatever progress we have made is likely to be imperiled if the present breach between criticism and history continues to widen. For that breach is much more than terminological. As we have seen, it depends upon and reinforces an attenuated view of the complex and interconnected ways of comprehending rhetorical transactions. Consequently, it must ultimately straiten rhetorical analysis and fetter the development of rhetorical theory.

What we need is not to expand further the rift between history and criticism, but to recognize and to capitalize upon their essential similarities. All rhetorical analysis deals with the past: the present is but a fleeting moment that can never be fully recaptured. All subjects for rhetorical study are inherently historical, whether they occurred one minute or one thousand years ago. From resolving questions of textual accuracy, to charting the evolution of rhetorical documents, to gauging the rhetorical temperament of their authors, to penetrating the dynamics of rhetorical situations, to explicating the formal properties and social functions of discourse, to rendering evaluative judgments, the rhetorician inescapably confronts a wide range of concerns that require rigorous historical interrogation. Seen from this point of view, historical understanding is not simply a prolegomenon to critical understanding, but an organic element of the whole process of rhetorical analysis.

At the center of that process, for historians and critics alike, is the quest to elucidate rhetorical transactions. Both share an abiding interest in the study of people as rhetorical animals, and both hold as controlling premises that language is a powerful means of social inducement and that people are, "by nature, subject to and capable of persuasion."[53] Moreover, what characterizes rhetorical criticism at its best is no less characteristic of rhetorical history at its best—a keen and penetrating focus on the functional attributes of rhetorical acts. Although accurate description is a necessary aspect of both history and criticism, it is not sufficient for signal attainment in either. Analysis, explanation, interpretation—these are the vital elements of rhetorical analysis, critical and historical alike. Rhetorical historians, like rhetorical critics, are concerned above all with what messages do rather than with what they are, and the central office of each is to explicate how rhetorical communication works.[54] To the extent that either critics or historians fulfill this office rigorously and resourcefully, they will produce scholarship essential to understanding the rhetorical dimensions of human experience.

Notes

1. Throughout this essay I use the term "history" to refer, not to past actuality, but to study of the past. I use "public address," "rhetorical communication," "public discourse," and the like to encompass the full range of verbal and nonverbal public acts of a rhetorical nature.

2. It should be carefully noted that my concern is strictly the relationship between history and criticism in rhetorical analysis, not the relationship between history and criticism in general.

3. Herbert Wichelns, "The Literary Criticism of Oratory," in *Studies in Rhetoric and Public Speaking in Honor of James Albert Winans*, ed. A. M. Drummond (New York: Century, 1925), pp. 209, 213, 199. In differentiating rhetoric from literature, Wichelns accepted, with some qualifications, the characterizations of each advanced during the previous two years in a brace of groundsetting essays by Hoyt H. Hudson: "The Field of Rhetoric," *Quarterly Journal of Speech Education*, 9 (1923), 167–180; "Rhetoric and Poetry," *Quarterly Journal of Speech Education*, 10 (1924), 143–154.

4. William Norwood Brigance, "Whither Research?" *Quarterly Journal of Speech*, 19 (1933), 557–558; Donald C. Bryant, "Some Problems of Scope and Method in Rhetorical Scholarship," *Quarterly Journal of Speech*, 23 (1937), 183–184; Lester Thonssen and A. Craig Baird, *Speech Criticism: The Development of Standards for Critical Appraisal* (New York: Ronald Press, 1948), pp. 11–12. Ernest J. Wrage, "Public Address: A Study in Social and Intellectual History," *Quarterly Journal of Speech*, 33 (1947), 451–457, and Leland M. Griffin, "The Rhetoric of Historical Movements," *Quarterly Journal of Speech*, 38 (1952), 184–188, both called for departures from standard approaches to the study of public address, but neither challenged the view that such study should be firmly grounded in historical scholarship. Indeed, Wrage saw the primary responsibility of the rhetorical critic as that of contributing to the history of ideas.

5. Thonssen and Baird, *Speech Criticism*, p. 315.

6. Anthony Hillbruner, *Critical Dimensions: The Art of Public Address Criticism* (New York: Random House, 1966), p. 26. This view, of course, can still be found in recent works such as Carroll C. Arnold, *Criticism of Oral Rhetoric* (Columbus: Charles E. Merrill, 1974), and Craig R. Smith, *Orientations to Speech Criticism* (Chicago: Science Research Associates, 1976). But it no longer commands the field, as it once did.

7. Loren D. Reid, "The Perils of Rhetorical Criticism," *Quarterly Journal of Speech*, 30 (1944), 416–422; Marie Hochmuth, "The Criticism of Rhetoric," in *A History and Criticism of Amer-*

ican Public Address, III, ed. Maries Hochmuth (New York: Longman's, Green, and Co., 1955), pp. 5–6. Cf. Irving J. Lee, "Four Ways of Looking at a Speech," *Quarterly Journal of Speech*, 28 (1942), 148–155; Wayne N. Thompson, "Contemporary Public Address as a Research Area," *Quarterly Journal of Speech*, 33 (1947), 274–283; Martin Maloney, "Some New Directions in Rhetorical Criticism," *Central States Speech Journal*, 4 (March 1953), 1–5; Barnet Baskerville, "The Critical Method in Speech," *Central States Speech Journal*, 4 (July 1953) 1–5; Virginia Holland, "Rhetorical Criticism: A Burkeian Method," *Quarterly Journal of Speech*, 39 (1953), 444–450; Wayland Maxfield Parrish, "The Study of Speeches," in *American Speeches*, ed. Parrish and Marie Hochmuth (New York: Longman's Green, and Co., 1954), pp. 1–20.

8. Malcolm O. Sillars, "Rhetoric as Act," *Quarterly Journal of Speech*, 50 (1964), 277; Anthony Hillbruner, "Criticism as Persuasion," *Southern Speech Journal*, 28 (1963), 260; W. Charles Redding, "Extrinsic and Intrinsic Criticism," in *Essays on Rhetorical Criticism*, ed. Thomas R. Nilsen (New York: Random House, 1968), p. 99. My characterizaiton of Hillbruner as a revisionist should be seen as equivocal, given the traditional tone and orientation of his 1965 *Critical Dimensions: The Art of Public Address Criticism* (cited in note 6 above). His "Criticism as Persuasion," however, sternly disapproved of conventional ways of studying and writing about public address.

The reorientation of rhetorical scholarship during the past two decades has been accompanied by a great outpouring of works dealing with one or another aspect of rhetorical analysis. Most of these works may be classified as revisionist inasmuch as they recommend alternatives to traditional ways of comprehending public address. Among those most germane to the discussion in this and the following paragraph are Albert J. Croft, "The Functions of Rhetorical Criticism," *Quarterly Journal of Speech*, 42 (1956), 283–291; Edwin Black, *Rhetorical Criticism: A Study in Method* (New York: Macmillan, 1965); Robert L. Scott and Donald K. Smith, "The Rhetoric of Confrontation," *Quarterly Journal of Speech*, 55 (1969), 1–8; Walter R. Fisher, "Method in Rhetorical Criticism," *Southern Speech Journal*, 35 (1969), 101–109; Herbert W. Simons, "Requirements, Problems, and Strategies: A Theory of Persuasion for Social Movements," *Quarterly Journal of Speech*, 56 (1970), 1–11; Samuel L. Becker, "Rhetorical Studies for the Contemporary World," in *The Prospect of Rhetoric*, ed. Lloyd F. Bitzer and Edwin Black (Englewood Cliffs: Prentice-Hall, 1971), pp. 21–43; "Report of the Committee on the Advancement and Refinement of Rhetorical Criticism," in ibid., pp. 220–227; Karlyn Kohrs Campbell, *Critiques of Contemporary Rhetoric* (Belmont: Wadsworth, 1972); *Explorations in Rhetorical Criticism*, ed. G. P. Mohrmann, Charles J. Stewart, and Donovan J. Ochs (University Park: Pennsylvania State University Press, 1973); and the papers collected in Nilsen, *Essays on Rhetorical Criticism*.

9. Bruce E. Gronbeck, "Rhetorical History and Rhetorical Criticism: A Distinction," *Speech Teacher*, 24 (1975), 309–320; Barnet Baskerville, "Must We All Be 'Rhetorical Critics'?" *Quarterly Journal of Speech*, 63 (1977), 107–116.

10. Witness the separation William N. Brigance makes, in his introduction to the first volume of *A History and Criticism of American Public Address* (New York: Longman's, Green, and Co., 1943), between "historical studies," which deal with "background," and "critical studies," which deal directly with the rhetoric of individual orators.

11. Parrish, "Study of Speeches," in Parrish and Hochmuth, *American Speeches*, p. 7; Gronbeck, "Rhetorical History," 310–311, 314. Similarly, see Hochmuth, "Criticism of Rhetoric," p. 5; Ernest G. Bormann, *Theory and Research in the Communicative Arts* (New York: Holt, Rinehart and Winston, 1965), p. 234; Lawrence W. Rosenfield, "The Anatomy of Critical Discourse," *Speech Monographs*, 35 (1968), 58; Redding, "Extrinsic and Intrinsic Criticism," in Nilsen, *Essays*, pp. 98–106; J. Jeffery Auer, "Implications of the Recommendations of the New Orleans Conference from the Perspective of Historical Scholarship," in *Conceptual Frontiers in Speech-Communication*, ed. Robert J. Kibler and Larry L. Barker (New York: Speech Association of America, 1969), p. 178.

12. R. C. Jebb, *The Attic Orators* (London: Macmillan, 1876), I, xiii.

13. It should be noted in this connection that Black does not indict neo-Aristotelianism because it compels critics to attend to the context of rhetorical acts, but because it adopts a "restricted view of context" as confined to a specific audience and an immediate occasion. Because "the work of rhetoric is fragmentary outside its environment," says Black, "the discovery of context" acquires "an enhanced importance in rhetorical criticism." One of Black's first steps in his study of John Jay Chapman's Coatesville Address, which he offers as an antidote to neo-Aristotelianism, is to set the Address in its proper context. That context, however, "is not the vacant grocery store" in which Chapman spoke on August 18, 1912. Rather, the Address must be understood as joining in the perduring "dialogue on the moral dimensions of the American experience." Thus the context of the Coatesville Address "is less a specific place than a culture.... It is a context whose place must be measured by a continent and whose time must be reckoned in centuries" (*Rhetorical Criticism*, pp. 39, 83–84).

14. J. G. A. Pocock, *Politics, Language, and Time: Essays on Political Thought and History* (New York: Atheneum, 1973), p. 12.

15. Thonssen and Baird, *Speech Criticism*, p. 16.

16. Baskerville, "Must We All Be Rhetorical Critics?" 114; Donald C. Bryant, *Rhetorical Dimensions in Criticism* (Baton Rouge: Louisiana State University Press, 1973), p. 38; Parrish, "Study of Speeches," in Parrish and Hochmuth, *American Speeches*, pp. 7–8. Similarly, see Bormann, *Theory and Research*, p. 238–242; Campbell, *Critiques*, pp. 29–30; Robert Cathcart *Post-Communication: Critical Analysis and Evaluation* (Indianapolis: Bobbs-Merrill, 1966), pp. 21–22.

17. Bryant, *Rhetorical Dimensions*, p. 38.

18. Cf. Parrish, "Study of Speeches," in Parrish and Hochmuth, *American Speeches*, p. 8. Although few rhetoricians forthrightly subscribe to such a presupposition, it is often implicit in their language—particularly in the images of measurement they commonly use when discussing rhetorical effect.

19. The value of dealing with such consequences is indicated by, respectively, Becker, "Rhetorical Studies," in Bitzer and Black, *Prospect of Rhetoric*, pp. 21–43; Black, *Rhetorical Criticism*, p. 35; Thomas R. Nilsen, "Criticism and Social Consequences," *Quarterly Journal of Speech*, 42 (1956), 173–178; Don M. Burks, "Persuasion, Self-Persuasion, and Rhetorical Discourse," *Philosophy and Rhetoric*, 3 (1970), 109–119; Michael C. McGee, "In Search of 'The People': A Rhetorical Alternative," *Quarterly Journal of Speech*, 61 (1975), 235–249; Stephen E. Lucas, *Portents of Rebellion: Rhetoric and Revolution in Philadelphia, 1765–1776* (Philadelphia: Temple University Press, 1976), pp. 254–262.

20. Representative eighteenth-century judgments of the impact of *Common Sense* and historical estimates of its circulation can be found in Moses Coit Tyler, *Literary History of the American Revolution* (1897; rpnt. ed., New York: Frederick Ungar, 1957), I, 469–474; Merrill Jensen, *The Founding of a Nation: A History of the American Revolution* (New York: Oxford University Press, 1968), pp. 668–669; Winthrop D. Jordan, "Familial Politics: Thomas Paine and the Killing of the King, 1776," *Journal of American History*, 60 (1973), 295–296. A succinct record of the printing history of *Common Sense* is available in Thomas R. Adams, *American Independence , the Growth of an Idea: A Bibliographical Study of the American Political Pamphlets Printed between 1764 and 1776 Dealing with the Dispute between Great Britain and Her Colonies* (Providence: Brown University Press, 1965), pp. 164–172.

21. Joseph Reed to Charles Pettit, March 30, 1776, in *Life and Correspondence of Joseph Reed*, ed. William B. Reed (Philadelphia: Lindsay and Blakiston, 1847), I, 182.

22. For full treatment and documentation of the issues discussed in this and the following paragraph see Lucas, *Portents of Rebellion*, pp. 167–175, 254–262.

23. Thomas Paine, quoted in Harry Hayden Clark, "Thomas Paine's Theories of Rhetoric," *Transactions of the Wisconsin Academy of Sciences, Arts, and Letters*, 28 (1933), 317.

24. Indeed, the nature of rhetorical influence, the degree to which assessing such influence is a vital task for rhetorical analysis, and the most profitable approaches to such assessment are all matters in need of thorough rethinking. This brief discussion is but a step in that direction.

25. Reid, "Perils of Rhetorical Criticism," 422; A. Craig Baird and Lester Thonssen, "Methodology in the Criticism of Public Address," *Quarterly Journal of Speech*, 33 (1947), 134; Baskerville, "Critical Method in Speech," 1; Hochmuth, "Criticism of Rhetoric," 4; Edwin Black, "Moral Values and Rhetorical Criticism," lecture presented at University of Wisconsin, July 1965, quoted in Rosenfield, "Anatomy of Critical Discourse," 54; Cathcart, *Post-Communication*, p. 89; Hillbruner, *Critical Dimensions*, p. 149; Rosenfield, "Anatomy of Critical Discourse," 54; Campbell, *Critiques*, pp. 21–22; Walter R. Fisher, "Rhetorical Criticism as Criticism," *Western Speech*, 38 (1974), 78. Not all of the above writers agree about the kinds of evaluations rhetorical critics ought to make, or about the best ways to reach them, but they are in fundamental agreement that critics need to engage in evaluation of some sort.

26. Hillburner, "Criticism as Persuasion," 260–261; Bormann, *Theory and Research*, pp. 227–229.

27. *Lectures in Criticism*, ed. Huntington Cairns, (Baltimore: Johns Hopkins University Press, 1949), pp. 1–8.

28. The report of the Committee on Rhetorical Criticism at the National Conference on Rhetoric, for instance, makes no mention of evaluation as an obligatory aspect of rhetorical criticism. In the view of the committee, "any critic, regardless of the subject of his inquiry, becomes a rhetorical critic when his work centers on suasory potential or persuasive effects, their source, nature, operation, and consequences" in Bitzer and Black, *Prospect*, p. 221.

29. Wayne Brockriede, "Rhetorical Criticism as Argument," *Quarterly Journal of Speech*, 60 (1974), 165; Bryant, *Rhetorical Dimensions*, p. 26; Phillip K. Tompkins, "The Rhetorical Criticism of Non-Oratorical Works," *Quarterly Journal of Speech*, 55 (1969), 431. Similarly, see *Methods of Rhetorical Criticism: A Twentieth-Century Perspective*, ed. Robert L. Scott and Bernard L. Brock (New York: Harper and Row, 1972), p. 341; Mark S. Klyne, "Toward a Pluralistic Rhetorical Criticism," in Nilsen, *Essays*, p. 147; Gary D. Keele, "Keele on Fisher," *Western Speech*, 38 (1974), 278–280.

30. Black, *Rhetorical Criticism*, pp. 5, 18. Also see the shifting stances on the same issue by Barnet Baskerville in the following essays: "Critical Method in Speech," 1; "Rhetorical Criticism, 1971: Retrospect, Prospect, Introspect," *Southern Speech Journal*, 37 (1971), 119–120; "Responses, Queries, and a Few Caveats," in Bitzer and Black, *Prospect*, p. 164; "Must We All Be Rhetorical Critics?" 110, 112, 115–116.

31. Redding, "Intrinsic and Extrinsic Criticism," in Nilsen, *Essays*, p. 107.

32. The distinction between implicit and explicit evaluation is a vital one that has seldom been recognized by rhetoricians. Their failure to recognize it helps, I think, to account for much of the ambiguity and ambivalence evident in the long-standing debate over the role of evaluation in rhetorical analysis.

33. Campbell, *Critiques*, p. 1.

34. Cairns *Lectures in Criticism*, p. 7; Scott and Brock, *Methods*, p. 9; Black, "Moral Values," quoted in Rosenfield, "Anatomy of Critical Discourse," 54. Also see Edwin Black, "The Second Persona," *Quarterly Journal of Speech*, 56 (1970), 109–110; Brockriede, "Criticism as Argument," 165; Baskerville, "Rhetorical Criticism, 1971," 119–120.

35. Nor was it the aim of the writers just quoted so to distinguish.

36. Cf. the conclusion of Morris Weitz with respect to much the same issue in literary criticism, in *Hamlet and the Philosophy of Literary Criticism* (Chicago: University of Chicago Press, 1964), p. 269.

37. Charles Beard, review of Maurice Mendelbaum's *The Problem of Historical Knowledge*, in *The Philosophy of History in Our Own Time*, ed. Hans Meyerhoff (New York: Double-day, 1959), p. 139; Charles Beard, "Written History as an Act of Faith," in ibid., p. 141; Friedrich Meinecke, "Values and Causalities in History," in *The Varieties of History*, 2d ed., ed. Fritz Stern (New York: Random House, 1972), p. 273. The positions enunciated by Beard and Meinecke are so common among historians and philosophers of history as to constitute first principles. Notable statements include Raymond Aron, *Introduction to the Philosophy of History: An Essay on the Limits of Historical Objectivity*, trans. George J. Irwin (Boston: Beacon *Press*, 1961); Charles Beard, "That Noble Dream," *American Historical Review*, 41 (1935), 74–87; Carl L. Becker, "What Are Historical Facts?" *Western Political Quarterly*, 8 (1955), 327–340; Edward Hallett Carr, *What is History?* (New York: Random House, 1961); R. G. Collingwood, *The Idea of History* (New York: Oxford University Press, 1946); Benedetto Croce, *History: Its Theory and Practice*, trans. Douglas Ainslee (New York: Harcourt, Brace, and Co., 1921); John Dewey, *Logic: The Theory of Inquiry* (New York: Henry Holt and Co., 1938), pp. 230–239; Patrick Gardiner, *The Nature of Historical Explanation* (New York: Oxford University Press, 1961); Herbert Muller, *The Uses of the Past: Profiles of Former Societies* (New York: Oxford University Press, 1952), chap. 2; Murray G. Murphey, *Our Knowledge of the Historical Past* (Indianapolis: Bobbs-Merrill, 1973).

38. Charles W. Eliot, *Educational Reform: Essays and Addresses* (New York: The Century Company, 1898), p. 105.

39. See, for instance, A. J. P. Taylor, *Rumours of Wars* (London: Hamish Hamilton, 1952), pp. 9–13; Isaiah Berlin, *Historical Inevitability* (London: Oxford University Press, 1954); C. V. Wedgwood, *Truth and Opinion: Historical Essays* (London: Collins, 1960), pp. 42–54; John Higham, "Beyond Consensus: The Historian as Moral Critic," *American Historical Review*, 67 (1962), 609–625; Page Smith, *The Historian and History* (New York: Alfred A. Knopf, 1964), pp. 218–231; Howard Zinn, *The Politics of History* (Boston: Beacon Press, 1970).

40. Such studies include Carroll C. Arnold, "Lord Thomas Erskine: Modern Advocate," *Quarterly*

Journal of Speech, 44 (1958), 17–30; Ross Scanlan, "Adolf Hitler and the Technique of Mass Brainwashing," in *The Rhetorical Idiom*, ed. Donald C. Bryant (Ithaca: Cornell University Press, 1958), pp. 201–220; Eugene E. White, "Puritan Preaching and the Authority of God," in *Preaching in American History*, ed. DeWitte Holland (Nashville: Abingdon Press, 1969), pp. 36–73; Robert P. Newman, "Under the Veneer: Nixon's Vietnam Speech of November 3, 1969," *Quarterly Journal of Speech*, 56 (1970), 168–178; James R. Andrews, "The Passionate Negation: The Chartist Movement in Rhetorical Perspective," *Quarterly Journal of Speech*, 59 (1973), 196–208; Richard B. Gregg, "A Rhetorical Re-Examination of Arthur Vandeberg's 'Dramatic Conversion,' January 10, 1945," *Quarterly Journal of Speech*, 61 (1975), 154–168; John Agnus Campbell, "The Polemical Mr. Darwin," *Quarterly Journal of Speech*, 61 (1975), 375–390; Michael Osborn, "The Evolution of the Archetypal Sea in Rhetoric and Poetic," *Quarterly Journal of Speech*, 63 (1977), 347–363; Barnet Baskerville, *The People's Voice: The Orator in American Society* (Lexington: University Press of Kentucky, 1979); Lloyd Bitzer and Theodore Rueter, *Carter vs Ford: The Counterfeit Debates of 1976* (Madison: University of Wisconsin Press, 1980).

41.   Black, *Rhetorical Criticism*, p. 62. The standard exposition of artistic criticisim in rhetoric remains Parrish's "The Study of Speeches," in Parrish and Hochmuth, *American Speeches*, pp. 1–20.

42.   Black, *Rhetorical Criticism*, p. 68.

43.   See, for example, Marc Bloch, *The Historian's Craft*, trans. Joseph R. Strayer (New York: Alfred A. Knopf, 1953), chap. 3; G. Kitson Clark, *The Critical Historian* (New York: Basic Books, 1967); Louis Gottschalk, *Understanding History: A Primer of Historical Method*, 2d ed. (New York: Alfred A. Knopf. 1969), chaps. 6–7; Homer C. Hockett, *The Critical Method in Historical Research and Writing* (New York: Macmillian, 1955), part I; Gregg Phifer, "The Historical Approach," in *An Introduction to Graduate Study in Speech and Theatre*, ed. Clyde W. Dow (East Lansing: Michigan State University Press, 1961), pp. 52–80.

44.   Jacques Barzum, *Clio and the Doctors: Psycho-History, Quanto-History and History* (Chicago: University of Chicago Press, 1974), pp. 39–41, 89–90. This viewpoint is well capsulized in Samuel Eliot Morison's dictum that historical method "is a product of common sense applied to circumstances" ("Faith of a Historian," *American Historical Review*, 56 [1951], 263). But cf. Lee Benson, *Toward the Scientific Study of History* (Philadelphia: Lippincott, 1972), esp. pp. 239–240, for a sharply worded contrary view.

45.   Fisher, "Method in Rhetorical Criticism," 107; G. P. Mohrmann and Michael C. Leff, "Lincoln at Cooper Union: A Rationale for Neo-Classical Criticism," *Quarterly Journal of Speech*, 60 (1974), 465; Kenneth Burke, *The Philosophy of Literary Form*, rev. ed. (New York: Vintage Press, 1957), p. 21; P. W. Bridgeman, "The Prospect for Intelligence," *Yale Review*, 34 (1945), 450, quoted in Thomas C. Cochran, "History and the Social Sciences," in *The Craft of American History: Selected Essays*, ed. A. S. Eisenstadt (New York: Harper and Row, 1966), II, 109.

46.   Linnea Ratcliff, "Rhetorical Criticism: An Alternative Perspective," *Southern Speech Journal*, 37 (1971), 125–135; Philip Wander and Steven Jenkins, "Rhetoric, Society, and the Critical Response," *Quarterly Journal of Speech*, 58 (1972), 441–450; James W. Chesebro and Caroline D. Hamsher, "Contemporary Rhetorical Theory and Criticism: Dimensions of the New Rhetoric," *Speech Monographs*, 42 (1975), 311–334.

47.   Muller, *Uses of the Past*, pp. 43–44. Also see the works cited in footnote 37 above. It should be stressed that this view is also shared by so-called objectivist historians. They agree that perception is inherently value-laden, but reject what Oscar Handlin calls "the deceptive path from acknowledging that no person. . . [is] entirely free of prejudice or capable of attaining a totally objective view of the past to the conclusion that all efforts to do so. . . [are] in vain and that, in the end, the past. . . [is] entirely a recreation emanating from the mind of the historian" (*Truth in History* [Cambridge: Harvard University Press, 1979], p. 410). Also see Ernest Nagel, *The Structure of Science* (London: Routledge and Kegan Paul, 1961), pp. 473–502, 547–606; Arthur O. Lovejoy, "Present Standpoints and Past History," *Journal of Philosophy*, 36 (1939), 477–489; Christopher Blake, "Can History Be Objective?" in *Theories of History*, ed. Patrick Gardiner (New York: Macmillan, 1959), pp. 329–343; Sidney Hook, "Objectivity and Reconstruction in History," in *Philosophy and History*, ed. Sidney Hook (New York: New York University Press, 1963), pp. 250–274; Peter Gay, *Style in History* (New York: McGraw Hill, 1974), pp. 185–217.

48.   This is not to endorse the extremely relativistic position that truth is unattainable, that every interpretation is hopelessly biased, and that every assessment is as good as another. "There is," as René Wellek points out, "a difference between the psychology of the investigator, his presumed bias, ideology, perspective, and the logical structure of his propositions. The genesis of a theory does not necessarily invalidate its truth. Men can correct their biases, criticize their presuppositions, rise above their temporal and local limitations, aim at objectivity, arrive at some knowledge and truth.... There are utterly fantastic interpretations, partial, distorted interpretations.... The concept of adequacy of interpretation leads clearly to the concept of the correctness of judgment. Evaluation grows out of understanding; correct evaluation out of correct understanding. There is a hierarchy of viewpoints implied in the very concept of adequacy of interpretation. Just as there is correct interpretation, at least as an ideal, so there is correct judgment, good judgment" (*Concepts of Criticism*, ed. Stephen G. Nichols, Jr., [New Haven: Yale University Press, 1963], pp. 14, 18). In the words of Abraham Kaplan, "everything depends on the conduct of the inquiry, on the way in which we arrive at our conclusions. Freedom from bias means having an open mind, not an empty one" (*The Conduct of Inquiry* [San Francisco: Chandler, 1964], p. 375). See also the second paragraph to follow in the present essay.

49.   On the rhetorical aspects of criticism consult Black, *Rhetorical Criticism*, pp. 6–9; Rosenfield, "Anatomy of Critical Discourse," 54–57; Arnold, *Criticism of Oral Rhetoric*, pp. 10–17, 278–282; Hillbruner, "Criticism as Persuasion"; Bryant, *Rhetorical Dimensions*, pp. 29–31; "Report of the Committee on...Rhetorical Criticism," in Bitzer and Black, *Prospect*, pp. 223–224. Among the historians who have dealt with the rhetorical nature of their craft are Gay, *Style in History*; Carl L. Becker, "The Art of Writing," in *Detachment and the Writing of History: Essays and Letters of Carl L. Becker*, ed. Phil L. Snyder, (Ithaca: Cornell University Press, 1958), pp. 121–144; Carl B. Cone, "Major Factors in the Rhetoric of Historians," *Quarterly Journal of Speech*, 33 (1947), 437–450; J. H. Hexter, "Historiography: The Rhetoric of History," in *International Encyclopedia of the Social Sciences*, ed. David L. Sills (New York: Free Press, 1968), VI, 368–373; Allan Nevins, *The Gateway to History*, rev. ed. (Chicago: Quadrangle Books, 1963), chap. 13; George M. Trevelyan, *Clio, A Muse, and Other Essays Literary and Pedestrian* (London: Longman's, Green and Co., 1914), chap. 1.

50.   Johann Gustav Droysen, *Outline of the Principles of History*, trans. E. Benjamin Andrews (Boston: Ginn and Co., 1893), p. 49.

51.   Everett Lee Hunt, "Rhetoric and Literary Criticism," *Quarterly Journal of Speech*, 21 (1935), 568.

52.   For a similar warning, though in a different context, see John Higham, "The Schism in American Scholarship," *American Historical Review*, 72 (1966), 1–21, from which the title of the present essay has been adapted.

53.   Karlyn Kohrs Campbell, "The Ontological Foundations of Rhetorical Theory," *Philosophy and Rhetoric*, 3 (1970), 97.

54.   Cf. Black, *Rhetorical Criticism*, p. 18; Bryant, *Rhetorical Dimensions*, p. 27; *Rhetoric: A Tradition in Transition*, ed. Walter R. Fisher (East Lansing: Michigan State University Press, 1974), pp. ix–x.

A Phenomenologically Oriented Approach to Rhetorical Criticism

RICHARD B. GREGG

Recently the dialogue concerning rhetorical criticism was stimulated and expanded with the appearance of a book on the subject by Edwin Black. The volume was written, as its author proclaims, "in the belief that variety is wanting in the methods of rhetoric," and "that the options available to the critic need to be multiplied...."[1] The book provides the genesis of a new frame of reference for criticism, not a systematic theory but an "orientation" to theory. In our present state of knowledge, writes Black, we should not hope to begin with a theory, but rather we can hope to evolve one after working with an orientation.[2]

In keeping with this spirit I would like to delineate a phenomenologically oriented approach to rhetorical criticism. The orientation to be expressed more closely approximates the interests of the psychologist concerned with the study of human behavior than it does the interests of the philosopher who seeks to discover the "essences" of things.[3] Also, rather than adopting the point of view and methodology of phenomenological psychology in its entirety, the orientation will be based on the primary postulate of the psychological approach and some of the implications of that postulate.

PHENOMENOLOGY, COMMUNICATION, AND THE CRITIC

The basic postulate about human behavior which will serve the rhetorical critic as well as the psychologist is that all behavior is determined by and pertinent to the perceptual field of the behaving organism, or, in other words, behavior is not so much a function of an external event as it is a product of the individual's perception of that event.[4] Phenomenological psychology concentrates its attention upon man's ability first to intellectualize and symbolize his environment into cognitive structures and then act upon the basis of those structures.

The phenomenological postulation is not confined to the phenomenologists alone. Carroll, for example, refers to the unifying theme in the work of Piaget as "the gradual unfolding of the individual's ability to construct an internal 'model' of the universe around him...."[5] Mowrer reconstructs the utility of the concept of mental imagery which was discarded by some behaviorists in the 1920s and 1930s.[6] Berelson and Steiner in a concluding note to their inventory of findings in the behavioral sciences point directly to the evidence accumulated bearing on man's behavior as influenced by his perception of reality.[7] The postulate seems to be firmly established and widely accepted.

Some attempt must now be made to arrive at an understanding of the components of a person's perceptual or cognitive reality. Boulding refers to cognitive reality when he describes the basic elements of a person's subjective knowledge of himself and the world around him. Boulding calls it a person's image of reality—an image in which a person sees himself as a being in time, located in the dimensions of space, grounded in past experience, acting in relationship to other persons, located in a world of nature and emotions. This subjective knowledge structure consists not only of images of fact but also of images of value which offer standards of judgement on some basis of good or bad.[8] The combination of what individuals perceive in any sense and what they think about what they perceive makes it clear that they deal with symbolic reality.

The relationship between a person's image of reality and his participation in communicative acts is as firmly established as the phenomenological postulate concerning human behavior. Langer's excellent analysis and synthesis of research on man's symbolic behavior traces the connection between the human ability to create symbols and the concomitant capacity to verbalize. In her opinion the decisive function in the making of language stems from the visual system in which the visual image is produced as a result of the human brain's mediating activity. Mental images in turn characteristically take on symbolic qualities which ultimately and logically demand and gain linguistic expression.[9] Speculating upon the origins of language, Langer concludes that:

> The great step from anthropoid to anthropos, animal to man, was taken when the vocal organs were moved to register the occurrence of an image, and stirred an equivalent occurrence in another brain, and the two creatures referred to the same thing. At that point the vocal habit that had long served for communion assumed the function of communication.[10]

One may want to question Langer's origin thesis, but the phenomenological pychologist understands the act of communication and its involvement with imagery and symbolic reality precisely as Langer does. According to Bemis and Phillips, a phenomenological view of communication is concerned with an individual's internal symbolic world and includes the idea that "each word and message has a cluster of images, some applicable to the society, some applicable to the individual, and some applicable to both."[11] The relationship between cognitive "realities" and communication is a reciprocal one, *i.e.*, the quality, intensity, shape, and force of images comprising an individual's symbolic reality will influence the character of his communication, and in a similar fashion a person' symbolic reality is to some extent shaped and colored by the communicative messages he receives. Boulding places a phenomenological view of communication in a rhetorical context when he refers to the fact that a public image is the result of a process of sharing messages within a universe of discourse,[12] and when he states that "The whole art of persuasion is the art of perceiving the weak spots in the images of others and of prying them apart with well constructed symbolic messages."[13]

At this juncture an outline, in the form of an initial summary, is possible for the approach to be taken by a critic as he begins his analytical task of explicating rhetorical discourse. Operating on the assumption that a person's perception and cognitive reality determine his attitudes and behavior, the critic focuses his energy upon discovering, defining, and describing those images which are active within the confines of the rhetorical act. He understands that the recipients of any rhetorical effort bring to the situation individual images of themselves and their reality which may in some form coalesce into shared group or public images. Such images will not be passive but will form a screen, actively sifting and sorting, interpreting and coloring, evaluating and judging, and finally accepting or rejecting all messages which pass through it. The rhetor in turn is one who attempts to manipulate images by the use of language. His choice of words and his manner of linguistic expression may reveal to some extent his perception of himself and his reality. But even if his discourse contains a fraudulent representation of his true beliefs, the critic knows that the rhetor's message will be involved with intentional cognitive structuring for some purpose.

COGNITIVE IMAGERY
IN COMMUNICATION

It remains now to demonstrate that the critical task just outlined can be accomplished and to attempt to gauge what advantages, if any, result from such an enterprise. The demonstration will be necessarily brief, but, it is hoped, suggestive.

The first question to be answered is whether it is possible to isolate and describe those images comprising cognitive reality which influence men and direct their energies. Various researchers have done so, among them Barbara Tuchman.[14] Her primary purpose is to provide an account of the activities of prominent anarchists during the last two decades before the First World War. To augment her analysis, Tuchman describes the anarchists' view of the contemporary world in which they lived and which they wanted to revolutionize. She reconstructs their vision of an ideal society in which men would cooperate because they wanted to, no government would be needed, and happiness would be achieved by all. The primary materials for her reconstruction are the writings and speeches of the anarchists themselves. She quotes, for example, Pierre Proudhon of France, who provides a clear picture of the anarchists' major enemy in the following words:

> *Government of man by man is slavery, its laws are cobwebs for the rich and chains of steel for the poor.... To be governed is to be watched, preached at, controlled, ruled, censored by persons who have neither wisdom or virtue. It is in every action and transaction to be registered, stamped, taxed, patented, licensed, assessed, measured, reprimanded, corrected, frustrated. Under pretext of the public good it is to be fined, harassed, vilified, beaten up, bludgeoned, disarmed, judged, condemned, imprisoned, shot, garrotted, deported, sold, betrayed, swindled, deceived, outraged, dishonored. That's government, that's its justice, that's its morality.*[15]

One can easily imagine how certain of the frustrated and poor, eager to find a scapegoat or an enemy to assume the mantle of sin and oppression, might respond to Proudhon's image of government. Tuchman describes how the anarchists, by verbal propaganda in all forms, painted a dismal cognitive world of the present to be swept away by a glorious society of the future. She also reconstructs the public image of the threat of anarchy, an image of sinister figures armed with bombs and guns and daggers leaving carnage and havoc in their wake, an image missing entirely the grand dream of hope which was a part of the anarchists' vision. She refers to press descriptions of the anarchists as "crypto-lunatics, degenerates, cowards, felons, 'odious fanatics prompted by perverted intellect and morbid frenzy.'"[16] The behavior of men in those times, based on their images of themselves and their adversaries, led to countless acts of violence and the assassination of six heads of state. Whereas Tuchman's analysis of the conitive imagery of the times serves incidentially to illustrate anarchist activity, the rhetorical critic would use a similar approach to explicate the rhetorical communication of the period and emphasize its significant relevance to human behavior.

An analysis of the rhetoric of Nazi Germany provides a clear example of the strategies of cognitive imagery. Because an abundance of Nazi governmental records, private diaries, speeches, and writing were recovered intact, scholars have succeeded in recreating the Nazi era with a high degree of accuracy. Rhetorical analyses of this fanatical episode in history seem particularly apropos since Hitler conceived the spoken and written word to be most significant weapons in the creation of the Third Reich.

The ideas expressed by Hitler, such as the belief in a master race, the hatred of Jews and Slavs, the contempt for democracy, the power of the absolute state, and the glorification of war, were not original with him, of course, nor were they created by the Nazis. Rather they were an integral part of German heritage, emanating, as Shirer says, "from that odd assortment of erudite but unbalanced philosophers, historians and teachers who captured the German mind during the century before Hitler. . . ."[17]

Viereck traces Nazism back to its ideational roots and finds it containing four major strains of thought: an exaggerated romanticisim, a science of racism, a vague economic socialism, and the alleged supernatural and unconscious forces of *Volk* activity.[18] The four strains may be illuminated by examining the words of such men as Fichte, who in his "addresses to the German Nation" in 1807 proclaimed the idea of a superior German *"Kultur"*; Hegel, who from his academic chair at the University of Berlin praised the power of the state and the virtues of war; and von Treitschke and Nietzsche, who stressed the principle of survival of the fittest in a jungle-like world.

Early in the nineteenth century an eccentric named Father Jahn orated his way through Germany praising Teutonic heroism and the spirit of the *Volk*. Composer Richard Wagner in his brilliant operas and erratic political writings created a *Weltanschauung* (world view) encompassing the concept of an unconscious race-force and a picture of the evils of Jewry. Hans Grimm contributed the notion of *Lebensraum* (national living space). Arthur de Gobineau and Houston Chamberlain concocted radical racial theories which lent themselves to Hitler's purposes. Out of all these ideas came Hilter's synthesis appearing in *Mein Kampf*, the second half of which is a development of the world view, or cognitive structure of reality, which later proved so captivating to Nazi officialdom. In the 1930's school children were indoctrinated with the Nazi world view, newspapers and churches supported it, and Goebbels propagandized it.

The power of Nazi rhetoric cannot be attributed solely to words; the German political and economic situation, which also had roots in earlier times, created tension and frustration among the population. But one cannot evade the fact that the coalescence of images appearing in the writings and speeches of Hitler and his Nazi leaders, images which gathered their force from ideas and themes already implanted in German tradition, was a potent force in securing that nation's willingness to follow the Fuhrer.[19]

Roberts' eyewitness account and analysis of one of the Nuremberg rallies assists in understanding the power of Hitler's imagery:

> At intervals, a curious tremor swept the crowd, and all around me individuals uttered a strange cry, a kind of emotional sigh, that invariably changed into a shout of "Heil Hitler.". . .Hitler's triumph was that of emotion and instinct over reason, a great upsurge of the subconscious in the German people. . . . He gave visions of ultimate expression to the repressed. . .some romance that would take away the drabness of their recent suffering.[20]

The significant phrase, "visions of ultimate expression," indicates the reaction to Hitler's world-view. Burke similarly concludes that an important attribute of Hitler's appeal was his presentation of a "world view" to people who had previously seen the world only piecemeal. The Nazi *Weltanschauung* included an image of the inborn dignity of a superior German race, of the evil Jew who became the perfect scapegoat for German ills, and of the promise of symbolic rebirth through the creation of a new German nation.[21] Hitler's rhetorical strategy can best be described as a strategy of combining existing images into a complete cognitive structure to capitalize on existent mental proclivities. A rhetorical analysis of that imagery is necessary for a complete understanding of Nazism.

The pages of American public address provide examples of cognitive structuring in a less fanatical context. Americans have been nourished on the idea that America, because of her natural abundance, the pioneering spirit and ingenuity of her people, and the democratic dreams of her leaders, is unique among the countries of the world. If the good life, the "great society," is going to be realized anywhere on earth, it will surely be here. Thomas Jefferson in his first inaugural address told the citizens of this nation that they possessed a "chosen country."[22] Only a short mental leap is required from this idea of national eminence to the corresponding notion that America has a chosen role to guide the world to the good life, to recast civilization in her image by example or otherwise. The rhetorical impact of this conceptualization is obvious in variations expressed in public discourse.

On the occasion of the dedication of the John Brown Memorial Park in 1910, Theodore Roosevelt proclaimed the history of America to be "the central feature of the history of the world; for the world has set its face hopefully toward our democracy. . . ." Therefore, said Roosevelt, each citizen bears the responsibility of doing well, not only for his own country but for all mankind.[23] Woodrow Wilson in his first inaugural address mentioned the image of American greatness several times,[24] and in his eloquent speech on the League of Nations delivered in Pueblo, Colorado, on September 25, 1919, projected his conceptualization of the American way of life upon the whole world. In that speech he premised his defense of and belief in the League on the notion that peaceful cooperation through resolution of disagreement by discussion based on a high moral code was the foremost goal of all nations.[25] Franklin Roosevelt, in his brief fourth inaugural address, found time to refer to the American faith "which has become the hope of all peoples in an anguished world."[26]

At least two implications of the image of American greatness emerge. First, the original vision of democratic greatness which gained expression in the work of the founding fathers must be adhered to, and, consequently, changes which are inevitable in a changing world must not be pictured as basic structural innovations but as modifications of the original and in keeping with the spirit of the Constitution. Thus, Franklin Roosevelt defended the New Deal by describing governmental policy as a necessary fulfillment of "old and tested American ideals" and metaphorically comparing his program to the White House renovations which still retained the building's original simplicity and strength.[27] John Dewey defended his concepts of education and the need for a new social order on the grounds that "they are a new version of the very same ideals that inspired the Declaration of Independence one hundred and sixty years ago."[28]

A second implication of the American image is the notion that "un-American" forces and ideals constitute "the enemy" to be avoided or defeated. A logical extension of this conception leads to the often used rhetorical strategy of identifying the people and ideas with which one disagrees with the conceptualization of the current popular enemy. For instance, both Al Smith and Herbert Hoover made public statements in 1936 equating the New Deal with the sinister designs of

Moscow.[29] Joseph McCarthy told the 25th Republican convention that the Truman policies were synonymous with Communist treason,[30] and two years later Senator Ralph Flanders placed McCarthy's tactics in league with Communist intentions.[31] The Commonwealth Club of California heard Thomas Brady defend the Southern position on segregation by charging that Communist-front organizers founded the NAACP,[32] and a month later Roy Wilkins charged that Communists and segregationists seemed to share the same objectives on the racial problem.[33]

From a phenomenological point of view the image of an American way of life over and against the image of an un-American enemy seems to be a significant thread running through American public discourse. The fact that such imagery appears so often attests to its emotional and motivational qualities.

THE CRITICAL APPROACH

The rhetorical critic who approaches his task phenomenologically is interested in these and other images which the rhetor constructs through his discourse and the methods he uses to construct them. He will attempt to discover the underlying value judgments present in discourse, for such judgments are a direct result of the rhetor's concept of reality. He will try to determine the degree to which the value judgments of an intended audience coincide with those of the rhetor, and if there is a disparity he will examine the rhetor's strategy for achieving audience identification on the level of values. The critic will examine the rhetor's allusions to physical reality and his interpretation of it and will try to gauge the possible reaction to such allusions. He will concentrate on the supporting and evidential material appearing in the discourse to determine its role in the development of cognitive structuring and the possible audience reaction to and interpretation of such material in light of its cognitive reality. And certainly the critic will analyze the language of the discourse, for in the rhetorical act the compact imagery of linguistic symbols is the vehicle for meaningful expression. The audience image of the rhetor must be evaluated. Finally and importantly, the critic must see the discourse as both a reaction to and an influence upon those existent societal images which comprise a major portion of the climate of opinion of the times.

To pre-judge the advantages and disadvantages of a phenomenological orientation to rhetorical criticism is difficult. But several advantages suggest themselves immediately and are worth considering. Black points out that one of the weaknesses of neo-Aristotelian criticism is its tendency to regard a discourse as a discrete entity with immediate effects being the only relevant ones and charges that, "There is little disposition among neo-Aristotelian critics to comprehend the discourse in a larger context, to see it, for example, as the movement study would, as part of a historical process of argument."[34] To evaluate a discourse on its own singular merits in terms of its immediate effect may be to overlook its more important long-range function of acting in conjunction with other discourses and events to solidify, alter, or break down the climate of opinion influencing policy and behavior. Thus, one would view Franklin Roosevelt's public statements before World War II as an attempt to get Americans to see that their frontiers of security extended beyond their shores and so to create public acceptance of Lend-Lease and assistance to Britain in sustaining and guarding her oceanic life-line. Alterations in public attitude lead to changes in the public dialogue and eventually to new courses of action. A phenomenological approach forces the critic to focus on the larger context.

A second advantage of a phenomenological orientation lies in the possibility that it may provide a more realistic insight into human motivation as it relates to communication. Contemporary psychologists have openly discussed the difficulties of constructing an adequate theory of motivation, and some have advocated that the concept be dropped from the psychological lexicon. At the 1962 Nebraska Symposium on Motivation, Kelly described a better way of talking about man's behavior: "We can start by saying that man copes with his environment by constructing it into similarities and contrasts." A system of constructs, says Kelly, "constitutes a ready-made format for future thinking [and]...means that a person has somewhat prepared himself to cope with all sorts of strange things that have not happened yet." Kelly concluded that "understanding a man's construct system is the first and most important step in understanding what is commonly known by that vaguest of psychological terms, 'motivation.'"[35] Phenomenological criticism, emphasizing the interplay of construct systems in the rhetorical act, is in keeping with Kelly's conclusion.

Finally, a phenomenological approach may provide a more realistic way of describing rhetorical strategems. A multitude of studies have been undertaken to determine the relative effectiveness of logical versus emotional appeals, well qualified evidence versus unqualified evidence versus no evidence, climactic versus anti-climactic order in argument, humor versus no humor, and other alternatives. Except for a qualified agreement that *ethos* appears to be an important factor in communication the results are inconclusive. Perhaps the reason is that researchers are neglecting the impact of the meat which fills in the spaces between the bones. To concentrate on evidence alone, without also examining the ideas being supported by the evidence, and ultimately the over-all conceptualizations supported or attacked by the ideas, seems a questionable method at best. A phenomenological approach demands a holistic analysis of the rhetorical act.

It would be naive to conclude that a phenomenological orientation is the only, or even the best, starting point for rhetorical criticism. But its promises make it a possible one.

Notes

1. Edwin Black, *Rhetorical Criticism: A Study in Method* (New York, 1965), p. viii.
2. *Ibid.*, p. 177.
3. The philosophical theory of phenomenology is constructed by Edmund Husserl, *Ideas Toward a Pure Phenomenology* (New York, 1931).
4. Arthur W. Combs and Donald Snygg, *Individual Behavior, A Perceptual Approach to Behavior* (New York. 1959), pp. 20–21.
5. John B. Carroll, *Language and Thought* (Englewood Cliffs, New Jersey, 1964), p. 79.
6. O. Hobart Mowrer, *Learning Theory and the Symbolic Processes* (New York, 1960), pp. 163, 174.
7. Bernard Berelson and Gary A. Steiner, *Human Behavior* (New York, 1964), pp. 662–667.
8. Kenneth Boulding, *The Image* (Ann Arbor, Mich., 1961), pp. 1–6.
9. Susanne K. Langer, "The Origins of Speech and Its Communicative Function," *Quarterly Journal of Speech*, XLVI (April 1960), 121–134.

10. *Ibid.*, p. 133.
11. James L. Bemis and Gerald M. Phillips, "A Phenomenological Approach to Communication Theory," *The Speech Teacher*, XIII (November 1964), 268.
12. Boulding, p. 132.
13. *Ibid.*, p. 134.
14. Barbara Tuchman, "The Anarchists," *The Atlantic Monthly*, May, 1963, pp. 91–110.
15. *Ibid.*, p. 92.
16. *Ibid.*, p. 110.
17. William L. Shirer, *The Rise and Fall of the Third Reich* (New York, 1960), p. 97.
18. Peter Viereck, *Meta-Politics* (New York, 1961), p. 4.
19. A recent analysis of Nazism which further confirms the considerable influence of nineteenth-century ideas on the populace of Hitler's Germany may be found in George L. Mosse, *The Crisis of German Ideology* (New York, 1964).
20. Stephen Roberts, *The House that Hitler Built* (New York, 1938), pp. 137–139.
21. Kenneth Burke, *The Philosophy of Literary Form* (New York, 1957), p. 165.
22. Thomas Jefferson, "First Inaugural Address," *American Prose and Poetry*, ed. Norman Foerster (New York, 1934), p. 214.
23. Theodore Roosevelt, "The New Nationalism," *Contemporary Forum*, ed. Ernest Wrage and Barnet Baskerville (New York, 1962), p. 28. Subsequent references to speeches will be found in this volume.
24. Woodrow Wilson, "First Inaugural Address," *Contemporary Forum*, pp. 41–43.
25. Woodrow Wilson, "In Support of the Proposed League of Nations," *Contemporary Forum*, pp. 76–86.
26. Franklin Roosevelt, "Fourth Inaugural Address," *Contemporary Forum*, p. 262.
27. Franklin Roosevelt, "Fireside Chat on the Accomplishments of the New Deal," *Contemporary Forum*, p. 166.
28. John Dewey, "Education and New Social Ideals," *Contemporary Forum*, p. 217.
29. Alfred E. Smith, "Come Back to Your Father's Home," *Comtemporary Forum*, pp. 168–178. Herbert Hoover, "A Holy Crusade for Liberty," *Contemporary Forum*, pp. 198–205.
30. Joseph McCarthy, "The Great Betrayal," *Contemporary Forum*, pp. 294–300.
31. Ralph E. Flanders, "Colossal Innocence in the United States Senate," *Contemporary Forum*, pp. 301–304.
32. Thomas Brady, "Segregation and the South," *Contemporary Forum*, p. 341.
33. Roy Wilkins, "Deep South Crisis," *Contemporary Forum*, p. 346.
34. Black, p. 33.
35. George A. Kelly, "Europe's Matrix of Decision," *Nebraska Symposium on Motivation*, ed. Marshall R. Jones (University of Nebraska Press, 1962), pp. 86–87.

The "Ideograph": A Link Between Rhetoric and Ideology

MICHAEL CALVIN MCGEE

In 1950, Kenneth Burke, apparently following Dewey, Mead, and Lippmann, announced his preference for the notion "philosophy of myth" to explain the phenomenon of "public" or "mass consciousness" rather than the then-prevalent concept "ideology."[1] As contemporary writers have pushed on toward developing this "symbolic" or "dramatistic" alternative, the concept "ideology" has atrophied.

Many use the term innocently, almost as a synonym for "doctrine" or "dogma" in political organizations;[2] and others use the word in a hypostatized sense that obscures or flatly denies the fundamental connection between the concept and descriptions of mass consciousness.[3] The concept seems to have gone the way of the dodo and of the neo-Aristotelian critic: As Bormann has suggested, the very word is widely perceived as being encrusted with the "intellectual baggage" of orthodox Marxism.[4]

Objecting to the use or abuse of any technical term would, ordinarily, be a sign of excessive crabbiness. But in this instance conceptualizations of "philosophy of myth," "fantasy visions," and "political scenarios," coupled with continued eccentric and/or narrow usages of "ideology," cosmetically camouflage significant and unresolved problems. We are presented with a brute, undeniable phenomenon: Human beings in collectivity behave and think differently than human beings in isolation. The collectivity is said to "have a mind of its own" distinct from the individual qua individual. Writers in the tradition of Marx and Mannheim explain this difference by observing that the only possibility of "mind" lies in the individual qua individual, in the human organism itself. When one appears to "think" and "behave" collectively, therefore, one has been tricked, self-deluded, or manipulated into accepting the brute existence of such fantasies as "public mind" or "public opinion" or "public philosophy." Symbolists generally want to say that this trick is a "transcendence," a voluntary agreement to believe in and to participate in a "myth." Materialists maintain that the trick is an insidious, reified form of "lie," a self-perpetuating system of beliefs and interpretations foisted on all members of the community by the ruling class. Burke, with his emphasis on the individuals who are tricked, concerns himself more with the structure of "motive" than with the objective conditions that impinge on and restrict the individual's freedom to develop a political consciousness. Neo-Marxians, with focus on tricksters and the machinery of trickery, say that the essential question posed by the fact of society is one of locating precise descriptions of the dialectical tension between a "true" and a "false" consciousness, between reality and ideology.[5]

Though some on both sides of the controversy would have it otherwise, there is no *error* in either position. Both "myth" and "ideology" presuppose a fundamental falsity in the common metaphor which alleges the existence of a "social organism." "Ideology," however, assumes that the exposure of falsity is a moral act: Though we have never experienced a "true consciousness," it is nonetheless theoretically accessible to us, and, because of such accessibility, we are morally remiss if we do not discard the false and approach the true. The falsity presupposed by "myth," on the other hand, is amoral because it is a purely poetic phenomenon, legitimized by rule of the poet's license, a "suspension of disbelief." A symbolist who speaks of "myth" is typically at great pains to argue for a value-free approach to the object of study, an approach in which one denies that "myth" is a synonym for "lie" and treats it as a falsehood of a peculiarly redemptive nature. Materialists, on the other hand, seem to use the concept "ideology" expressly to warrant normative claims regarding the exploitation of the "proletarian class" by self-serving plunderers. No error is involved in the apparently contradictory conceptions because, fundamentally, materialists and symbolists pursue two different studies: The Marxian asks how the "givens" of a human environment impinge on the development of political consciousness; the symbolist asks how the human symbol-using, reality-creating potential impinges on material reality, ordering it normatively, "mythically."

Errors arise when one conceives "myth" and "ideology" to be contraries, alternative and incompatible theoretical descriptions of the same phenomenon. The materialists' neglect of language studies and the consequent inability of Marxian theory to explain socially constructed realities is well-publicized.[6] Less well-described is the symbolists' neglect of the non-symbolic environment and the consequent inability of symbolist theory to account for the impact of material phenomena on the construction of social reality.[7] I do not mean to denigrate in any way the research of scholars attempting to develop Burke's philosophy of myth; indeed, I have on occasion joined that endeavor. I do believe, however, that each of us has erred to the extent that we have conceived the rubrics of symbolism as an *alternative* rather than *supplemental* description of political consciousness. The assertion that "philosophy of myth" is an alternative to "ideology" begs the question Marx intended to pose. Marx was concerned with "power," with the capacity of an elite class to control the state's political, economic, and military establishment, to dominate the state's information systems and determine even the consciousness of large masses of people. He was politically committed to the cause of the proletariat: If a norm was preached by the upper classes, it was by virtue of that fact a baneful seduction; and if a member of the proletarian class was persuaded by such an argument, that person was possessed of an "ideology," victimized and exploited. Not surprisingly, symbolists criticize Marx for his politics, suggesting that his is a wonderfully convenient formula which mistakes commitment for "historically scientific truth." By conceiving poetic falsity, we rid ourselves of the delusion that interpretation is scientific, but we also bury the probability that the myths we study as an alternative are thrust upon us by the brute force of "power." While Marx overestimated "power" as a variable in describing political consciousness, Burke, Cassirer, Polanyi, and others do not want to discuss the capacity even of a "free" state to determine political consciousness.[8]

If we are to describe the trick-of-the-mind which deludes us into believing that we "think" with/through/for a "society" to which we "belong," we need a theoretical model which accounts for both "ideology" and "myth," a model which neither denies human capacity to control "power" through the manipulation of symbols nor begs Marx's essential questions regarding the influence of "power" on creating and maintaining political consciousness. I will argue here that such a model must begin with the concept "ideology" and proceed to link that notion directly with the interests of symbolism.

I will elaborate the following commitments and hypotheses: If a mass consciousness exists at all, it must be empirically "present," itself a thing obvious to those who participate in it, or, at least, empirically manifested in the language which communicates it. I agree with Marx that the problem of consciousness is fundamentally practical and normative, that it is concerned essentially with describing and evaluating the legitimacy of public motives. Such consciousness, I believe, is always false, not because we are programmed automatons and not because we have a propensity to structure political perceptions in poetically false "dramas" or "scenarios," but because "truth" in politics, no matter how firmly we believe, is always an illusion. The falsity of an ideology is specifically rhetorical, for the illusion of truth and falsity with regard to normative commitments is the product of persuasion.[9] Since the clearest access to persuasion (and hence to ideology) is through the discourse used to produce it, I will suggest that ideology in practice is a political language, preserved in rhetorical documents, with the capacity to dictate decision and control public belief and behavior. Further, the political language which manifests ideology seems characterized by slogans, a vocabulary of "ideographs" easily mistaken for the technical terminology of political philosophy. An analysis of ideographic usages in political rhetoric, I believe, reveals interpenetrating systems or "structures" of public motives. Such structures appear to be "diachronic" and "synchronic" patterns of political consciousness which have the capacity both to control "power" and to influence (if not determine) the shape and texture of each individual's "reality."

HYPOTHETICAL CHARACTERISTICS
OF "IDEOGRAPHS"

Marx's thesis suggests that an ideology determines mass belief and thus restricts the free emergence of political opinion. By this logic, the "freest" members of a community are those who belong to the "power" elite; yet the image of hooded puppeteers twisting and turning the masses at will is unconvincing if only because the elite seems itself imprisoned by the same false consciousness communicated to the policy at large. When we consider the impact of ideology on freedom, and of power on consciousness, we must be clear that ideology is transcendent, as much an influence on the belief and behavior of the ruler as on the ruled. Nothing *necessarily* restricts persons who wield the might of the state. Roosevelts and Carters are as free to indulge personal vanity with capricious uses of power as was Idi Amin, regardless of formal "checks and balances." The polity can punish tyrants and maniacs after the fact of their lunacy or tyranny (if the polity survives it), but, in practical terms, the only way to shape or soften power at the moment of its exercise is prior persuasion. Similarly, no matter what punishment we might imagine "power" visiting upon an ordinary citizen, nothing *necessarily* determines individual behavior and belief. A citizen may be punished for eccentricity or disobedience after the fact of a crime, but, at the moment when defiance is contemplated, the only way to combat the impulse to criminal behavior is prior persuasion. I am suggesting, in other words, that social control in its essence is control over consciousness, the a priori influence that learned predispositions hold over human agents who play the roles of "power" and "people" in a given transaction.[10]

Because there is a lack of necessity in social control, it seems inappropriate to characterize agencies of control as "socializing" or "conditioning" media. No individual (least of all the elite who control the power of the state) is *forced* to submit in the same way that a conditioned dog is obliged to salivate or socialized children are required to speak English. Human beings are "conditioned," not directly to belief and behavior, but to a vocabulary of concepts that function as guides, warrants, reasons, or excuses for behavior and belief. When a claim is warranted by such terms as "law," "liberty," "tyranny," or "trial by jury," in other words, it is presumed that human beings will react predictably and autonomically. So it was that a majority of Americans were surprised, not when allegedly sane young men agreed to go halfway around the world to kill for God, country, apple pie, and no other particularly good reason, but, rather, when other young men displayed good common sense by moving to Montreal instead, thereby refusing to be conspicuous in a civil war which was none of their business. The end product of the state's insistence on some degree of conformity in behavior and belief, I suggest, is a *rhetoric* of control, a system of persuasion presumed to be effective on the whole community. We make a rhetoric of war to persuade us of war's necessity, but then forget that it is a rhetoric—and regard negative popular judgments of it as unpatriotic cowardice.

It is not remarkable to conceive social control as fundamentally rhetorical. In the past, however, rhetorical scholarship has regarded the rhetoric of control as a species of argumentation and thereby assumed that the fundamental unit of analysis in such rhetoric is an integrated set-series of propositions. This is, I believe, a mistake, an unwarranted abstraction: To argue is to test an affirmation or denial of claims; argument is the means of proving the truth of grammatical units, declarative sentences, that purport to be reliable signal representations of reality. Within the vocabulary of argumentation, the term "rule of law" makes no sense until it is made the subject or predicable of a proposition. If I say "The rule of law is a primary cultural value in the United States" or "Charles I was a cruel and capricious tyrant," I have asserted a testable claim that may be criticized with logically coordinated observations. When I say simply "the rule of law," however, my utterance cannot qualify logically as a claim. Yet I am conditioned to believe that "liberty" and "property" have an obvious meaning, a behaviorally directive self-evidence. Because I am taught to set such terms apart from my usual vocabulary, words used as agencies of social control may have an intrinsic force—and, if so, I may very well distort the key terms of social conflict, commitment, and control if I think of them as parts of a proposition rather than as basic units of analysis.

Though words only (and not claims), such terms as "property," "religion," "right of privacy," "freedom of speech," "rule of law," and "liberty" are more pregnant than propositions ever could be. They are the basic structural elements, the building blocks, of ideology. Thus they may be thought of as "ideographs," for, like Chinese symbols, they signify and "contain" a unique ideological commitment; further, they presumptuously suggest that each member of a community will see as a gestalt every complex nuance in them. What "rule of law" means is the series of propositions, all of them, that could be manufactured to justify a Whig/Liberal order. Ideographs are one-term sums of an orientation, the species of "God" or "Ultimate" term that will be used to symbolize the line of argument the meanest sort of individual *would* pursue, if that individual had the dialectical skills of philosophers, as a defense of a personal stake in and commitment to the society. Nor is one permitted to question the fundamental logic of ideographs: Everyone is conditioned to think of "the rule of law" as a *logical* commitment just as one is taught to think that "186,000 miles per second" is an accurate empirical description of the speed of light even though few can work the experiments or do the mathematics to prove it.[11]

The important fact about ideographs is that they exist in real discourse, functioning clearly and evidently as agents of political consciousness. They are not invented by observers; they come to be as a part of the real lives of the people whose motives they articulate. So, for example, "rule of law" is a more precise, objective motive than such observer-invented terms as "neurotic" or "paranoid style" or "*petit bourgeois*."

Ideographs pose a methodological problem *because* of their very specificity: How do we generalize from a "rule of law" to a description of consciousness that comprehends not only "rule of law" but all other like motives as well? What do we describe with the concept "ideograph," and how do we actually go about doing the specific cultural analysis promised by conceptually linking rhetoric and ideology?

Though both come to virtually the same conclusion, the essential argument seems more careful and useful in Ortega's notion of "the etymological man" than in Burke's poetically-hidden concept of "the symbol-using animal" and "logology":

> *Man, when he sets himself to speak, does so because he believes that he will be able to say what he thinks. Now, this is an illusion. Language is not up to that. It says, more or less, a part of what we think, and raises an impenetrable obstacle to the transmission of the rest. It serves quite well for mathematical statements and proofs.... But in proportion as conversation treats of more important, more human, more "real" subjects than these, its vagueness, clumsiness, and confusion steadily increase. Obedient to the inveterate prejudice that "talking leads to understanding," we speak and listen in such good faith that we end by misunderstanding one another far more than we would if we remained mute and set ourselves to divine each other. Nay, more: since our thought is in large measure dependent upon our language...it follows that thinking is talking with oneself and hence misunderstanding oneself at the imminent risk of getting oneself into a complete quandary.*[12]

All this "talk" generates a series of "usages" which unite us, since we speak the same language, but, more significantly, such "talk" *separates* us from other human beings who do not accept our meanings, our intentions.[13] So, Ortega claims, the essential demarcation of whole nations is language usage: "This gigantic architecture of usages is, precisely, society."[14] And it is through usages that a particular citizen's sociality exists:

> *A language, speech, is "what people say," it is the vast system of verbal usages established in a collectivity. The individual, the person, is from his birth submitted to the linguistic coercion that these usages represent. Hence the mother tongue is perhaps the most typical and clearest social phenomenon. With it "people" enter us, set up residence in us, making each an example of "people." Our mother tongue socializes our in-most being, and because of this fact every individual belongs, in the strongest sense of the word, to a society. He can flee from the society in which he was born and brought up, but in his flight the society inexorably accompanies him because he carries it within him. This is the true meaning that the statement "man is a social animal" can have.*[15]

Ortega's reference, of course, is to language generally and not to a particular vocabulary within language. So he worked with the vocabulary of greeting to demonstrate the definitive quality of linguistic usage when conceiving "society."[16] His reasoning, however, invites specification, attention to the components of the "architecture" supposedly created by usages.

Insofar as usages both unite and separate human beings, it seems reasonable to suggest that the functions of uniting and separating would be represented by specific vocabularies, actual words or terms. With regard to political union and separation, such vocabularies would consist of ideographs. Such usages as "liberty" define a collectivity, i.e., the outer parameters of a society, because such terms either do not exist in other societies or do not have precisely similar meanings. So, in the United States, we claim a common belief in "equality," as do citizens of the Union of Soviet Socialist Republics; but "equality" is not the same word in its meaning or its usage. One can therefore precisely define the difference between the two communities, in part, by comparing the usage of definitive ideographs. We are, of course, still able to interact with the Soviets despite barriers of language and usage. The interaction is possible because of higher-order ideographs—"world peace," "detente," "spheres of influence," etc.—that permit temporary union.[17] And, in the other direction, it is also true that there are special interests within the United States separated one from the other precisely by disagreements regarding the identity, legitimacy, or definition of ideographs. So we are divided by usages into subgroups: Business and labor, Democrats and Republicans, Yankees and Southerners are *united* by the ideographs that represent the political entity "United States" and *separated* by a disagreement as to the practical meaning of such ideographs.

The concept "ideograph" is meant to be purely descriptive of an essentially social human condition. Unlike more general conceptions of "Ultimate" or "God" terms, attention is called to the social, rather than rational or ethical, functions of a particular vocabulary. This vocabulary is precisely a group of *words* and not a series of symbols representing ideas. Ortega clearly, methodically, distinguishes a usage (what we might call "social" or "material" thought) from an *idea* (what Ortega would call "pure thought"). He suggests, properly, that *language gets in the way of thinking*, separates us from "ideas" we may have which cannot be surely expressed, even to ourselves, in the usages which imprison us. So my "pure thought" about liberty, religion, and property is clouded, hindered, made irrelevant by the existence in history of the ideographs "Liberty, Religion, and Property."[18] Because these terms are definitive of the society we have inherited, they are *conditions* of the society into which each of us is born, material ideas which we must accept to "belong." They penalize us, in a sense, as much as they protect us, for they prohibit our appreciation of an alternative pattern of meaning in, for example, the Soviet Union or Brazil.

In effect, ideographs—language imperatives which hinder and perhaps make impossible "pure thought"—are bound within the culture which they define. We can *characterize* an ideograph, say what it has meant and does mean as a usage, and some of us may be able to achieve an imaginary state of withdrawal from community long enough to speculate as to what ideographs *ought* to mean in the best of possible worlds; but the very nature of language forces us to keep the two operations separate: So, for example, the "idea" of "liberty" may be the subject of philosophical speculation, but philosophers can never be *certain* that themselves or their readers understand a "pure" meaning unpolluted by historical, ideographic usages.[19] Should we look strictly at material notions of "liberty," on the other hand, we distort our thinking by believing that a rationalization of a particular historical meaning is "pure," the truth of the matter.[20] Ideographs can *not* be used to establish or test truth, and vice versa, the truth, in ideal metaphysical senses, is a consideration irrelevant to accurate characterizations of such ideographs as "liberty." Indeed, if examples from recent history are a guide, the attempts to infuse usages with metaphysical meanings, or to confuse ideographs with the "pure" thought of philosophy, have resulted in the "nightmares" which Polanyi, for one, deplores.[21] The significance of ideographs is in their concrete history as usages, not in their alleged idea-content.

THE ANALYSIS OF IDEOGRAPHS

No one has ever seen an "equality" strutting up the driveway, so, if "equality" exists at all, it has meaning through its specific applications. In other words, we establish a meaning for "equality" by using the word as a description of a certain phenomenon; it has meaning only insofar as our description is acceptable, believable. If asked to make a case for "equality," that is to define the term, we are forced to make reference to its history by detailing the situations for which the word has been an appropriate description. Then, by comparisons over time, we establish an analog for the proposed present usage of the term. Earlier usages become precedent, touchstones for judging the propriety of the ideograph in a current circumstance. The meaning of "equality" does not rigidify because situations seeming to require its usage are never perfectly similar: As the situations vary, so the meaning of "equality" expands and contracts. The variations in meaning of "equality" are much less important, however, than the fundamental, categorical meaning, the "common denominator" of all situations for which "equality" has been the best and most descriptive term. The dynamism of "equality" is thus paramorphic, for even when the term changes its signification in particular circumstances, it retains a formal, categorical meaning, a constant reference to its history as an ideograph.

These earlier usages are vertically structured, related each to the other in a formal way, every time the society is called upon to judge whether a particular circumstance should be defined ideographically. So, for example, to protect ourselves from abuses of power, we have built into our political system an ideograph that is said to justify "impeaching" an errant leader: If the President has engaged in behaviors which can be described as "high crimes and misdemeanors," even that highest officer must be removed.

But what is meant by "high crimes and misdemeanors"? If Peter Rodino wishes to justify impeachment procedures against Richard Nixon in the Committee on the Judiciary of the House of Representatives, he must mine history for touchstones, precedents which give substance and an aura of precision to the ideograph "high crimes and misdemeanors." His search of the past concentrates on situations analogous to that which he is facing, situations involving actual or proposed "impeachment." The "rule of law" emerged as a contrary ideograph, and Rodino developed from the tension between "law" and "high crimes" an argument indicting Nixon. His proofs were historical, ranging from Magna Carta to Edmund Burke's impeachment of Warren Hastings. He was able to make the argument, therefore, only because he could organize a series of events, situationally similar, with an ideograph as the structuring principle. The structuring is "vertical" because of the element of *time*; that is, the deep meanings of "law" and "high crime" derive from knowledge of the way in which meanings have evolved over a period of time— awareness of the way an ideograph can be meaningful *now* is controlled in large part by what it meant *then*.[22]

All communities take pains to record and preserve the vertical structure of their ideographs. Formally, the body of nonstatutory "law" is little more than a literature recording ideographic usages in the "common law" and "case law."[23] So, too, historical dictionaries, such as the *O. E. D.*, detail etymologies for most of the Anglo-American ideographs. And any so-called "professional" history provides a record in detail of the events surrounding earlier usages of ideographs—indeed, the historian's eye is most usually attracted precisely to those situations involving ideographic applications.[24] The more significant record of vertical structures, however, lies in what might be called "popular" history. Such history consists in part of novels, films, plays, even songs; but the truly influential manifestation is grammar school history, the very first contact most have with their existence and experience as a part of a community.

To learn the meanings of the ideographs "freedom" and "patriotism," for example, most of us swallowed the tale of Patrick Henry's defiant speech to the Virginia House of Burgesses: "I know not what course others may take, but as for me, give me liberty or give me death!" These specific words, of course, were concocted by the historian William Wirt and not by Governor Henry. Wirt's intention was to provide a model for "the young men of Virigina," asking them to copy Henry's virtues and avoid his vices.[25] Fabricated events and words meant little, not because Wirt was uninterested in the truth of what really happened to Henry, but rather because what he wrote about was the definition of essential ideographs. His was a task of socialization, an exercise in epideictic rhetoric, providing the youth of his age (and of our own) with general knowledge of ideographic touchstones so that they might be able to make, or comprehend, judgments of public motives and of their own civic duty.

Though such labor tires the mind simply in imagining it, there is no trick in gleaning from public documents the entire vocabulary of ideographs that define a particular collectivity. The terms do not hide in discourse, nor is their "meaning" or function within an argument obscure: We might disagree metaphysically about "equality," and we might use the term differently in practical discourse, but I believe we can nearly always discover the functional meaning of the term by measure of its grammatic and pragmatic context.[26] Yet even a complete description of vertical ideographic structures leaves little but an exhaustive lexicon understood etymologically and diachronically—and no ideally precise explanation of how ideographs function *presently*.

If we find forty rhetorical situations in which "rule of law" has been an organizing term, we are left with little but the simple chronology of the situations as a device to structure the lot: Case One is distinct from Case Forty, and the meaning of the ideograph thus has contracted or expanded in the intervening time. But time is an irrelevant matter *in practice*. Chronological sequences are provided by analysts, and they properly reflect the concerns of theorists who try to describe what "rule of law" *may* mean, potentially, by laying out the history of what the term *has* meant. Such advocates as Rodino are not so scrupulous in research; they choose eight or nine of those forty cases to use as evidence in argument, ignore the rest, and impose a pattern of organization on the cases recommended (or forced) by the demands of a current situation. As Ortega argues with reference to language generally, key usages considered historically and diachronically are purely formal; yet in real discourse, and in public consciousness, they are *forces*:

> [A]ll that diachronism accomplishes is to reconstruct other comparative "pre-
> sents" of the language as they existed in the past. All that it shows us, then, is
> changes; it enables us to witness one present being replaced by another, the

succession of the static figures of the language, as the "film," with its motionless images, engenders the visual fiction of a movement. At best, it offers us a cinematic view of language, but not a dynamic understanding of how the changes were, and came to be, made. The changes are merely results of the making and unmaking process, they are the externality of language, and there is need for an internal conception of it in which we discover not resultant forms but the operating forces themselves.[27]

In Burke's terminology, describing a vertical ideographic structure yields a culture-specific and relatively precise "grammar" of one public motive. That motive is not captured, however, without attention to its "rhetoric."

Considered rhetorically, as *forces*, ideographs seem structured horizontally, for when people actually make use of them presently, such terms as "rule of law" clash with other ideographs ("principle of confidentiality" or "national security," for example), and in the conflict come to mean with reference to synchronic confrontations. So, for example, one would not ordinarily think of an inconsistency between "rule of law" and "principle of confidentiality." Vertical analysis of the two ideographs would probably reveal a consonant relationship based on genus and species: "Confidentiality" of certain conversations is a control on the behavior of government, a control that functions to maintain a "rule of law" and prevents 'tyranny" by preserving a realm of privacy for the individual.

The "Watergate" conflict between Nixon and Congress, however, illustrates how that consonant relationship can be restructured, perhaps broken, in the context of a particular controversy: Congress asked, formally and legally, for certain of Nixon's documents. He refused, thereby creating the appearance of frustrating the imperative value "rule of law." He attempted to excuse himself by matching a second ideograph, "principle of confidentiality," against normal and usual meanings of "rule of law." Before a mass television audience Nixon argued that a President's conversations with advisers were entitled to the same privilege constitutionally accorded exchanges between priest and penitent, husband and wife, lawyer and client. No direct vertical precedent was available to support Nixon's usage. The argument asked public (and later jurisprudential) permission to expand the meaning of "confidentiality" and thereby to alter its relationship with the "rule of law," making what appeared to be an illegal act acceptable. Nixon's claims were epideictic and not deliberative or forensic; he magnified "confidentiality" by praising the ideograph as if it were a person, attempting to alter its "standing" among other ideographs, even as an individual's "standing" in the community changes through praise and blame.[28]

Synchronic structural changes in the relative standing of an ideograph are "horizontal" because of the presumed consonance of an ideology; that is, ideographs such as "rule of law" are meant to be taken together, as a working unit, with "public trust," "freedom of speech," "trial by jury," and any other slogan characteristic of the collective life. If all the ideographs used to justify a Whig/Liberal government were placed on a chart, they would form groups or clusters of words radiating from the slogans originally used to rationalize "popular sovereignty"— "religion," "liberty," and "property." Each term would be a connector, modifier, specifier, or contrary for those fundamental historical commitments, giving them a meaning and a unity easily mistaken for logic. Some terms would be enshrined in the Constitution, some in law, some merely in conventional usage; but all would be constitutive of "the people." Though new usages can enter the equation, the ideographs remain essentially unchanged. But when we cause ideographs to *do work* in explaining, justifying, or guiding policy in specific situations, the relationship of ideographs changes. A "rule of law," for example, is taken for granted, a simple connector between "property" and "liberty," until a constitutional crisis inclines us to make it "come first." In Burke's vocabulary, it becomes the "title" or "god-term" of all ideographs, the center-sun about which every ideograph orbits. Sometimes circumstance forces us to sense that the structure is not consonant, as when awareness of racism exposes contradiction between "property" and "right to life" in the context of "open-housing" legislation. Sometimes officers of state, in the process of justifying particular uses of power, manufacture seeming inconsistency, as when Nixon pitted "confidentiality" against "rule of law." And sometimes an alien force frontally assaults the structure, as when Hitler campaigned against "decadent democracies." Such instances have the potential to change the structure of ideographs and hence the "present" ideology—in this sense, an ideology is dynamic and a *force*, always resilient, always keeping itself in some consonance and unity, but not always the *same* consonance and unity.[29]

In appearance, of course, characterizing ideological conflicts as synchronic *structural* dislocations is an unwarranted abstraction: An ideological argument could result simply from multiple usages of an ideograph. Superficially, for example, one might be inclined to describe the "bussing" controversy as a disagreement over the "best" meaning for "equality," one side opting for "equality" defined with reference to "access" to education and the other with reference to the goal, "being educated." An ideograph, however, is always understood in its relation to another; it is defined tautologically by using other terms in its cluster. If we accept that there are three or four or however many possible meanings for "equality," each with a currency and legitimacy, we distort the nature of the ideological dispute by ignoring the fact that "equality" is made meaningful, not within the clash of multiple usages, but rather in its relationship with "freedom." That is, "equality" defined by "access" alters the nature of "liberty" from the relationship of "equality" and "liberty" thought to exist when "equality" is defined as "being educated." One would not want to rule out the possibility that ideological disagreements, however rarely, could be simply semantic; but we are more likely to err if we assume the dispute to be semantic than if we look for the deeper structural dislocation which likely produced multiple usages as a disease produces symptoms. When an ideograph is at the center of a semantic dispute, I would suggest, the multiple usages will be either metaphysical or diachronic, purely speculative or historical, and in either event devoid of the force and currency of a synchronic ideological conflict.[30]

In the terms of this argument, two recognizable "ideologies" exist in any specific culture at one "moment." One "ideology" is a "grammar," a historically-defined diachronic structure of ideolograph-meanings expanding and contracting from the birth of the society to its "present." Another "ideology" is a "rhetoric," a situationally-defined synchronic structure of ideograph clusters constantly reorganizing itself to accommodate specific circumstances while maintaining its fundamental consonance and unity. A division of this sort, of course, is but an analytic convenience for talking about two *dimensions* (vertical and horizontal) of a single phenomenon: No present ideology can be divorced from past commitments if only because the very words used to express present dislocations have a history that establishes the category of their meaning. And no diachronic ideology can be divorced from the "here-and-now" if only because its entire *raison d'être* consists in justifying the form and direction of collective behavior. Both of these structures must be understood and described before one can claim to have constructed a theoretically precise explanation of a society's ideology, of its repertoire of public motives.

CONCLUSION

One of the casualties of the current "pluralist" fad in social and political theory has been the old Marxian thesis that governing elites control the masses by creating, maintaining, and manipulating a mass consciousness suited to perpetuation of the existing order.[31] Though I agree that Marx probably overestimated the influence of an elite, it is difficult *not* to see a "dominant ideology" which seems to exercise decisive influence in political life. The question, of course, turns on finding a way accurately to define and to describe a dominant ideology. Theorists writing in the tradition of Dewey, Burke, and Cassirer have, in my judgment, come close to the mark; but because they are bothered by poetic metaphors, these symbolists never conceive their work as description of a mass consciousness. Even these writers, therefore, beg Marx's inescapable question regarding the impact of "power" on the way we think. I have argued here that the concepts "rhetoric" and "ideology" may be linked without poetic metaphors, and that the linkage should produce a description and an explanation of dominant ideology, of the relationship between the "power" of a state and the consciousness of its people.

The importance of symbolist constructs is their focus on *media* of consciousness, on the discourse that articulates and propagates common beliefs. "Rhetoric," "sociodrama," "myth," "fantasy vision," and "political scenario" are not important because of their *fiction*, their connection to poetic, but because of their *truth*, their links with the trick-of-the-mind that deludes individuals into believing that they "think" with/for/through a social organism. The truth of symbolist constructs, I have suggested, appears to lie in our claim to see a legitimate social reality in a vocabulary of complex, high-order abstractions that refer to and invoke a sense of "the people." By learning the meaning of ideographs, I have argued, everyone in society, even the "freest" of us, those who control the state, seem predisposed to structured mass responses. Such terms as "liberty," in other words, constitute by our very use of them in political discourse an ideology that governs or "dominates" our consciousness. In practice, therefore, ideology is a political language composed of slogan-like terms signifying collective commitment.

Such terms I have called "ideographs." A formal definition of "ideograph," derived from arguments made throughout this essay, would list the following characteristics: An ideograph is an ordinary-language term found in political discourse. It is a high-order abstraction representing collective commitment to a particular but equivocal and ill-defined normative goal. It warrants the use of power, excuses behavior and belief which might otherwise be perceived as eccentric or antisocial, and guides behavior and belief into channels easily recognized by a community as acceptable and laudable. Ideographs such as "slavery" and "tyranny," however, may guide behavior and belief negatively by branding unacceptable behavior. And many ideographs ("liberty," for example) have a non-ideographic usage, as in the sentence, "Since I resigned my position, I am at liberty to accept your offer." Ideographs are culture-bound, though some terms are used in different signification across cultures. Each member of the community is socialized, conditioned, to the vocabulary of ideographs as a pre-requisite for "belonging" to the society. A degree of tolerance is usual, but people are expected to understand ideographs within a range of usage thought to be acceptable: The society will inflict penalties on those who use ideographs in heretical ways and on those who refuse to respond appropriately to claims on their behavior warranted through the agency of ideographs.

Though ideographs such as "liberty," "religion," and "property" often appear as technical terms in social philosophy, I have argued here that the ideology of a community is established by the usage of such terms in specifically rhetorical discourse, for such usages constitute excuses for specific beliefs and behaviors made by those who executed the history of which they were a part. The ideographs used in rhetorical discourse seem structured in two ways: In isolation, each ideograph has a history, an etymology, such that current meanings of the term are linked to past usages of it diachronically. The diachronic structure of an ideograph establishes the parameters, the category, of its meaning. All ideographs taken together, I suggest, are thought at any specific "moment" to be consonant, related one to another in such a way as to produce unity of commitment in a particular historical context. Each ideograph is thus connected to all others as brain cells are linked by synapses, synchronically in one context at one specific moment.

A complete description of an ideology, I have suggested, will consist of (1) the isolation of a society's ideographs, (2) the exposure and analysis of the diachronic structure of every ideograph, and (3) characterization of synchronic relationships among all the ideographs in a particular context. Such a description, I believe, would yield a theoretical framework with which to describe interpenetrating material and symbolic environments: Insofar as we can explain the diachronic and synchronic tensions among ideographs, I suggest, we can also explain the tension between *any* "given" human environment ("objective reality") and any "projected" environments ("symbolic" or "social reality") latent in rhetorical discourse.

Notes

1. Kenneth Burke, *A Rhetoric of Motives* (New York: Prentice-Hall, 1950), pp. 197–203; John Dewey, *The Public and Its Problems* (New York: Henry Holt, 1927); George H. Mead, *Mind, Self, and Society* (Chicago: Univ. of Chicago Press, 1934); and Walter Lippmann, *Public Opinion* (1922; rpt. New York: Free Press, 1965).

   Duncan groups the American symbolists by observing that European social theorists using "ideology" were concerned with "consciousness" (questions about the *apprehension* of society) while symbolists using poetic metaphors were concerned with a "philosophy of action" (questions about the way we do or ought *behave* in society). In rejecting the concept and theory of "ideology," Burke refused to consider the relationship between consciousness and action except as that relationship can be characterized with the agency of an a priori poetic metaphor, "dramatism." His thought and writing, like that of a poet, is therefore freed from truth criteria: Supposing his *form*, no "motive" outside the dramatistic terminology need be recognized or accounted for *in its particularity*. Though Burkeans are more guilty than

Burke, I think even he tends to redefine motives rather than account for them, to cast self-confessions in "scenarios" rather than deal with them in specific. One might say of "dramatism" what Bacon alleged regarding the Aristotelian syllogism, that it is but a form which chases its tail, presuming in its metaphoric conception the truth of its descriptions. See Hugh Dalziel Duncan, *Symbols in Society* (New York: Oxford Univ. Press, 1968), pp. 12–14; Richard Dewey, "The Theatrical Analogy Reconsidered," *The American Sociologist*, 4 (1969), 307–311; and R. S. Perinbanayagam, "The Definition of the Situation: an Analysis of the Ethnomethodological and Dramaturgical View," *Sociological Quarterly*, 15 (1974), 521–541.

2. See, e.g., Arthur M. Schlesigner, Jr., "Ideology and Foreign Policy: The American Experience," in George Schwab, ed., *Ideology and Foreign Policy* (New York: Cyrco, 1978), pp. 124–132; and Randall L. Bytwerk, "Rhetorical Aspects of the Nazi Meeting: 1926–1933," *Quarterly Journal of Speech*, 61 (1975), 307–318.

3. See, e.g., William R. Brown, "Ideology as Communication Process," *Quarterly Journal of Speech*, 64 (1978), 123–140; and Jürgen Habermas, "Technology and Science as 'Ideology,'" in *Toward a Rational Society*, trans. Jeremy J. Shapiro (1968; Boston: Beacon, 1970), pp. 81–122.

4. Bormann's distrust of "ideology" was expressed in the context of an evaluation of his "fantasy theme" technique at the 1978 convention of the Speech Communication Association. See "Fantasy Theme Analysis: An Exploration and Assessment," S. C. A. 1978 Seminar Series, Audio-Tape Cassettes. For authoritative accounts of the various "encrustations," see George Lichtheim, "The Concept of Ideology," *History and Theory*, 4 (1964–1965), 164–195; and Hans Barth, *Truth and Ideology*, trans. Frederic Lilge, 2nd ed. 1961 (Berkeley: Univ. of California Press, 1976).

5. See Kenneth Burke, *Permanence & Change*, 2nd ed. rev. (1954; rpt. Indianapolis: Bobbs-Merrill, 1965), pp. 19–36, 216–236; Karl Marx and Frederick Engels, *The German Ideology* (1847), trans. and ed. Clemens Dutt, W. Lough, and C. P. Magill, in *The Collected Works of Karl Marx and Frederick Engels*, 9+ vols. (Moscow: Progress Publishers, 1975–1977+), 5:3–5, 23–93; Karl Mannheim, *Ideology and Utopia*, trans. Louis Wirth and Edward Shils (1929; rpt. New York: Harvest Books, 1952); and Martin Seliger, *The Marxist Conception of Ideology: A Critical Essay* (Cambridge: Cambridge Univ. Press, 1977).

My purpose here is to expose the issue between symbolists (generally) and materialists (particularly Marxians). This of course results in some oversimplification: With regard to the brute problem of describing "consciousness," at least two schools of thought are not here accounted for, Freudian psychiatry and American empirical psychology. Freudians are generally connected with the symbolist position I describe here, while most of the operational conceptions of American empirical psychology (especially social psychology) may fairly be associated with Marxian or neo-Marxian description. Moreover, I treat the terms "ideology" and "myth" as less ambiguous than their history as concepts would suggest. My usage of the terms, and the technical usefulness I portray, reflects my own conviction more than the sure and noncontroversial meaning of either "myth" or "ideology."

6. See, e.g., Willard A. Mullins, "Truth and Ideology: Reflections on Mannheim's Paradox," *History and Theory*, 18 (1979), 142–154; William H. Shaw, "'The Handmill Gives You the Feudal Lord': Marx's Technological Determinism," *History and Theory*, 18 (1979), 155–176; Jean-Paul Sartre, *Critique of Dialectical Reason*, trans. Alan Sheridan-Smith (1960; Eng. trans. London: NLB, 1976), pp. 95–121; and Jean-Paul Sartre, *Search for a Method*, trans. Hazel E. Barnes (1958; Eng. trans. New York: Vintage, 1968), pp. 35–84.

7. See W. G. Runciman, "Describing," *Mind*, 81 (1972), 372–388; Perinbanayagam; and Herbert W. Simons, Elizabeth Mechling, and Howard N. Schreier, "Mobilizing for Collective Action From the Bottom Up: The Rhetoric of Social Movements," unpub. MS., Temple Univ., pp. 48–59, forthcoming in Carroll C. Arnold and John Waite Bowers, eds., *Handbook of Rhetorical and Communication Theory*.

8. Adolph Hitler, this century's archetype of absolute power—as well as absolute immorality—rose to dominance and maintained himself by putting into practice symbolist theories of social process. Hitler's mere existence forces one to question symbolist theories, asking whether "sociodramas" and "rhetorics" and "myths" are things to be studied scientifically or wild imaginings conjured up from the ether, deviltools playing upon human weakness and superstition, and therefore things to be politically eradicated. In the face of Hitler, most symbolists adopted a high moral stance of righteous wrath, concentrating on the evil of the man while underplaying the tools he used to gain and keep power. But subtly they modified their logics: Burke is most sensitive to the problem, but in the end he does little more than demonstrate the moral polemical power of dramatistic methods of criticism, becoming the "critic" of his early and later years rather than the "historian" and "theorist" of his middle years. Cassirer's reaction is more extreme, backing away from the logical implications of the symbolist epistemology he argued for before Hitler, begging the problem of power by characterizing the state itself as nothing but a "myth" to be transcended. Hitler was an inspiration to Polanyi, causing him to take up epistemology as a vehicle to discredit social philosophy generally. In the process Polanyi became an unabashed ideological chauvinist of his adopted culture. See, resp., Kenneth Burke, "The Rhetoric of Hitler's 'Battle,'" in *The Philosophy of Literary Form*, 3rd ed. (Berkeley: Univ. of California Press, 1973), pp. 191–220, and cf. Kenneth Burke, *Attitudes toward History* (1937; 2nd ed. rev. rpt. Boston: Beacon, 1961), pp. 92–107; Ernst Cassirer, *The Philosophy of Symbolic Forms*, trans. Ralph Manheim (1923–1929; Eng. trans. New Haven: Yale Univ. Press, 1953), 1:105–114; Ernst Cassirer, *The Myth of the State* (New Haven: Yale Univ. Press, 1946); Michael Polanyi, *The Logic of Liberty* (Chicago: Univ. of Chicago Press, 1951), pp. 93–110, 138–153; and Michael Polanyi, *Personal Knowledge: Towards a Post-Critical Philosophy* (1958; rpt. Chicago: Univ. of Chicago Press, 1962), pp. 69–131, 203–248, 299–324.

9. I am suggesting that the topic of "falsity" is necessary whenever one's conception of consciousness transcends the mind of a single individual. This is so because the transcendent consciousness, by its very conception, is a legitimizing agency, a means to warrant moral judgments (as in Perelman) or a means to create the fiction of verification when verification is logically impossible (as in Ziman and Brown). To fail to acknowledge the undeniable falsity of *any* description of mass or group consciousness is to create the illusion that one or another series of normative claims have an independent "facticity" about them. In my view Brown and Ziman are reckless with hypostatized "descriptions" of the consciousness of an intellectual elite, a "scientific community," which itself is in fact a creature of convention, in the specific terms of "description" a fiction of Ziman's and Brown's mind and a rhetorical vision for their readers. See Brown; Ch. Perelman and L. Olbrechts-Tyteca, *The New Rhetoric: A Treatise on Argumentation*, trans. John Wilkinson and Purcell Weaver (1958; Eng. trans. Notre Dame: Univ. of Notre Dame Press, 1969), pp. 31–35, 61–74; J. M. Ziman, *Public Knowledge: An Essay Concerning the Social Dimension of Science* (Cambridge: Cambridge Univ. Press, 1968), pp. 102–142; and contrast George Edward Moore, *Principia Ethica* (1903; rpt. Cambridge: Cambridge Univ. Press, 1965), esp. pp. 142–180; and Bruce E. Gronbeck, "From 'Is' to 'Ought': Alternative Strategies," *Central States Speech Journal*, 19 (1968), 31–39.

10. See Kenneth Burke, "A Dramatistic View of the Origins of Language and Postscripts on the Negative" in *Language as Symbolic Action* (Berkeley: Univ. of California Press, 1966), pp. 418–479, esp. pp. 453–463; Hannah Arendt, "What Is Authority?" in *Between Past and Future* (New York: Viking, 1968), pp. 91–141; Hannah Arendt, "Lying in Politics: Reflections on the Pentagon Papers," in *Crises of the Republic* (New York: Harcourt Brace Jovanovich, 1972), pp. 1–47; Jürgen Habermas, "Hannah Arendt's Communications Concept of Power," *Social Research*, 44 (1977), 3–24; J. G. A. Pocock, *Politics, Language and Time* (New York: Atheneum, 1973), pp. 17–25, 202–232; and Robert E. Goodwin, "Laying Linguistic Traps," *Political Theory*, 5 (1977), 491–504.

11. See Kenneth Burke, *A Grammar of Motives* (New York: Prentice-Hall, 1945), pp. 43–46, 415–418; Burke, *Rhetoric*, pp. 275–276, 298–301; Ernst Cassirer, *Language and Myth*, trans. Susanne K. Langer (1946; Eng. trans. 1946; rpt. New York: Dover, 1953), pp. 62–83; Richard M. Weaver, *The Ethics of Rhetoric* (1953; rpt. Chicago: Gateway, 1970), pp. 211–232; and Rosalind Coward and John Ellis, *Language and Materialism* (London: Routledge & Kegan Paul, 1977), pp. 61–152.

12. José Ortega y Gasset, *Man and People*, trans. Willard R. Trask (New York: Norton, 1957), p. 245.

13. *Ibid.*, pp. 192–221, 258–272.

14. *Ibid.*, p. 221.

15. *Ibid.*, p. 251.

16. *Ibid.*, pp. 176–191.

17. See Murray Edelman, *Political Language* (New York: Academic Press, 1977), pp. 43–49, 141–155; Schwab, pp. 143–157; and Thomas M. Franck and Edward Weisband, *Word Politics: Verbal Strategy Among the Superpowers* (New York: Oxford Univ. Press, 1972), pp. 3–10, 96–113, 137–169.

18. Ortega y Gasset, *Man and People*, pp. 243–252. Further, contrast Ortega and Marx on the

nature of "idea": José Ortega y Gasset, *The Modern Theme*, trans. James Cleugh (1931: rpt. New York: Harper, 1961), pp. 11–27; and Marx and Engels, pp. 27–37. See, also, Coward and Ellis, pp. 84–92, 122–135.

19. Ortega y Gasset, *Man and People*, pp. 57–71, 94–111, 139–191. Husserl's recognition of *praxis* and contradiction in his doctrine of "self-evidence" confirms Ortega's critique: Edmund Husserl, *Ideas: General Introduction to Pure Phenomenology*, trans. W. R. Boyce Gibson (1913; Eng. trans. 1931; rpt. London: Collier Macmillan, 1962), pp. 353–367. See, also, Schutz's and Luckmann's elaboration of the bases of Carnedean skepticism: Alfred Schutz and Thomas Luckmann, *The Structures of the Life-World*, trans. Richard M. Zaner and H. Tristram Engelhardt, Jr. (Evanston: Northwestern Univ. Press, 1973), pp. 182–229.

20. Michel Foucault, *The Archaeology of Knowledge*, trans. A. M. Sheridan Smith (1969; Eng. trans. New York: Pantheon, 1972), pp. 178–195; H. T. Wilson, *The American Ideology: Science, Technology and Organization as Modes of Rationality in Advanced Industrial Societies* (London: Routledge & Kegan Paul, 1977), pp. 231–253; and Roger Poole, *Towards Deep Subjectivity* (New York: Harper & Row, 1972), pp. 78–112.

21. Michael Polanyi and Harry Prosch, *Meaning* (Chicago: Univ. of Chicago Press, 1975), pp. 9, 22: "We have all learned to trace the collapse of freedom in the twentieth century to the writings of certain philosophers, particularly Marx, Nietzsche, and their common ancestors, Fichte and Hegel. But the story has yet to be told how we came to welcome as liberators the philosophies that were to destroy liberty.... We in the Anglo-American sphere have so far escaped the totalitarian nightmares of the right and left. But we are far from home safe. For we have done little, in our free intellectual endeavors, to uphold thought as an independent, self-governing force." Contrast this "personal knowledge" explanation with Max Horkheimer and Theodor W. Adorno, *Dialectic of Enlightenment*, trans. John Cumming (1944; Eng. trans. New York: Herder and Herder, 1972), pp. 255–256; and Jacques Ellul, *Propaganda: The Formation of Men's Attitudes*, trans. Konrad Kellen and Jean Lerner (1962; Eng. trans. New York: Vintage, 1973), pp. 52–61, 232–257.

22. See Peter Rodino's opening remarks in "Debate on Articles of Impeachment," U.S., Congress, House of Representatives, Committee on the Judiciary, 93rd Cong., 2nd sess., 24 July 1974, pp. 1–4.
    The "vertical/horizontal" metaphor used here to describe the evident structure of ideographs should not be confused with Ellul's idea (pp. 79–84) of the structural effects of "Propaganda." Lasky's analysis of "the English ideology" represents the "vertical" description I have in mind: Melvin J. Lasky, *Utopia and Revolution* (Chicago: Univ. of Chicago Press, 1976), pp. 496–575.

23. See Edward H. Levi, *An Introduction to Legal Reasoning* (Chicago: Univ. of Chicago Press, 1948), esp. pp. 6–19, 41–74; Perelman and Tyteca, pp. 70–74, 101–02, 350–357; and Duncan, pp. 110–123, 130–140.

24. Collingwood suggests that the content or ultimate subject matter of history should consist of explaining such recurrent usages ("ideographs") as "freedom" and "progress": R. G. Collingwood, *The Idea of History* (1946: rpt. London: Oxford Univ. Press, 1972), pp. 302–334. See, also, Herbert J. Muller, *The Uses of the Past* (New York: Oxford Univ. Press, 1952), pp. 37–38.

25. See William Wirt, *Sketches of the Life and Character of Patrick Henry*, 9th ed. (Philadelphia: Thomas Cowperthwait, 1839) dedication and pp. 417–443; Judy Hample, "The Textual and Cultural Authenticity of Patrick Henry's 'Liberty or Death' Speech," *Quarterly Journal of Speech*, 63 (1977), 298–310; and Robert D. Meade, *Patrick Henry: Portrait in the Making* (New York: Lippincott, 1957), pp. 49–58.

26. At least two strategies (that is, two theoretical mechanisms) have the capacity to yield fairly precise descriptions of functional "meaning" within situational and textual contexts: See Hans-Georg Gadamer, *Philosophical Hermeneutics*, trans. David E. Linge (Berkeley: Univ. of California Press, 1976), pp. 59–94; and Umberto Eco, *A Theory of Semiotics* (Bloomington: Indiana Univ. Press, 1976), pp. 48–150, 276–313.

27. Ortega y Gasset, *Man and People*, p. 247. Cf. Ferdinand de Saussure, *Course in General Linguistics*, trans. Wade Baskin, ed. Charles Bally and Albert Sechehaye in collaboration with Albert Riedlinger (1915; Eng. trans. 1959; rpt. New York: McGraw-Hill, 1966), pp. 140–190, 218–221.

28. See Richard M. Nixon, "Address to the Nation on the Watergate Investigation," *Public Papers of the Presidents of the United States* (Washington, D.C.: U.S. Government Printing Office, 1975), Richard Nixon, 1973, pp. 691–698, 710–725. Lucas' analysis of "rhetoric and revolu-

tion" (though it is more "idea" than "terministically" conscious) represents the "horizontal" description I have in mind: Stephen E. Lucas, *Portents of Rebellion: Rhetoric and Revolution in Philadelphia, 1765–1776* (Philadelphia: Temple Univ. Press, 1976).

29. See Jürgen Habermas, *Communication and the Evolution of Society*, trans. Thomas McCarthy (1976; Eng. trans. Boston: Beacon, 1979), pp. 1–68, 130–205.

30. See Foucault, pp. 149–165.

31. See Nicholas Abercrombie and Bryan S. Turner, "The Dominant Ideology Thesis," *British Journal of Sociology*, 29 (1978), 149–170.

Lincoln at Cooper Union:
A Rationale
for Neo-Classical Criticism

———————————— G. P. Mohrmann and Michael C. Leff ————————————

The last issue of this journal included our critique of Lincoln's Cooper Union Address, and we assume that the neo-classical origins of the analysis were apparent, even though methodological concerns were slighted. A more elaborate statement on methodology appeared in an earlier version, but the editors cautioned that the single article did not offer sufficient scope for both an explication of the rationale and its application. Accepting their advice, we deleted most of the theoretical material, but having offered the critique, we want to explore further its theoretical bases.

Our approach is neo-classical. That is, it is rooted in the rhetorical theory of antiquity. This is the same source that produced neo-Aristotelianism, "the dominant mode of rhetorical criticism of the present century in the United States."[1] Our critique shares most of the presuppositions that inform this traditional mode, but there is one essential difference. Treating "rhetorical discourses as discrete communications in specific contexts,"[2] neo-Aristotelianism is preoccupied with the particular. This orientation implies a rejection of formal criteria and almost forces the critic to rely on the criterion of empirical effect. On the other hand, we treat Lincoln's speech within the framework of the classical conception of oratorical genres. As opposed to the nominalism implicit in neo-Aristotelianism, genre theory permits an abstract conception of audience and of rhetorical situations. It, therefore, enables the critic to seek formal ends for critical judgment.

Our purpose, here, is to explore the potential of genre theory as a corrective to some defects in the neo-Aristotelian mode. We shall begin with reference to the development of neo-Aristotelianism, comment on its rejection of generic distinctions and note the limitations that this rejection imposes. We shall then suggest that the conception of genre can help invigorate critical inquiry based on classical models. We would emphasize, however, the provisional nature of our formulation; we do not consider it to be definitive, and we recognize that our version of neo-classicism has its own limitations.

NEO-ARTISTOTELIAN CRITICISM

Although the neo-Aristotelian position is most fully delineated when one moves from "The Literary Criticism of Oratory"[3] to *A History and Criticism of American Public Address*[4] to *Speech Criticism*,[5] Wichelns remains the commanding presence.

His essay "set the pattern and determined the direction"[6] of this approach, and the direction in which he moved took "certain Aristotelian conceptions as safe points of departure."[7] The most crucial of these was the centrality of audience. Of course, Aristotle and other classical theorists do not spell out a critical system, but "they do imply one. If a literary work may be said to have three references—to the universe, to the writer, and to the audience—Greek rhetorical theory, like the Renaissance criticism which descends from it, thinks the audience-reference by far the most important."[8] Seeking to revive the dormant rhetorical perspective, Wichelns makes this same reference the basis for the rhetorical analysis of oratory. The importance of this principle can scarcely be exaggerated; without it, modern speech criticsm would not have been possible. Nevertheless, Wichelns' determination to separate rhetoric from literature leads to a restricted conception of audience.

As the very title of this essay suggests, he thinks it important to distinguish between literary and rhetorical activity. The literary artist, he asserts, "is free to fulfill" (p. 56) his own law because literature is concerned "with permanent values" (p. 57). The rhetor, however is "perpetually in bondage to the occasion and the audience" (p. 56). Consequently, criticism of oratory must regard "a speech as a communication to a specific audience" and must be "concerned with effect" (p. 54). Permanence and universality are reserved for the literary critic, because "the result can only be confusion" when a speaker is "made to address a universal audience" (p. 57). Rhetorical criticism, then, finds its *raison d'etre* in the specifics of the particular situation, and it is in these terms that the critic must interpret the function of "personality," "proof," "arrangement," "delivery," or any other of Wichelns' topics (pp. 56–57), all of which originate in classical theory.

If Wichelns succeeds in establishing rhetorical criticism as an independent activity, his program also obscures formalistic aspects of the classical inheritance. Despite his many borrowings from Aristotle, Wichelns says nothing about oratorical genres. This is hardly accidental, for genre theory is notoriously abstract; it rejects time and place as bases for classification and groups historical situations into general categories. As a result, it raises questions about "the relation of the class and the individuals composing it, the one and the many, the nature of universals."[9] Such questions cannot be a part of Wichelns' program because they smack of literary judgment. It is only in literature that one hears "the voice of the human spirit addressing itself to men of all ages and times" (p. 57), a voice transcending particular situations.

Neo-Aristotelians attempt to modify and escape this particularism. For example, one reads that the consummate critic "appraises the entire event by assigning it comparative rank in the total enterprise of speaking"[10] and that a speech may be criticized "as a finished product having certain rhetorical features which conform agreeably to fixed principles or rules."[11] One reads also of touchstones. But to assign comparative rank or to note agreeable conformity to fixed principles demands some notion of permanence, and such standards simply are not available in a system oriented completely to the specific situation. Here, the appropriate standard is that of immediate effect, and this single criterion makes it difficult, if not impossible, to develop intrinsic artistic standards. The system supplies no logical mechanism for connecting apparently disparate events.

Since Aristotle speaks of oratorical genres, this would seem a likely source for neo-Aristotelian formalism, but neo-Aristotelians, caught up in Wichelns' severe nominalism, cannot exploit this possibility. They may refer to genres, but the distinctions do not become instrumental; limiting or dividing analyses, they do not control them.[12] Ironically, neo-Aristotelians slight the genres even as they embrace the taxonomic categories to which the genres gave purpose, with the result that critics tend to classify "certain grosser properties cast under the heads of the traditional modes and canons," to produce "a mechanical accounting or summing up of how well the speech fits an *a priori* mold."[13] Any critical system will exhibit certain *a priori* features, but it appears that the mold of traditional criticism has become mechanically taxonomic. Stripped of generic distinctions, the neo-classical taxonomy does not encourage interaction between the critical apparatus and the broader purposes of rhetorical discourse, and the critic glances off the relationship that has been accepted as the very excuse for his being—the relationship between speaker and audience. Seeking refuge, critics turn to biography or history, but neither is an adequate resolution. That the adducing of historical details offers no escape is reinforced if we turn to an essay representing "the neo-Aristotelian tradition at its best,"[14] Marie Hochmuth Nichols' "Lincoln's First Inaugural."[15]

The most noteworthy feature of this essay is its accumulation of historical detail. Avoiding generalization, Nichols invites the reader to participate in the ambiance of the situation by recounting the particulars that surround it. Disregard the reprinted text of the address, and two-thirds of the article is devoted to a "scrupulous documentation"[16] of the events immediately preceding and following the speech. Such documentation can be an important ancilla, but the final test is whether the critic uses the accumulated detail in ways that add to an understanding and appreciation of the rhetorical transaction. Nichols faces this responsibility in the final third of her essay, but she is unable to overcome the inherent limitations of Wichelns' program.

Adhering to his tenets, she evaluates the speech "as a speech, a medium distinct from other media, and with methods peculiarly its own" (p. 88). The special topics appropriate to this task are "Lincoln's selection of materials, his arrangement, his style, and his manner" (p. 90). What is to unify these lines of inquiry? It is the speaker's purpose. But Nichols warns against the casual assumption that "Lincoln's purpose is easily discernable in the occasion itself" (p. 89), and she implicity rejects generic considerations when she turns away from the fact that "this was an inaugural ceremony, with a ritual fairly well established" (p. 89). Genre is beside the point because Lincoln's purposes arise from the experiences "of the nation between his election as President and the day of his inauguration" (p. 89). These experiences focus on party, nation, and man, and they lead to this conclusion: "Clearly, he intended to take the occasion of the inauguration to declare the position of the Republican party in regard to the South, to announce his considered judgment in regard to the practical questions raised by the movement of secession, and, in all, to give what assurance he could of his personal integrity" (p. 90).

Compared to the specificity of the earlier historical documentation, the analysis following this statement of purpose is vague. For the most part, the critique is a summary. Including numerous quotations from the text and comparisons with earlier drafts, it certainly reproduces the flow of Lincoln's argument. Yet, it leaves the reader to his own devices in attempting to fathom the forms and topics of argument, the nature of evidence, the interaction among parts of the discourse, and the character of appeals to the audience. Summary simply does not explain how Lincoln "became the affectionate father, the benevolent and hopeful counselor" (p. 95). Moreover, the anlaysis of style does not probe deeply into the text itself; commentary becomes rigorous and specific only in terms of an external reference—in relation to the wording of earlier drafts. It is interesting to view the style through a consideration of the language Lincoln did not use, but a closer examination of that which he did use is needed to support the claim that his style produced "an image of great-heartedness, great humility and great faith" (p. 99).

To avoid misunderstanding, we want to underline that our purpose here is not to belittle this important essay. We merely want to emphasize that the critique exhibits a complete commitment to the unique context of the discourse. This commitment, in turn, produces an analysis that concentrates on external circumstances rather than on the internal development of the speech. The resulting limitations become strikingly apparent when Nichols attempts a general evaluation of the discourse.

Her position is unmistakably clear; the Inaugural Address is a rhetorical masterpiece. But what is the basis for this judgment? It cannot be found in either literary value or cultural force; these criteria are explicitly reserved for literary critics and historians (p. 88). Thus, everything comes down to effect, to the question of whether the discourse did what it was supposed to do. And this particular speech was supposed to ennunciate party policy, allay the fears of the seccessionists, and establish the orator's personal integrity. The reaction of the South, therefore, becomes the salient index. Yet, by this standard, the speech was the most abject of failures. It did not mollify the secessionists. In fact, Nichols argues convincingly that, after examining the Inaugural, "the South saw little hope from Lincoln" (p. 85). But she flees the inexorable conclusion. Ignoring immediate effect, she contends that "any fair-minded critic, removed from the passions of the times, must find himself much more in agreement with those observers of the day who believed the Inaugural met the 'requirements of good rhetoric" (p. 95). This will not do. It is patently inconsistent to focus exclusively on the unique and specific situation and then to ask that final evaluation be "removed from the passions of the times."

The problem we have just outlined seems insoluble within the terms of the neo-Aristotelian tradition. Certainly there is but cold comfort in Parrish's observation that "not failure, but low aim, is crime" in speechmaking (p. 100).[17] That only papers over the gap that necessarily yawns between a philosophical dedication to the particular and a desire for a more permanent frame of reference. Parrish correctly recognizes a need for abstract standards, but he does not offer an ultimate grounding for the formalism he proposes. That grounding, we believe, exists in the theory of genres. To explain our position, we must return to the ancients.

GENRE THEORY

As opposed to Wichelns, the dominant position in ancient rhetoric is not that situations are unique and particular, but that they fall into general categories, into "types" or "kinds." The influence of Aristotle is decisive. He describes the three familiar genres of deliberative, forensic and epideictic, maintaining that "rhetoric falls into three divisions [genē], determined by the three classes of listeners to speeches.'[18] Since it is the listener who "determines the speech's end and object,"[19] the audience is the central element in the system. Consequently, Aristotle paves the way for general acceptance of the proposition that "the important aspect of the speech situation is the speaker-audience relationship."[20] At the same time, however, Aristotle marks and emphasizes the similarities among certain kinds of audiences and certain speaking situations; his entire theory ultimately responds to an abstract classification of oratorical requirements.

Later classical rhetoricians thoroughly endorse this theory of genre, and we find Cicero, Quintilian, and other writers consistently treating inventional theory in terms of the three types of speaking. More importantly, the genres give meaning to the whole of the complex taxonomy in classical rhetoric. The five *officia* and their elaborate sub-structures are significant only insofar as they assist the speaker in achieving his goal. That goal, of course, is conditioned by the nature of the audience; the speaker, however, locates his audience with reference to the genre in which he must function. Without the genres, classical rhetorical theory loses contact with the audience, and the elaborate taxonomy becomes meaningless, a system bereft of any rhetorical purpose. For this reason, we believe that any critical program based on classical models must give serious consideration to genre theory.

The immediate advantage of generic criticism is that it permits the creation of intrinsic standards for rhetorical discourse without losing sight of the audience. Predicated upon the "expectations of the audience and the demands of the situation,"[21] the concept of genre assumes that certain types of situations provoke similar needs and expectations among audiences. Identifying and categorizing these situations are basic to inquiry, and the critic must uncover patterns of need and expectation that bind audiences together, even though they may be far removed in time and place. An adequate description of a genre, then, produces a general index of audience demands; it, therefore, locates the abstract rhetorical problems confronting the speaker and points to intrinsic standards for judging a particular kind of discourse.

To illustrate, we can expand upon the generic underpinning of our approach to the Cooper Union Address. This is a campaign speech, an oratorical form well-known to American audiences and easily distinguished from other types of public address. Nevertheless, this type does not fall within the tripartite Aristotelian division. The anomaly becomes evident when we consider the campaign speech in relation to audience and purpose, the basic components of the Aristotelian distinction. One who listens to a campaign speech is a judge of a future event, and he is urged to do something (i.e. to vote for a particular candidate). This corresponds to the function of the audience in deliberative oratory. The object of judgment, however, is not a policy, as it is in deliberative speaking, but a person, as it is in epideictic. Ends also are blurred; the deliberative orator examines the "expediency or the harmfulness of a proposed course of action"; and the epideictic orator must "praise or attack a man" in order to prove "him worthy of honour or the reverse."[22] Now, the end of campaign oratory is to make the candidate appear worthy and honorable. Nevertheless it makes no sense to argue that the campaign oration is a form of epideictic, since the speaker's goal is to effect a decision, and listeners are asked to judge, not merely to sit as spectators. Evidently, no one of the traditional genres is entirely satisfactory, and it follows that intelligent application of the neo-classical approach entails the description of a separate genre for campaign oratory.

In this instance, the problem in the traditional system appears to be an omission rather than an inherent defect, and we found it relatively easy to define the genre and remain consistent with Aristotelian principles. Finding Rosenthal's analysis of ethos suggestive, we approached the campaign oration as an instance of "personal persuasion," as discourse in which the central concern is the audience's attitude toward the candidate.[23] Given this condition, the campaign orator's first responsibility is, by definition, to promote himself as an individual. Both policies and character are in question, but policy is subsidiary to the purpose of creating an identification of thought and feeling between speaker and audience—a demand inherent in the situation. The ultimate objective is ingratiation. Translating all this into neo-classical terminology, we could describe the genre of campaign oratory as speaking in which listeners act as judges of a future event, an election: the end is to effect a judgment of the candidate, a judgment base on character and upon the treatment of issues.

This consideration of generic requirements helped to focus our analysis of the Cooper Union Address. In this case our description of the genre followed Aristotle rather closely. Other situations may demand more radical adjustments of the traditional system. Surely it is unreasonable to expect the tripartite division of antiquity to encompass all subsequent forms of public address. Genres are like institutions.[24] They exhibit a degree of stability over time, but they also grow, change, and decay in response to the conditions of society. Hence they "should not be viewed as static forms but as evolving phenomena."[25] The critic must retain the flexibility needed to adjust to changing circumstances. He must remember that generic distinctions should not force every item into a preconceived category; instead, their proper function is to uncover genuine points of similarity and difference among forms of discourse.

The discovery of these similarities and differences results in the establishment of generic constraints and the use of these constraints appears to solve the most troublesome problem in neo-Aristotelian criticism—the antithetical tension between the commitment to a particular situation and the need for formal standards of evaluation. Theoretically, the dissipating of this tension can make neo-classicism again available to the rhetorical critic. We intended that our critique of the Cooper Union Address specify some of the potential. The critique itself must stand as the sole witness to our success or failure, but the genesis deserves comment because it helps explain the rationale and points up both strengths and limitations.

THE USES OF NEO-CLASSICISM

The position we have taken in this essay and elsewhere clearly is at one with Black's call for "an alternative to neo-Aristotelianism,"[26] and the literature indicates that the search has been profitable. Nevertheless, it seemed that the common acceptance had become "any alternative to neo-Aristotelianism," and if neo-classicism had become mechanical, arbitrary rejection seemed a short-sighted reaction. To forsake traditional theory completely appeared a dubious course, and an examination of the original sources convinced us that a return to generic distinctions was the key to another useful alternative. And to a large extent genre theory anticipates the contention that the neo-classical taxonomy commits the critic to a static set of categories and deflects the true purpose of criticism. It specifically anchors a discourse in the context of other discourses and the demands of the audience, and it blunts the charge that the neo-classical orientation forces the critic to overlook "the effects of audience, situation and other contemporary discourses on the speaker's behavior."[27]

The system retains schematic features, but that seems an advantage rather than a disadvantage. If criticism is not totally whimsical and subjective, some schema must control the analysis. The critic may concentrate on archetypal metaphors, dramatistic elements, analogues from anthropology and mythology, but there must be standards for sifting and sorting the materials. In this light, the neo-classical taxonomy is but one of many schemata available, and it has the particularly appealing feature of attempting to deal with the entire rhetorical transaction on its own terms. Recently, the most important and instructive analyses have had a non-traditional bias, but many tend to isolate and emphasize a single element or concept. A complete neo-classical approach, however, centers directly on the rhetorical process and divides it into a simple but comprehensive set of constituents. Out of context, the categories can be domineering, but any other schema can become equally oppressive, and genre theory helps prevent a neo-classical tyranny. Keeping the taxonomy within proper bounds, it centers attention where it ought to be, on the speaker-audience relationship, and the system produced seems an excellent filter for the analysis for a particular speech. Examining the Cooper Union Address, for example, we did not feel prisoner to a crabbed and stultifying orthodoxy, nor find ourselves trapped in tangential concerns. We found, instead, that the system forced us to come to grips with the speech as a speech, and we found that it forced us to make choices.[28] Whether we made the proper ones is not as important as the fact that we were not enclosed within arbitrary and debilitating confines.

The system, of course, does have confines. Genre theory presumes types, and a critic ordinarily will use the type to explore the single example. Comparisons are possible, or criticism might center on a series from one genre, but the character of neo-classicism is most appropriate to the analysis of a single speech. If the system cannot address "picketing, sloganeering, chanting, singing, marching, gesturing," and similar communicative phenomena,[29] this limitation does no more than describe the scope of neo-classicism. A more serious problem attends the charge that the neo-classic critic suffers from a rationalistic bias.[30]

From the generic perspective, this bias is an institutional one. Rhetorical genres are grounded in established practices, and genre theory must assume the existence of stable conventions that govern public communication. Capitalizing upon this area of public agreement, genre theory can present a coherent and therefore "rational" account of rhetorical argument. This is advantageous under normal circumstances, but it is quite another matter when circumstances are not normal, in times of rapid change. Here is the most significant limitation to the critical program we are advocating.

This program necessarily works best in situations where the range of disagreement is limited, where there is a broad consensus about what can be argued and how it should be argued. Thus, even an observer as sympathetic as Booth must acknowledge that "the Aristotelian tradition is suited best to analyzing the cogency of...rhetoric, from the point of view of someone who is at least in some sense on the inside."[31] Our proposal, then, deals with an insider's rhetoric. Yet, everyone is aware of the outsider's, "the rhetoric of 'conversion,' of transformation—the rhetoric with the effect whether designed or not, of overturning personal ties and changing total allegiances."[32] This radical rhetoric may explicitly attack the stable conventions and institutions of a society; furthermore, it is likely to appear in a form that challenges the established norms of discourse, for attempts to subvert the establishment almost always involve an attempt to subvert its language.

In such situations, genre theory falters. Based on the presumption of stability, the system has no mechanism for explaining idiosyncratic and dramatic changes in ideology or style. The critic may adjust over time, but long-term flexibility is beside the point when one seeks to explain radical rhetorical *in situ*. Worse yet, adherence to a conventional typology can make the critic a captive of the institutional system that nascent rhetorical forms seek to destroy. The resultant analysis will condemn advocates of change because their rhetoric does not conform to conventional expectations, and the nature of that rhetoric may well go misunderstood. Nevertheless, even this limitation may prove to be of some value, if properly appreciated.

A time of rapid and drastic change is one, above all others, that may require stable points of reference. Surely it is hazardous always to evaluate new kinds of discourse in terms of the old, but there is no reason why old genres cannot be touchstones for understanding new developments. In other words, rhetorical criticism might "act on the premise that the study of historical change could greatly profit from a clearer view than we now have of what is changing."[33] We have yet to devise a critical rationale adequate to account for sudden shifts of ideology.

CONCLUSION

In concluding, we can do little more than repeat what we already have said. We simply propose the addition of genre theory as a means of introducing formalism into neo-classical criticism. Squarely within the tradition, this theory does not ask that critics abandon the centrality of the audience. In fact, genre theory acts as a corrective precisely because it allows for a broader conception of audience than is permitted in neo-Aristotelian criticism. If critics can identify situations that create generally similar audience demands, then they can abstract principles that will apply to a wide variety of discourses. Although these principles rest on audience analysis, the audience is conceived in generic terms, and the generalizations produced may offer formal grounds for evaluating speeches of a particular kind. These standards lack the more purely formal characteristics of certain literary genres, but they provide a point of entry into a discourse and focus the critical reaction.

Much remains to be done, of course. Our analysis of the campaign genre remains limited and tentative. To focus the neo-classical taxonomy, we established an *a priori* definition of the end for campaign oratory, and we were then able to construct very broad standards for rhetorical evaluation in a particular instance. Additional instances have to be accumulated before the genre can be described properly and more specific generic constraints developed. More generally, we have not examined genre theory in detail, nor have we attempted a systematic classification of modern rhetorical genres.

Fortunately, the evidence indicates a probing in those directions.[34] Much of the effort has been piecemeal, but this, after all, may prove the most satisfactory route. Modern rhetorical critics usually start with a settled theoretical position and then make an application, but in writing the two essays, we found ourselves attacking the problem from the opposite perspective. The experience was instructive, and perhaps it can be generalized. The progress of rhetorical criticism may depend more on the ability of critics to induce principles from actual critiques than on a concern with abstract issues.

Notes

1. Edwin Black, *Rhetorical Criticism* (New York: Macmillan, 1965), p. 27.
2. Black, p. 35.
3. Herbert A. Wichelns, "The Literary Criticism of Oratory," in *Methods of Rhetorical Criticism*, Robert L. Scott and Bernard L. Brock (New York: Harper and Row, 1972), pp. 27–60. Further references to the essay will be to this source.
4. William Norwood Brigance, ed., I & II (New York: McGraw-Hill, 1943); and Marie Kathryn Hochmuth, ed., III, *A History and Criticism of American Public Address* (New York: McGraw-Hill, 1955).
5. Lester Thonssen and A. Craig Baird, *Speech Criticism* (New York: Ronald Press, 1948).
6. Donald C. Bryant, ed., *The Rhetorical Idiom* (Ithaca, New York: Cornell Univ. Press, 1958), p. 5.
7. Thonssen and Baird, p. 15.
8. D. A. Russell, "Rhetoric and Criticism," *Greece and Rome*, 2nd Ser., 14 (Oct. 1967), 141–142.
9. René Wellek and Austin Warren, *Theory of Literature* (New York: Harcourt, Brace and World, 1956), p. 237.
10. Thonssen and Baird, p. 18.
11. Thonssen and Baird, p. 457.
12. Even a casual reading in *A History and Criticism of American Public Address* reveals that genres are not examined systematically.
13. Douglas Ehninger, "Rhetoric and the Critic," *Western Speech*, 29 (Fall 1965), 230.
14. Scott and Brock, p. 21.
15. Marie Hochmuth Nichols, "Lincoln's First Inaugural," in Scott and Brock, pp. 60–100. Further references to this essay will be to this source.
16. Black, p. 41.
17. Wayland Maxfield Parrish, "The Study of Speeches," in *American Speeches*, ed. Wayland Maxfield Parrish and Marie K. Hochmuth (New York: David McKay, 1954), p. 12. See Black, pp. 61–75.
18. *Rhetoric* (trans. W. Rhys Roberts), I. 3. 1358a, 36. For comment on a general formalism in Attic oratory see R. C. Jebb, *The Attic Orators* (1876; rpt. New York: Russell and Russell, 1962), I, xcii–civ.
19. *Rhetoric*, I. 3. 1358^b, 1.
20. Thonssen and Baird, p. 15.
21. Kathleen M. Hall Jamieson, "Generic Constraints and the Rhetorical Situation," *Philosophy and Rhetoric*, 6 (Summer 1973), 163.
22. *Rhetoric*, I. 3. 1358^b, 22–28.
23. Paul I. Rosenthal, "The Concept of Ethos and the Structure of Persuasion," *Speech Monographs*, 33 (June 1966), 114–126.
24. Wellek and Warren, p. 226.
25. Jamieson, p. 168.
26. Black, p. 132.

27. Joe A. Munshaw, "The Structures of History: Dividing Phenomena for Rhetorical Understanding," *Central States Speech Journal*, 24 (Spr. 1973), 30.

28. In our critique, we deliberately suppressed details of the analysis. For example, we slighted intricacies in the argument of the first section because the reporting would have been tedious for the reader and would have made the speech appear more formalistic than it really is. We slighted other matters as well. Except by implication, we did not explore Lincoln's use of the rhetorical question or the "our fathers" refrain. We could have extended the latter into each segment of the putative debate with the South, and we might have considered its echoic religious values for an audience all too familiar with the *Lord's Prayer*. We do not mean to imply that these facets of the speech would not be available to a critic of a different persuasion. We do insist, however, that genre and taxonomy brought them to our attention. That we did not report them indicates choices we made rather than any short-coming in the approach.

29. Lloyd F. Bitzer and Edwin Black, eds., *The Prospect of Rhetoric* (Englewood Cliffs, New Jersey: Prentice-Hall, 1971), p. 225.

30. See Black, pp. 91–131, and Karlyn K. Campbell, "The Ontological Foundations of Rhetorical Theory," *Philosophy and Rhetoric*, 3 (Spr. 1970), 97–108.

31. Wayne C. Booth, "The Scope of Rhetoric Today: A Polemical Excursion," in Bitzer and Black, p. 97.

32. Booth, p. 102.

33. Paul Hernadi, *Beyond Genre* (Ithaca, New York: Cornell Univ. Press, 1972), p. 8.

34. See Black, pp. 132–177; Forbes I, Hill, "Conventional Widsom—Traditional Form: The President's Message of November 3, 1969," *QJS*, 58 (Dec. 1972), 373–386; B. L. Ware and Wil A. Linkugel, "They Spoke in Defence of Themselves: On the Generic Criticism of Apologia," *QJS*, 59 (Oct. 1973), 273–283; and Jamieson. The last two articles include references to a number of related discussions.

Fantasy and Rhetorical Vision: The Rhetorical Criticism of Social Reality

—————————— ERNEST G. BORMANN ——————————

Recent research in small group communication reveals a process that can interrelate important features of communication and rhetorical theory. Just as some psychologists and sociologists have studied the small group in order to discover features of larger social structures, so can investigations of small group communication provide insight into the nature of public address and mass communication.

For several years the small group communication seminar at Minnesota has studied the decision-making process in group discussion.[1] The seminar began with two major lines of inquiry: content analysis of group meetings and extended case studies of individual groups. Careful case studies over periods of several months provided an understanding of group process and communication which was often more complete and useful than much of the quantitative data generated by using various category systems. To develop a method for process analysis which captured the richness of case studies while allowing generalization, the seminar studied the transcripts of the small group meetings as a rhetorical critic might analyze the text of a public speech.

Most of the attempts to make a rhetorical criticism of small group communication proved relatively barren until Robert Bales published *Personality and Interpersonal Behavior* in 1970.[2] What Bales and his associates had been discovering while working with natural groups in the classroom was very like what we had been working on at Minnesota. But Bales provided the key part to the puzzle when he discovered *the dynamic process of group fantasizing*. Group fantasizing correlates with individual fantasizing and extrapolates to speaker-audience fantasizing and to the dream merchants of the mass media. Rhetorical critics have long known that rhetoric and poetic have much in common yet, still, are different. Many have viewed persuasive discourse in dramatistic terms. Now Bales provides the critic with an account of how dramatizing communication creates social reality for groups of people and with a way to examine messages for insights into the group's culture, motivation, emotional style, and cohesion.

Bales and his associates originally developed twelve content analysis categories for the study of small groups.[3] One original category, "shows tension release," was later changed to "dramatizes." Continued work with the category of "dramatizes" led to the discovery of "group fantasy events." Some, but not all, of the communication coded as "dramatizes" would chain out through the group. The tempo of the conversation would pick up. People would grow excited, interrupt one another, blush, laugh, forget their self-consiousness. The tone of the meeting, often quiet and tense immediately prior to the dramatizing, would become lively, animated, and boisterous, the chaining process, involving both verbal and nonverbal communication, indicating participation in the drama.

What is the manifest content of a group fantasy chain? What do the group members say? The content consists of characters, real or fictitious, playing out a dramatic situation in a setting removed in time and space from the here-and-now transactions of the group. (The "here-and-now," a concept borrowed from sensitivity and encounter group practice, refers to what is immediately happening in the group. Thus a recollection of something that happened to the group in the *past* or a dream of what the group might do in the *future* could be considered a fantasy theme.)

How can a fantasy chain be interpreted? Often the drama is a mirror of the group's here-and-now situation and its relationship to the external environment. The drama played out somewhere else or in some other time often symbolizes a role collision or ambiguity, a leadership conflict, or a problem related to the task-dimension of the group. Just as an individual's repressed problems might surface in dream fantasies so those of a group might surface in a fantasy chain and a critic might interpret the manifest content with an eye to discovering the group's hidden agenda.

But the chaining can also be an expression in a given social field of the individual psychodynamics of the participants. A dramatic theme might relate to the repressed psychological problems of some or all of the members and thus pull them into participation.[4]

Bales' most important discovery for the integration of communication and rhetorical theory, however, was the process by which a zero-history group used fantasy chains to develop a common culture. The group tended to ignore comments coded as "dramatizes" which did not relate either to the group's here-and-now problems or to the individual psychodynamics of the participants. Those that did get the members of the group to empathize, to improvise on the same theme, or to respond emotionally not only reflected the members' common pre-occupations but served to make those commonalities public.

When group members respond emotionally to the dramatic situation they publicly proclaim some commitment to an attitude. Indeed, improvising in a spontaneous group dramatization is a powerful force for attitude change. Dramas also imply motives and by chaining into the fantasy the members gain motivations. Since some of the characters in the fantasies are good people doing laudable things the group collectively identifies in symbolic terms proper codes of conduct and the characteristics which make people credible message sources. A comparison with more direct here-and-now methods for establishing group norms clarifies the nature of fantasy chains. For instance, one way to discover a common ground in a zero-history group with a job to do is to confront the question directly. A member may say, "I think we all want to do a good job and we should all go to the library and do a lot of research. I know that I'm willing to do that." If the others enthusiastically respond with comments like, "Yes, that is a good idea." "Good, let's go to work," the problem is dealt with directly. The fantasy chain discovers the same common ground symbolically:

> *"Last semester my roommate took this course and he never worked so hard in his life."*
>
> *"Really?"*
>
> *"Yeah, it was really great though. He took field trips to hospital labs and everything."*
>
> *"Yeah, I know this girl who took the course and she said the same thing. She said you wouldn't believe how hard they worked. But she said she really got something out of it."*

Values and attitudes of many kinds are tested and legitimatized as common to the group by the process of fantasy chains. Religious and political dramas are tested. For example, if someone dramatizes a situation in which a leading political figure is a laughing stock and it falls flat that particular political attitude and value has been exhibited and not legitimatized. However, should the group chain out on that drama improvising on other laughable situations in which the politician has participated the group will have created a common character which they can allude to in subsequent meetings and elicit a smiling or laughing emotional response. (They have created an inside joke but they have also created an attitude towards a given political position.) As Bales describes it:

> *The culture of the interacting group stimulates in each of its members a feeling that he has entered a new realm of reality—a world of heroes, villains, saints, and enemies—a drama, a work of art. The culture of a group is a fantasy established from the past, which is acted upon in the present. In such moments, which occur not only in groups, but also in individual responses to works of art, one is "transported" to a world which seems somehow even more real than the everyday world. One may feel exalted, fascinated, perhaps horrified or threatened, or powerfully impelled to action, but in any case, involved. One's feelings fuse with the symbols and images which carry the feeling in communication and sustain it over time. One is psychologically taken into a psychodramatic fantasy world, in which others in the group are also involved. Then one is attached also to those other members.[5]*

My argument is that these moments happen not only in individual reactions to works of art, or in a small group's chaining out a fantasy theme, but also in larger groups hearing a public speech. The dramatizations which catch on and chain out in small groups are worked into public speeches and into the mass media and, in turn, spread out across larger publics, serve to sustain the members' sense of community, to impel them strongly to action (which raises the question of motivation), and to provide them with a social reality filled with heroes, villains, emotions, and attitudes.

The composite dramas which catch up large groups of people in a symbolic reality, I call a "rhetorical vision." Just as fantasy themes chain out in the group to create a unique group culture so do the fantasy dramas of a successful persuasive campaign chain out in public audiences to form a rhetorical vision.

A rhetorical vision is constructed from fantasy themes that chain out in face-to-face interacting groups, in speaker-audience transactions, in viewers of television broadcasts, in listeners to radio programs, and in all the diverse settings for public and intimate communication in a given society. Once such a rhetorical vision emerges it contains dramatis personae and typical plot lines that can be alluded to in all communication contexts and spark a response reminiscent of the original emotional chain. The same dramas can be developed in detail when the occasion demands to generate emotional response.

The relationship between a rhetorical vision and a specific fantasy theme within a message explains why so much "persuasive" communication simply repeats what the audience already knows.[6] Balance theories explain attitude and behavior change on the basis of dissonance or imbalance, and yet many strikingly successful speakers have not created dissonances but have rather given voice to what the listener already knows or feels and accepts.[7] One perceptive commentator on Hitler noted, for instance, that:

> One scarcely need ask with what arts he [Hitler] conquered the masses; he did not conquer them, he portrayed and represented them. His speeches are daydreams of this mass soul; they are chaotic, full of contradictions, if their words are taken literally, often senseless, as dreams are, and yet charged with deeper meaning.... The speeches begin always with deep pessimism and end in overjoyed redemption, a triumphant happy ending; often they can be refuted by reason, but they follow the far mightier logic of the subconscious, which no refutation can touch. Hitler has given speech to the speechless terror of the modern mass, and to the nameless fear he has given a name. That makes him the greatest mass orator of the mass age.[8]

The explanatory power of the fantasy chain analysis lies in its ability to account for the development, evolution, and decay of dramas that catch up groups of people and change their behavior. A rhetorical movement contains small group fantasy chains, public fantasy events, and a rhetorical vision in a complex and reciprocal set of relationships. The subsystems fit into a larger communication system as follows: A small group of people with similar individual psychodynamics meet to discuss a common preoccupation or problem. A member dramatizes a theme that catches the group and causes it to chain out because it hits a common psychodynamic chord or a hidden agenda item or their common difficulties vis-a-vis the natural environment, the socio-political systems, or the economic structures. The group grows excited, involved, more dramas chain out to create a common symbolic reality filled with heroes and villains. If the group's fantasy themes contain motives to "go public" and gain converts to their position they often begin artistically to create messages for the mass media for public speeches and so forth. When they need to develop a message for a specific context they often find themselves shaping the drama that excited them in their original discussions into suitable form for a different public.

Some of the dramas of their public rhetoric now catch members of the audience in the situation which Bales called, "individual responses to works of art, when one is 'transported' to a world which seems somehow even more real than the everyday world." Those so transported take up the dramas in small groups of acquaintances, and some of these derivative dramas again chain out as fantasy themes in the new groups; thus the rhetorical vision is propagated to a larger public until a rhetorical movement emerges.[9]

Individuals in rhetorical transactions create subjective worlds of common expectations and meanings. Against the panorama of large events and seemingly unchangeable forces of society at large or of nature the individual often feels lost and hopeless. One coping mechanism is to dream an individual fantasy which provides a sense of meaning and significance for the individual and helps protect him from the pressures of natural calamity and social disaster. The rhetorical vision serves much the same coping function for those who participate in the drama and often with much more force because of the supportive warmth of like-minded companions.

In most instances a viable rhetorical vision accounts plausibly for the evidence of the senses so those who pick up the dramatic action and find it personally satisfying are not troubled by contradictory evidence from common-sense experience. On occasion, however, small, highly dedicated groups of people generate and sustain rhetorical visions so out of joint with the common-sense and everyday experience of the majority of a community that their appeal is very limited. The analogy of the more bizarre rhetorical visions with pathological states in individuals caused one observer, Richard Hofstadter, to refer to the former as paranoid.[10]

What answer can be given, then, to the question of the relation between public fantasies and "reality" or action or substance? Writers in General Semantics often argue that the word is not the thing.[11] Scholars in many disciplines often go on to assume that since the word is not the thing any discrepancy between words and things must necessarily be resolved by assigning the greater importance to things and the words are, therefore, to be discounted as misleading or unimportant.

One line of historical analysis, for example, suggests that although the abolitionists often argued from theological grounds that slavery was a sin and that to save their eternal souls all persons must work for its elimination, the "real" reason the abolitionists fought with zeal to free the slaves was because they were members of a displaced social elite caught in a status crisis. The words of the abolitionists are discounted as being unimportant to the historical reality of the situation.[12]

Sociological analysis often starts from the premise that the words are generated out of the social context rather than that the words *are the social context*. Duncan laments the common view, "American sociologists simply do not believe that how we communicate determines how we relate as social beings. Most sociologists really think of symbols as photographs of some kind of reality that is 'behind' symbols.... Class *exists* and *then* is expressed, it does not arise *in* expression."[13]

When a critic makes a rhetorical analysis he or she should start from the assumption that when there is a discrepancy between the word and the thing the most important cultural artifact for understanding the events may not be the things or "reality" but the words or the symbols. Indeed, in many vital instances the words, that is, the rhetoric, are the social reality and to try to distinguish one symbolic reality from another is a fallacy widespread in historical and sociological scholarship which the rhetorical critic can do much to dispel.[14]

A critic can take the social reality contained in a rhetorical vision which he has constructed from the concrete dramas developed in a body of discourse and examine the social relationships, the motives, the qualitative impact of that symbolic world as though it were the substance of social reality for those people who participated in the vision. If the critic can illuminate how people who participated in the rhetorical vision related to one another, how they arranged themselves into social hierarchies, how they acted to achieve the goals embedded in their dreams, and how they were aroused by the dramatic action and the dramatis personae within the manifest content of their rhetoric, his insights will make a useful contribution to understanding the movement and its adherents.

How might the critic making a fantasy theme analysis proceed? There is not space to describe the technique in detail, but I shall raise some of the more general questions that a critic might choose to investigate. The critic begins by collecting evidence related to the manifest content of the communication, using video or audio tapes, manuscripts, recollections of participants, or his own direct observations. He discovers and describes the narrative and dramatic materials that have chained out for those who participate in the rhetorical vision. When a critic has gathered a number of dramatic incidents he can look for patterns of characterizations (do the same people keep cropping up as villains?) of dramatic situations and actions (are the same stories repeated?) and of setting (where is the sacred ground and where the profane?). The critic must then creatively reconstruct the rhetorical vision from the representative fantasy chains much as a scholar would delineate a school of drama on the basis of a number of different plays.

Once the critic has constructed the manifest content of the rhetorical vision he can ask more specific questions relating to elements of the dramas. Who are the dramatis personae? Does some abstraction personified as a character provide the ultimate legitimatization of the drama? God? The People? The Young? (What are young people really trying to tell us?). Who are the heroes and the villains? How concrete and detailed are the characterizations? Motives attributed? How are the members of the rhetorical community characterized? For what are the insiders praised, the outsiders or enemies castigated? What values are inherent in the praiseworthy characters?

Where are the dramas set? In the wilderness? In the countryside? In the urban ghetto? Is the setting given supernatural sanction?

What are the typical scenarios? What acts are performed by the ultimate legitimatizer? The neutral people? The enemy? Which are sanctioned and praised; which censored? What lifestyles are exemplified as praiseworthy?

What meanings are inherent in the dramas? Where does the insider fit into the great chain of being? How does the movement fit into the scheme of history? What emotional evocations dominate the dramas? Does hate dominate? Pity? Love? Indignation? Resignation? What motives are embedded in the vision? Would the committed work for or resist legal action? Violence? Would they resign this life to get ready for an afterlife?

How does the fantasy theme work to attract the unconverted? How does it generate a sense of community and cohesion from the insider?

How artistic is the development of the fantasy theme? How skillful the characterization? How artistic the use of language? How rich the total panorama of the vision? How capable is the drama to arouse and interpret emotions?

A critic need not, of course, raise all of such questions for a given piece of criticism but for some in-depth critiques of a single message the critic might ask more questions and search for more details. A brief analysis of one important rhetorical vision from American history illustrates the way a critic might proceed.

The point relating to the way fantasy themes help people transcend the everyday and provide meaning for an audience is made graphically by the rhetorical vision embedded in the preaching of Puritan ministers to their small congregations huddled in unheated, crude, and undecorated meeting houses in the wilderness in the early years of the Massachusetts Bay Colony. The daily routine of the people was one of back-breaking drudgery. The niceties of life were almost nonexistent; music, the arts, decoration of home or clothing, largely unavailable. A discursive description of the emigration and the daily externals of life would be very grim. But the Puritans of Colonial New England led an internal fantasy life of mighty grandeur and complexity. They participated in a rhetorical vision that saw the migration to the new world as a holy exodus of God's chosen people. The Biblical drama that supported their vision was that of the journey of the Jews from Egypt into Canaan. John Cotton's sermon delivered when Winthrop's company was leaving for Massachusetts was on the text, "Moreover I will appoint a place for my People Israell, [sic] and I will plant them, that they may dwell in a place of their own, and move no more."[15]

The Puritan rhetorical vision saw them as conquering new territories for God, saving the souls of the natives, and, most importantly, as setting up in the wilderness a model religious community, a new Israel, patterned after the true meaning of the scriptures to light the way for the reformation still to be accomplished in old England and in all of Europe.

Such a vision gave to every social and political action a sense of importance. Every intrusion of nature or of other communities upon their inner reality also was given added significance. A time of troubles such as a drought or an Indian raid became evidene of God's displeasure and served as a motive to drive the Puritans to higher effort and greater striving to please God.

The Puritan vision also gave meaning to each individual within the movement. The scenario places each member of the audience firmly in the role of protagonist. Cotton Mather wrote to students preparing to be ministers that, "the *Gaining* of one Soul to GOD by your Ministry, will be of more Account with you than any *Gain* of this World; than all the *Wealth* in the World."[16]

In creating fantasy themes for specific sermons the minister would use all his art of assertion, imperatives, and descriptive language to search out the hiding places and bring each member of the congregation center stage to play out the drama of salvation or damnation. Turn and dodge as the listener might, the skillful minister kept driving the auditors to the recognition of their personal spiritual dramas. The odds against success were enormous, the fruits of victory unbelievably sweet, the results of defeat incredibly awesome and terrifying. Thomas Hooker, a first generation minister, does an excellent job of presenting the Puritan rhetorical vision in the following fantasy theme:

> *Imagine thou sawest the Lord Jesus coming in the clouds, and heardest the last trump blow,* Arise ye dead, and come to judgment: *Imagine thou sawest the Judg [sic] of all the World sitting upon the Throne, thousands of Angels before him, and ten thousand ministring unto him, the Sheep standing on his right hand, and the Goats at the left: Suppose thou heardest that dreadful Sentence, and final Doom pass from the Lord of Life (whose Word made Heaven and Earth, and will shake both)* Depart from me ye cursed; *How would thy heart shake and sink, and die within thee in the thought thereof, wert thou really perswaded it was thy portion? Know, that by thy dayly continuance in sin, thou dost to the utmost of thy power execute that Sentence upon thy soul: It's thy life, thy labor, the desire of thy heart, and thy dayly practice to depart away from the God of all Grace and Peace, and turn the Tombstone of everlasting destruction upon thine own soul.*[17]

For the members of the community who participated in the Puritan rhetorical vision the events in the meeting house were significant far beyond the crude externals of their living conditions. In their private prayers and in public worship they participated in a social reality resonant with high drama and rich symbolism.

An audience observing the drama from the outside might find it lacking in suspense, find it inartistic because the basic assumption upon which it rested was the deus ex machina. Man was completely dependent upon God for election to sainthood. The plot was similar to the pattern of the classical Greek plays. Reading the sermons today, we find the action static, the protagonist an insect squirming helplessly in the hands of an all-powerful Diety. But for the listener who chained out on the fantasy and imaginatively took the central role, the suspense might well become unbearable. Each hour might bring eternal salvation or eternal death. In his famous revival sermon Jonathan Edwards said, "And it would be no wonder if some persons, that now sit here, in some seats of this meetinghouse, in health, quiet and secure, should be there [in hell] before tomorrow morning."[18]

The predominant emotion which the Puritan vision evoked was that of awe. The focus is upon an afterlife with high potential for ecstasy or terror, almost beyond the power of the ministers to fantasize. The rhetoric contained powerful pragmatic motivations. The preoccupation with time, the fear of death before God's call to election, impelled the participant in the fantasy to do as much as soon as possible to put herself or himself in the proper posture for election to sainthood. The minutes wasted might be those very ones when his time had come.

One basic action line contained the motive power for much of the Puritan's tough and unrelenting effort to do good and to make good in the material world, namely that a time of troubles was God's punishment for the evil ways of an individual or a community, but that out of punishment would arise an understanding of guilt and a rebirth and regeneration so that the punishment would really serve as a means to salvation. By a zealous striving in the new direction, the guilt of their sins revealed by God's punishment would be propitiated. Insofar as they were cleansed by the experience in the sight of God, the new venture would increase and prosper. When they began again to fall from God's grace they could anticipate more hardships. To some extent, therefore, since in their view nothing happened by chance, the prospering of worldly affairs was evidence of their ability to please God. (Without this dramatic line one might well expect that a vision that emphasized the afterlife would result in contemplative inaction in this life).

The fantasy themes in which good Puritans took each setback and difficulty as a sign from God and made good use of them to become better persons contained strong motives for action and reform.[19] Contemplation, inactivity, impracticality, and apathy were undesirable in the context of the scenario. Working, striving, acting in a hardheaded way, involvement, were all positive values. The drama began with a rite of self-abasement which loaded the participant with a high charge of guilt and turned to a plan of action which was providentially the path to salvation furnished by God. By working hard and doing the right thing they released the charge of guilt, and success became the final evidence that their conscience need no longer be troubled. The rhetoric used failure as evidence that they had not tried hard enough, or been good enough and must therefore work even harder and be even better.

Two common fantasy themes expressed the Puritan rhetorical vision. The first was the pilgrim making his slow, painful, and holy way, beset by many troubles and temptations. The second was the Christian soldier fighting God's battles and overcoming all adversaries in order to establish the true church. The first emphasized the abasement, sacrifice, and dedication of the Puritans to things of the other world; the second emphasized their militancy. Those who participated in the rhetorical vision exhibited an active and if need be, violent, bloody temper. When they could not convert the Indians they fought them and they fought, as well, their fellow Englishmen in the old country for the true faith.

The motivations embedded in the Puritan rhetorical vision, therefore, required great energy and overt activity. Morison, writing a history of Harvard, noted that Emmanuel College, Cambridge was a Puritan stronghold and produced many of the early leaders who emigrated to Massachusetts. Emmanuel College also had an active group of Cambridge neo-Platonists. Morison regrets that "the tolerant and generous philosophy of these men...could not have set the tone of Harvard College." But even as he regrets it, he recognized that "Harvard must have been puritan, or not have existed. A neo-Platonist could not be a man of action, a pioneer, an emigrant, any more than a Hindu. The kingdom of God was within him, not in Massachusetts Bay."[20]

Of course to do justice to a fantasy theme analysis of the rhetorical vision of the Puritans would require a monograph. However, even this sketch can point to some of the insights that a fantasy theme analysis could provide. If we view the Puritans as organisms grubbing away in the wilderness to keep alive or create material wealth or to achieve status or to reach self-actualization we find the enterprise relatively mean and trivial. However, if we examine the internal fantasy of the community as revealed in the sermons of their ministers, we discover the characters of the drama, their emotional values, their actions and their relationship to an over-reaching supernatural power. We come to a new understanding of the grubbing in the wilderness and we have an opportunity to be in possession of much more of the Puritan experience.

Of course, nature does intrude upon our fantasies. Factual descriptions of our common-sense perceptions of the world are also part of the manifest content of rhetorical discourse. A total rhetoric consists of both discursive material and fantasy themes. Cassirer provides the rhetorical critic with an approach to the relationship between discursive material and fantasy themes when he writes, " . . . myth, art, language and science appear as symbols; not in the sense of mere figures which refer to some given reality by means of suggestion and allegorical renderings, but in the sense of forces each of which produces and posits a world of its own."[21] In Langer's words Cassirer was helped, "by a stroke of insight: the realization that *language*, man's prime instrument of reason, reflects his mythmaking tendency more than his rationalizing tendency. Language, the symbolization of thought, exhibits two entirely different modes of thought. Yet in both modes the mind is powerful and creative. It expresses itself in different forms, *one of which is discursive logic, the other creative imagtion*."[22]

When the authentic record of events is clear and widely understood the competing visions must take it into account. If two teams play a game and team A beats team B by 5 to 4, the two teams may chain out different fantasies about the game. Team A may participate in a drama to the effect that justice has been done and the best team has won by superior play. Team B may fantasize that they did not really lose and that the game was stolen from them by an inept official or by dirty play on the part of their opponents. However, the outcome of the grame as represented in the authentic record by a score of 5 to 4 is accounted for and incorporated into the explanatory system of both fantasies.

Whenever occasions are so chaotic and indiscriminate that the community has no clear observational impression of the facts, people are given free rein to fantasize within the assumptions of their rhetorical vision without inhibition. On such occasions fantasy themes become the main explanatory systems for the events. Rumors are illustrations of the principle in action.[23]

The conventional wisdom of communication theorists that "meanings are in people not messages" is much too simple for the critic who wishes to study the rhetorical vision of a movement, an organization, or a community.[24] In a very important way meanings *are* in messages. When the members of a group chain out a fantasy they emerge from the meeting with new meanings, that may not have existed before, else how can we account for novelty and innovation? The new meanings are embedded in the messages created during the meeting. The members have appropriated them by sharing in their creation through public dramatization. (One might as well say the meanings associated with *Hamlet* are in the people who know the play rather than in the productions or the manuscripts. The trouble with that view, of course, is that until the first production of *Hamlet* very few people had the meanings. Unless the meanings relating to *Hamlet* are to some extent in the communication transactions associated with a performance of the play, the new meanings could never have been created.)

The emotions associated with the meanings are, also, partly in the message as well as in the people participating in a fantasy chain. The rhetorical vision provides its participants with an emotional evocation. Thus, the critical analysis of emotional appeals is illuminated by the process of fantasy theme analysis. Physiological studies of emotions reveal that changes in blood chemistry, heart rate, endocrine secretion, palm sweat, and so forth vary little from emotion to emotion.[25] Whether an individual's aroused physiological state is interpreted as hate, fear, anger, joy, or love is partly determined by the drama that accompanies the emotional state.

Finally, and most importantly, motives are in the messages. The rhetorical vision of a group of people contains their drives to action. People who generate, legitimatize and participate in a public fantasy are, in Bales' words, "powerfully impelled to action" by that process. Motives do not exist to be expressed in communication but rather arise in the expression itself and come to be embedded in the drama of the fantasy themes that generated and serve to sustain them. Motives are thus available for direct interpretation by a community of scholars engaged in rhetorical criticism.[26]

When an actor assumes a role in a drama he gains with the part constraining forces (the dramatic action of the unfolding plot) which impel him to do and to say certain things. When a person appropriates a rhetorical vision he gains with the supporting dramas constraining forces which impel him to adopt a life style and to take certain action. The born-again Christian is baptized and adopts a life style and behavior modeled after the heroes of the dramas that sustain that vision. The devout Puritan in Massachusetts was driven by his vision. Likewise the convert to one of the counterculture in the 1960s would let his hair and beard grow, change his style of dress, and his method of work, and so forth. Concurrently a person might participate in a number of narrower visions related to such issues as foreign policy, taxation, civil rights, and women's rights.

One widespread explanation of human motivation posits a fixed schedule of motives that most people have within them. When one uses a schedule of motives as a check-list in preparing persuasive discourse or in critically analyzing it, several shortcomings become apparent. While the schedule is fixed, human behavior is not, thus, accounting for action by attributing a motive to the actor tends to work only after the fact. For instance, when a person chooses a martyr's death the notion that the most fundamental of human motives is self-preservation does not predict the behavior. After the fact the critic can select some other motive from the schedule and argue that it has clearly become more compelling for the martyr than self-preservation.

When a critic begins instead with the approach that each rhetorical vision contains as part of its substance the motive that will impel the people caught up in it, then he can anticipate the behavior of the converts. If the critic discovers that a person faced with the choice of martyrdom participates in a rhetorical vision that includes the fantasy of persons assuring themselves eternal salvation by dying for God's purposes, he can anticipate the act itself.

The notion that motives are hidden within individuals makes them difficult to study in a critical way, and that same inaccessibility makes it possible for people involved in argument and conflict to attribute motives to their friends and enemies. Indeed, a person who tries to get a fantasy to chain out often uses the technique of attributing motives to characters in a dream. A speaker can characterize a hero by attributing praise-worthy motivation, or create a bad image by suggesting unsavory motives. Almost every major evangelist in American history has become a central character in several rhetorical visions, which alternately portray him as a villain seeking money, power, and notoriety, or as a selfless hero trying to better the human condition and do God's will. Those whose rhetorical vision in the 1960s contained the draft resister as hero saw him motivated by a high moral commitment to do good for humanity and those whose fantasy saw him as a villain often attributed to him a cowardly motive to save his own skin.

For the scholar, at any rate, to view motives as embedded in the rhetorical vision rather than hidden in the skulls and viscera of people makes it possible to check the critic's insights by going directly to the rhetoric rather than relying on inferences about psychological entities unavailable for analysis.

Not only does the fantasy analysis of rhetorical visions provide at least as great if not greater power of prediction than the fixed schedule of motives approach but, more importantly, once we participate in the rhetorical vision of a community or movement, even if we keep an aesthetic distance, we have come vicariously to experience a way of life that would otherwise be less accessible to us, we have enlarged our awareness, we have become more fully human. Certainly the discovery and appreciation of rhetorical visions should be one possible function of criticism.

Notes

1. For a description of the Minnesota Studies and a report of the major conclusions of the research see Ernest G. Bormann, *Discussion and Group Methods: Theory and Practice* (New York: Harper and Row, 1969).

2. (New York: Holt, Rinehart).

3. The original categories and the method of independent coders making a content analysis are presented in Robert F. Bales, *Interaction Process Analysis: A Method for the Study of Small Groups* (Cambridge, Mass.: Addison-Wesley, 1950). Changing the category from "show of tension release" to "dramatizes" did not change the essential procedure of coding items.

4. Bales, *Personality and Interpersonal Behavior*, pp. 136–155.

5. *Ibid.*, p. 152.

6. See for example A. J. M. Sykes, "Myth in Communication," *The Journal of Communication*, 20 (Mar. 1970), 17–31 and A. J. M. Sykes, "Myth and Attitude Change," *Human Relations*, 18 (Nov. 1965), 323–337.

7. Exposition of typical balance theories can be found in Theodore M. Newcomb, *The Acquaintance Process* (New York: Holt, Rinehart, 1961) and Fritz Heider, *The Psychology of Interpersonal Relations* (New York: Wiley, 1958).

8. Konrad Heiden, *Der Fuehrer: Hitler's Rise to Power*, trans. Ralph Manheim (Boston: Houghton Mifflin, 1944), p. 106.

9. A study that traces the conscious attempts of some participants to chain out group fantasies that individuate a rhetorical vision to radicalize the uncommitted is James W. Chesebro, John F. Cragan, and Patricia McCullough, "The Small Group Techniques of the Radical-Revolutionary: A Synthetic Study of Consciousness Raising," *Speech Monographs*, in press. The investigators discovered that in the opening phases of the consciousness raising sessions members dramatized events and characters prominent in the national rhetorical vision of Gay Liberation. After the dramatization of the national vision had formed a common bond the participants turned to dramatizing personl experience narratives.

10. Richard Hofstadter, *The Paranoid Style in American Politics and Other Essays* (New York: Knopf, 1965).

11. See Wendell Johnson, *People in Quandaries: The Semantics of Personal Adjustment* (New York: Harper and Row, 1946) and S. I. Hayakawa, *Language in Thought and Action* (New York: Harcourt, Brace and World, 1964).

12. For a quick survey of some representative historical accounts of the Abolitionists see "Introduction" in Richard O. Curry, ed., *The Abolitionists: Reformers or Fanatics?* (New York: Holt, Rinehart, 1965), pp. 1–9. See also David Donald, "Abolition Leadership: A Displaced Social Elite," *ibid.*, pp. 42–48.

13. "The Search for a Social Theory of Communication in American Sociology," Frank E. X. Dance, ed., *Human Communication Theory: Original Essays* (New York: Holt, Rinehart, 1967), p. 237.

14. Not all social scientists start from the assumption that rhetoric differs from social reality. Hugh Dalziel Duncan's work is illustrative of one who viewed symbolic forms as social reality. A group of sociologists exploring what they often referred to as the sociology of knowledge also assumed that social reality was smybolic. See, for example, Peter L. Burger and Thomas Luckmann, *The Social Construction of Reality: A Treatise in the Sociology of Knowledge* (1966: rpt. Garden City, N.Y.: Doubleday Anchor Books, 1967). See also Wallace J. Thies, "Public Address and the Sociology of Knowledge," *Journal of the Wisconsin Speech Communication Association*, 1 (1971), 28–41.

15. John Cotton, "God's Promise to His Plantations," *Old South Leaflets*, Vol. 3, No. 53.

16. Cotton Mather, *Manductuo Ad Ministerium: Directions for a Candidate of the Ministry* (1726; rpt. New York: Published for the Facsimile Text Society by Columbia Univ. Press, 1938), p. 114.

17. Perry Miller and Thomas H. Johnson, eds., *The Puritans*, I (1938; rpt. New York: Harper Torchbooks, 1963), p. 298.

18. Wayland Maxfield Parrish and Marie Hochmuth, eds., *American Speeches* (New York: Longmans, Green, 1954), p. 88.

19. Cotton Mather's advice to stammerers is typical of the Puritan vision which saw each affliction as an opportunity to improve in God's eyes. The stutterer should *"fetch Good out of Evil*...and make a very *pious Improvement* of your very *humbling Chastisement* which a sovereign GOD has laid upon you," quoted in Ernest G. Bormann, "Ephphatha, or, Some Advice to Stammerers," *Journal of Speech and Hearing Research*, 12 (Sept. 1969), 457.

20. Samuel Eliot Morison, *The Founding of Harvard College* (Cambridge: Harvard Univ. Press, 1935), pp. 99–100.

21. Ernest Cassirer, *Language and Myth*, trans. Susanne K. Langer (New York: Harper, 1946), p. 8.

22. Cassirer, pp. viii–ix.

23. See, for example, Tamotsu Shibutani, *Improvised News: A Sociological Study of Rumor* (Indianapolis: Bobbs-Merrill, 1966).

24. A seminar in organizational communication at the University of Minnesota taught by Professor David Smith in 1972 analyzed organizational myths (rhetorical visions) of all or part of four organizations in the Metropolitan Twin Cities area. Included in the study was a religious organization, a division of a major computer facility, a small family-owned business supply company, and a station of the University of Minnesota hospitals. The investigators used interviews to elicit narratives about the organizations and then submitted the resulting dramas to fantasy theme analysis.

25. For a representative analysis of emotions by a psychologist see Norman L. Munn, *Psychology: The Fundamentals of Human Adjustment*, 5th ed. (Boston: Houghton Mifflin, 1966), pp. 189–221.

26. My notion is not the same as Kenneth Burke's concept as interpreted by Richard E. Crable and John J. Makay, "Kenneth Burke's Concept of Motives in Rhetorical Theory," *Today's Speech*, 20 (Win. 1972), 11–18. Crable and Makay present a survey of various commentaries on Burke's view of motives in rhetorical theory and provide an interpretation of their own. Much closer to my view of motivation is that developed by Karlyn Kohrs Campbell, "The Ontological Foundations of Rhetorical Theory," *Philosophy and Rhetoric*, 3 (Spr. 1970), 97–108. She writes, for instance, of theorists who "contend that human motivation is distinct from that of other beings because the nature and structure of language are themselves motivating forces and because the interaction between man and his language profoundly transforms his physical, biological, and animal needs, drives and desires.... In addition, the interaction between man and language is viewed as a process which destroys all purely 'animal' or 'biological' motives." (p. 104)

Select Bibliography of Recent Critical Studies

Although the following Bibliography is extensive, it is not exhaustive. The bibliography presents a sample of critical studies, published over the last decade that illustrates the rich variety of critical purposes, approaches and objects for study that are open to the rhetorical critic.

Andrews, James R. "Rhetoric in the Creation of Social Reality: Radical Consciousness and Whig Strategy in Parliamentary Reform." *Quarterly Journal of Speech*, 69 (1983), 401–412.

Appel, Edward C. "The Perfected Drama of Rev. Jerry Falwell." *Communication Quarterly*, 35 (1987), 26–38.

Balthrop, V. William. "Culture, Myth, and Ideology as Public Argument: An Interpretation of the Ascent and Demise of Southern Culture." *Communication Monographs*, 51 (1984), 339–352.

Bass, Jeff D. "The Appeal to Efficiency as Narrative Closure: Lyndon Johnson and the Dominican Crisis, 1965." *Southern Speech Communication Journal*, 50 (1985), 103–120.

Bate, Barbara, and Lois S. Self. "The Rhetoric of Career Success Books for Women." *Journal of Communication*, 33 (1983), 149–165.

Benson, Thomas W. "The Rhetorical Structure of Frederick Wiseman's *Primate*." *Quarterly Journal of Speech*, 71 (1985), 204–217.

Birdsell, David S. "Ronald Reagan on Lebanon and Grenada: Flexibility and Interpretation in the Application of Kenneth Burke's Pentad." *Quarterly Journal of Speech*, 73 (1987), 267–279.

Black, Edwin. "Ideological Justifications." *Quarterly Journal of Speech*, 70 (1984), 144–150.

Blair, Carole. "From 'All of President's Men' to Every Man for Himself: The Strategies of Post-Watergate Apologia." *Central States Speech Journal*, 35 (1984), 250–260.

Bormann, Ernest G., Becky Swanson Kroll, Kathleen Waters, and Douglas McFarland. "Rhetorical Visions of Committed Voters: Fantasy Theme Analysis of a Large Sample Survey." *Critical Studies in Mass Communication*, 1 (1984), 287–310.

Bormann, Ernest G. *The Force of Fantasy: Restoring the American Dream*. Carbondale: Southern Illinois University Press, 1985.

Bostdorff, Denise M. "Making Light of James Watt: A Burkean Approach to the Form and Attitude of Political Cartoons." *Quarterly Journal of Speech*, 73 (1987), 43–59.

Boyd, Newell D. "Gladstone, Midlothian and Stump Oratory." *Central States Speech Journal*, 30 (1979), 144–155.

Boyd, Newell D. "The Emergence of the Welsh Bounder: David Lloyd George's Oratorical Attacks During the Anglo–Boer War." *Communication Monographs*, 52 (1985), 78–91.

Braden, Waldo W., and Harold Mixon. "Epideictic Speaking in the Post-Civil War South and the Southern Experience." *Southern Speech Communication Journal*, 54 (1988), 40–57.

Branham, Robert, and W. Barnett Pearce. "A Contract for Civility: Edward Kennedy's Lynchburg Address." *Quarterly Journal of Speech*, 73 (1987), 424–443.

Brown, Stephen H. "Edmund Burke's *Letter to a Noble Lord*: A Textual Study in Political Philosophy and Rhetorical Action." *Communication Monographs*, 55 (1988), 215–229.

Brummett, Barry. "Perfection and the Bomb: Nuclear Weapons, Teleology, and Motives." *Journal of Communication*, 39 (1989), 85–95.

Burgchardt, Carl R. "Two Faces of American Communism: Pamphlet Rhetoric of the Third Period and the Popular Front." *Quarterly Journal of Speech*, 66 (1980), 375–391.

Burgchardt, Craig R. "Discovering Rhetorical Imprints: LaFollette, 'Iago,' and the Melodramatic Scenario." *Quarterly Journal of Speech*, 71 (1985), 441–456.

Bytwerk, Randall L. "The SST Controversy: A Case Study of the Rhetoric of Technology." *Central States Speech Journal*, 30 (1979), 187–198.

Campbell, John Angus. "Scientific Revolution and the Grammar of Culture: The Case of Darwin's *Origin*." *Quarterly Journal of Speech*, 72 (1986), 351–376.

Campbell, J. Louis III. "Jimmy Carter and the Rhetoric of Charisma." *Central States Speech Journal*, 30 (1979), 174–186.

Campbell, J. Louis III. 'All Men are Created Equal': Waiting for Godot in the Culture of Inequality." *Communication Monographs*, 55 (1988), 143–161.

Campbell, Karlyn Kohrs. "Stanton's 'The Solitude of Self': A Rationale for Feminism." *Quarterly Journal of Speech*, 66 (1980), 304–312.

Campbell, Karlyn Kohrs. "Style and Content in the Rhetoric of Early Afro-American Feminists." *Quarterly Journal of Speech*, 72 (1986), 434–445.

Campbell, Karlyn Kohrs, and Kathleen Hall Jamieson. "Inaugurating the Presidency." *Presidential Studies Quarterly*, 15 (1985), 394–411.

Carlson, A. Cheree. "Albert J. Beveridge as Imperialist and Progressive: The Means Justify the Ends." *Western Journal of Speech Communication*, 52 (1988), 46–62.

Carlson, A. Cheree. "Gandhi and the Comic Frame: 'Ad Bellum Purificandum'." *Quarterly Journal of Speech*, 72 (1986), 446–455.

Carlson, A. Cheree. "John Quincy Adams 'Armistad Address': Eloquence in a Generic Hybrid." *Western Journal of Speech Communication*, 49 (1985), 14–26.

Carlson, A. Cheree and John E. Hocking. "Strategies of Redemption at the Vietnam Veterans' Memorial." *Western Journal of Speech Communication*, 52 (1988), 203–215.

Carlton, Charles. "The Rhetoric of Death: Scaffold Confessions in Early Modern England." *Southern Speech Communication Journal*, 49 (1983), 66–79.

Carpenter, Ronald H. *The Eloquence of Frederick Jackson Turner*. San Marino, CA: The Huntington Library, 1983.

Carpenter, Ronald H. "Admiral Mahan, 'Narrative Fidelity,' and the Japanese Attack on Pearl Harbor." *Quarterly Journal of Speech*, 72 (1986), 290–305.

Carpenter, Ronald H. "On American History Textbooks and Integration in the South: Woodrow Wilson and the Rhetoric of *Division and Reunion 1829–1889*." *Southern Speech Communication Journal*, 51 (1985), 1–23.

Carpenter, Ronald H. "Woodrow Wilson as Speechwriter for George Creel: Presidential Style in Discourse as an Index of Personality." *Presidential Studies Quarterly*, 19 (1989), 117–126.

Carter, David A. "The Industrial Workers of the World and the Rhetoric of Song." *Quarterly Journal of Speech*, 66 (1980), 365–374.

Chester, Edward W. "Beyond the Rhetoric: A New Look at Presidential Inaugural Addresses." *Presidential Studies Quarterly*, 10 (1980), 571–582.

Chester, Edward W. "Shadow or Substance? Critiquing Reagan's Inaugural Address." *Presidential Studies Quarterly*, 11 (1981), 172–176.

Clark, E. Culpepper. "Pitchfork Ben Tillman and the Emergence of Southern Demagoguery." *Quarterly Journal of Speech*, 69 (1983), 423–433.

Clark, Thomas. "An Exploration of Generic Aspects of Contemporary American Campaign Orations." *Central States Speech Journal*, 30 (1979), 122–133.

Condit, Celeste Michelle. "The Function of Epideictic: The Boston Massacre Orations as Exemplar." *Communication Quarterly*, 33 (1985), 284–298.

Condit, Celeste Michelle, and J. Ann Selzer. "The Rhetoric of Objectivity in the Newspaper Coverage of a Murder Trial." *Critical Studies in Mass Communication*, 2 (1985), 197–216.

Cooper, Martha, and John J. Makay. "Knowledge, Power and Freud's Clark Conference Lectures." *Quarterly Journal of Speech*, 74 (1988), 416–433.

Corcoran, Farrel. "The Bear in the Back Yard: Myth, Ideology, and Victimage Ritual in Soviet Funerals." *Communication Monographs*, 50 (1983), 305–320.

Crable, Richard E., and Steven L. Vibbert. "Mobil's Epideictic Advocacy: 'Observations' of Prometheus Bound." *Communication Monographs*, 50 (1983), 380–394.

Daniels, Tom D., Richard J. Jensen, and Allen Lichtenstein. "Resolving the Paradox in Politicized Christian Fundamentalism." *Western Journal of Speech Communication*, 49 (1985), 248–266.

Darsey, James. "The Legend of Eugene Debs: Prophetic *Ethos* as Radical Argument." *Quarterly Journal of Speech*, 74 (1988), 434–452.

Depoe, Stephen P. "Arthur Schlesinger, Jr.'s 'Middle Way Out of Vietnam': The Limits of 'Technocratic Realism' as the Basis for Foreign Policy Dissent." *Western Journal of Speech Communication*, 52 (1988), 147–166.

Diffley, Kathleen. "'Erecting Anew the Standard of Freedom': Salmon P. Chase's 'Appeal of the Independent Democrats' and the Rise of the Republican Party." *Quarterly Journal of Speech*, 74 (1988), 401–415.

DiMare, Lesley A. "Functionalizing Conflict: Jesse Jackson's Rhetorical Strategy at the 1984 Democratic National Convention." *Western Journal of Speech Communication*, 51 (1987), 218–226.

Dowling, Ralph E., and Gabrielle Marraro. "Grenada and the Great Communicator: A Study in Democratic Ethics." *Western Journal of Speech Communication*, 50 (1986), 350–367.

Doyle, Marsha Vanderford. "The Rhetoric of Romance: A Fantasy Theme Analysis of Barbara Cartland Novels." *Southern Speech Communication Journal*, 51 (1985), 24–48.

Duffy, Bernard K. "The Anti-Humanist Rhetoric of the New Religious Right." *Southern Speech Communication Journal*, 49 (1984), 339–360.

Enholm, Donald K., David Curtis Skaggs, and W. Jeffrey Welsh. "Origins of the Southern Mind: The Parochial Sermons of Thomas Cardock of Maryland, 1744–1770." *Quarterly Journal of Speech*, 73 (1987), 200–218.

Erickson, Keith V. "Jimmy Carter: The Rhetoric of Private and Civic Piety." *Western Speech*, 44 (1980), 235–251.

Fischli, Ronald. "Anita Bryant's Stand Against 'Militant Homosexuality': Religious Fundamentalism and the Democratic Process." *Central States Speech Journal*, 30 (1979), 262–271.

Foss, Karen A., and Stephen W. Littlejohn. "*The Day After*: Rhetorical Vision in an Ironic Frame." *Critical Studies in Mass Communication*, 3 (1986), 317–336.

Foss, Sonja K. "Equal Rights Amendment Controversy: Two Worlds in Conflict." *Quarterly Journal of Speech*, 65 (1979), 275–288.

Foss, Sonja K. "Ambiguity as Persuasion: The Vietnam Veterans Memorial." *Communication Quarterly*, 34 (1986), 326–339.

Fulkerson, Richard P. "The Public Letter as a Rhetorical Form: Structure, Logic, and Style in King's 'Letter from Birmingham Jail.'" *Quarterly Journal of Speech*, 65 (1979), 121–136.

Fulmer, Hal W. "Mythic Imagery and Irish Nationalism: Henry Grattan Against Union, 1800." *Western Journal of Speech Communication*, 50 (1986), 144–157.

Gilbert, Robert E. "The Eisenhower Campaign of 1952: War Hero as Television Candidate." *Political Communication and Persuasion*, 3 (1985), 293–312.

Glenn, Gary D. "Rhetoric and Religion in the 1984 Campaign." *Political Communication and Persuasion*, 5 (1988), 1–14.

Goldzwig, Steven. "James Watt's Subversion of Values: An Analysis of Rhetorical Failure." *Southern Speech Communication Journal*, 50 (1985), 305–326.

Goldzwig, Steven. "A Rhetoric of Public Theology: The Religious Rhetor and Public Policy." *Southern Speech Communication Journal*, 52 (1987), 128–150.

Goodnight, G. Thomas. "Ronald Reagan's Reformulation of the Rhetoric of War: Analysis of the 'Zero Option', 'Evil Empire', and 'Star Wars' Addresses." *Quarterly Journal of Speech*, 72 (1986), 390–414.

Grade, Rebecca Drake. "Origin of the 'Lost casue' Argument: Analysis of Civil War Letters." *Southern Speech Communication Journal*, 49 (1984), 420–430.

Graves, Michael P. "Functions of Key Metaphors in Early Quaker Sermons, 1671–1700." *Quarterly Journal of Speech*, 69 (1983), 364–378.

Green, Lawrence D. "'We'll Dress Him Up in Voices': The Rhetoric of Disjunction in *Troilus and Cressida*." *Quarterly Journal of Speech*, 70 (1984), 23–40.

Griffin, Keith H. "The Light That Failed: A Rhetorical Analysis of Walter Hines Page as a Ceremonial Orator." *Southern Speech Communication Journal*, 46 (1980), 228–250.

Griffin, Leland M. "When Dreams Collide: Rhetorical Trajectories in the Assassination of President Kennedy." *Quarterly Journal of Speech*, 70 (1984), 111–131.

Gronbeck, Bruce E. "Functional and Dramaturgical Themes of Presidential Campaigning." *Presidential Studies Quarterly*, 14 (1984), 486–499.

Gross, Alan G. "Public Debates as Failed Social Dramas; The Recombinant DNA Controversy." *Quarterly Journal of Speech*, 70 (1984), 397–409.

Gustainis, J. Justin, and Dan F. Hahn. "While the Whole World Watched: Rhetorical Failures of Anti-War Protest." *Communication Quarterly*, 36 (1988), 203–216.

Gwin, Stanford P. "Slavery and English Polarity: The Persuasive Campaign of John Bright Against English Recognition of the Confederate States of America." *Southern Speech Communication Journal*, 49 (1984), 406–419.

Hahn, Dan F. "One's Reborn Every Minute: Carter's Religious Appeal in 1976." *Communication Quarterly*, 28 (1980), 56–62.

Hahn, Dan F. "Archetype and Signature in Johnson's 1965 State of the Union." *Central States Speech Journal*, 34 (1983), 236–246.

Hahn, Dan F. and . Justin Gustainis. "Anatomy of an Enigma: Jimmy Carter's 1980 State of the Union Address." *Communication Quarterly*, 33 (1985), 43–49.

Hahn, Dan F. "The Rhetoric of Jimmy Carter, 1976–1980." *Presidential Studies Quarterly*, 14 (1984), 265–288.

Hammerback, John C., and Richard J. Jensen. "The Rhetorical Worlds of Cesar Chavez and Reies Tijerina." *Western Speech*, 44 (1980), 176–189.

Hammerback, John C., Richard J. Jensen, and Jose Angel Gutierrez. *A War of Words: Chicano Protest in the 1960s and 1970s*. Westport, CT: Greenwood Press, 1985.

Harrell, Jackson, B. L. Ware, and Wil Linkugel. "Failure of Apology in American Politics: Nixon on Watergate." *Speech Monographs*, 42 (1975), 245–261.

Hart, Roderick P. "The Language of the Modern Presidency." *Presidential Studies Quarterly*, 14 (1984), 249–264.

Hart, Roderick P., Patrick Jerome, and Karen McComb. "Rhetorical Features of Newscasts About the President." *Critical Studies in Mass Communication*, 1 (1984), 260–286.

Heisey, D. Ray, and J. David Trebing. "Authority and Legitimacy: A Rhetorical Case Study of the Iranian Revolution." *Communication Monographs*, 53 (1986), 295–310.

Henry, David. "The Rhetorical Dynamics of Mario Cuomo's 1984 Keynote Address: Situation, Speaker, Metaphor." *Southern Speech Communication Journal*, 53 (1988), 105–120.

Hikins, James W. "The Rhetoric of 'Unconditional Surrender' and the Decision to Drop the Atomic Bomb." *Quarterly Journal of Speech*, 69 (1983), 379–400.

Hogan, J. Michael. "Public Opinion and American Foreign Policy: The Case of Illusory Support for the Panama Canal Treaties." *Quarterly Journal of Speech*, 71 (1985), 302–317.

Hogan, J. Michael. *The Panama Canal in American Politics: Domestic Advocacy and the Evolution of Policy*. Carbondale: Southern Illinois University Press, 1986.

Hogan, J. Michael. "Wallace and the Wallacites: A Reexamination." *Southern Speech Communication Journal*, 50 (1984), 24–48.

Hogan, J. Michael. "Theodore Roosevelt and the Heroes of Panama." *Presidential Studies Quarterly*, 19 (1989), 79–94.

Hollihan, Thomas A. "Propagandizing in the Interest of War: A Rhetorical Study of the Committee on Public Information." *Southern Speech Communication Journal*, 49 (1984), 241–257.

Hollihan, Thomas A. "The Public Controversy Over the Panama Canal Treaties: An Analysis of American Foreign Policy Rhetoric." *Western Journal of Speech Communication*, 50 (1986), 368–387.

Holmberg, Carl Bryan. "Sir Joshua Reynold's Nonliterary, Preromantic Rhetoric." *Southern Speech Communication Journal*, 49 (1984), 289–308.

Ingold, Beth A. J., and Theodore Otto Windt, Jr.. "Trying to 'Stay the Course': President Reagan's Rhetoric During the 1982 Elections." *Presidential Studies Quarterly*, 14 (1984), 87–97.

Ivie, Robert L. "Metaphor and the Rhetorical Invention of Cold War 'Idealists'." *Communication Monographs*, 54 (1987), 165–182.

Ivie, Robert L. "Speaking 'Common Sense' About the Soviet Threat: Reagan's Rhetorical Stance." *Western Journal of Speech Communication*, 48 (1984), 39–50.

Jablonski, Carol J. "Promoting Radical Change in the Roman Catholic Church: Rhetorical Requirements, Problems, and Strategies of the American Bishops." *Central States Speech Journal*, 31 (1980), 282–289.

Jablonski, Carol J. "Rhetoric, Paradox, and the Movement for Women's Ordination in the Roman Catholic Church." *Quarterly Journal of Speech*, 74 (1988), 164–183.

Jamieson, Kathleen Hall. *Packaging the Presidency: A History and Criticism of Presidential Campaign Advertising*. New York: Oxford University Press, 1984.

Japp, Phyllis M. "Esther of Isaiah?: The Abolitionist-Feminist Rhetoric of Angelina Grimke." *Quarterly Journal of Speech*, 71 (1985), 335–348.

Jensen, J. Vernon. "Robert G. Ingersoll: 'True Believer' Unbeliever." *Central States Speech Journal*, 35 (1984), 105–112.

Jensen, Richard J., and John C. Hammerback. "Radical Nationalism Among Chicanos: The Rhetoric of Jose Angel Gutierrez." *Western Speech*, 44 (1980), 202–212.

Jensen, Richard J., and Cara J. Abeyta. "The Minority in the Middle: Asian-American Dissent in the 1960s and 1970s." *Western Journal of Speech Communication*, 51 (1987), 402–416.

Jensen, Richard J. and John C. Hammerback. "From Muslim to Mormon: Eldridge Cleaver's Rhetorical Crusade." *Communication Quarterly*, 34 (1986), 24–40.

Johannesen, Richard L. "The Jeremiad and Jenkin Lloyd Jones." *Communication Monographs*, 52 (1985), 156–172.

Johannesen, Richard L. "Ronald Reagan's Economic Jeremiad." *Central States Speech Journal*, 37 (1986), 79–89.

Kahl, Mary. "*Blind Ambition* Culminates in *Lost Honor*: A Comparative Analysis of John Dean's Apologetic Strategies." *Central States Speech Journal*, 35 (1984), 239–250.

Kaplan-Tuckel, Barbara. "Disraeli on Jewish Disabilities: Another Look." *Central States Speech Journal*, 30 (1979), 156–163.

Kaufer, David S. "The Ironist and Hypocrite as Presidential Symbols: A Nixon-Kennedy Analog." *Communication Quarterly*, 27 (1979), 20–26.

King, Robert L. "Transforming Scandel into Tragedy: A Rhetoric of Political Apology." *Quarterly Journal of Speech*, 71 (1985), 289–301.

Klope, David C. "Defusing a Foreign Policy Crisis: Myth and Victimage in Reagan's 1983 Lebanon/Grenada Address." *Western Journal of Speech Communication*, 50 (1986), 336–349.

Klumpp, James F., and Thomas A. Hollihan. "Debunking the Resignation of Earl Butz: Sacrificing an Official Racist." *Quarterly Journal of Speech*, 65 (1979), 1–11.

Kuseski, Brenda K. "Kenneth Burke's 'Five Dogs' and Mother Teresa's Love." *Quarterly Journal of Speech*, 74 (1988), 323–333.

Lake, Randall A. "Order and Disorder in Anti-Abortion Rhetoric: A Logological View." *Quarterly Journal of Speech*, 70 (1984), 425–443.

Lee, Ronald. "The New Populist Campaign for Economic Democracy: A Rhetorical Exploration." *Quarterly Journal of Speech*, 72 (1986), 274–289.

Lessl, Thomas M. "Science and the Sacred Cosmos: The Ideological Rhetoric of Carl Sagan." *Quarterly Journal of Speech*, 71 (1985), 175–187.

Lewis, William F. "Telling America's Story: Narrative Form and the Reagan Presidency." *Quarterly Journal of Speech*, 73 (1987), 280–302.

Logue, Calvin M. and Howard Dorgan, eds. *A New Diversity in Contemporary Southern Rhetoric*. Baton Rouge: Louisiana State University Press, 1987.

Lyne, John, and Henry F. Howe. " 'Punctuated Equilibria': Rhetorical Dynamics of a Scientific Controversy." *Quarterly Journal of Speech*, 72 (1986), 132–147.

McCants, David A. "The Role of Patrick Henry in the Stamp Act Debate." *Southern Speech Communication Journal*, 46 (1981), 205–227.

McGee, Michael Calvin. "Secular Humanism: A Radical Reading of 'Culture Industry' Productions." *Critical Studies in Mass Communication*, 1 (1984), 1–33.

Makay, John J., and Alberto Gonzalez. "Dylan's Biographical Rhetoric and the Myth of the Outlaw Hero." *Southern Speech Communication Journal*, 52 (1987), 165–180.

Manoff, Robert Karl. "Modes of War and Modes of Social Address: The Text of SDI." *Journal of Communication*, 39 (1989), 59–84.

Martin, Donald R., and Vicky Gordon Martin. "Barbara Jordan's Symbolic Use of Language in the Keynote Address to the National Women's Conference." *Southern Speech Communication Journal*, 49 (1984), 319–330.

Martin, Martha Anne. "Ideologues, Ideographs, and 'The Best Man': From Carter to Reagan." *Southern Speech Communication Journal*, 49 (1983), 12–25.

Medhurst, Martin J. "Argument and Role: Monsignor John A. Ryan on Social Justice." *Western Journal of Speech Communication*, 52 (1988), 75–90.

Medhurst, Martin J. "Eisenhower's 'Atoms for Peace' Speech: A Case Study in the Strategic Use of Language." *Communication Monographs*, 54 (1987), 204–220.

Medhurst, Martin J. "Postponing the Social Agenda: Reagan's Strategy and Tactics." *Western Journal of Speech Communication*, 48 (1984), 262–276.

Medhurst, Martin J. "Truman's Rhetorical Reticence, 1945–1947: An Interpretive Essay." *Quarterly Journal of Speech*, 74 (1988), 52–70.

Mister, Steven M. "Reagan's Challenger Tribute: Combining Generic Constraints and Situational Demands." *Central States Speech Journal*, 37 (1986), 158–165.

Mohrmann, G. P. "Place and Space: Calhoun's Fatal Security." *Western Journal of Speech Communication*, 51 (1987), 143–158.

Moore, Mark P. "Reagan's Quest for Freedom in the 1987 State of the Union Address." *Western Journal of Speech Communication*, 53 (1989), 52–65.

Oliver, Robert T. *The Influence of Rhetoric in the Shaping of Great Britain*. Newark: University of Delaware Press, 1986.

Oliver, Robert T. *Public Speaking in the Reshaping of Great Britain*. Newark: University of Delaware Press, 1987.

Olson, Lester C. "Benjamin Franklin's Pictorial Representations of the British Colonies in America: A Study in Rhetorical Iconology." *Quarterly Journal of Speech*, 73 (1987), 18–42.

Oravec, Christine. "Conservationism vs. Preservationism: The 'Public Interest' in the Hetch Hetchy Controversy." *Quarterly Journal of Speech*, 70 (1984), 444–458.

Osborne, Leonard L. "Rhetorical Pattern in President Kennedy's Major Speeches: A Case Study." *Presidential Studies Quarterly*, 10 (1980), 332–335.

Palmerton, Patricia R. "The Rhetoric of Terrorism and Media Response to the 'Crisis in Iran'." *Western Journal of Speech Communication*, 52 (1988), 105–121.

Pearce, W. Barnett, Stephen W. Littlejohn, and Alison Alexander. "The New Christian Right and the Humanist Response: Reciprocated Diatribe." *Communication Quarterly*, 35 (1987), 171–192.

Perry, Steven. "Rhetorical Functions of the Infestation Metaphor in Hitler's Rhetoric." *Central States Speech Journal*, 34 (1983), 229–235.

Peterson, Tarla Rai. "The Rhetorical Construction of Institutional Authority in a Senate Subcommittee Hearing on Wilderness Legislation." *Western Journal of Speech Communication*, 52 (1988), 259–276.

Peterson, Tarla Rai. "The Will to Conservation: A Burkeian Analysis of Dust Bowl Rhetoric and American Farming Motives." *Southern Speech Communication Journal*, 52 (1986), 1–21.

Philipsen, Gerry. "Mayor Daley's Council Speech: A Cultural Analysis." *Quarterly Journal of Speech*, 72 (1986), 247–260.

Pilota, Joseph, John W. Murphy, Elizabeth Wilson, and Tricia Jones. "The Contemporary Rhetoric of the Social Theories of Law." *Central States Speech Journal*, 34 (1983), 211–220.

Preston, C. Thomas. "Reagan's 'New Beginning': Is it the 'New Deal' of the Eighties?" *Southern Speech Communication Journal*, 49 (1984), 198–211.

Railsback, Celeste C. "The Contemporary American Abortion Controversy: Stages in the Argument." *Quarterly Journal of Speech*, 70 (1984), 410–424.

Rasmussen, Karen, and Sharon D. Downey. "Dialectical Disorientation in *Agnes of God*." *Western Journal of Speech Communication*, 53 (1989), 66–84.

Ritter, Kurt W. "American Political Rhetoric and the Jeremiad Tradition: Presidential Nomination Acceptance Addresses, 1960–1976." *Central States Speech Journal*, 31 (1980), 153–171.

Ritter, Kurt W. "Drama and Legal Rhetoric: The Perjury Trials of Alger Hiss." *Western Journal of Speech Communication*, 49 (1985), 83–102.

Ross, David. "The Projection of Credibility as a Rhetorical Strategy in Anwar el-Sadat's Address to the Israeli Parliament." *Western Speech*, 44 (1980), 74–80.

Rowland, Robert C., "On Limiting the Narrative Paradigm: Three Case Studies." *Communication Monographs*, 56 (1989), 39–54.

Rowland, Robert C., and Roger A. Payne. "The Context-Embeddedness of Political Discourse: A Re-Evaluation of Reagan's Rhetoric in the 1982 Midterm Election Campaign." *Presidential Studies Quarterly*, 14 (1984), 500–511.

Rowland, Robert C., and Rodger A. Payne. "The Effectiveness of Reagan's 'Star Wars' Address: The Three Audiences of Defense Policy Rhetoric." *Political Communication and Persuasion*, 4 (1987), 161–178.

Rushing, Janice Hocker. "*E.T.* as Rhetorical Transcendence." *Quarterly Journal of Speech*, 71 (1985), 188–203.

Rushing, Janice Hocker. "Evolution of 'The New Frontier' in *Alien* and *Aliens*: Patriarchal Co-optation of the Feminine Archetype." *Quarterly Journal of Speech*, 75 (1989), 1–24.

Rushing, Janice Hocker. "Mythic Evolution of 'The New Frontier' in Mass Mediated Rhetoric," *Critical Studies in Mass Communication*, 3 (1986), 265–296.

Rushing, Janice Hocker. "Ronald Reagan's 'Star Wars' Address: Mythic Containment of Technical Reasoning." *Quarterly Journal of Speech*, 72 (1986), 415–433.

Ryan, Halford Ross. "Baldwin vs. Edward VIII: A Case Study in *Kategoria* and *Apologia*." *Southern Speech Communication Journal*, 49 (1984), 125–134.

Scheele, Henry Z. "Ronald Reagan's 1980 Acceptance Address: A Focus on American Values." *Western Journal of Speech Communication*, 48 (1984), 51–61.

Scult, Allen, Michael Calvin McGee, and J. Kenneth Kurtz. "Genesis and Power: An Analysis of the Biblical Story of Creation." *Quarterly Journal of Speech*, 72 (1986), 113–131.

Sedano, Michael Victor. "Chicanismo: A Rhetorical Analysis of Themes and Images of Selected Poetry from the Chicano Movement." *Western Speech*, 44 (1980), 190–201.

Short, C. Brant. "Comic Book Apologia: The 'Paranoid' Rhetoric of Congressman George Hansen." *Western Journal of Speech Communication*, 51 (1987), 189–203.

Short, C. Brant. *Ronald Reagan and the Public Lands*. College Station: Texas A & M University Press, 1989.

Smith, Craig Allen. "An Organic Systems Analysis of Persuasion and Social Movement: The John Birch Society, 1958–1966." *Southern Speech Communication Journal*, 49 (1984), 155–176.

Smith, Craig Allen. "Leadership, Orientation, and Rhetorical Vision: Jimmy Carter, The 'New Right,' and the Panama Canal." *Presidential Studies Quarterly*, 16 (1986), 317–328.

Smith, Craig Allen. "Mister Reagan's Neighborhood: Rhetoric and National Unity." *Southern Speech Communication Journal*, 52 (1987), 219–239.

Smith, Craig Allen, and Kathy B. Smith. "Presidential Values and Public Priorities: Recurrent Patterns in Addresses to the Nation, 1963–1984." *Presidential Studies Quarterly*, 15 (1985), 743–753.

Smith, Craig Allen. "The Audiences of the 'Rhetorical Presidency': An Analysis of Presidential-Constituent Interactions, 1963–1981." *Presidential Studies Quarterly*, 13 (1983), 613–622.

Smith, Craig R. "Ronald Reagan's Attempt to Build a National Majority." *Central States Speech Journal*, 30 (1979), 98–102.

Smith, Craig R. "Daniel Webster's July 17th Address: A Mediating Influence in the 1850 Compromise." *Quarterly Journal of Speech*, 71 (1985), 349–361.

Smith, Stephen A. "Sounds of the South: The Rhetorical Saga of Country Music Lyrics." *Southern Speech Communication Journal*, 45 (1980), 164–172.

Smith, Stephen A. "Redemptive Rhetoric: The Continuity Motif in the Rhetoric of Right to Life." *Central States Speech Journal*, 31 (1980), 52–62.

Snow, Melinda. "Martin Luther King's 'Letter from Birmingham Jail' as Pauline Epistle." *Quarterly Journal of Speech*, 71 (1985), 318–334.

Solomon, Martha. "Ideology as Rhetorical Constraint: The Anarchist Agitation of 'Red Emma' Goldman." *Quarterly Journal of Speech*, 74 (1988), 184–200.

Solomon, Martha. "The Rhetoric of Dehumanization: An Analysis of Medical Reports of the Tuskegee Syphilis Project." *Western Journal of Speech Communication*, 49 (1985), 233–247.

Solomon, Martha. "Villianless Quest: Myth, Metaphor, and Dream in 'Chariots of Fire'." *Communication Quarterly*, 31 (1983), 274–281.

Solomon, Martha. *Emma Goldman*. Boston: Twayne Publishers, 1987.

Starosta, William J. "Roots for an Older Rhetoric: On Rhetorical Effectiveness in the Third World." *Western Speech*, 43 (1979), 278–287.

Thompson, Wayne N. "Barbara Jordan's Keynote Address: Fulfilling Dual and Conflicting Purposes." *Central States Speech Journal*, 30 (1979), 272–277.

Thompson, Wayne N. "Barbara Jordan's Keynote Address: The Juxtaposition of Contradictory Values." *Southern Speech Communication Journal*, 44 (1979), 223-232.

Turner, Kathleen J. *Lyndon Johnson's Dual War: Vietnam and the Press*. Chicago: The University of Chicago Press, 1985.

Vartabedian, Robert A. "Nixon's Vietnam Rhetoric: A Case Study of Apologia as Generic Paradox." *Southern Speech Communication Journal*, 50 (1985), 366–381.

Walzer, Arthur E. "Logic and Rhetoric in Malthus' *Essay on the Principle of Population, 1798*." *Quarterly Journal of Speech*, 73 (1987), 1–17.

Wander, Philip. "The Aesthetics of Fascism." *Journal of Communication*, 33 (1983), 70–78.

Wander, Philip. "The Rhetoric of American Foreign Policy." *Quarterly Journal of Speech*, 70 (1984), 339–361.

Warnick, Barbara. "A Rhetorical Analysis of Episteme Shifts: Darwin's *Origins of the Species*." *Southern Speech Communication Journal*, 49 (1983), 26–42.

Weaver, Bruce J. "Debate and the Destruction of Friendship: An Analysis of Fox and Burke on the French Revolution." *Quarterly Journal of Speech*, 67 (1981), 57–68.

Weiler, Michael. "The Rhetoric of Neo-Liberalism." *Quarterly Journal of Speech*, 70 (1984), 362–378.

Witherspoon, Patricia D. "'Let us Continue': The Rhetorical Initiation of Lyndon Johnson's Presidency." *Presidential Studies Quarterly*, 17 (1987), 531–540.

Young, Marilyn J., and Michael K. Launer. "KAL 007 and the Superpowers: An International Argument." *Quarterly Journal of Speech*, 74 (1988), 271–295.

Zarefsky, David. "The Great Society as a Rhetorical Proposition." *Quarterly Journal of Speech*, 65 (1979), 364–378.

Zarefsky, David. "Conspiracy Arguments in the Lincoln-Douglas Debates." *Journal of the American Forensics Association*, 21 (1984), 63–75.

Zarefsky, David. "The Lincoln-Douglas Debates Revisited: The Evoluation of Public Argument." *Quarterly Journal of Speech*, 72 (1986), 162–184.

Zarefsky, David, Carol Miller-Tutzauer, and Frank E. Tutzauer. "Reagan's Safety Net for the Truly Needy: The Rhetorical Uses of Definition." *Central States Speech Journal*, 35 (1984), 113–119.

Zarefsky, David. *President Johnson's War on Poverty: Rhetoric and History*. University: The University of Alabama Press, 1986.

Select Bibliography of Works on Critical Theory and Practice

The following bibliography samples work on the theory and practice of rhetorical criticism.

Andrews, James R. *A Choice of Worlds: The Practice and Criticism of Public Discourse*. New York: Harper Row, 1973.

Baskerville, Barnet. "Must We All Be 'Rhetorical Critics'?" *Quarterly Journal of Speech*, 63 (1977), 107–116.

Bennett, W. Lance, and Murray Edelman. "Toward a New Political Narrative." *Journal of Communication*, 35 (1985), 156–171.

Bitzer, Lloyd F. "The Rhetorical Situation." *Philosophy and Rhetoric*, 1 (1968), 1–14.

Black, Edwin. *Rhetorical Criticism: A Study in Method*. New York: MacMillan, 1965: rpt. Madison, Wisconsin: University of Wisconsin Press, 1978.

Black, Edwin. "Secrecy and Disclosure as Rhetorical Forms." *Quarterly Journal of Speech*, 74 (1988), 133–150.

Bock, Douglas G. "Axiology and Rhetorical Criticism: Some Dimensions of the Critical Judgment." *Western Speech*, 37 (1973), 87–96.

Booth, Wayne C. *The Rhetoric of Fiction*. Chicago: University of Chicago Press, 1961.

Brown, William R. "Power and the Rhetoric of Social Intervention." *Communication Monographs*, 53 (1986), 180–199.

Brummett, Barry. "Burke's Representative Anecdote as a Method in Media Criticism." *Critical Studies in Mass Communication*, 1 (1984), 161–176.

Brummett, Barry. "Consensus Criticism." *Southern Speech Communication Journal*, 49 (1984), 111–124.

Bryant, Donald C. *Rhetorical Dimensions of Criticism*. Baton Rouge: Louisiana State University Press, 1973.

Burgess, Parke. "The Rhetoric of Moral Conflict: Two Critical Dimensions." *Quarterly Journal of Speech*, 56 (1970), 120–130.

Burke, Kenneth. *A Grammar of Motives*. Englewood Cliffs. N.J.: Prentice-Hall, 1946.

Burke, Kenneth. *A Rhetoric of Motives*. Englewood Cliffs, N.J.: Prentice-Hall, 1950.

Campbell, Karlyn Kohrs. "Criticism: Ephemeral and Enduring." *Speech Teacher*, 23 (1974), 9–14.

Campbell, Karlyn Kohrs. "The Nature of Criticism in Rhetorical and Communicative Studies." *Central States Speech Journal*, 30 (1979), 4–13.

Campbell, Karlyn Kohrs, and Kathleen Hall Jamieson, eds. and intro. essay. *Form and Genre*. Falls Church, Va.: Speech Communication Association, n.d.

Chesebro, James W. "The Symbolic Construction of Social Realities: A Case Study in the Rhetorical Criticism of Paradox." *Communication Quarterly*, 32 (1985), 164–171.

Chesebro, James W., and Caroline D. Hamsher. "Contemporary Rhetorical Theory and Criticism: Dimensions of the New Rhetoric." *Speech Monographs*, 42 (1975), 311–334.

Clark, Robert D. "Biography and Rhetorical Criticism" (A Review Essay). *Quarterly Journal of Speech*, 44 (1958), 182–186.

Condit, Celeste Michelle. "Crafting Virtue: The Rhetorical Construction of Public Morality." *Quarterly Journal of Speech*, 73 (1987), 79–97.

Conrad, Charles. "Phases, Pentads, and Dramatistic Critical Process." *Central States Speech Journal*, 35 (1984), 94–104.

Corbett, Edward P. J., ed. *Rhetorical Analyses of Literary Works*. New York and London: Oxford University Press, 1969.

Crable, Richard E. "Ethical Codes, Accountability, and Argumentation." *Quarterly Journal of Speech*, 64 (1978), 23–32.

Cragen, John F. "Rhetorical Strategy: A Dramatistic Interpretation and Application." *Central States Speech Journal*, 26 (1975), 4–11.

Croft, Albert J. "The Functions of Rhetorical Criticism." *Quarterly Journal of Speech*, 42 (1956), 283–291.

Denton, Robert E., Jr. and Gary C. Woodward. *Political Communication in America*. New York: Praeger, 1985.

Devlin, L. Patrick, ed. *Political Persuasion in Presidential Campaigns*. New Brunswick, NJ: Transaction Books, 1987.

Ericson, Jon M. "Evaluative and Formulative Functions in Speech Criticism." *Western Speech*, 32 (1968), 173–176.

Eubanks, Ralph T. "Axiological Issues in Rhetorical Inquiry." *Southern Speech Communication Journal*, 44 (1978), 11–24.

Farrell, Thomas B. "Narrative in Natural Discourse: On Conversation and Rhetoric." *Journal of Communication*, 35 (1985), 109–127.

Farrell, Thomas B. "Rhetorical Resemblance: Paradoxes of a Practical Art." *Quarterly Journal of Speech*, 72 (1986), 1–19.

Fisher, Walter R. "Method in Rhetorical Criticism." *Southern Speech Communication Journal*, 35 (1969), 101–109.

Fisher, Walter R. *Human Communication as Narration: Toward a Philosophy of Reason, Value, and Action*. Columbia, SC: University of South Carolina Press, 1987.

Fisher, Walter R. "Clarifying the Narrative Paradigm." *Communication Monographs*, 56 (1989), 55–58.

Fisher, Walter R. "Narration as a Human Communication Paradigm: The Case of Public Moral Argument." *Communication Monographs*, 51 (1984), 1–22.

Fisher, Walter R. "The Narrative Paradigm: An Elaboration." *Communication Monographs*, 52 (1985), 347–367.

Fisher, Walter R. "The Narrative Paradigm: In the Beginning." *Journal of Communication*, 35 (1985), 74–89.

Francesconi, Robert. "The Implication of Habermas's Theory of Legitimation for Rhetorical Criticism." *Communication Monographs*, 53 (1986), 16–35.

Griffin, Leland M. "The Rhetoric of Historical Movements." *Quarterly Journal of Speech*, 38 (1952), 184–188.

Grossberg, Lawrence. "Marxist Dialectics and Rhetorical Criticism." *Quarterly Journal of Speech*, 65 (1979), 235–249.

Hagen, Michael R. "Kenneth Burke and Generative Criticism of Speeches." *Central States Speech Journal*, 22 (1971), 252–257.

Harrell, Jackson, and Wil A. Linkugel. "On Rhetorical Genre: An Organizaing Principle." *Philosophy and Rhetoric*, 11 (1978), 262–281.

Hart, Roderick P. *Verbal Style and the Presidency: A Computer — Based Analysis*. Orlando: Academic Press, 1984.

Hillbruner, Anthony. "Creativity and Contemporary Critics." *Western Speech*, 24 (1960), 5–11.

Hillbruner, Anthony. "Criticism as Persuasion." *Southern Speech Communication Journal*, 28 (1963), 260–267.

Hillbruner, Anthony. "The Moral Imperative of Criticism." *Southern Speech Communication Journal*, 40 (1975), 228–247.

Hunt, Everett Lee. "Rhetoric and Literary Criticism." *Quarterly Journal of Speech*, 21 (1935), 564–568.

Jamieson, Kathleen M. Hall. "Generic Constraints and the Rhetorical Situation." *Philosophy and Rhetoric*, 6 (1973), 162–170.

Klumpp, James F., and Thomas A. Hollihan. "Rhetorical Criticism as Moral Action." *Quarterly Journal of Speech*, 75 (1989), 84–96.

Kneupper, Charles W. "Rhetoric, Public Knowledge and Ideological Argumentation." *Journal of American Forensic Association*, 21 (1985), 183–195.

Lee, Ronald. "Moralizing and Ideologizing: An Analysis of Political Illocutions." *Western Journal of Speech Communication*, 52 (1988), 291–307.

Leff, Michael C., ed. "Rhetorical Criticism: The State of the Art," *Western Speech*, 44 (1980). This symposium contains the following essays: G. P. Mohrmann, "Elegy in a Critical Grave-Yard"; Suzanne Volmar Riches, and Malcolm O. Sillars, "The Status of Movement Criticism"; Walter R. Fisher, "Genre: Concepts and Applications in Rhetorical criticism"; Thomas B. Farrel, "Critical Models in the Analysis of Discourse"; Bruce E. Gronbeck, "Dramaturgical Theory and Criticism: The State of the Art (or Science?)"; Edwin Black, "A Note on Theory and Practice in Rhetorical Criticism"; Michael C. Leff, "Interpretation and the Art of the Rhetorical Critic."

Lucaites, John Louis, and Celeste Michelle Condit. "Re-Constructing Narrative Theory: A Functional Perspective." *Journal of Communication*, 35 (1985), 90–108.

Maloney, Martin. "Some New Directions in Rhetorical Criticism." *Central States Speech Journal*, 4 (1953), 1–5.

McGee, Michael Calvin. "Another Philippic: Notes on the Ideological Turn in Criticism." *Central States Speech Journal*, 35 (1984), 43–50.

McGee, Michael Calvin, and John S. Nelson. "Narrative Reason in Public Argument." *Journal of Communication*, 35 (1985), 139–155.

Miller, Carolyn R. "Genre as Social Action." *Quarterly Journal of Speech*, 70 (1984), 151–167.

Mohrmann, G. P., Charles J. Stewart, and Donovan J. Ochs, eds. *Explorations in Rhetorical Criticism*. University Park, Penn.: The Pennsylvania State University Press, 1973.

Moore, Mark P. "The Rhetoric of Ideology: Confronting A Critical Dilemma." *Southern Speech Communication Journal*, 54 (1988), 74–92.

Murphy, James J., ed. *Demosthenes' "On the Crown."* New York: Random House, 1967.

Murphy, Richard. "The Speech as Literary Genre." *Quarterly Journal of Speech*, 44 (1958), 117–127.

[Nichols], Marie Hochmuth. "The Criticism of Rhetoric." In her *A History and Criticism of American Public Address*. Vol. III. New York: Longmans, Green, 1955, pp. 1–23.

Nichols, Marie Hochmuth. *Rhetoric and Criticism*. Baton Rouge: Louisiana State University Press, 1963.

Nilsen, Thomas R. "Criticism and Social Consequences." *Quarterly Journal of Speech*, 42 (1956), 173–178.

Nilsen, Thomas R., ed. *Essays on Rhetorical Criticism*. New York: Random House, 1968.

Nilsen, Thomas R. "Interpretive Functions of the Critic." *Western Speech*, 21 (1957), 70–76.

Nothstine, William L. "'Topics' as Ontological Metaphors in Contemporary Rhetorical Theory and Criticism." *Quarterly Journal of Speech* 74 (1988), 151–163.

Rathbun, John W. "The Problems of Judgment and Effect in Historical Criticism." *Western Speech*, 33 (1969), 146–159.

Reid, Loren. "The Perils of Rhetorical Criticism." *Quarterly Journal of Speech*, 30 (1944), 416–422.

Rosenfield, Lawrence W. "The Anatomy of Critical Discourse." *Speech Monographs*, 35 (1968), 50–69.

Rueckert, William H., ed. *Critical Responses to Kenneth Burke*. Minneapolis: University of Minnesota Press, 1969.

Scott, Robert L., and Bernard L. Brock. *Methods of Rhetorical Criticism: A Twentieth Century Perspective*. New York: Harper & Row, 1972; rev. ed. Detroit: Wayne State University Press, 1980.

Sholle, David J. "Critical Studies: From the Theory of Ideology to Power/Knowledge." *Critical Studies in Mass Communication*, 5 (1988), 16–41.

Simmons, Herbert W. and Aram A. Aghazarian, eds. *Form, Genre, and the Study of Political Discourse*. Columbia, SC: University of South Carolina Press, 1986.

Thonssen, Lester, A. Craig Baird, and Waldo W. Braden. *Speech Criticism*. 2d ed. New York: Ronald Press, 1970.

Thurow, Glen E., and Jeffrey D. Wallin, eds. *Rhetoric and American Statesmanship*. Durham, NC: Carolina Academic Press, 1984.

Tracy, Karen, Donna Van Dusen, and Susan Robinson. "'Good' and 'Bad' Criticism: A Descriptive Analysis." *Journal of Communication*, 37 (1987), 46–59.

Wander, Philip, and Steven Jenkins. "Rhetoric, Society, and the Critical Response." *Quarterly Journal of Speech*, 58 (1972), 441–450.

Warnick, Barbara. "A Ricoeurian Approach to Rhetorical Criticism." *Western Journal of Speech Communication*, 51 (1987), 227–244.

White, Eugene, ed. *Rhetoric in Transition: Studies in the Nature and Uses of Rhetoric*. University Park: The Pennsylvania State University Press, 1980.

Wichelns, Herbert A. "The Literary Criticism of Oratory." *Studies in Rhetoric and Public Speaking in Honor of James A. Winans*. New York: Century, 1925, pp. 181–216.

Windt, Theodore Otto, Jr. "Presidential Rhetoric: Definition of a Field of Study." *Presidential Studies Quarterly*, 16 (1986), 102–116.

Wrage, Ernest J. "The Ideal Critic." *Central States Speech Journal*, 8 (1957), 20–23.

Wrage, Ernest J. "Public Address: A Study in Social and Intellectual History." *Quarterly Journal of Speech*, 33 (1947), 451–457.

Index